Introduction to Finance

Pearson

At Pearson, we have a simple mission: to help people make more of their lives through learning.

We combine innovative learning technology with trusted content and educational expertise to provide engaging and effective learning experience that serve people wherever and whenever they are learning.

We enable our customers to access a wide and expanding range of market-leading content from world-renowned authors and develop their own tailor-made book. From classroom to boardroom, our curriculum materials, digital learning tools and testing programmes help to educate millions of people worldwide — more than any other private enterprise.

Every day our work helps learning flourish, and wherever learning flourishes, so do people.

To learn more, please visit us at: www.pearson.com/uk

Introduction to Finance

Selected chapters from:

CORPORATE FINANCE AND INVESTMENT: DECISIONS AND STRATEGIES

Ninth Edition

Richard Pike, Bill Neale and Saeed Akbar
with Philip Linsley

Pearson

Harlow, England • London • New York • Boston • San Francisco • Toronto • Sydney • Dubai • Singapore • Hong Kong
Tokyo • Seoul • Taipei • New Dehli • Cape Town • São Paulo • Mexico City • Madrid • Amsterdam • Munich • Paris • Milan

Pearson
KAO Two
KAO Park
Harlow
Essex CM17 9SR

And associated companies throughout the world

Visit us on the World Wide Web at:
www.pearson.com/uk

© Pearson Education Limited 2019

Compiled from:

Corporate Finance and Investment: Decisions and Strategies
Ninth Edition
Richard Pike, Bill Neale and Saeed Akbar
with Philip Linsley
ISBN 978-1-292-20854-1
© Prentice Hall Europe 1993, 1999 (print)
© Pearson Education Limited 2003
© Pearson Education Limited 2012, 2015, 2018 (print and electronic)

All rights reserved. No part of this publication may be reproduced, stored in a retrieval system, or transmitted in any form or by any means, electronic, mechanical, photocopying, recording or otherwise, without either the prior written permission of the publisher or a licence permitting restricted copying in the United Kingdom issued by the Copyright Licensing Agency Ltd, Barnard's Inn, 86 Fetter Lane, London, EC4A 1EN.

ISBN 978-1-78764-324-6

Printed and bound in Great Britain by CPI Group.

Contents

Chapter 1 W1
The financial environment — 1

1.1	Introduction	2
1.2	Financial markets	2
1.3	The financial services sector	4
1.4	The London Stock Exchange (LSE)	9
1.5	Are financial markets efficient?	11
1.6	Reading the financial pages	16
1.7	Taxation and financial decisions	18

Chapter 2 W2
Present values, and bond and share valuation — 31

2.1	Introduction	32
2.2	Measuring Wealth	32
2.3	Time-value of money	32
2.4	Financial arithmetic for capital growth	33
2.5	Present value	35
2.6	Present value arithmetic	39
2.7	Valuing bonds	42
2.8	Valuing shares: the dividend valuation model	45
2.9	Problems with the dividend growth model	47

Chapter 3 W2
Analysing investment risk — 59

3.1	Introduction	60
3.2	Expected net present value (ENPV): Betterway plc	61
3.3	Attitudes to risk	61
3.4	Types of risk	63
3.5	Measurement of risk	64
3.6	Risk description techniques	68
3.7	Adjusting the NPV formula for risk	72
3.8	Risk analysis in practice	74
3.9	Capital investment options	75

Chapter 4 W3
Relationships between investments: portfolio theory — 87

4.1	Introduction	88
4.2	Portfolio analysis: the basic principles	89
4.3	How to measure portfolio risk	90
4.4	Portfolio analysis where risk and return differ	93
4.5	Different degrees of correlation	95
4.6	Worked example: gerrybild plc	97
4.7	Portfolios with more than two components	99
4.8	Can we use this for project appraisal? some reservations	101

Chapter 5 W4
Setting the risk premium: the Capital Asset Pricing Model (CAPM) — 106

5.1	Introduction	107
5.2	Security valuation and discount rates	107
5.3	Concepts of risk and return	108
5.4	International portfolio diversification	112
5.5	Systematic risk	115
5.6	Completing the model	119
5.7	Using the CAPM: assessing the required return	121
5.8	Worked example	126
5.9	The underpinnings of the CAPM	127
5.10	Portfolios with many components: the capital market line	128
5.11	How it all fits together: the key relationships	130
5.12	Reservations about the CAPM	132
5.13	Testing the CAPM	133
5.14	Factor models	134
5.15	The Arbitrage Pricing Theory	136
5.16	Fama and French's three-factor model	137
5.17	The four- and five-factor models	138
5.18	Issues raised by the CAPM: some food for managerial thought	139

Chapter 6
The required rate of return on investment — 147

6.1	Introduction	148
6.2	The required return in all-equity firms: the DGM	148
6.3	The required return in all-equity firms: the CAPM	152
6.4	Using 'tailored' discount rates	154
6.5	Worked example: Tieko plc	161
6.6	Another problem: taxation and the CAPM	162
6.7	Problems with 'tailored' discount rates	163
6.8	A critique of divisional hurdle rates	164

Chapter 7
Enterprise value and equity value — 170

7.1	Introduction	171
7.2	The valuation problem	171
7.3	Valuation using published accounts	172
7.4	Valuing the earnings stream: P:E ratios	178
7.5	EBITDA – a halfway house	180
7.6	Valuing cash flows	182
7.7	The DCF approach	184
7.8	Valuation of unquoted companies	187
7.9	Shareholder value analysis	188
7.10	Using value drivers	190
7.11	Worked example: Safa plc	191
7.12	Economic Value Added (EVA)	194

Chapter 8
Identifying and valuing options — 202

8.1	Introduction	203
8.2	Share options	203
8.3	Option pricing	211
8.4	Application of option theory to corporate finance	218
8.5	Capital investment options (real options)	219
8.6	Why conventional NPV may not tell the whole story	221

Chapter 9
Returning value to shareholders: the dividend decision — 228

9.1	Introduction	229
9.2	The strategic dimension	231
9.3	The legal dimension	232
9.4	The theory: dividend policy and firm value	232
9.5	Objections to dividend irrelevance	240
9.6	The information content of dividends: Dividend smoothing	245
9.7	Worked example	246
9.8	Alternatives to cash dividends	248
9.9	The dividend puzzle	253
9.10	Conclusions	255

Chapter 10
Capital structure and the required return — 263

10.1	Introduction	264
10.2	Measures of gearing	265
10.3	Operating and financial gearing	270
10.4	Financial gearing and risk: Lindley plc	272
10.5	The 'traditional' view of gearing and the required return	276
10.6	The cost of debt	279
10.7	The overall cost of capital	281
10.8	Worked example: damstar plc	284
10.9	More on Economic Value Added (EVA)	287
10.10	Financial distress	287
10.11	Two more issues: signalling and agency costs	291
10.12	Conclusions	291

Chapter 11
Does capital structure really matter? — 299

11.1	Introduction	300
11.2	The Modigliani–Miller message	300
11.3	MM's propositions	305
11.4	Does it work? Impediments to arbitrage	305
11.5	MM with corporate income tax	306
11.6	Capital structure theory and the CAPM	309
11.7	Linking the Betas: ungearing and re-gearing	312
11.8	MM with financial distress	313
11.9	Calculating the WACC	315
11.10	The Adjusted Present Value Method (APV)	318
11.11	Worked example: Rigton plc	319
11.12	Further issues with the APV	320
11.13	Which discount rate should we use?	321
11.14	Valuation of a geared firm	321
11.15	Performance evaluation in a geared firm: The EVA revisited	323

Chapter 12
Acquisitions and re-structuring — 333

12.1	Introduction	334
12.2	Takeover activity	335
12.3	Motives for takeover	340
12.4	Alternative bid terms	346
12.5	Evaluating a bid: the expected gains from takeovers	348
12.6	Worked example: ML plc and CO plc	349
12.7	The importance of strategy	351
12.8	The strategic approach	352
12.9	Post-merger activities	357
12.10	Assessing the impact of mergers	360
12.11	Value gaps	368
12.12	Corporate restructuring	371
12.13	Private equity	376

Chapter 13 W8
Managing currency risk — 389

13.1	Introduction	390
13.2	The structure of exchange rates: spot and forward rates	391
13.3	Foreign exchange exposure	393
13.4	Should firms worry about exchange rate changes?	396
13.5	Economic theory and exposure management	399
13.6	Exchange rate forecasting	404
13.7	Devising a foreign exchange management (FEM) strategy	407
13.8	Internal hedging techniques	410
13.9	Simple external hedging techniques	414
13.10	More complex techniques	416
13.11	More complex techniques: Futures and swaps	419
13.12	Conclusions	422

Chapter 14
Foreign investment decisions — 429

14.1	Introduction	430
14.2	Advantages of MNCS over national firms	432
14.3	Foreign market entry strategies	434
14.4	Additional Complexities Of Foreign Investment	437
14.5	The discount rate for Foreign Direct Investment (FDI)	438
14.6	Evaluating FDI	440
14.7	Worked example: Sparkes plc and Zoltan kft	440
14.8	Exposure to foreign exchange risk	443
14.9	How MNCS manage operating exposure	447
14.10	Hedging the risk of foreign projects	449
14.11	Political and country risk	450
14.12	Managing political and country risk (PCR)	452
14.13	Financing FDI	454
14.14	The WACC for FDI	457
14.15	Applying the APV to FDI	457
14.16	Worked example: applying the APV	458

Chapter 15 W10
Key issues in modern finance: a review — 465

15.1	Introduction	466
15.2	Understanding individual behaviour	467
15.3	Understanding corporate behaviour	468
15.4	Understanding how markets behave	472
15.5	Behavioural finance	479

Appendix A
Solutions to self-assessment activities — 489

Appendix B
Solutions to selected questions — 501

Glossary — 523

References — 537

Index — 553

1
The financial environment

Serco finance director departs as company seeks emergency funding

Scandal-hit outsourcing company Serco – the business embroiled in controversy over billing the government for electronically tagging prisoners who had died – has parted company with its finance director after unveiling plans to raise an emergency £170m by selling new shares.

Serco, which runs services ranging from prisons to rail franchises and London's cycle hire scheme, said it would be 'uncomfortably close' to breaching its banking agreements and intended to sell nearly 50m new shares to raise cash.

The company commented: 'The proposed equity placing has a single purpose: to give us the opportunity to conduct a thorough review of the strategy of the business whilst remaining within the terms of our debt facilities.' The company, which has already warned it will take a big hit to profits as a result of the tagging scandal, said its performance this year had been 'more challenging than expected'.

Source: Copyright Guardian News & Media Ltd 2018.

Learning objectives

By the end of this chapter, the reader should understand the nature of financial markets and the main players that operate within them. Particular focus is placed on the following topics:

- The functions of financial markets.
- The operation of the Stock Exchange.
- The extent to which capital markets are efficient.
- How taxation affects corporate finance.

Enhanced ability to read financial statements and the financial pages in a newspaper should also be achieved.

1.1 INTRODUCTION

The corporate financial manager, whether in Serco or any company, has the important task of ensuring that sufficient funds are available to meet all the likely needs of the business. To do this properly, this person requires a clear grasp of both the future financial requirements of the business and the workings of the financial markets. This chapter provides an overview of these markets, and the major institutions within them, paying particular attention to the London Stock Exchange.

1.2 FINANCIAL MARKETS

financial market
Any market in which financial assets and liabilities are traded

A **financial market** is any mechanism for trading financial assets or securities. A **security** is a legal contract giving the right to receive future benefits under a stated set of conditions. Examples of financial securities range from the mortgage on a house or lease on a car to securities that are traded on financial markets, termed marketable securities.

Frequently, there is no physical marketplace, traders conducting transactions via computer. London is widely regarded as the leading European financial centre and is the largest by volume of dealing. Figure 1.1 shows the main financial markets, which are further explained here.

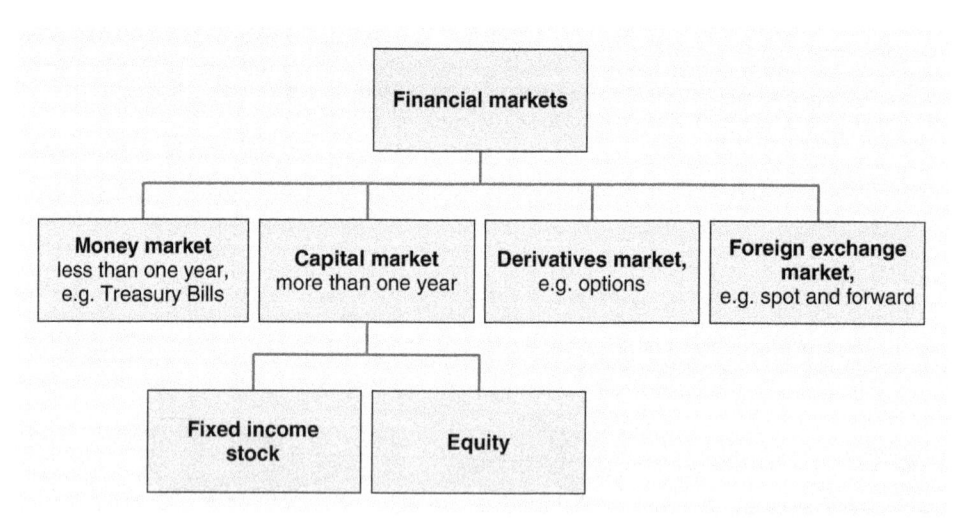

```
                        Financial markets
                               |
    ┌──────────────┬───────────┴──────────┬──────────────────┐
 Money market   Capital market      Derivatives market   Foreign exchange
 less than one  more than one year    e.g. options        market,
 year,                                                   e.g. spot and forward
 e.g. Treasury                |
 Bills              ┌─────────┴─────────┐
                Fixed income         Equity
                   stock
```

Figure 1.1 Financial markets

money market
The market for short-term money, broadly speaking for repayment within about a year

securities/capital market
The market for long-term finance

spot
The spot, or cash market, is where transactions are settled 'immediately' (in practice, within two days)

forward
The forward market is where contracts are made for future settlement at a price specified now

1 The **money market** channels wholesale funds, usually for less than one year, from lenders to borrowers. The market is largely dominated by the major banks and other financial institutions, but local government and large companies also use it for short-term lending and borrowing purposes. The official market is where approved institutions deal in financial instruments with the Central Bank. Other money markets include the inter-bank market, where banks lend short-term funds to each other, and the Euro-currency market, where banks lend and borrow in foreign currencies.

2 The **securities** or **capital market** deals with long-dated securities such as shares and loan stock. The London Stock Exchange is the best-known institution in the UK capital market, but there are other important markets, such as the bond market (for long-dated government and corporate borrowing) and the Eurobond market.

3 The foreign exchange market is a market for buying and selling one currency against another. Deals are either on a **spot** basis (for immediate delivery) or on a **forward** basis (for future delivery).

derivatives
Securities that are traded separately from the assets from which they are derived

future
A tradable contract to buy or sell a specified amount of an asset at a specified price at a specified future date

option
The right but not the obligation to buy or sell a particular asset

4 Futures and options exchanges provide means of **hedging** (i.e. protecting) or speculating against movements in shares, currencies and interest rates. These are called **derivatives** because they are derived from the underlying security. A **future** is an agreement to buy or sell an asset (foreign currency, shares, etc.) at an agreed price at some future date. An **option** is the right, but not the obligation, to buy or sell such assets at an agreed price at, or within, an agreed time period. Examples of futures and options exchanges are Euronext NYSE Liffe, which operates exchanges in Europe (www.euronext.com) and the Chicago Mercantile Exchange in the United States (www.cmegroup.com).

The financial markets provide mechanisms through which the corporate financial manager has access to a wide range of sources of finance and instruments.

Capital markets function in two important ways:

1 *Primary market* – providing new capital for business and other activities, usually in the form of share issues to new or existing shareholders (equity) or loans.
2 *Secondary market* – trading existing securities, thus enabling share or bond holders to dispose of their holdings when they wish. An active secondary market is a necessary condition for an effective primary market, as no investor wants to feel 'locked in' to an investment that cannot be realised when desired.

Imagine what business life would be like if these capital markets were not available to companies. New businesses could start up only if the owners had sufficient personal wealth to fund the initial capital investment; existing businesses could develop only through re-investing profits generated; and investors could not easily dispose of their shareholdings. In many parts of the world where financial markets are embryonic or even non-existent, this is exactly what does happen. *The development of a strong and healthy economy rests very largely on efficient, well-developed financial markets.*

Financial markets promote savings and investment by providing mechanisms whereby the financial requirements of lenders (suppliers of funds) and borrowers (users of funds) can be met. Figure 1.2 shows in simple terms how businesses finance their operations.

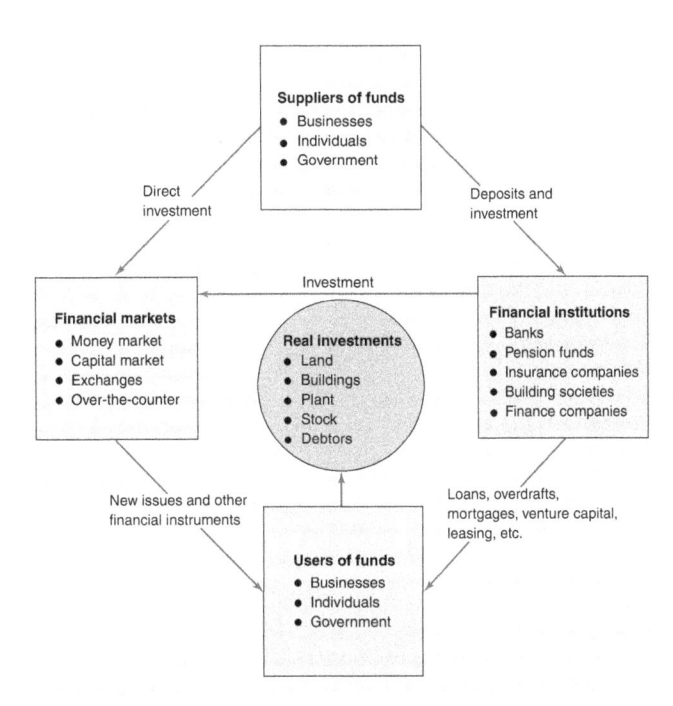

Figure 1.2 Financial markets, institutions, suppliers and users

financial intermediaries
Institutions that channel funds from savers and depositors with cash surpluses to people and organisations with cash shortages

Financial institutions (e.g. pension funds, insurance companies, banks, building societies, unit trusts and specialist investment institutions) act as **financial intermediaries**, collecting funds from savers to lend to their corporate and other customers through the money and capital markets, or directly through loans, leasing and other forms of financing.

Businesses are major users of these funds. The financial manager raises cash by selling claims to the company's existing or future assets in financial markets (e.g. by issuing shares, debentures or Bills of Exchange) or borrowing from financial institutions. The cash is then used to acquire fixed and current assets. If those investments are successful, they will generate positive cash flows from business operations. This cash surplus is used to service existing financial obligations in the form of dividends, interest, etc., and to make repayments. Any residue is re-invested in the business to replace existing assets or to expand operations.

We focus in this chapter on the financial institutions and financial markets shown in Figure 1.2.

■ Financial institutions provide essential services

The needs of lenders and borrowers rarely match. Hence, there is an important role for financial intermediaries, such as banks, if the financial markets are to operate efficiently. Financial intermediaries perform the following functions:

1 *Re-packaging, or pooling, finance:* gathering small amounts of savings from a large number of individuals and repackaging them into larger bundles for lending to businesses. The banks have an important role here.
2 *Risk reduction:* placing small sums from numerous individuals in large, well-diversified investment portfolios, such as unit trusts.
3 *Liquidity transformation:* bringing together short-term savers and long-term borrowers (e.g. building societies and banks). Borrowing 'short' and lending 'long' is acceptable only where relatively few savers will want to withdraw funds at any given time. The financial difficulties faced by Northern Rock in the United Kingdom in 2007, and the Greek and Italian banks more recently, show that this is not always the case.
4 *Cost reduction:* minimising transaction costs by providing convenient and relatively inexpensive services for linking small savers to larger borrowers.
5 *Financial advice:* providing advisory and other services for both lender and borrower.

1.3 THE FINANCIAL SERVICES SECTOR

The financial services sector can be divided into three groups of institutions: those engaged in (1) deposit-taking, (2) contractual savings and (3) other investment funds.

■ Deposit-taking institutions

retail banks
Retail banks accept deposits from the general public who can draw on these accounts by cheque (or ATM) and lend to other people and organisations seeking funds

Retail banks have three important roles: they manage nationwide networks of High Street branches and online facilities; they operate a national payments system by clearing cheques and by receiving and paying out notes and coins; and they accept deposits in varying amounts from a wide range of customers. The cheque-clearing system in Great Britain is managed by the Cheque and Credit Clearing Company (www.chequeandcredit.co.uk). Because of the decline in cheque usage, a target date of 2018 had been set to close central cheque clearing. However, in 2011 the Payments Council withdrew its plans, partly because of security concerns concerning alternatives. (Useful websites: www.bba.org.uk, www.lendingstandardsboard.org.uk)

The balance sheet of any clearing bank reveals that the main sterling assets are advances to the private sector, other banks, the public sector in the form of Treasury

Bills and government stock, local authorities and private households. Nowadays, the main instruments of lending by retail banks are overdrafts, term loans and mortgages.

In the European Union the Capital Requirements Directive (CRD) came into existence in 2007. The CRD enacted the Basel II Accord which aims to ensure banks hold sufficient capital to meet the market, credit and operational risks they face. Consequently, Basel II is endeavouring to ensure that banks and other credit institutions are financially sound and can withstand losses that may occur in the course of business. It also aims to improve risk management practices and market discipline. To strengthen the banking system in the wake of the 2007 financial crisis, the Basel Committee on Banking Supervision has agreed a Basel III Accord, although this will not come into effect until 2018.

Wholesale banks

Wholesale banking (or investment banking) developed out of the need to finance the enormous growth in world trade in the 19th century. **Accepting houses** were formed whose main business was to accept Bills of Exchange (promising to pay a sum of money at some future date) from less well-known traders, and from **discount houses** which provided cash by discounting such bills. **Investment banks** nowadays concentrate on dealing with institutional investors, large corporations and governments. They have three major activities, frequently organised into separate divisions: corporate finance, mergers and acquisitions, and fund management.

Investment banks' activities include *giving financial advice to companies and arranging finance* through syndicated loans and new security issues. Investment banks are also members of the Issuing Houses Association, an organisation responsible for the *flotation of shares* on the Stock Exchange. This involves advising a company on the correct mix of financial instruments to be issued and on drawing up a prospectus and underwriting the issue. They also play a leading role in the *development of new financial products*, such as swaps, options and other derivative products, that have become very widely traded in recent years.

Another area of activity for wholesale banks is advising companies on corporate *mergers, acquisitions and restructuring*. This involves both assisting in the negotiation of a 'friendly' merger of two independent companies and developing strategies for 'unfriendly' takeovers, or acting as an adviser for a company defending against an unwanted bidder.

Finally, investment banks fulfil a major role as *managers of the investment portfolios* of some pension funds, insurance companies, investment and **unit trusts**, and various charities. Whether in arranging finance, advising on takeover bids or managing the funds of institutional investors, merchant banks exert considerable influence on both corporate finance and the capital market. Investment banks effectively grew out of merchant banks and, to all intents and purposes, provide similar services. The 1933 Glass–Steagall Act was implemented in the United States to enforce the separation of retail banks and investment banks. This Act was repealed approximately 50 years later. Following the 2007 financial crisis, the Independent Commission on Banking was set up and, in September 2011, recommended a clear boundary between retail and investment banking and to remove some risk from the banking sector.

The growth of *overseas banking* has been closely linked to the development of Eurocurrency markets and to the growth of multinational companies. Over 500 foreign banks operate in London. A substantial amount of their business consists of providing finance to branches or subsidiaries of foreign companies.

Following criticisms of the banks after the financial crisis, different governments have acted to reduce the possibility of a future crisis. A key action in the United Kingdom has been the development of the Banking Reform Bill, which came into force in 2015. This requires UK banks to separate investment banking and retail banking activities by ring-fencing any deposits of individuals and SMEs.

---

accepting houses
Accepting houses are specialist institutions that discount or 'accept' Bills of Exchange, especially short-term government securities

discount houses
Discount houses bid for issues of short-term government securities at a discount and either hold them to maturity or sell them on in the money market

investment banks
Investment banks are wholesale banks that arrange specialist financial services like mergers and acquisition funding, and finance of international trade fund management

unit trust
Investment business attracting funds from investors by issuing units of shares or bonds to invest in

Introduction to Finance

building societies
Financial institutions whose main function is to accept deposits from customers and lend for house purchases

Building societies (www.bsa.org.uk) are a form of savings bank specialising in the provision of finance for house purchases in the private sector. As a result of deregulation of the financial services industry, building societies now offer an almost complete set of private banking services, and the distinction between them and the traditional banks is increasingly blurred. Indeed, many societies have given up their mutual status to become public limited companies with varying degrees of success.

Self-assessment activity 1.1

What are financial intermediaries and what economic services do they perform?
(Answer in Appendix A)

Institutions engaged in contractual savings

pension funds
Financial institutions that manage the pension schemes of large firms and other organisations

self-administered schemes
A pension fund that invests clients' contributions directly into the stock market and other investments

insured schemes
A pension fund that uses an insurance company to invest contributions and to insure against actuarial risks (e.g. members living longer than expected)

insurance companies
Financial institutions that guarantee to protect clients against specified risks, including death, and general risks in return for the payment of an annual premium

portfolios
Combinations of securities of various kinds invested in a diversified fund

Pension funds accumulate funds to meet the future pension liabilities of a particular organisation to its employees. Funds are normally built up from contributions paid by the employer and employees. They can be divided into **self-administered schemes**, where the funds are invested directly in the financial markets, and **insured schemes**, where the funds are invested by, and the risk is covered by, a life assurance company. Pension schemes have enormous and rapidly growing funds available for investment in the securities markets. Pension funds enjoy major tax advantages. Subject to certain restrictions, individuals enjoy tax relief on their subscriptions to a fund. Together with insurance companies, pension funds make up the major purchasers of company securities.

Insurance companies' activities (www.abi.org.uk) can be divided into long-term and general insurance. Long-term insurance business consists mainly of *life assurance* and *pension provision*. Policyholders pay premiums to the companies and are guaranteed either a lump sum in the event of death, or a regular annual income for some defined period. With a guaranteed premium inflow and predictable aggregate future payments, there is no great need for liquidity, so life assurance funds are able to invest heavily in long-term assets, such as ordinary shares.

General insurance business (e.g. fire, accident, motor, marine and other insurance) consists of contracts to cover losses within a specified period, normally 12 months. As liquidity is important here, a greater proportion of funds is invested in short-term assets, although a considerable proportion of such funds is invested in securities and property.

The investment strategy of both pension fund managers and insurance companies tends to be long term. They invest in **portfolios** of company shares and government stocks, direct loans and mortgages.

Other investment funds

As we shall see in Section 1.4, private investors, independently managing their own investment portfolios, are a dying breed. Increasingly, they are being replaced by financial institutions that manage widely diversified portfolios of securities, such as unit trusts and investment trusts (www.investmentfunds.org.uk). These pool the funds of large numbers of investors, enabling them to achieve a degree of diversification not otherwise attainable owing to the prohibitive transactions costs and time required for active portfolio management. However, there are important differences between these institutions.

Investment trusts

Investment trusts are limited companies, whose shares are usually quoted on the London Stock Exchange, and set up specifically to invest in securities. The company's share price depends on the value of the securities held in the trust but also on supply and demand. As a result, these shares often sell at values different from their net asset values, usually at a discount.

They are traditionally 'closed-ended' in the sense that the company's articles restrict the number of shares, and hence the amount of share capital, that can be issued. However, several open-ended investment companies (OEICs) have now been launched. To realise their holdings, shareholders can sell their shares on the stock market.

Unit trusts

Unit trusts are investment syndicates, established by trust deed and regulated by trust law. Investors' funds are pooled into a portfolio of investments, each investor being allocated tranches or 'units' according to the amount of the funds they subscribe. They are mainly operated by banks and insurance companies, which appoint managers whose conduct is supervised by a set of trustees.

Unit prices are fixed by the managers but reflect the value of the underlying securities. Prices reflect the costs of buying and selling, via an initial charge. Managers also apply annual charges, usually about 1 per cent of the value of the fund. Unit-holders can realise their holdings only by selling units back to the trust managers.

They are 'open-ended' in the sense that the size of the fund is not restricted and the managers can advertise for funds.

Private equity funds

Private equity funds are typically limited partnerships where institutional investors make a commitment which is then drawn down over the term of the fund, as shown in Figure 1.3. The equity capital is invested either into companies that are already private or into public companies which are then taken private.

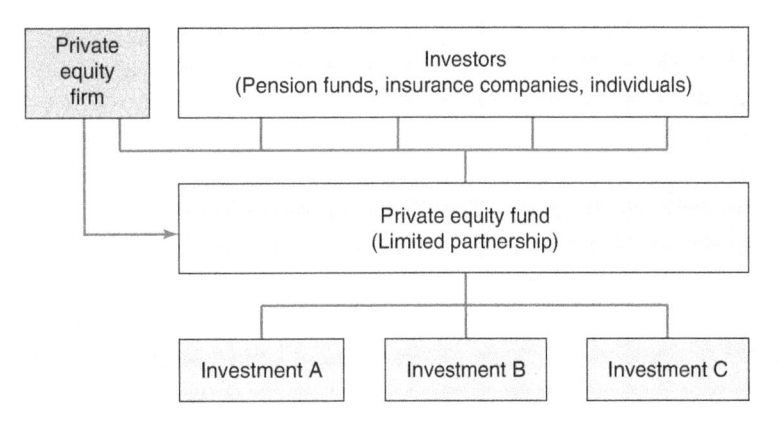

Figure 1.3 **Private equity firm**

Hedge funds

A hedge fund is a fund used by wealthy individuals and institutions. They are exempt from many of the rules and regulations governing other institutions, which allows them to accomplish aggressive investing strategies that are unavailable to others. These include:

- *Arbitrage*– simultaneous buying and selling of a financial instrument in different markets to profit from differences in prices.
- **Short selling** – selling a security one does not own with the expectation of buying it in the future at a lower cost.
- *Leverage*– borrowing money for investment purposes.
- *Hedging*– using derivative instruments to offset potential losses on the underlying security.

Hedge fund managers receive their remuneration in the form of a management fee plus incentive fees tied to the fund's performance.

short selling
Selling securities not yet owned (and generally borrowed) in the expectation of being able to buy them later at a lower price

Disintermediation and securitisation

disintermediation
Business-to-business lending that eliminates the banking intermediary

securitisation
The capitalisation of a future stream of income into a single capital value that is sold on the capital market for imme-diate cash

While financial intermediaries play a vital role in the financial markets, **disintermediation** is an important new development. This is the process whereby companies borrow and lend funds directly between themselves without recourse to banks and other institutions. Allied to this is the process of **securitisation**, the development of new financial instruments to meet ever-changing corporate needs (i.e. financial engineering). Some assets generate predictable cash returns and offer security. Debt can be issued to the market on the basis of the returns and suitable security. Securitisation usually also involves a credit-rating agency assessing the issue and giving it a credit rating. Securitisation can also be used to create value through 'unbundling' traditional financial processes. For example, a conventional loan has many elements, such as loan origination, credit status evaluation, financing and collection of interest and principal. Rather than arranging the whole process through a single intermediary, such as a bank, the process can be 'unbundled' and handled by separate institutions, which may lower the cost of the loan. Securitisation was a particular feature of the 2007 financial crisis.

Fund houses take on banks over lending

When Busaba Eathai, a Thai restaurant chain, borrowed money to finance its expansion across the UK, it was not a bank that was handed its business. The eatery bypassed Europe's long-dominant source of loans and instead turned to an alternative lender: an asset manager.

Muzinich, the New York-based fixed income specialist with $25bn under management, provided Busaba with a private debt deal of £16m in June. Using the loan, the chain plans to open two new restaurants – in St Albans and Oxford Circus – in October.

Similar stories are playing out across Europe, where small and medium-sized businesses (SMEs) are increasingly turning to fund managers to borrow money. But the rise in lending by fund houses has sparked fears that some asset managers lack the expertise required to both source and understand the risks of the loans they provide, leaving their investors vulnerable to future losses. There are also concerns that lending by asset managers is a form of so-called shadow banking that is not regulated stringently enough.

Figures show the private debt market is growing rapidly. It includes loans made directly to companies as well as property financing and mezzanine financing, a hybrid between debt and equity. Between 2006 and 2014, it nearly tripled in size to $441bn, according to research from Brown Brothers Harriman, the US bank.

The asset class owes much of this growth to the financial crisis. Rules introduced to shore up bank balance sheets left lenders reluctant to lend large sums to SMEs.

This opened up a new market for asset managers, particularly in Europe, where banks traditionally dominated lending. In the US, about three-quarters of business financing is estimated to come from alternative lenders. But this figure is only around 20 per cent in Europe, according to Brown Brothers.

Fund houses have embraced the asset class because of rising demand from institutional investors, which have struggled to generate returns due to low interest rates and volatile markets. Many funds are targeting much higher returns than that generated by traditional fixed income products. Fund houses are able to achieve this by charging borrowers higher interest rates than banks typically do. Borrowers are willing to pay more either because they have struggled to get a loan from a bank or because asset managers will be more flexible around the length of the loan or its structure.

However, there are concerns that the performance of private debt funds could come under pressure. With more fund managers operating in this area, there is rising competition to find companies to lend to.

The level of capital that asset managers have to lend, so-called dry powder, reached a record high of $202bn in August, as fund houses and investors piled into the sector.

Source: Mooney, A. (2016) Fund houses take on banks over lending. *Financial Times*, 2 September. © The Financial Times Limited 2018. All rights reserved.

Securitisation and disintermediation have permitted larger companies to create alternative, more flexible forms of finance. This, in turn, has forced banks to become more competitive in the services offered to larger companies. Recent, more exotic, forms of securitisation include pubs, gate receipts from a football club, future income from a pop star's recordings, and even the football World Cup competition.

1.4 THE LONDON STOCK EXCHANGE (LSE)

The capital market is the market where long-term securities are issued and traded. The London Stock Exchange is the principal trading market for long-dated securities in the United Kingdom (www.londonstockexchange.com).

A stock exchange has two principal economic functions: to <u>enable companies to raise new capital</u> (the primary market), and to *facilitate the trading of existing shares* (the secondary market) through the negotiation of a price at which title to ownership of a company is transferred between investors.

■ A brief history of the London Stock Exchange

The world's first joint-stock company – the Muscovy Company – was founded in London in 1553. With the growth in such companies, there arose the need for shareholders to be able to sell their holdings, leading to a growth in brokers acting as intermediaries for investors. In 1760, after being ejected from the Royal Exchange for rowdiness, a group of 150 brokers formed a club at Jonathan's Coffee House to buy and sell shares. By 1773, the club was renamed the Stock Exchange.

The Exchange developed rapidly, playing a major role in financing UK companies during the Industrial Revolution. New technology began to have a major impact in 1872, when the Exchange Telegraph tickertape service was introduced.

For over a century, the Exchange continued to expand and become more efficient, but fundamental changes did not occur until 27 October 1986 – the 'Big Bang' – the most important of which were:

1. All firms became brokers/dealers able to operate in a dual capacity – either buying securities from, or selling them to, clients without the need to deal through a third party. Firms could also register as market-makers committed to making firm bid (buying) and offer (selling) prices at all times.
2. Ownership of member firms by an outside corporation was permitted, enabling member firms to build a large capital base to compete with competition from overseas.
3. Minimum scales of commission were abolished to improve competitiveness.
4. Trading moved from being conducted face-to-face on a single market floor to being performed via computer and telephone from separate dealing rooms. Computer-based systems were introduced to display share price information, such as **SEAQ** (Stock Exchange Automated Quotations).

SEAQ
A computer-based quotation system on the London Stock Exchange where market-makers report bid and offer prices and trading volumes

In 2007, the Exchange launched a new trading system with greater capacity and speed of trading. Today, the London Stock Exchange is viewed as one of the leading and most competitive places to do business in the world, second only to New York in total market value terms.

The LSE has two tiers. The bigger market is the <u>Official Main Market</u>, providing a quotation for some 2.600 companies from 60 countries. To obtain a full listing, companies have to satisfy rigorous criteria relating to size of issued capital, financial record, trading history and acceptability of board members. These details are set out in a document called the company's 'listing particulars'. The **Financial Conduct Authority (FCA)** regulates admission of securities to the Official List. The UK Listing Authority (UKLA) is the division of the FCA responsible for approving applications to the Official List, and companies seeking to have securities listed must comply with the FCA Listing Rules.

Financial Conduct Authority (FCA)
A regulatory body for maintaining confidence in the financial markets

Alternative Investment Market (AIM)
Where smaller, younger companies can acquire a stock market listing

The second tier is the **Alternative Investment Market (AIM)**. It attempts to minimise the cost of entry and membership by keeping the rules and application process as simple as possible. A nominated adviser (or NOMAD) firm (typically a stockbroker or bank) both introduces the new company to the market and acts as a mentor, ensuring that it complies with market rules. However, the requirement to observe existing obligations in relation to publication of price-sensitive information and annual and interim accounts remains. The AIM is unlikely to appeal to private investors unless they are prepared to invest in relatively high-risk businesses.

While the vast majority of share trading takes place through the Stock Exchange, it is not the only trading arena. For some years, there has been a small but active over-the-counter (OTC) market, where organisations trade their shares, usually on a 'matched bargain' basis, via an intermediary.

Self-assessment activity 1.2

What type of company would be most likely to trade on:

(a) the main securities market?
(b) the Alternative Investment Market?
(c) the over-the-counter market?

(Answer in Appendix A)

Regulation of the market

Investor confidence in the workings of the stock market is paramount if it is to operate effectively. Even in deregulated markets, there is still a requirement to provide strong safeguards against unfair or incompetent trading and to ensure that the market operates as intended. The mechanism for regulating the whole UK financial system was established by the Financial Services Act 1986 (FSA86), which provided a structure based on 'self-regulation within a statutory framework' and established the Financial Services Authority (FSA), responsible to the Treasury. Its objectives were to sustain confidence in the UK financial services industry and to monitor, detect and prevent financial crime (**www.fsa.gov.uk**). This involved the regulation of the financial markets, investment managers and investment advisers.

The severe impact of the financial crisis resulted in the UK government identifying two primary policy issues: 'Improving regulation of the financial sector to protect customers and the economy' and 'Creating stronger and safer banks'. The idea underlying the first policy issue was that an appropriately regulated financial services sector was needed if the economy was to prosper. Consequently, the government undertook a major review of the regulation of the financial services sector to ensure the sector better managed its risks. This has led to the enactment of the Financial Services Act which came into force in April 2013. Formerly, under the tripartite system of regulation, responsibility was divided between the Financial Services Authority (FSA), the Bank of England and the Treasury. The new regulatory system comprises the Financial Policy Committee (FPC), the Prudential Regulation Authority (PRA) and the Financial Conduct Authority (FCA). The FPC is responsible for the macro-prudential regulation of risks that might impact the whole financial system. The PRA is responsible for micro-prudential regulation of financial firms, ensuring banks have appropriate amounts of capital and liquidity. The role of the FCA is to protect consumers by promoting competition and regulating financial services firms.

The strategic objective of the FCA is to ensure that the relevant markets function well, and this is underpinned by three operational objectives:

- to secure an appropriate degree of protection for consumers;
- to protect and enhance the integrity of the UK financial system;
- to promote effective competition in the interests of consumers.

The new regulatory system still has a connection to the Bank of England as the FPC is a committee of the Court of Directors of the Bank of England and the PRA is a subsidiary of the Bank of England. Other bodies overseeing aspects of the workings of the capital markets include the Competition and Markets Authority, and the Panel on Takeovers and Mergers.

Self-assessment activity 1.3

To what extent does an effective primary capital market depend on a healthy secondary market?
(Answer in Appendix A)

Share ownership in the United Kingdom

Back in 1963, over half (54 per cent) of all UK equities were held by private individuals. This proportion had dropped to 12 per cent by the end of 2014 (www.ons.gov.uk). Today, share ownership is dominated by financial institutions (the pension funds, insurance groups and investment and unit trusts) and 'rest of the world' investors. Financial institutions, acting for millions of pensioners and employees, policyholders and small investors, have vast power to influence the market and the companies they invest in. Institutional investors employ a variety of investment strategies, from passive index-tracking funds, which seek to reflect movements in the stock market, to actively managed funds.

Institutional investors have important responsibilities, and this can create a dilemma: on the one hand, they are expected to speak out against corporate management policies and decisions that are deemed unacceptable environmentally, ethically or financially. But public opposition to the management could well adversely affect share price. Institutions therefore have a conflict between their responsibilities as major shareholders and their investment role as managers seeking to outperform the markets.

Successive governments have promoted a 'share-owning democracy', particularly through privatisation programmes. However, individuals tend to hold small, undiversified portfolios, which exposes them to a greater degree of risk than from investing in a diversified investment portfolio. There are also a growing number of socially aware investors and a Social Stock Exchange was also recently launched in the United Kingdom.

Towards a European stock market?

The European Union is meant to be about removing barriers and providing easier access to capital markets. Until recently, this was still a pipe dream, with some 30 stock exchanges within the EU, most of which had different regulations. With the introduction of a single currency, there is strong pressure towards a single capital market. But does this mean a single European stock exchange, with one set of rules for share listing and trading?

Euronext is a pan-European stock exchange based in Paris with subsidiaries in France, Belgium, the Netherlands, Portugal and the United Kingdom. Euronext merged with NYSE Group in 2007 to form NYSE Euronext, arguably the first global stock exchange.

allocative efficiency
The most efficient way that a society can allocate its overall stock of resources

1.5 ARE FINANCIAL MARKETS EFFICIENT?

operating/technical efficiency
The most cost-effective way of producing an item, or organising a process

social efficiency
The extent to which a socio-economic system accords with prevailing social and ethical **standards**

pricing/information efficiency
The extent to which available information is impounded into the current set of share prices

If financial managers are to achieve corporate goals, they require well-developed financial markets where transfers of wealth from savers to borrowers are efficient in both pricing and operational cost.

Efficiency can mean many things. The *economist* talks about **allocative efficiency** – the extent to which resources are allocated to the most productive uses, thus satisfying society's needs to the maximum. The *engineer* talks about **operating** or **technical efficiency** – the extent to which a mechanism performs to maximum capability. The *sociologist* and the *political scientist* talk about **social efficiency** – the extent to which a mechanism conforms to accepted social and political values. The most important concept of efficiency for our purposes is **pricing** or **information efficiency**. This refers to the extent to which available information is built into the structure of share prices. If information relevant for assessing a company's future earnings prospects (including both past information and relevant information relating to future expected events) is widely and cheaply available, then this will be impounded into share prices by an efficient market. As a result, the market should allow all participants to compete on an equal basis in a so-called **fair game**.

fair game
A competitive process in which all participants have equal access to information and therefore similar chances of success

We often hear of the shares of a particular company being 'under-valued' or 'over-valued', the implication being that the stock market pricing mechanism has got it wrong and that analysts know better. *In an efficient stock market, current market prices fully reflect available information* and it is impossible to outperform the market consistently, except by luck.

Consider any major European stock market. On any given trading day, there are hundreds of analysts – representing the powerful financial institutions which dominate the market – closely tracking the daily performance of the share price of, say, Sky plc, the broadcasting company. They each receive at the same time new information from the company – a major acquisition, a labour dispute or a revised profits forecast. This information is rapidly evaluated and reflected in the share price by their decisions to buy or sell Sky shares. *The measure of efficiency is seen in the extent and speed with which the market reflects new information in the share price*.

arbitrage
The process whereby astute entrepreneurs identify and exploit opportunities to make profits by trading on differentials in price of the same item as between two locations or markets

The Law of One Price suggests that equivalent securities must be traded at the same price (excluding differences in transaction costs). If this is not the case, **arbitrage** opportunities arise whereby a trader can buy a security at a lower price and simultaneously sell it at a higher price, thereby making a profit without incurring any risk. In an efficient market, arbitrage activity will continue until the price differential is eliminated.

■ The efficient markets hypothesis (EMH)

Information can be classified as historical, current or forecast. Only current or historical information is certain in its effect on price. The more information that is available, the better the situation. Informed decisions are more likely to be correct, although the use of inside information to benefit from investment decisions (insider dealing) is illegal in the United Kingdom.

Company information is available both within and without the organisation. Those within the organisation will obviously be better informed about the state of the business. They have access to sensitive information about future investment projects, contracts under negotiation, forthcoming managerial changes, etc. The additional knowledge will vary according to a person's level of responsibility and place in the organisational hierarchy.

Outsider investors fall into two categories: individual investors and the institutions. Of these two groups, the institutions are the better informed, as they have greater access to senior management and may be represented on the board of directors.

Different amounts of financial information are available to different groups of people. There is unequal access to the information, called '**information asymmetry**', which may affect a company's share price. If you are one of the well-informed, this gives you the opportunity to keep one step ahead of the market. Otherwise, you may lose out. The share price reflects who knows what about the company. You should note, however, that in the United Kingdom, share dealings by company directors are tightly circumscribed; for example, they can only buy and sell at specific times, and details of all such trades must be publicly disclosed.

Market efficiency evolved from the notion of perfect competition, which assumes free and instantly available information, rational investors and no taxes or transaction costs. Of course, such conditions do not exist in capital markets, so just how do we assess their level of efficiency? Market efficiency, as reflected by the efficient markets hypothesis (EMH), may exist at three levels:

weak form
A weak-form efficient share market does not allow investors to look back at past share price movements and identify clear, repetitive patterns

1 The **weak form** of the EMH states that current share prices fully reflect *all information contained in past price movements*. If this level of efficiency holds, there is no value in

trying to predict future price movements by analysing trends in past price movements. Efficient stock market prices will fluctuate more or less randomly, any departure from randomness being too expensive to determine. Share prices are said to follow a **random walk**.

random walk theory
Share price movements are independent of each other so that tomorrow's share price cannot be predicted by looking at today's

2. The **semi-strong form** of the EMH states that current market prices reflect not only all past price movements, but also *all publicly available information*. In other words, there is no benefit in analysing existing information, such as that given in published accounts, dividend and profits announcements, appointment of a new chief executive or product breakthroughs, after the information has been released. The stock market has already captured this information in the current share price.

semi-strong form
A semi-strong efficient share market incorporates newly released information accurately and quickly into the structure of share prices

3. The **strong form** of the EMH states that current market prices reflect *all relevant information* – even if privately held. The market price reflects the 'true' or intrinsic value of the share based on the underlying future cash flows. The implications of such a level of market efficiency are clear: no one can consistently beat the market and earn abnormal returns. Few would go so far as to argue that stock markets are efficient at this level, although some investors are often good at predicting what is happening inside companies before the information is officially released.

strong form
In a strong-form efficient share market, all information including inside information is built into share prices

You will have noticed that as the EMH strengthens, the opportunities for profitable speculation reduce. Competition between well-informed investors drives share prices to reflect their intrinsic values.

The EMH and fundamental and technical analysis

intrinsic worth
The inherent or fundamental value of a company and its shares

Investment analysts who seek to determine the **intrinsic worth** of a share based on underlying information undertake **fundamental analysis**. The EMH implies that fundamental analysis will not identify under-priced shares unless the analyst can respond more quickly to new information than other investors, or has inside information.

fundamental analysis
Analysis of the fundamental determinants of company financial health and future performance prospects, such as endowment of resources, quality of management, product innovation record, etc.

Another approach is **technical analysis**, its advocates being labelled **chartists** - because of their reliance upon graphs and charts of price movements. Chartists are less interested in estimating the intrinsic value of shares, preferring to develop trading rules based on patterns in share price movement over time, or 'breakout' points of change. Charts are used to predict 'floors' and 'ceilings', marking the end of a share price trend. Figure 1.4 shows how charts are used to detect patterns of 'resistance' (for shares on the way up) and 'support' (for shares on the way down). This approach can often prove to be a 'self-fulfilling prophecy'. In the short term, if analysts predict that share prices will rise, investors will start to buy, thus creating a bull market and resulting in upward pressure on prices.

technical analysis
The detailed scrutiny of past time series of share price movements attempting to identify repetitive patterns

chartists
Analysts who use technical analysis

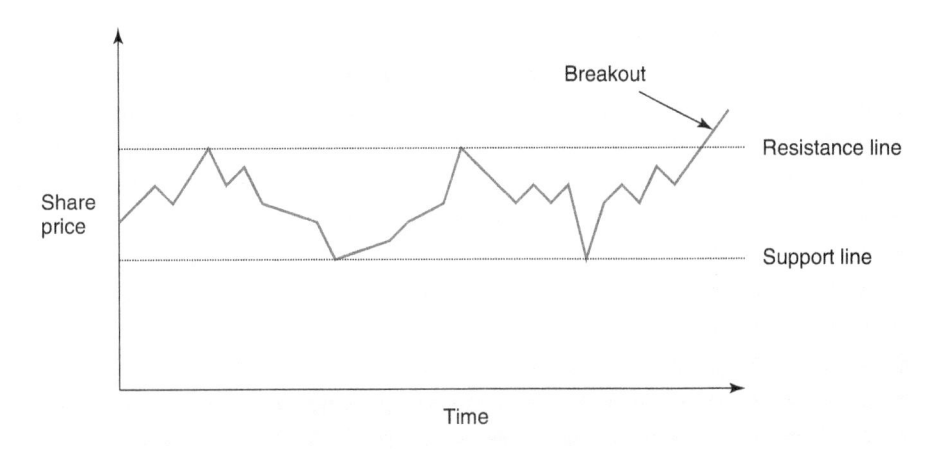

Figure 1.4 Chart showing possible breakout beyond resistance line

Even in its weak form, the EMH questions the value of technical analysis; future price changes cannot be predicted from past price changes. However, the fact that many analysts, using fundamental or technical analysis, make a comfortable living from their investment advice suggests that many investors find comfort in the advice given.

Considerable empirical tests on market efficiency have been conducted over many years. In the United States and the United Kingdom, at least until the 1987 stock market crash, the evidence broadly supported the semi-strong form of efficiency. More specifically, it suggests the following:

1 *There is little benefit in attempting to forecast future share price movements by analysing past price movements.* As the EMH seems to hold in its weak form, the value of charts must be questioned.
2 For quoted companies that are regularly traded on the stock market, analysts are *unlikely to find significantly over- or under-valued shares through studying publicly held information.* Studies indicate (e.g. Ball and Brown, 1968) that most of the information content contained in annual reports and profit announcements is reflected in share prices anything up to a year before release of the information, as investors make judgements based on press releases and other information during the year. However, analysts with specialist knowledge, paying careful attention to smaller, less well-traded shares, may be more successful. Equally, analysts able to respond to new information slightly ahead of the market may make further gains. The semi-strong form of the EMH seems to hold fairly well for most quoted shares.
3 The strong form of the EMH does not hold, so superior returns can be achieved by those with 'inside knowledge'. However, it is the duty of directors to act in the shareholders' best interests, and it is a criminal offence to engage in insider trading for personal gain. The fact that cases of **insider trading** have led to the conviction of senior executives shows that market prices do not fully reflect unpublished information.

insider trading
Dealing in shares using information not publicly available

Recent governments have encouraged greater market efficiency in several ways:

- Stock market deregulation and computerised dealing have enabled speedier adjustment of share prices in response to global information.
- Mergers and takeovers have been encouraged as ways of improving managerial efficiency. Poorly performing companies experience depressed share prices and become candidates for acquisition.
- Governments have seen privatisation of public utilities as a means of subjecting previously publicly owned organisations to market pressures.

How people trade in London

The Big Bang in 1986 gave the London Stock Exchange a huge advantage over most of its competitors. The result was strong growth in trading activity and international participation. But the Big Bang was only a partial revolution – automating the distribution of price information, but stopping short of automating the trading function itself.

Since 1986, global equity markets have become increasingly complex, with investors constantly looking for greater choice and lower costs. The London Stock Exchange made various attempts to retain its reputation as one of the most efficient stock markets. It took a major step by moving from a quote-based trading system, under which share dealing is conducted by telephone, to order-driven trading, termed SETS – the Stock Exchange Electronic Trading Service. The aim was to improve efficiency and reduce costs by automating trading and narrowing the spread between buying and selling prices. This it achieves by the automatic matching of orders placed electronically by prospective buyers and sellers.

The system works as follows. Instead of agreeing to trade at a price set by a market-maker, prospective buyers and sellers can:

(a) advertise through their broker the price at which they would like to deal, and wait for the market to move; or
(b) execute immediately at the best price available.

An investor wishing to buy or sell will contact his or her broker and agree a price at which the investor is willing to trade. The broker enters the order in the order book, which is then displayed to the entire market along with other orders. Once the order is executed, the trade is automatically reported to the Exchange. Time will tell whether it does lead to greater efficiency, but it is hoped that it will offer users more attractive, transparent and flexible trading opportunities.

Implications of market efficiency for corporate managers

In quoted companies, managers and investors are directly linked through stock market prices, corporate actions being rapidly reflected in share prices. This indicates the following:

1 Investors are not easily fooled by glossy financial reports or 'creative accounting' techniques, which boost corporate reported earnings but not underlying cash flows.
2 Corporate management should endeavour to make decisions that maximise shareholder wealth.
3 The timing of new issues of securities is not critical. Market prices are a 'fair' reflection of the information available and accurately reflect the degree of risk in shares.
4 Where corporate managers possess information not yet released to the market, there is an opportunity for influencing prices. For example, a company may retain information so that, in the event of an unwelcome takeover bid, it can offer positive signals such as an updated earnings forecast.

We return to the issue of market efficiency in discussing behavioural finance in Chapter 15.

Media – old and new – still move the markets

Newspapers report the news. They should never aim to be part of the story themselves. But in the stock market, that division is hard to sustain. A rigorous statistical study by academics at Warwick Business School has shown that we at the Financial Times regularly move the markets we write about. The research is part of a growing effort to understand how to interpret people's use of data, and the trails they leave on the internet through search engines and social media, to predict how they, and markets, will behave.

The study looked at 1,821 FT issues published in the six years from 2007 to 2012 – years that included a historic stock collapse and a dramatic rebound. The researchers counted all mentions of the 31 stocks that were part of the Dow Jones Industrial Average during this period and linked their mentions in the paper to their share price performance the next day. It showed a strong correlation – a mention in the morning's FT meant a greater volume of trading.

Interestingly, their study involved the printed edition when much of the news on which the FT reported would already have appeared online the previous day. So the news continued to have an impact on the next day. As there are now many sources that should move markets more swiftly than a printed newspaper, this also implies that it was the news itself, rather than any editorial choice about publishing stories, that moved prices.

How does the news about mentions in the FT, an externally driven event, affect these findings? It could go in one of two ways. As many stories are about share price moves that have just happened, the fact that the effect continues on the next day bears out that stock tend to have momentum once they have started moving.

But trading in reaction to news could also bear out the notion of market efficiency – that prices adjust to incorporate all known information and follow a 'random walk' in response to new news. The bubbles of the past two decades have shown that there is a lot wrong with the 'random walk' as a theory – but it is reassuring to confirm that traders do respond to news from the real world.

Source: Authers, J. (2014) It's true! The FT – and social media – really do move markets. *Financial Times*, 3 January. © The Financial Times Limited 2018. All rights reserved.

Self-assessment activity 1.4

Consider why a dealing rule like 'Always buy in early December' should be doomed to failure. This rule is designed to exploit the so-called 'end-of-year effect' claiming that share prices 'always' rise at the end of the year.

(Answer in Appendix A)

Self-assessment activity 1.5

Share prices of takeover targets invariably rise before the formal announcement of a takeover bid. What does this suggest for the EMH?

(Answer in Appendix A)

1.6 READING THE FINANCIAL PAGES

Corporate finance is changing so quickly that it is essential for students of finance to read the financial pages in newspapers on a regular basis. In this section, we explain the main information contained in the Share Service pages of the *Financial Times*, and in other newspapers.

The FTSE Index

Every day, shares move up or down with the release of information from within the firm, such as a revised profits forecast, or from an external source, such as the latest government statistics on inflation or unemployment. To indicate how the whole share market has performed, a share index is used, the most common being the **FTSE 100** – familiarly known as 'Footsie'. This index is based on the share prices of the 100 most valuable UK-quoted companies (sometimes termed 'blue chips'), mostly those with capitalisations above £3 billion, with each company weighted in proportion to its total market value. All the world's major stock markets have similar indices (for example, the Nikkei Index in Japan, the Dow Jones Index in the United States and the CAC 40 in France).

Every share index is constructed on a base date and base value. The FTSE 100 started with a base value of 1,000 at the end of 1983 and reached a peak of 6,930 at the end of 1999. By February 2008, the index stood at around 6,029. Despite the collapse in world markets in 2000, and the subsequent slow recovery in confidence (punctuated by a fresh collapse at the time of the Iraq war), this still represented an annual compound growth rate of about 8 per cent, well above both the rate of inflation and the yield on low-risk investments over the same period. Moreover, it includes only capital appreciation – inclusion of dividend income would raise this percentage to about a 12 per cent return. However, the difficulties arising from the fallout of the 2007 financial crisis caused the index to fall to 3,530 in March 2009, although it had recovered to pass 7,700 by January 2018.

The FTSE Actuaries Share Indices reveal share movements by sector. Their total gives the All-Share Index, representing the more frequently traded quoted companies.

Other FT indices

In recent years, the Stock Exchange has introduced several new indices, including:

- FTSE 350 provides the benchmark for investors who wish to focus on the more actively traded large and medium-sized UK companies, and covers 95 per cent of trading by value.
- FTSE Small Cap offers investors a daily measure of the performance of smaller companies.
- FTSE All-Share AIM covers companies on the Alternative Investment Market (AIM).

Using the published information

Financial managers and investors need to study the performance of the shares of their company, both against the appropriate sector as a whole and also against competitors within that sector. Two performance statistics that are most commonly reported are the **dividend yield** and **price:earnings ratio**.

Dividend yield

dividend yield
Gross dividend per ordinary share (including both interim and final payments) divided by current share price

Dividend yield is the gross, or pre-tax, dividends of companies and whole sectors in the last year as a percentage of their market value. Generally, sectors with low dividend yields are those with companies where the market expects high growth. Often, we observe that the dividend yield for leading shares, and also on the overall index, is well below the return investors could currently earn on a safe investment in Treasury Bills. However, following the financial crisis, interest rates have been at extremely low levels and dividend yields have been above treasury rates in recent years.

Price:earnings (P:E) ratio

The P:E ratio is a much-used performance indicator. It is the share price divided by the most recently reported earnings, or profit, per share. So, for the sector, it is the total market value of the companies represented in the sector divided by total sector earnings. The P:E ratio is a measure of the market's confidence in a particular company or industry. A high P:E usually indicates that investors have confidence that profits will grow strongly in future, perhaps after a short-term setback, although irregular events like a rumoured takeover bid will raise the P:E ratio if they lead to a higher share price.

Let us now turn to the performance of individual companies. Table 1.1 is an extract from the London Share Service pages in the *Financial Times*, giving the food and drug retailing sector. Transactions and prices of stocks are published continuously through SEAQ (the Stock Exchange Automatic Quotation).

Table 1.1 Share price information for the retail sector (selected companies)

	Price	Change	52 week high	52 week low	Yield	P/E	Average Vol.
Greggs	555.00	+19.00	565.00	388.40	3.64%	22.45	0.11m
Marks & Spencer	425.20	0.00	520.50	415.90	4.00%	13.20	3.86m
Morrisons	178.89	−4.51	312.30	178.70	7.09%	–	8.98m
Next	6,505.00	+40.00	6,907.90	4,514.96	1.99%	18.17	0.36m
Sainsbury	311.90	−3.30	428.00	301.50	5.48%	8.54	5.59m
Tesco	281.15	−3.15	386.40	278.50	5.19%	11.98	18.24m

FT *Source: Financial Times*, 1 July 2014. © Financial Times.

yield
Income from a security as a percentage of market price

price:earnings (P:E) ratio
The ratio of price per ordinary share to earnings (i.e. profit after tax) per share (EPS)

Tesco's closing share price of 281.15p is down 3.15p from the previous day's trading. The current price is 105p below its highest price over the past year. The **yield** of 5.19 per cent is the dividend yield, i.e. the dividend expressed as a proportion of the current share price. The **price:earnings (P:E) ratio** of 11.98 suggests that it would take 12 years for investors to get their money back in profit terms. Why should anyone be willing to wait that long? Remember that the calculation compares the last reported earnings per share with the current share price.

1.7 TAXATION AND FINANCIAL DECISIONS

Few financial decisions are immune from taxation considerations. *Corporate and personal taxation affects both the cash flows received by companies and the dividend income received by shareholders.* Consequently, financial managers need to understand the tax consequences of investment and financing decisions. Taxation may be important in three key areas of financial management:

1. *Raising finance.* There are clear tax benefits in raising finance by issuing debt rather than equity capital. Interest on borrowings attracts tax relief, thereby reducing the company's tax bill, while a dividend payment on equity capital does not attract tax relief. The tax system is thereby biased in favour of debt finance.
2. *Investment in fixed assets.* Spending on certain types of fixed asset attracts a form of tax relief termed **capital allowances**. This relief is intended to stimulate certain types of investment, such as in industrial plant and machinery. The taxation implications of an investment decision can be very important.
3. *Paying dividends.* Until 1973, in the United Kingdom, company profits were effectively taxed twice – first on the profits achieved and then again on those profits paid to shareholders in the form of dividends. Such a 'classical' tax system (which still exists in certain countries) is clearly biased in favour of retaining profits rather than paying out large dividends. The UK taxation system is more neutral, the same tax bill being paid (for companies making profits) regardless of the dividend policy.

capital allowances
Tax allowances for capital expenditure

Finally, the corporate financial manager should understand not only how taxation affects the company, but also how it affects the company's shareholders (**www.hmrc.gov.uk**). For example, some financial institutions (e.g. pension funds) pay no tax; some shareholders pay tax at 20 per cent, while others pay higher-rate income tax at 40 to 45 per cent. Therefore, due to variations in tax rates, some investors may prefer capital gains to dividends. In 2017 the dividend tax-free allowance was £2,000.

Self-assessment activity 1.6

Explain why it is important to consider the tax implications of financial and investment decisions.

(Answer in Appendix A)

SUMMARY

This chapter has introduced readers to the financial and tax environment within which financial and investment decisions take place and the way a stock exchange operates in our economy. We have also covered an overview of market efficiency and the extent to which capital markets are efficient. The effects of taxation and tax rates on financing and investing decisions was also briefly covered in this chapter.

Key points

- Financial markets consist of numerous specialist markets where financial transactions occur (e.g. the money market, capital market, foreign exchange market, derivatives markets).
- Financial institutions (e.g. banks, building societies, pension funds) provide a vital service by acting as financial intermediaries between savers and borrowers.
- Securitisation and disintermediation have permitted larger companies to create alternative, more flexible forms of finance.

- The London Stock Exchange operates two tiers: the Main Market for larger established companies, and the Alternative Investment Market which mainly caters for very young companies.
- An efficient capital market is one where investors are rational and share prices reflect all available information. The efficient markets hypothesis has been examined in its various forms (weak, semi-strong and strong). In all but the strong form, it seems to hold up reasonably well, but it is increasingly unable to explain 'special' circumstances.
- Taxation can play a key role in financial management, particularly in raising finance, investing in fixed assets and paying dividends.

Further reading

Boakes (2010) provides a clear explanation of how to read the financial pages. More extensive discussions on financial markets are available in Pilbeam (2010), Valdez and Molyneux (2012), Stoakes (2013), Oehmke and Zawadowski (2017), and Kirilenko, Kyle, Samadi and Tuzun (2017).

Two classic review articles on market efficiency were written by Fama (1991), while Rappaport (1987) examines the implications for managers. Tests of capital market efficiency are found in Keane (1983), Ross *et al.* (2010) and Copeland *et al.* (2013). Ball (2009) discusses what the global financial crisis may tell us about market efficiency, as do Choudhry and Jayasekera (2013). Discussion on short-termism in the City is found in Marsh (1990) and Ball (1991). Lim and Brooks (2011) survey the empirical literature on stock market efficiency in a thorough review article. Oehmke and Zawadowski (2017) provide evidence on credit default swaps as alternative trading venues, whereas Kirilenko, Kyle, Samadi and Tuzun (2017) explore issues in High Frequency Trading in US financial markets. Similarly, Díaz and Escribano (2017) cover issues in relation to different components of market liquidity.

Useful websites

www.moneysupermarket.com
www.moneynet.co.uk
www.fool.com

Appendix
FINANCIAL STATEMENT ANALYSIS

statement of financial position/balance sheet
A financial statement that lists the assets held by a business at a point in time and explains how they have been financed (i.e. by owners' capital and by third-party liabilities)

profit and loss account/ income statement
A financial statement that details for a specific time period the amount of revenue earned by a firm, the costs it has incurred, the resulting profit and how it has been distributed ('appropriated')

Most readers will previously have undertaken a module in accounting and be familiar with financial statements. This appendix provides a summary of the key elements in analysing financial statements and the main ratios involved in interpreting accounts.

Investors, whether shareholders or bank managers, ask three basic questions when they examine the accounts of a business:

- *Financial Position* – what is the current financial position, or state of affairs, of the business? This question is addressed by examining the **balance sheet**, also referred to as the **statement of financial position**.
- *Financial Performance* – how well has the business performed over the period of time we are interested in, for example, the past year? This question is addressed by looking at the **profit and loss account**, otherwise termed the **income statement**.
- *Future Prospects* – what are the likely future prospects of the business for which we are considering investment? A bank manager would probably request a cash flow forecast, showing the expected cash receipts and payments for the coming year.

cash flow statement
A financial statement that explains the reasons for cash inflows and outflows of a business and highlights the resulting change in cash position

However, published accounts are historical documents, and the shareholder will have to settle for the **cash flow statement** for the past year. Clues as to the expected future prospects may be found in the Chairman's Statement frequently published with the accounts.

We will examine the three financial statements, drawing on the abridged accounts of a fictitious company called *Foto-U*, a business specialising in offering instant photographs through photo booths in public places throughout Europe.

Statement of financial position

Imagine it is possible to take a financial snapshot of *Foto-U* on 31 March 2015, the end of its trading year. What we would see are the very things we find in the balance sheet. Looking at *Foto-U*'s statement of financial position in Table 1.2, we see three main categories – assets, creditors (or liabilities) and shareholders' equity. This statement demonstrates the 'accounting equation': the money invested in the business by shareholders and creditors is represented by the assets in which they have been invested.

Where the cash came from = *Where the cash went*
(sources of funds) *(uses of funds)*

Shareholders' funds of £78m + Liabilities (Creditors) £120m = Assets £198m

non-current assets
Assets that remain in the balance sheet for more than one accounting period

current assets
Assets that will leave the balance sheet in the next accounting period

intangible
Intangible assets cannot be seen or touched, e.g. the image and good reputation of a firm

tangible
Tangible assets can quite literally be seen touched, e.g. machinery and buildings

net book value
The original cost of buying an asset less accumulated depreciation charges to date

net current assets
Current assets less current liabilities

shareholders' equity
The value of the owners' stake in the business – identically equal to net assets, or equity

Generally Accepted Accounting Principles (GAAP)
The set of legal regulations and accounting standards that dictate 'best practice' in constructing company accounts

The more permanent assets (typically those with a life beyond a year) are termed **non-current assets** while the less permanent are termed **current assets**. For *Foto-U*, **intangible** non-current assets refer to patents and goodwill, the latter arising from acquiring another company and paying more for it than the balance sheet value of its underlying assets. **Tangible** non-current assets include land and buildings, photo booths, plant and machinery, vehicles, and fixtures and fittings. Their values are not stated at what they could be sold for, but at their **net book value** – what they originally cost less an estimate of the extent to which they have depreciated in value with use or age.

Current assets represent the less permanent items (typically less than a year) the business owns at the statement of financial position date. Our snapshot for *Foto-U* captures three items – inventories (also termed stocks), receivables (also termed debtors) and cash and cash equivalents. Unlike non-current assets, these items are continuously changing (or 'turning over') as trading takes place. Trade creditors and bank overdraft, where the amount has to be settled within one year, are deducted from the current assets to give the **net current assets** figure, commonly termed **working capital**. This is the amount of money likely to be turned into cash over the coming weeks. Creditors to be paid after more than a year (non-current liabilities) are typically in the form of medium/long-term loans. Finally, **shareholders' equity** represent the capital originally paid in by shareholders plus any reserves created since then. The most common reserve will be the profit retained in the business rather than paid to the shareholders as dividends.

Does the statement of financial position show the worth of the business?

Although the shareholders' equity for *Foto-U* of £78 million is the difference between what it *owns*, in the form of various assets, and what it *owes* to third parties, it would not be correct to say that this is what their investment is worth. The market value for the company is based on what investors are willing to pay for it. But the assets and liabilities are valued according to **Generally Accepted Accounting Principles (GAAP)**. We cannot explore them all here, but one principle is that

Table 1.2 *Foto-U* plc

Statement of Financial Position as at 31 March 2017

	2017 £m	2016 £m
Non-current assets		
Intangible assets	15	10
Tangible assets	117	92
	132	102
Current assets		
Inventories	25	24
Receivables	29	25
Cash and cash equivalents	12	5
	66	54
Total assets	198	156
Current liabilities		
Payables*	60	62
Non-current liabilities		
Borrowings	60	23
Total liabilities	120	85
Net assets	78	71
Shareholders' equity		
Called-up share capital	2	2
Reserves	76	69
Total shareholders' equity	78	71
*The payables figures include trade creditors	40	42

Income Statement for the year ended 31 March 2017

	2017	2016
Turnover – continuing operations	200	190
Cost of sales (including depreciation of £27m)	(157)	(160)
Gross profit	43	30
Administration expenses	(21)	(20)
Operating profit (Earnings before interest and taxes)	22	10
Interest payable	(2)	(2)
Profit before taxation	20	8
Tax on profit	(6)	(4)
Profit after tax attributable to shareholders	14	4

Cash Flow Statement for the year ended 31 March 2017

	2017	2016
Net cash inflow from operations	42	46
Servicing of finance	(2)	(2)
Taxation	(6)	(4)
Capital expenditure	(57)	(33)
Dividends paid	(7)	(3)
Financing	37	2
Increase in cash in the year	7	6

Other data: *Foto-U* has 200 million shares in issue.
Share price at 31 March 2017 is 120p (50p for 2016).
Dividends declared and paid are £7 million (£3 million last year)

assets are usually valued at their historical cost less a provision for such things as depreciation, in the case of non-current assets, and bad or doubtful debts, in the case of debtors. The key difference is that book values, based on GAAP, are backward-looking, while market values are forward-looking, based on expected future profits and cash flows.

To get some idea of the difference between the market and book values of the shareholders' funds, we can look at the share price listed on the Stock Exchange on the balance sheet date. For *Foto-U*, the share price at the balance sheet date was 120p. There are 200 million issued shares, so the **market capitalisation** is:

(200 million shares × 120p a share) = £240 million

> **market capitalisation**
> The market value of a firm's equity, i.e. number of ordinary shares issued times market price

Comparing the market value with the book value for shareholders' equity, we find a ratio of approximately 3:1 (£240m/£78m). We should not be surprised to find that the market value is so much higher. Successful businesses are much more than a collection of assets less liabilities. They include creative people, successful trading strategies, profitable brands and much more. Generally, we can say that the greater the market-to-book value ratio, the more successful the business.

■ The income statement or profit and loss account

To gain an impression of how well *Foto-U* has performed over the past year, we need to turn to the profit and loss account or income statement. This shows the sales income less the costs of trading. Shareholders are primarily interested in the **profit after tax (PAT)** available for distribution to them in the form of dividends. *Foto-U* has made a PAT of £14 million.

> **profit after tax (PAT)**
> Profit available to pay dividends to shareholders after tax has been paid

Investors also want to know how much profit (or earnings) has been made from its trading, before the cost of financing is deducted. **Earnings before interest and taxes (EBIT)** for *Foto-U* is:

> **earnings before interest and taxes (EBIT)**
> Earnings (i.e. profits) before interest and taxation

EBIT = total revenues − operating costs (including depreciation)
     = £200m − £178m
     = £22m

This is also termed **operating profit**.

> **operating profit**
> Revenues less total operating costs, both variable and fixed – as distinct from financial costs such as interest payments

Profit is not the sole consideration for investors. They are perhaps more interested in how much cash has been created through successful trading. This can be estimated by adding back the depreciation (a non-cash cost) previously deducted in calculating EBIT. This is termed **earnings before interest, taxes, depreciation and amortisation (EBITDA)** (amortisation is just a fancy name for depreciating intangible assets). For our company, this is:

> **earnings before interest, tax, depreciation & amortisation (EBITDA)**
> A rough measure of operating cash flow, effectively, operating profit with depreciation added back. It differs from the 'Net Cash Inflow from Operating Activities' shown in cash flow statements due to working capital movements

EBITDA = EBIT + Depreciation
       = £22m + £27m
       = £49m

■ The cash flow statement

The third financial statement in a published set of accounts is the cash flow statement. This statement is valuable because it reveals the main sources of cash and how it has been applied. For *Foto-U*, the main two sources of cash during the year are additional finance raised from new loans and net cash from operations (basically, the EBITDA referred to above plus a few other adjustments for non-cash items). The main applications of this cash generated from trading are investment in capital expenditure, and dividends. The final line on this statement shows that, during the year, cash and cash equivalent has increased by £7 million.

A financial health check using ratios

Accountants and bank managers have formulated dozens of financial ratios to help diagnose the financial health of the business, its position, performance and prospects. We shall restrict our focus to those key financial ratios that every finance manager and investor should be acquainted with. Some of the most widely used financial ratios are summarised in Table 1.3 and discussed briefly in this section.

Table 1.3 *Foto-U* key ratios

Ratio	Form	2017	2016
Profitability			
Gross profit margin	%	21.5	15.8
Net profit margin	%	11.0	5.3
Return on total assets (ROTA)	%	11.1	6.4
Activity ratios			
Net asset turnover	times	1.01	1.22
Debtors	days	53	48
Stock	days	58	54
Supplier credit period	days	93	96
Liquidity and financing ratios			
Current ratio	times	1.1	0.9
Quick (acid test) ratio	times	0.7	0.5
Gearing	%	43.5	24.5
Interest cover	times	11	5
Investor ratios			
Return on shareholders' funds	%	17.9	5.6
Dividend per share	pence	3.5	1.5
Earnings per share	pence	7	2
Dividend cover	times	2	1.3
Price:earnings	times	17.1	25
Dividend yield	%	2.9	3

Profitability ratios

To assess the performance of *Foto-U*, we study a number of profitability ratios.

Profit margin

This ratio shows how much profit is generated from every £ of sales. It can be considered in the form of a percentage at both the gross and net profit levels.

Gross profit margin

$$\frac{\text{Gross profit}}{\text{Sales}} \times 100 = \frac{43}{200} \times 100$$
$$= 21.5\% \quad (15.8\% \text{ last year})$$

Net profit margin

$$\frac{\text{EBIT}}{\text{Sales}} \times 100 = \frac{22}{200} \times 100$$
$$= 11\% \quad (5.3\% \text{ last year})$$

(EBIT is earnings before interest and tax, i.e. operating profit.)

Return on total assets (ROTA)

This ratio, also termed the primary ratio, examines the rate of profit the business makes on the capital invested in it. *Foto-U* has total assets of £198 million.

$$\text{ROTA} = \frac{\text{EBIT}}{\text{Total assets}} \times 100 = \frac{22}{198} \times 100$$

$$= 11.1\% \quad (6.4\% \text{ last year})$$

Activity ratios

Here we examine how efficiently *Foto-U* manages its assets in terms of the level of sales obtained from the assets invested.

Asset turnover

$$\frac{\text{Sales}}{\text{Total Sales}} = \frac{200}{198}$$

$$= 1.01 \text{ times} \quad (1.22 \text{ last year})$$

This can also be expressed in terms of each type of asset, but here, we usually express it in terms of days. For example, the average number of days it takes for debtors to pay is given by debtor days.

Debtor days

$$\frac{\text{Receivables}}{\text{Credit sales}} \times 365 = \frac{29}{200} \times 365$$

$$= 53 \text{ days} \quad (48 \text{ days last year})$$

Note also that we have used the asset figure at the year-end. A more accurate picture is given by finding the average asset value based on the values at the start and end of the year.

Similar calculations can be made for stock and creditors, but with one important difference. Stock and trade creditors are valued in the statement of financial position at original cost, so instead of using sales, we use cost of sales, i.e. what it cost the firm to build these stocks.

Stockholding period

$$\frac{\text{Inventory}}{\text{Cost of sales}} \times 365 = \frac{25}{157} \times 365$$

$$= 58 \text{ days} \quad (54 \text{ days last year})$$

Supplier credit days

$$\frac{\text{Trade payables}}{\text{Cost of sales}} \times 365 = \frac{40}{157} \times 365$$

$$= 93 \text{ days} \quad (96 \text{ days last year})$$

It is preferable to use purchases rather than cost of sales, although this figure is not always available.

Liquidity and financing ratios

To assess whether the company is able to meet its financial obligations as they fall due, we need to compare short-term assets with short-term creditors. Two such ratios are commonly employed.

Current ratio

$$\frac{\text{Current assets}}{\text{Current liabilities}} = \frac{66}{60}$$

$$= 1.1 \text{ times} \quad (0.9 \text{ times last year})$$

Acid-test ratio (quick assets)
For most firms, it is not easy to convert stock into cash with any great speed. The acid-test ratio (quick assets) is a more prudent liquidity ratio which excludes stock entirely.

$$\frac{\text{Current assets} - \text{stock}}{\text{Current liabilities}} = \frac{60 - 25}{60}$$

$$= 0.7 \text{ times } (0.5 \text{ times last year})$$

As a general rule of thumb, we would typically expect the current ratio to be 2 and the quick assets to match creditors (i.e. a quick ratio of 1). However, this guide may differ from industry to industry depending on the trade credit periods granted to customers and claimed from suppliers.

Gearing ratio
A rather different question asks how the capital employed in the business is financed. The gearing ratio shows the proportion of capital employed funded by long-term borrowings.

$$\frac{\text{Long-term borrowings}}{\text{Debt} + \text{Equity capital}} \times 100 = \frac{60}{138} \times 100$$

$$= 43.5\% \ (24.5\% \text{ last year})$$

An equally acceptable way of expressing the gearing ratio is by the Debt/Equity ratio.

$$\frac{\text{Long-term borrowings}}{\text{Shareholders' equity}} = \frac{60}{78} = 0.77{:}1$$

Interest cover
Another way of considering gearing is to look to the profit and loss account by assessing the degree of profits cover the firm has to meet its interest payments.

$$\frac{\text{Earnings before interest and taxes}}{\text{Interest payable}} = \frac{22}{2}$$

$$= 11 \text{ times (5 times last year)}$$

An interest cover of 11 times is very safe. But were it to fall to, say, below three or four, concern may arise that taxation and dividends cannot be paid.

Investor ratios
Shareholders are more interested in the return they obtain on *their* investment rather than the return the company makes on the total business.

Return on shareholders' funds (return on equity)
This indicates how profitable the company has been for its shareholders.

$$\frac{\text{Earnings after tax and preference dividends}}{\text{Shareholders' equity}} \times 100 = \frac{14}{78} \times 100$$

$$= 17.9\% \quad (5.6\% \text{ last year})$$

Shareholders will also be interested in the earnings per share (what dividend could be paid) and dividend per share (what dividend is paid) for the year.

Earnings per share (EPS)

$$\frac{\text{Earnings after tax and preference dividends}}{\text{Number of ordinary shares in issue}} = \frac{14}{200}$$

$$= 7 \text{ pence per share}$$
$$(2 \text{ pence last year})$$

In practice, the EPS calculation is usually more complex than this, but the notes to the accounts will explain the calculation.

Dividend per share (DPS)

$$\frac{\text{Total ordinary dividend}}{\text{Number of ordinary shares in issue}} = \frac{7}{200}$$

$$= 3.5 \text{ pence per share (1.5 pence last year)}$$

Dividend cover

This links the DPS and the EPS to indicate how many times the dividend *could* be paid, and, hence, how safe it is, in terms of exposure to a fall in EPS.

$$\frac{\text{Earnings per share}}{\text{Dividend per share}} = \frac{7}{3.5}$$

$$= 2 \text{ times (1.3 times last year)}$$

The final two ratios relate earnings and dividends to stock market performance as reflected in the current share price. If the current share price for *Foto-U* is 120p, we can calculate the price:earnings ratio and dividend yield.

Price/earnings ratio (P/E)

$$\frac{\text{Current share price}}{\text{Earnings per share}} = \frac{120}{7}$$

$$= 17.1 \text{ times (25 time last year)}$$

The share price, of course, is based on investors' expectations of *future* profits. A high P:E ratio indicates that investors expect future profits to grow – the higher the P:E, the greater the profit growth expectation.

Dividend yield

$$\frac{\text{Dividend per share (p)}}{\text{Share price (p)}} \times 100 = \frac{3.5}{120} \times 100$$

$$= 2.9\% \text{ (3\% last year)}$$

■ Interpretation of the accounts and ratios

The financial manager or investor needs to put together all the clues suggested by ratio analysis and reading the accounts to gain insights into the financial position, performance and prospects of the company. This will probably involve looking at the trend of financial indicators, not simply comparison with the previous year, together with comparison with industry and competitor data. It certainly requires a reasonable grasp of the business, its objectives and strategies. Table 1.4 offers a brief report to senior management of *Foto-U* by the finance manager on the company's published accounts.

Table 1.4 *Foto-U* annual corporate performance report

To: Senior Management of *Foto-U*
From: Finance Manager

Subject: **Annual corporate performance**
30 April 2017

I have reviewed the published accounts for the past year to establish how successful *Foto-U* was in financial terms.

Profitability. The Return on Total Assets has improved over the year from 6.4% to 11.1%. This is a significant improvement and well above the risk-free return we would expect from investing in say building society deposits, but we need also to compare the return against that achieved by our competitors. ROTA is a combination of two subsidiary ratios – net profit margin and asset turnover:

	ROTA	=	Net profit margin	×	Asset turnover
2016	6.4%	=	5.3%	×	1.22 times
2017	11.1%	=	11%	×	1.01 times

Both the gross and net profit margins have improved significantly as a result of the £10 million growth in sales over the year without any increase in costs. However, this growth has come at the expense of a poorer utilisation of our assets, as reflected in the significant decline in asset turnover. This is mainly attributable to a major capital expenditure programme during the year, the benefits of which will not be fully experienced for at least another year. A further factor is the increase in working capital. Last year, we actually managed to have negative working capital (i.e. our trade creditors and overdraft financed more than our current assets). This year, there has been a slight deterioration in all elements of working capital:

- We take five more days to collect cash from customers
- Stockholding period has increased by four days
- We pay suppliers a little quicker.

Liquidity. Our current and quick asset ratios are both well below the typical level for the industry of 1.8 and 1.0 respectively. However, this is largely due to the fact that our suppliers have been willing to grant us extended credit periods of about three months. Realistically, we cannot expect this to continue. Were they to demand payment within, say, 45 days, it is difficult to see where we would be able to find the cash. It is not good financial management for us to rely on the generous credit of suppliers over whom we have no control, and we need to address this issue urgently. Linked to this, we have just raised a large medium-term loan in order to fund our capital expenditure in the coming year. Our gearing ratio has now nearly doubled and we will have to find cash both for additional interest payments and, eventually, the loan repayments. Unless the new investment very rapidly produces higher profits and cashflow, I am concerned that we could be in serious financial difficulty, despite the strong level of profits. Perhaps it is time to consider asking shareholders to invest more capital in the business, or to reduce dividend payments.

Investment attractiveness. The company's share price has progressed from 50 pence to 120 pence over the year. No doubt this is due to the growth in sales, profits and dividends in the year. Many of the investment performance indicators have improved, particularly earnings per share and return on shareholders' funds, the latter looking much healthier at nearly 18%. However, the price:earnings ratio has slipped a little, suggesting that investors do not expect the company's profits and share price to continue to grow at quite the same rate as this year.

In summary, *Foto-U* has improved its performance over the past year, but there remain concerns regarding its liquidity. Management is urged to give urgent attention to this matter.

QUESTIONS

Questions with a coloured number have solutions in Appendix B on page 501.

1. When a company seeks a listing for its shares on a stock exchange, it usually recruits the assistance of an investment bank.
   (a) Explain the role of an investment bank in a listing operation with respect to the various matters on which its advice will be sought by a company.
   (b) Identify the conflicts which might arise if the investment bank were part of a group providing a wide range of financial services.

   (CIMA)

2. (a) Briefly outline the major functions performed by the capital market and explain the importance of each function for corporate financial management. How does the existence of a well-functioning capital market assist the financial management function?
   (b) Describe the efficient markets hypothesis and explain the differences between the three forms of the hypothesis which have been distinguished.
   (c) Company A has 2 million shares in issue and Company B 6 million. On day 1 the market value per share is £2 for A and £3 for B. On day 2, the management of B decides, at a private meeting, to make a cash takeover bid for A at a price of £3.00 per share. The takeover will produce large operating savings with a value of £3.2 million. On day 4, B publicly announces an unconditional offer to purchase all shares of A at a price of £3.00 per share with settlement on day 15. Details of the large savings are not announced and are not public knowledge. On day 10, B announces details of the savings which will be derived from the takeover.

   Required
   Ignoring tax and the time-value of money between days 1 and 15, and assuming the details given are the only factors having an impact on the share prices of A and B, determine the day 2, day 4 and day 10 share prices of A and B if the market is:

   1. semi-strong form efficient, and
   2. strong form efficient.

   in each of the following separate circumstances:

   (i) the purchase consideration is cash as specified above, and
   (ii) the purchase consideration, decided upon on day 2 and publicly announced on day 4, is one newly issued share of B for each share of A.

   (ACCA)

3. You are an accountant with a practice that includes a large proportion of individual clients, who often ask for information about traded investments. You have extracted the following data from a leading financial newspaper.

   (i)
Stock	Price	P:E ratio	Dividend yield (% gross)
Buntam plc	160p	20	5
Zellus plc	270p	15	3.33

   (ii) Earnings and dividend data for Crazy Games plc are given below:

	2013	2014	2015	2016	2017
EPS	5p	6p	7p	10p	12p
Div. per share (gross)	3p	3p	3.5p	5p	5.5p

   The estimated before tax return on equity required by investors in Crazy Games plc is 20 per cent.

Required

Draft a report for circulation to your private clients which explains:
- **(a)** the factors to be taken into account (including risks and returns) when considering the purchase of different types of traded investments;
- **(b)** the role of financial intermediaries, and their usefulness to the private investor;
- **(c)** the meaning and the relevance to the investor of each of the following:
    - **(i)** Gross dividend (pence per share)
    - **(ii)** EPS
    - **(iii)** Dividend cover

Your answer should include calculation of, and comment upon, the gross dividends, EPS and dividend cover for Buntam plc and Zellus plc, based on the information given above.

(ACCA)

4 Beta plc has been trading for 12 years and during this period has achieved a good profit record. To date, the company has not been listed on a recognised stock exchange. However, Beta plc has recently appointed a new chairman and managing director who are considering whether or not the company should obtain a full stock exchange listing.

Required
- **(a)** What are the advantages and disadvantages which may accrue to the company and its shareholders of obtaining a full stock exchange listing?
- **(b)** What factors should be taken into account when attempting to set an issue price for new equity shares in the company, assuming it is to be floated on a stock exchange?

(Certified Diploma)

5 Collingham plc produces electronic measuring instruments for medical research. It has recorded strong and consistent growth during the past 10 years since its present team of managers bought it out from a large multinational corporation. They are now contemplating obtaining a stock market listing.

Collingham's accounting statements for the last financial year are summarised below. Fixed assets (i.e. non-current assets), including freehold land and premises, are shown at historic cost net of depreciation. The debenture is redeemable in two years, although early redemption without penalty is permissible.

Profit and Loss Account (Income Statement) for the year ended 31 December 2018 (£m)

Turnover	80.0
Cost of sales	(70.0)
Operating profit	10.0
Interest charges	(3.0)
Pre-tax profit	7.0
Corporation Tax (after capital allowances)	(1.0)
Profits attributable to ordinary shareholders	6.0
Dividends	(0.5)
Retained earnings	5.5

Statement of Financial Position as at 31 December 2018 (£m)

Assets employed		
Fixed: Land and premises	10.0	
Machinery	20.0	30.0
Current: Stocks	10.0	
Debtors	10.0	
Cash	3.0	23.0
Current liabilities: Trade creditors	(15.0)	

Bank overdraft	(5.0)	(20.0)
Net current assets		3.0
Total assets less current liabilities		33.0
14% Debentures		(5.0)
Net assets		28.0
Financed by:		
Issued share capital (par value 50p):		
Voting shares		2.0
Non-voting 'A' shares		2.0
Profit and Loss Account		24.0
Shareholders' funds		28.0

The following information is also available regarding key financial indicators for Collingham's industry.

Return on (long-term) capital employed	22% (pre-tax)
Return on equity	14% (post-tax)
Operating profit margin	10%
Current ratio	1.8:1
Acid test	1.1:1
Gearing (total debt/equity)	18%
Interest cover	5.2
Dividend cover	2.6
P:E ratio	13:1

Required

(a) Briefly explain why companies like Collingham seek stock market listings.
(b) Discuss the performance and financial health of Collingham in relation to that of the industry as a whole.
(c) In what ways would you advise Collingham:
   (i) to restructure its balance sheet prior to flotation?
   (ii) to change its financial policy following flotation?

Practical assignment

Select two companies from one sector in the Financial Times share information service. Analyse the share price and other data provided and compare this with the FT All-Share Index data for the sector. Suggest why the P:E ratios for the companies differ.

2

Present values, and bond and share valuation

The fatal attraction of profits and share prices

It is easy to put a value on a company. All you need to do is foresee the future. If not, it is impossible. And that is where the problems start. The value of a company is tied up in the future. It is worth the total cash flows that it produces in the future, discounted for the time value of money – the fact that a dollar today is worth much more than a dollar in 10 years.

The mathematics is not that difficult if you know the company's future cash flows, the cost of its equity and debt, and the relative proportions of debt and equity into the future. The problem is that all these four variables are unknown at the time you have to decide how much a company is worth.

This is why the art of valuing stocks is so imprecise, allowing investors to win and lose so much on the stock market. It is also why astute corporate financiers can get away with so much. With 'true' valuation unknowable, it is far easier to prompt buyers to pay ridiculous prices in acquisitions, or for managers to take damaging decisions that seem to enhance value in the short term.

FT *Source:* Authers, J. (2010) The fatal attraction of profits and share prices. *Financial Times*, 30 October. © The Financial Times Limited 2018. All rights reserved.

Learning objectives

Having completed this chapter, you should have a sound grasp of the time-value of money and discounted cash flow concepts. In particular, you should understand the following:

- The time-value of money.
- The financial arithmetic underlying compound interest and discounting.
- Present value formulae for single amounts, annuities and perpetuities.
- The valuation of bonds and shares.

Skills developed in discounted cash-flow analysis, using both formulae and tables, will help enormously in subsequent chapters.

2.1 INTRODUCTION

Managers are expected to make sound long-term decisions and to manage resources in the best interests of the owners. To assess whether investment ideas are wealth-creating, we need to have a clear understanding of cash flow and the time-value of money. Capital investment decisions, security and bond value analyses, financial structure decisions, lease vs. buy decisions and the tricky question of the required rate of return can be addressed only when you understand exactly what the old expression 'time is money' really means.

In this chapter, we will consider the measurement of wealth and the fundamental role it plays in the decision-making process; the time-value of money, which underlies the discounted cash flow concept; and the net present value approach for analysing investment decisions. The time value of money is one of the most important concepts in Corporate Finance and will be utilised throughout this text. This chapter explains issues in relation to the timings of cash flows and its impact on investing and financing decisions for investors and organisations.

2.2 MEASURING WEALTH

'Cash is King' seems to be the message for businesses today. Spectacular business collapses in recent years demonstrate that reliance on sales, profits or earnings per share as measures of performance can be dangerous.

Businesses go 'bust' because they run out of the cash required to fulfil their financial obligations. Of course, there are always reasons why this happens – recession, an overambitious investment programme, rapid growth without adequate long-term finance – but, basically, corporate survival and success come down to cash flow and value creation.

Boo.com, the internet fashion retailer, thought it had a promising future at the start of 2000. It had raised $135 million to set up the new business and invest in marketing to break into the competitive fashion retail sector. But less than six months later, it had virtually run out of cash and was forced into liquidation. The Chief Executive confessed: 'My mistake has been not to have an accountant who was a strong financial controller.'

The assumed objective of the firm is to create as much wealth as possible for its shareholders. A successful business is one that creates value for its owners. Wealth is created when the market value of the outputs exceeds the market value of the inputs, i.e. the benefits are greater than the costs. Expressed mathematically:

$$V_j = B_j - C_j$$

The value (V_j) created by decision j is the difference between the benefits (B_j) and the costs (C_j) attributable to the decision. This leads to an obvious decision rule: accept only those investment or financing proposals that enhance the wealth of shareholders, i.e. accept if $B_j - C_j > 0$.

time-value of money
Money received in the future is usually worth less than today because it could be invested to earn interest over this period

Nothing could be simpler in concept – the problems emerge only when we probe more deeply into how the benefits and costs are measured and evaluated. One obvious problem is that benefits and costs usually occur at different times and over a number of years. This leads us to consider the **time-value of money**.

2.3 TIME-VALUE OF MONEY

An important principle in financial management is that the value of money depends on *when the cash flow occurs* – £100 *now* is worth more than £100 at some *future* time. There are a number of reasons for this:

1 *Risk*. One hundred pound now is certain, whereas £100 receivable next year is less certain. This 'bird-in-the-hand' principle affects many aspects of financial management that will be covered in later chapters.

2 *Inflation.* Under inflationary conditions, the value of money, in terms of its purchasing power over goods and services, declines.
3 *Personal consumption preference.* Most of us have a strong preference for immediate rather than delayed consumption.

More fundamental than any of the above, however, is the time-value of money. Money – like any other desirable commodity – has a price. If you own money, you can 'rent' it to someone else, say a banker, and earn interest. A business which carries unnecessarily high cash balances incurs an **opportunity cost** – the lost opportunity to earn money by investing it to earn a higher return. The investor's overall return, which reflects the time-value of money, therefore comprises:

opportunity cost
The value forgone by opting for a particular course of action

(a) the risk-free rate of return rewarding investors for forgoing immediate consumption, plus
(b) compensation for risk and loss of purchasing power.

Self-assessment activity 2.1

Imagine you went to your bank manager asking for a £50,000 loan, for five years, to start up a burger bar under a McDonald's franchise. Which of the considerations in the previous paragraph would the bank manager consider?

(Answer in Appendix A)

Before proceeding further, we need to understand the essential financial arithmetic for the time-value of money. Einstein once said 'compound interest is the 8th wonder of the world. He who understands it, earns it. He who doesn't, pays it.' The next section of the chapter considers compound interest and associated ideas.

2.4 FINANCIAL ARITHMETIC FOR CAPITAL GROWTH

■ Simple and compound interest

The future value (FV) of a sum of money invested at a given annual rate of interest will depend on whether the interest is paid only on the original investment (simple interest), or whether it is calculated on the original investment plus accrued interest (compound interest). Suppose you win £1,000 on the National Lottery and decide to invest it at 10 per cent for five years' simple interest. (In the present economic climate an interest rate of just 1 per cent is more realistic but this example is purely to illustrate the principle). The future value will be the original £1,000 capital plus five years' interest of £100 a year, giving a total future value of £1,500.

compound interest
Interest paid on the sum which accumulates, i.e. the principal plus interest

With compound interest, the interest is paid on the original capital plus accrued interest, as shown in Table 2.1. The process of compounding provides a convenient way of adjusting for the time-value of money. An investment made now in the capital market of V_0 gives rise to a cash flow of $V_0(1 + i)^2$ after two years, and so on. In general, the

Table 2.1 Compound interest on £1,000 over five years (at 10%)

Year	Starting balance £	+	Interest £	=	Closing balance £
1	1,000		100		1,100
2	1,100		110		1,210
3	1,210		121		1,331
4	1,331		133		1,464
5	1,464		146		1,610

future value of V_0 invested today at a compound rate of interest of i per cent for n years will be:

$$FV_{(i,n)} = V_0(1 + i)^n$$

where $FV_{(i,n)}$ is the future value at time n, V_0 is the original sum invested, sometimes termed the principal (note that the 0 subscript refers to the time period, i.e. today), and i is the annual rate of interest.

Using this formula in the above example, we obtain the same future value as in Table 2.1.

$$FV_5 = £1{,}000(1 + 0.10)^5 = £1{,}610$$

Note that the effect of compound interest yields a higher value than simple interest, which yielded only £1,500.

More frequent compounding and annual percentage rates

annual percentage rate
The true annual interest rate charged by the lender which takes account of the timing of interest and principal payments

Unless otherwise stated, it is assumed that compounding or discounting is an annual process; cash payments of benefits arise either at the start or the end of the year. Frequently, however, the contractual payment period is less than one year. Building societies and government bonds pay interest semi-annually or quarterly. Interest charged on credit cards is applied monthly. To compare the true costs or benefits of such financial contracts, it is necessary to determine the **annual percentage rate** (APR), or effective annual interest rate, taking into account any costs such as one-off fees. In the United Kingdom, lenders are required to disclose the APR before the loan is finalised. Taking compounding to its limits, we can adopt a continuous discounting approach.*

Examples of more frequent compound interest

Returning to our earlier example of £1,000 invested for five years at 10 per cent compound interest, we now assume 5 per cent payable every six months.

After the first six months, the interest is £50, which is reinvested to give interest for the second half year of (£1,050 × 5%) = £52. The end-of-year value is therefore (£1,050 + £52) = £1,102. We can still use the compound interest formula, but with i as the six-monthly interest rate and n the six-monthly, rather than annual, interval:

After 1 year, $FV_1 = £1{,}000(1 + 0.05)^2$
$= £1{,}102$

After 5 years, $FV_5 = £1{,}000(1 + 0.05)^{10}$
$= £1{,}629$

Note that this value is higher than the £1,610 value based on the earlier annual interval calculation. In converting the annual compounding formula to another interest payment

---

*When the number of compounding periods each year approaches infinity, the future value is found by:

$$FV_n = V_0 e^{in}$$

where i is the annual interest rate, n is the number of years and e is the value of the exponential function. Using a scientific calculator, this is shown as 2.71828 (to five decimal places).

Using the same example as before:

$FV_4 = V_0 e^{in} = £1{,}000 e^{(0.1)5}$
$= £1{,}648.72$ (slightly more than compounding on a weekly basis)

frequency, the trick is simply to divide the annual rate of interest (i) and multiply the time (n) by the number of payments each year.

If, in the above example, interest is calculated at weekly intervals over five years, the future value will be:

$$FV_5 = £1,000\left(1 + \frac{0.10}{52}\right)^{52(5)} = £1,648$$

We calculate here the APRs based on a range of interest payment frequencies for a 22 per cent per annum loan. By charging compound interest on a daily basis, the effective annual rate is 24.6 per cent, some 2.6 per cent higher than on an annual basis.

Annually	$(1 + 0.022) - 1$	$= 0.22$ or 22%
Semi-annually	$\left(1 + \frac{0.22}{2}\right)^2 - 1$	$= 0.232$ or 23.2%
Monthly	$\left(1 + \frac{0.22}{12}\right)^{12} - 1$	$= 0.244$ or 24.4%
Daily	$\left(1 + \frac{0.22}{365}\right)^{365} - 1$	$= 0.246$ or 24.6%

2.5 PRESENT VALUE

present value
The current worth of future cash flows

discounting
The process of reducing cash flows to present values

An alternative way of assessing the worth of an investment is to invert the compounding process to give the **present value** of the future cash flows. This process is called **discounting**.

The time-value of money principle argues that, given the choice of £100 now or the same amount in one year's time, it is always preferable to take the £100 now because it could be invested over the next year at, say, a 10 per cent interest rate to produce £110 at the end of one year. If 10 per cent is the best available annual rate of interest, then one would be indifferent to (i.e. attach equal value to) receiving £100 now or £110 in one year's time. Expressed another way, the *present value* of £110 received one year hence is £100.

We obtained the present value (PV) simply by dividing the future cash flow by 1 plus the rate of interest, i, i.e.

$$PV = \frac{£110}{(1 + 0.10)} = \frac{£110}{(1.1)} = £100$$

Discounting is the process of adjusting future cash flows to their present values. It is, in effect, compounding in reverse.

Recall that earlier we specified the future value as:

$$FV_n = V_0(1 + i)^n$$

Dividing both sides by $(1 + i)^n$, we find the present value:

$$V_0 = \frac{FV_n}{(1 + i)^n}$$

which can be read as the present value of the future cash flow FV receivable in n years' time given a rate of interest i. This is the process of discounting future sums to their present values.

Let us apply the present value formula to compute the present value of £133 receivable three years hence, discounted at 10 per cent:

$$PV_{(10\%, 3\text{ yrs})} = \frac{£133}{(1 + 0.10)^3} = \frac{£133}{1.33} = £100$$

The message is: do not pay more than £100 today for an investment offering a certain return of £133 after three years, assuming a 10 per cent market rate of interest.

> **Calculator tip**
>
> Your calculator should have a power function key, usually x^y. Try the following steps for the previous example.
>
> | | |
> |---|---|
> | Input | 1.1 |
> | Press | x^y function key |
> | Input | 3 |
> | Press | = |
> | Display | 1.331 |
> | Press | 1/x |
> | Multiply | 133 |
> | Press | = |
> | Answer | 99.9 |

Self-assessment activity 2.2

Calculate the present value of £623 receivable in eight years' time plus £1,092 receivable eight years after that, assuming an interest rate of 7 per cent.

(Answer in Appendix A)

■ Discount tables

Much of the tedium of using formulae and power functions can be eased by using discount tables or computer-based spreadsheet packages. In the previous example, the discount factor for £1 for a 10 per cent discount rate in three years' time is:

$$\frac{1}{(1.10)^3} = \frac{1}{1.33} = 0.751$$

We call this the present value interest factor (PVIF) and express it as $\text{PVIF}_{(10\%, 3\text{yrs})}$ or $\text{PVIF}_{(10,3)}$.

Multiplying the cash flow of £133 by the discount factor yields the same result as before:

$$PV = £133 \times 0.751 = £100 \text{ (subject to rounding)}$$

annuity
A constant annual cash flow for a prescribed period of time

With a constant annual cash flow, termed an **annuity**, we can shorten the discounting operation. Thus, if £133 is to be received in each of the next three years, the present value is:

$$PV = £133 \times \text{PVIFA}_{(10\%, 3\text{ yrs})}$$
$$= £133 \times 2.4868 = £331$$

It is standard practice to write interest factors as: Interest factor (rate, period).

Examples:

$\text{PVIF}_{(8,10)}$ is the present value interest factor at 8 per cent for 10 years.
$\text{PVIFA}_{(10,4)}$ is the present value interest factor for an annuity at 10 per cent for four years.

Example of present values: Soldem Pathetic FC Ltd

Soldem Pathetic Football Club has recently been bought up by a wealthy businessman who intends to return the club to its former glory days. He also wants to pay a good dividend to the shareholders of the newly formed quoted company by making sound investments in quality players. One such player the manager would dearly like in his squad is Shane Moony, currently on the market for around £9 million. The chairman reckons that, quite apart from the extra income at the turnstiles from buying him, he could be sold for £11 million by the end of the year, given the way transfer prices are moving. Should he bid for Moony?

Assuming a 10 per cent rate of interest as the reward that the other shareholders demand for accepting the delayed payoff, the present value (PV) of £11 million receivable one year hence is:

$$PV = \text{discount factor} \times \text{future cash flow} = \frac{1}{1.10} \times £11 \text{ million}$$
$$= £10 \text{ million}$$

How much better off will the club be if it buys Moony? The answer is, in present value terms:

$$£10 \text{ million} - £9 \text{ million} = £1 \text{ million}$$

net present value
The present value of the future net benefits less the initial cost

We call this the **net present value** (NPV). The decision to buy the player makes economic sense; it promises to create wealth for the club and its shareholders, even excluding the likely additional gate receipts. Of course, Moony could break a leg in the very first game for his new club and never play again. In such an unfortunate situation, the club would achieve a negative NPV of £9 million, the initial cost. Alternatively, he could be insured against such injury, in which case there would be premiums to pay, resulting in a lower net present value.

Another way of looking at this issue is to ask whether the investment offers a return greater than could have been achieved by investing in financial, rather than human, assets. The return over one year from acquiring Moony's services is:

$$\text{Return} = \frac{\text{Profit}}{\text{Investment}} = \frac{£11m - £9m}{£9m} \times 100 = 22.2\%.$$

If the available rate of interest is 10 per cent, the investment in Moony is a considerably more rewarding prospect.

In the highly simplified example of Soldem Pathetic, we assumed that the future value was certain and the interest rate was known. Of course, a spectrum of interest rates is listed in the financial press. This variety of rates arises predominantly because of uncertainty surrounding the future and imperfections in the capital market. To simplify our understanding of the time-value of money concept, let us 'assume away' these realities. The lender knows with certainty the future returns arising from the proposal for which finance is sought, and can borrow or lend on a perfect capital market. The latter assumes the following:

1. Relevant information is freely available to all participants in the market.
2. No transaction costs or taxes are involved in using the capital market.
3. No participant (borrower or lender) can influence the market price for funds by the scale of its activities.
4. All participants can lend and borrow at the same rate of interest.

Under such conditions, the corporate treasurer of a major company like Shell can raise funds no more cheaply than the chairman of Soldem Pathetic. A single market rate of interest prevails. Borrowers and lenders will base time-related decisions on this unique market rate of interest. The impact of uncertainty will be discussed in later chapters; for now, these simplistic assumptions will help us to grasp the basics of financial arithmetic.

■ The effect of discounting

Figure 2.1 shows how the discounting process affects present values at different rates of interest between 0 and 20 per cent. The value of £1 decreases very significantly as the rate and period increase. Indeed, after 10 years, for an interest rate of 20 per cent, the present value of a cash flow is only a small fraction of its nominal value.

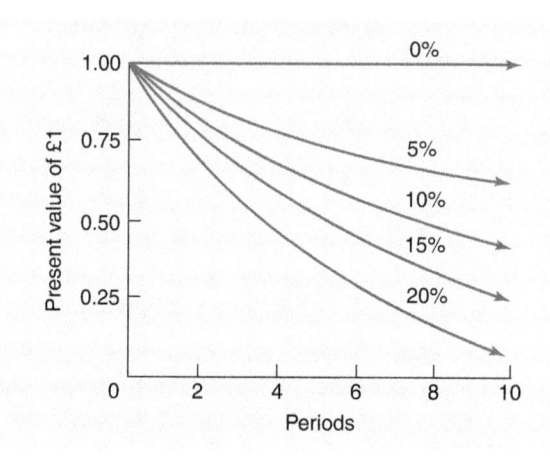

Figure 2.1 The relationship between present value of £1 and interest over time

Table 2.2 summarises the discount factors for three rates of interest. It is useful to develop a 'feel' for how money changes with time for these rates of interest. The 15 per cent discount rate is particularly useful, because this is a popular discount rate for evaluating capital projects. It also happens to be easy to remember: every five years the discounted value halves. Thus, with a 15 per cent discount rate, after five years the value of £1 is 50p, after 10 years 25p, etc.

Table 2.2 Present value of a single future sum

Year	10%	15%	20%
0	£1.00	£1.00	£1.00
5	0.60	0.50	0.40
10	0.40	0.25	0.16
15	0.24	0.12	0.06
20	0.15	0.06	0.03
25	0.09	0.03	0.01

Self-assessment activity 2.3

Your company is just about to sign a deal to purchase a fleet of lorries for £1 million. The payment terms are a £500,000 down payment and £500,000 at the end of five years. No one present has a calculator or discount tables to hand. If the cost of capital for the company is 15 per cent, what is the present value cost of the purchase?

(Answer in Appendix A)

2.6 PRESENT VALUE ARITHMETIC

We have seen that the present value of a future cash flow is found by multiplying the cash flow by the present value interest factor. The present value concept is not difficult to apply in practice. This section explains the various present value formulae, and illustrates how they can be applied to investment and financing problems. Throughout, we shall use the symbol X to denote annual cash flow in pound and i to denote the interest, or discount, rate (expressed as a percentage). Recall that PVIF is the present value interest factor and PVIFA is the PVIF for an annuity.

Present value

We know that the present value of X receivable in n years is calculated from the expression:

$$PV_{(i,n)} = \frac{X_n}{(1+i)^n}$$

$$= X \text{ times PVIF}_{(i,n)}$$

Example

Calculate the present value of £1,000 receivable in 10 years' time, assuming a discount rate of 14 per cent:

$$PVIF_{(14\%, 10 \text{ yrs})} = \frac{1}{(1.14)^{10}} = 0.26974$$

$$PV = £1,000 \times 0.26974 = £269.74$$

The present value of £1,000 receivable 10 years hence, discounted at 14 per cent, is thus £269.74.

Self-assessment activity 2.4

Calculate the present value of £1,000 receivable 12 years hence, assuming the discount rate is 12 per cent.

(Answer in Appendix A)

Example: Pay cash up front or by instalments?

Mary has agreed to purchase a new car for £18,500. She is considering whether to pay this amount in full now or by instalments involving £9,000 now and payments of £5,000 at the start of each of the next two years.

Her first thought is that by paying through instalments, she pays £19,000 which is £500 more than the single payment option. She then recalls that the time-value of money principle argues that all future cash flows should be converted to present values to make a valid comparison. She estimates that the rate she could earn on her savings is 6 per cent. The calculations are:

		Present value
Down payment	£9,000	£9,000
Second payment	£5,000/1.06	£4,717
Third payment	£5,000/(1.06)²	£4,450
Total present value		£18,167

Continued

Mary decides that it is better to go for the deferred payment package as it will cost her £18,167 in present value terms which is £333 cheaper than outright purchase.

In practice, most managers will use spreadsheets to do present value calculations, particularly when they involve multiple cash flows. We illustrate this using Microsoft Excel™ below.

1	A	B	C	D
2	Year	Cash flow	Present value	Formula in column C
3	0	−£9,000	−£9,000	=PV(B9,A3,0,B3)
4	1	−£5,000	−£4,717	=PV(B9,A4,0,B4)
5	2	−£5,000	−£4,450	=PV(B9,A5,0,B5)
6				
7	Total present value		−£18,167	=SUM(C3:C5)
8				
9	Discount rate	0.06		

Valuing perpetuities

perpetuity
A constant annual cash flow for an infinite period of time

Frequently, an investment pays a fixed sum each year for a specified number of years. A series of annual receipts or payments is termed an annuity. The simplest form of annuity is the infinite series or **perpetuity**. For example, certain government stocks offer a fixed annual income, but there is no obligation to repay the capital. The present value of such stocks (called irredeemables) is found by dividing the annual sum received by the annual rate of interest:

$$\text{PV perpetuity} = \frac{X}{i}$$

Example

Uncle George wishes to leave you in his will an annual sum of £10,000, starting next year. Assuming an interest rate of 10 per cent, how much of his estate must be set aside for this purpose? The answer is:

$$\text{PV perpetuity} = \frac{£10,000}{0.10} = £100,000$$

Suppose that your benevolent uncle now wishes to compensate for inflation, estimated to be at 5 per cent per annum. The formula can be adjusted to allow for growth at the rate of g per cent p.a. in the annual amount. (The derivation of the present value of a growing perpetuity is found in Appendix II at the end of the chapter.)

$$\text{PV} = \frac{X}{i - g}$$

As long as the growth rate is less than the interest rate, we can compute the present value required:

$$\text{PV} = \frac{£10,000}{0.10 - 0.05} = £200,000$$

This formula plays a key part in analysing financial decisions and will be developed further when we consider the valuation of assets, shares and companies.

Valuing annuities

An annuity is an investment paying a fixed sum each year for a specified period of time. Examples of annuities are many credit agreements and house mortgages.

The life of an annuity is less than that of a perpetuity, so its value will also be somewhat less. In fact, the formula for calculating the present value of an annuity of £A is found by calculating the present value of a perpetuity and deducting the present value of that element falling beyond the end of the annuity period. This gives the somewhat complicated formula (see Appendix II at the end of the chapter for the derivation) for the present value of an annuity (PVA):

$$PVA_{(i,n)} = A\left(\frac{1}{i} - \frac{1}{i(1+i)^n}\right)$$
$$= A \times PVIFA_{(i,n)}$$

In words, the present value of an annuity for n years at i per cent is the annual sum multiplied by the appropriate present value interest factor for an annuity.

Suppose an annuity of £1,000 is issued for 20 years at 10 per cent.

$$PVA_{(10\%, 20\ yrs)} = £1,000 \times PVIFA_{(10,20)}$$
$$= £1,000 \times 8.5136 = £8,513.60$$

Self-assessment activity 2.5

Calculate the present value of £250 receivable annually for 21 years plus £1,200 receivable after 22 years, assuming an interest rate of 11 per cent.

(Answer in Appendix A)

Calculating interest rates

Sometimes, the present values and future cash flows are known, but the rate of interest is not given. A credit company may offer to lend you £1,000 today on condition that you repay £1,643 at the end of three years. To find the compound rate of interest on the loan, we solve the present value formula for i:

$$PV_{(i,n)} = PVIF_{(i,n)} \times FV$$

Rearranging the formula:

$$PVIF_{(i,3)} = \frac{PV}{FV} = \frac{£1,000}{£1,643} = 0.60864$$

internal rate of return
The rate of return that equates the present value of future cash flows with initial investment outlay

This calculation is fundamental to investment and finance decisions and is termed the **internal rate of return**.

Alternatively, it is also possible to solve the present value formula for i:

$$PV = \frac{FV}{(1+i)^n}$$
$$(1+i)^n = FV/PV$$
$$i = (FV/PV)^{1/n} - 1$$

In the above example:

$$i = (1,643/1,000)^{1/3} - 1 = 0.18\ \text{or}\ 18\%$$

Who wants to be a millionaire?

An advertisement in the financial press read: 'How to become a millionaire? Invest £9,138 in the M&G Recovery unit trust in 1969 and wait for 25 years.' So, for those of us who missed out on this investment, let us grudgingly calculate its annual return:

$$i = (FV/PV)^{1/n} - 1$$
$$= (£1 \text{ million}/£9{,}138)^{1/25} - 1$$
$$= 20.66\%$$

By investing in a unit trust earning an annual rate of return of around 21 per cent, £9,138 turns you into a millionaire in 25 years' time. All you have to do is find an investment giving 21 per cent for 25 years!

2.7 VALUING BONDS

discounted cash flow (DCF) analysis
The process of analysing financial instruments and decisions by discounting cash flows to present values

bonds
A debt obligation with a maturity of more than a year

principal
The principal or face value or par value is the amount of the debt excluding interest

Now that we have explored the essential financial arithmetic of discounting, we can apply it to **discounted cash flow (DCF) analysis** in the analysis and valuation of financial instruments and investment projects. This chapter will cover the valuation of shares and **bonds**. When a company wants to make long-term investments, it may look to raising a long-term loan to finance it. One way of doing this is by issuing corporate bonds, promising investors that it will make a series of fixed interest payments and then repay the initial loan. A bond is a long-term (more than one year) loan which promises to pay interest and repay the loan in accordance with agreed terms. Governments, local authorities, companies and other organisations frequently seek to raise funds by issuing fixed interest bonds, offering a specific payment schedule for interest and repayment of **principal**. The return offered to the investor will depend on the creditworthiness of the issuer. For example, a UK government bond is seen as less risky than an unsecured corporate bond where the risk of default (the inability to meet its payment obligations) is higher. Accordingly, the return required for the corporate bond would typically be higher.

Once issued, bonds are traded in the bond markets. Although a bond has a par, or nominal, value – typically £100 – its actual value will vary according to the cash flows it pays (interest and repayments) and the prevailing rate of interest for this type of bond. This is the present value of the future interest and repayments.

$$V_0 = PV(\text{interest payments}) + PV(\text{redemption value})$$

Example: Bondo Ltd

coupon rate
The nominal annual rate of interest expressed as a percentage of the principal value

Bondo Ltd issues a two-year bond with a 10 per cent **coupon rate** and interest payable annually. The bond is priced at its face value of £100:

$$£100 = \frac{£10}{1.10} + \frac{£10 + £100}{(1.10)^2}$$

The bond value above includes the present value of the first year's interest plus the present value of the two elements of the Year 2 cash flow (i.e. interest and redemption value).

Bond prices are subject to interest rate risk, increasing when interest rates fall and dropping when market interest rates rise. Typically, the longer the term of the bond, the greater the exposure to interest rate risk.

discount
The amount below the face value of a financial instrument at which it sells

Assume that the market interest rate unexpectedly rises to 12 per cent. The bond is now priced in the market at a **discount** at the lower value of £96.62, reflecting the fact that the 10 per cent interest rate is now less attractive to investors:

$$£96.62 = \frac{£10}{1.12} + \frac{£10 + £100}{(1.12)^2}$$

Assume now that the market interest rate falls to 8 per cent. The bond would now be viewed as more attractive and lead it to be priced at a **premium**:

premium
The amount above the face value of a financial instrument at which it sells

$$£103.57 = \frac{£10}{1.08} + \frac{£10 + £100}{(1.08)^2}$$

From the above example, we may conclude that bonds will sell:

- at a <u>discount</u> when the <u>coupon rate is below the market interest rate</u>, and
- at a <u>premium</u> when the <u>coupon rate is above the market interest rate</u>.

yield to maturity
The interest rate at which the present value of the future cash flows equals the current market price

In the Bondo Ltd. example, the market interest was known. It may be that we know the bond prices and wish to calculate the **yield to maturity**. This measures the average rate of return to an investor who holds the bond until maturity. Here, we use the same formula but the unknown is the interest rate:

$$£103.57 = \frac{£10}{1+i} + \frac{£10 + £100}{(1+i)^2}$$

Thus, where the market price is £103.57, we solve the equation (using a computer or trial and error) to find that 8 per cent is the yield to maturity. The bond has a 10 per cent coupon and is priced at £103.57 to yield 8 per cent.

Example: Valuing a bond in Millie Meter plc

Some time ago you purchased an 8 per cent bond in the fashion chain Millie Meter. Today, it has a par value of £100 and two years to maturity. Interest is payable half-yearly. What is it worth?

Assuming the current comparable rate of interest is 8 per cent, the value should equal the par value of £100.

$$V_0 = \frac{4}{(1.04)} + \frac{4}{(1.04)^2} + \frac{4}{(1.04)^3} + \frac{4}{(1.04)^4} + \frac{100}{(1.04)^4} = £100$$

Notice that because payments are made half-yearly, both the interest and discount rate are half the annual figures.

In reality, the required rate of return demanded by investors may be different from the original coupon rate. Let us say it is 10 per cent. As this is higher than the coupon rate, the bond value for Millie Meter will fall *below* its par value:

$$V_0 = \frac{4}{(1.05)} + \frac{4}{(1.05)^2} + \frac{4}{(1.05)^3} + \frac{4}{(1.05)^4} + \frac{100}{(1.05)^4} = £96.45$$

This example shows that an investor would have to pay £96.45 for a bond offering a 4 per cent coupon rate (i.e. based on the par value of £100) plus the redemption value in two years' time, assuming that the market rate of interest for this type of security is 10 per cent.

For actively traded bonds there is little need to value them in this way because, if the bond market is efficient, it is already done for you. All you need do is to look at the latest quoted price. However, the required rate of return is less easy to obtain. Who says, in the above example, that 10 per cent is the return expected by the market for this type of bond? The answer is simple. If we know the current bond price, we put this in the above equation to find that discount rate which equates price with the discounted future cash flows – 10 per cent in the previous example.

US stocks and bonds delay epic reckoning

Bull market milestones always matter, especially when they arrive with a red flag.

Perennially optimistic investors may be heartened at the sight of the S&P 500 and Dow Jones Industrial Average entering uncharted territory this week.

Usually a peak in equities reflects a combination of robust earnings growth, an improving macro outlook and excessive investor optimism over the ability of companies to grow their businesses.

If you are looking for an explanation as to why US equities are exploring record territory, much of the answer lies in the ever-shrinking yields on government debt.

In the wake of Brexit, the universe of negative-yielding debt has expanded further, while UK and US long-term bond benchmarks have plumbed all-time lows, with investors snapping up 30-year Treasury paper on Wednesday.

A dual rally in share and bond prices to record levels should not normally occur. Rising equity values signal optimism over the economy and earnings, contradicting the dour message sent by sinking yields.

The lower bond yields fall, so the attraction of securing some form of fixed return only intensifies. Declining yields boost the value of future cash flows for companies, and in an uncertain world, US blue-chips have a certain lustre that has not escaped the attention of investors.

Expanding equity multiples reflect how the market has become a proxy for yield seekers and, unsurprisingly, the big gainers among S&P sectors this year have been utilities and telecoms, which are packed with dividend payers.

The distortions rendered by a world of negative and near-zero interest rates, along with central banks deploying quantitative easing policies, have dominated financial markets in recent years. Periods of sliding bond yields are accompanied by robust buying of shares in dividend-paying companies. Indeed many companies have taken advantage of low borrowing costs to help fund shareholder-friendly activities of buybacks and increasing dividends.

That debt binge is now being followed by weakening earnings and a high multiple for the S&P — trading at forward 12-month P/E ratio of 16.6 versus a 10-year average of 14.3, according to FactSet.

Such a combination should temper bullish inclinations for US shares. However, set against that, there is a relief factor of Brexit jitters easing, Japan inching towards a fiscal stimulus package and no Fed tightening on the horizon.

The bottom line for investors is that both US equities and bonds trade at expensive levels and face a reckoning of epic proportions at some juncture.

Plenty of juice remains in US bond yields that can be squeezed a lot lower from their present levels, helping drive equity prices higher.

FT *Source:* Mackenzie, M. (2016) US stocks and bonds delay epic reckoning. *Financial Times*, 14 July. © The Financial Times Limited 2018. All rights reserved.

■ Factors affecting interest rates

It is common in financial management to talk about 'the interest rate ruling in the money market'. However, it is important to realise that there is never a single prevailing rate. At any time, there is a spectrum of interest rates on offer – along this spectrum the rates depend on the identity of the borrower, e.g. firm or government, and hence the degree of risk faced by the lender, the amount lent or borrowed and the period over which the loan is made available. The last of these aspects is referred to as the **term structure of interest rates**. This shows how the yields offered for loans of different maturities vary as the term of the loan increases. We discuss this, together with the **yield curve**, in Appendix I to this chapter.

term structure of interest rates
Pattern of interest rates on bonds of the same risk with different lengths of time to maturity

2.8 VALUING SHARES: THE DIVIDEND VALUATION MODEL

Bond valuation is relatively straightforward because the cash flows and life of the bond are known in advance. When we consider valuing shares, we realise that the share may exist for as long as the company exists, and the cash flows to the shareholder are far from certain. The main cash flow arising to a shareholder will be the dividend payment, but this can be paid only if the company has built up sufficient profits, and the dividend policy pursued by companies may vary. Shareholders attach value to shares because they expect to receive a stream of dividends and hope to make an eventual capital gain. Although shareholders are legally entitled to the earnings of a company, in the case of a company with a dispersed ownership body, their influence on the dividend payout is limited by their ability to exert their voting power on the directors. Other things being equal, shareholders prefer higher to lower dividends, but issues such as capital investment strategy and taxation may cloud the relationship between dividend policy and share value. With this reservation in mind, we now develop the **dividend valuation model (DVM)**. *This is appropriate for valuing shares of companies rather than whole enterprises.* This is because minority shareholders have little or no control over dividend policy, and thus it is reasonable to project past dividend policy, especially as companies and their owners are known to prefer a steadily rising dividend pattern rather than more erratic payouts. Conversely, if control changes hands, the new owner can appropriate the earnings as it chooses.

■ Valuing the dividend stream

The DVM states that the value of a share now, P_0, is the sum of the stream of future discounted dividends plus the value of the share as and when sold, in some future year, n:

$$P_0 = \frac{D_1}{(1 + k_e)} + \frac{D_2}{(1 + k_e)^2} + \frac{D_3}{(1 + k_e)^3} + \cdots + \frac{D_n}{(1 + k_e)^n} + \frac{P_n}{(1 + k_e)^n}$$

However, since the new purchaser will, in turn, value the stream of dividends after year n, we can infer that the value of the share at any time may be found by valuing all future expected dividend payments over the lifetime of the firm.

Zero growth

If the lifespan is assumed to be infinite and the annual dividend is constant, we have:

$$P_0 = \sum_{t=1}^{\infty} \frac{D_t}{(1 + k_e)^t} = \frac{D_1}{k_e} \quad \text{where } D_1 = D_2 = D_3, \text{ etc.}$$

This is another application of valuing a perpetuity.

For example, the shares of Nogrow Ltd, whose owners require a return of 15 per cent, and which is expected to pay a constant annual dividend of 30p per share through time, would be valued thus:

$$P_0 = \frac{30\text{p}}{0.15} = £2.00 \text{ per share}$$

In reality, the assumptions underlying this basic model are suspect. The annual dividend is unlikely to remain unchanged indefinitely, and it is difficult to forecast a varying stream of future dividend flows. To a degree, the forecasting problem is moderated by the effect of applying a risk-adjusted discount rate because more distant dividends are more heavily discounted. For example, discounting at 20 per cent, the present value of a dividend of £1 in 15 years' time is only 6p, while £1 received in 20 years adds only 3p to the value of a share. In other words, for a plausible cost of equity, we lose little by assuming a time-horizon of, say, 15 years. Even so, reliable valuations still require estimates of dividends over the intervening years, and, by the same token, any errors will have a magnified effect during this period.

Allowing for future dividend growth

Dividends fluctuate over time, largely because of variations in the company's fortunes, although most firms attempt to grow dividends more or less in line with the company's longer-term earnings growth rate. For reasons explained in Chapter 9, financial managers attempt to 'smooth' the stream of dividends. For companies operating in mature industries, the growth rate will roughly correspond to the underlying growth rate of the whole economy. For companies operating in activities with attractive growth opportunities, dividends are likely to grow at a faster rate, at least over the medium term.

Allowing for dividend growth: the DGM

The constant dividend valuation model can be extended to cover constant growth, thus becoming the dividend growth model (DGM). This states that the value of a share is the sum of all discounted dividends, growing at the annual rate g:

$$P_0 = \frac{D_0(1+g)}{(1+k_e)} + \frac{D_0(1+g)^2}{(1+k_e)^2} + \frac{D_0(1+g)^3}{(1+k_e)^3} + \cdots + \frac{D_0(1+g)^n}{(1+k_e)^n}$$

If D_0 is this year's recently paid dividend,* $D_0(1+g)$ is the dividend to be paid in one year's time, (D_1), and so on.

Such a series growing to infinity has a present value of:

$$P_0 = \frac{D_0(1+g)}{(k_e - g)} = \frac{D_1}{(k_e - g)}$$

The growth version of the model is often used in practice by security analysts (it is popularly known as 'the dividend discount model'), at least as a reference point, but it makes some key assumptions. Dividend growth is assumed to result from earnings growth, generated solely by new investment that is financed by retained earnings. Such investment is, of course, worthwhile only if the anticipated rate of return, R, is in excess of the cost of equity, k_e. Furthermore, it is assumed that the company will retain a constant fraction of earnings and invest these in a continuous stream of projects all offering a return of R. It also breaks down if g exceeds k_e.

Example: Growmore Ltd

Growmore Ltd has just paid a dividend of 6p per share. The dividend grows at a steady rate of 5 per cent per year and the cost of equity is 12 per cent. Using the dividend growth model, the price per share is:

$$P_0 = D_1/(k_e - g)$$
$$= 6p \times 1.05/(0.12 - 0.05)$$
$$= 6.3p/0.07$$
$$= 90p$$

---

*If the dividend has recently been paid – i.e. the next dividend will be paid in, say, a year's time – the shares are said to be 'ex-dividend'. They trade without entitlement to a dividend for some considerable time.

Where did Growmore's dividend growth rate, g, come from? It is a compound of the proportion of profits retained in the company and the return it expects to make on those reinvested profits. If we term the retention ratio b, and return on invested capital R, we can say:

$$g = (b \times R)$$

If Growmore regularly reinvested 40 per cent of its earnings and expected to get a 15 per cent return on the reinvested earning, the dividend growth rate would be 6 per cent:

$$g = (b \times R)$$
$$= 0.40 \times 0.15$$
$$= 0.06 \text{ or 6 per cent}$$

An alternative approach to estimating the dividend growth rate is to determine the historical rate of growth in dividend over a number of years.

In Chapter 9, we examine more fully the issues of whether and how a change in dividend policy can be expected to alter share value. For the moment, we are mainly concerned with the mechanics of the DGM and rely simply on the assumption that any retained earnings are used for worthwhile investment. If this applies, the value of the equity will be higher with retentions-plus-reinvestment than if the investment opportunities were neglected, i.e. the decision to retain earnings benefits shareholders because of company access to projects that offer returns higher than the owners could otherwise obtain.

Self-assessment activity 2.6

XYZ plc currently earns 16p per share. It retains 75 per cent of its profits to reinvest at an average return of 18 per cent. Its shareholders require a return of 15 per cent. What is the ex-dividend value of XYZ's shares? What happens to this value if investors suddenly become more risk-averse by seeking a return of 20 per cent?

(Answer in Appendix A)

2.9 PROBLEMS WITH THE DIVIDEND GROWTH MODEL

The DGM, while possessing some convenient properties, has some major limitations.

What if the company pays no dividend?

The company may be faced with highly attractive investment opportunities that cannot be financed in other ways. According to the model, such a company would have no value at all! Total retention is fairly common, either because the company has suffered an actual or expected earnings collapse, or because, as in some European economies (e.g. Switzerland), the expressed policy of some firms is to pay no dividends at all. The cash-rich American computer software firm Microsoft paid its first dividend only in 2003, while two other computer firms, Dell and Apple, began paying dividends only in 2012. Yet we observe that shares in such companies do not have zero values. Indeed, nothing could be further from the truth.

For inveterate non-dividend payers, the market is implicitly valuing the liquidating dividend when the company is ultimately wound up. Until this happens, the company is adding to its reserves as it reinvests, and continually enhancing its assets, its earning power and its value. In effect, the market is valuing the stream of future earnings that are legally the property of the shareholders.

■ Will there always be enough worthwhile projects in the future?

The DGM implies an ongoing supply of attractive projects to match the earnings available for retention. It is most unlikely that there will always be sufficient attractive projects available, each offering a constant rate of return, R, sufficient to absorb a given fraction, b, of earnings in each future year. While a handful of firms do have very lengthy lifespans, corporate history typically parallels the marketing concept of the product life cycle – introduction, (rapid) growth, maturity, decline and death – with paucity of investment opportunities a very common reason for corporate demise. It is thus rather hopeful to value a firm over a perpetual lifespan. However, remember that the discounting process compresses most of the value into a relatively short lifespan.

■ What if the growth rate exceeds the discount rate?

The arithmetic of the model shows that if $g > k_e$, the denominator becomes negative and value is infinite. Again, this appears nonsensical, but, in reality, many companies do experience periods of very rapid growth. Usually, however, company growth settles down to a less dramatic pace after the most attractive projects are exploited, once the firm's markets mature and competition emerges. There are two ways of redeeming the model in these cases. First, we may regard g as a long-term average or 'normal' growth rate. This is not totally satisfactory, as rapid growth often occurs early in the life cycle and the value computed would thus understate the worth of near-in-time dividends. Alternatively, we could segment the company's lifespan into periods of varying growth and value these separately. For example, if we expect fast growth in the first five years and slower growth thereafter, the expression for value is:

$P_0 = [$ Present value of dividends during Years 1–5 $]$
$\quad\quad + [$ Present value of all further dividends $]$

Note that the second term is a perpetuity beginning in Year 6, but we have to find its present value. Hence it is discounted down to Year 0 as in the following expression:

$$P_0 = \frac{D_0(1 + g_f)}{(1 + k_e)} + \frac{D_0(1 + g_f)^2}{(1 + k_e)^2} + \cdots + \frac{D_0(1 + g_f)^5}{(1 + k_e)^5} + \left(\frac{D_5(1 + g_s)}{(k_e - g_s)} \times \frac{1}{(1 + k_e)^5}\right)$$

$$= \sum_{t=1}^{5} \frac{D_0(1 + g_f)}{(1 + k_e)^t} + \sum_{t=6}^{\infty} \frac{D_5(1 + g_s)}{(1 + k_e)^t}$$

where g_f is the rate of fast growth during Years 1–5 and g_s is the rate of slower growth beginning in Year 6 (i.e. from the end of Year 5).

The DGM may be used to examine the impact of changes in dividend policy, i.e. changes in b. Detailed analysis of this issue is deferred to Chapter 9.

Example: the case of unequal growth rates

Consider the case of dividend growth of 25 per cent for Years 1–5 and 7 per cent thereafter. Assuming shareholders require a return of 10 per cent, and that the dividend in Year 0 is 10p, the value of the share is calculated as follows:

		For Years 1–5	
Year	Dividend (p)	Discount factor at 10%	PV (p)
1	10(1.25) = 12.5	0.909	11.4
2	10(1.25)² = 15.6	0.826	12.9
3	etc. = 19.5	0.751	14.6
4	= 24.4	0.683	16.7
5	= 30.5	0.621	18.9
			Total 74.5

For later years, we anticipate a perpetual stream growing from the Year 5 value at 7 per cent p.a. The present value of this stream as at the end of Year 5 is:

$$\frac{D_6}{k_e - g_s} = \frac{D_5(1 + 7\%)}{(10\% - 7\%)} = \frac{30.5p(1.07)}{0.03} = \frac{32.64p}{0.03} = £10.88$$

This figure, representing the PV of all dividends following Year 5, is now converted into a Year 0 present value:

$$PV_0 = £10.88(PVIF_{10,5}) = (£10.88 \times 0.621) = £6.76$$

Adding in the PV of the dividends for the first five years, the PV of the share right now is:

$$PV_0 = (£0.745 \times £6.76) = £7.51$$

However, we may note here that valuation of the dividend stream implies a known dividend policy. Because dividends are controlled not by shareholders but by the firm's directors, the DGM is more applicable to the valuation of small investment stakes in companies than to the valuation of whole companies, as in takeover situations. When company control changes hands, control of dividend policy is also transferred. It seems particularly unrealistic, therefore, to assume an unchanged dividend policy when valuing a company for takeover. However, the growth formula can be used to value the earnings stream, i.e. by assuming all earnings are paid as dividend as, in effect, they would be if the enterprise became a 100 per cent-owned subsidiary of an acquiring firm.

SUMMARY

This chapter has examined the meaning of wealth and its fundamental importance in financial management. For most investments, there is a time-lag between the initial investment outlay and the receipt of benefits. Consideration, therefore, must be given to both the timing and size of the costs and benefits. Whenever there is an alternative opportunity to use funds committed to a project (e.g. to invest in the capital market), cash today is worth more than cash received tomorrow. These concepts were then applied to valuing bonds and shares.

Key points

- Money, like any other scarce resource, has a cost. We allow for the time-value of money by discounting. The higher the interest cost for a future cash flow, the lower its present value.
- Discount tables take away much of the tedium of discounting – but computer spreadsheets eliminate it altogether.
- Standard discount factors are:

    PVIF = the present value interest factor;

    PVIFA = the present value interest factor for an annuity.

    Conventional shorthand is:

    Interest factor (rate of interest, number of years)

    e.g. $PVIFA_{(10,3)}$ reads 'the present value interest factor for an annuity at 10 per cent for three years'.

- Bonds are valued by discounting the interest payments and final repayment by the market interest rate for comparable bonds. The yield to maturity is the interest rate that equates the present value of bond payments to the bond price.

- Shares are more difficult to value because the future dividends are difficult to forecast. The dividend growth model offers a valuation approach where the dividend growth rate is constant.
- The value of a share can be found by discounting all future expected dividend payments.
- The retention of earnings for worthwhile investment enhances future earnings, dividends and, therefore, the current share price.
- The dividend valuation model must be treated with caution. It embodies many critical assumptions.
- The term structure of interest rates shows how yields on bonds vary as the durations of loans increase.

Further reading

Early writers on discounted cash flow include Fisher (1930) and Dean (1951). Ross, Westerfield and Jordan (2010) have good chapters on bond and share valuation. Huang, Mian and Sankaraguruswamy (2009) discuss the information content of analysts' investment recommendations in relation to their revision of the target share prices, whereas Daa and Schaumburg (2011) explain the relationship between the analysts' target price forecasts and relative shares valuations. Similarly, Black, Stock and Yadav (2016) explore different dimensions of liquidity for the pricing of corporate bonds.

Useful websites

Discounted cash flow: www.investopedia.com

Annual percentage rate: www.moneyextra.com

www.investinginbonds.com

www.yieldcurve.com

Appendix I
THE TERM STRUCTURE OF INTEREST RATES AND THE YIELD CURVE

We saw in Section 2.7 that the interest rate depends on a number of factors, one of which is duration of the investment or loan. This relationship is called the **term structure of interest rates**. It shows how the yields offered for loans of different maturities vary as the term of the loan increases.

Relating this to bonds issued by the state, or government stock, the term structure shows the rate of return expected, or yield, by today's purchaser of stock who plans to hold to **maturity**, or redemption, i.e. when the stock will be repaid, or redeemed, by the government. It also shows how the yield varies for different lengths of time to maturity. In graphical terms, it is shown by a relationship called the **yield curve**.

yield curve
A graph depicting the relationship between interest rates and length of time to maturity

Normally, we find that yields to maturity increase as the term increases. In other words, rates of interest on 'longs' are higher than on 'shorts', as the blue curve in Figure 2.2 shows. Notice that the relevant yield is the gross redemption yield, which includes both interest payments and any capital gain or loss at redemption.

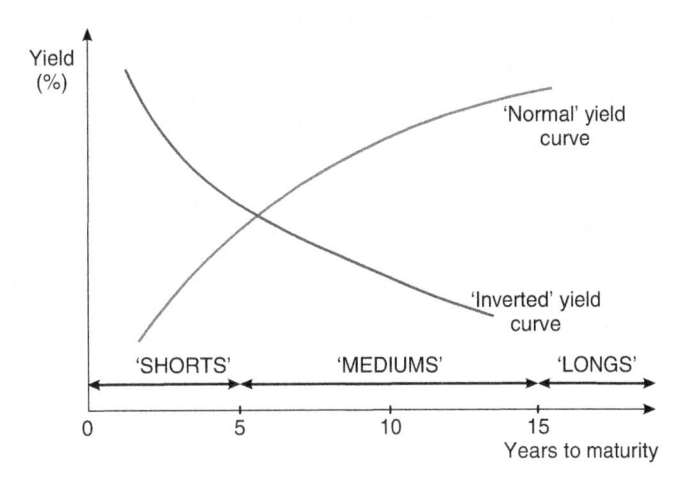

Figure 2.2 The term structure of interest rates

By tradition, short-dated stocks, with up to five years to maturity, are called *shorts*; *mediums* have between 5 and 15 years before repayment, and *longs* will be paid beyond 15 years. Notice that longs include a number of irredeemables or perpetuities which quite literally will never be repaid but will attract interest forever. These are also called undated stocks. Figure 2.3 presents the actual yield curves for UK Gilts and US Treasuries at 19 June 2017. Here we see that both stocks follow the normal shape of the yield curve. For example, the six-month yield for UK Gilts is 0.23 per cent, while the 30-year yield is 1.72 per cent.

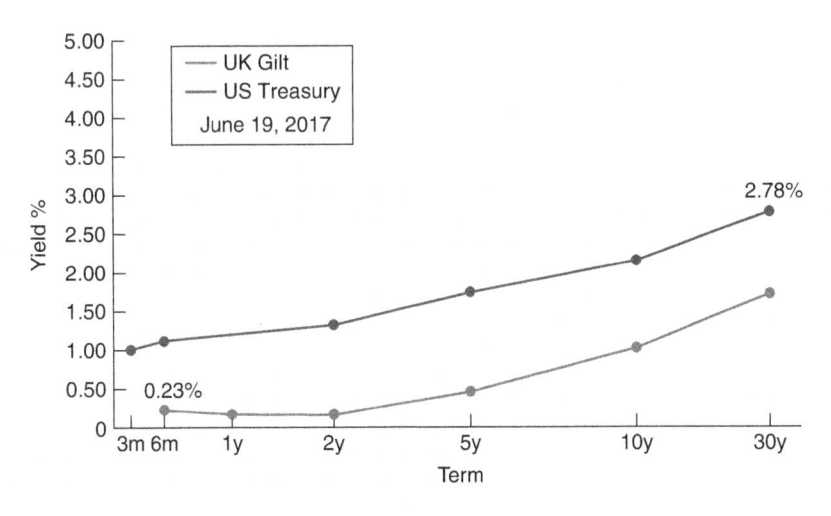

Figure 2.3 Yield curves
Source: From www.yieldcurve.com © Moorad Choudhry 2015. Reproduced with permission. Visit www.yieldcurve.com.

19 June 2017

UK Gilt 19 June 2017	6 month 0.23	1 year 0.17	2 year 0.16	5 year 0.46	10 year 1.02	30 year 1.72
US Treasury 19 June 2017	3 month 1.01	6 month 1.12	2 year 1.32	5 year 1.74	10 year 2.15	30 year 2.78

Explaining the shape of the yield curve

Three theories have been proposed to explain the shape of the yield curve – the expectations theory, the liquidity preference theory and the market segmentation theory. These are not mutually exclusive explanations – the influences incorporated in each theory all tend to operate at any one time but with different degrees of pressure. Sometimes, investors' expectations (e.g. about future inflation) are predominant, while at other times, investors' desire for liquidity may govern the shape of the curve.

Expectations theory

This theory asserts that investors' expectations about future interest rates exert the dominant influence. When the curve rises with years to maturity, this suggests that people expect interest rates to rise in the future. This is reflected in the relative demand for short-dated and long-dated securities – investors expect to be able to earn higher rates in the future so they defer buying long-dated stocks, preferring to invest in shorts. This pushes up the price on shorts, and thus lowers the yields on them, and conversely, for longer-dated stock.

> **Key US yield curve measure flattest since US election**
>
> An important measure of the US yield curve on Wednesday narrowed to its lowest level since the US election, the latest indication that the optimism over Donald Trump's pro-growth agenda continues to unwind.
>
> The difference between the yield on the two-year and the yield on the 10-year Treasury has dropped to just over 1 percentage point, its lowest level since November 8.
>
> The indicator is a measure of the 'slope' of the Treasury curve. A steeper curve suggests a more positive view of future economic conditions, meaning interest rates will rise more quickly. A flatter curve implies a more shallow trajectory for future interest rates.
>
> The move comes as investors rush into haven assets like Treasuries, with the benchmark 10-year yield falling seven basis points on Wednesday morning to 2.26 per cent, its lowest level this month.
>
> Market measures of inflation expectations have also fallen on Wednesday, with the 10-year breakeven rate at its lowest level of the year. A further sign of the capitulation of so-called 'Trumpflation', that had pegged higher growth and inflation on the prospect of the new administrations economic agenda.

FT Source: Rennison, J. (2017) Key US yield curve measure flattest since US election. *Financial Times*, 17 May. © The Financial Times Limited 2018. All rights reserved.

Liquidity preference theory

Most investors, being risk-averse, prefer to hold cash rather than securities – cash is effectively free of risk (although banks do go bust!), while even the shortest-dated government stocks carry a degree of risk. Here, by risk, we mean not the risk of default, but the risk of not being able to find a willing buyer of the stock at an acceptable price, i.e. liquidity risk. Consequently, investors need to be compensated for having to wait for the return of their money. Preference for liquidity now, and risk avoidance, thus explains the shape of the yield curve. The longer the time to maturity, the greater the risk of illiquidity and the higher the compensation required.

Market segmentation theory

In developed markets, there is a wide range of investors with different needs and time-horizons who, therefore, focus on different segments of the yield curve. For example, some financial institutions, such as banks, are anxious to protect their ability to allow investors to withdraw their deposits freely – for them, shorts are very attractive as they need liquidity. Conversely, pension funds have far longer-term liabilities and wish to match the maturity stream of their assets to these quite predictable liabilities. For them, longs are more suitable.

According to this view, the 'short' market is quite distinct from the 'long' market, and the two ends could behave quite differently under similar market conditions. For example, if the government is expected to be a net repayer of its debt in the future, this suggests a shortage of longs. This is likely to increase the demand for those stocks presently available and thus reduce their yields. This would explain the case of the 'inverted', i.e. downward-sloping, yield curve, shown by the red curve in Figure 2.2.

Appendix II
PRESENT VALUE FORMULAE

Formula for the present value of a perpetuity

This formula derives from the present value formula:

$$PV = \frac{X}{1+i} + \frac{X}{(1+i)^2} + \frac{X}{(1+i)^3} + \cdots$$

Let $X/(1+i) = a$ and $1/(1+i) = b$. We now have:

(i) $PV = a(1 + b + b^2 + \cdots)$

Multiplying both sides by b gives us:

(ii) $PVb = a(b + b^2 + b^3 + \cdots)$

Subtracting (ii) from (i), we have:

$PV(1 - b) = a$

Substituting for a and b,

$$PV\left(1 - \frac{1}{1+i}\right) = \frac{X}{1+i}$$

Multiplying both sides by $(1 + i)$ and rearranging, we have:

$$PV = \frac{X}{i}$$

Formula for the present value of a growing perpetuity

In the previous formula in this section, we obtained:

$PV(1 - b) = a$

Redefining $b = (1 + g)/(1 + i)$ and keeping $a = X/(1 + i)$:

$$PV\left(1 - \frac{1+g}{1+i}\right) = \frac{X}{1+i}$$

Multiplying both sides by $(1 + i)$ and rearranging, we have:

$$PV = \frac{X}{i - g}$$

■ The present value of annuities

The above perpetuities were special cases of the annuity formula. To find the present value of an annuity, we can first use the perpetuity formula and deduct from it the years outside the annuity period. For example, if an annuity of £100 is issued for 20 years at 10 per cent, we would find the present value of a perpetuity of £100 using the formula:

$$PV = \frac{X}{i} = \frac{100}{0.10} = £1{,}000$$

Next, find the present value of a perpetuity for the same amount, starting at Year 20, using the formula:

$$PV = \frac{X}{i(1 + i)^t} = \frac{£100}{0.10(1 + 0.10)^{20}} = £148.64$$

The difference will be:

$$PV \text{ of annuity} = \frac{X}{i} - \frac{X}{i(1 + i)^t}$$
$$= £1{,}000 - £148.64 = £851.36$$

The present value of an annuity of £100 for 20 years discounted at 10 per cent is £851.36. The formula may be simplified to:

$$PV \text{ of annuity} = X\left(\frac{1}{i} - \frac{1}{i(1 + i)^t}\right)$$

Appendix III
THE P:E RATIO AND THE CONSTANT DIVIDEND VALUATION MODEL

If we examine the P:E ratio more closely, we find it has a close affinity with the growth version of the DVM. The P:E ratio is defined as price per share (PPS) divided by earnings per share (EPS). In its reciprocal form, it measures the **earnings yield** of the firm's shares:

earnings yield
The earnings per share (EPS) divided by market share price

$$\frac{1}{\text{P:E}} = \frac{\text{EPS}}{\text{PPS}} = \frac{\text{Earnings}}{\text{Company value}} = \frac{E}{V}$$

This equals the dividend yield plus retained earnings (bE) per share. As in the DGM, the growth version of the DVM, we define the fraction of earnings retained as b. We can then write:

$$\frac{E}{V} = \frac{D}{V} + \frac{bE}{V}$$

The ratio E/V is the overall rate of return *currently* achieved. If this equals R, the rate of return on reinvested funds, then bE/V is equivalent to the growth rate g in the DGM. In other words, the earnings yield, E/V, comprises the dividend yield plus the growth rate or 'capital gains yield' for a company retaining a constant fraction of earnings and investing at the rate R. The two approaches thus look very similar. However, this apparent similarity should not be overemphasised for three important reasons:

1. The earnings yield is expressed in terms of the current earnings, whereas the DGM deals with the *prospective* dividend yield and growth rate, i.e. the former is historic in its focus, while the latter is forward-looking.
2. The DGM relies on discounting cash returns, while the earnings figure is based on accounting principles. It does not follow that cash flows will coincide with accounting profit, not least due to depreciation adjustments.
3. For the equivalence to hold, the current rate of return, E/V, would have to equal the rate of return expected on future investments.

Despite these qualifications, it is still common to find the earnings yield presented as the rate of return required by shareholders, and hence the cut-off rate for new investment projects. Unfortunately, this confuses a historical accounting measure with a forward-looking cash flow concept.

QUESTIONS

Questions with a coloured number have solutions in Appendix B on page 501.

1. Explain the difference between accounting profit and cash flow.

2. Calculate the present value of a 10-year annuity of £100, assuming an interest rate of 20 per cent.

3. A firm is considering the purchase of a machine which will cost £20,000. It is estimated that annual savings of £5,000 will result from the machine's installation, that the life of the machine will be five years and that its residual value will be £1,000. Assuming the required rate of return to be 10 per cent, what action would you recommend?

4. Brymo Ltd issued bonds two years ago that pay interest on an annual basis at 8 per cent. The bonds are due for repayment in two years' time. They will be redeemed at £110 per £100 nominal value. A yield of 10 per cent is required by investors for such bonds. What is the expected market value?

5. The gross yield to redemption on government stocks (gilts) are as follows:

    | Treasury 8.5% 2000 | 7.00% |
    | Exchequer 10.5% 2005 | 6.70% |
    | Treasury 8% 2015 | 6.53% |

    (a) Examine the shape of the yield curve for gilts, based upon the information above, which you should use to construct the curve.
    (b) Explain the meaning of the term 'gilts' and the relevance of yield curves to the private investor.

6. Calculate the net present value of projects A and B, assuming discount rates of 0 per cent, 10 per cent and 20 per cent.

	A (£)	B (£)
Initial outlay	1,200	1,200
Cash receipts:		
Year 1	1,000	100
Year 2	500	600
Year 3	100	1,100

    Which is the superior project at each discount rate? Why do they not all produce the same answer?

7. Brosnan plc generates cash flows of £5 million p.a. after allowing for tax and depreciation, which is used for reinvestment. It has issued 10 million shares. Shareholders require a 12 per cent return.

    Required
    Value each share:
    (i) assuming all cash flows are distributed as dividend.
    (ii) assuming 50 per cent of cash flows are retained, with a return on retained earnings of 15 per cent.
    (iii) as for (ii), but assuming 10 per cent return on reinvestment.
    (iv) assuming that cash flows grow at 7.5 per cent for each of the first three future years, then at 5 per cent thereafter.
    Note: assume all cash flows are perpetuities.

8 Insert the missing values in the following table:

	P_0	D_0	D_1	g	b	R	k_e
(i)	£8.44	£0.35	?	8.5%	0.5	17%	13.0%
(ii)	£4.98	£0.20	£0.219	?	0.6	16%	14.0%
(iii)	?	£0.10	£0.108	8.0%	0.4	20%	15.0%
(iv)	£2.75	?	£0.220	10.0%	0.5	20%	18.0%
(v)	£10.20	£0.60	£0.610	2.0%	?	10%	8.0%
(vi)	£0.60	£0.05	£0.054	8.0%	0.8	20%	?
(vii)	£1.47	£0.12	£0.133	10.5%	0.7	?	19.5%

Note: answers may have some minor rounding errors.

9 Leyburn plc currently generates profits before tax of £10 million, and proposes to pay a dividend of £4 million out of cash holdings to its shareholders. The rate of Corporation Tax is 30 per cent. Recent dividend growth has averaged 8 per cent p.a. It is considering retaining an extra £1 million in order to finance new strategic investment. This switch in dividend policy will be permanent, as management believe that there will be a stream of highly attractive investments available over the next few years, all offering returns of around 20 per cent after tax. Leyburn's shares are currently valued 'cum-dividend'. Shareholders require a return of 14 per cent. Leyburn is wholly equity-financed.

Required
(a) Value the equity of Leyburn assuming no change in retention policy.
(b) What is the impact on the value of equity of adopting the higher level of retentions? (Assume the new payout ratio will persist into the future.)

Practical assignment

List three decisions in a business with which you are familiar where cash flows arise over a lengthy time period and where discounted cash flow (DCF) may be beneficial. To what extent is DCF applied (formally or intuitively)? What are the dangers of ignoring the time-value of money in these particular cases?

3

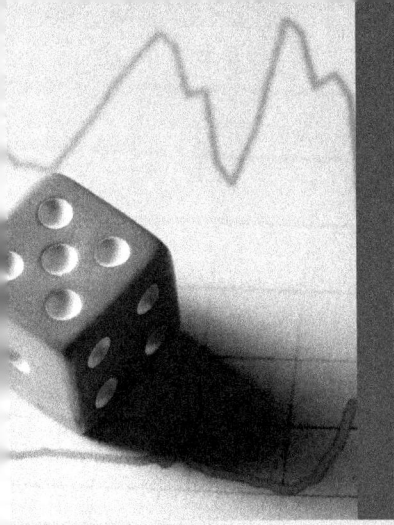

Analysing investment risk

We all lose if failure is punished too harshly

We are all fascinated by entrepreneurs going broke. Perhaps it is envy at work, possibly morbid curiosity, in some cases a desire to see justice served – or is it simply that such tales are full of human drama?

I would like to believe that educated citizens know such speculators are a vital element in the capitalist system. Without the risk-takers, innovation would be stunted, job-creation inhibited, tax proceeds reduced and society generally poorer. But often there is a fine line between winning and losing in business. And systems that punish failure too harshly discourage those who would seek opportunities – thereby making everyone a loser.

As a case study, Steve Oliver is the founder of MusicMagpie. His company is an online retailer of second-hand CDs, DVDs and computer games with almost £100m in revenue, selling in 140 countries That achievement was built using experience gained from a previous flop – Music Zone, that went into administration in 2007. If financiers, suppliers and other stakeholders had demonised him, his recent comeback would not have happened.

Whether in energy exploration or drug discovery, there will be more defeats than victories. But as Winston Churchill said: 'Success is not final, failure is not fatal. It is the courage to continue that counts.'

FT *Source:* Johnson, L. (2013) We all lose if failure is punished too harshly. *Financial Times*, 12 November. © The Financial Times Limited 2018. All rights reserved.

Learning objectives

The aim of this chapter is to enable the reader:

- To explain uncertainty and risk.
- To understand how uncertainty affects investment decisions.
- To explore managers' risk attitudes.
- To appreciate the levels at which risk can be viewed.
- To be able to measure the expected NPV and its variability.
- To appreciate the main risk-handling techniques and apply them to capital budgeting problems.
- To understand the various forms of real options that can further enhance a project's value.

3.1 INTRODUCTION

As the introductory case study shows, Steve Oliver, the founder of MusicMagpie, knows a thing or two about risk: you win some, you lose some! The finance director of a major UK manufacturer for the motor industry remarked, 'We know that, on average, one in five large capital projects flops. The problem is: we have no idea beforehand which one!'

Stepping into the unknown – which is what investment decision-making effectively is – means that mistakes will surely occur. Only about 50 per cent of small businesses are still trading three years after start-up. Sir Richard Branson, head of Virgin Atlantic, once said, 'the safest way to become a millionaire is to start as a billionaire and invest in the airline industry'!

This does not mean that managers can do nothing about project failures. In this and subsequent chapters, we examine how project risk is assessed and controlled. The various forms of risk are defined and the main statistical methods for measuring project risk within single-period and multi-period time-spans are described. A variety of risk analysis techniques will then be discussed. These fall conveniently into methods intended to describe risk and methods incorporating project riskiness within the net present value formula. The chapter concludes by examining the various forms of investment options and how they can add value to a project.

Defining terms

At the outset, we need to clarify our terms:

- *Certainty*. Perfect certainty arises when expectations are single-valued: that is, a particular outcome will arise rather than a range of outcomes. Is there such a thing as an investment with certain payoffs? Probably not, but some investments come fairly close. For example, an investment in three-month Treasury Bills will, subject to the Bank of England keeping its promise, provide a precise return on redemption.
- *Risk and uncertainty*. Although used interchangeably in everyday parlance, these terms are not quite the same. Risk refers to the set of unique unfavourable consequences for a given decision that can be assigned probabilities, while uncertainty implies that it is not fully possible to identify outcomes or to assign probabilities. Perhaps the worst cases of uncertainty are the 'unknown unknowns' – outcomes from events that we did not even consider.

The purest example of risk is the 50 per cent chance of obtaining a 'head' from tossing a coin. For most investment decisions, however, empirical experience is hard to find. Managers are forced to estimate probabilities where objective statistical evidence is not available. Nevertheless, a manager with little prior experience of launching a particular product in a new market can still subjectively assess the risks involved based on the information that person has. Because subjective probabilities may be applied to investment decisions in a manner similar to objective probabilities, the distinction between risk and uncertainty is not critical in practice, and the two terms are often used synonymously.

Investment decisions are only as good as the information upon which they rest. Relevant and useful information is central in projecting the degree of risk surrounding future economic events and in selecting the best investment option.

Self-assessment activity 3.1

Why is risk assessment important in making capital investment decisions?

(Answer in Appendix A)

3.2 EXPECTED NET PRESENT VALUE (ENPV): BETTERWAY PLC

To what extent is the net present value criterion relevant in the selection of risky investments? Consider the case of Betterway plc, contemplating three options with very different degrees of risk. The distribution of possible outcomes for these options is given in Table 3.1. Notice that A's cash flow is totally certain.

Table 3.1 Betterway plc: expected net present values

Investment	NPV outcomes (£)		Probability		Weighted outcomes (£)
A	9000	×	1	=	9,000
B	−10,000	×	0.2	=	−2,000
	10,000	×	0.5	=	5,000
	20,000	×	0.3	=	6,000
			1.0	ENPV =	9,000
C	−55,000	×	0.2	=	−11,000
	10,000	×	0.5	=	5,000
	50,000	×	0.3	=	15,000
			1.0	ENVP =	9,000

expected net present value (ENPV)
The average of the range of possible NPVs weighted by their probability of occurrence

Clearly, while the NPV criterion is appropriate for investment option A, where the cash flows are certain, it is no longer appropriate for the risky investment options B and C, each with three possible outcomes. The whole range of possible outcomes may be considered by obtaining the **expected net present value (ENPV)**, which is the mean of the NPV distribution when weighted by the probabilities of occurrence. The ENPV is given by the equation:

$$\overline{X} = \sum_{i=1}^{N} p_i X_i$$

where $\overline{X}$ is the expected value of event X, X_i is the possible outcome i from event X, p_i is the probability of outcome i occurring and N is the number of possible outcomes.

The NPV rule may then be applied by selecting projects offering the highest expected net present value. In our example, all three options offer the same expected NPV of £9,000. Should the management of Betterway view all three as equally attractive? The answer to this question lies in their attitudes towards risk, for while the *expected* outcomes are the same, the *possible* outcomes vary considerably. Thus, although the expected NPV criterion provides a single measure of profitability, which may be applied to risky investments, it does not, by itself, provide an acceptable decision criterion.

3.3 ATTITUDES TO RISK

Business managers prefer less risk to more risk for a given return. In other words, they are *risk-averse*. In general, a business manager derives less utility, or satisfaction, from gaining an additional £1,000 than he or she forgoes in losing £1,000. This is based on the concept of diminishing marginal utility, which holds that, as wealth increases, marginal utility declines at an increasing rate. Thus, the utility function for risk-averse managers is concave, as shown in Figure 3.1. As long as the utility function of the decision-maker can be specified, this approach may be applied in reaching investment decisions.

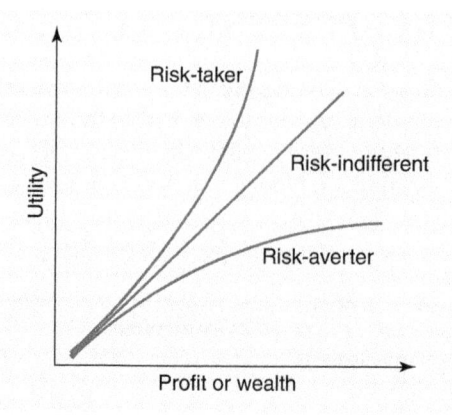

Figure 3.1 **Risk profiles**

Example: Carefree plc's utility function

Mike Cool, the managing director of Carefree plc, a business with a current market value of £30 million, has an opportunity to relocate its premises. It is estimated that there is a 50 per cent probability of increasing its value by £12 million and a similar probability that its value will fall by £10 million. The owner's utility function is outlined in Figure 3.2. The concave slope shows that the owner is risk-averse. The gain in utility (ΔU_F) as a result of the favourable outcome of £42 million is less than the fall in utility (ΔU_A) resulting from the adverse outcome of only £20 million.

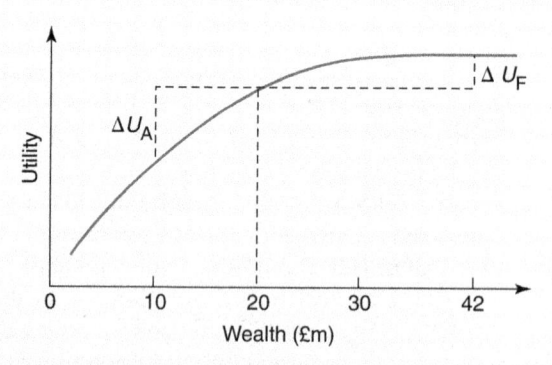

Figure 3.2 **Risk-averse investor's utility function**

The conclusion is that, although the investment proposal offers £1 million expected additional wealth (i.e. $[0.5 \times £12m] + [0.5 \times -£10m]$), the project should not be undertaken because total expected utility would fall if the factory were relocated.

While decision-making based upon the expected utility criterion is conceptually sound, it has serious practical drawbacks. Mike Cool may recognise that he is risk-averse but is unable to define, with any degree of accuracy, the shape of his utility function. This becomes even more complicated in organisations where ownership and management are separated, as is the case for most large companies. Thus, while utility analysis provides a useful insight into the problem of risk, it does not provide us with operational decision rules.

3.4 TYPES OF RISK

Risk may be classified into a number of types. A clear understanding of the different forms of risk is useful in the evaluation and monitoring of capital projects:

1 *Business risk* – the variability in operating cash flows or profits before interest. A firm's business risk depends, in large measure, on the underlying economic environment within which it operates. But variability in operating cash flows can be heavily affected by the cost structure of the business, and hence its **operating gearing**. A company's break-even point is reached when sales revenues match total costs. These costs consist of fixed costs – that is, costs that do not vary much with the level of sales – and variable costs. The decision to become more capital-intensive generally leads to an increase in the proportion of fixed costs in the cost structure. This increase in operating gearing leads to greater variability in operating earnings.

2 *Financial risk* – the risk, over and above business risk, that results from the use of debt capital. Financial gearing is increased by issuing more debt, thereby incurring more fixed-interest charges and increasing the variability in net earnings. Financial risk is considered more fully in later chapters.

3 *Portfolio or market risk* – the variability in shareholders' returns. Investors can significantly reduce their variability in earnings by holding carefully selected investment portfolios. This is sometimes called '**relevant**' risk, because only this element of risk should be considered by a well-diversified shareholder. Chapters 4 and 5 examine such risk in greater depth.

operating gearing
The proportion of fixed costs in the firm's operating cost structure

financial gearing
Includes both capital gearing and income gearing

relevant risk
The component of total risk taken into account by the stock market when assessing the appropriate risk premium for determining capital asset values

Project risk can be viewed and defined in three different ways: (1) in isolation, (2) in terms of its impact on the business and (3) in terms of its impact on shareholders' investment portfolios.

In this chapter, we assess project risk in isolation before moving on to estimate its impact on investors' portfolios (i.e. market risk) in Chapter 5.

Operating gearing example: Hifix and Lofix

Hifix and Lofix are two companies identical in every respect except cost structure. While Lofix pays its workforce on an output-related basis, Hifix operates a flat-rate wage system. The sales, costs and profits for the two companies are given under two economic states, normal and recession, in Table 3.2. While both companies perform equally well under normal trading conditions, Hifix, with its heavier fixed cost element, is more

Table 3.2 Effects of cost structure on profits (£000)

	Hifix		Lofix	
	Normal	Recession	Normal	Recession
Sales	200	120	200	120
Variable costs	−100	−60	−160	−96
Fixed costs	−80	−80	−20	−20
Profit/loss	20	−20	20	4
Change in sales		−40%		−40%
Change in profits		−200%		−80%

Continued

vulnerable to economic downturns. This can be measured by calculating the degree of operating gearing:

$$\text{Operating gearing} = \frac{\text{percentage change in profits}}{\text{percentage change in sales}}$$

$$\text{For Hifix} = \frac{-200\%}{-40\%} = 5$$

$$\text{For Lofix} = \frac{-80\%}{-40\%} = 2$$

The degree of operating gearing is far greater for the firm with high fixed costs than for the firm with low fixed costs.

Self-assessment activity 3.2

Which type of risk do the following describe?

1 Risks associated with increasing the firm's level of borrowing.
2 The variability in the firm's operating profits.
3 Variability in the cash flows of a proposed capital investment.
4 Variability in shareholders' returns.

(Answer in Appendix A)

3.5 MEASUREMENT OF RISK

A well-known politician (not named to protect the guilty) once proclaimed, 'Forecasting is very important – particularly when it involves the future!' Estimating the probabilities of uncertain forecast outcomes is difficult. But with the little knowledge the manager may have concerning the future, and by applying past experience backed by historical analysis of a project and its setting, the manager may be able to construct a probability distribution of a project's cash outcomes. This can be used to measure the risks surrounding project cash flows in a variety of ways. If we assume that the range of possible outcomes from a decision is distributed normally around the expected value, risk-averse investors can assess project risk using expected value and standard deviation. We shall consider three statistical measures: the <u>standard deviation</u>, <u>semi-variance</u> and <u>coefficient of variation</u> for single-period cash flows.

■ Measuring risk for single-period cash flows: Snowglo plc

Standard deviation

We have seen that expected value overlooks important information on the dispersion (risk) of the outcomes. We also know that different people behave differently in risky situations. Figure 3.3 shows the NPV distributions for projects A and B. Both projects have the same expected NPV, indicated by M, but project A has greater dispersion. The risk-averse manager in Snowglo will choose B since that person wants to minimise risk. The risk-taker will choose A because the NPV of project A has a chance (W) of being higher than X (which project B cannot offer), but also a chance (L) of being lower than Y. Hereafter, we make the reasonable assumption that most people are risk-averse, an assumption which is borne out by intuition, experience and empirical evidence.

Analysing Investment Risk

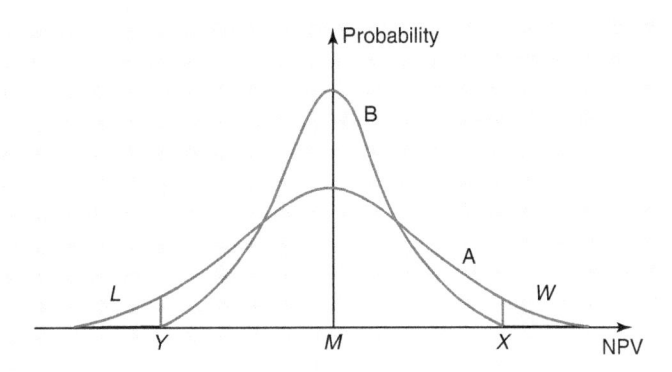

Figure 3.3 Variability of project returns

The standard deviation is a measure of the dispersion of possible outcomes; the wider the dispersion, the higher the standard deviation.

The expected value, denoted by $\overline{X}$, is given by the equation:

$$\overline{X} = \sum_{i=1}^{N} p_i X_i$$

and the standard deviation of the cash flows by:

$$\sigma = \sqrt{\sum_{i=1}^{N} p_i (X_i - \overline{X})^2}$$

Table 3.3 shows the information on two projects for Snowglo plc.

Table 3.3 Snowglo plc project data

State of economy	Probability of outcome	Cash flow (£) A	Cash flow (£) B
Strong	0.2	700	550
Normal	0.5	400	400
Weak	0.3	200	300

Table 3.4 provides the workings for projects A and B.

Applying the formulae, we obtain an expected cash flow of £400 for both project A and project B. If the decision-maker had a neutral risk attitude, he or she would view the two projects equally favourably. But as the decision-maker is likely to be risk-averse, it is appropriate to examine the standard deviations of the two probability distributions. Here we see that project A, with a standard deviation twice that of project B, is more risky and hence less attractive. This could have been deduced in this case simply by observing the distribution of outcomes and noting that the same probabilities apply to both projects. But observation cannot always tell us by how much one project is riskier than another.

Semi-variance

While deviation above the mean may be viewed favourably by managers, it is 'downside risk' (i.e. deviations below expected outcomes) that is mainly considered in the

Table 3.4 Project risk for Snowglo plc

Economic state	Probability (a)	Outcome (b)	Expected value (c = a × b)	Deviation (d = b − $\bar{X}$)	Squared deviation (e = d²)	Variance (f = a × e)
Project A						
Strong	0.2	700	140	300	90,000	18,000
Normal	0.5	400	200	0	0	0
Weak	0.3	200	60	−200	40,000	12,000
			$\bar{X}_A = 400$		Variance = σ_A^2	= 30,000
					Standard deviation = σ_A	= 173.2
Project B						
Strong	0.2	550	110	150	22,500	4,500
Normal	0.5	400	200	0	0	0
Weak	0.3	300	90	−100	10,000	3,000
			$\bar{X}_B = 400$		Variance = σ_B^2	= 7,500
					Standard deviation = σ_B	= 86.6

Alternatively:

$\bar{X}_A = 700(0.2) + 400(0.5) + 200(0.3) = 400$

$\sigma_A = \sqrt{[0.2(700 - 400)^2 + 0.5(400 - 400)^2 + 0.3(200 - 400)^2]}$

$= 173.2$

$\bar{X}_A = 550(0.2) + 400(0.5) + 300(0.3) = 400$

$\sigma_B = \sqrt{[0.2(550 - 400)^2 + 0.5(400 - 400)^2 + 0.3(300 - 400)^2]}$

$= 86.6$

decision process. <u>Downside risk</u> is best measured by the semi-variance, a special case of the variance, given by the formula:

$$SV_i = \sum_{j=1}^{K} p_j(X_j - \bar{X})^2$$

where SV_i is the semi-variance of decision i, j is each outcome value less than the expected value and K is the number of outcomes that are less than the expected value.

Applying the semi-variance to the example in Table 3.4, the downside risk relates exclusively to the 'weak' state of the economy:

$SV_A = 0.3(200 - 400)^2 = £12,000$

$SV_B = 0.3(300 - 400)^2 = £3,000$

Once again, project B is seen to have a much lower degree of risk. In both cases, the semi-variance accounts for 40 per cent of the project variance.

Coefficient of variation (CV)

Where projects differ in scale, a more valid comparison is found by applying a relative risk measure such as the coefficient of variation. The lower the CV, the lower the relative degree of risk. This is calculated by dividing the standard deviation by the expected value of net cash flows, as in the expression:

$CV = \sigma / \bar{X}$

The Snowglo example (Table 3.4) gives the following coefficients:

	Standard deviation (1)	Expected value (2)	Coefficient of variation (1 ÷ 2)
Project A	£173.2	£400	0.43
Project B	£86.6	£400	0.22

Both projects have the same expected value, but project B has a significantly lower degree of risk. Next, we consider the situation where the two projects under review are different in scale:

	Standard deviation		Expected value		Coefficient of variation
Project F	£1,000	÷	£10,000	=	0.10
Project G	£2,000	÷	£40,000	=	0.05

Although the absolute measure of dispersion (the standard deviation) is greater for project G, few people in business would regard it as more risky than project F because of the significant difference in the expected values of the two investments. The coefficient of variation reveals that G actually offers a lower amount of risk per £1 of expected value.

Self-assessment activity 3.3

Project X has an expected return of £2,000 and a standard deviation of £400. Project Y has an expected return of £1,000 and a standard deviation of £400. Which project is more risky?

(Answer in Appendix A)

Mean–variance rule

Given the expected return and the measure of dispersion (variance or standard deviation), we can formulate the **mean–variance rule**. This states that one project will be preferred to another if either of the following holds:

1 Its expected return is *higher* and the variance is *equal* to or *less* than that of the other project.
2 Its expected return *exceeds* or is *equal* to the expected return of the other project and the variance is *lower*.

This is illustrated by the mean–variance analysis depicted in Figure 3.4. Projects A and D are preferable to projects C and B, respectively, because they offer a higher return for

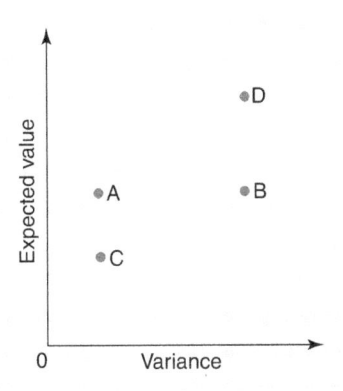

Figure 3.4 Mean–variance analysis

the same degree of risk. In addition, A is preferable to B because for the same expected return, it incurs lower risk. These choices are applicable to all risk-averse managers regardless of their particular utility functions. However, it is not possible to say whether Project D (high risk – high return) is superior to Project A (lower risk – lower return). This will depend on the preferences of the management team. This important issue will be discussed in Chapters 4 and 5.

So far, our analysis of risk has assumed single-period investments. We have conveniently ignored the fact that, typically, investments are multi-period. The analysis of project risk where there are multi-period cash flows is discussed in the Appendix to this chapter.

Self-assessment activity 3.4

What do you understand by the following?

(a) risk
(b) uncertainty
(c) risk-aversion
(d) expected value
(e) standard deviation
(f) semi-variance
(g) mean–variance rule

(Answer in Appendix A)

■ Risk-handling methods

There are two broad approaches to handling risk in the investment decision process. The first attempts to *describe* the riskiness of a given project, using various applications of probability analysis or some simple method. The second aims to *incorporate* the investor's perception of project riskiness within the NPV formula.

We turn first to the various techniques available to help describe investment risk.

Airline profits threatened by volcanic ash

The success of investment projects in the airline sector in 2010 was affected by a risk that few had ever considered – volcanic ash. This is a good example of those 'unknown unknowns' which, like a volcano, can erupt and seriously damage otherwise good projects. When the Eyjafjallajokull volcano in Iceland erupted, its plume of ash meant that all planes in Europe were grounded. When the volcano last erupted in 1821, it spewed ash into the atmosphere for two years. How many tour operators and airlines today could survive large-scale flight cancellations over such a sustained period? The International Air Transport Association estimated the cost to the industry in April 2010 alone as $1.7 billion.

Undoubtedly, aerospace engine developers will be considering new capital projects which can help reduce the risk from volcanic ash to acceptable levels.

3.6 RISK DESCRIPTION TECHNIQUES

■ Sensitivity analysis

sensitivity analysis
Analysis of the impact of changes in assumptions on investment returns

In principle, **sensitivity analysis** is a very simple technique used to isolate and assess the potential impact of risk on a project's value. It aims not to quantify risk, but to identify the impact on NPV of changes to key assumptions. Sensitivity analysis provides the decision-maker with answers to a whole range of 'what if' questions. For example, what is the NPV if selling price falls by 10 per cent? What is the IRR if the project's life is only three years, not five years as expected? What is the level of sales revenue required to break even in net present value terms?

Sensitivity graphs permit the plotting of net present values (or IRRs) against the percentage deviation from the expected value of the factor under investigation. The sensitivity graph in Figure 3.5 depicts the potential impact of deviations from the expected values of a project's variables on NPV. When everything is unchanged, the NPV is £2,000. However, NPV becomes zero when market size decreases by 20 per cent or price decreases by 5 per cent. This shows that NPV is very sensitive to price changes. Similarly, a 10 per cent increase in the capital cost will bring the NPV down to zero, while the discount rate must increase to 25 per cent in order to render the project uneconomic. Therefore, the project is more sensitive to capital investment changes than to variations in the discount rate. The sensitivity of NPV to each factor is reflected by the slope of the sensitivity line – the steeper the line, the greater the impact on NPV of changes in the specified variable.

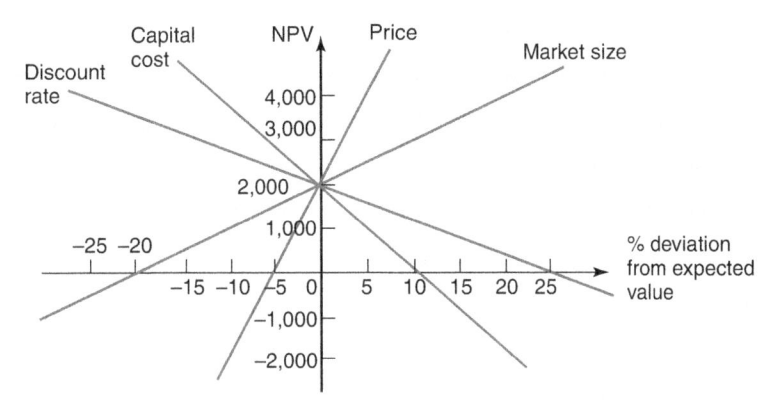

Figure 3.5 **Sensitivity graph**

Sensitivity analysis is widely used because of its simplicity and ability to focus on particular estimates. It can identify the critical factors that have greatest impact on a project's profitability. It does not, however, actually *evaluate* risk; the decision-maker must still assess the likelihood of occurrence for these deviations from expected values.

Break-even sensitivity analysis: UMK plc

The accountant of UMK plc has put together the cash flow forecasts for a new product with a four-year life, involving capital investment of £200,000. It produces a net present value, at a 10 per cent discount rate, of £40,920. His basic analysis is given in Table 3.5. Which factors are most critical to the decision?

Investment outlay

This can rise by up to £40,920 (assuming all other estimates remain unchanged) before the decision advice alters. This is a percentage increase of:

$$\frac{£40,920}{£200,000} \times 100 = 20.5\%$$

Continued

Table 3.5 UMK cost structure

Unit data	£	£
Selling price		20
Less: Materials	(6)	
Labour	(5)	
Variable costs	(1)	
		(12)
Contribution		8
Annual sales (units)	12,000	
Total contribution		96,000
Less: Additional fixed costs		(20,000)
Annual net cash flow		76,000
Present value (4 years at 10%)		
76,000 × 3.17		240,920
Less: Capital outlay		(200,000)
Net present value		40,920

Annual cash receipts

The break-even position is reached when annual cash receipts multiplied by the annuity factor equal the investment outlay. The break-even cash flow is therefore the investment outlay divided by the annuity factor:

$$\frac{£200,000}{3.17} \times £63,091$$

This is a percentage fall of $\frac{£76,000 - £63,091}{£76,000} = 17.0\%$

Annual fixed costs could increase by the same absolute amount of £12,909, or

$$\frac{£12,909}{£20,000} \times 100 = 64.5\%$$

Annual sales volume: the break-even annual contribution is £63,091 + £20,000 = £83,091. Sales volume required to break even is £83,091/£8 = 10,386, which is a percentage decline of:

$$\frac{12,000 - 10,386}{12,000} \times 100 = 13.5\%$$

Selling price can fall by:

$$\frac{£96,000 - £83,091}{12,000} = £1.07 \text{ per unit}$$

a decline of $\frac{£1.07}{£20} \times 100 = 5.4\%$

Variable costs per unit can rise by a similar amount:

$$\frac{£1.07}{£12} \times 100 = 8.9\%$$

Discount rate

The break-even annuity factor is £200,000/£76,000 = 2.63. Reference to the present value annuity tables for four years shows that 2.63 corresponds to an IRR of 19 per cent. The error in cost of capital calculation could be as much as nine percentage points before it affects the decision advice.

Sensitivity analysis, as applied in the UMK plc example, discloses that selling price and variable costs are the two most critical variables in the investment decision. The decision-maker must then determine (subjectively or objectively) the probabilities of such changes occurring, and whether he or she is prepared to accept the risks.

Scenario analysis and stress testing

Sensitivity analysis considers the effects of changes in key variables only one at a time. It does not ask the question: 'How bad could the project look?' Enthusiastic managers can sometimes get carried away with the most likely outcomes and forget just what might happen if critical assumptions – such as the state of the economy or competitors' reactions – are unrealistic. Scenario analysis seeks to establish 'worst' and 'best' scenarios, so that the whole range of possible outcomes can be considered. It encourages 'contingent thinking', describing the future by a collection of possible eventualities.

Shell was an early adopter of scenario analysis in the 1970s and continues to use this approach as the company explains below (see the 'Scenario analysis at Shell' box).

Stress testing is closely related to scenario analysis and, usually, involves assessing how resilient a company is to severe or crisis events. The term is now closely associated with the banking sector where regulators, governments and other stakeholders are very concerned to evaluate whether a bank has adequate capital should another financial crisis occur.

Simulation analysis

Monte Carlo simulation
Method for calculating the probability distribution of possible outcomes

An extension of scenario analysis is simulation analysis. **Monte Carlo simulation** is an operations research technique with a variety of business applications. The computer generates hundreds of possible combinations of variables according to a pre-specified probability distribution. Each scenario gives rise to an NPV outcome which, along with other NPVs, produces a probability distribution of outcomes.

Scenario analysis at Shell

Shell has been developing scenarios to explore the future since the early 1970s. Scenarios are stories that consider 'what if?' questions. Whereas forecasts focus on probabilities, scenarios consider a range of plausible futures and how these could emerge from the realities of today. They recognise that people hold beliefs and make choices that lead to outcomes. Our scenarios team considers changes such as in the global economic environment, geopolitics, resource stresses such as water, greenhouse gases, and energy supply and demand to help business leaders make better decisions.

Scenarios help decision makers reconcile apparent contradictions or uncertainties, such as how political change in one region impacts global society. They also have the potential to improve awareness around issues that could become increasingly important to society, such as increased urbanisation, greater connectivity or loss of trust in institutions.

By exploring plausible, as well as predictable outcomes, scenarios challenge conventional wisdom. Organisations using scenarios find it easier to recognise impending disruptions in their own operating environment, such as political changes, demographic shifts or recessions. They also increase their resilience to sudden changes caused by unexpected crises like natural disasters or armed conflicts.

In an industry often defined by uncertainty and volatility, Shell is stronger thanks to the forward planning capacity that scenarios bring.

Source: Based on Shell Scenarios.

www.shell.com.

One of the first writers to apply the simulation approach to risky investments was Hertz (1964), who described the approach adopted by his firm in evaluating a major expansion of the processing plant of an industrial chemical producer. This involved constructing a mathematical model that captured the essential characteristics of the investment proposal throughout its life as it encountered random events.

A simulation model might consider the following variables, which are subject to random variation.

Market factors	Investment factors	Cost factors
Market size	Investment outlay	Variable costs
Market growth rate	Project life	Fixed costs
Selling price of product	Residual value	
Market share captured by the firm		

Comparison is then possible between mutually exclusive projects whose NPV probability distributions have been calculated in this manner (Figure 3.6). It will be observed that project A, with a higher expected NPV and lower risk, is preferable to project B.

In practice, few companies use this risk analysis approach, for the following reasons:

1 The simple model described above assumes that the economic factors are unrelated. Clearly, many of them (e.g. market share and selling price) are statistically interdependent. To the extent that interdependency exists among variables, it must be specified. Such interrelationships are not always clear and are frequently complex to model.
2 Managers are required to specify probability distributions for the exogenous variables. Few managers are able or willing to accept the demands required by the simulation approach.

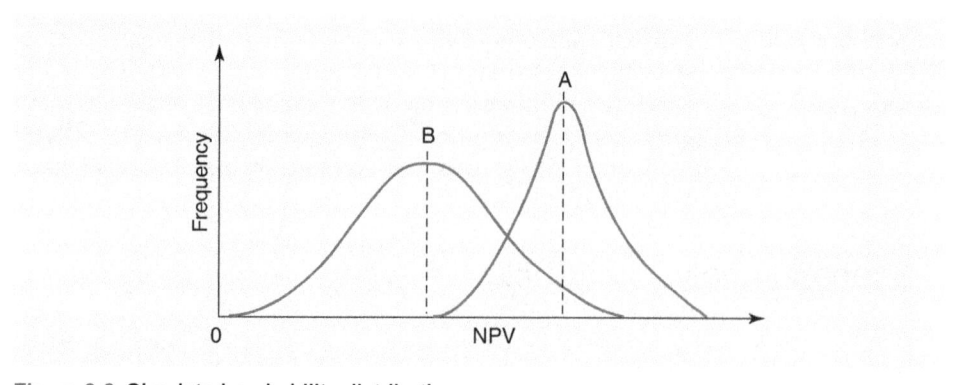

Figure 3.6 Simulated probability distributions

Self-assessment activity 3.5

What do you understand by Monte Carlo simulation? When might it be useful in capital budgeting?

(Answer in Appendix A)

3.7 ADJUSTING THE NPV FORMULA FOR RISK

Two approaches are commonly used to incorporate risk within the NPV formula.

■ Certainty equivalent method

This conceptually appealing approach permits adjustment for risk by incorporating the decision-maker's risk attitude into the capital investment decision. The certainty equivalent method adjusts the numerator in the net present value calculation by multiplying the expected annual cash flows by a certainty equivalent coefficient. The revised formula becomes:

$$\overline{NPV} = \sum_{t=1}^{N} \frac{\alpha \overline{X}_t}{(1+i)^t} - I_0$$

where $\overline{NPV}$ is the expected net present value; α is the certainty equivalent coefficient, which reflects management's risk attitude; $\overline{X}_t$ is the expected cash flow in period t; i is the riskless rate of interest; n is the project's life and I_0 is the initial cash outlay.

The numerator ($\alpha \overline{X}_t$) represents the figure that management would be willing to receive as a certain sum each year in place of the uncertain annual cash flow offered by the project. The greater is management's aversion to risk, the nearer the certainty equivalent coefficient is to zero. Where projects are of normal risk for the business, and the cost of capital and risk-free rate of interest are known, it is possible to determine the certainty equivalent coefficient.

Example

Calculate the certainty equivalent coefficient for a project with a one-year life and an expected cash flow of £5,000 receivable at the end of the year. Shareholders require a return of 12 per cent for projects of this degree of risk, and the risk-free rate of interest is 6 per cent.

The present value of the project, excluding the initial cost and using the 12 per cent discount rate, is:

$$PV = \frac{£5,000}{1 + 0.12} = £4,464$$

Using the present value and substituting the risk-free interest rate for the cost of capital, we obtain the certainty equivalent coefficient:

$$\frac{\alpha \times £5,000}{1 + 0.06} = £4,464$$

$$\alpha = \frac{(£4,464)(1.06)}{£5,000}$$

$$= 0.9464$$

The management is, therefore, indifferent as to whether it receives an uncertain cash flow one year hence of £5,000 or a certain cash flow of £4,732 (i.e. £5,000 × 0.9464).

■ Risk-adjusted discount rate

Whereas the certainty equivalent approach adjusted the numerator in the NPV formula, the risk-adjusted discount rate adjusts the denominator:

$$\overline{NPV} = \sum_{t=1}^{N} \frac{\overline{X}_t}{(1+k)^t} - I_0$$

where k is the risk-adjusted rate based on the perceived degree of project risk.
The higher the perceived riskiness of a project, the greater the risk premium to be added to the risk-free interest rate. This results in a higher discount rate and, hence, a lower net present value.

Although this approach has a certain intuitive appeal, its relevance depends very much on how risk is perceived to change over time. The risk-adjusted discount rate involves the impact of the risk premium growing over time at an exponential rate, implying that the riskiness of the project's cash flow also increases over time. Figure 3.7 demonstrates this point. Although the expected cash flow from a project may be constant over its 10-year life, the riskiness associated with the cash flows increases with time. However, if risk did not increase with time, the risk-adjusted discount rate would be inappropriate.

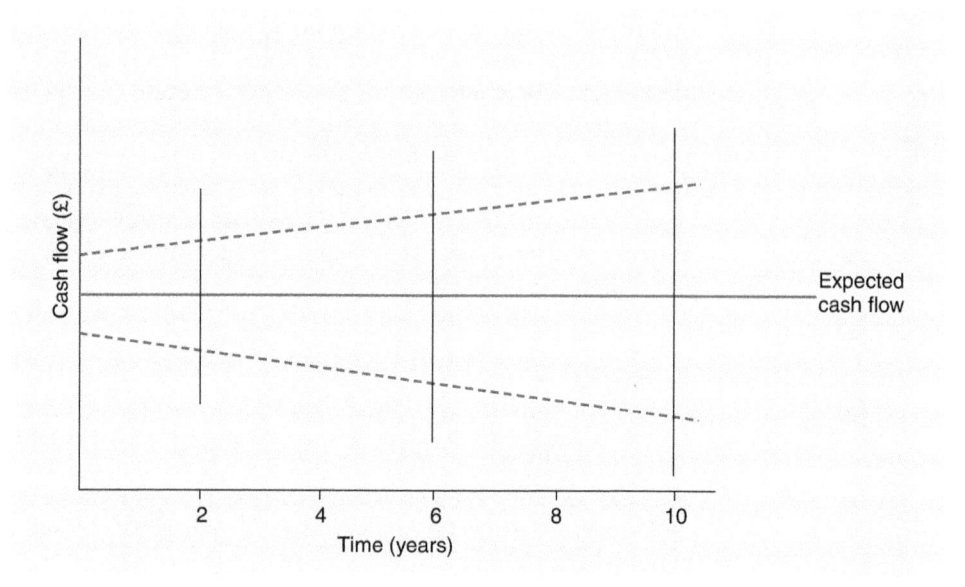

Figure 3.7 **How risk is assumed to increase over time**

Adjusting the discount rate: Chox-Box Ltd

Chox-Box Ltd is a manufacturer of confectionery currently appraising a proposal to launch a new product that has had very little pre-launch testing. It is estimated that this proposal will produce annual cash flows in the region of £100,000 for the next five years, after which product profitability declines sharply. As the proposal is seen as a high-risk venture, a 12 per cent risk premium is incorporated in the discount rate. The risk-adjusted cash flow, before discounting at the risk-free discount rate, is therefore £89,286 in Year 1 (£100,000/1.12), falling to £56,742 in Year 5 (£100,000/1.12^5).

To what extent does this method reflect the actual riskiness of the annual cash flows for Years 1 and 5? Arguably, the greatest uncertainty surrounds the initial launch period. Once the initial market penetration and subsequent repeat orders are known, the subsequent sales are relatively easy to forecast. Thus, for Chox-Box, a single risk-adjusted discount rate is a poor proxy for the impact of risk on value over the project's life, because risk does not increase exponentially with the passage of time, and, in some cases, actually declines over time. The Eurotunnel project provides another illustration of this. By far the greatest risks were in the initial tunnelling and development phases.

A deeper understanding of the relationship between the certainty equivalent and risk-adjusted discount rate approaches may be gained by reading the Appendix to this chapter.

3.8 RISK ANALYSIS IN PRACTICE

To what extent do companies employ the techniques discussed in this chapter? Table 3.6 shows changes since 1980.

Table 3.6 Risk analysis in large UK firms

	1980 (%)	1992 (%)	2003 (%)
Sensitivity analysis	42	86	89
Reduced payback period	30	59	75
Risk-adjusted rate	41	64	82
Probability analysis	10	47	77
Beta analysis	–	20	43

Source: Pike (1996), Alkaraan and Northcott (2006).

Although the surveys are quite dated, they demonstrate that use of sensitivity analysis has increased significantly over the period and is now used in nearly all larger firms. Similar increases here occurred in the use of risk-adjusted discount rates and shortening the payback period. However, the greatest increase has taken place in the use of probability analysis and beta analysis (see Chapters 5 and 6 which cover the Capital Asset Pricing Model).

It is important to remember that investment appraisal and the associated risk analysis is not simply a financial exercise. There is a human aspect to this that means that the processes may not be wholly rational. For example, managers in a firm have to compete with one another for funding of capital projects. Duchin and Sosyura (2013) have examined this aspect of capital projects in a US setting and find that divisional managers are more likely to receive funding for capital projects if they are socially connected to the CEO. Social connections may arise because the manager and CEO have worked together previously or are in the same alumni networks. This is potentially important as funds should ideally be allocated to those projects that will provide the best returns and taking into account the risk of the project, not based on whether a manager is connected to the CEO. The findings of Greene *et al.* (2009) suggest that multinational firms appear to be better at capital budgeting than purely domestic companies. The key reason proposed is that the managers' skills in multinational firms are stronger than in domestic firms. Yim *et al.* (2015) examined risk indicators for reworking on previously failed projects and named those projects as rework projects. The main objective of this research project was to examine differences and/or similarities between the risks associated with the original and rework projects. Their results indicate some differences in the type of risks associated with the rework projects, and regard urgency of the project, quality of the project and changes in technology as the additional risks specifically associated with the rework projects.

3.9 CAPITAL INVESTMENT OPTIONS

In financial markets, 'options' are a type of financial instrument that gives the holder of the option the right to do something in the future but, very importantly, the holder has no obligation to do this thing. For example, the holder may have the right to sell a share in Marks & Spencer plc in three months' time at £5, but is not obliged to do so. Therefore, the holder of the option has flexibility. They can choose to do something or choose not to do something. Capital investment options (sometimes termed **real options**) are option-like features found in capital budgeting decisions. While discounted cash flow techniques are very useful tools of analysis, they are generally more suited to financial assets, because they assume that assets are held rather than managed. The main difference between evaluating financial assets and real assets is that investors in, say, shares are generally *passive*. Unless they have a fair degree of control, they can only monitor performance and decide whether to hold or sell their shares.

real options
Options to invest in real assets such as capital projects

Corporate managers, on the other hand, play a far more *active* role in achieving the planned net present value on a capital project. When a project is slipping behind forecast, they can take action to try to achieve the original NPV target. In other words, they can create options – actions to mitigate losses or exploit new opportunities presented by capital investments. Managerial flexibility to adapt its future actions creates an asymmetry in the NPV probability distribution that increases the investment project's value by improving the upside potential while limiting downside losses.

We will consider three types of option: the abandonment option, the timing option and strategic investment options.

■ Abandonment option

Major investment decisions involve heavy capital commitments and are largely irreversible: once the initial capital expenditure is incurred, management cannot turn the clock back and do it differently. The costs associated with divestment are usually very high. Most capital projects divested early will realise little more than scrap value. In the case of a nuclear power plant, the decommissioning cost could be phenomenal. Because management is committing large sums of money in pursuit of higher, but uncertain, payoffs, the **option to abandon**, without incurring enormous costs if things look grim, can be very valuable. To ignore this is to undervalue the project.

> **option to abandon**
> Choice to allow an option to expire. With a capital investment, abandonment should take place where the value for which an asset can be sold exceeds the present value of its future benefits from continuing its operations

The development of new drugs in the pharmaceutical industry provides an example of an abandonment option. The research process for the development of a new drug takes considerable time, is very costly and offers no guarantee that it will be successful. Therefore, a pharmaceutical company may need to decide to abandon a research project at some point in its life. However, this might also create an opportunity to derive some value from the research carried out up to that point. For example, the company could potentially sell on the intellectual capital to another firm. Consequently, pharmaceutical companies can view drug development as having optionality, for at any time during the research process, the company has the option to either continue development (and invest more in the research project) or to stop development and sell the intellectual capital.

Related to abandonment options are contraction options. For example, a company may find that the market it sells into starts to decline, and because of this the company needs less space for warehousing its products. If it has leased the warehouse premises, then at the outset it may have been written into the lease that it can 'return' spare space to the landlord. Similarly, the company may have outsourced some of its production, and as the market declines, it is able to decrease production levels simply because part of the contractual agreement with the other company is that it can request less product when required. Another example of a contraction option is an oil company that decides to either slow down or close down oil production temporarily because the price of oil has dropped. It can then recommence production when the price of oil has risen sufficiently.

Life in the post-Opec era

The oil price is back where it was some months ago – with Brent crude struggling to stay above $50 a barrel. This is despite an extension of the Opec quota deal and the support of Russia. The fall in prices shows a lack of confidence in the cartel's ability to reassert total control of the market. The open question is, what happens next?

In the short to medium term, oil supply looks strong and certainly stronger than demand. In the longer term, the analysis is more complicated. Some in the industry and parts of the financial market believe that the longer prices stay low, the sharper will be the correction. On this view, low prices discourage new investment and that means that new production will be limited. Meanwhile demand, especially from emerging economies such as India, will keep rising.

Clearly, the headline investment numbers in the oil industry have fallen in the last two years. Most of the majors have cut spending on exploration and new project development. Companies are cutting costs and simplifying operations for a lower price environment. Cost discipline and ever-advancing technology are proving very effective. Those who expected the US shale industry or indeed North Sea oil to go out of business when prices fell from their peak of $115 three years ago have been proved wrong. Margins have been reduced but very few companies have gone out of business. US shale is now in most cases profitable at $50 a barrel, as is much of the North Sea.

The same approach is being taken to new developments. Certainly, projects have been postponed, feeding the view that future production will be limited. But in many cases the delay is designed to allow project managers to take 10, 20 or even 40 per cent out of costs. The fall in the total money invested reflects that and, rather than a sign of collapse, the numbers can be read as a measure of improved productivity.

If the supply forecasts could be too low the demand numbers certainly look too high. No one knows for sure, which is what makes the outlook so interesting.

FT *Source*: Butler, N. (2017) Life in the post-Opec era. *Financial Times*, 5 June. © The Financial Times Limited 2018. All rights reserved.

Example: Topvision plc

An established television manufacturer, Topvision plc, has decided to market a new product using technology new to the company, and is currently evaluating an £11 million capital project to enable its manufacture. The project has an infinite life and the discount rate is 10 per cent. Only two outcomes are possible, each with a 50 per cent probability:

At best outcome: annual cash benefits of £3 million, yielding an NPV of:

−£11 million (capital outlay) + £3 million/0.10 (PV of annual benefits)

= £19 million

At worst outcome: annual cash benefits of −£1 million giving an NPV of:

−£11 million − £1 million/0.10

= −£21 million

This yields an expected NPV of:

50% × £19 million + 50% × −£21 million = −£1 million.

On this basis the project would not be acceptable. However, on further consideration, management recognises that it would be able to identify which of the two outcomes would prevail by the end of the first year. This means that it has the option to abandon the project at that time.

The 'at worst' outcome now becomes a one-year project:

−£11 million − £1 million/1.10 = −£11.91 million

Exercising the abandonment option now suggests an expected NPV for the project of:

50% × £19 million + 50% × −£11.91 million

= £3.545 million.

The option to abandon the project after Year 1 turns the expected NPV from −£1 million to +£3.545 million, and it now indicates that the project should be accepted. Arguably, project abandonment after one year would also realise a higher scrap value, further improving the 'at worst' outcome and strengthening the case for investment.

A further example: Cardiff Components Ltd

Cardiff Components Ltd is considering building a new plant to produce components for the nuclear defence industry. Proposal A is to build a custom-designed plant using the latest technology but applicable only to nuclear defence contracts. A less profitable scheme, Proposal B, is to build a plant using standard machine tools, giving greater flexibility in application and having a much higher salvage value than Proposal A.

The outcome of a general election to be held one year hence has a major impact on the decision. If the current government is returned to office, its commitment to nuclear defence is likely to give rise to new orders, making Proposal A the better choice. If the current opposition party is elected, its commitment to run down the nuclear defence industry would make Proposal B the better course of action. Proposal B has, in effect, an option attached to it, giving the flexibility to abandon the proposed operation in favour of some other activity. We underestimate NPV if we assume that the project must last for the prescribed project life, no matter what happens in the future.

A similar type of option is the option to redeploy. A utility company may have the option to switch between various fuels to produce electricity. This dual plant may cost more than one that is only capable of burning a single fuel, but the value of the redeployment option should be considered in reaching a decision.

■ Timing option

timing/delay option
The option to invest now or defer the decision until conditions are more favourable

The Cardiff Components example not only introduces an abandonment option, it also raises the **timing or delay option**. Management may have viewed the investment as a 'now or never' opportunity, arguing that in highly competitive markets there is no scope for delay. However, most project decisions have three possible outcomes – accept, reject or defer until economic and other conditions improve. In effect, this amounts to viewing the decision as an option that is about to expire on the new plant. If a positive NPV is expected, the option will be exercised; otherwise, the option lapses and no investment is made.

An immediate investment would yield either a negative NPV – in which case it would not be taken up – or a positive NPV. Delaying the decision by a year to gain valuable new information is a more valuable option. Managements sometimes delay taking up apparently wealth-creating opportunities because they believe that the option to wait and gather new information is sufficiently valuable.

A further example of a timing option could be a supermarket that buys land but delays building the supermarket until it considers the time appropriate. The reason for delaying the build may be because the supermarket believes there is currently insufficient market demand for its goods or because people living close by will react adversely to the development of a new supermarket at the present time. Of course, there also exists an abandonment option, as the land has value in its own right and the supermarket can decide to sell the land if it judges it is strategically the better thing to do.

■ Strategic investment options

follow-on opportunities
Options that arise following a course of action

Certain investment decisions give rise to **follow-on opportunities** that are wealth-creating. New technology investment, involving large-scale research and development, is particularly difficult to evaluate. Managers refer to the high level of intangible benefits associated with such decisions. What they really mean is that these investments offer further investment opportunities (e.g. greater flexibility), but that, at this stage, the precise form of such opportunities cannot be quantified.

Valuation calculations applied to strategic investment options raise as many questions as they answer. For example, how much of the risk for the follow-on project depends upon the outcome of the initial project? But option pricing does offer insights into the problem of valuing 'intangibles' in capital budgeting, particularly where they create options not otherwise available to the firm. Real options will be further discussed in Chapter 8 where the main focus will be on their valuation. For example, a company may initially choose to establish only a small operation in an overseas country and, in effect, test the market. Subsequently, if there is strong demand for its products or services, then it can choose to expand the operation. This idea of follow-on options can apply not only to establishing an operation in a new market, but also to establishing a company's brand name in a new market. A company can undertake a marketing campaign in an overseas country, and if a positive reaction occurs, it can choose to commence selling into that market.

The use of real options in practice

The evidence suggests that, in practice, only a small number of companies are using a real options approach to appraise projects. For example, Baker *et al.*'s (2011) survey of Canadian firms found that only 16.8 per cent of respondents used real options approaches. When the managers of the sample firms ranked their use of capital budgeting techniques, net present value, internal rate of return and payback period were frequently used, but the barrier to using real options was a lack of knowledge and expertise. This was despite those firms that were using real options citing the primary reasons for doing so were that it enabled them to incorporate flexibility into managerial decision-making, and that it aided in the development of the strategic vision of the company.

Similarly, Horn, Kjærland, Molnar and Steen (2015) conducted a survey from the Chief Financial Officers of the 1,500 largest companies from Norway, Denmark and Sweden, comprising 500 companies from each country. Their results suggest that only 6 per cent of the sample companies use real options as their capital budgeting method, whereas the most used method recorded, the net present value method, was used by 74 per cent of the responding companies. As 70 per cent of the respondents showed no familiarity with the real options method for capital budgeting, they regard the complex nature of real options as the main reason behind the limited use of this method.

In light of these research findings, we argue that due to its complex nature and lack of required knowledge and expertise in organisations, the real options method is rarely used in capital budgeting decisions.

SUMMARY

Risk is an important element in virtually all investment decisions. Because most people in business are risk-averse, the identification, measurement and, where possible, reduction of risk should be a central feature in the decision-making process. The arguments presented in this chapter suggest that firms are increasingly conducting risk analysis. This does not mean that the risk dimension is totally ignored by other firms; rather, they choose to handle project risk by less objective methods such as experience, feel or intuition.

We have defined what is meant by risk and examined a variety of ways of measuring it. The probability distribution, giving the probability of occurrence of each possible outcome following an investment decision, is the concept underlying most of the methods discussed. Measures of risk, such as the standard deviation, indicate the extent to which actual outcomes are likely to vary from the expected value.

Key points

- The expected NPV, although useful, does not show the whole picture. We need to understand managers' attitudes to risk and to estimate the degree of project risk.

- Three types of risk are relevant in capital budgeting: project risk in isolation, the project's impact on corporate risk and its impact on market risk. The last two are addressed more fully in Chapters 5 and 6.

- The standard deviation, semi-variance and coefficient of variation each measure, in slightly different ways, project risk.
- Sensitivity analysis and scenario analysis are used to locate and assess the potential impact of risk on project performance. Simulation is a more sophisticated approach which captures the essential characteristics of the investment that are subject to uncertainty.
- The NPV formula can be adjusted to consider risk. Adjustment of the cash flows is achieved by the certainty equivalent method. The risk-adjusted discount rate increases the risk premium for higher-risk projects.
- Capital investment decisions may have options attached such as the option to abandon, delay or expand. Conventional NPV analysis that ignores these options can seriously understate a project's value.

Further reading

Books on real options include Guthrie (2009), Mun (2016), and Peters (2016). Useful research contributions on risk and risk analysis are given in Pike (1988, 1996), Pike and Ho (1991), Mao and Helliwell (1969), Bierman and Hass (1973), Caliskana and Doukas (2015), Buchner and Wagner (2017), and O'Brien and Szerszen (2017). Risk analysis has become increasingly incorporated into risk management so that a very wide range of risk-related issues are considered across the company. Significant numbers of risk management books are now in publication. Some recent books that cover many related areas are McNeil, Frey and Embrechts (2015), Hull (2015), and Hopkin (2017).

Appendix
MULTI-PERIOD CASH FLOWS AND RISK

For simplicity, we have so far assumed single-period investments and conveniently ignored the fact that investments are typically multi-period. As risk is to be specifically evaluated, cash flows should be discounted at the risk-free rate of interest, reflecting only the time-value of money. To include a risk premium within the discount rate, when risk is already considered separately, amounts to double-counting and typically understates the true net present value. The expected NPV of an investment project is found by summing the present values of the expected net cash flows and deducting the initial investment outlay. Thus, for a two-year investment proposal:

$$\overline{NPV} = \frac{\overline{X}_1}{1+i} + \frac{\overline{X}_2}{(1+i)^2} - I_0$$

where $\overline{NPV}$ is the expected NPV, $\overline{X}_1$ is the expected value of net cash flow in Year 1, $\overline{X}_2$ is the expected value of net cash flow in Year 2, I_0 is the cash investment outlay and i is the risk-free rate of interest.

A major problem in calculating the standard deviation of a project's NPVs is that the cash flows in one period are typically dependent, to some degree, on the cash flows of earlier periods. Assuming for the present that cash flows for our two-period project are statistically independent, the total variance of the NPV is equal to the discounted sum of the annual variances.

For example, the Bronson project, with a two-year life, has an initial cost of £500 and the possible payoffs and probabilities outlined in Table 3.7. Applying the standard deviation and expected value formulae already discussed, we obtain an expected NPV of £268 and standard deviation of £206.

Table 3.7 Bronson project payoffs with independent cash flows

Probability	Year 1 cash flow (£)	Year 2 cash flow (£)
0.1	100	200
0.2	200	400
0.4	300	600
0.2	400	800
0.1	500	1,000
Expected value	£300	£600
Variance (σ^2)	£12,000	£48,000
Standard deviation	£110	£219

Assuming a risk-free discount rate of 10 per cent, the expected NPV is:

$$\overline{\text{NPV}} = \frac{300}{(1.10)} + \frac{600}{(1.10)^2} - 500 = £268$$

The standard deviation of the entire proposal is found by discounting the annual variances to their present values, applying the equation:

$$\sigma = \sqrt{\sum_{t=1}^{N} \frac{\sigma_t^2}{(1+i)^{2t}}}$$

In our simple case, this is:

$$\sigma = \sqrt{\frac{\sigma_1^2}{(1+i)^2} + \frac{\sigma_2^2}{(1+i)^4}} = \sqrt{\frac{12,000}{(1.1)^2} + \frac{48,000}{(1.1)^4}} = £206$$

The project therefore offers an expected NPV of £268 and a standard deviation of £206.

■ Perfectly correlated cash flows

At the other extreme from the independence assumption is the assumption that the cash flows in one year are entirely dependent upon the cash flows achieved in previous periods. When this is the case, successive cash flows are said to be perfectly correlated. Any deviation in one year from forecast directly affects the accuracy of subsequent forecasts. The effect is that, over time, the standard deviation of the probability distribution of net present values increases. The standard deviation of a stream of cash flows perfectly correlated over time is:

$$\sigma = \sum_{t=1}^{N} \frac{\sigma_t}{(1+i)^t}$$

Returning to the example in Table 3.7, but assuming perfect correlation of cash flows over time, the standard deviation for the project is:

$$\sigma = \frac{£109}{1.1} + \frac{£219}{(1.1)^2}$$
$$= £280$$

Thus, the risk associated with this project is £280, assuming perfect correlation, which is higher than that for independent cash flows. Obviously, this difference would be considerably greater for longer-lived projects.

In reality, few projects are either independent or perfectly correlated over time. The standard deviation lies somewhere between the two. It will be based on the formula for the independence case, but with an additional term for the covariance between annual cash flows.

Interpreting results

While decision-makers are interested to know the degree of risk associated with a given project, their fundamental concern is whether the project will produce a positive net present value. Risk analysis can go some way to answering this question. If a project's probability distribution of expected NPVs is approximately normal, we can estimate the probability of failing to achieve at least zero NPV. In the previous example, the expected NPV was £268. This is standardised by dividing it by the standard deviation using the formula:

$$Z = \frac{X - \overline{\text{NPV}}}{\sigma}$$

where X in this case is zero and Z is the number of standardised units. Thus, in the case of the independent cash flow assumption, we have:

$$Z = \frac{0 - £268}{£206}$$

$$= -1.30 \text{ standardised units}$$

Reference to normal distribution tables reveals that there is a 0.0968 probability that the NPV will be zero or less. Accordingly, there must be a (1 − 0.0968) or 90.32 per cent probability of the project producing an NPV in excess of zero.

It is probably unnecessary to attempt to measure the standard deviation for every project. Even the larger European companies tend to use probability analysis sparingly in capital project analysis. Unless cash flow forecasting is wildly optimistic, or the future economic conditions underlying all investments are far worse than anticipated, the bad news from one project should be compensated by good news from another project.

Sometimes, however, a project is of such great importance that its failure could threaten the very survival of the business. In such a case, management should be fully aware of the scale of its exposure to loss and the probability of this occurring.

Probability of failure: Microloft Ltd

Microloft Ltd, a local family-controlled company specialising in attic conversions, is currently considering investing in a major expansion giving wider geographical coverage. The NPV from the project is expected to be £330,000 with a standard deviation of £300,000. Should the project fail (perhaps because of the reaction by major competitors), the company could afford to lose £210,000 before the bank manager 'pulled the plug' and put in the receiver. What is the probability that this new project could put Microloft out of business?

We need to find the value of Z where X is the worst NPV outcome that Microloft could tolerate:

$$Z = \frac{X - \overline{\text{NPV}}}{\sigma}$$

$$= \frac{-£210 - £330}{£300} = -1.8$$

Assuming the outcomes are normally distributed, probability tables will show a 3.6 per cent chance of failure from accepting the project. A family-controlled business, like Microloft, may decide that even this relatively small chance of sending the company on to the rocks is more important than the attractive returns expected from the project.

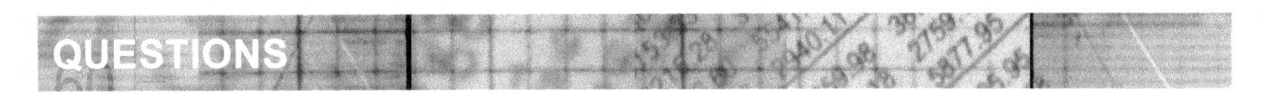

QUESTIONS

Questions with a coloured number have solutions in Appendix B on page 501.

1. Explain the importance of risk in capital budgeting.

2. Explain the distinction between project risk, business risk, financial risk and portfolio risk.

3. The 'woodpulp' project has an initial cost of £13,000 and the firm's risk-free interest rate is 10 per cent. If certainty equivalents and net cash flows (NCFs) for the project are as in the following table, should the project be accepted?

Year	Certainty equivalents	Net cash flows (£)
1	0.90	8,000
2	0.85	7,000
3	0.80	7,000
4	0.75	5,000
5	0.70	5,000
6	0.65	5,000
7	0.60	5,000

4. Meedas Enterprises has a proposal costing £800. Using a 10 per cent cost of capital, compute the expected NPV, standard deviation and coefficient of variation, assuming independent interperiod cash flows.

Probability	Year 1 net cash flow (£)	Year 2 net cash flow (£)
0.2	400	300
0.3	500	400
0.3	600	500
0.2	700	600

5. Corbyn plc is considering launching a new product involving capital investment of £180,000. The machine has a four-year life and no residual value. Sales volumes of 6,000 units are forecast for each of the four years. The product has a selling price of £60 and a variable cost of £36 per unit. Additional fixed overheads of £50,000 will be incurred. The cost of capital is 12.5 per cent p.a. Present a report to the directors of Corbyn plc giving:
   (a) the net present values;
   (b) the percentage amount each variable can deteriorate before the project becomes unacceptable;
   (c) a sensitivity graph.

6. Devonia (Laboratories) Ltd has recently carried out successful clinical trials on a new type of skin cream, which has been developed to reduce the effects of ageing. Research and development costs in relation to the new product amount to £160,000. In order to gauge the market potential of the new product, an independent firm of market research consultants was hired at a cost of £15,000. The market research report submitted by the consultants indicates that the skin cream is likely to have a product life of four years and could be sold to retail chemists and large department stores at a price of £20 per 100-ml container. For each of the four years of the new product's life, sales demand has been estimated as follows:

Number of 100-ml containers sold	Probability of occurrence
11,000	0.3
14,000	0.6
16,000	0.1

If the company decides to launch the new product, production can begin at once. The equipment necessary to make the product is already owned by the company and originally cost £150,000. At the end of the new product's life, it is estimated that the equipment could be sold for £35,000. If the company decides against launching the new product, the equipment will be sold immediately for £85,000 as it will be of no further use to the company.

The new skin cream will require two hours' labour for each 100-ml container produced. The cost of labour for the new product is £4.00 per hour. Additional workers will have to be recruited to produce the new product. At the end of the product's life, the workers are unlikely to be offered further work with the company and redundancy costs of £10,000 are expected. The cost of the ingredients for each 100-ml container is £6.00. Additional overheads arising from the product are expected to be £15,000 p.a.

The new skin cream has attracted the interest of the company's competitors. If the company decides not to produce and sell the skin cream, it can sell the patent rights to a major competitor immediately for £125,000.

Devonia (Laboratories) Ltd has a cost of capital of 12 per cent.

Ignore taxation.

Required

(a) Calculate the expected net present value (ENPV) of the new product.
(b) State, with reasons, whether or not Devonia (Laboratories) Ltd should launch the new product.
(c) Discuss the strengths and weaknesses of the expected net present value approach for making investment decisions.

(Certified Diploma)

7 Plato Pharmaceuticals Ltd has invested £300,000 to date in developing a new type of insect repellent. The repellent is now ready for production and sale, and the marketing director estimates that the product will sell 150,000 bottles per annum over the next five years. The selling price of the insect repellent will be £5 per bottle, and the variable costs are estimated to be £3 per bottle. Fixed costs (excluding depreciation) are expected to be £200,000 per annum. This figure is made up of £160,000 additional fixed costs and £40,000 fixed costs relating to the existing business which will be apportioned to the new product.

In order to produce the repellent, machinery and equipment costing £520,000 will have to be purchased immediately. The estimated residual value of this machinery and equipment in five years' time is £100,000. The company calculates depreciation on a straight-line basis.

The company has a cost of capital of 12 per cent. Ignore taxation.

Required

(a) Calculate the net present value of the product.
(b) Undertake sensitivity analysis to show by how much the following factors would have to change before the product ceased to be worthwhile:
 (i) the discount rate;
 (ii) the initial outlay on machinery and equipment;
 (iii) the net operating cash flows;
 (iv) the residual value of the machinery and equipment.
(c) Discuss the strengths and weaknesses of sensitivity analysis in dealing with risk and uncertainty.
(d) State, with reasons, whether or not you feel the project should go ahead.

(Certified Diploma)

8 The managing director of Tigwood Ltd believes that a market exists for 'microbooks'. He has proposed that the company should market 100 best-selling books on microfiche, which can be read using a special microfiche reader that is connected to a television screen. A microfiche containing an entire book can be purchased from a photographic company at 40 per cent of the average production cost of best-selling paperback books.

The average cost of producing paperback books is estimated at £1.50, and the average selling price of paperbacks is £3.95 each. Copyright fees of 20 per cent of the average selling price of the paperback books would be payable to the publishers of the paperbacks plus an initial lump sum that is still being negotiated but is expected to be £1.5 million. No tax allowances are available on this lump-sum payment. An agreement with the publishers would be signed for a period of six years. Additional variable costs of staffing, handling and marketing are 20p per microfiche, and fixed costs are negligible.

Tigwood Ltd has spent £100,000 on market research and expects sales to be 1,500,000 units per year at an initial unit price of £2.

The microfiche reader would be produced and marketed by another company.

Tigwood would finance the venture with a bank loan at an interest rate of 16 per cent per year. The company's money (nominal) cost of equity and real cost of equity are estimated to be 23 per cent p.a. and 12.6 per cent p.a., respectively. Tigwood's money weighted average cost of capital and real weighted average cost of capital are 18 per cent p.a. and 8 per cent p.a., respectively. The risk-free rate of interest is 11 per cent p.a. and the market return is 17 per cent p.a.

Corporation Tax is at the rate of 35 per cent, payable in the year the profit occurs. All cash flows may be assumed to be at the year end, unless otherwise stated.

Required

(a) Calculate the expected net present value of the microbooks project.
(b) Explain the reasons for your choice of discount rate in the answer to part (a). Discuss whether this rate is likely to be the most appropriate to use in the analysis of the proposed project.
(c) (i) Using sensitivity analysis, estimate by what percentage each of the following would have to change before the project was no longer expected to be viable:
  initial outlay;
  annual contribution;
  the life of the agreement;
  the discount rate.
 (ii) What are the limitations of this sensitivity analysis?
(d) What further information would be useful to help the company decide whether to undertake the microbook project?

(ACCA)

9 The general manager of the nationalised postal service of a small country, Zedland, wishes to introduce a new service. This service would offer same-day delivery of letters and parcels posted before 10 a.m. within a distance of 150 km. The service would require 100 new vans costing $8,000 each and 20 trucks costing $18,000 each. One hundred and eighty new workers would be employed at an average annual wage of $13,000, and five managers on average annual salaries of $20,000 would be moved from their existing duties, where they would not be replaced.

Two postal rates are proposed. In the first year of operation, letters will cost $0.525 and parcels $5.25. Market research undertaken at a cost of $50,000 forecasts that demand will average 15,000 letters and 500 parcels per working day during the first year, and 20,000 letters and 750 parcels per working day thereafter. There is a five-day working week. Annual running and maintenance costs on similar new vans and trucks are estimated to be $2,000 per van and $4,000 per truck, respectively, in the first year of operation. These costs will increase by 20 per cent p.a. (excluding the effects of inflation). Vehicles are depreciated over a five-year period on a straight-line basis. Depreciation is tax-allowable, and the vehicles will have negligible scrap value at the end of five years. Advertising in Year 1 will cost $500,000, and in Year 2 $250,000. There will be no advertising after Year 2. Existing premises will be used for the new service, but additional costs of $150,000 per year will be incurred.

All the above cost data are current estimates and exclude any inflation effects. Wage and salary costs and all other costs are expected to rise because of inflation by approximately 5 per cent p.a. during the five-year planning horizon of the postal service. The government of Zedland will not permit annual price increases within nationalised industries to exceed the level of inflation.

Nationalised industries are normally required by the government to earn at least an annual after-tax return of 5 per cent on average investment and to achieve, on average, at least zero net present value on their investments.

The new service would be financed half by internally generated funds and half by borrowing on the capital market at an interest rate of 12 per cent p.a. The opportunity cost of capital for the postal service is estimated to be 14 per cent p.a. Corporate taxes in Zedland, to which the postal service is subject, are at the rate of 30 per cent for annual profits of up to $500,000 and 40 per cent for the balance in excess of $500,000. Tax is payable one year in arrears. All transactions may be assumed to be on a cash basis and to occur at the end of the year, with the exception of the initial investment, which would be required almost immediately.

Required

(a) Acting as an independent consultant, prepare a report advising whether the new postal service should be introduced. Include a discussion of other factors that might need to be taken into account before a final decision was made. State clearly any assumptions that you make.

(b) Monte Carlo simulation has been suggested as a possible method of estimating the net present value of a project. Briefly assess the advantages and disadvantages of using this technique in investment appraisal.

(ACCA)

Practical assignment

Describe the types of risk associated with investment decisions in a firm known to you. (If necessary, read the Annual Report of a major company, like BP plc, to familiarise yourself with a company.) Suggest how these risks should be formally assessed within their investment appraisal process.

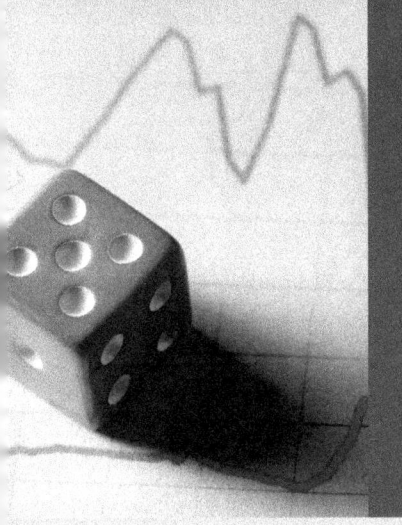

4

Relationships between investments: portfolio theory

Netwealth benefits from rise in UK and international equities

Netwealth, the wealth manager led by Charlotte Ransom, a former Goldman Sachs partner, reported returns ranging from 2.9 per cent to 25.6 per cent across its seven portfolios in the year to the end of May, with the best gains generated from investments in UK and international equities.

Iain Barnes, head of portfolio management, said the performance of Netwealth's highest-risk sterling-denominated portfolio was 'pretty much in line with the FTSE 100, but with lower levels of volatility'. The lowest-risk portfolio, which generated 2.9 per cent net of fees, is Netwealth's most conservative strategy, focused on cash and short-dated gilts.

Launched just over a year ago, Netwealth has joined a clutch of investment platforms, such as Nutmeg and Wealthify, that aim to dislodge longer-established groups. It offers online wealth management services and, for higher fees, access to financial advice.

Sources: Thompson, J. (2017) Netwealth benefits from rise in UK and international equities. *Financial Times*, 3 June.
© The Financial Times Limited 2018. All rights reserved.

Learning objectives

This chapter is designed to explore the financial equivalent of the maxim 'don't put all your eggs in one basket'. In particular, it will help the reader:

- To understand the rationale behind the diversification decisions of shareholders and companies.
- To explain the mechanics of portfolio construction with a user-friendly approach to the key statistics, using numerical examples.
- To explore why optimal portfolio selection is a matter of personal choice.
- To examine the drawbacks of portfolio analysis as an approach to project appraisal.

A good grasp of the principles of portfolio analysis is an essential underpinning to understanding the Capital Asset Pricing Model, to be covered in Chapter 5.

4.1 INTRODUCTION

diversification
Extension of a firm's activities into new and unrelated fields. Although this may generate cost savings, e.g. via shared distribution systems, as a by-product, the fundamental motive for diversification is to reduce exposure to fluctuations in economic activity

portfolio
A combination of investments – securities or physical assets – into a single 'bundled' investment. A well-diversified portfolio has the potential capacity to lower the investor's exposure to the risk of fluctuations in the overall economy

contra-cyclical
A term applied to an investment whose returns fluctuate in opposite ways to general trends in business activity, i.e. contrary to the cycle

portfolio effect
The tendency for the risk on a well-diversified holding of investments to fall below the risk of most, and sometimes all, of its individual components

This chapter deals with the theory underlying **diversification** decisions. Diversification is a strategic device for dealing with risk. Whereas Chapter 3 examined ways to analyse the risk of individual projects, here, we study how the financial manager can exploit interrelationships between projects to adjust the risk–return characteristics of the whole enterprise. In the process, we will show why many firms develop a wide spread of activities or **portfolios**. The term 'portfolio' is usually applied to combinations of securities, but we will show that the principles underlying security portfolio formation can be applied to combinations of any type of asset, including investment projects.

Many firms diffuse their efforts across a range of products, market segments and customers in order to spread the risks of declining trade and profitability. If a firm can reduce its reliance on particular products or markets, it can more easily bear the impact of a major reverse in any single market. However, firms do not reduce their exposure to the threat of new products or new competitors for entirely negative reasons. Diversification can generate some major strategic advantages: for example, the wider the spread of activities, the greater the access to star-performing sectors of the economy. Imagine an economy divided into five sectors, with one star performer each year whose identity is always random. A company operating in a single sector is likely to miss out in four years out of five. In such a world, it is prudent to have a stake in every sector by building a portfolio of all five activities.

Diversification is designed to even out the bumps in the time profile of profits and cash flows. The ideal form of diversification is to engage in activities that behave in exactly opposite ways. When sales and earnings are relatively low in one area, the adverse consequences can be offset by participation in a sector where sales and profits are relatively high. With perfect synchronisation, the time profile of overall returns will describe the pattern shown in Figure 4.1. This shows the returns from two activities: A, which moves in parallel with the economy as a whole; and B, which moves in an *exactly* opposite way. The equal and opposite fluctuations in the returns from these two activities would result in a perfectly level profile for a diversified enterprise comprising both activities. In generally adverse economic conditions, the returns from activity A, closely following the economy as a whole, will be depressed, but involvement in activity B has an exactly compensating effect. The reverse applies when the economy is expanding. The returns from B are said to be **contra-cyclical**, and the dampening effect on the variability of returns is called a **portfolio effect**.

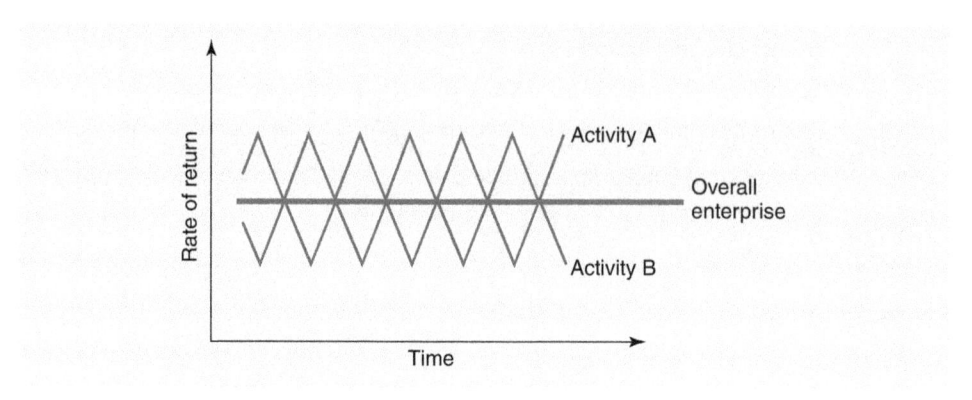

Figure 4.1 Equal and offsetting fluctuations in returns

For firms planning to diversify, there are two important messages. First, it is not enough simply to spread your activities. Different activities are subject to different types of risk, which are not always closely related. For an internationally diversified firm, the factors affecting domestic operations may be quite different from those affecting overseas operations. If changes in these influences are random and relatively uncorrelated, diversification may significantly reduce the variability of company earnings. Second, to generate an appreciable impact on overall returns, <u>diversification must usually be substantial in relation to the whole enterprise</u>. Hence, two key messages of portfolio diversification are: *look for unrelated activities* and *engage in significant diversification*.

4.2 PORTFOLIO ANALYSIS: THE BASIC PRINCIPLES

The theory of diversification was developed by Markowitz (1952). It can be reduced to the maxim 'don't put all your eggs in one basket'. This is a simple motto, but one that many investors persistently ignore. How often do we read heart-rending stories of small investors who have lost all their savings in some shady venture or other? Why do more than 50 per cent of private investors persist in holding a single security in their investment portfolios? Perhaps they are unaware of the advantages of spreading their risks, or have not understood the arguments. Perhaps they are not risk-averse or are simply irrational.* Rational, risk-averse investors appreciate that not all investments perform well at the same time, that some may never perform well, and that a few may perform spectacularly well. Since no one can predict which investments will fall into each category in any one period, it is rational to <u>spread one's funds over a wide set of investments</u>.

A simple example will illustrate the remarkable potential benefits of diversification.

■ Achieving a perfect portfolio effect

An investor can undertake one or both of the two investments, Apple and Pear. Apple has a 50 per cent chance of achieving an 8 per cent return and a 50 per cent chance of returning 12 per cent. Pear has a 50 per cent chance of generating a return of 6 per cent and a 50 per cent chance of yielding 14 per cent. The two investments are in sectors of the economy that move in direct opposition to each other. The investor expects the return on Apple to be relatively high when that on Pear is relatively low, and vice versa. What portfolio should the investor hold?

First of all, note that the expected value (EV) of each investment's return is identical:

Investment Apple: EV = (0.5 × 8%) + (0.5 × 12%) = (4% + 6%) = 10%
Investment Pear: EV = (0.5 × 6%) + (0.5 × 14%) = (3% + 7%) = 10%

At first glance, it may appear that the investor would be indifferent between Apple and Pear or, indeed, any combination of them. However, there is a wide variety of possible expected returns according to how the investor 'weights' the portfolio. Moreover, a badly weighted portfolio can offer wide variations in returns in different time periods.

For example, when Pear is the star performer, a portfolio comprising 20 per cent of Apple and 80 per cent of Pear will offer a return of:

$$\frac{\text{Apple}}{(0.2 \times 8\%)} + \frac{\text{Pear}}{(0.8 \times 14\%)} = \frac{\text{Portfolio}}{(1.6\% + 11.2\%)} = 12.8\%$$

When Apple is the star, the return is only:

$$(0.2 \times 12\%) + (0.8 \times 6\%) = (2.4 + 4.8\%) = 7.2\%$$

---

*A common reason is probably that they have applied for shares in a privatisation, or been given shares in a building society demutualisation! The biggest demutualisation was that by the Halifax Building Society (now part of the Lloyds Group). 'The Halifax' gave free shares to 7.5 million customers in June 1997.

Although there should be as many good years for Apple as for Pear, resulting over the long term in an average return of 10 per cent, *in the shorter term*, the investor would be over-exposed to the risk of a series of bad years for Pear. Happily, there is a portfolio which removes this risk entirely.

Consider a portfolio invested two-thirds in Apple and one-third in Pear. When Apple is the star, the return on the portfolio (R_p) is a weighted average of the returns from the two components:

$$R_p = (2/3 \times 12\%) + (1/3 \times 6\%) = (8\% + 2\%) = 10\%$$

Conversely, when Pear is the star, the portfolio offers a return of:

$$R_p = (2/3 \times 8\%) + (1/3 \times 14\%) = (5.33\% + 4.67\%) = 10\%$$

With this combination, the risk-averse investor cannot go wrong! The portfolio completely removes variability in returns as there are only two possible states of the economy. Any rational risk-averse investor should select this combination of Apple and Pear to eliminate risk for a guaranteed 10 per cent return. Here, the portfolio effect is perfect, like that shown in Figure 4.1. However, not every investor would necessarily opt for this particular portfolio. Super-optimists might load their funds entirely on to Pear, hoping for 14 per cent returns every year. This may work for a year or two, but the chances of achieving a consistent return of 14 per cent year after year are very low. The chance of achieving 14 per cent in the first year is 50 per cent, but the chance of getting 14 per cent in *each* of the first two years is (50 per cent) × (50 per cent) = 25 per cent and so on. Diversification is usually the safest (and often the most profitable) policy. We will study later in the chapter how different portfolio weightings affect the overall risk and return.

In this example, the opportunity to eliminate all risk arises from the *perfect negative correlation*[*] between the two investments, but this attractive property can only be exploited by weighting the portfolio in a particular way.

Regrettably, cases of perfect negative correlation between the returns from securities are rare. Most investment returns exhibit varying degrees of positive correlation, largely according to how they depend on overall economic trends. This does not rule out risk-reducing diversification benefits, but suggests they may be less pronounced than in our example. As we will see, *the extent to which portfolio combination can achieve a reduction in risk depends on the degree of correlation between returns*. Later in the chapter, we will examine rather more realistic cases, but first we need to explore more fully the nature and measurement of portfolio risk.

Self-assessment activity 4.1

What are the two required conditions for total elimination of portfolio risk?

(Answer in Appendix A)

4.3 HOW TO MEASURE PORTFOLIO RISK

We have just seen the importance of the degree of correlation between the returns from two investments. We saw also how the return from a portfolio could be expressed as a weighted average of the individual asset returns, the weights being the proportions of the portfolio accounted for by each of the various components. A similar relationship

---

[*]Readers lacking a grounding in elementary statistics may want to consult an introductory text such as C. Morris, *Quantitative Approaches in Business Studies* (Pearson Education, 2008), in order to study the concept of correlation. Correlation is measured on a scale of −1 (perfect negative correlation) through zero to +1 (perfect positive correlation).

applies before the event: that is, if we consider the *expected value* of the return from the portfolio. The expected return on a portfolio (ER_p) comprising two assets, A and B, whose individual expected returns are ER_A and ER_B, respectively, is given by:

$$ER_p = \alpha ER_A + (1 - \alpha)ER_B \qquad (4.1)$$

where α and $(1 - \alpha)$ are the respective weightings of assets A and B, with $\alpha + (1 - \alpha) = 1$.

The riskiness of the portfolio expresses the extent to which the actual return may deviate from the expected return. This may be expressed by the variance of the return, σ_p^2, or by its standard deviation, σ_p.

Portfolio risk

The (rather fearsome!) expression for the standard deviation of a two-asset investment portfolio, σ_p, is:

$$\sigma_p = \sqrt{[\alpha^2 \sigma_A^2 + (1 - \alpha)^2 \sigma_B^2 + 2\alpha(1 - \alpha)\text{cov}_{AB}]} \qquad (4.2)$$

where

$\alpha =$ the proportion of the portfolio invested in asset A

$(1 - \alpha) =$ the proportion of the portfolio invested in asset B

$\sigma_A^2 =$ the variance of the return on asset A

$\sigma_B^2 =$ the variance of the return on asset B

$\text{cov}_{AB} =$ the covariance of the returns on A and B.

covariance
A statistical measure of the extent to which the fluctuations exhibited by two (or more) variables are related

correlation coefficient
A relative measure of co-movement that locates assets on a scale between −1 and +1. Where returns move exactly in unison, perfect positive correlation exists, and where exactly opposite movements occur, perfect negative correlation exists. Most investments fall in between, mainly with positive correlation

co-movement/ co-variability
The tendency for two variables, e.g. the returns from two investments, to move in parallel

We need now to explain the meaning of the covariance. The **covariance**, like the **correlation coefficient**, is a measure of the interrelationship between random variables, in this case, the returns from the two investments A and B. In other words, it measures the extent to which their returns move together, i.e. their **co-movement** or **co-variability**. When the two returns move together, it has a positive value; when they move away from each other, it has a negative value; and when there is no co-variability at all, its value is zero. However, unlike the correlation coefficient, whose value is restricted to a scale ranging from −1 to +1, the covariance can assume any value. It measures co-movement in *absolute* terms, whereas the correlation coefficient is a *relative* measure.

The correlation coefficient between the return on A and the return on B, r_{AB}, is simply the covariance, normalised or standardised, by the product of their standard deviations:

$$\text{Correlation coefficient between A's and B's returns} = r_{AB} = \frac{\text{cov}_{AB}}{\sigma_A \times \sigma_B}$$

The covariance, cov_{AB}, between the returns on the two investments, A and B, is given by:

$$\text{cov}_{AB} = \sum_{i=1}^{N} [p_i(R_A - ER_A)(R_B - ER_B)] \qquad (4.3)$$

where R_A is the realised return from investment A, ER_A is the expected value of the return from A, R_B is the realised return from investment B, ER_B is the expected value of the return from B, and p_i is the probability of any pair of values occurring.

Equation 4.3 tells us first to calculate, for each pair of simultaneously occurring outcomes, their deviations from their respective expected values; next, to multiply these deviations together and then to weight the resulting product by the relevant probability for each pair. Finally, the sum of all weighted products of paired divergences between expected and actual outcomes defines the covariance. This relationship is more easily understood with a numerical example. Table 4.1 shows possible returns from two assets

Table 4.1 Returns under different states of the economy

State of the economy	Probability	Return from A	Return from B
E_1	0.25	−10%	+60%
E_2	0.25	−10%	−20%
E_3	0.25	+50%	−20%
E_4	0.25	+50%	+60%

Table 4.2 Calculating the covariance

R_A	ER_A	R_B	ER_B	$(R_A - ER_A)$	$(R_B - ER_B)$	Product	Probability	Weighted product
−10	20	+60	20	−30	+40	−1200	0.25	−300
−10	20	−20	20	−30	−40	+1200	0.25	+300
+50	20	−20	20	+30	−40	−1200	0.25	−300
+50	20	+60	20	+30	+40	+1200	0.25	+300
								covariance$_{AB}$ = 0

Note: Although the rate of return figures are percentages, they have been treated as integers to clarify exposition.

under four different economic conditions, with associated probabilities. First, do Self-assessment activity 4.2. Then, check through the calculation in Table 4.2.

Self-assessment activity 4.2

With the figures in Table 4.1, check that the expected values for both A and B are 20 per cent, and that their respective standard deviations are 30 per cent and 40 per cent, using the formulae presented in Chapter 3.

(Answer in Appendix A)

In this case, there is no co-variability at all between the returns from the two assets. If the return from A increases, it is just as likely to be associated with a fall in the return from B as a concurrent increase. If the covariance (which measures the degree of co-movement in absolute terms) is zero, we will find the correlation coefficient (the relative measure of co-movement) is also zero. We may now demonstrate this:

$$\text{Correlation coefficient between A's and B's returns} = r_{AB} = \frac{\text{cov}_{AB}}{(\sigma_A \times \sigma_B)} = \frac{0}{(30 \times 40)} = 0$$

The case of zero covariance is a very convenient one, as we can see from looking at the expression for portfolio risk, σ_p (Equation 4.2).

$$\sigma_p = \sqrt{[\alpha^2 \sigma_A^2 + (1-\alpha)^2 \sigma_B^2 + 2\alpha(1-\alpha)\text{cov}_{AB}]}$$

When the covariance is zero, the third term is zero, and portfolio risk reduces to:

$$\sigma_p = \sqrt{[\alpha^2 \sigma_A^2 + (1-\alpha)^2 \sigma_B^2]}$$

With zero covariance, portfolio risk is thus smaller for any portfolio compared to cases where the covariance is positive. Even better, when the covariance is negative, the third term becomes negative and risk falls even further. In general, the lowest achievable portfolio risk declines as the covariance diminishes: if it is negative, all the better. There is, however, no limit on the covariance value. If we re-express portfolio risk in terms of the correlation coefficient, we can be more specific about the greatest achievable degree of risk reduction. The formula relating covariance and correlation coefficient (Equation 4.3) can be rewritten as:

$$\text{cov}_{AB} = (r_{AB} \times \sigma_A \times \sigma_B)$$

Substituting into the expression for portfolio risk (Equation 4.2), we derive:

$$\sigma_P = \sqrt{[\alpha^2 \sigma_A^2 + (1-\alpha)^2 \sigma_B^2 + 2\alpha(1-\alpha) r_{AB} \sigma_A \sigma_B]}$$

Inspection of this formula shows that when the correlation coefficient is negative, portfolio risk can be lowered by combining assets A and B. From a risk-minimising perspective, the most advantageous value of the coefficient is minus one, since when the portfolio is suitably weighted, the standard deviation of the portfolio return can be reduced to zero. We thus have a formulaic demonstration of the result intuitively obtained in the Apple and Pear example at the start of the chapter. Whether one works in terms of the covariance or the correlation coefficient is generally a matter of preference, but sometimes it is dictated by the information available.

The optimal portfolio

An obvious question to ask is: which is the best portfolio to hold? In this example, the two investments have the same expected values, so any portfolio we construct by combining them will also offer this expected value. The optimal portfolio is therefore the one that offers the lowest level of risk. Although very few decision-makers are outright risk-minimisers, any rational risk-averse manager will adopt the risk-minimising action where every alternative offers an equal expected payoff.

The minimum risk portfolio with two assets

The expression for finding the weightings required to minimise the risk of a portfolio comprising two assets, A and B, where α_A^* = the proportion invested in asset A is:

$$\alpha_A^* = \frac{\sigma_B^2 - \text{cov}_{AB}}{\sigma_A^2 + \sigma_B^2 - 2\text{cov}_{AB}} \quad (4.4)$$

Substituting the figures for the AB example into Equation 4.4, we find:

$$\alpha_A^* = \frac{40^2}{30^2 + 40^2} = \frac{1{,}600}{2{,}500} = 0.64$$

This formula tells us that, to minimise risk, we should place 64 per cent of our funds in A and 36 per cent in B.

Self-assessment activity 4.3

Verify that the standard deviation of this risk-minimising portfolio is 24 per cent.

(Answer in Appendix A)

In the next section, we analyse the more likely, and more interesting, case where both the risks and expected returns of the two components differ.

4.4 PORTFOLIO ANALYSIS WHERE RISK AND RETURN DIFFER

Suppose we are offered the two investments, Z and Y, whose characteristics are shown in Table 4.3. Which should we undertake? Or should we undertake some combination? To answer these questions, we need to consider the possible available combinations of risk and return. Notice that correlation is negative.

Table 4.3 Differing returns and risks

Asset	Expected return (%)	Standard deviation (%)
Z	15	20
Y	35	40

Correlation coefficient$_{ZY}$ = −0.25; Covariance$_{ZY}$ = (−0.25) × (20) × (40) = −200

Table 4.4 Portfolio risk–return combinations

Z weighting (%)	Y weighting (%)	Expected return (%)	Standard deviation (%)
100	0	15	20
75	25	20	16
50	50	25	20
25	75	30	29
0	100	35	40

Let us assume that the two assets can be combined in any proportions, i.e. the two assets are perfectly divisible, as with security investments. There is an infinite number of possible combinations of risk and return. However, for simplicity, we confine our attention to the restricted range of portfolios whose risk and return characteristics are shown in Table 4.4.

If we wanted to minimise risk, we would invest solely in asset Z, since this has the lowest standard deviation. However, as we move from the all-Z portfolio to the combination 75 per cent of Z plus 25 per cent of Y, the risk of the whole portfolio diminishes and the expected return *increases*. Eventually, however, for portfolios more heavily weighted towards Y, the effect of Y's higher risk outweighs the beneficial effect of negative correlation, resulting in rising overall risk.

Figure 4.2 traces the full range of available opportunities (or **opportunity set**), shaped rather like the nose cone of an aircraft. The profile ranges from point A, representing total investment in Y, through to point C, representing total investment in Z, having described a U-turn at B.

opportunity set
The set of investment opportunities (i.e. risk–return combinations) available to the investor to select from

Self-assessment activity 4.4

Verify that the portfolio at B, involving 75 per cent of Z and 25 per cent of Y, is the minimum risk combination.

(Answer in Appendix A)

efficient frontier
Traces out all the available portfolio combinations that either minimise risk for a stated expected return or maximise expected return for a specified measure of risk

optimal portfolio
The risk–return combination that offers maximum satisfaction to the investor, i.e. his/her most-preferred risk–return combination

Not all combinations are of interest to the rational risk-averse investor. Comparing segment AB with the segment BC, we find that combinations lying along the latter are inefficient. For any combination along BC, we can achieve a higher return for the same risk by moving to the combination vertically above it on AB. Point S is clearly superior to T and, applying similar logic to the whole of BC, we are left with the segment AB summarising all efficient portfolios, i.e. those that maximise return for a given risk. AB is thus called the **efficient frontier**. Points along AB are said to dominate corresponding points along BC.

However, we cannot specify an **optimal portfolio**, except for the outright risk-minimiser, who would select the portfolio at B, and for the maximiser of expected return, who would settle at point A (all Y). A risk-averse person might select any portfolio along AB, depending on his or her degree of risk aversion: that is, what

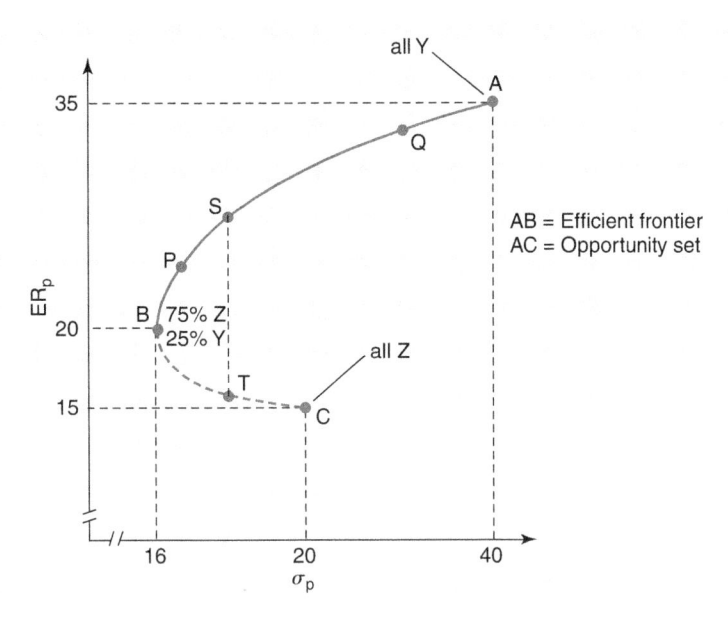

Figure 4.2 Available portfolio risk–return combinations when assets, risks and expected returns are different

additional return they would require to compensate for a specified increase in risk. For example, a highly risk-averse person might locate at point P, while the less cautious person might locate at point Q.

This is a crucial result. The most desirable combination of risky assets depends on the decision-maker's attitude towards risk. If we knew the extent of their risk-aversion – that is, how large a premium is required for a given increase in risk – we could specify the best portfolio.

Self-assessment activity 4.5

What is meant by an efficient frontier in portfolio analysis?

(Answer in Appendix A)

4.5 DIFFERENT DEGREES OF CORRELATION

Using arbitrary values for the correlation coefficient, we have found that negative correlation offers a handsome portfolio effect, and, to a lesser degree, also zero correlation. It is useful now to consider more carefully the general relationship between risk, correlation and return. To do this, we look at the full range of possible degrees of correlation, extending from perfect negative to perfect positive.

Say we are dealing with two investments, A and B, with asset A offering the higher expected return but also carrying greater risk. These are shown in Figure 4.3.

Consider the following degrees of correlation:

1 *Perfect positive.* In this case, it is not possible to achieve a portfolio effect at all. Combinations of A and B locate along the straight line AB. To achieve lower risk levels, we would simply invest more in asset B, while the risk-minimising 'portfolio' is simply asset B alone.

2 *Perfect negative.* In this case, combinations along AXB all become possible. With the returns from the two assets moving in perfect opposition to each other, it is possible to eliminate risk by adding B to A, but only by weighting the portfolio correctly is it possible fully to exploit the beneficial effect of correlation. Maximum risk-reduction

is achieved at point X where the portfolio risk is zero. Combinations along XB are clearly inefficient.

3 *Intermediate values.* For correlation coefficients between +1 and −1, it is still possible to generate a portfolio effect. The lower the correlation, i.e. the further away from +1, the greater the portfolio effect achievable. Two examples are shown in Figure 4.3 as dotted curves between A and B. The characteristic 'bow' shapes result from a progressively lower correlation bending the profile from its original position until we start observing 'nose cones' as identified earlier.

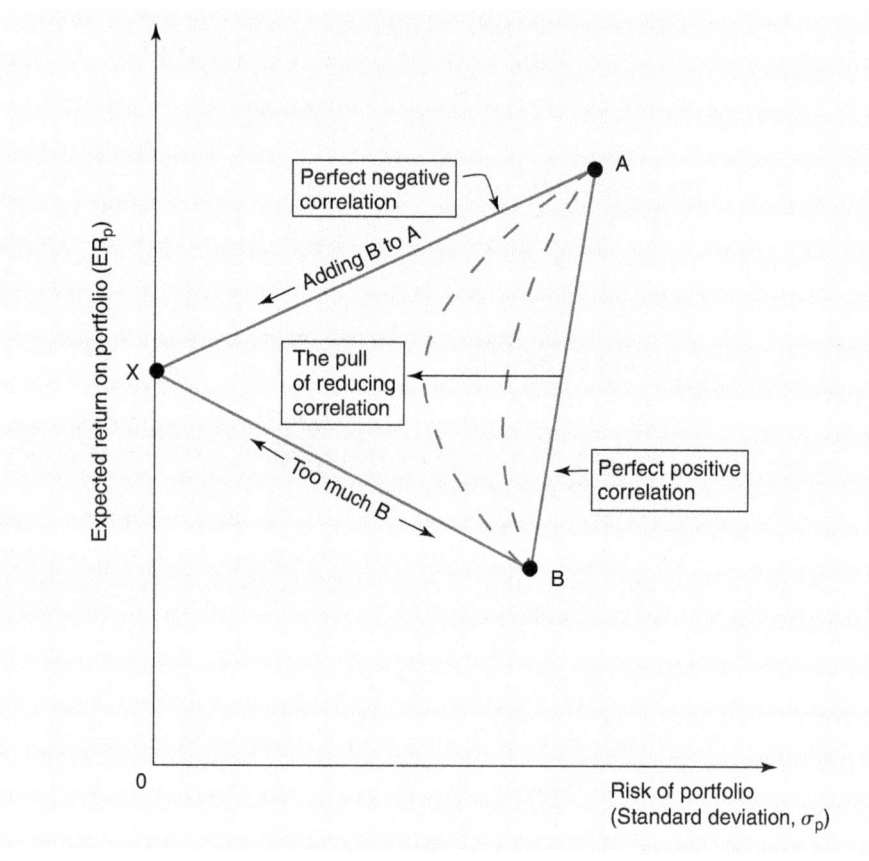

Figure 4.3 The effect on the efficiency frontier of changing correlation

Keeping the family fortune relatively intact

Family-controlled companies loom large in Asia, many tracing their origins to the 19th-century migration of mercantilist entrepreneurs from China. Many younger generation Asian family members have seen the need to diversify their family's businesses or risk oblivion.

One such family is Eu Yan Sang, a Singapore business founded in 1910 that has been transformed from a sleepy seller of traditional Chinese medicine into one with a global presence in the fast-growing 'health and wellness' sector. That turnaround was engineered by one of the city-state's best known entrepreneurs, Richard Eu, great-grandson of the founding patriarch. When he took over in the 1990s Eu Yan Sang was barely profitable from a few shops in Singapore and Malaysia. Last year net profit was S$21m ($16.8m), from sales of modern, high-margin products.

'The family businesses that have survived did not just stick to their core business,' says Annie Koh, associate professor of finance at Singapore Management University. Others are seizing opportunities to expand regionally as they outgrow their home market. Some businesses are also moving further afield as they diversify, buying assets in the US and Europe. This year Eu Yan Sang bought a 22.5 per cent stake in Oriental & Western, a maker of food supplements and anti-ageing creams based in Oxfordshire, England.

Source: Grant, J. (2013) Keeping the family fortune relatively intact. *Financial Times*, 22 September. © The Financial Times Limited 2018. All rights reserved.

4.6 WORKED EXAMPLE: GERRYBILD PLC

Gerrybild plc is a firm of speculative housebuilders that builds in advance of firm orders from customers. It has a given amount of capital to purchase land and raw materials and to pay labour for development purposes. It is considering two design types – a small two-bedroomed terraced town house and a large four-bedroomed 'executive' residence. The project could last a number of years, and its success depends largely on general economic conditions, which will influence the demand for new houses. Some information is available on past sales patterns of similar properties in roughly similar locations – the demand is relatively higher for larger properties in buoyant economic conditions, and higher for smaller properties in relatively depressed states of the economy. Since there appears to be a degree of inverse correlation between demand, and, therefore, net cash flows, from the two products, it seems sensible to consider diversified development. Table 4.5 shows annual net present value estimates for various economic conditions.

Table 4.5 Returns from Gerrybild

		Estimated NPV £ per:	
State of the economy	Probability	Large house	Small house
E_1	0.2	20,000	20,000
E_2	0.3	20,000	30,000
E_3	0.4	40,000	20,000
E_4	0.1	40,000	30,000

To analyse this decision problem, we need, first, to calculate the risk–return parameters of the investment, and, second, to assess the degree of correlation. This information may be obtained by performing a number of statistical operations:

1 *Calculation of expected values*. A shortcut is available, since some outcomes may occur under more than one state of the economy. Grouping data where possible:

EV_L = Expected value of a large house = (0.5 × £20,000) + (0.5 × £40,000)
= £30,000

EV_S = Expected value of a small house = (0.6 × £20,000) + (0.4 × £30,000)
= £24,000

2 *Calculation of project risks*. We now apply the usual expression for the standard deviation. The calculations for each activity are shown in Table 4.6. Clearly, the relative money-spinner, the large house project, is also the more risky activity.

3 *Calculation of co-variability*. Table 4.7 presents the calculation of the covariance in tabular form, following the steps itemised in Section 4.3.

The covariance of −£20 million suggests a strong element of inverse association. This is confirmed by the value of the correlation coefficient:

$$r_{LS} = \frac{cov_{LS}}{\sigma_L \times \sigma_S} = \frac{-£20,000,000}{(£10,000)(£4,899)} = -0.41$$

There are clearly significant portfolio benefits to exploit. To offer concrete advice to the builder, we would require information on his risk–return preferences, but we can still specify the available set of portfolio combinations. Rather than compute the full set of

Table 4.6 Calculation of standard deviations of returns from each investment

Outcome (£)	Probability	EV (£)	Deviation (£)	Squared deviation (£ million)	Weighted squared deviation (£ million)
Large houses					
20,000	0.5	30,000	−10,000	100	50.0
40,000	0.5	30,000	+10,000	100	50.0
					σ_L^2 = Variance = 100.0
					hence $\sigma_L = \sqrt{100\text{ m}}$
					= 10,000
					i.e. £10,000
Small houses					
20,000	0.6	24,000	−4,000	16	9.6
30,000	0.4	24,000	+6,000	36	14.4
					σ_S^2 = Variance = 24.0
					hence $\sigma_S = \sqrt{24\text{ m}}$
					= 4,899
					i.e. £4,899

Table 4.7 Calculation of the covariance

Outcomes (£)						
R_L	R_S	Probability	$(R_L - EV_L)$ (£)	$(R_S - EV_S)$ (£)	Product (£m)	Weighted product (£m)
20,000	20,000	0.2	−10,000	−4,000	40	+8
20,000	30,000	0.3	−10,000	+6,000	60	−18
40,000	20,000	0.4	+10,000	−4,000	40	−16
40,000	30,000	0.1	+10,000	+6,000	60	+6
						$\text{cov}_{LS} = -20$
						i.e. −£20 million

opportunities, we will identify the minimum risk portfolio, to enable construction of the overall risk–return profile.

■ The minimum risk portfolio

Using Equation 4.4, and defining α_L^* as the proportion of the portfolio (i.e. proportion of the available capital) devoted to large houses to minimise risk, we have:

$$\alpha_L^* = \frac{(\sigma_S^2 - \text{cov}_{LS})}{(\sigma_S^2 + \sigma_L^2 - 2\text{cov}_{LS})} = \frac{£24\text{m} + £20\text{m}}{£24\text{m} + £100\text{m} + £40\text{m}}$$

$$= \frac{£44\text{m}}{£164\text{m}} = 0.27$$

If Gerrybild wanted to minimise risk, it would have to invest 27 per cent of its capital in developing large houses and 73 per cent in developing small houses.

Self-assessment activity 4.6

Verify that the lowest achievable portfolio standard deviation is £3,496 and the expected NPV per house built from the minimum risk portfolio is £25,620.

(Answer in Appendix A)

■ The opportunity set

We now have assembled sufficient information to display the full range of opportunities available to Gerrybild. The opportunity set ABC is shown in Figure 4.4 as the familiar nose cone shape. If Gerrybild is risk-averse, only segment AB is of interest, but precisely where along this segment it will choose to locate depends on the attitude towards risk of its decision-makers.

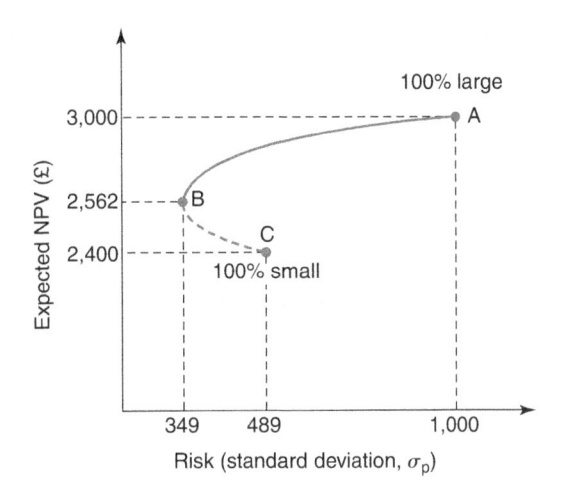

Figure 4.4 Gerrybild's opportunity set

Self-assessment activity 4.7

Using Figure 4.4, distinguish between risk-minimisation and risk-aversion.

(Answer in Appendix A)

4.7 PORTFOLIOS WITH MORE THAN TWO COMPONENTS*

Having so far looked only at simple two-asset portfolios, it is now useful to extend the analysis to more comprehensive combinations (see Figure 4.5). Imagine three assets are available, A, B and C, for each of which we have estimates of expected return and standard deviation, and also the covariance (and hence correlation) between each pair of assets. Imagine further that, whereas A and B are quite closely correlated, B and C are less so, and that correlation between A and C is even weaker.

---

*As one might imagine, the mathematics of more complex portfolios becomes more awkward to handle as the number of components increases. The interested reader may wish to consult a more rigorous treatment, such as that given by Copeland, Weston and Shastri (2013). We will rely on an intuitive approach.

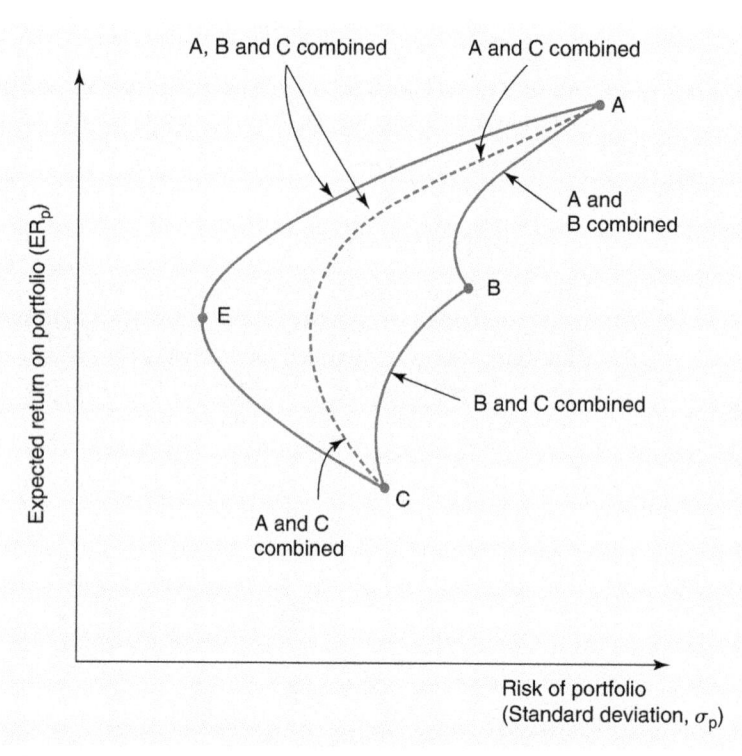

Figure 4.5 Portfolio combinations with three assets

Using a technique called Quadratic Programming, developed by Sharpe (1963), we can specify all available portfolios comprising one, two or three assets. Although there are only seven possible configurations of whole investments (A, B and C alone, A plus B, B plus C, A plus C and all three together), there are myriad combinations if we allow for divisibility of assets. The full range of available portfolios, i.e. risk–return combinations, is shown by the opportunity set in the form of an envelope, or 'bat-wing'.

The corners represent individual assets, while two-asset combinations are shown by the solid curves AB and BC and the dotted profile AC. Notice that by combining A and C, the investor can exploit their relative lack of correlation by accessing relatively more attractive portfolios in terms of their respective returns for particular levels of risk. The opportunity set thus moves inwards as assets with lower correlation are included. However, he can now access even more attractive combinations of A and C by combining all three assets. Points inside the envelope, or along the outer boundary, represent all possible combinations of A, B and C.

Notice that the investor now has access to a far wider range of investment combinations. If he is limited to combinations of only two assets, say A and B, as we saw in earlier analyses, he is restricted to risk–return combinations along AB or BC, depending on which two assets are combined. However, if access is opened up to include a third asset, the expanded range of combinations now available allows him to select far superior mixes of risk and return. For example, combinations within the envelope and on its upper bound, AEC, are superior to most of the two-asset portfolios available along AB and BC.

As before, we can differentiate between efficient and inefficient combinations. Clearly, all points lying beneath the upper edge AE and those along the segment EC are inefficient. The efficient set is therefore AE, identical in shape to our earlier profile, except that we are dealing with three-asset combinations (enabling investors to achieve lower levels of risk for specified returns by diversifying away yet more risk). Similar principles would apply if we were dealing with 30 or 300 assets, although the information requirements would become progressively more formidable.

Generally, we can conclude that the more assets that are available, the wider the range of choice open to the investor, and the greater the opportunities to achieve more desirable combinations of risk and return. The more assets under consideration, the nearer to the vertical axis lies the envelope of portfolios. Hence, the higher is the return achievable for a given risk, or conversely, the lower is the risk achievable for a specified expected return.

Notice also that the earlier conclusion about the optimal portfolio remains valid – it still depends on the particular investor's risk–return preferences.

Self-assessment activity 4.8

Draw an envelope of portfolios for the case where four assets are available to invest in, either individually or as portfolios.

(Answer in Appendix A)

The case for putting all your eggs in one basket

To date, portfolio diversification remains the most important lesson taught to students of investment and risk management. However, if we look at the portfolios of the rich and famous, they are, surprisingly, mostly concentrated.

Several great investors have very concentrated portfolios. Warren Buffett, George Soros, Rakesh Jhunjhunwala and many others are renowned proponents of portfolio concentration. Warren Buffett famously stated that 'diversification is protection against ignorance. It makes little sense if you know what you are doing.' In Mr Buffett's view, studying one or two industries in great depth, learning their ins and outs and using that knowledge to profit on those industries is more lucrative than spreading a portfolio across a broad array of sectors so that gains from certain sectors offset losses from others.

To Mr Buffett, over-diversification presented a 'low-hazard, low-return' situation and thus he dismissed it. A concentrated portfolio pivots on the absolute conviction of the investor in his or her stocks and his or her risk appetite.

A diversified portfolio, on the other hand, works well if the investor is optimistic about the stock, but wary of the associated risk. Investors like the first billion-dollar Indian investor, Mr Jhunjhunwala, walk a fine line between the two.

Mr Buffett, echoing Benjamin Graham, the father of 'value' investing, says he does not just buy an insignificant thing that bounces by a small percentage every day on the stock market. He buys part of a real business and thinks like the owner of a business would.

Mr Buffett says: 'Wide diversification is only required when investors do not understand what they are doing.' Bruce Berkowitz, founder of Fairholme Capital and a leading 'value' proponent, adds that just a handful of significant positions are enough to do unbelievably well in a lifetime.

Source: Bang, N.P and Sakaldeepi, K. (2013) Concentration: the case for putting all your eggs in one basket. *Financial Times*, 29 September. © The Financial Times Limited 2018. All rights reserved.

4.8 CAN WE USE THIS FOR PROJECT APPRAISAL? SOME RESERVATIONS

The Gerrybild example illustrates some drawbacks with the portfolio approach to handling project risk.

1. Most projects can be undertaken only in a very restricted range of sizes or even on an 'all-or-nothing' basis. This does not entirely undermine the portfolio approach – it simply means that the range of combinations available is much narrower. Besides, enterprises are often undertaken on a joint venture basis (e.g. in large, high-risk activities like Eurotunnel and the proposed Hinkley B power station), where the various parties have some freedom to select the extent of their participation.
2. A more severe problem is the implication of constant returns to scale. Our analyses imply that if a smaller version of a project is undertaken, the percentage returns, or

the absolute return per pound invested, will remain unchanged. For example, if the return on a whole project is 20 per cent, the return from doing 30 per cent of the same project is still 20 per cent. This may apply for investment in securities but is unlikely for investment projects, where there is often a minimum size below which there are zero or negative returns and, thereafter, increasing returns to scale.

3 We should be wary of any approach that relies on subjective assessments of probabilities, and wary of the probabilities themselves. In the case of repetitive activities, such as replacement of equipment, about which a substantial data bank of costs and benefits has been compiled, the probabilities may have some basis in reality. In other cases, such as major new product developments, probabilities are largely based on inspired guesswork. Different decision analysts may well formulate different 'guesstimates' about the chances of particular events occurring. However, the subjective nature of probabilities used in practice need not be a deterrent if the estimates are well supported by reasoned argument, and therefore instil confidence.

4 Since attitudes to risk determine choice, we need to know the decision-maker's utility function, which summarises his or her preferences for different monetary amounts, if we wanted to pinpoint the optimal (as distinct from the risk-minimising) portfolio. The difficulties of obtaining information about an individual manager's utility function (let alone for a group) are formidable, as Swalm (1966) has shown. Besides, we should really be seeking to apply the risk–return preferences of shareholders rather than those of managers.

5 The portfolio approach to analysing project risk seems unduly management-oriented. Managers formulate the assessments of alternative payoffs, assess the relevant probabilities and determine what combinations of activities the enterprise should undertake. Managers are considerably less mobile and less well diversified than shareholders, who can buy and sell securities more or less at will. Managers can hardly shrug off a poor investment outcome if it jeopardises the future of the enterprise or, more pertinently, their job security. Most managers are more risk-averse than shareholders, resulting in the likelihood of sub-optimal investment decisions. Here, we see another manifestation of the agency problem – how do we get managers to accept the levels of risk that owners are prepared to tolerate?

These may appear to be highly damaging criticisms of the portfolio approach, especially as it applies to investment decisions. However, although having limited operational usefulness for many investment projects, it provides the infrastructure of a more sophisticated approach to investment decision-making under risk, the **Capital Asset Pricing Model (CAPM)**. This is based on an examination of the risk–return characteristics and resulting portfolio opportunities of securities, rather than physical investment opportunities.

Capital Asset Pricing Model (CAPM)
The CAPM is a model designed to explain how the stock market values capital assets, including ordinary shares, by assessing their relative risk–return properties

The CAPM explains how individual securities are valued, or priced, in efficient capital markets. Essentially, this involves discounting the future expected returns from holding a security at a rate that adequately reflects the degree of risk incurred in holding that security. A major contribution of the CAPM is the determination of the premium for risk demanded by the market from different securities. This provides a clue as to the appropriate discount rate to apply when evaluating risky projects. The CAPM is analysed in the next chapter.

SUMMARY

This chapter examined some reasons why firms diversify their activities, and it considered the extent to which the theory of portfolio analysis can provide operational guidelines for diversification decisions. It covered the rationale behind the diversification decisions of shareholders and organisations and explored the mechanics of portfolio construction with the use of numerical examples. The real nature of optimal portfolio selection as a matter of personal choice is explained with real-life examples. The chapter also provided an overview of limitations of portfolio analysis as an approach to project appraisal.

Key points

- Both firms and individuals diversify investments – firms build portfolios of business activities, and individuals build portfolios of securities.
- An important motive for business diversification is to reduce fluctuations in returns.
- Variations in returns can be totally eliminated only if the investments concerned have perfect negative correlation and if the portfolio is weighted so as to minimise risk.
- The expected return from a portfolio is a weighted average of the returns expected from its components, the weights being determined by the proportion of capital invested in each activity or security. For a portfolio comprising the two assets, A and B:

$$ER_P = \alpha ER_A + (1 - \alpha)ER_B$$

- Portfolio risk is given by a square-root formula that includes a measure of co-variability:

$$\sigma_P = \sqrt{[\alpha^2 \sigma_A^2 + (1 - \alpha)^2 \sigma_B^2 + 2\alpha(1 - \alpha)\text{cov}_{AB}]}$$

- The degree of co-variability between the returns expected from the components of the portfolios can be measured by the covariance, cov_{AB}, or by the correlation coefficient, r_{AB}. The lower the degree of co-variability, the lower is the risk of the portfolio (for given weightings).
- The available risk–return combinations for mixing investments are shown by the opportunity set.
- Some combinations can be rejected as inefficient. Rational risk-averting investors focus only on the efficient set.
- The optimal portfolio for any investor depends on their attitude to risk, that is, how risk-averse they are.
- In practice, there are serious difficulties in applying the portfolio techniques to physical investment decisions.

Further reading

The classic works on portfolio theory are by Markowitz (1952), Sharpe (1964) and Tobin (1958) (all of whom have won Nobel Prizes for Economics). See also Sharpe, Alexander and Bailey (1998), Levy and Sarnat (1994a) and Copeland, Weston and Shastri (2013) for more developed analyses, and also proofs and derivations of the formulae used in this chapter. Finally, Markowitz's Nobel address (Markowitz, 1991) is well worth reading. Rubinstein (2002) gives a '50 years on' assessment of the impact of the CAPM. A special issue of the journal *ABACUS* (Volume 49, January 2013) debates the importance, relevance and validity of CAPM. Driessena and Laeven (2007) highlighted the benefits of international portfolio diversification in different countries. More recently, Alexander, Baptista, and Yan (2017) examined optimal portfolio construction through the application of simulated and empirical data.

QUESTIONS

Questions with a coloured number have solutions in Appendix B on page 501.

1. The returns on investment in two projects, X and Y, have standard deviations of 30 per cent and 45 per cent, respectively. The correlation coefficient between the returns on the two investments is 0.2. What is the standard deviation of a portfolio containing equal proportions of the two investments?

2. Determine the risk-minimising portfolios for the following two-asset portfolios:
   (i) $ER_A = 8\%; ER_B = 10\%; \sigma_A = 3\%; \sigma_B = 7\%; r_{AB} = -0.6$
   (ii) $ER_A = 20\%; ER_B = 12\%; \sigma_A = 12\%; \sigma_B = 6\%; r_{AB} = -0.5$
   (iii) $ER_A = 11\%; ER_B = 5\%; \sigma_A = 15\%; \sigma_B = 1\%; r_{AB} = 0$

3. Tomb-zapper plc manufactures computer video games. It is considering whether to expand production at its existing site in 'Silicon Glen' in Scotland, or to start production in a 'greenfield site' in China, where labour costs are considerably lower than in Europe. The IRRs for each project depend on average rates of growth in the world economy over the 10-year lifespan of the project. These are expected to be:

World growth	Probability	IRR China	IRR Scotland
Rapid	0.3	50%	10%
Stable	0.4	25%	15%
Slow	0.3	0%	16%

Tomb-zapper wants to exploit the less-than-perfect correlation between the returns from the two projects, without over-committing itself to the China investment.

Required
(a) What is the expected return and standard deviation of return for each separate project?
(b) Determine the expected return and standard deviation of an expansion programme that involves 25 per cent of available funds in China and 75 per cent in the Scottish location.

4. Nissota, a Japanese-based car manufacturer, is evaluating two overseas locations for a proposed expansion of production facilities at a site in Ireland and another on Humberside. The likely future return from investment in each site depends to a great extent on future economic conditions. Three scenarios are postulated, and the internal rate of return from each investment is computed under each scenario. The returns with their estimated probabilities are shown in the following table:

	Internal rate of return (%)	
Probability	Ireland	Humberside
0.3	20	10
0.3	10	30
0.4	15	20

There is zero correlation between the returns from the two sites.

Required
(a) Calculate the expected value of the IRR and the standard deviation of the return from investment in each location.
(b) What would be the expected return and the standard deviation of the following split investment strategies:
   (i) committing 50 per cent of available funds to the site in Ireland and 50 per cent to Humberside?
   (ii) committing 75 per cent of funds to the site in Ireland and 25 per cent to the Humberside site?

5 The management of Gawain plc is evaluating two projects whose returns depend on the future state of the economy as shown in the following table:

Probability	IRR$_A$(%)	IRR$_B$(%)
0.3	27	35
0.4	18	15
0.3	5	20

The project (or projects) accepted would double the size of Gawain.

Required

(a) Explain how a portfolio should be constructed to produce an expected return of 20 per cent.
(b) Calculate the correlation between projects A and B, and assess the degree of risk of the portfolio in (a).
(c) Gawain's existing activities have a standard deviation of 10 per cent. How does the addition of the portfolio analysed in (a) and (b) affect risk?

Practical assignment

Select a company with a reasonably wide portfolio of activities. Such companies do not always give segmental earnings figures, but they usually divulge sales figures for their component activities. By looking at the annual reports for three or four years, you can obtain a series of annual sales figures for each activity.

Assess the degree of past volatility of the sales of each sub-unit and their degree of inter-correlation. Also, see whether you can assess the extent of the correlation between each segment and the overall enterprise. How well diversified does your selected company appear to be? What qualifications should you make in your analysis?

5

Setting the risk premium: the Capital Asset Pricing Model (CAPM)

'Modern' portfolio theory

Overheard on the 6:41 from Bognor Regis to London Bridge:

Student 1: We did modern portfolio theory (MPT) yesterday. It was hard but I really enjoyed it.
Student 2: Yeah? What did it tell you?
Student 1: Well, for starters, you should own shares in both sun lotion manufacturers and umbrella manufacturers.
Student 2: Yeah, but what if the weather's just cloudy and dry?
Student 1: Dunno.

One answer offered by Modern Portfolio Theory (MPT) is that the canny marketing men at All Weather Products plc will produce both products, just in case the weather takes a turn for either the better or the worse. So, it wins both ways. Another is that shares in AWP will fluctuate in value according to the financial rather than the meteorological weather, as they are protected from climatological vicissitudes. The rise of the large investment management houses was driven by MPT (no longer so modern now), which enjoyed its heyday in the 1980s. Investors were urged by its proponents to contemplate the benefits of diversification. Quantitative analysts drew up efficient frontier curves that purported to show how to achieve any given target rate of investment return at the lowest possible risk.

Investment was not just about picking stocks but about choosing the perfect combination of baskets among which to distribute one's nest eggs. Diversification takes two forms: owning a range of asset classes (bonds, shares, property, commodities and so on), and owning a range of investments within each class. To do justice to the portfolio theory requires a significant input from analysts and fund managers, which plays into the hands of the largest investment groups.

Unfortunately, having a big roster of investment professionals and having a critical mass of talented ones are very different things. As investment groups grew, their performance did not improve. In one respect, it declined markedly, in that large size became a guarantee of ordinariness. With a small number of honourable exceptions, the leading fund managers delivered strikingly similar investment portfolios and, hence, returns for their customers. Portfolio theory is just that – a theory. It flounders on the constraints of time and resource that challenge all investors. Sometimes, it is better to pick a small number of out-of-favour investments and wait for the weather to turn in their favour than condemn your performance to the depressing law of the average.

Source: Copyright Guardian News & Media Ltd 2018

Learning objectives

This chapter explores the rate of return required by shareholders of an all-equity-financed company, building on the principles of portfolio theory covered in Chapter 4. Its specific aims are:

- To explain what type of risk is relevant for valuing capital assets.
- To explain what a 'Beta coefficient' is.
- To determine the appropriate risk premium to incorporate into a discount rate, whether for investment in securities or in capital projects.
- To examine the case for *corporate* diversification.
- To examine some criticisms of the CAPM.

An understanding of the significance of Beta coefficients is particularly important in appreciating how financial managers should view risk.

5.1 INTRODUCTION

In Chapters 3 and 4, we examined various methods of handling risk and uncertainty in project appraisal, ranging from sensitivity analysis through to diversification that seeks to exploit the (normally) less-than-perfect correlation between the returns from risky investments. Most of these approaches aim to identify the sources and extent of project risk and to assess whether the expected returns sufficiently compensate investors for bearing the risk. Utility theory suggests that, as risk increases, rational risk-averse people require higher returns, justifying the common practice of adjusting discount rates for risk. However, none of these approaches offers an explicit guide to measuring the *precise* reward that investors should seek for incurring a particular level of risk.

The CAPM theory was originally devised by Sharpe (1964) to explain how the capital market sets share prices. This theory stipulates the relationship between risk and required returns and is based on the presumption that rational investors hold diversified portfolios. It provides the infrastructure of much of modern financial theory and research and offers important insights into measuring risk and setting risk premiums. In particular, it shows how the study of security prices can help in assessing required rates of return on investment projects. However, as we shall see, like most theories, the CAPM has not gone unchallenged.

5.2 SECURITY VALUATION AND DISCOUNT RATES

Asset value is governed by two factors – the stream of expected benefits from holding the asset and their 'quality', or likely variability. For example, the value of a single-project company is assessed by discounting a project's future cash flows at a discount rate reflecting their risk. The value, V_0, of a company newly formed by issuing 1 million shares to exploit a one-year project offering a single net cash flow of £10 million, at a 25 per cent discount rate, is:

$$V_0 = \frac{£10\text{m}}{(1.25)} = £8\text{m}$$

This suggests a market price per share of (£8m/1m shares) = £8. This would be the value established by an efficient capital market taking account of all known information about the company's future prospects.

Sometimes, the 'correct' discount rate is unclear to the firm. A major contribution of the CAPM is to explain how discount rates are established and, hence, how securities are valued. However, from the capital market value of a company, we can 'work backwards' to infer what discount rate underlies the market price. In the example, if we observe a market price of £8, this suggests a required return of 25 per cent.

By implication, if the market sets a value on a security that implies a particular discount rate, it is reasonable to conclude that any further activity *of similar risk* to current operations should offer about the same rate. This argument depends critically on market prices being unbiased indicators of the intrinsic worth of companies, i.e. that the efficient markets hypothesis applies.

Generally, a discount rate is based on the amalgam of three components:

1. Allowance for the time value of money – the compensation required by investors for having to wait for their payments.
2. Allowance for price level changes – the additional return required to compensate for the impact of inflation on the real value of capital.
3. Allowance for risk – the promised reward that provides the incentive for investors to expose their capital to risk.

Introduction to Finance

Aside from expected inflation (or assuming that it is 'correctly' built into the structure of interest rates), discount rates have two components – <u>the rate of return required on totally risk-free assets</u>, such as government securities, and <u>a risk premium</u>.

5.3 CONCEPTS OF RISK AND RETURN

In this section, we examine risk and return concepts relevant for security valuation.

■ The returns from holding shares

Investors hold securities because they expect positive returns. While security investors like positive returns, they are usually risk-averse. Purchasers of ordinary shares are attracted by two elements: first, the anticipated dividend(s) payable during the holding period; and second, the expected capital gain. Taken together, these elements make up the **Total Shareholder Return (TSR)**.

> **Total Shareholder Return (TSR)**
> The overall return enjoyed by investors, including dividend and capital appreciation, expressed as a percentage of their initial investment. Related to individual years, or to a lengthier time period, and then converted into an annualised, or equivalent annual return

Total Shareholder Return (TSR)

In general, for any holding period, t, and company, j, the TSR is the percentage return, R_{jt}, from holding its shares:

$$R_{jt} = \frac{D_{jt} + (P_{jt} - P_{jt-1})}{P_{jt-1}} \times 100$$

where D_{jt} is the dividend per share paid by company j in period t, P_{jt} is the share price for company j at the end of period t and P_{jt-1} is the share price for company j at the start of period t.

To illustrate this calculation, consider the following figures for a firm, for the calendar year 2017:

Share price at end of December 2016 = £11.61

Share price at end of December 2017 = £12.25

Net dividend paid during 2017 = 70p per share

The percentage return over this year was:

$$\frac{70p + (£12.25 - £11.61)}{£11.61} \times 100 = \frac{(70p) + 64p}{£11.61} \times 100 = 11.5\%$$

However, these TSR data relate to just one year and may be influenced in either direction by random factors. A more meaningful measure of shareholder return would remove these short-term fluctuations, adverse or favourable. This is done by taking the overall return over a specific period, commonly five years, and converting this into an average annual or annualised equivalent rate of return. It is standard practice to make this calculation by assuming that dividends are re-invested in ordinary shares, i.e. the cash proceeds are used to buy shares at the prevailing market price at the date of dividend payment.

To illustrate this, figures from D.S. Smith, the UK packaging firm, are shown in Figure 5.1. For the period 2010–17, its TSR growth comfortably outstripped growth in the FTSE 250 index of which D.S. Smith is a member.

Firms increasingly use TSR, usually in relation to other firms, as a performance benchmark as part of the executive reward scheme. For example, under its so-called Performance Share Plan, D.S. Smith bases a part of executive rewards on company TSR performance in relation to that of the constituents of the FTSE Industrial Goods and Services Supersector.

Setting the Risk Premium: The Capital Asset Pricing Model (CAPM)

Total shareholder return from May 2010

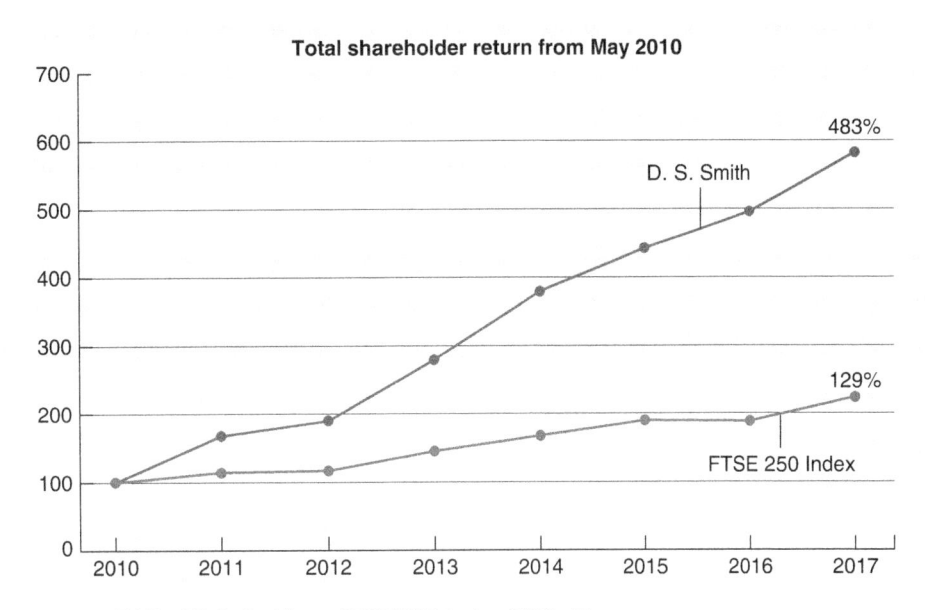

Figure 5.1 TSR of D.S. Smith vs. FTSE 250 Index 2010–17

Source: D.S. Smith *Annual Report* 2017.

Self-assessment activity 5.1

Determine the TSR for the year 201X in the following case:

- Share price, 1 January: £2.20
- Share price, 31 December: £2.37
- Interim dividend paid: £0.035 per share
- Final dividend paid: £0.065 per share

(Answer in Appendix A)

The risks of holding ordinary shares

In Chapter 4, we saw the power of portfolio combination in reducing the risk of a collection of investments. Risk was measured by the variance or standard deviation of the return on the combination. This measure can also be applied to portfolios of securities, with some remarkable results, as shown in Figure 5.2.

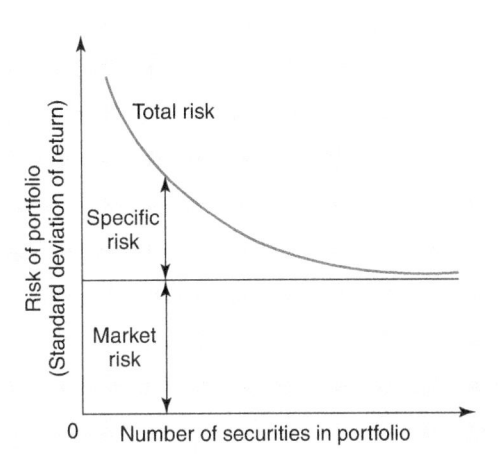

Figure 5.2 Specific vs. market risk of a portfolio

As the number of securities held in the portfolio increases, the overall variability of the portfolio's return, or its total risk, as measured by its standard deviation, diminishes very sharply for small portfolios but falls more gradually for larger combinations. This reduction in risk is achieved because exposure to the risk of volatile securities can be offset by the inclusion of low-risk securities *or even ones of higher risk*, so long as their returns are not closely correlated.

■ Specific and systematic risk

Not all the risk of individual securities is relevant for assessing the risk of a portfolio of risky shares. In assessing the risk of a share portfolio, an investor should consider only those risk factors that are specifically related to the companies which are part of the risky portfolio. However, if an investor's intention is to calculate the total risk associated with particular securities (or portfolio of securities), then the investor has to consider both firm-specific and external factors.

The total risk of securities (and also portfolios of securities) has two different components:

1. *Specific risk*: the variability in return due to factors unique to the individual firm.
2. *Systematic risk*: the variability in return due to dependence on factors that influence the return on all securities traded in the market.

specific risk
The variability in the return on a security due to exposure to risks relating to that security in isolation, e.g. risk of losing market share due to poor marketing decisions

Specific risk refers to the expected impact on sales and earnings of random events – industrial relations problems, equipment failure, R&D achievements, etc. In a portfolio of shares, such factors tend to cancel out as the number of securities included increases.

systematic risk
Variability in a security's return due to exposure to risks affecting all firms traded in the market (hence, **market risk**), e.g. the impact of exchange rate changes

Systematic risk refers to the impact of movements in the macro-economy, such as fiscal changes, swings in exchange rates and interest rate movements, all of which cause reactions in security markets. These are captured in the movement of an index reflecting security prices in general, such as the FTSE in the United Kingdom or the DAX index in Germany. No firm is entirely insulated from these factors, and even portfolio diversification cannot provide total protection. Because these factors affect all firms in the market, such risk is often called 'market-related' (or just 'market') risk.

Returning to Figure 5.2, we see that the reduction in the total risk of a portfolio is achieved by gradual elimination of the risks unique to individual companies, leaving an irreducible, undiversifiable risk floor.

market portfolio
Includes all securities traded on the stock market weighted by their respective capitalisations. Usually, a more limited portfolio such as the FT All Share Index is used as a proxy

Fosback (1985) found that substantial reductions in specific risk can be achieved with quite small portfolios, with the bulk of risk reduction being achieved with a portfolio of some 25–30 securities. To eliminate unique risk totally would involve holding a vast portfolio comprising all the securities traded in the market. This construct, called the '**market portfolio**', has a pivotal role in the CAPM, but for the individual investor, it is neither practicable nor cost-effective, in view of the dealing fees required to construct and manage it. However, since relatively small portfolios can capture the lion's share of diversification benefits, it is only a minor simplification to use a well-diversified portfolio as a proxy for the overall market, such as the FTSE 100, which covers approximately 80 per cent of the market capitalisation of all UK quoted companies (with just the top 10 firms representing about 43 per cent of the total). (www.ftse.com, 30 June 2017).

Self-assessment activity 5.2

How many shares would an investor have to hold in order to *totally* eliminate specific risk?

(Answer in Appendix A)

Implications

Three major implications now follow:

1 *It is clear that risk-averse investors should diversify.* Yet, in reality, over half of UK investors hold just one security (usually, shares in a privatised company). However, the major players in capital markets, holding well over two-thirds of all quoted UK ordinary shares (according to the Office of National Statistics, 31 December 2014, www.ons.gov.uk*) are financial institutions such as banks, pension funds and insurance companies, which do hold highly diversified portfolios.

2 *Investors should not expect rewards for bearing specific risk.* Since the risk unique to particular companies can be diversified away, the only relevant consideration in assessing risk premiums is the risk that cannot be dispersed by portfolio formation. If bearing unique risk was rewarded, astute investors prepared to build portfolios would snap up securities with high levels of unique risk to diversify it away, while still hoping to enjoy disproportionate returns, at least in the short term. The value of such securities would rise and the returns on them would fall until only systematic risks were rewarded.

3 *Securities have varying degrees of systematic risk.* Few securities exhibit patterns of returns rising or falling exactly in line with the overall market. This is partly because in the short term, unique random factors affect different companies in different ways. Yet even in the long term, when such factors tend to even out, very few securities track the market. Some appear to outperform the market by offering superior returns, and some appear to underperform it. However, performance relative to the market should not be too hastily judged, because the returns on different securities do not always depend on general economic factors in the same way.

For example, in an expanding economy, retail sales tend to increase sharply, but sales in less responsive sectors like water and defence are barely altered. Share prices of retailers usually increase quite sharply in an expanding economy, but the share prices of water companies and armaments suppliers respond far less dramatically. Retail sales are said to be 'more highly geared to the economy'. Systematic or market risk varies between companies, so we find different companies valued by the market at different discount rates. Already, we begin to see that the CAPM, based on the premise that rational investors can and do hold efficiently diversified portfolios, may show us how these discount rates might be assessed. Clearly, we need to measure systematic risk. This is covered in Section 5.5.

Self-assessment activity 5.3

Give three examples of systematic and unique factors respectively that cause the returns on holding ordinary shares to vary over time.

(Answer in Appendix A)

---

*At the end of December 2014, UK financial institutions held 29.2 per cent, foreign investors 53.8 per cent and private investors just 11.9 per cent, with the balance of 5.1 per cent held by the public sector and 'others', such as charities. The majority of foreign shareholdings (which have risen from 16 per cent in 1994) is reckoned to represent institutional, rather than private, holdings.

Too many stocks spoil the portfolio

Diversification of a portfolio is a good thing. Right? Whether you reach that conclusion intuitively from the simple adage 'don't put all your eggs in one basket' or have heard of modern portfolio theory, you know it makes sense.

Unsurprisingly, the covariance of a portfolio of FTSE 100 stocks falls as the number of stocks in the portfolio increases, but the covariance – or risk – does not fall in a straight line. The risk falls sharply as the portfolio increases in number from just one stock, but by the time it has reached about 20 to 30 stocks most of the reduction in risk that can be attained has already been achieved. The problem is that increasing the number of stocks beyond this not only fails to achieve any significant further risk reduction, it also leads to other problems.

It is important to invest in good companies. But there is a severe limit to the number of good companies available and the more stocks you own the more you are likely to have to compromise on quality. It is also a fact that the more stocks you own, the less you know about each of them, and I have never found a theory of investment that suggests that the less you know about something, the more likely you are to generate superior returns.

There is even a term for this: 'diworsification', which was coined by the legendary fund manager Peter Lynch in his book *One Up on Wall Street*. He suggested that a business that diversifies too widely risks destroying itself, because management time, energy and resources are diverted from the original investment. Similarly, adding more investments to a portfolio can lead to diworsification.

Source: Smith, T. (2013) Too many stocks spoil the portfolio. *Financial Times*, 12 April. © The Financial Times Limited 2018. All rights reserved.

5.4 INTERNATIONAL PORTFOLIO DIVERSIFICATION

Most investors tend to adopt a local perspective when deciding which shares to buy. That is, they are inclined to invest in shares listed on their domestic stock market, thus demonstrating a 'home bias' when building portfolios. The prime reason cited for this home bias is that it is 'behavioural', being rooted in a preference for the familiar. Investors feel reassured when investing in the local stock market and perceive investing in other stock markets as high risk. This is despite financial markets having undergone a process of liberalisation since 1945, resulting in investors now facing increasingly greater possibilities to create portfolios that include international shares. Some argue that investors should grasp this opportunity and adopt a strategy of constructing international, rather than domestic, share portfolios. The implied rationale is that because correlations between different financial markets are quite low, albeit apparently increasing, investors can benefit from international diversification through reducing risk. For example, Odier and Solnik (1993) calculated the following correlation coefficients of the UK stock market with other markets over the 1980–90 period: United States 0.6, Switzerland 0.5 and Germany 0.4. More recently, in 2014, correlation coefficients for the UK stock market with these markets were estimated as: United States 0.66, Switzerland 0.82 and Germany 0.87 (www.bespokeinvest.com). The overall effect of international diversification upon the risk of a portfolio is illustrated in Figure 5.3.

Whilst international diversification can have a beneficial effect upon the risk–return profile of an investor's portfolio, it introduces currency risk. However, it has generally been found that even if currency risk is left unhedged, it is preferable to invest internationally rather than just domestically.

Correlation coefficients between different stock markets do not remain static, however. As financial globalisation has continued, and stock markets have become more integrated, the question arises as to whether inter-market correlation has increased. This is significant for investors as increased correlation coefficients erode the benefits of international diversification, and eventually a point is reached where it has no value. For example, Chiou (2008) analysed the two time periods 1988 to

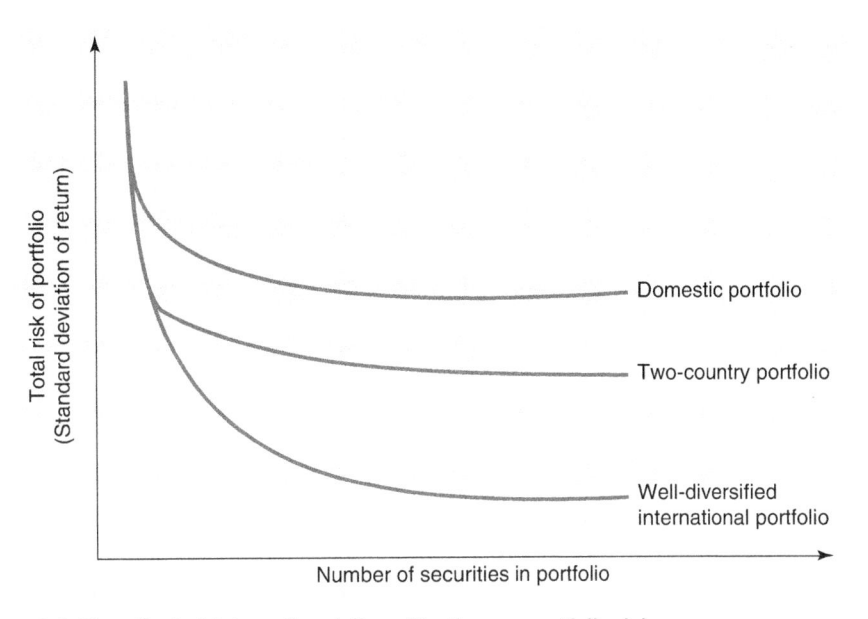

Figure 5.3 The effect of international diversification on portfolio risk

1996 and 1996 to 2004, concluding that the advantages of global diversification have reduced somewhat. Chiou's findings also suggest these advantages are not evenly spread as investors based in emerging markets (particularly Latin America and East Asia) gain more from international diversification than investors based in developed countries. Driessen and Laeven's (2007) analysis of the effects of global diversification upon local investors in a diverse sample of 52 countries supports Chiou's findings. For the period 1985–2002, they concluded that correlations between markets have increased as a result of greater market integration. However, they still find international diversification beneficial for all investors, and particularly so for investors in developing countries. Within developing countries, the gains from global diversification are greatest for those countries with higher levels of country risk. Similarly, while examining the dynamics of diversification opportunities between developed and emerging markets, Todorov (2017) also argues that, on average, diversification opportunities in markets have decreased between 1995 and 2014.

If home bias still deters investors from purchasing international stocks, an alternative strategy is for investors to maintain a sense of the familiar by diversifying regionally. Driessen and Laeven, in considering this strategy, suggested that regional diversification is beneficial, although not as advantageous as international diversification.

Another important issue concerns whether stock market correlations alter in periods of extreme volatility. For example, when a stock market crash occurs, it is plausible that with all markets falling simultaneously, the correlation coefficients between markets will increase substantially. If this does occur, the benefits of diversification diminish, and this at a time when these benefits are most needed. For this reason, studies examining correlations during bull and bear markets have been undertaken. For example, Longin and Solnik (2001) examined the period 1959–96 (which incorporates highly volatile episodes such as the 1987 Crash and the Gulf War crisis in the early 1990s), and Flavin and Panopoulou (2009) studied the period 1973–2005 which encompasses significant events such as the dotcom bubble. Longin and Solnik's principal conclusion from examining the five largest stock markets is that correlation increases in bear markets but not in bull markets. This has been supported by other research (for example, by Campbell *et al.*, 2002; Meric *et al.*, 2002).

By contrast, Flavin and Panopoulou find that the benefits of international diversification are unaffected regardless of whether the market conditions are 'calm' or 'turbulent'. A particular difficulty in comparing the results of these types of study is that methods used to calculate correlations differ. In Flavin and Panopoulou's work, statistical correlations are not even considered – instead, they investigate whether market linkages remain static over time. Their underlying argument is that if market linkages remain unchanged, this implies market contagion does not occur and international diversification will still deliver value for investors even when markets are highly unstable.

This discussion regarding international diversification neglects the issue of industry diversification. If, as already suggested, inter-market correlations have risen in recent years, country factors will have become less important for diversification. Concurrently, industry factors have risen in importance for investors' diversification strategies, and studies now suggest that industry diversification is of greater significance than country diversification. Therefore, investors need to consider purchasing shares in companies across a range of different industries to benefit their portfolios. The impact of industry and country diversification upon portfolio risk is shown in Figure 5.4.

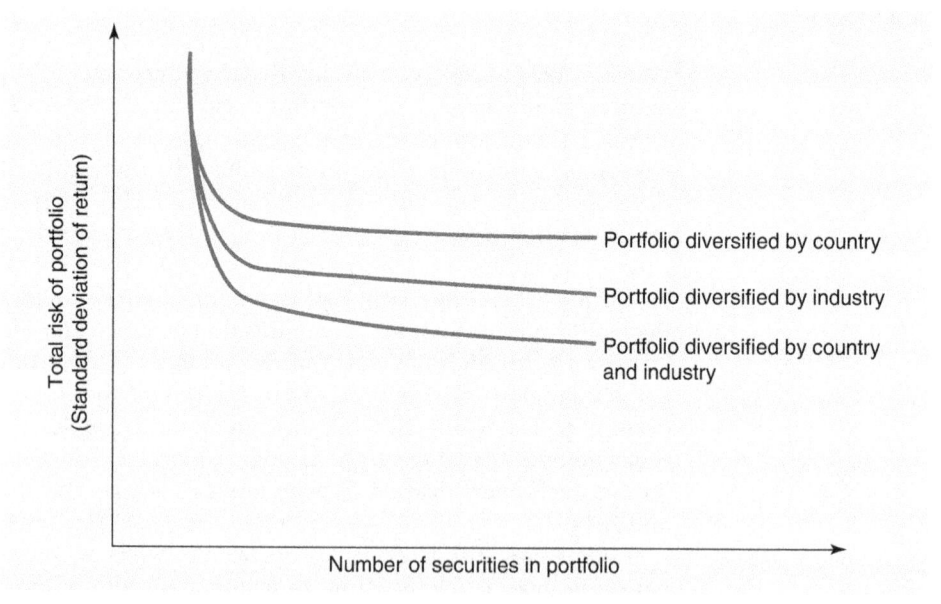

Figure 5.4 **The effects of industry and country diversification on portfolio risk**

Source: Republished with permission of CFA Institute, from The Increasing Importance of Industry Factors in The financial analysts journal, Stefano Cavaglia, Christopher Brightman, and Michael Aked, 56, 2000; permission conveyed through Copyright Clearance Center, Inc.

When investors create portfolios, it is important to remember that shares are only one type of asset that they may decide to purchase. Property, commodities, bonds and other alternative assets can all form part of a portfolio. The risk–return profiles of these assets may differ substantially from the risk–return profiles of shares; more significantly, the correlation between returns on shares and alternative assets may be relatively low or even negative. This applies for bonds and shares where the correlation between their returns is normally found to be either very small or negative. Consequently, although bonds offer lower returns than shares, the relative lack of correlation can make them attractive to hold as a part of a diversified portfolio.

Heavy exposure to domestic assets divides US advisers

US financial advisers are divided over how heavily their clients should be exposed to domestic securities, as investors risk missing out on benefiting from fast-growing foreign economies.

Of the total funds looked after by advisers in the FT 300 list, 72 per cent are held in products that invest in US equities and fixed income. Since the US represents around 50 per cent of the global equity market and around 40 per cent of the global bond market, some investment professionals have warned of the over-reliance on domestic securities. Home country bias is prevalent in other markets, according to a report published by Vanguard, the asset manager, in December. For example, while the UK represents around 7 per cent of the global equity market, local investors dedicate 26 per cent of their equity allocations to UK stocks. Japan represents 7 per cent of the global equity market and local investors have around 55 per cent of their equity allocations in Japanese shares.

'Investors are more comfortable with what they know well,' says David Cariani, chief investment officer at Reilly Financial Advisors, adding that wealth managers and investors in the US 'prefer to avoid countries with less rule of law and minimal investor protections'. He says there are two other main reasons US investors' portfolios are overweight in US assets: the role of the dollar and investment performance.

The currency that investments are denominated in is a crucial factor because it affects an investment portfolio's net returns. The expenses and liabilities of US investors are in US dollars, 'so it makes sense' to avoid adding too much risk from exchange rate volatility, which is a by-product of investing in foreign markets. On performance, Mr Cariani says US assets have generally been more appealing over the long term. He points to the 6.7 per cent annual return of the US S&P 500 index over the 15 years to December, compared to the 5.9 per cent return for the MSCI All Country World Index ex-US over the same period.

John Frownfelter, managing director of investment products at SEI Investments, stresses that balance is needed in an investment portfolio. 'By focusing assets in one country, even a large one like the US, you're foregoing potential diversification benefits associated with owning a broader set of securities,' he says.

Mr Cariani, notes that 'The S&P 500 generates roughly half of its sales overseas,' adding that it is possible to build a portfolio that is 50 per cent exposed to US markets and 50 per cent to international markets while investing in only US securities. However, he also points out that not all sectors are represented equally. For example, utilities are physically constrained to operating locally, so it would be necessary to add foreign investments to gain utility exposure globally, he says. 'The result is that construction of a globally-diversified portfolio is now more complicated than ever, requiring managers to dig deeper into the details to understand exactly which exposures they are taking on.'

Source: De Ramos, R.R. (2017) Heavy exposure to domestic assets divides US advisers. *Financial Times*, 22 June. © The Financial Times Limited 2018. All rights reserved.

5.5 SYSTEMATIC RISK

As specific risk can be diversified away by portfolio formation, rational investors expect to be rewarded only for bearing systematic risk. Since systematic risk indicates the extent to which the expected return on individual shares varies with that expected on the overall market, we have to assess the extent of this co-movement. This is given by the slope of a line relating the expected return on a particular share, ER_j, to the return expected on the market, ER_m. It is important to appreciate that 'returns' in this context include both changes in market price and also dividends. For the overall market, dividend returns may be measured by the average dividend yield on the market index.

characteristics line (CL)
Relates the periodic returns on a security to the returns on the market portfolio. Its slope is the Beta of the security. The regression model used to estimate Betas is called the **market model**

Beta coefficients
Relate the responsiveness of the returns on individual securities to variations in the return on the overall market portfolio

Example: Walkley Wagons

The case of Walkley Wagons is shown in Table 5.2. Investors anticipate four possible future states of the economy. For every percentage point increase in the expected market return (ER_m), the expected return on Walkley shares (ER_j) rises by 1.2 percentage points. Walkley thus outperforms a rising market. The graphical relationship between ER_j and ER_m, shown in Figure 5.5, is known as the **characteristics line (CL)**. Its slope of 1.2 is the **Beta coefficient**. Beta indicates how the return on Walkley is *expected* to vary alongside given variations in the return on the overall stock market.

Table 5.2 **Possible returns from Walkley Wagons**

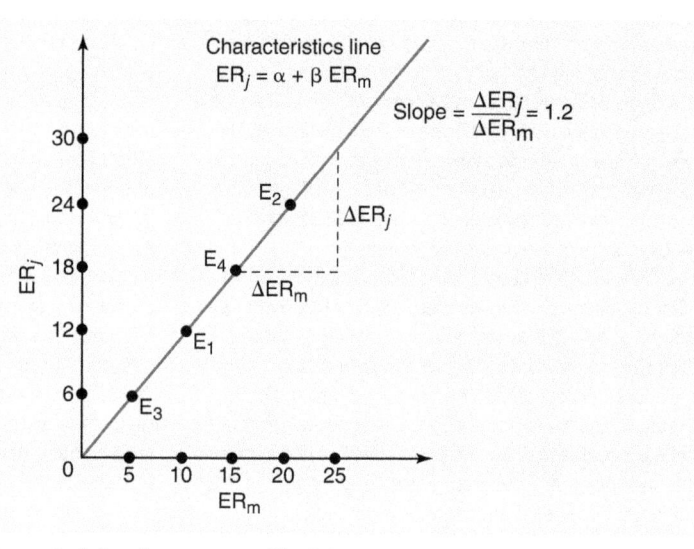

State of economy	$ER_m(\%)$	$ER_j(\%)$
E_1	10	12
E_2	20	24
E_3	5	6
E_4	15	18

Figure 5.5 **The characteristics line: no specific risk**

The market model

In practice, because it is not easy to record people's expectations, the measurement of Beta cannot be done by looking forward. We have to measure Beta using *past* observations of the actual values of both the return on the individual company's shares, and also for the overall market, i.e. R_j and R_m, respectively. So long as the past is accepted as a reliable indication of likely future events (i.e. people's expectations are moulded by examination of the frequency distribution of past recorded outcomes), observed Betas can be taken to indicate the extent to which R_j may vary for specified variations in R_m. A regression line* is fitted to a set of recorded relationships, as in Figure 5.6. The hypothesised relationship is:

$$R_j = \alpha_j + \beta_j R_m$$

and the fitted line is given by:

$$R_j = \hat{\alpha}_j + \hat{\beta}_j R_m + u$$

market model
A device relating the expected (in practice, *actual*) return from individual securities to the expected/*actual* return from the overall stock market

where $\hat{\alpha}_j$ and $\hat{\beta}_j$ are estimates of the 'true' values of α and β, and u is a term included to capture random influences, that are assumed to average zero. This regression model is called the **market model**.

The intercept term, α_j, deserves explanation. This is the return on security j when the return on the market is zero, i.e. the return with the impact of market or systematic

---

*Readers unfamiliar with the technique of regression analysis might refer to C. Morris, *Quantitative Approaches in Business Studies* (Pearson, 2008).

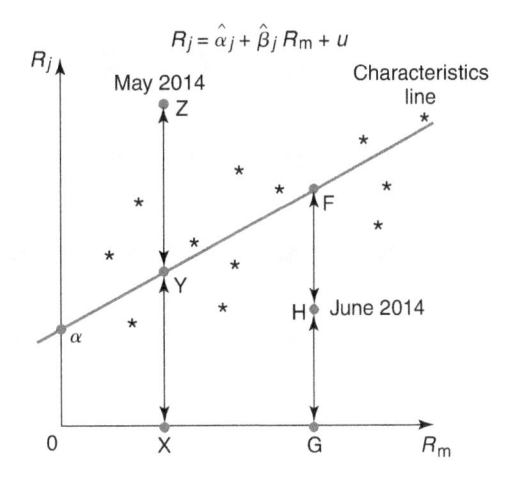

Figure 5.6 The characteristics line: with specific risk

risk stripped out. Consequently, it indicates what return the security offers for specific risk. We might expect this to average out at zero over time, given the random character of sources of specific risk. However, it is by no means uncommon empirically to record non-zero values for α. Notice that, in Figure 5.5, α is zero.

Self-assessment activity 5.4

You read in the financial press that the 'experts' are predicting overall stock market returns of 25 per cent next year. What return would you expect from holding Walkley Wagons ordinary shares?

(Answer in Appendix A)

■ Systematic and unsystematic returns

Figure 5.6 shows an imaginary set of monthly observations relating to a given year, say 2014, to which has been fitted a regression line. Clearly, unlike the *expected* values displayed in Figure 5.5, most values actually lie off the line of best fit. These divergences are due to the sort of random, unsystematic factors suggested in Section 5.3. For example, observation Z relates to the returns in May 2014. The overall return on security j in this month, XZ, can be broken down into the market-related return, XY, due to co-movement with the overall stock market, and the non-market return; or 'excess return', YZ, due to unsystematic factors, which in this month have operated favourably. The opposite appears to have applied in June 2014, indicated by point H. The market-related return 'should' have been FG, but the actual return of GH was dampened by unfavourable random factors represented by FH. *This analysis implies that variations in R_j along the characteristics line stem from market-related factors, which systematically affect all securities, and that variations* **around** *the line represent the impact of factors specific to company j. The systematic relationship is captured by β.*

Self-assessment activity 5.5

What is the significance of variations around the characteristics line? Relate this to a particular company, say, British Airways (now merged with Iberia to form International Airlines Group).

(Answer in Appendix A)

Beta values: the key relationships

Beta is the slope of a regression line. The slope coefficient relating R_j to R_m equals the covariance of the return on security j with the return on the market (cov_{jm}) divided by the variance of the market return (σ_m^2):

$$\text{Beta}_j = \frac{\text{cov}_{jm}}{\sigma_m^2}$$

Since the covariance is equal to the correlation coefficient times the product of the respective standard deviations ($r_{jm}\sigma_j\sigma_m$) (see Chapter 4), Beta is also equivalent to:

$$\text{Beta}_j = \frac{r_{jm}\sigma_j\sigma_m}{\sigma_m^2} = \frac{r_{jm}\sigma_j}{\sigma_m}$$

Beta is thus the correlation coefficient multiplied by the ratio of individual security risk to market risk. If the security concerned has the same total risk as the market, Beta equals the correlation coefficient. For a given correlation, the greater the security's systematic risk in relation to the market, the greater is Beta. Conversely, the lower the degree of correlation, for a given risk ratio, the lower the Beta. Therefore, while Beta does not measure risk in absolute terms, it is a risk indicator, reflecting the extent to which the return on the single asset moves with the return on the market, i.e. it is a measure of relative risk. To obtain a risk measure in absolute terms, we have to examine the total risk of the security in more detail, using a statistical technique called **analysis of variance**. This is explained in the Appendix to this chapter.

analysis of variance
A statistical technique for isolating the separate determinants of the fluctuations recorded in a variable over time

■ Systematic risk: Beta measurement in practice

Betas are regularly calculated by several agencies. The Risk Measurement Service (RMS) operated by the London Business School (LBS) is one of the best known in the United Kingdom. The RMS is a quarterly updating service, based on monthly observations extending back over five years, which computes the Betas of all firms listed both on the main market and also on AIM. For each of the preceding 60 months, R_j is calculated for every security and regressed against R_m. An extract from the RMS showing selected companies is given in Table 5.3.

Table 5.3 Beta values of selected companies

Company name	FTSE-ICB classification	Market capit'n*	Beta	Variability	Specific risk	Std err of Beta	R-sq'rd
British American Tobacco	Tobacco	97.585	1.14	18	14	0.16	37
GKN	AutoPart	5.599	1.20	20	16	0.18	16
ITV	BroadEnt	7.302	1.01	24	22	0.21	21
National Grid	MultUtil	32.679	0.80	16	15	0.17	21
Sainsbury	RetFood	5.511	0.86	21	20	0.20	15
Smiths Group	Div Inds	6.316	0.93	18	15	0.17	25
Tate & Lyle	FoodProd	3.076	0.77	23	22	0.21	10
Tullow Oil	Exp&Prod	2.084	1.05	49	48	0.27	4
Whitbread	RestBars	7.275	1.06	22	20	0.20	21

Note: capitalisation in £billion
Source: Data from London Business Risk Measurement Service, July-September 2017.

The Beta values of securities can fall into three categories: 'defensive', 'neutral' and 'aggressive'. An aggressive security has a Beta greater than 1. Its returns move by a greater proportion than the market as a whole. In the case of GKN, with a Beta of 1.20, for every percentage point change in the market's return, the return on GKN's shares changes by 1.20 points. Such stocks are highly desirable in a rising market, although the excess return is not guaranteed due to the possible impact of company-specific factors. A defensive share is National Grid, with a Beta of 0.80, movements in whose returns tend to understate those of the whole market. The nearest stock to a neutral one, whose returns parallel those on the market portfolios, is ITV, with a Beta of 1.01. A truly neutral stock, of course, has a Beta of 1.0.

Notice that the total risk of each security is shown as 'variability', e.g. 20 for GKN. This is a standard deviation. Notice also that this invariably exceeds 'Specific risk', e.g. 16 for GKN. The difference indicates the market risk that cannot be diversified away. (See the Appendix to this chapter for a fuller explanation.)

Self-assessment activity 5.6

Suggest why Beta values tend to cluster in a range of roughly 0.60 to 1.30.

(Answer in Appendix A)

5.6 COMPLETING THE MODEL

security market line (SML)
An upward-sloping relationship tracing out all combinations of expected return and systematic risk, available in an efficient market. All traded securities locate on this schedule. In effect, this is the capital market line adjusted for systematic risk

To recap, the CAPM suggests that only systematic risk is relevant in assessing the required risk premiums for individual securities, and we have established that Beta values reflect the sensitivity of the returns on securities to movements in the market return. However, the size of the risk premium on individual securities (or on efficient portfolios) will depend on the extent to which the return on the investment concerned is correlated with the return on the market. For a security that is perfectly correlated with the market, the market risk premium would be suitable; otherwise, the required return depends on the Beta.

The CAPM concludes that when an efficient capital market is in equilibrium, i.e. all securities are correctly priced, the relationship between risk and return is given by the **security market line (SML)**, as depicted in Figure 5.7.

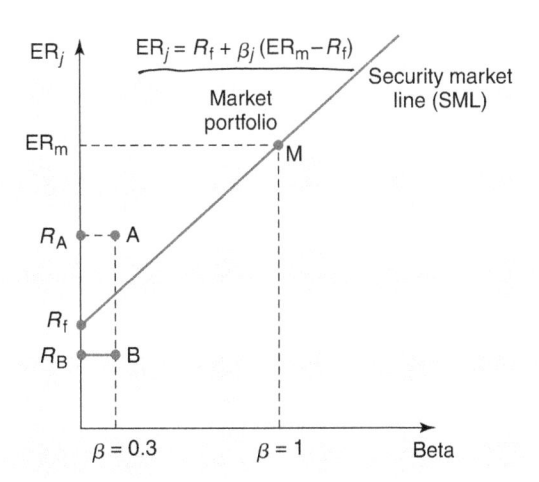

Figure 5.7 The security market line

Self-assessment activity 5.7

Why is the Beta of the overall market equal to 1.0?

(Answer in Appendix A)

■ The security market line

The equation of the SML states that the required return on a share is made up of the return on a risk-free asset, plus a premium for risk that is related to the market's own risk premium, but which varies according to the Beta of the share in question:

$$ER_j = R_f + \beta_j(ER_m - R_f)$$

If Beta is 1, the required return is simply the average return for all securities, i.e. the return on the benchmark market portfolio. Otherwise, the higher the Beta, the higher are both the risk premium and the total return required. *A relatively high Beta does not, however, guarantee a relatively high return.* The actual return depends partly on the behaviour of the market, which acts as a proxy for general economic factors. Similarly, expected returns for the individual security hinge on the expected return for the market. In a 'bull', or rising, market, it is worth holding high Beta (aggressive) securities. Conversely, defensive securities offer some protection against a 'bear', or falling, market. *However, holding a single high Beta security is foolhardy, even on a rising market. Undiversified investments, whatever their Beta values, are prey to specific risk factors. Portfolio formation is essential to diversify away the risks unique to individual companies.*

Self-assessment activity 5.8

As explained, the SML is an equilibrium relationship that traces out the set of required returns for securities of different levels of risk which an efficient capital market would demand.

How would you interpret securities such as A and B on Figure 5.7 that lie off the SML, yielding current returns of R_A and R_B, respectively?

(Answer in Appendix A)

Risk-free status of government bonds comes under scrutiny

In recent weeks, some market commentators have asked a question that would once have seemed unthinkable. Should government bonds still be viewed as risk free? If a negative answer is anywhere near possible it has huge implications.

The question has become more urgent following the recent credit downgrade of Greece on concerns over its public debt burden. For institutional investors and other market participants, government debt is assumed to be the sole risk-free asset and has therefore been the cornerstone of capital allocation and diversified investment portfolios for many years.

This is because government debt is at the base of much of the applied theory of finance and portfolio management that institutional investment has been built on. For example, the risk-free asset is the foundation of the capital asset pricing model (CAPM), the capital market line (CML) and parts of modern portfolio theory. As government debt has always been freely assumed to be risk free in practice, government debt is therefore key to diversified portfolio construction as well as capital and asset allocation. This is also the case with many of today's asset liability structures for pension funds.

The CAPM holds that an investor earns a premium for taking risk greater than that available from the risk-free rate. This premium comes from the beta of the investment (or its market return). The convention is to use the yield on local government debt as the risk-free rate, which has a beta of zero. If, however, the beta on government paper has a positive measure, then it is worth pondering the implications for investors who use these models. If the reference risk-free rate has risk, then the application of models such as the CAPM and the CML may need revisiting.

Source: Gordon, M. (2010) Risk-free status of government bonds comes under scrutiny. *Financial Times*, 7 January. © The Financial Times Limited 2018. All rights reserved.

5.7 USING THE CAPM: ASSESSING THE REQUIRED RETURN

We may now apply the CAPM formula to derive the rate of return required by shareholders in a particular company. To do this, we require information on three components: the risk-free rate, the risk premium on the market portfolio and the Beta coefficient.

Specifying the risk-free rate

Treasury Bills
Short-dated (up to three months) securities issued by the Bank of England on behalf of the UK government to cover short-term financing needs

No asset is totally risk-free. Even governments default on loans and defer interest payments. However, in a stable political and economic environment, government stock is about the nearest we can get to a risk-free asset. Most governments issue an array of stock. These range from very short-dated securities, such as Treasury Bills in the United Kingdom, maturing in 1 to 3 months, to long-dated stock, maturing in 15 years or more and even, exceptionally, undated stock, such as the 3.5 per cent War Loan with no stated redemption date.

Alternatively, it is tempting to try to match up the life of the investment project with the corresponding government stock when assessing the risk-free rate. For example, when dealing with a 10-year project, we might look at the yield on 10-year government stock.

This may be unsatisfactory for several reasons. First, although the *nominal* yield to maturity is guaranteed, the *real* yield may well be undermined by inflation at an unknown rate. Second, there is an element of risk in holding even government stock. This is reflected in the 'yield curve', which normally rises over time to reflect the increasing liquidity risk of longer-dated stock. Third, although the yield to maturity is given, a forced seller of the stock might have to take a capital loss during the intervening period, since bond values fluctuate over time with variations in interest rates.

Usually, a better way to specify R_f is to take the shortest-dated government stock available, normally three-month Treasury Bills, for which these risks are minimised. The current yield appears in the financial press. This is about the same as the LIBOR, the London Interbank Offered Rate, the rate of interest at which banks lend to each other overnight. However, this rate is not always reliable as an indicator of long-term expectations; for example, following the global financial crisis in 2008, interest rates have been artificially kept down in Europe and the United States partly for political reasons. When the short-term money market is operating inefficiently, it seems sensible to take the long-term rate. Either way, it should be noted that inflation should be catered for via the risk-free rate because it *ought* to reflect the market's inflationary expectations.

Finding the risk premium on the market portfolio

The risk premium on the market portfolio, $(ER_m - R_f)$, is an expected premium. Therefore, having assessed R_f, we need to specify ER_m by finding a way of capturing the market's expectations about future returns. An approximation can be obtained by looking at past returns, which, taken over lengthy periods, are quite stable. The usual approach with ordinary shares is to analyse the actual total returns on equities as compared with total returns on fixed-interest government stocks over some previous time period. The results are likely to differ according to the period taken and the type of government stock used as the reference level (e.g. short-term securities such as Treasury Bills or long-term gilts). However, studies seem to come up with quite stable results. For example, Dimson and Brealey (1978), Day *et al.* (1987) and Dimson (1993) for the periods 1918–77, 1919–84 and 1919–92, respectively, showed average annual returns above the risk-free rate of 9.0, 9.1 and 8.7 per cent (before taxes) for the market index in the United Kingdom.

Similar estimates have been obtained in the United States. Mehra and Prescott (1985) found that, after adjusting for inflation, equities delivered average *real* returns of 7 per cent p.a. over a quarter of a century, compared with 1 per cent for Treasury bonds – a real risk premium of 6 per cent. Mehra and Prescott found this premium 'puzzling' on the grounds that it seemed too large a premium for bearing non-diversifiable market risk, especially given international opportunities for diversification. Fama and French (2002) found the equity risk premium averaged 8.3 per cent p.a. over 1950–99, this being well in excess of the 4.1 per cent p.a. average for 1872–1949.

Dimson (1993) reported similar premia in Japan (9.8 per cent, 1970–92), Sweden (7.7 per cent, 1919–90) and the Netherlands (8.5 per cent, 1947–89), although the last two estimates were in real terms, i.e. relative to domestic inflation.

However, for shorter periods, say five or 10 years (more akin to project lifetimes), returns are highly volatile and sometimes negative. Clearly, people neither require nor expect negative returns for holding risky assets! It therefore seems more sensible to take the long-term average and to accept that, in the short term, markets exhibit unpredictable variations.

Johnson *et al.* (2007) conducted a survey with 116 finance-related academics in US higher educational institutions. The results show that a majority of the respondents expect that the equity risk premium in the next 30 years will be between 3 and 7 per cent. Graham and Harvey (2007) report that over a period of six years (2000–6), chief financial officers (CFOs) of US companies reduced their equity risk premium rate from an average of 4.65 per cent to 2.93 per cent.

The most recent survey on equity risk premium used by companies in different parts of the world is that of Fernandez *et al.* (2017), covering 41 different countries. Their results show a risk premium figure of 5.7 per cent in the United States and Germany, 5.9 per cent in the United Kingdom and Finland, 6.0 per cent in Canada and Japan, 7.5 per cent in China, 7.3 per cent in Australia, 5.6 per cent in New Zealand and between 6.0 and 7.5 per cent among other European countries. In addition, they reported equity risk premium figures between 6.0 and 17.4 per cent in several other (non-European) countries which were part of their study sample. However, as shown in Tables 5.4 and 5.5, these long-term averages can hide distinctly disappointing returns in some years.

The investment banking arm of Barclays Bank, Barclays Capital (www.investment-bank.barclays.com), publishes an annual analysis of equity and gilt-edged returns for various time periods called the 'Equity Gilt Study'. Table 5.4 is an extract from the 2016 report detailing real investment returns on equities, government bonds and cash deposits. Data in Table 5.4 indicate that, in 2015, real investment returns on equities were −0.1 per cent in the United Kingdom and −2.4 per cent in the United States, compared to government bond returns of −0.5 per cent and −1.6 per cent, respectively. These findings indicate, that, compared to previous years, 2015 was a difficult year for both UK and US investors because equity and government bond returns collapsed during that year.

However, we might expect to see a more 'normal' future financial environment in most countries, with interest rates returning to more 'normal' historical levels. Equity returns have already recovered from the lows of 2015, but ongoing, historically low rates will depress the long-period average.

However, Barclays Capital conclude that, although on average equity returns are likely to fall in the near future, 'the estimated equity risk premium remains in the 500–600bp (5%–6%) range, broadly consistent with historical experience . . . and if the low-volatility environment persists . . . the search for return will push investors more forcefully into equities'.

Table 5.4 Real investment returns by asset class in the United Kingdom and the United States (% pa)

UK Real investment returns (% pa)

Last:	2015	10 years	20 years	50 years	116 years*
Equities	−0.1	2.3	3.7	5.6	5
Gilts	−0.6	3	4.3	2.9	1.3
Corporate Bonds	−0.5	1.8			
Index-Linked	−3.4	2.5			
Cash	−0.7	−1.1	0.9	1.4	0.8
Inflation	1.2	3	2.8	5.9	3.9

Source: Barclays Research.

US Real investment returns (% pa)

Last:	2015	10 years	20 years	50 years	90 years*
Equities	−2.4	4.9	5.8	5.3	6.6
Government Bonds	−1.2	4.6	4.8	3.4	2.6
TIPS	−8.7	2.9			
Corporate Bonds	−5.3	4.2	4.4		
Cash	−0.7	−0.7	0.2	0.8	0.5
Inflation	0.7	1.9	2.2	4.1	2.9

Note: * Entire sample.

Source: Centre for Research into Security Prices (CRSP), Barclays Research, Equity Gilt Study, 2016, Used with permission from the Barclays Bank PLC

Table 5.5 shows Barclays Research and CRSP data for *real* investment returns for different types of assets in the United Kingdom and the United States. The data are *real* geometric annualised returns, i.e. they exclude the effect of inflation.

In one of the most thorough analyses of the equity risk premium, Dimson, Marsh and Staunton (2002) updated and largely corroborated earlier results in a study of the equity risk premium for 16 countries, over a full century (1900–2000). They suggested that some earlier studies (including the earlier Dimson studies!) might have over-estimated the equity premium by excluding the First World War era, when equity returns were poor, and by confining the study to the performance of surviving firms, thus excluding the relatively poor performers that had expired.

They found:

- The average global real return on equity was 4.6 per cent.
- Germany had offered the highest risk premium at 6.7 per cent.
- Denmark offered the lowest risk premium at just 2 per cent.
- In the United States, for every 20-year period examined, equities outperformed bonds.
- Only four countries – Germany, the Netherlands, Sweden and Switzerland – exhibited any 20-year periods over which bonds outperformed equities.
- It is reasonable to expect a real equity premium of no more than 5 per cent or so in the United Kingdom in the future.

Dimson *et al.* (2002) have also discussed the 'puzzle' raised by Mehra and Prescott (1985) regarding the size of the equity premium. They suggest that, given the persistent

Table 5.5 Real investment returns in the United Kingdom and the United States

(a) Real investment returns (% pa): UK 1905–2015

	Equities	Gilts	Index-Linked	Cash
1905–15	−0.20	−2.20		−0.50
1915–25	3.90	−1.10		0.80
1925–35	8.70	10.80		4.70
1935–45	2.40	0.30		−2.30
1945–55	5.30	−5.40		−3.00
1955–65	7.30	−1.00		1.80
1965–75	0.10	−5.40		−1.40
1975–85	11.00	5.20		1.50
1985–95	9.90	6.80		5.20
1995–2005	5.00	5.60	5.20	2.90
2005–15	2.30	3.00	2.50	−1.10

Source: Barclays Research.

(b) Real investment returns (% pa): USA 1925–2015

	Equities	Government Bond	Corporate Bond	Cash
1925–35	6.70	7.70		4.60
1935–45	6.00	1.60		−2.60
1945–55	10.60	−2.40		−2.70
1955–65	9.50	0.00		1.00
1965–75	−2.80	−2.50		−0.10
1975–85	8.00	2.20		2.00
1985–95	10.10	7.90	7.70	2.00
1995–2005	6.60	5.00	4.60	1.00
2005–15	4.90	4.60	4.20	−0.70

Source: Centre for Research into Security Prices (CRSP), Barclays Research, Equity Gilt Study, 2016, Used with permission from the Barclays Bank PLC

worldwide out-performance by equities, the risk element in equity investment, at least in developed, efficient markets, is overplayed. McGrattan and Prescott (2003) have revisited this puzzle. They found that in the United States, after taking into account certain factors ignored by Mehra and Prescott (1985) – e.g. taxes, regulatory constraints, diversification costs and focusing on long-term rather than short-term saving instruments – the puzzle is solved. Allowing for all these factors, they found that the difference between average equity and debt returns during peacetime is less than 1 per cent p.a., with the average real equity return just under 5 per cent, and the average real return on debt instruments a little under 4 per cent, a far lower premium than other writers have suggested.

In a later paper, Dimson *et al.* (2008) present data suggesting that past estimates of the equity premium have been overstated by some writers (thus resolving part of the 'puzzle'), partly due to 'survivorship bias' in the time series employed. After adjusting for non-repeatable factors that favoured equities in the past, they infer that investors expect an equity premium on the world index, relative to bills, of around 3–3.5 per cent, on the basis of geometric means, and on an arithmetic mean basis, a premium of around 4.5–5 per cent.

Whether the real equity premium is entering a period of long-term decline is still a matter of some debate. However, subsequent analysis will build in a risk premium for equities, i.e. the risk premium of the overall market portfolio, of 5 per cent, a 'guesstimate', that is, supported by a substantial weight of recent evidence.

Finding Beta

Beta values appear to be fairly stable over time, so we can use Beta values based on past recorded data, such as those provided by the RMS, with a fair degree of confidence. This is acceptable so long as the company is not expected to alter its risk characteristics in the future: for example, by a takeover of a company in an unrelated field or a spin-off of unwanted activities.

The required return

We now demonstrate the calculation of the required return for the 'aggressive' share GKN, using the equation for the SML:

$$ER_j = R_f + \beta_j(ER_m - R_f)$$

The Beta recorded by the RMS was 1.20 (Table 5.3). At the same date, the yield on long-term UK gilts was about 3 per cent.[*] For GKN, this results in the following required return, assuming a market risk premium of 5 per cent:

$$ER = 3\% + 1.2(5\%) = 9.0\%$$

Application to investment projects

As GKN shareholders appear to require a return of 9.0 per cent, it may seem reasonable to use this rate as a cut-off for new investments. However, two warnings are in order.

First, the discount rate applicable to new projects often depends on the nature of the activity. For example, if a new project takes GKN away from its present spheres of activity into, say, food retailing, its systematic risk will alter, as suggested by the Beta for Sainsbury of 0.86. The relevant premium for risk hinges on the systematic risk of food retailing rather than that of engineering. This suggests that we 'tailor' risk premiums, and thus discount rates, to particular activities. This aspect is examined in the next chapter.

Self-assessment activity 5.9

What is the implied discount rate for investment by GKN into food retailing?

(Answer in Appendix A)

Second, the appropriate discount rate may depend upon the method of financing used. Until now, we have implicitly been dealing with an all-equity-financed company whose premium for risk is a reward purely for the business risk inherent in the company's activity. In reality, most firms are partially debt-financed, exposing shareholders to financial risk. Using debt capital increases the risk to shareholders because of the legally preferred position of creditors. Defaulting on the conditions of the loan (e.g. failing to pay interest) can result in liquidation if creditors apply to have the company placed into receivership. The more volatile the earnings of the firm, the greater the risk of default.

Financial risk raises the Beta of the equity, as shareholders demand additional returns to compensate. The Beta of the equity becomes greater than the Beta of the underlying activity. In Chapter 11, we shall see that observed Betas have two components, one to

---

[*]The general level of interest rates at this time was artificially depressed for political reasons since certain actions have been taken to manage the economic situation following the financial crisis.

reflect business risk and one to allow for financial risk. The Betas recorded by the RMS are actually equity Betas, so the required return computed for GKN is the shareholders' required return, part of which is to compensate for financial risk. However, when a company borrows, only the method of financing changes; nothing happens to alter the riskiness of the basic activity. The cut-off rate reflecting the basic risk of physical investment projects is often lower than the shareholders' own required return.

5.8 WORKED EXAMPLE

An investor holds the following portfolio of four risky assets and a deposit in a risk-free asset. The table shows their respective portfolio weightings and the current returns on the assets, together with their Beta coefficients.

Asset	Weighting (%)	Current return (%)	Beta
A	20	12.0	1.5
B	10	18.0	2.0
C	15	14.0	1.2
D	25	8.0	0.9
Risk-free asset	30	5.0	0

The *overall* return on the market portfolio of risky assets is 11 per cent, and this is expected to continue for the foreseeable future.

Required

(a) What is the current return on the whole portfolio, and its Beta value?
(b) Which of the four risky assets (if any) appear to be inefficient/efficient/super-efficient?
(c) In view of the answer to part (b), what predictions would you make regarding future asset values and, hence, their rates of return as the market moves to full equilibrium?
(d) What is the equilibrium return on this portfolio? (Assume the weightings remain unchanged.)

Answers

(a) The portfolio return is a weighted average of the individual asset returns, viz:

$$R_p = (0.2 \times 12\%) + (0.1 \times 18\%) + (0.15 \times 14\%) + (0.25 \times 8\%) + (0.3 \times 5\%)$$
$$= 2.4\% + 1.8\% + 2.1\% + 2.0\% + 1.5\%$$
$$= 9.8\%$$

The portfolio Beta is a weighted average of the individual asset Betas, viz:

$$Beta_p = (0.2 \times 1.5) + (0.1 \times 2.0) + (0.15 \times 1.2) + (0.25 \times 0.9) + (0.3 \times 0)$$
$$= 0.3 + 0.2 + 0.18 + 0.225 + 0$$
$$= 0.905$$

These results imply that the investor is relatively risk-averse, choosing to combine risky assets and the risk-free asset in such a way as to undershoot the overall market return of 11 per cent and the market Beta of 1.0.

(b) Efficient assets lie on the security market line, thus offering a return consistent with their Beta values. If we compare the actual with the required returns for each asset, we can judge the status of each one. The table shows this evaluation.

Asset	Risk-free rate (%)	Beta	Market premium (%)	Required return (%)	Actual return	Assessment
A	5	1.5	(11% − 5%) = 6%	5 + (1.5 × 6) = 14%	12%	Inefficient
B	5	2.0	6%	5 + (2.0 × 6) = 17%	18%	Super-efficient
C	5	1.2	6%	5 + (1.2 × 6) = 12.2%	14%	Super-efficient
D	5	0.9	6%	5 + (0.9 × 6) = 10.4%	8%	Inefficient

Super-efficient assets offer in excess of what their Beta values warrant. The opposite is true for inefficient assets. Assets A and D are thus inefficient, and B and C are super-efficient.

(c) Super-efficient assets are very attractive while they offer abnormal returns, and conversely, for inefficient assets. Investors will therefore scramble to buy the former and to sell the latter, triggering windfall gains for those lucky enough to be holding the former and losses for those holding the latter. Prices will adjust until every asset offers a return consistent with its Beta value. Hence, we would predict a rise in price for assets B and C, depressing their returns, i.e. the equilibrium return will be lower than the current return, and price falls for assets A and D until their expected returns increase accordingly.

(d) The equilibrium portfolio return is:

$$R_p = (0.2 \times 14.0\%) + (0.1 \times 17.0\%) + (0.15 \times 12.2\%) + (0.25 \times 10.4\%) \\ + (0.3 \times 5\%) \\ = 2.8\% + 1.7\% + 1.83\% + 2.6\% + 1.5\% \\ = 10.43\%$$

Thus, the equilibrium portfolio return is a little above its initial level and closer to the market return.

5.9 THE UNDERPINNINGS OF THE CAPM

In the previous sections, we have concentrated on developing the operational aspects of the CAPM, without explaining the underlying theoretical relationships. The underlying theory is explained in Sections 5.9 and 5.10 and brought together in Section 5.11, which you may omit at this stage. Section 5.12 discusses some general issues raised by the CAPM.

All theories rely on assumptions in order to simplify the analysis and expose the important relationships between key variables. In economics and related sciences, it is generally accepted that the validity of a theory depends on the empirical accuracy of its predictions rather than on the realism of its assumptions (Friedman, 1953). However, if we find that the predictions fail to correspond with reality, and we are satisfied that this is not due to measurement errors or random influences, then it is appropriate to reassess the assumptions. The ensuing analysis, based on an amended set of assumptions, may lead to the generation of alternative predictions that accord more closely with reality.

■ The assumptions of the CAPM

The most important assumptions are as follows:

1. All investors aim to maximise the utility they expect to enjoy from wealth-holding.
2. All investors operate on a common single-period planning horizon.
3. All investors select from alternative investment opportunities by looking at expected return and risk.

4   All investors are rational and risk-averse.
5   All investors arrive at similar assessments of the probability distributions of returns expected from traded securities.
6   All such distributions of expected returns are normal.
7   All investors can lend or borrow unlimited amounts at a similar common rate of interest.
8   There are no transaction costs entailed in trading securities.
9   Dividends and capital gains are taxed at the same rates.
10 All investors are price-takers: that is, no investor can influence the market price by the scale of his or her own transactions.
11 All securities are highly divisible, i.e. they can be traded in small parcels.

Several of these assumptions are patently untrue, but it has been shown that the CAPM stands up well to relaxation of many of them. Incorporation of apparently more realistic assumptions does not materially affect the implications of the analysis. A full discussion of these adjustments is beyond our scope, but van Horne (2001) offers an excellent analysis.

5.10 PORTFOLIOS WITH MANY COMPONENTS: THE CAPITAL MARKET LINE

capital market line (CML)
Traces out the efficient combinations of risk and return available to investors when combining a risk-free asset with the market portfolio

The theory behind the CAPM revolves around the concept of the 'risk–return trade-off'. This suggests that investors demand progressively higher returns as compensation for successive increases in risk. The derivation of this relationship, known as the **capital market line (CML)**, relies on the portfolio analysis techniques examined in Chapter 4.

The reader may find it useful to re-read Section 4.7, where we explained the derivation of the efficient set available to an investor who can invest in a large number of assets. One conclusion of this analysis was that the only way to differentiate between the many portfolios in the efficient set was to examine the investor's risk–return preferences, i.e. there was no definable optimal portfolio of equal attractiveness to all investors.

■ Introducing a risk-free asset

risk-free assets
Securities with zero variation in overall returns

The above conclusion applies only in the absence of a **risk-free asset**. A major contribution of the CAPM is to introduce the possibility of investing in such an asset. If we allow for risk-free investment, the range of opportunities widens much further. For example, in Figure 5.8, which is based on Figure 8.5 which showed an efficient frontier of AE, consider the line from R_f, the return available on the risk-free asset, passing through point T on the efficiency frontier. This represents all possible combinations of the risk-free asset and the portfolio of risky securities represented by T. To the left of T, both portfolio return and risk are less than those for T, and conversely for points to the right of T. This implies that between R_f and T, the investor is tempering the risk and return on T with investment in the risk-free asset (i.e. lending at the rate R_f), while above T, the investor is seeking higher returns even at the expense of greater risk (i.e. borrowing in order to make further investment in T).

However, the investor can improve portfolio performance by investing along the line R_fV, representing combinations of the risk-free asset and portfolio V. The investor can do better still by investing along R_fWZ, the tangent to the efficient set. This schedule describes the best of all available risk–return combinations. No other portfolio of risky assets when combined with the risk-free assets allows the investor to achieve higher returns for a given risk. The line R_fWZ becomes the new efficient boundary.

Portfolio W is the most desirable portfolio of risky securities as it allows access to the line R_fWZ. If the capital market is not already in equilibrium, investors will

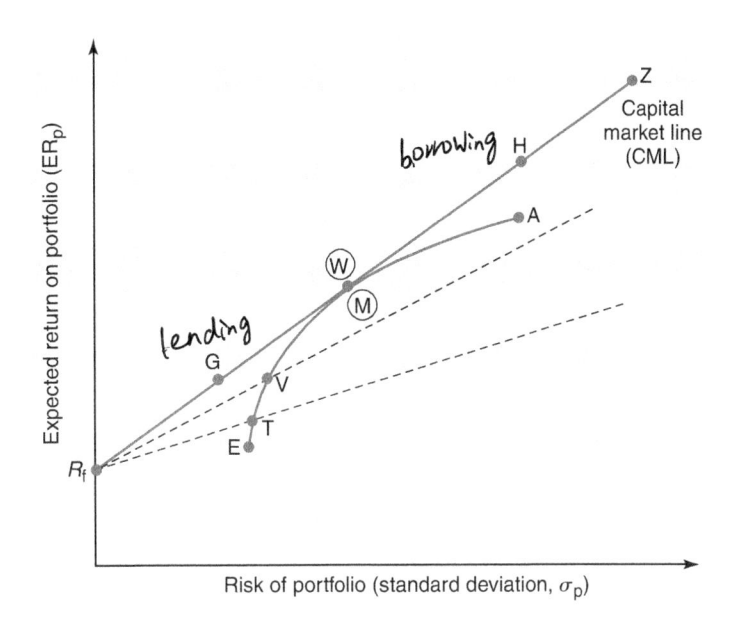

Figure 5.8 The capital market line

compete to buy the components of W and tend to discard other investments. As a result, realignment of security prices will occur, the prices of assets in W will rise and hence their returns will fall; and conversely, for assets not contained in W. The readjustment of security prices will continue until all securities traded in the market appear in a portfolio like W, where the line drawn from R_f touches the efficient set. *This adjusted portfolio is the 'market portfolio' (re-labelled as M), which contains all traded securities, weighted according to their market capitalisations. For rational risk-averting investors, this is now the only portfolio of risky securities worth holding.*

There is now a definable optimal portfolio of risky securities, portfolio M, which all investors should seek, and which does not derive from their risk–return preferences. This proposition is known as the **separation theorem** – the most preferred portfolio is separate from individuals' attitudes to risk. The beauty of this result is that we need not know all the expected returns, risks and covariances required to derive the efficient set in Figure 5.8. We need only define the market portfolio in terms of some widely used and comprehensive index.

However, having invested in M, if investors wish to vary their risk–return combination, they need only to move along $R_f MZ$, lending or borrowing according to their risk–return preferences. For example, a relatively risk-averse investor will locate at point G, combining lending at the risk-free rate with investment in M. A less cautious investor may locate at point H, borrowing at the risk-free rate in order to raise his or her returns by further investment in M, but incurring a higher level of risk. However, we would still need information on attitudes towards risk to *predict* how individual investors behave.

The line $R_f MZ$ is highly significant. It describes the way in which rational investors – those who wish to maximise returns for a given risk or minimise risk for a given return – seek compensation for any additional risk they incur. In this sense, $R_f MZ$ describes an optimal risk–return trade-off that all investors and thus the whole market will pursue; hence, it is called the capital market line (CML).

The trade-off schedule $R_f MZ$ is, in fact, a more fully developed version of the upward-sloping relationship in that earlier diagram.

separation theorem
A model that shows how individual perceptions of the optimal portfolio of risky securities is independent of (i.e. separate from) individuals' different risk–return preferences

The capital market line

The CML traces out all optimal risk–return combinations for those investors astute enough to recognise the advantages of constructing a well-diversified portfolio. Its equation is:

$$\text{ER}_p = R_f + \left[\frac{(\text{ER}_m - R_f)}{\sigma_m}\right]\sigma_p$$

Its slope signifies the rate at which investors travelling up the line will be compensated for each extra unit of risk, i.e. $(\text{ER}_m - R_f)/\sigma_m$ units of additional return.

For example, imagine investors expect the following:

$R_f = 10\%$

$\text{ER}_m = 20\%$

$\sigma_m = 5\%$

so that

$$\left[\frac{\text{ER}_m - R_f}{\sigma_m}\right] = \left[\frac{20 - 10\%}{5\%}\right] = 2$$

Every additional unit of risk that investors are prepared to incur, as measured by the portfolio's standard deviation, requires compensation of two units of extra return. With a portfolio standard deviation of 2 per cent, the appropriate return is:

$\text{ER}_p = 10\% + (2 \times 2\%) = 14\%$

for $\sigma_p = 3\%$, $\text{ER}_p = 16\%$; for $\sigma_p = 4\%$, $\text{ER}_p = 18\%$; and so on.

Anyone requiring greater compensation for these levels of risk will be sorely disappointed.

To summarise, we can now assess the appropriate risk premiums for combinations of the risk-free asset and the market portfolio, and therefore the discount rate to be applied when valuing such portfolio holdings. The final link in the analysis of risk premiums is an explanation of how the discount rates for individual securities are established and hence how these securities are valued. This was already provided by the discussion of the SML in Section 5.6.

5.11 HOW IT ALL FITS TOGETHER: THE KEY RELATIONSHIPS

The CAPM sometimes looks complex. However, its essential simplicity can be analysed by reducing it to the three panels of Figure 5.9.

Panel I shows the CML, derived using the principles of portfolio combination developed in Chapter 4. The CML is a tangent to the envelope of efficient portfolios of risky assets, the point of tangency occurring at the market portfolio, M. Any combination along the CML (except M itself) is superior to any combination of risky assets alone. In other words, investors can obtain more desirable risk–return combinations by mixing the risk-free asset and the market portfolio to suit their preferences, i.e. according to whether they wish to lend or borrow.

The slope of the CML, given by $[(\text{ER}_m - R_f)/\sigma_m]$ defines the best available terms for exchanging risk and return. It is desirable to hold a well-diversified portfolio of securities in order to eliminate the specific risk inherent in individual securities like C. When holding single securities, investors cannot expect to be rewarded for total risk (e.g. 15 per cent for C) because the market rewards investors only for bearing the undiversifiable or systematic risk. The extent to which risk can be eliminated depends on the covariance of the share's return with the return on the overall market. Hence, the degree of correlation with the return on the market influences the reward from holding a security and thus its price.

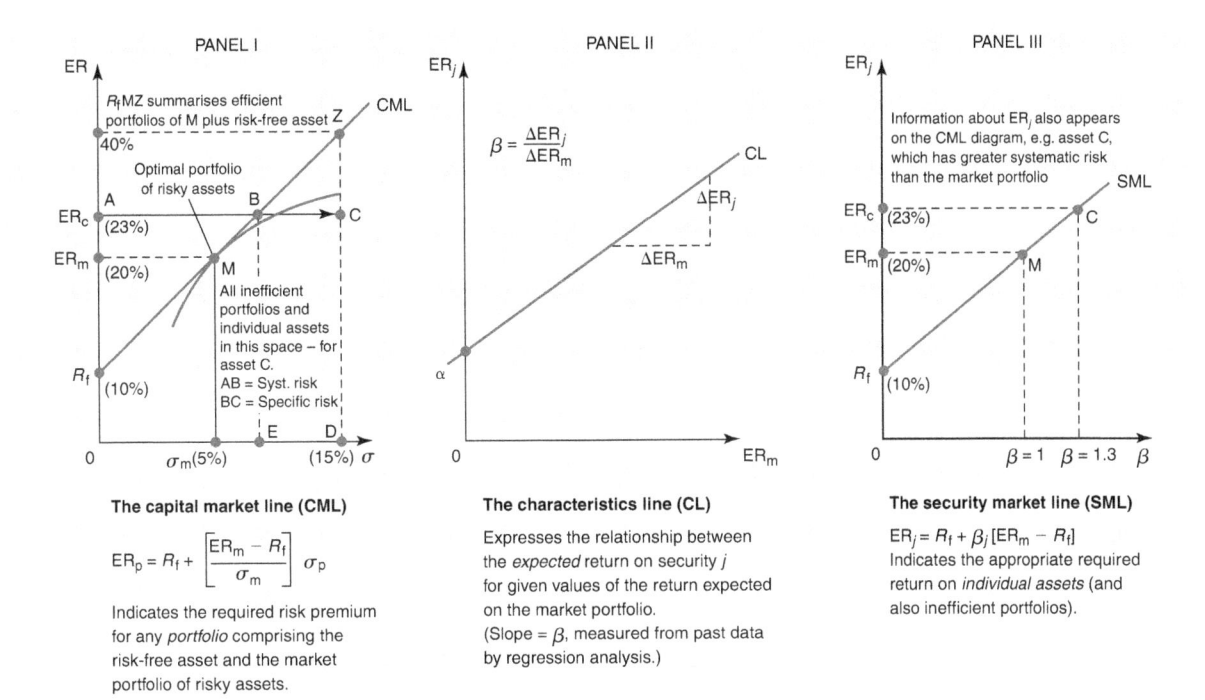

Figure 5.9 The CAPM: the three key relationships

PANEL I — The capital market line (CML)

$$ER_p = R_f + \left[\frac{ER_m - R_f}{\sigma_m}\right]\sigma_p$$

Indicates the required risk premium for any *portfolio* comprising the risk-free asset and the market portfolio of risky assets.

R_fMZ summarises efficient portfolios of M plus risk-free asset. Optimal portfolio of risky assets. All inefficient portfolios and individual assets in this space – for asset C. AB = Syst. risk; BC = Specific risk. ER_c (23%), ER_m (20%), R_f (10%), σ_m(5%), (15%).

PANEL II — The characteristics line (CL)

$$\beta = \frac{\Delta ER_j}{\Delta ER_m}$$

Expresses the relationship between the *expected* return on security *j* for given values of the return expected on the market portfolio.
(Slope = β, measured from past data by regression analysis.)

PANEL III — The security market line (SML)

$$ER_j = R_f + \beta_j[ER_m - R_f]$$

Indicates the appropriate required return on *individual assets* (and also inefficient portfolios).

Information about ER_j also appears on the CML diagram, e.g. asset C, which has greater systematic risk than the market portfolio. ER_c (23%), ER_m (20%), R_f (10%), $\beta = 1$, $\beta = 1.3$.

The characteristics line in Panel II shows how the return on an individual share, such as that represented by point C, is expected to vary with changes in the return on the overall market. Its slope, the Beta, indicates the degree of systematic risk of the security.

The security market line in Panel III shows the market equilibrium relationship between risk and return, which holds when all securities are 'correctly' priced. Clearly, the higher the Beta, the higher the required return. Although Beta is not a direct measure of systematic risk, it is an important indicator of relevant risk.

The decomposition of the overall variability, or variance, of the share's return into systematic and unsystematic components is explained in the Appendix to this chapter. It can be demonstrated by focusing on security C in Panel III of Figure 5.9. Security C lies to the north-east of the market portfolio because its Beta of 1.3 exceeds that of the overall market. If the market as a whole is expected to generate a return of 20 per cent, and the risk-free rate is 10 per cent, C's expected return is:

$$ER_C = 10\% + 1.3(20\% - 10\%) = 10\% + 13\% = 23\%$$

This reward compensates only for systematic risk, rather than for the share's total risk. Looking at Panel I of the total risk of C, represented by distance OD, only OE is relevant.

The risk–return trade-off, given by the slope of the CML, is $(20\% - 10\%)/5\% = 2$, since the risk of the market itself is 5 per cent. For C, with overall risk of 15 per cent, we would not expect to obtain compensation at this rate (i.e. $2 \times 15\% = 30\%$ giving an overall return of 40 per cent), because much of the total risk can be diversified away.

Observe that a variety of required return figures could have emerged from our calculation – in fact, anything along the perpendicular ZD in Panel I of Figure 5.9, depending on the extent to which security C is correlated with the market portfolio. The nearer C lies to Z, the greater the correlation and the higher the required return, and conversely, should C be nearer to D. This reflects the changing balance between the two risk components along ZD.

If the market rewarded total risk, the return offered on security C would be the risk-free rate of 10 per cent supplemented by the risk–return trade-off ($2 \times$ the total security risk of 15 per cent), yielding a total of 40 per cent. However, because the total risk is partly diversifiable, the market offers a return of just 23 per cent for security C. This relationship is indicated on Panel I of Figure 5.9 by the distances AB and BC, representing respectively the systematic and specific risk components of security C's total risk (not to scale).

Self-assessment activity 5.10

You expect the stock market to rise in the next year or so. Could you beat the market portfolio by holding, say, the five securities with the highest Betas?

(Answer in Appendix A)

5.12 RESERVATIONS ABOUT THE CAPM

The CAPM analyses the sources of asset risk and offers key insights into what rewards investors should expect for bearing these risks. However, certain limitations detract from its applicability.

■ It relies on a battery of 'unrealistic' assumptions

It is often easy to criticise theories for the lack of realism of their assumptions, and certainly, many of those embodied in the CAPM, especially concerning investor behaviour, do not seem to reflect reality. However, if the aim is to provide predictions that can be tested against real-world observations, the realism of the underlying assumptions is secondary. Obviously, if the predictions themselves do not accord reasonably closely with reality, then the theory is undoubtedly suspect.

■ Single time period

A key assumption of the CAPM is that investors adopt a one-period time-horizon for holding securities. Whatever the length of the period (not necessarily one year), the rates of return incorporated in investor expectations are rates of return over the whole holding period, assumed to be common for all investors. This provides obvious problems when we come to use a required return derived from a CAPM exercise in evaluating an investment project. Quite simply, we may not compare like with like. If an investor requires a return of, say, 25 per cent, over a five-year period, this is rather different from saying that the returns from an investment project should be discounted at 25 per cent p.a. Attempts have been made, notably by Mossin (1966), to produce a multi-period version of the CAPM, but its mathematical complexity takes it out of the reach of most practising managers, especially those inclined to scepticism about the CAPM itself.

The problem for active managers

Traditional active asset management has been under siege for some time, squeezed by the move to low-cost passive strategies on one hand and to expensive hedge funds and other alternative investments on the other.

According to a new paper from the 300 Club, a group of investment professionals, this trend is due to the far-reaching and unfortunate influence of the investment theories that underlie current practice, namely the efficient market hypothesis (EMH) and capital asset pricing model (CAPM).

These have persuaded people that active management does not work and 'spawned today's $4tn index fund industry', says the paper, written by Amin Rajan, chief executive of Create-Research and club member.

Mr Rajan maintains the theories have also contributed to the pervasive view among policy makers and others that the market knows best and interfering with its working through regulation is bound to cause distortions.

The paper does not go so far as to blame the financial crisis entirely on the ideas the theories promote (that investors are rational, market prices reflect all available information; price levels align with fundamental values over time and individual stock selection contributes little to portfolio returns), but it sees them as contributing factors.

It concludes that neither theory has much empirical support. They have been refined 'to the point where their principal inferences – that markets are efficient and active management does not work – are no longer tenable'.

Mr Rajan hopes that by questioning the tenets and implications of the EMH and CAPM, a new theory will emerge.

Source: Skypala, P. (2012) The problem for active managers. *Financial Times*, 29 April. © The Financial Times Limited 2018. All rights reserved.

5.13 TESTING THE CAPM

Many writers have observed that, in principle, the CAPM is untestable, since it is based on investors' expectations about future returns, and expectations are inherently awkward to measure. Hence, tests of the CAPM have to examine past returns and take these as proxies for future expected returns. This is based on the key premise that if a long enough period is examined, mistaken expectations are likely to be corrected, and people will come to rely on past average achieved returns when formulating expectations. Greatly simplified, the essence of the research methods is as follows.

Research usually proceeds in two stages. First, using time series analysis over a lengthy period applied to a large sample of securities (say 750), researchers estimate both the Beta for each security and its average return. Relying heavily on market efficiency, these estimates are taken to be estimates of the *ex ante* expected return, i.e. it is assumed that rational investors will be strongly influenced by past returns and their variability when formulating future expectations.

Second, the researcher tries to locate the SML to investigate whether it is upward-sloping, as envisaged by the CAPM. The 750 pairs of estimates for Beta and the average return for each security are used as the input into a cross-section regression model of the form:

$$R_i = a_1 + a_2\beta_i + u_i$$

where R_i is the expected return from security i, a_1 is the intercept term (i.e. the risk-free rate), a_2 is the slope of the SML and u_i is an error term.

If the CAPM is valid, the measured SML would appear as in the steeper line on Figure 5.10, with an intercept approximating to recorded data for the risk-free rate: for example, the realised return on Treasury Bills.

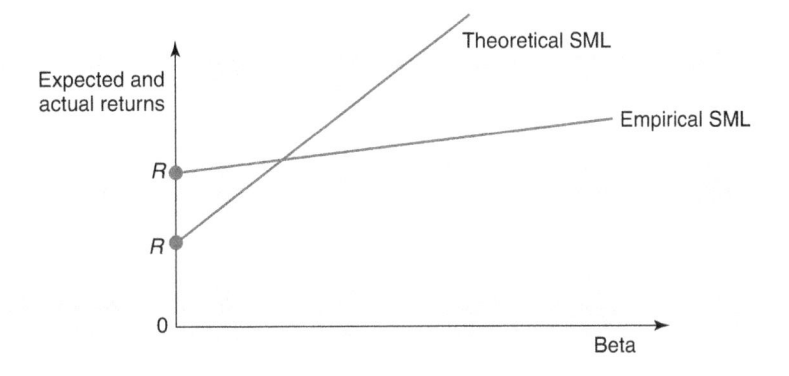

Figure 5.10 Theoretical and empirical SMLs

Several early studies (e.g. Black *et al.*, 1972; Fama and McBeth, 1973) did seem to support the positive association between Beta and average stock returns envisaged by the CAPM for long periods up to the late 1960s. However, evidence began to emerge that the empirical SML was much flatter than implied by the theory and that the intercept was considerably higher than achieved returns on 'risk-free' assets.

Some researchers have continued to test the validity of the CAPM, but others, following Ross (1976), have concluded that some of the 'rogue' results stem from intrinsic difficulties concerning the CAPM that make it inherently untestable. In the process, they have developed an alternative theory, based on the **Arbitrage Pricing Theory (APT)**, discussed in Section 5.15.

Other reasons why the CAPM is thought to be nigh impossible to test adequately are as follows:

1 It relies on specification of a risk-free asset – there is some doubt whether such an asset really exists.
2 It relies on analysing security returns against an efficient benchmark portfolio, the market portfolio, usually proxied by a widely used index. Because no index captures all stocks, the index portfolio itself could be inefficient, as compared with the full market portfolio, thus distorting empirical results.
3 The model is unduly restrictive in that it includes only *securities* as depositories of wealth. A full 'capital asset pricing model' would include all forms of asset, such as real estate, paintings or rare coins – in fact, any asset that offers a future return. Hence, the CAPM is only a *security* pricing model.

> **Arbitrage Pricing Theory (APT)**
> An extension of the CAPM to include more than one factor (hence, an example of a **multi-factor model**) used to explain the returns on securities. Each factor has its own Beta coefficient

Fama and French (1992) made a thorough test of the CAPM, finding no US evidence for the 'correct' relationship between security returns and Beta over the period 1963–90. The cross-section approach supported neither a linear nor a positive relationship. It appeared that average stock returns were explained better by company size as measured by market capitalisation, large firms generally offering lower returns, and by the ratio of book value of equity to market value, returns being positively associated with this variable. They concluded that rather than being explained by a single variable, Beta, security risk was multi-dimensional.

In the United Kingdom, Beenstock and Chan (1986) and Poon and Taylor (1991) did not find any significant positive relationships between security returns and Beta. Similarly, the observations of Levis (1985) for a sample covering the period 1958–82 indicate that smaller firms tend to outperform larger firms (although erratically). Strong and Xu (1997) attempted to replicate the Fama and French analysis in a UK context. Specifically, they investigated whether Beta could explain security returns and whether it was outweighed by 'the size effect'. For the period 1960–92, they found a positive risk premium associated with Beta in isolation, but this became insignificant when Beta was combined with other variables in a multiple regression. For the whole period, market value dominated Beta, but over 1973–92, it was itself insignificant compared with book-to-market value of equity, and gearing. However, the explanatory power of various combinations of variables used was poor, never exceeding an R^2 of 8 per cent. Overall, there appeared to be a size effect, but it did not operate in as clear or as stable a fashion as in the Fama and French study of US data.

5.14 FACTOR MODELS

It is not too surprising that some of the studies listed in the previous section do not support the notion that Beta is the most important determinant of the return on quoted securities. In the CAPM, the only independent variable driving individual security returns is the return on the market, i.e. there is a single factor at work. In reality, everyone knows there are many factors at work, but the researcher is hoping that their various impacts will all be rolled up into this single market factor.

However, the returns on a share react to general industry or sector changes in addition to general market changes. These aspects are all confused in Beta. This helps explain why the CAPM is such a poor explanatory model. The explanatory power of a regression model like the CAPM is measured by the R-squared, or Coefficient of Determination, which is measured on a scale of zero to $+1$. These are shown in Table 5.3 in the final column. While expert opinions vary on this, it is commonly accepted that an R-squared of above 50 per cent indicates a strong relationship, i.e. a high degree of explanatory power. The highest figure shown in the table is 41 per cent for GKN. The interpretation we have to put on this is that there are other, perhaps many other, factors at work impacting on security returns.

Whereas the CAPM is a single-factor model, many researchers like Fama and French (1992) have attempted to develop multi-factor models. A multi-factor model will include two elements:

- a list of factors that have been identified as having a significant influence on security returns;
- a measure of the sensitivity of the return on particular securities to changes in these factors.

In the CAPM, there is only the one factor, the return on the market portfolio, and the sensitivity is measured by each security's Beta. As in the CAPM, which distinguishes between specific and market-related risk, there are two types of risk – factor risk and non-factor risk. Thus, variations in the returns on stocks can be explained by variations in the identified factor(s) (analogous to market risk) and variations due to background 'noise', i.e. changes in factors not included in the model (analogous to specific risk).

■ A two-factor model

In the United Kingdom, 60 per cent of the economy is represented by consumer expenditure, which is largely driven by income growth and the 'feel-good factor' from rising house prices. Also bear in mind that the stock market is generally supposed to herald movements in the overall economy one to two years ahead. Therefore, a model devised to explain stock market returns in terms of income growth and house prices would be quite plausible.

This would be a two-factor model of the following form:

$$R_j = a + b_1 F_1 + b_2 F_2 + e_j$$

where R_j is the return on stock j in the usual sense, a is the intercept term, F_1 and F_2 are the two identified factors, income growth and house prices, b_1 and b_2 are the sensitivity coefficients and e_j is an error term.

The values of the parameters a, b_1 and b_2 would be found by multiple regression analysis, while the error term is assumed to average zero. Say the values established by empirical investigation are:

$a = 0.01$
$b_1 = 2.0$
$b_2 = 0.2$

This means that for every 1 per cent point change in income growth (F_1), individual security returns change by twice as much, i.e. by two percentage points. Similarly, for every 1 per cent point change in the house price index (F_2), security returns change by 0.2 of a percentage point.

It should be stressed that the explanatory factors in the equation would be common to all firms, but the sensitivity coefficients, the 'Betas', would vary according to how closely 'geared' the returns on each firm were to each factor. For example, if one identified factor was the sterling/dollar exchange rate, we would expect to see much higher sensitivity for a firm exporting to, or operating in, the United States, compared to one conducting most of its operations in the domestic arena.

5.15 THE ARBITRAGE PRICING THEORY

The most fully developed multi-factor model is the Arbitrage Pricing Theory (APT), developed by Ross (1976). Unlike the CAPM, APT does not assume that shareholders evaluate decisions within a mean–variance framework. Rather, it assumes the return on a share depends partly on macroeconomic factors and partly on events specific to the company. Instead of specifying a share's returns as a function of one factor (the return on the market portfolio), it specifies the returns as a function of multiple macroeconomic factors upon which the return on the market portfolio depends.

The expected risk premium of a particular share would be:

$$ER_j = R_f + \beta_1(ER_{factor\,1} - R_f) + \beta_2(ER_{factor\,2} - R_f) + \ldots + e_j$$

where ER_j is the expected rate of return on security j, $ER_{factor\,1}$ is the expected return on macroeconomic factor 1, β_1 is the sensitivity of the return on security j to factor 1 and e_j is the random deviation based on unique events impacting on the security's returns. The bracketed terms are thus risk premiums, as found in the CAPM.

Diversification can eliminate the specific risk associated with a security, leaving only the macroeconomic risk as the determinant of required security returns. A rational investor will arbitrage (hence the name) between different securities if the current market prices do not give sufficient compensation for variations in one or more factors in the APT equation.

The APT model does not specify what the explanatory factors are; they could be the stock market index, Gross National Product, oil prices, interest rates and so on. Different companies will be more sensitive to certain factors than others.

In theory, a riskless portfolio could be constructed (i.e. a 'zero Beta' portfolio) which would offer the risk-free rate of interest. If the portfolio gave a higher return, investors could make a profit without incurring any risk by borrowing at the risk-free rate to buy the portfolio. This process of 'arbitrage' (i.e. taking profits for zero risk) would continue until the portfolio's expected risk premium was zero.

The Arbitrage Pricing Theory avoids the CAPM's problem of having to identify the market portfolio. But it replaces this problem with possibly more onerous tasks. First, there is the requirement to identify the macroeconomic variables. US research indicates that the most influential factors in explaining asset returns in the APT framework are changes in industrial production, inflation, personal consumption, money supply and interest rates (McGowan and Francis, 1991).

Tests of the APT, especially for the United Kingdom, are still in their relative infancy. However, in an early test, Beenstock and Chan (1986) found that, for the period 1977–83, the first few years of the UK 'monetarist experiment', share returns were largely explained by a set of monetary factors – interest rates, the sterling M3 measure of money supply and two different measures of inflation, all highly interrelated variables. Clare and Thomas (1994) reported results from analysing 56 portfolios, each containing 15 shares sorted by Beta and by size of company by value. For the Beta-ordered portfolios, the key factors were oil prices, two measures of corporate default risk, the Retail Price Index (RPI), private-sector bank lending, current account bank balances and the yield to redemption on UK corporate loan stock. Using portfolios ordered by size, the key factors reduced to one measure of default risk and the RPI. Again, there was much intercorrelation among variables, but the return on the stock market index, although included in the initial tests, appeared in none of these final lists.

Once the main factors influencing share returns are established, there remain the problems of estimating risk premiums for each factor and measuring the sensitivity of individual share returns to these factors. For this reason, the APT is currently only in the prototype stage and yet to be accepted by practitioners.

5.16 FAMA AND FRENCH'S THREE-FACTOR MODEL

An approach that marries the APT to the multi-factor approach is the three-factor model developed in a series of papers by Fama and French (1993, 1995, 1996). This has the distinctive merit of an empirical grounding, being based on their paper of 1992. In Section 5.13, we noted that they found that US stock returns were explained better by company size and by the ratio of book value of equity to market value than merely by movements in the return on the whole market, magnified or moderated by Beta, as in the CAPM.

These two additional explanatory variables are utilised in the three-factor model. It states that stock returns above the risk-free rate (i.e. the equity premium) are determined by:

- The risk premium on the market portfolio.
- The difference between the return on a portfolio of small company shares and the return on a portfolio of large company shares (small less big, or SLB).
- The difference between the return on a portfolio of high book-to-market value stocks and the return on a portfolio of low book-to-market value stocks (high less low, or HLL).

The three-factor equation can be written thus:

$$\text{Expected return on stock}_j =$$
$$ER_j = R_f + \text{Risk premium} = R_f + [\text{Beta}_1(ER_m - R_f) + \text{Beta}_2(SLB) + \text{Beta}_3(HLL)]$$

The logic behind the formulation of the model is that the average small company and its stock is assumed to be more risky than the average large firm and its stock and thus commands a higher risk premium. Larger firms are generally more stable as they are more diversified by products and markets, and have better credit ratings, partly because their stock of assets is larger. Similarly, a stock with a high book value relative to market value is assumed to be more risky than one with a low book value relative to market value. The former owes its higher valuation rating to a greater growth potential and/or greater endowment of intangible assets such as intellectual capital.

To make the model operational, information is required on the risk premiums related to each factor, and for the various Beta factors. For example, imagine that empirical evidence suggests that, in past years, the risk premium on the market portfolio has averaged 5 per cent, the risk premium for a small company stock compared to a larger firm has averaged 6 per cent, and the risk premium for the stock of a typical firm with a high book-to-market value compared to market price has averaged 4 per cent.

When the risk-free rate is 3 per cent, for a firm of average risk, i.e. average sensitivity to each of these three factors, and thus with Beta values of 1.0 across the board, the overall expected return will be:

$$ER_j = 3\% + [(1.0 \times 5\%) + (1.0 \times 6\%) + (1.0 \times 4\%)] = 3\% + 15\% = 18\%$$

In practice, firms exhibit varying sensitivities to these factors depending on their product and market profiles, for example, and thus carry Beta values different from one. Assume that Firm X has a low sensitivity to market movements (Beta = 0.4), a relatively high sensitivity in respect of relative size (Beta = 1.2) and a relatively low sensitivity to the book versus market value factor (Beta = 0.8), then its expected return is:

$$ER_j = 3\% + [(0.4 \times 5\%) + (1.2 \times 6\%) + (0.8 \times 4\%)] = 3\% + 12.4\% = 15.4\%$$

There has been extensive research in recent years based on Fama and French's highly influential approach. Most studies reinforce the view that Beta alone cannot adequately explain stock market returns, although they do not always agree on the most powerful determinants. In the process of analysis, a number of anomalies that the Fama and French model is unable to explain have emerged, for example, a negative relationship between returns and growth in assets, which appears counter-intuitive – why do firms invest in new projects if the returns are persistently negative? Among the most recent claimants to have developed a better 'three-factor model' is the model developed by Chen and Zhang (2010). This appears to account for many such anomalies and gives a good explanation of stock returns over a lengthy period as well as recording a non-significant alpha coefficient. Even so, their model does include the sensitivity of stock returns to the market excess returns (i.e. Beta as in the CAPM), as the first factor. The others are: the difference between the returns on a portfolio of low-investment stocks, and the returns on a portfolio of high-investment stocks; and the difference between the returns on a portfolio of stocks with high returns on assets, and the returns on a portfolio with low returns on assets. No doubt, such work will continue.

5.17 THE FOUR- AND FIVE-FACTOR MODELS

In addition to several other earlier studies, the findings of Fama and French (1992, 1993, 1995, 1996) persuaded several researchers in this area to construct and empirically investigate factor models. First, Carhart (1997) presented a four-factor model that added momentum to the Fama and French (1993) three-factor model. The author regards the four-factor model as a model of market equilibrium and find the evidence which is consistent with market efficiency, and that explains the role of size, book-to-market ratio and momentum factors. In another study, Fama and French (2006b) explained the CAPM anomalies by linking it to the dividend discount model. They found no clear evidence to support of the role of earnings and growth in assets, as predictors of stock returns.

Fama and French (2015) added operating income and growth in firms' assets as the two additional factors to their three-factor model and then tested the explanatory power of their new five-factor model. Their findings support the theoretical underpinning of their five-factor model and present the evidence suggesting that performance of their five-factor model is robust to the way its factors are constructed. Fama and French (2017) tested their five-factor model with data from four different regions, including America, Europe, Asia and Japan. The authors argued that their five-factor model generally provides the strongest evidence about all metrics across all regions, and they support the use of their five-factor model over and above the three and four factor models.

In the UK context, Racicot and Rentz (2016) re-tested the Fama and French five-factor model by using a more robust qualitative analysis with UK data. They found favourable evidence only for the market factor, whereas the rest of the factors were identified as insignificant in predicting stock returns in the United Kingdom. Similarly, in addition to the application of a more robust analysis, Racicot and Rentz (2017) added liquidity as the sixth factor to the FF's five-factor model, and again found the evidence suggesting that only the market factor is significantly associated with UK stock returns. For all other factors, including liquidity, no significant relationship was found with UK stock returns.

5.18 ISSUES RAISED BY THE CAPM: SOME FOOD FOR MANAGERIAL THOUGHT

The CAPM raises a number of important issues, which have fundamental implications for the applicability of the model itself and the role of diversification in the armoury of corporate strategic weapons.

■ Should we trust the market?

Legally, managers are charged with the duty of acting in the best interests of shareholders, i.e. maximising their wealth (although company law does not express it *quite* like this). This involves investing in all projects offering returns above the shareholders' opportunity cost of capital. The CAPM provides a way of assessing the rate of return required by shareholders from their investments, albeit based partly on past returns. If the Beta is known and a view is taken on the future returns on the market, then the apparently required return follows. This becomes the cut-off rate for new investment projects, at least for those of similar systematic risk to existing activities. This implies that managers' expectations coincide with those of shareholders or, more generally, with those of the market. If, however, the market as a whole expects a higher return from the market portfolio, some projects deemed acceptable to managers may not be worthwhile for shareholders.

The subsequent fall in share price would provide the mechanism whereby the market communicates to managers that the discount rate applied was too low. The CAPM relies on efficiently set market prices to reveal to managers the 'correct' hurdle rate and any mistakes caused by misreading the market. The implication that one can trust the market to arrive at correct prices, and hence required rates of return, is problematic for many practising managers, who are prone to believe that the market incorrectly values the companies that they operate. Managers who doubt the validity of the EMH are unlikely to accept a CAPM-derived discount rate.

■ Should companies diversify?

The CAPM is based on the premise that rational shareholders form efficiently diversified portfolios, realising that the market will reward them only for bearing market-related risk. The benefits of diversification can easily be obtained by portfolio formation, i.e. buying securities at relatively low dealing fees. The implication of this is that *corporate diversification is perhaps pointless as a device to reduce risk because companies are seeking to achieve what shareholders can do themselves, probably more efficiently*. Securities are far more divisible than investment projects and can be traded much more quickly when conditions alter. So why do managers diversify company activities?

An obvious explanation is that managers have not understood the message of the EMH/CAPM, or doubt its validity, believing instead that shareholders' best interests are enhanced by reduction of the total variability of the firm's earnings. For some shareholders, this may indeed be the case, as a large proportion of those investing directly on the stock market hold undiversified portfolios.

Many small shareholders were attracted to equity investment by privatisation issues or by Personal Equity Plans and their successor, ISAs (Individual Savings

Accounts). Larger shareholders sometimes tie up major portions of their capital in a single company in order to take, or retain, an active part in its management. In such cases, market risk, based on the co-variability of the return on a company's shares with that on the market portfolio, is an inadequate measure of risk. The appropriate measure of risk for capital budgeting decisions probably lies somewhere between total risk, based on the variance, or standard deviation, of a project's returns, and market risk, depending on the degree of diversification of shareholders.

A more subtle explanation of why managers diversify is the divorce of ownership and control. Managers who are relatively free from the threat of shareholder interference in company operations may pursue their personal interests above those of shareholders. If an inadequate contract has been written between the manager–agents and the shareholder–principals, managers may be inclined to promote their own job security. This is understandable, since shareholders are highly mobile between alternative security holdings, but managerial mobility is often low. *To managers, the distinction between systematic risk and specific risk may be relatively insignificant, since they have a vested interest in minimising total risk in order to increase their job security.* If the company flounders, it is of little comfort for them to know that their personal catastrophe has only a minimal effect on well-diversified shareholders.

As we will see in Chapter 12, there are many motives for diversification beyond merely reducing risk. However, it is common to justify diversification to shareholders purely on these grounds, at least under certain types of market imperfection. When a company fails, there are liquidation costs to bear as well as the losses entailed in selling assets at 'knock-down' prices. These costs may result in both creditors and shareholders failing to receive full economic value in the asset disposal. Although this will not devastate a well-diversified shareholder, the resulting hole in his or her portfolio will require filling in order to restore balance. Company diversification may reduce these risks and also the costs of portfolio disruption and readjustment.

■ The conglomerate discount

Conglomerate companies are made up of businesses that operate in different industry or business sectors. Therefore, conglomerate companies are, by definition, diversified. The value of conglomerates is typically less than the value that would be assigned to the different parts of the business if they were operating separately from one another. Consequently, in stock markets there is often talk of a 'conglomerate discount' applying to the shares, and this is illustrated in the examples below of Akzo and Sony.

Akzo faces tough battle after fending off PPG

After vanquishing the enemy, Akzo Nobel now faces more battles on other fronts. The Dutch paintmaker's resistance to a three-month takeover assault finally succeeded last week, when its US rival PPG Industries gave up its pursuit of a €26.9bn deal that would have created an industry leader.

But Akzo's victory may yet be pyrrhic. Chief executive Ton Büchner faces the considerable tasks of splitting the company into two and achieving increased financial targets that were promised as part of the defence. At the same time, he must repair strained relationships with a number of investors who were angered by the Amsterdam-based group's handling of the episode.

The immediate task at hand is to win back the support of several large shareholders, who publicly criticised Akzo over its refusal to enter negotiations with its suitor.

But for its part, Akzo has acknowledged some mistakes. 'We highly value shareholder perspectives and regret that a number of shareholders believe we have insufficiently explained our considerations in respect of PPG's proposals,' said Mr Büchner. 'We will be seeking and listening to feedback with an aim to improving these important relationships.'

One area where investors will be expecting early signs of progress is the planned separation of Akzo's speciality chemicals business, which makes everything from table salt to bleaching agents on an annual revenue of €4.8bn. A 'dual-track' process is under way whereby the business could either be sold or spun off as a discrete listed entity. Akzo expects to complete this process within a year, and if the company opts for a sale of the business the resulting cash is expected to be returned to investors. The planned separation of the speciality chemicals unit will leave Akzo focused on paints and coatings, and analysts say the company's share price could therefore shed its current *'conglomerate' discount*.

However, Akzo's management will be under pressure to create value at least commensurate with the level of PPG's bid. Its third and final stock-and-cash offer valued Akzo's shares at €96.75 each — a premium of 50 per cent to the undisturbed price. The stock closed at €75.75 on Friday. Akzo management responded to PPG's pursuit with a bumper shareholder payout, including a special dividend, of €1.6bn this year. It has also set higher financial targets.

Source: Pooler, M. (2017) Akzo faces tough battle after fending off PPG. *Financial Times*, 4 June. © The Financial Times Limited 2018. All rights reserved.

Sony: ghosts in the machine

The chief executive of Sony is seeking kudos as a ghost-buster by promising to lift operating profits above ¥500bn ($4.4bn) this financial year. Weak profitability has haunted the Japanese electronics and media group for a decade. But investors should beware a spectre Mr Hirai cannot dispel: Sony's conglomerate status.

The company's interests range from silicon chips and consumer electronics to a US movie studio whose remake of Ghostbusters flopped in 2016. Sony's full-year results, released after market close on Friday, made for poor viewing too. A $962m impairment for Sony Pictures contributed to a 17.4 per cent drop in profits before tax, to ¥251.6bn. But the shares popped 3 per cent on Monday, in response to plans for a financial sequel with greater appeal.

The 73 per cent uplift to operating profits envisaged this year would take operating margins to about 6.25 per cent. Erstwhile chief executive Howard Stringer only beat the 5 per cent hurdle once in seven years. On that basis, the return on common equity of the group could be expected to come in at about 11 per cent, beating a 10 per cent target.

There is scope for Sony to do even better. The ¥500bn forecast includes a ¥40bn cushion for group cost overruns that may not be needed. Mr Hirai has reined in costs and risked the wrath of traditionalists by ditching Sony's Vaio laptop and PC business in 2014. As a result, the shares have handsomely outperformed the QE-fattened Topix index over three years. His rosy short-term forecast would look more durable if it did not depend on better trading from movies and chips. The first business is hit-and-miss. The second is highly cyclical.

Mr Hirai is splitting Sony into distinct subsidiaries to dispel an illusion common within large diversified groups that profitability is a collective responsibility with no individual comeback. However, the group will suffer from a *conglomerate discount* so long as its activities remain so widely spread. The shares are rated in line with Panasonic rather than Nintendo. A full break-up is unlikely. However, Mr Hirai might at least vacuum up and expel some more troublesome little spooks in the mould of Vaio. The underperforming components division would be a good place to start.

Source: Sony: ghosts in the machine. *Financial Times*, 1 May. © The Financial Times Limited 2018. All rights reserved.

Self-assessment activity 5.11

What reasons may there be for a conglomerate discount existing?

(Answer in Appendix A)

SUMMARY

We have examined the nature of the risks affecting the holders of securities and have begun to discuss whether the return required by shareholders, as implied by market valuations, can be used as a cut-off rate for new investment projects.

Key points

- Security risk can be split into two components: risk specific to the company in question, and the variability in return due to general market movements.
- Rational investors form well-diversified portfolios to eliminate specific risk.
- The most efficient portfolio of risky securities is the market portfolio, although investors may mix this with investment in the risk-free asset in order to achieve more preferred risk–return combinations along the capital market line.
- The risk premium built into the required return on securities reflects a reward for systematic risk only.
- The risk premium on a particular share depends on the risk premium on the overall market and the extent to which the return on the security moves with that of the whole market, as indicated by its Beta coefficient.
- This premium for risk is the second term in the equation for the security market line:

    $$ER_j = R_f + \beta_j(ER_m - R_f).$$

- Practical problems in using the CAPM centre on measurement of Beta, specification of the risk-free asset and measurement of the market's risk premium.
- In an all-equity-financed company, the return required by shareholders can be used as a cut-off rate for new investment if the new project has systematic risk similar to the company's other activities.
- There is some debate about whether managers should diversify company activities merely in order to lower risk.
- Empirical studies seem to throw increasing doubt on the CAPM.
- The main proposed alternative, the Arbitrage Pricing Theory (APT), relies on fewer restrictive assumptions but is still in the prototype stage.

Further reading

Because this a wide and rapidly moving field, we give more than our customary commentary on some of these references in order to provide more context.

Copeland *et al.* (2013) offer a rigorous treatment of the derivation of the formulae used in this chapter. Brealey *et al.* (2013) offer an alternative, less mathematical treatment. You should also read the famous critique of the CAPM by Roll (1977). Fama and French (1992), although a difficult paper, is essential reading for obtaining an in-depth understanding of these issues. In the UK context, Strong and Xu (1997) have attempted to replicate the original Fama and French paper.

An excellent text on Modern Portfolio Theory is Elton *et al.* (2014), covering the basic theory and including an up-to-date survey of empirical work. There is a very good resumé of the Fama and French analysis in Ross *et al.* (2015). Meanwhile, all these arguments have not gone unchallenged – see, for example, the two articles by Black (1993a, 1993b) and that by Shanken *et al.* (1995).

Fama and French (1995, 2002) have updated their earlier work, reaching essentially similar conclusions. Fama and French (2002) has also entered the debate on the equity premium, whereas Fama and French (2006b) explained the CAPM anomalies by linking it to the dividend discount model but found no clear evidence about the role of earnings and growth in assets in predicting of stock returns. Chen and Zhang (2010) have staked a claim to a 'better' three-factor model. More recently, Fama and French (2015) added operating income and growth in firms' assets as two additional factors to their three-factor model and then tested the explanatory power of their new five-factor model. Similarly, Fama and French (2017) test their five-factor model with data from four different regions, including America, Europe, Asia and Japan. Racicot and Rentz (2016) re-tested this five-factor model with UK data and found favourable evidence only for the market factor. Similarly, Racicot and Rentz (2017) added liquidity to the five-factor model but found only the market factor as significantly associated with UK stock returns.

The validity, and future, of CAPM is very much under debate. Finance researchers have different standpoints in these debates, and a 2013 special issue of the journal *ABACUS* provides an excellent coverage of these. The CAPM debates are also extensively covered in Levy (2012).

Appendix
ANALYSIS OF VARIANCE

The total risk of a security (σ_T), comprising both unsystematic risk (σ_{USR}) and systematic risk (σ_{SR}), is measured by the variance of returns, which can be separated into the two elements. Imagine an asset with total risk of $\sigma_T^2 = 500$, of which 80 per cent (400) is explained by systematic risk factors, the remainder resulting from factors specific to the firm:

$$\sigma_T^2 = 500 = \sigma_{SR}^2 + \sigma_{USR}^2 = 100 + 400$$

In terms of standard deviations, $\sigma_{SR} = \sqrt{400} = 20$ and $\sigma_{USR} = \sqrt{100} = 10$. Notice that we cannot express the overall standard deviation by summing the two component standard deviations – variances are additive, standard deviations are not – the square root of the total risk is $\sqrt{500} = 22.4$, rather than the sum of σ_{SR} and σ_{USR} (20 + 10 = 30).

In regression models, the extent to which the overall variability in the dependent variable is explained by the variability in the independent variable is given by the R-squared (R^2) statistic, the square of the correlation coefficient. The R^2 is thus a measure of 'goodness of fit' of the regression line to the recorded observations. If all observations lie on the regression line, R^2 equals 1, and the variations in the market return fully explain the variations in the return on security j. In this case, all risk is market risk. It follows that the lower is R^2, the greater the proportion of specific risk of the security. For investors wishing to diversify away specific risk, such securities are highly attractive. Notice that an R^2 of 1 does not entail a Beta of 1, as Figure 5.11 illustrates. All three securities have R^2 of 1, but they have different degrees of market risk, as indicated by their Betas.

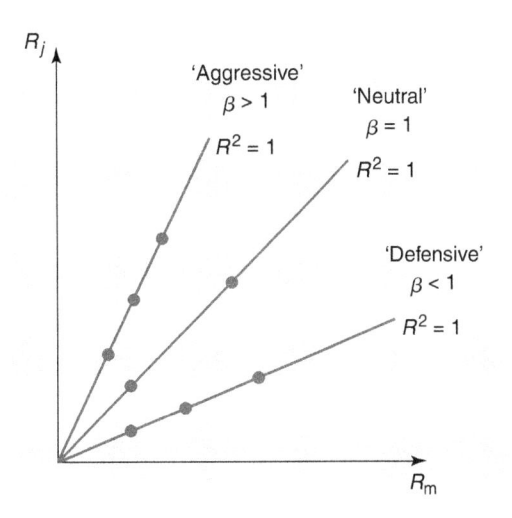

Figure 5.11 Alternative characteristics lines

In the example mentioned earlier, the R^2 of 80 per cent would correspond to a correlation coefficient, r_{jm}, of $\sqrt{0.8} = 0.89$. Looking at the standard deviations, we can infer that 0.89 of the standard deviation is market risk, i.e. $(0.89 \times 22.4) = 19.94$, while the specific risk $= (1 - r_{jm}) \times 22.4 = (0.11 \times 22.4) = 2.46$. Let us re-emphasise these relationships:

Market, or systematic, risk is:

$R^2 \times$ the overall variance, σ_T^2; or ($r_{jm} \times$ the overall standard deviation, σ_T)
$(0.8 \times 500) = 400$; or $(0.89 \times 22.4\%) = 19.94\%$

Specific risk is:

$(1 - R^2) \times$ overall variance, σ_T^2; or $(1 - r_{jm}) \times$ overall standard deviation σ_T
$(0.2 \times 500) = 100$; or $(0.11 \times 22.4\%) = 2.46\%$.

The reader may find it useful to test out these relationships using the data provided in Table 5.3 ('Variability' is total risk expressed as a standard deviation). However, not all cases work out neatly owing to rounding errors.

QUESTIONS

Questions with a coloured number have a solution in Appendix B on page 501.

1. The ordinary shares of Paddy plc have a Beta of 1.23. The risk-free rate of interest is 5 per cent, and the risk premium achieved on the market index over the past 20 years has averaged 11.5 per cent p.a. What is the future expected return on Paddy Plc's shares?
   If you believe that overall market returns will fall to 8 per cent in future years, how does your answer change?

2. Supply the missing links in the table:

	ER_j	R_f	β	ER_m
(i)	19%	?	1.10	18%
(ii)	17%	5%	?	12%
(iii)	?	4%	0.75	10%
(iv)	15%	7%	0.65	?

3. Locate the security market line (SML) given the following information: $R_f = 8\%$, $ER_m = 12\%$.

4. Which of the following shares are over-valued?

	Beta	Current rate of return
A	0.7	7%
B	1.3	13%
C	0.9	9%

   The risk-free rate is 5 per cent, and the return on the market index is 10 per cent.

5. The market portfolio has yielded 12 per cent on average over past years. It is expected to offer a risk premium in future years of 7 per cent. The standard deviation of its return is 8 per cent. The risk-free rate is 5 per cent.
   (i) What is the expected return from the market portfolio?
   (ii) Draw a diagram to show the location of the capital market line.
   (iii) What is the expected return on a portfolio comprising 50 per cent invested in the market portfolio and 50 per cent invested in the risk-free asset?
   (iv) What is the risk of the portfolio in (iii)?
   (v) What is the market trade-off between portfolio risk and return suggested by these figures?

6. The following figures relate to monthly observations of the percentage return on a widely used stock market index (R_m) and the return on a particular ordinary share (R_j) over a period of six months.

Month	R_m	R_j
1	5	4
2	-10	-8
3	12	9.6
4	3	2.4
5	-4	-3.2
6	7	5.6

   (a) Plot these data on a graph and deduce the value of the Beta coefficient.
   (b) To what extent are variations in R_m due to specific risk factors?
   (c) Calculate the systematic risk of the security. (NB: systematic risk = $\beta^2 \sigma_m^2$)

7 Z plc is a long-established company with interests mainly in retailing and property development. Its current market capitalisation is £750 million. The company trades exclusively in the United Kingdom, but it is planning to expand overseas either by acquisition or joint venture within the next two years. The company has built up a portfolio of investments in UK equities and corporate and government debt. The aim of developing this investment portfolio is to provide a source of funds for its overseas expansion programme. Summary information on the portfolio is given here.

Type of security	Value £ million	Average % return over the last 12 months
UK equities	23.2	15.0
US equities	9.4	13.5
UK corporate debt	5.3	8.2
Long-term government debt	11.4	7.4
Three-month Treasury bonds	3.2	6.0

Approximately 25 per cent of the UK equities are in small companies' shares, some of them trading on the Alternative Investment Market. The average return on all UK equities, over the past 12 months, has been 12 per cent. On US equities, it has been 12.5 per cent.

Ignore taxation throughout this question.

Required

Discuss the advantages and disadvantages of holding such a portfolio of investments in the circumstances of Z plc.

(CIMA, November 1997)

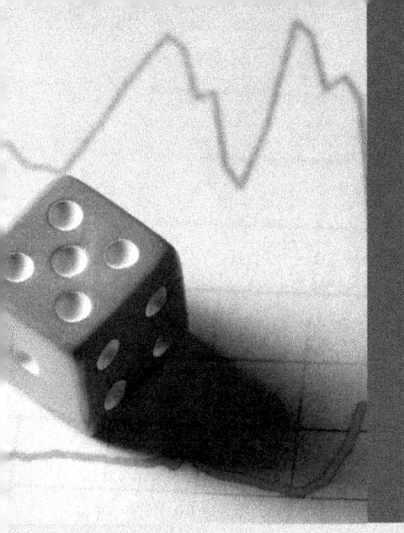

6

The required rate of return on investment

Cost of equity

Calculating a cost of equity in practice can be difficult, and there are several different approaches that can be used. The following is taken from the 2016 cost of capital survey conducted by the accounting firm KPMG.

- **Risk-free rate:** The average risk-free rate used by the survey firms was recorded as 1.5 per cent. In this survey, 45 per cent of companies used the yield on government bonds with a period of 30 years or more in the calculation of the risk-free rate. This rate is at the lowest point in financial history.
- **Market risk premium:** The average market risk premium used by the surveyed firms was recorded as 6.4 per cent. The market risk premium is usually determined retrospectively based on a comparison between observable long-term stock yields and risk-free bond yields over a specific period.
- **Beta factor:** The average beta factor used by the surveyed companies was recorded as 0.85. The majority of the surveyed companies used an industry peer group to derive their beta factors.
- **Cost of equity:** The average cost of equity used by the surveyed companies was recorded as 8.2 per cent. This is a little lower than the 2015 rate of 8.4 per cent.

Source: Based on KPMG Cost of Capital Study, 2016

Learning objectives

This chapter applies the models developed in earlier chapters for measuring the required rate of return on investment projects. After reading this chapter, you should:

- Understand how the Dividend Growth Model can be used to set the hurdle rate.
- Understand how the Capital Asset Pricing Model also can be used for this purpose.
- Be able to apply the required rate of return to firm valuation.
- Appreciate that different rates of return may be required at different levels of a firm.
- Be aware of the practical difficulties in specifying discount rates for particular activities.
- Appreciate how taxation may influence discount rates.

6.1 INTRODUCTION

No company can expect prolonged existence without achieving returns that at least compensate investors for their opportunity costs. Shareholders who receive a poor rate of return will vote with their wallets, depressing share price. If its share price underperforms the market (allowing for Beta), a company is ripe for reorganisation, takeover or both. A management team, motivated if only by job security, must earn acceptable returns for shareholders. This chapter deals with assessing such rates of return and showing how they can be used in valuing firms. Different returns may be required for different activities, according to their riskiness. Multi-division companies, which operate in a range of often unrelated activities, may require tailor-made 'divisional cut-off rates' to reflect the risk of particular activities.

The return that a company should seek on its investment depends not only on its inherent business risk, but also on its **capital structure** – its particular mix of debt and equity financing. However, because determining this rate for a geared company is complex, we defer treatment of the impact of gearing until Chapters 10 and 11. Here, *we focus on the return required by the shareholders in an all-equity company*.

capital structure
A firm's mixture of debt and equity resulting from decisions on financing its operations

Shareholders seek a return to cover the cost of waiting for their returns, plus compensation for inflation, plus a premium to cover the exposure to risk of their capital, depending on the risk of the business activity.

Two widely-adopted approaches are the Dividend Growth Model (DGM), encountered in Chapter 2, and the Capital Asset Pricing Model (CAPM), developed in the last chapter. Under each approach, we determine the return that shareholders demand on their investment holdings. We then consider whether this return should dictate the hurdle rate on new investment projects.

6.2 THE REQUIRED RETURN IN ALL-EQUITY FIRMS: THE DGM

■ The DGM revisited

In Chapter 2, we discussed the value of shares in an all-equity firm which retained a constant fraction, b, of its earnings in order to finance investment. If retentions are expected to achieve a rate of return, R, this results in a growth rate of $g = bR$. The share price is:

$$P_0 = \frac{D_0(1 + g)}{(k_e - g)} = \frac{D_1}{(k_e - g)}$$

where D_0 and D_1 represent this year's and next year's dividends per share, respectively, and k_e is the rate of return required by shareholders.

■ The cost of equity

cost of equity
The minimum rate of return a firm must offer its owners to compensate for waiting for their returns, and also for bearing risk

Rearranging the expression, we find the shareholders' required return is:

$$k_e = \frac{D_1}{P_0} + g$$

The shareholders' required return is thus a compound of two elements, the *prospective* dividend yield and the expected rate of growth in dividends.

It is important to appreciate that this formula for k_e is based on the *current* market value of the shares, and that it incorporates specific expectations about growth, dependent on current assumptions about both the retention ratio, b, and the expected rate of return on new investment, R. With b and R constant, the rate of growth, g, is also constant. These are highly restrictive assumptions. Often, the nearest we can get to assessing the likely growth rate is to project the past rate of growth, 'tweaking' it if we believe that a faster or slower rate may occur in future.

For example, assume Arthington plc is valued by the market at £3 per share, having recently paid a dividend of 20p per share, and has recorded dividend growth of 12 per cent p.a. Projecting this past growth rate into the future, we can infer that shareholders require a return of 19.5 per cent, viz:

$$k_e = \frac{20p\,(1.12)}{300p} + 0.12 = (0.075 + 0.12) = 0.195, \text{ i.e. } 19.5\%$$

If people felt this growth was unsustainable, then perhaps it might be 'nudged down' to a more achievable 10 per cent, say. In this case, the k_e becomes 17.3 per cent, a rather less demanding target.

Self-assessment activity 6.1

Determine the required return by shareholders in the following case:

Share price = £1.80 (ex div)
Past growth = 3%
EPS = £0.36
Dividend cover = 3 times

(Answer in Appendix A)

■ Whitbread plc (www.whitbread.co.uk)

Let us relate this approach to a real company. Table 6.1 shows the dividend payment record and end-of-financial year share prices for Whitbread, the leisure conglomerate, for the years 2007–17.

Table 6.1 The dividend return on Whitbread plc shares 2007–17

Year	DPS (p)
2007–8	36.00
2008–9	36.55
2009–10	38.00
2010–11	44.50
2011–12	51.25
2012–13	57.40
2013–14	68.80
2014–15	82.15
2015–16	90.35
2016–17	95.80

Source: Whitbread plc, *Annual Report*/Thomson Reuters Datastream.

The dividend per share (DPS) grew from 36.00p in 2007–8 to 95.80 p by 2016–17. Using discount tables, we find the average annual compound growth rate is about

11.5 per cent.* Applying this rate to the share price of 3,919p ruling at the date of analysis (21 July 2017), we find:

$k_e = [95.8 (1.115)]/3919] + 0.115$

$k_e = 0.0273 + 0.115 = 0.1423$, or 14.2%

■ Some problems

Apart from the restrictive assumptions of the Dividend Growth Model, some further warnings are in order.

1 The dividend growth depends on the time period used

The choice of time period can have a significant impact on the results. Too short a period and the estimate of growth is distorted by random factors, and too long a period exposes the result to the impact of structural changes in the business, e.g. divestment and acquisitions.

The calculation of g, and hence k_e, should certainly be based on a sufficiently long period to allow random distortions to even out. We may still feel that past growth is an unreliable guide to future performance, especially for a company in a mature industry, growing roughly in line with the economy as a whole. If past growth is considered unrepresentative, we may interpose our own forecast, but this would involve second-guessing the market's growth expectations, which is tantamount to challenging the EMH.

2 The calculated k_e depends on the choice of reference date for measuring share price

Our calculation used the price at the end of the accounting period, but this pre-dates the announcement of results and payment of dividend. Arguably, we should use the ex-dividend price, as this values all future dividends, beginning with those payable in one year's time. This would reduce the distortion to share price caused by the pattern of dividend payment (i.e. the share price drops abruptly when it goes 'ex-dividend', beyond which purchasers of the share will not qualify for the declared dividend). However, the eventual ex-dividend price may well reflect different expectations from those ruling at the company financial year-end.

Conversely, in an efficient capital market, share prices gradually increase as the date of dividend payment approaches, so that, especially for companies that pay several dividends each year, some distorting effect is always likely to be present. Our practical advice is to take the ruling share price as the basis of calculation, but to moderate the calculation according to whether a dividend is in the offing. For example, if a 5p dividend is expected in two months' time, a prospective fall in share price of 5p should be allowed for. In our assessment, the error caused by using an out-of-date share price is likely to outweigh that from using a valuation incorporating a forthcoming dividend.

3 The calculation is at the mercy of short-term movements in share price

If, as many observers believe, capital markets are becoming more volatile, possibly undermining their efficiency in valuing companies, the financial manager may feel disinclined to rely on current market prices. Managers are generally reluctant to accept

---

*The growth rate, g, is found from the expression:

$36.00/(1 + g)^9 = 95.80$, or $(1 + g)^9 = 95.80/36.00$
$1 + g = 1.1150$
$g = 1.1150 - 1 = 0.1150$, or 11.5%

The growth rate can be found directly from compound interest tables, or by inverting the expression from the present value tables, i.e. $1/(1 + g)^9 = 0.3758$; hence g approximates to 11.50 per cent.

the EMH and commonly assert that the market undervalues 'their companies'. However, there remains a need for a benchmark return to guide managers. One might examine, over a period of years, the actual returns received by shareholders in the form of both dividends and capital gains. One way of conducting such a calculation is to focus on average annual rates of return, based on the analysis adopted in Chapter 5, as applied to D.S. Smith plc. This evens out short-term fluctuations. However, it does not follow that the achieved return matches the required return.

4 Taxation

A project's NPV can be found on a post-tax or a pre-tax basis. If the NPV model is used on a pre-tax basis, both denominator and numerator must be on a pre-tax basis, and vice versa. If, for example, we wish to work in post-tax terms, the standard NPV expression for a one-off end-of-year cash flow, X, is:

$$\text{NPV} = \frac{X(1-T)}{(1+k_T)}$$

where T is the rate of Corporation Tax and k_T is the required return adjusted for tax. If shareholders seek a return of, say, 10 per cent after tax at 30 per cent, the company has to earn a pre-tax return of $10\%/(1-30\%) = 14.3$ per cent. In principle, computation on a pre-tax basis should generate the same NPV as that produced by a post-tax calculation, so long as the discount rate is suitably adjusted. However, this relationship is complicated by access to capital allowances. As a result, it is usual to compute NPVs on a post-tax basis.

The rate of tax applicable to corporate earnings might appear to be the rate of Corporation Tax. However, the picture is clouded by the prevailing type of tax regime (e.g. whether classical or an **imputation tax system**), and by the forms in which shareholders receive income (i.e. the balance between dividend income and capital gains, and the relevant rates of tax on these two forms of income). In other words, it is important to consider the interaction between the system of corporate taxation and the system of personal taxation.

imputation tax systems
Taxation systems that offer shareholders tax credits (fully or partially) in respect of company tax already paid when assessing their income tax liability on dividends paid out

Under an imputation tax, a shareholder receives a tax credit for the income tax component incorporated into the profits tax. Shareholders subject to tax at the standard rate face no further tax liability, while higher-rate taxpayers face a supplementary tax demand. To add to the complexity, some imputation systems allow investors to reclaim all the tax paid on their behalf (full imputation), while others involve a discrepancy between the rate of Corporation Tax and the relevant rate of income tax (partial imputation). The UK system is a modified partial imputation system under which a tax credit is granted but is not repayable to non-tax payers. The current rate of tax imputed for UK residents is 10 per cent of the gross dividends, although the first £2,000 (2017–18) of dividend income is tax-free. Beyond this threshold, tax is collected in arrears. Higher-rate tax payers face higher tax demands on their dividend income.

When we calculated k_e using the DGM, the computation was based on the net-of-tax dividend payment, so it may appear that we have met the requirement to allow for taxation. However, the UK tax system imposes two possible tax distortions. First, the relative tax treatment of capital gains and dividend income has differed over time, and second, as we have just seen, different shareholders are subject to tax in different ways.

A major problem facing a company is divining the tax status of its shareholders. Inspection of the shareholder register may provide much information, but there is no easy solution to this problem. The share price is set by the market by the interaction of the supply and demand for its shares as expressed by thousands of investors. Although each may well be in a different tax position, the resulting share price is the result of investors assessing whether the shares represent good value or not for them. In other words, the market automatically takes into account the *average* tax positions of its participants.

Under this view, it is not the function of the company to gauge the tax requirements of the investor and to adjust the discount rate accordingly. This is impossible in a capital market with large numbers of investors. The market imposes a required return for particular companies, and then it is up to individual investors to make their own arrangements regarding taxation. The market-determined rate of return can be regarded as the return that the company must make on its investments. This becomes the after-tax return that the company should use to discount the after-tax cash flows from capital projects. (The only adjustment that the company should make is to allow for the tax shield on debt, as explained in Chapter 10.)

To summarise: in principle, we could discount pre-tax cash flows, but the identification of the appropriate pre-tax required return is complicated by the existence and timing of capital allowances. Hence, a post-tax computation is preferable. Theoretically, we ought to allow for investors' personal tax positions as well as Corporation Tax (i.e. discount project cash flows net of both Corporation Tax and investors' personal tax liabilities). But this requires such detailed knowledge of the relevant tax rates applicable to shareholders as to render it impracticable. As a result, it is usual to discount post-Corporation Tax cash flows at the market-expressed required return, assuming that shareholders have made their own tax arrangements. This means that shareholders will gravitate to those companies whose dividend policies most suit their tax positions. This personal **clientèle effect** is discussed further in Chapter 9.

clientèle effect
The notion that a firm attracts investors by establishing a set dividend policy that suits a particular group of investors

Self-assessment activity 6.2

Specify the two situations under which the DGM breaks down completely. (You may have to revisit Chapter 2.)

(Answer in Appendix A)

6.3 THE REQUIRED RETURN IN ALL-EQUITY FIRMS: THE CAPM

In Chapter 5, we saw how the security market line (SML) traces out the systematic risk–return characteristics of all the securities traded in an efficient capital market. The SML equation is:

$$ER_j = R_f + \beta_j(ER_m - R_f)$$

ER_j is the return required on the shares of company j and is therefore the same as k_e, R_f is the risk-free rate of return and ER_m is the expected return on the market portfolio. We saw in Chapter 5 that, in order to utilise the CAPM, we needed either to measure, or to make direct assumptions about, these items. (Refer back to the discussion in Chapter 5 of measurement difficulties and the application to GKN.)

However, despite these problems, the CAPM has major advantages over the DGM. The DGM usually involves extrapolating past rates of growth and accepting the validity of the market's valuation of the equity at any time. If we suspect that past growth rates are unlikely to be replicated and/or that a company's share price is over- or under-valued, we might doubt the validity of an estimate of k_e derived from the DGM.

The CAPM does not require growth projections; nor does it totally depend on the instantaneous efficiency of the market. Recall that the Beta is derived from a regression model relating the returns from holding the shares of a particular company to the returns on the market over a lengthy period. Taking, say, monthly observations over five years (60 in all) effectively irons out short-term influences. This requires semi-strong market efficiency for the period and a reasonably consistent relationship between security returns and the returns on the market portfolio.

■ Applying the CAPM to Whitbread plc

The London Business School quotes a Beta of 1.06 for Whitbread. In July 2017, the yield on long-term UK 30 years gilts was about 2 per cent. Using a market risk premium of about 6 per cent, yields the following required return:

$$ER_j = R_f + \beta(ER_m - R_f) = 0.02 + 1.06\,(6\%)$$
$$= 0.02 + 0.0636$$
$$= 0.087362, \text{ or } 8.7\%$$

This is well below the DGM result of 14.2 per cent. As the two approaches, in principle, should yield about the same result, some reconciliation is required. At the time of this calculation, market interest rates were historically very low, at least in money terms, generating expectations of low interest rates for the future. It is doubtful whether Whitbread can sustain 11.5 per cent annual dividend growth in the future, so it might be more prudent to use a rate nearer to that of the industry as a whole.

It appears that estimates of k_e obtained by either method are susceptible to the date of the calculation and prevailing expectations for the future. More fundamentally, whereas the DGM looks at past performance over a number of years, the CAPM is essentially a forward-looking, one-period model, although it is commonly used for long-term purposes.

Counting the cost

Lex Column

There are few more essential items in the corporate finance tool-kit than a company's cost of capital – the return its investors expect as compensation for putting their funds in one business rather than another. Estimating the cost of capital, however, involves as much art and guesswork as it does science, and the results can vary widely.

A few years ago, those companies that publish a figure for their cost of capital – usually those which have adopted a form of economic profit or economic value added performance framework – often came out with figures 1–2 percentage points higher than those implied by market values, or estimated by stock market analysts. As at today the gap has in many cases reversed. Lloyds TSB, for example, calculates its economic profit using a cost of equity of 9.96 per cent (https://www.gurufocus.com, 25/8/2017). Yet its share price appears to imply, even if you assume it will halve its dividend, a cost of equity in excess of 10 per cent.

Why does this matter? To create value for shareholders, companies need to make returns greater than their cost of capital. If companies are underestimating cost of capital, they will make acquisitions or invest in projects that destroy value. Conversely, if the market is setting the hurdle too high, investors will miss out on value-creating investments.

CAPM

Computing the cost of debt is fairly straightforward, at least for companies whose bonds are traded. The cost of equity is more complicated. The standard formula remains the capital asset pricing model, or CAPM, devised separately by William Sharpe, John Lintner and Jack Treynor. Though many academic studies have raised doubts about its empirical validity, three out of four chief financial officers use CAPM.

CAPM's starting point is the risk-free rate – typically a 10-year government bond yield. To this is added a premium, which equity investors require to compensate them for the extra risk they accept. This equity risk premium is multiplied by a factor, known as beta, to reflect a company's volatility and correlation with the market as a whole. Beta is designed to capture the risk that an investor cannot diversify away by holding

Continued

a portfolio of other shares; a company whose share price tends to rise and fall more than the market will have a high beta. There are difficulties with all three of these elements. Government bond yields are currently very low, by historical standards. A company contemplating a long-term investment can lock in these low rates for its debt, but if interest rates then rise so will its cost of equity. It may generate the cash flows it anticipated from its investment, but these will no longer cover its cost of capital. It may be appropriate to use a somewhat higher normalised risk-free rate. Yet it looks as though many equity analysts have taken insufficient account of the fall of risk-free rates in their cost of capital estimates.

The equity risk premium is the element that has generated most controversy. In the early 1990s, most companies used numbers in excess of 6 per cent, drawing on data from Ibbotson Associates and others. Then market analysts started to use equity risk premiums of 3–4 per cent and these numbers began to filter into corporate use. Historical performance data compiled by Elroy Dimson, Paul Marsh and Mike Staunton give a world equity premium over bonds of 3.8 per cent over the last 103 years. Marakon Associates, the strategic consultancy, derives an equity risk premium of 5.3 per cent, rather higher than the recent average, from the implied internal rate of return of 1,190 stocks, but of 3.6 per cent on the basis of dividend yield and growth. Splitting the difference, that gives an estimate of about 4.5 per cent.

Beta

Beta can be even trickier to calculate. Ideally, companies would use a forward-looking beta but estimates depend on historical trading data. Yet as McKinsey analysts pointed out in a recent study, the TMT bubble of 1998–2001 has dramatically lowered the apparent betas of unaffected sectors. They calculate an improbably low current beta of 0.02 for the food, beverage and tobacco sector, against an average of 0.85 for 1990–7.

Individual company betas can also deliver counter-intuitive results. An accident-prone company may have a very low beta, because its mishaps mean it shows less correlation with the overall market.

Take Allianz as an example: the German insurer bases its embedded value calculations on an 8.15 per cent risk discount rate for Europe and the US. This is based on a 5 per cent long-term view of risk-free rates, a 3.5 per cent equity risk premium and a beta of 0.9. This beta, in particular, might raise an eyebrow, since the vulnerability of the company's capital base to equity market declines would prompt most investors to call it a high beta stock. Substituting a historical German equity risk premium of 5.7 per cent – according to Dimson, Marsh and Staunton – and a Bloomberg-calculated beta of 1.14 would yield a cost of equity of 11.5 per cent.

The finer points of CAPM mattered less when nominal interest rates were high. Take a company whose cash flows are growing at 3 per cent: using a 12 per cent cost of capital to discount these cash flows, only one third of its value lies more than 10 years out but, at 7 per cent, more than half is accounted for by these more distant years. Small adjustments to the cost of capital will also have a larger impact on the overall valuation at these lower rates. This effect weighs even more on non-financial companies with a significant amount of debt on their balance sheets, as their weighted average cost of capital will be lower than their cost of equity.

In most corporate investment decisions, the odd half point makes little difference, though in pricing acquisitions the precise cost of capital may be more significant. With equity markets still jittery, however, companies are better off setting a higher hurdle rate for investment than a straightforward CAPM calculation would imply. That might not be consistent with academic theory but it will, in practice, make them choose more carefully between their business units in allocating capital and lead to less wasteful investment than in the past.

Source: *Financial Times*, 24 March 2003. © Financial Times, and updated August 2017.

6.4 USING 'TAILORED' DISCOUNT RATES

Applying the discount rates derived using the CAPM to investment projects assumes that new projects fall into the same risk category as the company's other operations. This might be a reasonable assumption for minor projects in existing areas and perhaps for replacements, but it hardly seems justifiable for major new product developments or acquisitions of companies in unrelated areas. If the expected return is positively related to risk, firms that rely on a single discount rate may tend to over-invest in risky projects to the detriment of less risky, though still attractive, projects. Many multi-divisional companies are effectively portfolios of diverse activities of different degrees of risk. The Beta of the firm as a whole is thus the weighted average of its component activity Betas. Each division contributes to the firm's overall business risk in a way similar to that in which individual shares contribute to the systematic risk of a portfolio of securities. The dangers of using a uniform discount rate are shown in Figure 6.1.

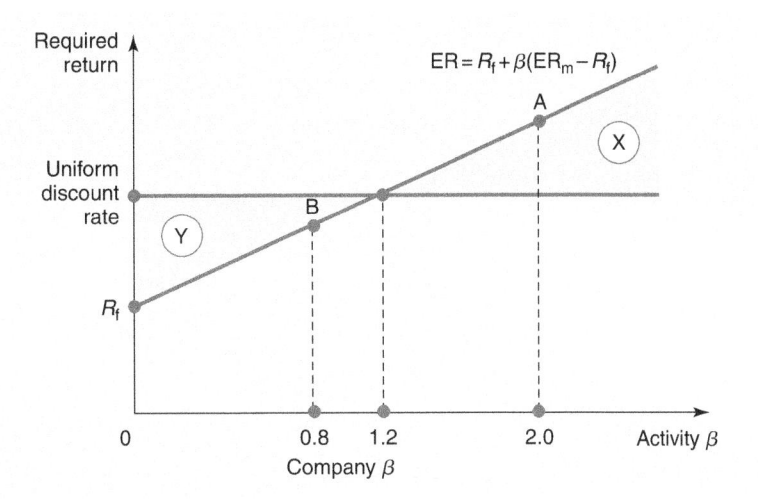

Figure 6.1 Risk premiums for activities of varying risk

Figure 6.1 shows the relationship between the rate of return required on a particular project and that expected on the market portfolio, linked by the Beta. The overall portfolio of company activities may have a Beta of, say, 1.2, which is a weighted average of the Betas of component activities. For example, activity A has a greater-than-average degree of risk, with a Beta of 2.0, and thus a higher-than-average discount rate would be applicable when appraising new projects in this area, while the reverse applies for activity B, which has a Beta of only 0.8. Clearly, to appraise all new projects using a discount rate based on the overall company Beta of 1.2 would invite serious errors. For example, in area X, application of the uniform discount rate would result in accepting some projects that should be rejected because they offer too low a return for their level of risk, while in area Y, some worthwhile, low-risk projects would be rejected. Firms should use 'tailor-made' cut-off rates for activities involving a degree of risk different from that of the overall company.

Self-assessment activity 6.3

What are the discount rates applicable to the firm as a whole and activities A and B in Figure 6.1, assuming a risk-free rate of 5 per cent, and a market risk premium of 6 per cent?

(Answer in Appendix A)

Figure 6.2 shows the three levels, or tiers, of risk found in the multi-activity enterprise, each requiring a different rate of return.

In Chapter 11, we will find that there is a fourth tier of risk that uniquely applies to ordinary shareholders. In a geared firm, that faces financial risk, the returns achieved by shareholders are more volatile than the firm's operating cash flows due to the interest payments that must be paid on debt. In response to this higher risk, shareholders demand a higher return. In other words, the Beta of the shares exceeds the Beta of the firm's business activities. To arrive at the activity Beta, we would need to 'ungear' the Beta of the shares.

If the company is entirely equity-financed, the risks that shareholders incur coincide with those incurred by the company as a whole, i.e. those related to trading and

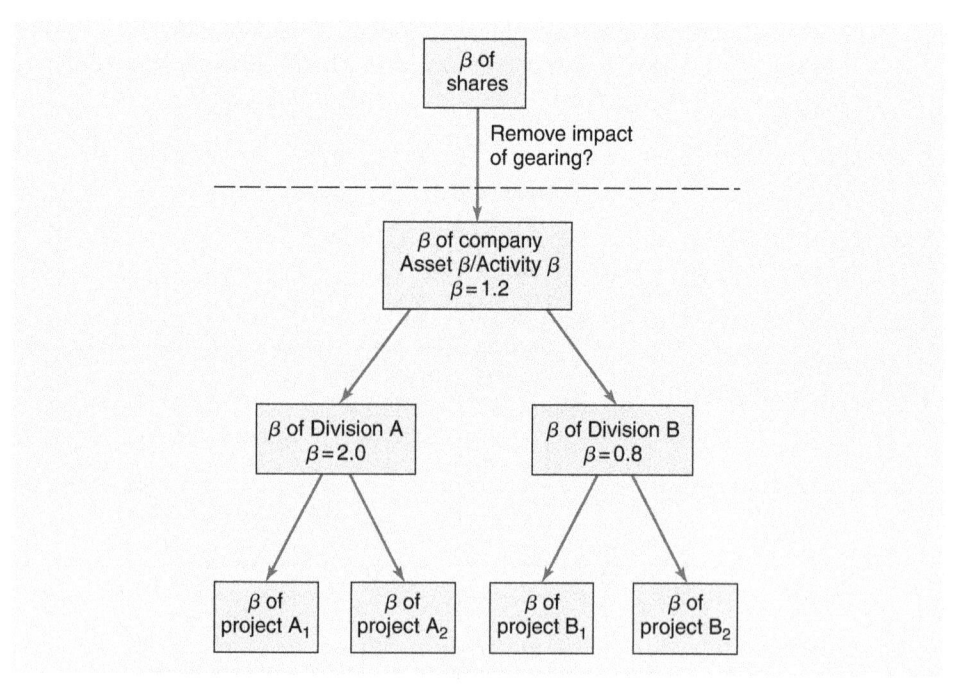

Figure 6.2 The Beta pyramid

operational factors. In this case, the Beta of the ordinary shares coincides with that of the company itself.

Many companies are structured into separate strategic sub-units or divisions, organised along product or geographical lines. In such companies, it is unlikely that every activity faces identical systematic risk. So different discount rates should be applied to evaluate 'typical' projects within each division.

However, even within divisions, rarely do two projects have identical risk. Hence, different discount rates are required when new projects differ in risk from existing divisional activities.

Segmental Betas

The company Beta is a weighted average of component divisional Betas. For a company with two divisions, A and B, the overall Beta is a weighted average given by:

$$\text{Company } \beta = \left(\beta_A \times \frac{V_A}{V_A + V_B}\right) + \left(\beta_B \times \frac{V_B}{V_A + V_B}\right)$$

where the weights represent the proportion of company value accounted for by each segment. A similar expression would apply for each division, where the corresponding weights would represent the contribution to divisional value accounted for by each component activity. Figure 6.2 illustrates these concepts in the form of a 'Beta pyramid'.

Self-assessment activity 6.4

What is the company Beta for the firm shown in Figure 6.1 if activities A and B constitute 65 per cent and 35 per cent of its assets, respectively?

(Answer in Appendix A)

Let us use Whitbread plc to illustrate the derivation of the appropriate discount rate at different levels of an organisation. It is organised into two broad product divisions, as shown in Table 6.2, which lists the operating divisions. These titles suggest quite different activities, although a firm's own description of its division is not always a reliable guide to the nature of those activities.

We performed a CAPM calculation earlier in relation to the equity of Whitbread, obtaining a result of 8.7 per cent. Should we apply this rate to all investments undertaken by Whitbread? The answer is 'no', if we believe there are risk differences between the divisions, in which case we should calculate tailor-made discount rates.

Table 6.2 Divisional Betas for Whitbread plc

Activity	% share of sales	Surrogate company	Beta	Weighted Beta
Hotels and Restaurants	61.43	Millennium and Copthorne	0.78	0.479
Costa	38.57	Wetherspoon	0.66	0.443
	100			0.922

*There are no UK coffee shops quoted on the LSE. Wetherspoon, although it provides a wider range of products (but including coffee), is arguably subject to similar operating risks to a coffee retail operation.
Source: Whitbread plc *Annual Report* 2016–17; Thomson Reuters Datastream, 21 July 2017.

■ The divisional cut-off rate

We need now to consider what are suitable Betas for the two Whitbread divisions. However, no Betas are recorded for company divisions, simply because no market trades securities representing title to a firm's divisional assets. Instead, we need to look for two surrogate companies and use their ungeared Betas as the 'stand-in' estimates for the Betas of the Whitbread divisions. This involves using what Fuller and Kerr (1981) called the **pure play technique**. It relies on the principle that: 'the risk of a division of a conglomerate company is the same as the risk of an undiversified firm in the same line of business (adjusted for financial risk)'.

pure play technique
Adoption of the Beta value of another firm for use in evaluating investment in an unquoted entity such as an unquoted firm, or a division of a larger firm

Consulting the RMS, we look for suitable surrogate companies whose Betas we can use as proxies for those of the Whitbread divisions. The dangers of doing this should not be understated. Ideally, the surrogate should be a close match for the relevant Whitbread division, i.e. they should conduct the same activity or mix of activities in the same proportions, and should also be ungeared. (If they use debt finance, the gearing effect on their Betas should be stripped out, as explained in Chapter 11.) In principle, the weighted averages of these Beta values will coincide with the overall Beta of Whitbread plc if we have selected good surrogates. The weightings ought to be based on market values, but as these are unknown for company divisions, book values of net operating assets could be used. Not all companies reveal divisional asset values, so a proxy measure such as sales or operating profits may have to be used. For Whitbread, share of sales has been used. This is only a valid proxy for assets if the sales-to-assets ratio is similar from division to division, which is quite unlikely. (Actually, the respective shares of operating profit were 85 per cent for Hotels and Restaurants, and 15 per cent for Costa.)

Table 6.2 shows that the weighted average Beta for Whitbread is 0.922. This differs from the Whitbread Beta we observed previously – the discrepancy could be due to:

■ The chosen surrogates are not close enough matches for Whitbread's two activities.
■ Differences in gearing. As we will see in Chapter 11, gearing has the effect of raising Beta values as shareholders seek an extra premium to compensate for the financial risk that gearing imposes. The RMS Beta values are all equity Betas – they include

the effect of gearing, and, of course, different firms may have different gearing ratios. Hence, if we take a Beta from a low-geared firm and apply it to a high-geared one, our weighted average calculation will understate the true Beta of the focus firm, and vice versa. Ideally, we should compare like with like: either strip out the effect of gearing altogether, and work in terms of pure equity (or activity) Betas; or ungear the Betas of the surrogates, and then re-gear them to reflect the gearing of the focus firm. These issues we defer to Chapter 11.

- Differences in how the Betas are calculated in the databases.

The following cameo shows an example of restructuring by Whitbread.

Self-assessment activity 6.5

Re-work the Whitbread weighted average Beta calculation, using share of operating profits as weightings (given above).

(Answer in Appendix A)

Whitbread smells self-service success

Andy Harrison is bringing the stripped-down service delivery he learnt at EasyJet to Whitbread, with a £59.5m deal that will launch the company's Costa Coffee division into the self-serve market.

The hotels and restaurants group said on Wednesday it would buy Coffee Nation, an operator of 900 self-service coffee machines across the UK, for 14 times the smaller group's earnings last year.

The machines will be relabelled 'Costa Express' – a new brand – and serve as a platform for growth in the UK's 'emerging self-serve coffee bar sector', according to the group. It aims to expand to 3,000 stations over the next five years.

Mr Harrison, who joined as chief executive last autumn after five years at the low-cost carrier, said Coffee Nation's use of freshly ground beans and fresh milk in its machines would give Costa access to new types of locations and help it attract hurried customers without compromising on quality.

'There are 6bn cups of coffee sold through traditional vending machines. That tells us there's a huge customer demand for speed and convenience,' he said.

The deal was announced alongside a fourth-quarter trading update showing like-for-like sales slowing at both Costa and Whitbread's hotel and restaurant division, which contributes 87 per cent of group profits.

Total sales rose 12.4 per cent in the quarter, on the back of 24 per cent growth at Costa and 12 per cent at Premier Inns. The company said full-year results would be in line with market expectations. The shares fell 90p to £16.44.

Investec Growth & Acquisition Finance, which alongside Milestone Capital and members of Coffee Nation's management team sold the self-serve operator, said the deal had returned double the amount it had invested in 2008 as part of a secondary management buy-out.

According to the Whitbread's 2016–17 annual report, Costa currently operates over 6,800 Costa Express self-serve units.

Source: Jacobs, R. (2011) Whitbread smells self-service success. *Financial Times*, 3 March. © The Financial Times Limited 2018. All rights reserved.

■ The project cut-off rate

If any division undertakes a new venture that takes it outside its existing risk parameters, clearly, we must look for different rates of return – in effect, we need to obtain estimates for individual project Betas. Without access to internal records, our analysis can only be indicative, but the following principles offer broad guidance.

Essentially, we look for sources of risk that make the individual project more or less chancy relative to existing operations. There are two broad reasons why projects have different risks to the divisions where they are based – different revenue sensitivity and different operating gearing.

Revenue sensitivity

Imagine Whitbread is looking at developing a new coffee shop brand. The sales generated by the projected facility may vary with changes in economic activity to a greater or lesser degree than existing sales in the relevant division. For example, we may expect that, for a specified rise in the level of GDP, whereas overall retail sales of Whitbread existing outlets increase by 7 per cent, the sales of the new brand rise by 9 per cent.

The revenue sensitivity factor

revenue sensitivity factor (RSF)
The sensitivity to economic fluctuations of a project's sales in relation to that of the division to which it is attached

This magnifying effect is measured by the **revenue sensitivity factor (RSF)**. The RSF is calculated as follows:

$$\text{RSF} = \frac{\text{Sensitivity of project sales to economic changes}}{\text{Sensitivity of divisional sales to economic changes}} = \frac{9\%}{7\%} = 1.29$$

This relationship may stem from the nature of the product – if it is pitched at discretionary spenders (e.g. people who frequent more 'upmarket' outlets), it may be more closely geared to the economy as a whole.

Operating gearing

This concerns the extent to which the project cost structure comprises fixed charges. The higher the proportion of fixed costs in the cost structure, the greater the impact of a change in economic conditions on the operating cash flow of the project, thus magnifying the revenue sensitivity effect. Again, the project may exhibit a degree of operating gearing different from that of the division as a whole.

To illustrate the impact of operating gearing, consider the figures in Table 6.3, where the firm applies a 50 per cent mark-up on variable cost. An increase in sales revenue of 50 per cent will lead to an increase in net operating cash flow of 67 per cent because of the gearing effect. There is thus a magnifying factor of 1.34. This so-called **project gearing factor (PGF)** may well differ from the gearing factor(s) found elsewhere in the division.

project gearing factor (PGF)
The proportionate increase in a project's operating cash flow in relation to a proportionate increase in the project's sales

Table 6.3 The effect of operating gearing (£m)

Sales revenue	Variable costs	Fixed cash costs	Operating cash flow
90	60	5	25
60	40	5	15

operating gearing factor (OGF)
The operating gearing factor of an individual project in relation to that of the division to which it is attached

To measure the relative level of gearing, the **operating gearing factor (OGF)** is used. This is defined as:

$$\text{OGF} = \frac{\text{Project gearing factor}}{\text{Divisional gearing factor}}$$

If the divisional gearing factor is 1.80, for example, the project's OGF = 1.34/1.80 = 0.74.

The second step in assessing the project discount rate brings together these two sources of relative project risk into a project risk factor (PRF).

■ The project risk factor

This is the compound of the revenue sensitivity factor and the operating gearing factor:

Project risk factor = RSF × OGF

In our example, this is equal to (1.29 × 0.74) = 0.95. In this case, the project is less risky than the 'average' project within the division and merits the application of a lower Beta. Based on the Beta for Whitbread's surrogate for the Costa operation, shown in Table 6.2, this is given by

Project Beta = (0.95 × 0.66) = 0.63

The final step calculates the required return using the basic CAPM equation, based on a 2.0 per cent risk-free rate and a market risk premium of 6 per cent:

Required return = 0.02 + 0.63 (0.06)
Required return = 0.02 + 0.038
Required return = 0.058%, or 5.8%

Self-assessment activity 6.6

Determine the required return on a project whose revenue sensitivity is 50 per cent and operating gearing 80 per cent compared to the division where it is located. The divisional Beta is 1.2, the risk-free rate is 5 per cent and the market risk premium is 6 per cent.

(Answer in Appendix A)

■ Project discount rates in practice

Considering the informational requirements for obtaining reliable tailor-made discount rates for particular investment projects, few firms go to these lengths. A far more common practice is to seek an overall divisional rate of return, which becomes the average cut-off rate, but is then adjusted for risk on a largely intuitive basis, according to the perceived degree of risk of the project. For example, many firms group projects into 'risk categories' such as the classification in Table 6.4. For each category, a target or required return is established as the cut-off rate.

Table 6.4 Subjective risk categories

Project type	Required return (%)
Replacement	12
Cost saving/application of advanced manufacturing technology	15
'Scale' projects, i.e. expansion of existing activities	18
New project development:	
Imitative products	20
Conceptually new products, i.e. no existing competitors	25

Imagine the divisional required return is 18 per cent, the rate applicable to projects that replicate the firm's existing activities. Around this benchmark are clustered activities of varying degrees of risk, and as the perceived riskiness increases, the target return rises in tandem.

In all these cases, we are discussing a discount rate derived from the ungeared Beta. In other words, we are separating out the inherent profitability of the project from any financing costs and benefits. Analysis of financing complications is deferred to Chapters 10 and 11.

6.5 WORKED EXAMPLE: TIEKO PLC

Tieko plc is a diversified conglomerate that is currently financed entirely by equity. Its five activities and their respective share of corporate assets are shown in the following table. Also shown are the Beta coefficients of highly similar surrogate firms operating in the same markets as the Tieko divisions.

Division	% share of book value of Tieko assets	Beta of a close substitute
Electronics	30	1.40
Property	20	0.70
Defence equipment	30	0.20
Durables	20	1.05

The yield on short-term government stock is currently 6 per cent, and people expect the stock market portfolio to deliver an average annual return of 13 per cent in future years.

Required

In each of the following (separate) situations, determine Tieko's company Beta and the return required by shareholders:

(i) As it is currently structured. Also, calculate the hurdle rates for the four divisions.
(ii) If Tieko sells the defence division for book value and returns the cash proceeds to shareholders as a Special Dividend.
(iii) If Tieko sells the defence division for book value and places the cash proceeds on deposit.
(iv) If Tieko acquires a telecommunications firm that has a Beta of 1.60, and total assets equal in value to the defence division.

Solution

In each case, the Beta value is a weighted average of the Betas of the component activities, with each division's share of total assets providing the weights.

(i) At present, the Beta is:

$(0.3 \times 1.4) + (0.20 \times 0.70) + (0.30 \times 0.20) + (0.20 \times 1.05)$
$= (0.42 + 0.14 + 0.06 + 0.21) = 0.83$

Using the CAPM formula, the required return for the firm as a whole is thus:

$6\% + 0.83\,[13\% - 6\%] = (6\% + 5.8\%) = 11.8\%$

The separate divisional hurdle rates are as shown in the following table.

Division	Risk-free rate	Beta	Market premium	Required return
Electronics	6%	1.40	7%	6% + 1.40(7%) = 15.80%
Property	6%	0.70	7%	6% + 0.70(7%) = 10.90%
Defence equipment	6%	0.20	7%	6% + 0.20(7%) = 7.40%
Durables	6%	1.05	7%	6% + 1.05(7%) = 13.35%

(ii) If Tieko 'downsizes' to 70 per cent of its previous size, the weightings for the three remaining divisions become:

Electronics 3/7 = 0.429
Property 2/7 = 0.285
Durables 2/7 = 0.285

The overall Beta becomes:

$(0.429 \times 1.4) + (0.285 \times 0.70) + (0.285 \times 1.05)$
$= (0.60 + 0.20 + 0.30) = 1.10$

Clearly, Tieko has become more risky and the required return increases to

$6\% + 1.10\,[13\% - 6\%] = 6\% + 7.7\% = 13.7\%$

(iii) If it retains the cash, then the total assets remain unchanged, but the Beta will alter as the Beta of cash is zero – it is uncorrelated with the risky securities quoted on the stock market.

The overall Beta becomes:

$(0.3 \times 1.4) + (0.20 \times 0.70) + (0.30 \times 0) + (0.20 \times 1.05)$
$= (0.42 + 0.14 + 0 + 0.21) = 0.77$

Having disposed of its least risky division and replaced it with risk-free cash, Tieko has become much less risky. As a result, its overall required return decreases to:

$6\% + 0.77\,[13\% - 6\%] = (6\% + 5.39\%) = 11.39\%$

(iv) If Tieko expands by adding another division of equal size to the electronics arm, i.e. a 30 per cent expansion, the new weightings are:

Electronics 3/13 = 0.230
Property   2/13 = 0.154
Defence   3/13 = 0.230
Durables   2/13 = 0.154
Telecomms   3/13 = 0.230

The overall Beta becomes:

$(0.230 \times 1.4) + (0.154 \times 0.70) + (0.230 \times 0.20) + (0.154 \times 1.05) + (0.230 \times 1.60)$
$= (0.322 + 0.108 + 0.046 + 0.162 + 0.368) = 1.006$

The required return increases to:

$6\% + 1.006\,[13\% - 6\%] = (6\% + 7.04\%) = 13.04\%$

After this expansion, Tieko has a Beta very similar to that of the market portfolio (1.0). It has thus managed to diversify itself into a portfolio of activities of virtually average risk.

6.6 ANOTHER PROBLEM: TAXATION AND THE CAPM

Empirical studies of the risk premium usually reveal gross-of-personal-tax results. To adjust for tax, one might consider the tax status of interest income from the risk-free asset, normally taken as government stock of some form, and the tax status of the return on the market portfolio.

Franks and Broyles (1979) recommended two adjustments. First, adjust the risk-free rate for the shareholders' rate of personal tax, then adjust the risk premium according to the relative proportions of excess return earned in dividend and in capital gain formed. There are practical difficulties in doing this. However, take for illustration 20 per cent as an average rate of capital gains tax (CGT) and 25 per cent as an average rate of tax on dividends. If we then assume half of the return on equities was from dividends and half from capital gain, this yields a weighted average tax rate (WAT) of

$(0.5 \times 0.20) + (0.5 \times 0.25) = 22.5\%$. Consequently, the calculation of the post-tax required return on Whitbread's ordinary shares (ER_W) would be:

$ER_w = R_f[1 - \text{present income tax rate}] + \beta[\text{market risk premium}][1 - \text{WAT}]$

$ER_w = 0.02[1 - 0.2] + 1.06\,[0.06][1 - 0.225]$

$ER_w = 0.016 + 1.1296\,[0.06][0.775]$

$ER_w = 0.016 + 0.04929$

$ER_w = 0.06529$, i.e. 6.5%

There are obvious problems in taking average rates of tax over periods when tax regimes have altered. Wilkie (1994) argues that such a calculation is conceptually flawed, being based on the assumption that individuals would have invested in a tax-inefficient vehicle (government stock) – although many do! Most personal investors would have been subject to higher rates of income tax and thus would have taken steps anyway to shelter their income from tax. Finally, he points out that the securities market historically has been dominated by tax-exempt investors, in terms of both the percentages of market value held and, more crucially, the flow of new funds to the market, which dictates market prices. He concludes that little accuracy is lost by using the gross-of-tax risk premium, and ignoring any tax effect on the risk-free rate, especially as future tax rates on investment income are likely to be lower than past rates, following widespread tax cuts in the 1990s.

6.7 PROBLEMS WITH 'TAILORED' DISCOUNT RATES

The pure play technique is an appealing device for estimating discount rates for specific activities, but it suffers from a number of practical difficulties.

1. *Selecting the proxy.* To select a proxy, the firm needs to examine the range of apparently similar candidates operating in the relevant sector. However, no two companies have the same business risk due to diversity of markets, management skills and other operating characteristics. How one chooses between a range of 'fairly similar' candidates is essentially an issue of judgement.
2. *Divisional interdependencies.* In practice, it is difficult to make a rigid demarcation of divisional costs and incomes, since most divisionalised companies share facilities, ranging from the highest decision-making level to joint research and development, joint distribution channels and joint marketing activities. Indeed, access to shared facilities often provides the initial motive for forming a diversified conglomerate, enabling the elimination of duplicated services and the exploitation of scale economies. If carefully evaluated and implemented, the merging of activities should create value and reduce business risk. Only when a merger has no operating impact across divisional lines can it be suggested that business risk itself is unaffected. Even so, there may well be synergies at the peak decision-making level.
3. *Differential growth opportunities.* Using a cut-off rate based on another firm suggests that the division in question has the same growth prospects as the surrogate. However, opportunities to grow are determined by dividend policy, the extent of capital rationing and the interaction between divisions, e.g. competition for scarce investment capital. In reality, because the firm's own decision processes help to determine the potential for growth, it is not accurate to assume that growth opportunities are externally derived.
4. *Joint ventures.* The use of differential discount rates may destroy the incentive to cooperate on projects that straddle divisional boundaries. For example, a joint venture whose expected return lies between the cut-off rates of the two divisions will be attractive to one and unacceptable to the other. Here, some form of mediation is

required at peak level, which reassures the 'loser' of the decision that subsequent performance will be assessed after adjusting for having to operate with a project that it did *not* want, or without a project that it *did* wish to undertake.

Regulator turns screw on UK water operators

Ofwat (the UK water regulator) has turned the screw on water industry operators across England and Wales by demanding they accept lower rates of return on equity and capital in the next five-year regulatory period, which will run to 2020.

The regulator confirmed yesterday that companies should expect their weighted average cost of capital to be pegged to no more than 3.85 per cent.

WACC is a blended measure of the return on the mix of debt and equity needed to underpin investment and spending plans.

The regulator has concluded that an acceptable cost of debt to companies is in the range of 2.2 per cent to 2.8 per cent for the period.

It also set an acceptable average cost of equity at nearly 1 percentage point below companies' average claim of 6.6 per cent. The 'current total equity return expectations should be below historical evidence on returns', it said.

The guidelines suggested that an increase of half a percentage point in WACC – close to the spread between Ofwat's guidance of 3.85 per cent and average companies' assumption of 4.3 per cent – equated to an increase in annual bills of about £10.

FT *Source:* Kavanagh, M. (2014) Water operators hit by Ofwat's demands. *Financial Times*, 27 January. © The Financial Times Limited 2018. All rights reserved.

6.8 A CRITIQUE OF DIVISIONAL HURDLE RATES[*]

Modern strategic planning has moved away from crude portfolio planning devices such as the Boston Consulting Group's market share/market growth matrix towards capital allocation methods that emphasise the creation of shareholder value. Central to value-based approaches is discounting projected cash flows to determine the value to shareholders of business units and their strategies. *A key feature of the DCF approach is the recognition that different business strategies involve different degrees of risk and should be discounted at tailored risk-adjusted rates.*

However, critics such as Reimann (1990) suggest that differential rates will increase the likelihood of internal dissension, whereby a manager of a 'penalised' division may resent the requirement to earn a rate of return significantly higher than some of his colleague-competitors. This resentment may be worsened by the observation that longer-term developments, especially in advanced manufacturing technology and other risky, but potentially high value-added activities, may be 'unfairly' discriminated against. As a result, managers may be reluctant to propose some potentially attractive projects.

As we saw in Chapter 3, risk-adjusted discount rates have the effect of compounding risk differences, making ostensibly riskier projects appear to increase in risk over time. One school of thought contends that in order to avoid this risk penalty, the attempt to tailor discount rates to divisions should be modified, if not abandoned. For example, instead of using differential discount rates, firms might use a more easily understood and acceptable, company-wide discount rate for projects of 'normal' risk, but appraise high-risk/high-return projects using different approaches.

Underlying these arguments is the familiar assertion that diversification by firms differs crucially from shareholder diversification, so that applying the CAPM to the former could be misleading. If an investor adds a new share to an existing portfolio, the systematic risk of the portfolio will alter according to the Beta of the new security. If its Beta is

---

[*]This section relies heavily on arguments used by Reimann (1990).

higher than that of the existing portfolio, then the portfolio Beta increases, and vice versa. With corporate diversification, however, we are not dealing with a basket of shares of unrelated companies, which may be freely traded on the market. A firm that diversifies rarely adds totally unrelated activities to its core operations. It may add value if the new activity possesses synergy, or detract from value if the market views the combination as merely a bundle of disparate, unwieldy activities that are hard to manage.

Systematic risk can be altered by strategic diversification decisions at two levels. At the corporate level, decisions concerning business and product mixes, and operating and financial gearing, can affect market risk. The effect of both types of gearing can be magnified by the business cycle, so that a firm which engages in contra-cyclical diversification may dampen oscillations in shareholder returns and thus reduce market risk. At the business level, market risk can be reduced by tying up outlets and supplier sources (i.e. by increasing market power), and by developing business activities that enjoy important interrelationships, such as common skills or technologies (i.e. by exploiting economies of scale).

Many managers feel that the emphasis on hurdle rates is probably misplaced insofar as accurate cash flow forecasts are more important to creating business value than the particular discount rate applied to them. This probably helps explain the continuing popularity of the payback method, and the relative reluctance in the United Kingdom, to adopt CAPM-based approaches. It may also explain why so many successful firms place great emphasis on post-auditing capital projects in order to sharpen up the cash flow forecasting and project appraisals of subordinate staff. Furthermore, there is (US) evidence (Pruitt and Gitman, 1987; Pohlman *et al.*, 1988) that senior managers manifest their suspicion of subordinates' cash flow predictions by deflating the figures presented to them when projects are submitted for approval.

In view of these arguments, there may be a case for reconsidering the merits of using certainty equivalents – adjusting the cash flow estimates and then discounting at the risk-free rate. However, this has not been widely adopted. Apart from the difficulty of specifying the risk-free asset, there is the problem of determining the certainty equivalent factors, which involves specifying the probabilities of different possible cash flows as a basis for assessing their utility values. While techniques are available for doing this (Swalm, 1966; Chesley, 1975), it has not been practicable in most firms.

Reimann (1990) suggests a 'management by exception' approach. The firm should establish and continuously update a corporate cost of capital, based on CAPM principles. This should be applied as a common hurdle rate for the majority of business activities, which, he argues, typically exhibit very similar degrees of risk. At the business level, major emphasis should be given to careful cash flow estimation, based on evaluation of long-term strategic opportunities and competitive advantage. A key element should be a multiple scenario approach, whereby the implications of 'best', 'worst' and 'most likely' states of the world are examined. For projects that, by their very nature, have a demonstrably greater level of risk, other procedures may be appropriate. Rather than adjust the corporate discount rate, Reimann suggests the risk adjustment be made to the cash flow estimates by the business unit executives themselves, i.e. those with closest knowledge both of the market and of competitors' behaviour patterns. Again, a multiple scenario approach should be adopted. This avoids the effect of compounding risk differences over time and thus penalising longer-term projects, which may have a demotivating effect on staff engaged in pursuing high-risk activities.

This discussion may seem to downgrade the importance of DCF and CAPM approaches in project appraisal. However, it is really intended to remind you that apparently neat mathematical models rarely hold the whole answer. If the rigid application of a numerical routine leads managers to question the basis of the routine itself (one which we believe offers powerful guidance in many situations) and to exhibit dysfunctional behaviour, it is far better to modify the routine itself to reflect real-world practicalities.

SUMMARY

We have considered the relative merits of using the DGM and the CAPM to derive the rate of return required by shareholders. The case for and against using tailor-made discount rates for particular business segments and projects was also discussed.

Key points

- The return required on new investment depends primarily on two factors: degree of risk and the method of financing the project.
- The return required by shareholders can be estimated using either the DGM or the CAPM.
- The DGM relies on several critical assumptions: in particular, sustained and constant growth, and the instantaneous reliability of the share price set by the market.
- The CAPM relies on a Beta estimate obtained after smoothing short-term distortions, but the estimated k_e may be affected by random influences on the risk-free rate.
- Application of a uniform company-wide discount rate to all company projects can lead to accepting projects that should be rejected and to rejecting projects that should be accepted.
- To resolve the problem of risk differences between divisions of a company, the Beta of a surrogate firm (adjusted for gearing) can be used to establish divisional cut-off rates.
- If individual projects within the division also differ in risk, the divisional Beta can be adjusted for differences in revenue sensitivity and/or differences in operating gearing.
- Not all academics and business people accept the need to define discount rates so carefully, preferring instead to concentrate on the problems of cash flow estimation.
- Reimann argues that a divisional cut-off rate should be used as a rough benchmark for projects, but alternative methods of risk analysis should be applied to explore more fully the risk characteristics and the acceptability of investment proposals.

Further reading

Analyses of the 'tailored' discount rate can be found in Dimson and Marsh (1982) and Andrews and Firer (1987). Gup and Norwood (1982), Harrington (1983) and Weaver (1989) all provide practical illustrations of how US corporations apply divisional discount rates, while Reimann (1990) gives a critique of the whole approach.

Recent articles reviewing required returns include those by King (2009), who surveys costs of equity for banks, van Binsbergen *et al.* (2010), who examine costs of debt, and DeLong and Magin (2009), who examine the US equity premium. Ferris *et al.* (2017) examined the association between managerial social capital and cost of equity. Chakravarty and Rutherford (2017) reported a negative association between the 'busy-ness' (i.e. range of activities) of board members and the cost of debt in their sample firms, suggesting that firms with busy board members had a lower cost of debt. Donaldson *et al.* (2010) used fundamental financial information in the estimation of equity premiums, while Li and Tsiakas (2017) generate a model for predicting the equity premium.

QUESTIONS

Questions with a coloured number have solutions in Appendix B on page 501.

1. The ordinary shares of Rasal plc have a market price of £10.50, following a recent dividend payment of £0.80 per share. Dividend growth has averaged 4.5 per cent p.a. over the past five years. What is the rate of return required by shareholders implied by the current share price?

2. Insert the missing values in the following table:

	k_e	P_0	g	D_0
(i)	11%	£8.00	3%	?
(ii)	14%	?	4%	£0.350
(iii)	?	£5.00	6%	£0.155
(iv)	12%	£4.60	?	£0.250

3. Mack plc has paid out dividends per share over the past few years, as follows:

2014	11.0p
2015	12.5p
2016	14.0p
2017	17.0p
2018	20.0p

In March 2018, the market price per share of Mack is £5.00 ex-dividend. What is the rate of return required by investors in Lofthouse's equity implied by the Dividend Growth Model?

4. The all-equity-financed Lasar plc has a Beta of 0.8. What rate of return should it seek on new investment:
   (i) with similar risk to existing activities?
   (ii) with 25 per cent greater systematic risk compared to existing activities?
   (iii) with 25 per cent lower systematic risk compared to existing activities?

   The risk-free rate of interest is 6 per cent, and the expected return on the market portfolio is 11 per cent.

5. Salas Ltd is an unquoted company that operates four divisions, all focused on single activities as shown in the following table. Salas identifies a proxy quoted company for each activity in order to calculate cut-off rates for new investment.

Division	Proxy Beta	Assets employed (£m)
Construction (C)	0.7	3.00
Engineering (E)	1.1	8.00
Road haulage (R)	0.8	4.00
Packaging (P)	0.6	5.00

The risk-free rate is 7 per cent, and the expected return on the market portfolio is 15 per cent.

Required
(i) Calculate the required return at each division.
(ii) Calculate Salas' overall required rate of return.

6 Megacorp plc, an all-equity-financed multinational, is contemplating expansion into an overseas market. It is considering whether to invest directly in the country concerned by building a greenfield site factory. The expected payoff from the project would depend on the future state of the economy of Erewhon, the host country, as shown here:

State of Erewhon economy	Probability	IRR from project (%)
E_1	0.1	10
E_2	0.2	20
E_3	0.5	10
E_4	0.2	20

Megacorp's existing activities are expected to generate an overall return of 30 per cent with a standard deviation of 14 per cent. The correlation coefficient of Megacorp's returns with that of the new project is −0.36, Megacorp's returns have a correlation coefficient of 0.80 with the return on the market portfolio, and the new project has a correlation coefficient of −0.10 with the UK market portfolio.

- The Beta coefficient for Megacorp is 1.20.
- The risk-free rate is 12 per cent.
- The risk premium on the UK market portfolio is 15 per cent.
- Assume Megacorp's shares are correctly priced by the market.

Required

(a) Determine the expected rate of return and standard deviation of the return from the new project.
(b) If the new project requires capital funding equal to 25 per cent of the value of the existing assets of Megacorp, determine the risk–return characteristics of Megacorp after the investment.
(c) What effect will the adoption of the project have on the Beta of Megacorp?

Ignore all taxes.

7 PFK plc is an undiversified and ungeared company operating in the cardboard packaging industry. The Beta coefficient of its ordinary shares is 1.05. It now contemplates diversification into making plastic containers. After evaluation of the proposed investment, it considers that the expected cash flows can be described by the following probability distribution:

State of economy	Probability	Internal rate of return (%)
Recession	0.2	−5
No growth	0.3	8
Steady growth	0.3	12
Rapid growth	0.2	30

The overall risk (standard deviation) of parent company returns is 20 per cent and the risk of the market return is 12 per cent. The risk-free rate is 5 per cent and the FTSE 100 Index is expected to offer an *overall* return of 10 per cent per annum in the foreseeable future.

The new project will increase the value of PFK's assets by 33 per cent.

Required

(a) Calculate the risk–return characteristics of PFK's proposed diversification.
(b) It is believed that the plastic cartons activity has a covariance value of 40 with the company's existing activity.
  (i) Calculate the *total* risk of the company *after* undertaking the diversification.
  (ii) Calculate the new Beta value for PFK, given that the diversification lowers its overall covariance with the market portfolio to 120.
  (iii) Deduce the Beta value for the new activity.
  (iv) What appears to be the required return on this new activity?
(c) Discuss the desirability, from the shareholders' point of view, of the proposed diversification.

You may ignore taxes.

8 Lancelot plc is a diversified company with three operating divisions – North, South and West. The operating characteristics of North are 50 per cent more risky than South, while West is 25 per cent less risky than South. In terms of financial valuation, South is thought to have a market value twice that of North, which has the same market value as West. Lancelot is all-equity-financed with a Beta of 1.06. The overall return on the FT All-Share Index is 25 per cent, with a standard deviation of 16 per cent.

Recently, South has been under-performing and Lancelot's management plan to sell it and use the entire proceeds to purchase East Ltd, an unquoted company. East is all-equity-finan1ced, and Lancelot's financial strategists reckon that, while East is operating in broadly similar markets and industries to South, East has a revenue sensitivity of 1.4 times that of South, and an operating gearing ratio of 1.6 compared to the current operating gearing in South of 2.0.

Assume no synergistic benefits from the divestment and acquisition. You may ignore taxation.

Required

(a) Calculate the asset Betas for the North, South and West divisions of Lancelot. Specify any assumptions that you make.
(b) Calculate the asset Beta for East.
(c) Calculate the asset Beta for Lancelot after the divestment and acquisition.
(d) What discount rate should be applied to any new investment projects in East division?
(e) Indicate the problems in obtaining a 'tailor-made' project discount rate such as that calculated in section (d).

Note: More questions on required rates of return can be found in Chapter 11, where the additional complexities of gearing are discussed.

7

Enterprise value and equity value

Snapchat owner closes up 44% for $28.3bn valuation

The US broke its long drought of big technology initial public offerings on Thursday as shares in Snap soared 44 per cent on their market debut despite questions about corporate governance and profitability for the messaging service Snapchat.

The IPO was priced at $17 with the shares opening at $24, valuing the group at $28.3bn. making Snap worth about two and a half times social media rival Twitter, and about the same as food manufacturer Kellogg, video games maker Electronic Arts and electronics company Panasonic. But it is dwarfed by its two main rivals for advertising dollars: Google, at $580bn, and Facebook, at $395bn.

The enthusiasm for Snap came despite the decision by some portfolio managers to shun the stock over concerns about the company's decision to issue shares with no voting rights, a first in the US, and to ensure control for the co-founders even if they leave the company. In addition, some analysts questioned whether an app with no profits and fierce competition from other social media groups warranted such a lofty valuation. Last year, the company recorded a net loss of $515m, on revenue of $405m.

Brian Wieser, an analyst at Pivotal Research, said Snap was 'significantly overvalued' because of the competitive environment it faces, a mostly unproven business model and the risks to shareholders that they will be diluted because of 'aggressive' share issuance to employees. Mr Wieser issued a 'sell' rating on the stock and a price target of just $10.

John Colley, a professor at Warwick Business School, noted that the company faces significant challenges in competing with Facebook and Google, generates substantial losses, and is suffering from slowing growth. 'Snap Inc is benefiting from institutions and individuals being awash with cash,' he said. 'The top-end valuation reflects high liquidity rather than a great prospect. There is far more cash than opportunities, which means pursuit of long-odds risky options such as Snapchat.'

FT *Source:* Bullock, N. and Kuchler, H. (2017) Snapchat owner closes up 44% for $28.3bn valuation. *Financial Times*, 3 March. © The Financial Times Limited 2018. All rights reserved.

Learning objectives

The ultimate effectiveness of financial management is judged by its contribution to enterprise value. This chapter aims:

- To provide an understanding of the main methods of fundamental analysis and valuation of companies and shares.
- To stress that valuation is an imprecise art, requiring a blend of theoretical analysis and practical skills.
- To explain and critically evaluate the limitations of different valuation methods.
- To identify and explain different valuation methods of intangible assets.
- To explore different valuation methods for valuing unquoted companies.
- To explain and critically evaluate shareholder value analysis (SVA).
- To identify and explain the key value drivers.

A sound grasp of the principles of valuation is essential for most areas of financial management.

7.1 INTRODUCTION

The concept of value is at the heart of financial management, yet the introductory case on Snapchat demonstrates that valuation of companies is by no means an exact science. Inability to make precisely accurate valuations complicates the task of financial managers.

The financial manager controls capital flows into, within and out of the enterprise, attempting to achieve maximum value for shareholders. The test of the financial manager's effectiveness is the extent to which these operations enhance shareholder wealth. The financial manager needs a thorough understanding of the determinants of value to anticipate the consequences of alternative financial decisions. If there is an active and efficient market in the company's shares, it should provide a reliable indication of value. However, managers may feel that the market is unreliable and may wish to undertake their own valuation exercises. Indeed, some managers behave and talk as though they doubt the Efficient Markets Hypothesis (EMH), as outlined in Chapter 1.

In addition, financial managers must undertake valuations in specific situations, for example, when valuing a proposed acquisition, or assessing the value of their own company when faced with a takeover bid. Directors of unquoted companies may also need to apply valuation principles if they intend to invite a takeover approach from a larger firm or if they decide to obtain a market quotation.

Valuation skills thus have an important strategic dimension. When advising on the desirability of alternative financial strategies, the financial manager needs to assess the value to the firm of pursuing each option. This chapter examines the major difficulties in valuation and explains the main methods available.

7.2 THE VALUATION PROBLEM

Anyone who has ever attempted to buy or sell a second-hand car or house will appreciate that value, like beauty, is in the eye of the beholder. Value is whatever the highest bidder is prepared to pay. With a well-established market in the asset concerned, and if the asset is fairly homogeneous, valuation is relatively simple. *So long as the market is reasonably efficient, the market price can be trusted as a fair assessment of value.*

Problems arise in valuing unique assets, or assets that have no recognisable market, such as the shares of most unquoted companies. Even with a ready market, valuation may be complicated by a change of use or ownership. For example, the value of an incompetently managed company may be less than the same enterprise after a shake-up by replacement managers. But by how much would value increase? Valuing the firm under new management would require access to key financial data not readily available to outsiders. Similarly, a conglomerate that has grown haphazardly may be worth more when broken up and sold to the highest bidders. But who are the prospective bidders, and how much might they offer? Undoubtedly, valuation in practice involves considerable informed guesswork. (Inside information often helps as well!)

Regarding the introductory Snapchat case, we do not know how the valuation was arrived at, but we can see that even the 'experts' can get it wrong. This illustrates an important lesson – the only certain thing about a valuation is that it will be 'wrong'! However, this is no excuse for hand-wringing. A key question is whether the valuations were reasonable in the light of the information then available.

net asset value (NAV)
The value of the owners' stake in a firm, found by deducting total liabilities (i.e. debts) from total assets

price–earnings multiples
The price–earnings multiple, or ratio (PER), is the ratio of earnings (i.e. *profit after tax*) per share (EPS) to market share price

discounted cash flow
Future cash flows adjusted for the time-value of money

The three basic valuation methods are **net asset value**, **price–earnings multiples** and **discounted cash flow**. None of these is foolproof, and they often give different answers. Moreover, different approaches may be required when valuing whole companies from those appropriate to valuing part-shares of companies. In addition, the value of a whole company (i.e. the value of its entire stock of assets) may differ from the value of the shareholders' stake. This applies when the firm is partly financed by debt capital.

Enterprise value vs. equity value: Innogy plc

To persuade the present owners to sell, a bidder must offer an acceptable price for their equity and expect to take on responsibility for the company's debt. Consider the purchase by RWE Ag, the German multi-utility group of the British electricity supplier Innogy, itself a spin-off from the privatised company International Power. RWE's logic was to complement its previous acquisition of Thames Water in order to gain access to 10 million customer accounts to which it could offer gas, electricity and water. The overall deal was valued at around £5 billion, comprising some £3 billion of equity and £2 billion of debt.

Innogy's stock of assets was financed partly by equity and partly by debt. To obtain ownership of all the assets, i.e. the whole company, RWE was obliged to offer £3 billion to the shareholders to induce them to sell, *and* either pay off the debt or assume responsibility for it. Although RWE chose the latter route, either course of action made the total cost of the acquisition £5 billion.

Obviously, to make the acquisition worthwhile to RWE, its own (undisclosed) valuation would presumably have exceeded £5 billion. We thus encounter several different concepts of value:

Enterprise value → { Value of whole company to the buyer: probably more than £5 billion
Cost to acquire whole company: £5 billion }

Equity value → { Value of equity stake required to clinch sale: £3 billion
Value of equity stake perceived by owners: possibly below £3 billion }

net asset value approach
Calculation of the equity value in a firm by netting the liabilities against the assets

The distinction between company or enterprise value and the value of the owners' stake is clarified by considering the first method of valuation, the **net asset value approach**, which is based on scrutiny of company accounts.

Self-assessment activity 7.1

Using the Innogy example, distinguish between the value of a whole company and the value of the equity stake. When would these two measures coincide?

(Answer in Appendix A)

7.3 VALUATION USING PUBLISHED ACCOUNTS

Using the asset value stated in the accounts has obvious appeal for those impressed by the apparent objectivity of published accounting data. The balance sheet shows the recorded value for the total of fixed assets* (sometimes, but not invariably, including intangible assets) and current assets, namely stocks and work-in-progress, debtors, and other holdings of liquid assets such as cash and marketable securities. After deducting the debts of the company, both long- and short-term, from the total asset value (i.e. the value of the whole company), the residual figure is the net asset value (NAV), i.e. the value of net assets, or the book value of the owners' stake in the company or, simply, 'owners' equity'.

The statement of financial position for D.S. Smith plc, the paper and packaging group, is shown in Table 7.1. The 'Consolidated Statement of Financial Position' pinpoints the NAV, the net assets figure, £1,355 million, which, by definition, must

---
*Also called 'non-current assets' following the adoption of IFRSs.

Table 7.1 Consolidated statement of financial position of D.S. Smith plc as at 30 April 2017

	£m	£m
Assets		
Non-current assets		
Intangible assets	1,178	
Property, plant and equipment	1,866	
Equity accounted investment	9	
Other investments	3	
Deferred tax assets	79	
Other receivables	3	
Derivative financial instruments	19	
Total non-current assets		3,157
Current assets		
Inventories	406	
Income tax receivable	10	
Trade and other receivables	766	
Cash and cash equivalents	139	
Derivative financial instruments	13	
Assets held for sale	2	
Total current assets		1,336
Total assets		**4,493**
Liabilities		
Non-current liabilities		
Interest-bearing borrowings	−1,144	
Employee benefits	−181	
Other payables	−14	
Provisions	−5	
Deferred tax liabilities	−133	
Derivative financial instruments	−11	
Total non-current liabilities		−1,488
Current liabilities		
Bank overdrafts	−16	
Interest-bearing loans and borrowings	−119	
Trade and other payables	−1,358	
Income tax liabilities	−120	
Provisions	−24	
Derivative financial instruments	−13	
Total current liabilities		−1,650
Total liabilities		−3,138
Net assets [Total assets − Total liabilities]		**1,355**
Equity		
Issued capital	95	
Share premium	728	
Reserves	530	
Total equity attributable to owners of the parent	1,353	
Non-controlling interests	2	
Total equity [shareholders' funds]		**1,355**

Source: D.S. Smith plc Annual Report 2017.

coincide with shareholders' funds, i.e. the value of the shareholders' stake net of all liabilities (and, in this case, net of a small minority item, i.e. residual ownership in an acquired firm). The net (book) value of assets of the whole company is £4,493 million (i.e. non-current assets of £3,157 million + current assets of £1,336 million). However, the NAV is a very unreliable indicator of value in most circumstances. Most crucially, it derives from a valuation of the separate assets of the enterprise, although the accountant will assert that the valuation has been made on a 'going concern basis', i.e. as if the bundle of assets will continue to operate in their current use. Such a valuation often, but not invariably, understates the earning power of the assets, particularly for profitable companies.

On 2 May 2017, the market value of D.S. Smith's equity was £4,158 million (share price of £4.40 times the number of ordinary shares outstanding, 945 million). Hence, the equity of the firm as a going concern with its existing and expected strategies, management and skills, all of which determine its ability to generate profits and cash flows, was worth far more than its net assets. Although not the case here, if the profit potential of a company is suspect, then asset value assumes great importance. The value of the assets in their best alternative use (e.g. selling them off) might then exceed the market value of the business, providing a signal to the owners to disband the enterprise and shift the resources into those alternative uses. Sometimes, we can adjust the NAV to take into account more up-to-date or more relevant information, thus obtaining the **adjusted NAV**.

adjusted NAV
The NAV as per the accounts, adjusted for any known or suspected deviations between book values and market, or realisable values

Self-assessment activity 7.2

For D.S. Smith plc, identify:

(i) the value of the whole firm, i.e. enterprise value;
(ii) the value of its total liabilities;
(iii) the value of the owners' equity.

(Answer in Appendix A)

The cameo that follows highlights examples in the utility sector, where some of these utility companies' assets appear to be valued more than the market value of their shares.

European utilities slash asset valuations

European utilities wrote off a record amount of value from their assets last year, bringing the total cost of impairments to more than €100bn in the past six years.

Data compiled by analysts show that 12 of Europe's biggest energy companies had to reduce the value of their assets – many of them power stations – by just over €30bn in 2015.

This brings the total value of write-downs in the sector to €104bn since the beginning of 2010 – the cost of building the new UK nuclear power station at Hinkley Point nearly five times over. The impairments swept across the sector as the tumbling price of wholesale power, coupled with an increase in renewables, left coal- and gas-fired power plants worth much less than previously calculated.

Since the beginning of the decade, more than 50 gigawatts of gas-fired capacity in Europe – equivalent to 50 nuclear plants – have been closed or moth-balled by 10 of the continent's biggest utilities.

Companies forced to make impairments include Eon and RWE, the German utilities, and EDF of France. Several of these companies, including Engie and EDF, have recently announced dividend cuts.

Jefferies' research suggests there may be further write-downs to come, but hitting goodwill more than the value of physical assets. Goodwill appears on the balance sheet when a company makes a purchase, and is the premium the purchaser paid above the actual market value of the company or asset that has been acquired.

Eight of the largest European utilities have reduced the goodwill on their balance sheets by €24bn over the past six years. But they also show they still carry €80bn, partly as a result of the M&A spree before the recent downturn.

One company – RWE – was carrying €12bn of goodwill by end-2015, representing a remarkable 170 per cent of the company's current market capitalisation of €7.1bn.

Source: Stacey, K. (2016) European utilities slash asset valuations. *Financial Times*, 22 May. © The Financial Times Limited 2018. All rights reserved.

Problems with the NAV

The NAV, even as a measure of break-up value, may be defective for several reasons.

1 Fixed asset values are based on historical cost

Book values of non-current assets, e.g. £3,157 million for D.S. Smith, are expressed net of depreciation, the result of writing down asset values over their assumed useful lives. Depreciating an asset, however, is not an attempt to arrive at a market-oriented assessment of value but an attempt to spread out the historical cost of an asset over its expected lifetime so as to reflect the annual cost of using it. It would be an amazing coincidence if the historical cost less accumulated depreciation were an accurate measure of the current value of an asset to the owners, especially at times of generally rising prices. Some companies try to overcome this problem by periodic valuations of assets, especially freehold property. Indeed, property companies are *required* to conduct an annual 'impairment' review. However, outside the property sector, few companies do this annually, and even when they do, the resulting estimate is valid only at the stated dates. Whichever way we look at it, fixed asset values are always out of date!

A more sophisticated approach (but thus far stoutly resisted by the accounting profession) is to adopt **current cost accounting (CCA)**. Under CCA, assets are valued at their **replacement cost**, i.e. what it would cost the firm now to obtain assets of similar vintage. For example, if a machine cost £1 million five years ago, and asset prices have inflated at 10 per cent p.a., the cost of a new asset would be about £1.6 million, i.e. £1m $\times (1.10)^5$. The historical cost less five years' depreciation on a straight-line basis, and assuming a 10-year life, would be £0.5 million. However, the cost of acquiring an asset of similar vintage would be around £0.8 million.

There are obvious problems in applying CCA. For example, estimating current cost requires knowledge of the rate of inflation of identical assets, and of the impact of changing technology on replacement values. Nevertheless, the replacement cost measure is often far closer to a market value than historical cost less depreciation. Ideally, companies should revalue assets annually, but the time and costs involved are generally considered prohibitive.

Asset values may also fall. Directors are legally required to state in the annual report if the market value of assets is materially different from book value. It is better to 'bite the bullet' and actually reduce the value of poorly performing assets in the accounts. In July 2007, Metronet, the five-firm consortium formed to upgrade London's underground system with capital of £350 million, collapsed owing over £2 billion, amidst allegations of management incompetence and poor cost control, with the job well short of completion. All five of its constituent shareholders made it clear that no extra funding would be forthcoming, but Bombardier, the Canadian conglomerate, went further by totally writing off its £70 million investment.

The highest write-off to date was the $50 billion write-down in 2003 by Worldcom (later renamed MCI) of assets acquired during an acquisition spree, following which several executives saw the inside of jails after convictions for false accounting. Write-offs are, in effect, an admission that profits have been overstated in the past, i.e. depreciation has been too low. Firms tend to increase write-offs during difficult trading times on the principle of unloading all the bad news in one go. The 2012 Duff and Phelps survey of goodwill write-downs recorded that US companies wrote off $29bn in 2011. This compares to write-offs totalling $188bn in 2008, the year of the financial crisis.

2 Stock values are often unreliable

Under **Generally Accepted Accounting Practice (GAAP)**, stocks are valued at the lower of cost or net realisable value. Such a conservative figure may hide appreciation in the value of stocks, e.g. when raw material and fuel prices are rising. Conversely, in

---

current cost accounting (CCA)
Attempts to capture the effect of inflation on asset values (and liabilities) by recording them at their current replacement cost, i.e. the cost of obtaining an identical replacement

replacement cost
The cost of replacing the existing assets of a firm with assets of similar vintage capable of performing similar functions

Generally Accepted Accounting Principles (GAAP)
The set of legal regulations and accounting standards that dictate 'best practice' in constructing company accounts

some activities, fashions and tastes change rapidly, and although the recorded stock value might have been reasonably accurate at the balance sheet date, it may look inflated some time later.

Uber registers $2.8bn loss in 2016 expansion drive

Uber recorded a $2.8bn loss in 2016 in the middle of an aggressive global expansion, cementing its place as the most heavily-loss-making private company in the history of Silicon Valley. Yet the San Francisco-based transportation company also grew rapidly over the year, reporting net revenues of $6.5bn for 2016. This makes Uber significantly larger than companies such as Yahoo, Twitter, Snapchat or Airbnb in terms of revenue.

In previous quarters, Uber's financials have been closely scrutinised by investors and often leaked to the press. On Friday, the company took the highly unusual step of directly confirming its audited revenues and losses for the fourth quarter and full year.

As the most highly-valued private technology company in the world, the group has raised eyebrows over how quickly it has burnt through cash as it has expanded into more than 70 countries and pumped money into incentive payments for drivers.

Analysts said that Uber's full-year losses, and its revenues, were both higher than expected.

'The cash burn is slowing down,' said Rohit Kulkarni, head of research at Sharespost, a brokerage for private company shares. 'This is a pretty strong step toward demonstrating that this company is serious about profitability,' he added.

Uber's valuation will be tested when the company undertakes an initial public offering, which is not expected before 2018, and could be several years away.

After record fund-raising last year, Uber has $7bn in cash on hand, with an additional $2.3bn available in untapped lines of credit, a person close to the company confirmed. That means it could still operate for at least three more years on its current burn rate, even if it did not raise any additional funds.

Source: Hook, L. (2017) Uber registers $2.8bn loss in 2016 expansion drive. *Financial Times*, 15 April. © The Financial Times Limited 2018. All rights reserved.

---

3 The debtors' figure may be suspect

Similar comments may apply to the recorded figure for debtors. Not all debtors can be easily converted into cash, since debtors may include an element of dubious or bad debts, although some degree of provision is normally made for these.

The debtors' collection period, supplemented by an ageing profile of outstanding debts, should provide clues to the reliability of the debtors' position.

4 A further problem: valuation of intangible assets

Even if these problems can be overcome, the resulting asset valuation is often less than the market value of the firm. 'People businesses' typically have few fixed assets and low stock levels. Based on the accounts, several leading quoted advertising agencies and consultancies have tiny or even negative NAVs.

However, they often have substantial market values because the people they employ are 'assets' whose interactions confer earning power – the quality that ultimately determines value. This may be seen most clearly in the case of professional football clubs, few of which place a full value for players on their Balance Sheets (only acquired players are valued).

Valuation of brands

However, some other companies have attempted to close the gap between economic value and NAV by valuing certain intangible assets under their control, such as brand names.

The brand valuation issue came to the fore in 1988 when the Swiss confectionery and food giant Nestlé offered to buy Rowntree, the UK chocolate manufacturer, for more than double its then market value. This generated considerable discussion about whether and why the market had undervalued Rowntree, and perhaps other companies that had invested heavily in brands, either via internal product development or by acquisition.

Later that year, Grand Metropolitan Hotels (now Diageo) decided to capitalise acquired brands in its accounts and was followed by several other owners of 'household name' brands, such as Rank Hovis McDougall, which capitalised 'home-grown' brands.

Decisions to enter the value of brands in balance sheets were partly a consequence of the prevailing official accounting guidelines, relating to the treatment of assets acquired at prices above book value, often termed 'goodwill'. These guidelines enabled firms to write off goodwill directly to reserves, thus reducing capital, rather than carrying it as an asset to be depreciated against income in the profit and loss account, as in the United States and most European economies. UK regulations allowed companies to report higher earnings per share, but with reduced shareholder funds, thus raising the reported return on capital, especially for merger-active companies. Such write-offs were stopped by a new accounting standard, FRS10, which also prevented capitalisation of 'home-grown' brands. FRS10 obliged UK firms to follow US practice by depreciating goodwill. Under IFRSs, adopted by all listed UK firms, acquired goodwill only needs to be depreciated if there is judged to be a 'substantial impairment' in the value of the asset.

Brand valuation raises the value of the intangible assets in the balance sheet and thus the NAV. Some chairpeople have presented the policy as an effort to make the market more aware of the 'true value' of the company. Under strong-form capital market efficiency, the effect on share price would be negligible, since the market would already be aware of the economic value of brands. However, under weaker forms of market efficiency, if placing a balance sheet value on brands provides genuinely new information, it may become an important vehicle for improving the stock market's ability to set 'fair' prices.

Methods of brand valuation

Many methods are available for establishing the value of a brand, all of which purport to assess the value to the firm of being able to exploit the profit potential of the brand.

1 Cost-based methods
At its simplest, the value of a brand is the historic cost incurred in creating the intangible asset. However, there is no obvious correlation between expenditure on the brand and its economic value, which derives from its future economic benefits. For example, do failed brands on which much money has been spent have any value? Replacement cost could be used, but it is difficult to estimate the costs of re-creating an asset without measuring its value initially. Alternatively, one may look at the cost of maintaining the value of the brand, including the cost of advertising and quality control. However, it is difficult to differentiate between expenditure incurred in merely maintaining the value of an asset and investment expenditure which enhances its value.

2 Methods based on market observation
Here, the value of the brand is determined by looking at the prices obtained in transactions involving comparable assets, for example, in mergers and acquisitions. This may be based on a direct price comparison, or by separating the market value of the company from its net tangible assets, or by looking at the P:E multiple at which the deal took place, compared to similar unbranded businesses. Although the logic is more acceptable, the approach suffers from the infrequency of transactions involving similar brands, given that individual brands are supposedly unique.

3 Methods based on economic valuation
In general, the value of any asset is its capitalised net cash flows. If these can be readily identified, this approach is viable, but it requires separation of the cash flows associated with the brand from other company cash inflows. The 'brand contribution

method' looks at the earnings contributed by the brand over and above those generated by the underlying or 'basic' business. The identification, separation and quantification of these earnings can be done by looking at the financial ratios (e.g. profit margin, ROI), of comparable non-branded goods and attributing any differential enjoyed by the brand itself as stemming from the value of the brand, i.e. the incremental value over a standard or 'generic' product.

For example, if a brand of chocolates enjoys a price premium of £1 per box over a comparable generic product, and the producer sells 10 million boxes per year, the value of the brand is imputed as (£1 × 10m) = £10m p.a., which can then be discounted accordingly to derive its capital value. Alternatively, looking at comparative ROIs as between the branded manufacturer and the generic, we may find a 5 per cent differential. If capital employed by the former is £100 million, this implies a profit differential of £5 million, which is then capitalised accordingly.

Such approaches raise many questions about the comparability of the manufacturers of branded and non-branded goods, the lifespan assumed, and the appropriate discount rate. Adjustments should also be made for brand maintenance costs, such as advertising, that result in cash outflows.

4 Brand strength methods

Other, more intuitive, methods have been devised which purport to capture the 'strength' of the brand. This involves assessing factors like market leadership, longevity, consumer esteem, recall and recognition, and then applying a subjectively determined multiplier to brand earnings in order to derive a value. Although appealing, the subjectivity of these approaches divorces them from commercial reality.

No broad measure of agreement has yet been reached about the best method to use in brand valuation, or whether the whole exercise is meaningful. Indeed, a report commissioned by the ICAEW (1989), which rejected brand valuation for balance sheet purposes, was said to have been welcomed by its sponsors. The report claimed that brand valuation 'is potentially corrosive to the whole basis of financial reporting', arguing that balance sheets do not purport to be statements of value!

The role of the NAV

Generally speaking, the NAV, even when based on reliable accounting data, only really offers a guide to the lower limit of the value of owners' equity, but even so, some form of adjustment is often required. Assets are often revalued as a takeover defence tactic. The motive is to raise the market value of the firm and thus make the bid more expensive and difficult to finance. However, the impact on share price will be minimal unless the revaluation provides new information, which largely depends on the perceived quality and objectivity of the 'expert valuation'.

We conclude that while the NAV may provide a useful reference point, it is unlikely to be a reliable guide to valuation. This is largely because it neglects the capacity of the assets to generate earnings. We now consider the commonest of the earnings-based methods of valuation, the use of price-to-earnings multiples.

7.4 VALUING THE EARNINGS STREAM: P:E RATIOS

It is well known that accounting-based measures of earnings are suspect for several reasons, including the arbitrariness of the depreciation provisions (usually based on the historic cost of the assets) and the propensity of firms to designate unusually high items of cost or revenue as 'exceptional' (i.e. unlikely to be repeated in magnitude in future years). Yet we find that one of the commonest methods of valuation in practice is based on accounting profit. This method uses the **price-to-earnings multiple** or **P:E ratio**.

price-to-earnings multiple/P:E ratio
Another way of expressing the PER

The meaning of the P:E ratio

As we saw in Chapter 1, the P:E ratio is simply the market price of a share divided by the last reported earnings per share (EPS). P:E ratios are cited daily in the financial press and vary with market prices. A P:E ratio measures the price that the market attaches to each £1 of company earnings, and thus (superficially at least) is a sort of payback period. For example, for its financial year 2016, Severn Trent Water plc reported EPS of 145.9p. Its share price opened on 10 August 2017 at 2,286p, producing a P:E ratio of 15.7. Allowing for daily variations, the market seemed to indicate that it was prepared to wait about 16 years to recover the share price, on the basis of the latest earnings. So, would a higher P:E ratio signify a willingness to wait longer? Not necessarily, because companies that sell at relatively high P:E ratios do so because the market values their perceived ability to grow their earnings from the present level. Contrary to some popular beliefs, a high P:E ratio does not signify that a company *has* done well, but that it is *expected* to do better in the future. It is possible to identify companies with exceptionally high P:E ratios. For example, also in August 2017, Amazon had a P:E ratio of approximately 510, due largely to widespread expectations of rapid growth fuelled by a high level of retentions.

The P:E ratio varies directly with share price, but it also *derives from* the share price, i.e. from market valuation, so how does this help with valuation? Investment analysts typically have in mind what an 'appropriate' P:E ratio should be for particular share categories and individual companies, and look for disparities between sectors and companies.

On 10 August 2017, GlaxoSmithKline (GSK) plc, the UK pharmaceuticals firm, was selling at a massive P:E ratio of 80.2 with an EPS of 18.8p, while another comparable firm, Astra Zeneca (AZ) plc, was selling at a P:E ratio of 16.3, reporting an EPS of 277p. Did this imply that their current respective share prices – 1,508p for GSK and 4,506p for AZ – were out of line? Was there an arbitrage opportunity here by selling GSK and buying AZ?

Maybe so, but there is an element of circularity here. Acting in this way would have presumed that AZ is correctly valued and that GSK was overvalued, despite the apparent similarity to the outsider between these two 'Big Pharma' majors. There may have been sound reasons why they should have been valued differently. The reason for the significant difference at this juncture was that GSK had recently written down its 'pipeline' of drugs due to disappointing clinical trials, so that its EPS was temporarily depressed but expected to recover in the future.

Using P:E ratios to detect under- or overvaluation implies that markets are slow or inefficient processors of information, but there are reliable, rough benchmarks that can be utilised. The industry benchmark is established by one or more transactions, against which other deals in the same industry can be judged and exceptions identified. In some industries, analysts use benchmarks other than the earnings figure implicit in the P:E ratio. Some examples are multiples of billings in advertising, sale price per room in hotels, price per subscriber in mail-order businesses, price per bed in nursing homes, and the more grisly 'stiff ratio' (value per funeral) in the undertaking business. At the height of the 'dotcom boom', some analysts attempted to explain the stratospheric valuations of internet companies in terms of number of 'hits' or visits to the site in question. More analysts are now utilising multiples based on cash flow. This development hints at the major problem with using P:E ratios – it relies on accounting profits rather than the expected cash flows which confer value on any item.

Following the Cookie-cutter cameo that discusses the asset-based and P:E ratio approaches, and their value to investors, we will consider cash-flow-oriented approaches to valuation.

Cookie-cutter approach to value investing is a mistake

Since the US election prompted financial markets to reconsider the outlook for growth and inflation, we have heard numerous commentators boldly declare the return of value investing as a winning strategy. Shares possessing 'value characteristics' have duly outperformed those defined as growth stocks. While the 'return of value' as a thesis is an attractive story to peddle, especially when trying to lure money back into higher-cost actively managed funds, it is built on a number of spurious premises.

Howard Marks, the distressed debt investor, has spoken of the tendency of modern financial theory to assign importance to things that are easily quantifiable, or what he calls 'machinable' inputs, at the expense of caring about things that are harder to know.

Value investment, as pioneered by Columbia Business School professors Ben Graham and David Dodd, is, by its very nature, impossible to grind down into a small number of neat ratios. It requires many hours of painstaking and often tedious fundamental analysis. Anyone who believes that the long-proven benefits of bottom-up research can be replaced by a cookie-cutter approach is likely to be making a significant blunder.

The first mistake made by those who choose to define value investment in this way is to misunderstand what value investors are really trying to achieve. Defining a value investment as possessing certain predefined characteristics, such as low price-to-earnings or price-to-book ratios, is an easy way to find precisely that: companies that trade on low valuation multiples. But the value investor is not simply trying to find stocks that trade on low p/e multiples. The true value investor is trying to dig out securities that are, for one reason or another, mis-priced and mis-understood by the wider market. Whether a share trades on a low or high earnings multiple is meaningless in, and of, itself. More important is how accurately the price that it can be bought for reflects its intrinsic value.

Declaring that a stock that trades on a low p/e or price-to-book multiple is 'cheap' can only be understood in conjunction with fundamental analysis of its accounts and assets.

Businesses are complex and dynamic. Using these multiples on their own to assess the merits of an investment can be deeply misleading. Large amounts of depreciation may be obscuring the true earnings power of a highly cash-generative business. Such nuances are not discernible from looking at a p/e multiple.

Similarly, the nature of company assets and how they are accounted for change over time. The market value of the S&P 500 made up of intangible assets stood at just 17 per cent in 1975, but reached 87 per cent by 2015, according to Ocean Tomo. Under current rules, US companies do not specifically record these types of assets on their balance sheets. Such assets often dominate the earnings and investment of large companies and this should be taken into account when people make historical comparisons about price-to-book multiples.

Investors like seeking simple ways of looking at the world, when it is a messy and complicated place. Declaring the return of value because stocks displaying a few crude valuation characteristics have bounced does a serious disservice to a great investment tradition. The truth is that value investing never went away in the first place.

Source: Johnson, M. (2017) Cookie-cutter approach to value investing is a mistake. *Financial Times*, 7 February. © The Financial Times Limited 2018. All rights reserved.

Self-assessment activity 7.3

XYZ plc, which is unquoted, earns profit before tax of £80 million. It has issued 100 million shares. The rate of Corporation Tax is 30 per cent.

A similar listed firm sells at a P:E ratio of 15:1. What value would you place on XYZ's shares?

(Answer in Appendix A)

7.5 EBITDA – A HALFWAY HOUSE

Earnings Before Interest, Tax, Depreciation & Amortisation (EBITDA)
A rough measure of operating cash flow, effectively, operating profit with depreciation added back. It differs from the 'Net Cash Inflow from Operating Activities' shown in cash flow statements due to working capital movements

Cash flows and profits differ due to application of accruals accounting principles, but value depends upon cash generating ability rather than 'profitability'. An intermediate concept is that of **EBITDA**, an unattractive acronym standing for **Earnings Before Interest, Taxes, Depreciation and Amortisation**. EBITDA is equivalent to operating profit with depreciation and amortisation (the writing-down of intangible assets) added back. As such, it is a measure of the basic operating cash flow before deducting tax, but it ignores working capital movements.

Many companies use EBITDA as a measure of performance, especially when related to capital employed. However, being a *performance* measure, it can only be used in valuation if we look at the way in which the market values other companies' EBITDAs. As with P:E ratios, comparison with other companies is needed as a reference point.

The calculation 'EV/EBITDA' (where EV denotes Enterprise Value) is now commonly used to determine a market price for a company and to compare companies. Firms, such as Deloitte (see Table 7.2), provide analyses detailing this measure for companies. Enterprise value is calculated by adding to the market value of equity the market value of debt, minority interests and preferred equity and deducting cash and cash equivalents.

Table 7.2 EV/EBITDA for companies in carton-board and corrugated sector

Company	EV/EBITDA as at 27 July 2017
D.S. Smith	11.4
Graphic Packaging	9.72
Mondi	8.50
Smurfit Kappa	8.41
Sonoco	8.88

Source: https://www.gurufocus.com, 27 July 2017.

The 'relative valuation' implicit in the use of EBITDA can be seen in the 'Cashmere if you can' extract from the *Financial Times*.

Cashmere if you can

'My first bunny' is a soft toy made of real rabbit hair with a polyester interior. It will set you back a mere £2,045. This is just one of the products made by Loro Piana – The Italian cashmere brand in which LVMH has just invested €2bn for an 80 per cent stake. LVMH chairman and chief executive Bernard Arnault really is living up to his nickname 'the wolf in cashmere'.

With a market capitalisation of €67bn this is a bolt-on deal for the French luxury goods group that has been homing-in on premium luxury brands, e.g. Hermes. And the price looks fair. Including debt, the enterprise value of €2.7bn values the Italian brand on 19 times this year's earnings before interest, tax, depreciation and amortisation.

Granted, that is steep when considering LVMH trades on a multiple of 10 times, and its peer group on 11 times. But then, Loro Piana's earnings are expected to grow by at least 18 per cent each year on average over the next two years – seven percentage points faster than the group, according to Morgan Stanley. Loro Piana's closest peer Brunello Cucinelli trades on an EV/EBITDA multiple of 20 times.

All that makes Mr Arnault look quite the opportunist. LVMH bought Italy's family-owned jeweller Bulgari two years ago. Last week, it bought a majority stake in Milanese coffee house Cova; a decade ago, it took control of Fendi. After all, it costs dearly to finance a global distribution and marketing operation for luxury goods and as sales slow closer to home, the need to expand intensifies. Analysts reckon that it now takes annual revenues of €1bn–€2bn to compete globally. The pride that exists within Italy's family-run luxury groups has prevented them from merging to form the country's own sizeable luxury conglomerate. Like the rabbit and the wolf, Italy's loss is definitely the French luxury conglomerates' gain.

Source: Column, L. (2013) LVMH: the rabbit and the wolf. Financial Times, 10 July. © The Financial Times Limited 2018. All rights reserved.

Like a P:E multiple, an EBITDA multiple used in valuation stems from the value which the market attaches to other companies' EBITDAs, which invites the question of how it values those other companies, i.e. the EBITDA multiple is led by the valuation. Moreover, even when used crudely as a rough-and-ready comparison of value, one should appreciate that it is still based on accounting earnings. Although gross of depreciation and special items, it is still subject to different accounting practices between firms at the operating level, e.g. stock valuation.

Continuing to focus on income-generating methods, we now examine the genuine article, discounted cash flow.

7.6 VALUING CASH FLOWS

The value of any asset depends upon the stream of benefits that the owner expects to enjoy from his or her ownership. Sometimes, these benefits are intangible, as in the case of Van Gogh's *Sunflowers*, which simply gives aesthetic pleasure to people looking at it. In the case of financial assets, the benefits are less subjective. Ownership of ordinary shares, for example, entitles the holder to receive a stream of future cash flows in the form of dividends plus a lump sum when the shares are sold on to the next purchaser; or, if held until the demise of the company, a liquidating dividend when it is finally wound up. In the case of an all-equity-financed company, the earnings over time should be compared on an equivalent basis by discounting them at the minimum rate of return required by shareholders or the **cost of equity capital** (henceforth denoted as k_e).

■ Valuing a newly-created company: Navenby plc

Navenby plc is to be formed by public issue of 10 million £1 shares. It proposes to purchase and let out residential property in a prime location. It has been agreed that, after five years, the company will be liquidated and the proceeds returned to shareholders. The fully subscribed book value of the company is £10 million, the amount of cash offered for the shares. However, this takes no account of the investment returns likely to be generated by Navenby. In the prospectus inviting investors to subscribe, the company announced details of its £10 million investment programme. It has concluded a deal with a builder to purchase a block of properties on very attractive terms, as well as instructing a letting agency to rent out the properties at a guaranteed income of £1.3 million p.a. Based upon past property price movements, Navenby's management estimate 70 per cent capital appreciation over the five-year period. All net income flows (after management fees of £300,000 p.a.) will be paid out as dividends.

In the absence of risk and taxation, Navenby is easy to value. Its value is the sum of discounted future expected cash flows (including the residual asset value) from the project, i.e. (£1.3m − £300,000) p.a., plus the eventual sale proceeds:

	Year				
	1	2	3	4	5
Net rentals p.a. (£m)	+1.0	+1.0	+1.0	+1.0	+1.0
Sale proceeds (£m)					+17.0

If shareholders require, say, a 12 per cent return for an activity of this degree of risk, the present value (PV) of the project is found using the relevant annuity* (PVIFA) and single payment* (PVIF) discount factors, introduced in Chapter 2, as follows:

$$PV = (£1.0m \times PVIFA_{(12,5)}) + (£17.0m \times PVIF_{(12,5)})$$
$$= (£1.0m \times 3.6048) + (£17.0m \times 0.5674)$$
$$= (£3.61m + £9.64m) = £13.25m$$

The value of the company is £13.25 million, and shareholders are better off by £3.25 million. In effect, the managers of Navenby are offering to convert subscriptions of

---

*Remember the notation convention – interest rate first, time period second. Hence, $PVIF_{(12,5)}$ refers to the PV factor at 12 per cent for five years.

£10 million into cash flows worth £13.25 million. If there is general consensus that these figures are reasonable estimates, and if the market efficiently processes new information, then Navenby's share price should be (£13.25m/10m) = £1.325 when information about the project is released. If so, Navenby will have created wealth of £3.25 million for its shareholders.

Self-assessment activity 7.4

Navenby has a value of £13.25 million, but a major part of this reflects the eventual resale value of the assets. What final asset value would enable investors to just break even?

(Answer in Appendix A)

The general valuation model (GVM)

general valuation model
A family of valuation models that rely on discounting future cash flows to establish the value of the equity or of the whole enterprise

In analysing Navenby, we applied the general valuation model, which states that the value of any asset is the sum of all future discounted net benefits expected to flow from the asset:

$$V_0 = \sum_{t=0}^{n} \frac{X_t}{(1 + k_e)^t}$$

where X_t is the net cash inflow or outflow in year t, k_e is the rate of return required by shareholders and n is the time period over which the asset is expected to generate benefits.

It should be noted that for a newly formed company, such as Navenby, the valuation expression can be written in two ways:

value = cash subscription + NPV of proposed activities

or

value = present value of all future cash inflows less outflows

These are equivalent expressions. The value of Navenby is £13.25 million, and the net present value of the investment is £3.25 million, i.e. it would be rational to pay up to £3.25 million to be allowed to undertake the investment opportunity. Valuation of Navenby is relatively straightforward partly because the company has only one activity, but primarily because most key factors are known with a high degree of precision (although not the residual value). In practice, future company cash flows and dividends are far less certain.

The oxygen of publicity

Many corporate managers are somewhat parsimonious in their release of information to the market. Their motives are often understandable, such as reluctance to divulge commercially sensitive information. As a result, many valuations are largely based on inspired guesswork. The value of a company quoted on a semi-strong efficient share market can only be the product of what information has been released, supplemented by intuition.

Yet company chairpeople are often heard to complain that the market persistently undervalues 'their' companies. Some, for example Richard Branson (Virgin) and Andrew Lloyd-Webber (Really Useful Group), in exasperation, even mounted buy-back operations to re-purchase publicly held shares. The 'problem', however, is often of their own making. The market can only absorb and process that information which is offered to it. Indeed, information-hoarding may even be interpreted adversely. If information about company performance and future prospects is jealously guarded, we should not be surprised when the valuation appears somewhat enigmatic.

7.7 THE DCF APPROACH

The previous section implies that we should rely on a discounted cash flow approach. After all, it is rational to attach value to future cash proceeds rather than to accounting earnings, which are based on numerous accounting conventions, including the deduction of a non-cash charge for depreciation. Given that depreciation is not a cash item, surely all we need do is to take the reported profit after tax (PAT) figure and add back depreciation to arrive at cash flow and then discount accordingly?

As a first approximation, we could thus value a company by valuing the stream of annual cash flows as measured by:

Cash flow = (operating profit + depreciation)
= (cash revenues-cash operating costs)

The depreciation charge is added back because it is merely an accounting adjustment to reflect the fall in value of assets. If firms did replace capacity as it expired, in principle, this investment should equate to depreciation. In practice, however, only by coincidence does the annual depreciation charge accurately measure the annual capital expenditure required to maintain production, and thus earnings capacity. Moreover, most companies need investment funds for growth purposes as well as for replacement. The value of growing companies depends not simply on the earning power of their existing assets, but also on their growth potential: in other words, the NPV of the cash flows from all future non-replacement investment opportunities.

This suggests a revised concept of cash flow. To obtain an accurate assessment of value, we should assess total ongoing investment needs and set these against anticipated revenue and operating cost flows; otherwise, we might overvalue the company.

■ Valuation and free cash flow (FCF)

The inflow remaining net of investment outlays is referred to as **free cash flow** (i.e. 'free' of 'must-do' outlays such as interest, tax and investment). The most common definition of this is:

Free cash flow = [revenues − operating cost] − [interest payments] − [taxes]
+ [depreciation] − [investment expenditure]

Using this measure, the value of the owners' stake in a company is the sum of future discounted free cash flows:

$$V_0 = \sum_{t=1}^{n} \frac{FCF}{(1 + k_e)^t}$$

Self-assessment activity 7.5

What is the free cash flow for the following firm?

Operating profit (after depreciation of £2m)	= £25m
Interest paid	= £1m
Tax rate	= £30%
Investment expenditure	= £3m

(Answer in Appendix A)

This approach removes the problem of confining investment financing to retentions, as in the **Dividend Growth Model**. However, we encounter significant forecasting problems in having to assess the growth opportunities and their financing needs in all future years.

Unfortunately, the accounting data for revenues and operating costs upon which this approach is based may fail to reflect cash flows due to movements in the various items of working capital. For example, a sales increase may raise reported profits, but if made on lengthy credit terms, the benefit to cash flow is delayed. Indeed, the net effect may be negative if suppliers of additional raw materials insist on payment before debtors settle.

It is important to mention another distortion. Stock-building, either in advance of an expected sales increase or simply through poor inventory control, can seriously impair cash flow, although the initial impact on profit reflects only the increased stockholding costs.

For these and similar reasons, accurate estimation of cash flow involves forecasting not merely all future years' sales, relevant costs and profits, but also all movements in working capital. Alternatively, one may assume that these factors will have a net cancelling effect, which may be reasonable for longer-term valuations but much less appropriate for short time-horizon valuations, as in the case of high-risk activities. Figure 7.1 provides a schema to show the calculation of FCF, and how it relates to other cash flow concepts.

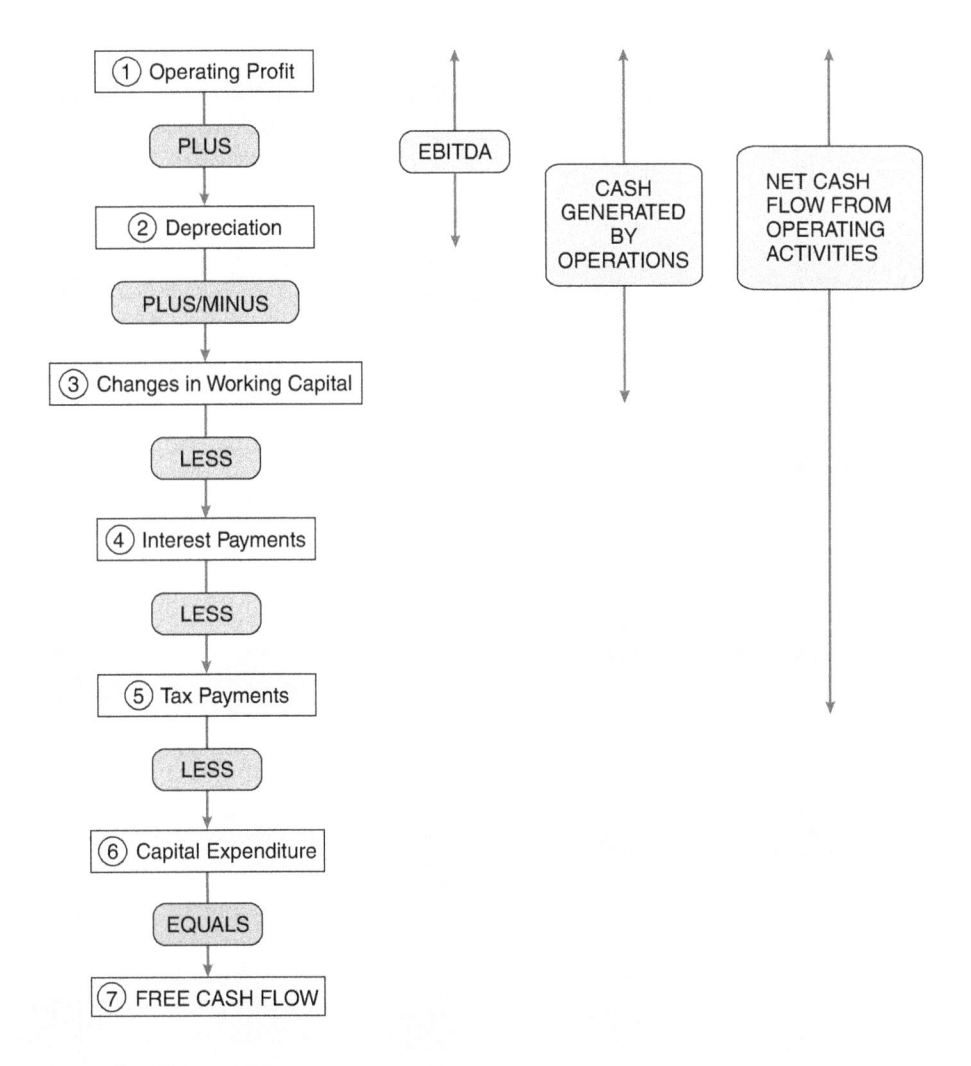

```
① Operating Profit
      PLUS                           EBITDA
② Depreciation                                    CASH             NET CASH
   PLUS/MINUS                                     GENERATED        FLOW FROM
                                                  BY               OPERATING
③ Changes in Working Capital                      OPERATIONS       ACTIVITIES
      LESS
④ Interest Payments
      LESS
⑤ Tax Payments
      LESS
⑥ Capital Expenditure
      EQUALS
⑦ FREE CASH FLOW
```

Notes: ① + ② is roughly equivalent to EBITDA.

① + ② + ③ corresponds to 'cash generated by operations' found on a UK firm's cash flow statement.

① + ② + ③ + ④ + ⑤ corresponds to 'net cash flow from operating activities' found on a UK firm's cash flow statement.

Item ⑥ is sometimes confined to Replacement Capital Expenditure.

Figure 7.1 Calculating free cash flow (FCF)

A warning!

The term 'free cash flow' is used in a wide variety of ways in practice. Here, we use it to signify cash left in the company after meeting all operating expenditures, all mandatory expenditures such as tax payments, and investment expenditure. It focuses on what remains for the directors to spend either as dividend payments, repayment of debts, acquisition of other companies or simply to build up cash balances. This broad definition is necessary because the cash inflow figure is defined to include revenues from both existing and future operations. Consequently, the investment expenditure required to generate enhancements in revenue must be allowed for. By the same token, a growth factor should be incorporated in the operating profit figures to reflect the returns on this investment.

A narrower definition could be used to confine cash inflows to those relating to existing operations and investment, and expenditures to those required simply to make good wear and tear, i.e. replacement outlays. This has the merit of expressing the cash flow before strategic investment, over which directors have full discretion. It also avoids financing complications, e.g. where a company wishes to invest more than its free cash flows, thus requiring additional external finance, which may distort the actual cash flow figure, as reflected in the cash flow statement.

The data in Table 7.3 relating to D.S. Smith plc are consistent with the first, broader definition, which is probably in widest use in the United Kingdom.

Table 7.3 D.S. Smith plc: cash flow

	2017 £m	2016 £m
Continuing operations		
Operating profit before amortisation and exceptional items	443	379
Depreciation	148	127
Adjusted EBITDA	591	506
Working capital movement	124	56
Provision and employee benefits	(25)	(37)
Other	9	2
Cash generated from operations before exceptional cash items	**699**	**527**
Capital expenditure	(244)	(229)
Proceeds from sale of property, plant and equipment and other investments	18	28

Source: D.S. Smith Annual Report 2017.

However, company accounts are, by definition, backward-looking, so focusing on last year's cash flow may yield a very restricted, static vision of the business. This neglects the strategic opportunities and their costs and benefits, which are truly responsible for imparting a major portion of value in practice. Failure to capture these longer-term strategic opportunities could yield a valuation well short of the market's assessment.

The problem of defining free cash flows is compounded by examination of UK company reports. Listed UK companies are obliged to present cash flow statements which report the net change in cash and near-cash holdings over the year. This is a backward-looking statement which says more about past liquidity changes than future cash flows. Some firms do report a figure for 'free cash flow', but often without defining it. Jupe and Rutherford (1997) analysed the reports of 222 of the 250 largest listed UK companies. They found that just 21 disclosed a free cash flow figure, although only 14 used the term itself, and few of these supplied either a definition or a breakdown.

Analysis of the comments of 13 companies appeared to reveal the use of 13 different definitions. Clearly, this is an area where care is required in definition and usage.

Finally, it is appropriate to remind readers of the inherent difficulties in valuing an unquoted firm which are highlighted in the following extract from the *Financial Times*. This echoes the warning given at the very start of the chapter.

> ## Social guess-working
>
> **Lex Column**
>
> Have investors learnt anything from the dotcom bust? As the latest technology darlings – including Facebook, Twitter and LinkedIn – prepare to go public, almost everyone seems to believe the hype. That Facebook is worth $50bn or Twitter $10bn is recounted as fact. True, some social networks do actually make a profit. But there are still precious few numbers to analyse and business models are no more proven than for dotcoms a decade ago.
>
> To illustrate the ridiculousness of trying to value these things consider LinkedIn. Its S-1 registration statement (with US regulators) provides rudimentary financial statements from which to model the company. Revenues, operating costs, capital expenditure and depreciation and amortisation schedules are available for the past five years. It is then a hop to forecast earnings before interest, tax, depreciation and amortisation and, thus, future free cash flows. Discount these cash flows (made easier because there is no debt) and you've got a valuation.
>
> But who on earth knows what forecasts to make? Private secondary markets supposedly value LinkedIn at $2.5bn–$3bn. To arrive at the bottom of that range requires sales to expand 60, 50 then 40 per cent over the next three years, before tailing off to a terminal growth rate of 3 per cent in 2019. EBITDA as a proportion of revenues has to double to 20 per cent and stay there. What is more, the elevated current high level of investment (23 per cent of sales) has to fall sharply and quickly.
>
> That sounds like punchy stuff. If sales growth tapers off faster than expected, or if systems spending becomes a bottomless pit, you can halve that valuation for starters. But what if LinkedIn's platform easily copes with millions of new members? Double EBITDA margins to 40 per cent and a $5bn company is easily within reach. Who knows? No wonder it's easier to simply quote the same price tag as everyone else.

Source: Social networks Lex column: Social network valuation. Financial Times, 16 February 2011. © The Financial Times Limited 2018. All rights reserved.

7.8 VALUATION OF UNQUOTED COMPANIES

The inexact science of valuing a company or its shares is made considerably simpler if the firm's shares are traded on a stock market. If trading is regular and frequent, and if the market has a high degree of information efficiency, we may feel able to trust market values, at least as a guide. If so, the models of valuation merely provide a check, or enable us to assess the likely impact of altering key parameters such as dividend policy or introducing more efficient management.

With unquoted companies, the various models have a leading rather than a supporting role but give by no means definitive answers. Attempts to use the models inevitably suffer from information deficiencies, which may be only partially overcome. For example, in using a P:E multiple, a question arises concerning the appropriate P:E ratio to apply. Many experts advocate using the P:E ratio of a 'surrogate' quoted company, one that is similar in all or most respects to the unquoted subject. One possible approach is to take a sample of 'similar' quoted companies and find a weighted average P:E ratio using their various market capitalisations as weights.

188 Introduction to Finance

However, the shares of a quoted company are, by definition, more marketable than those of unquoted firms, and marketability usually attracts a premium, suggesting a lower P:E ratio for the unquoted company. Any adjustment for this factor is bound to be arbitrary, and different valuation experts might well apply quite different adjustment factors.

Furthermore, a major problem in valuing and acquiring unquoted companies is the need to tie in the key managers for a sufficient number of years to ensure the recovery of the investment. The cost of such 'earn-outs', or '**golden handcuffs**', could be a major component of the purchase consideration.

golden handcuffs
An exceptionally good remuneration package paid to executives to prevent them from leaving

In principle, all the valuation approaches explained in this chapter are applicable to valuing unquoted companies, so long as suitable surrogates can be found, or if reliable industry averages are available. If surrogate data cannot be used, valuation becomes even more subjective. In these circumstances, it is not unusual to find valuers convincing themselves that company accounts are objective and reliable indicators of value. While accounts may offer a veneer of objectivity, we need hardly repeat the pitfalls in their interpretation.

7.9 SHAREHOLDER VALUE ANALYSIS

During the 1980s, based on the work of Rappaport (1986), an allegedly new approach to valuation emerged, called **shareholder value analysis (SVA)**. In fact, it is not really novel, but a rather different way of looking at value, based on the NPV approach.

shareholder value analysis (SVA)
A way of assessing the inherent value of the equity in a company, taking into account the sources of value creation and the time-horizon over which the firm enjoys competitive advantages over its rivals

The key assumption of SVA is that a business is worth the net present value of its future cash flows, discounted at the appropriate cost of capital. Many leading US corporations (e.g. Westinghouse, Pepsi and Disney) and a growing number of European companies (e.g. Philips, Siemens) embraced SVA because it provides a framework for linking management decisions and strategies to value creation. The focus is on how a business can plan and manage its activities to increase value for shareholders and, at the same time, benefit other stakeholders.

How is this achieved? Figure 7.2 shows the relationship between decision-making and shareholder value. Key decisions – whether strategic, operational, investment or financial – with important cash flow and risk implications are specified. Managers

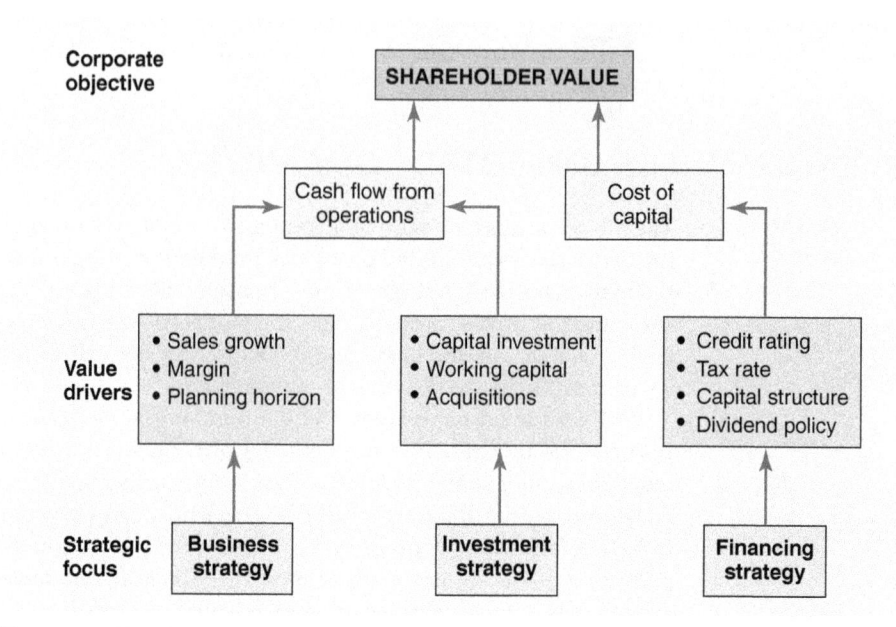

Figure 7.2 Shareholder value analysis framework

value drivers
Factors that have a powerful influence on the value of a business, and the investors' equity stake

should focus on decisions influencing the **value drivers**, the factors that have greatest impact on shareholder value. Typically, these include the following:

1 *Sales growth and margin.* Sales growth and margins are influenced by competitive forces (e.g. threat of new entrants, power of buyers and suppliers, threat of substitutes and competition in the industry). The balance between sales, growth and profits should be based not only on profit impact, but also on value impact.
2 *Working capital and fixed capital investment.* Over-emphasis on profit, particularly at the operating level, may result in neglect of working capital and fixed asset management. In Section 7.7, the free cash flow approach advocated using cash flows after meeting fixed and working capital requirements.
3 *The cost of capital.* A firm should seek to make financial decisions that minimise the cost of capital, given the nature of the business and its strategies. As will be seen later, this does not simply mean taking the source of finance that is nominally the cheapest.
4 *Taxation* is a fact of business life, especially as it affects cash flows and the discount rate. Managers need to be aware of the main tax impacts on both investment and financial decisions. (This is not always negative.)

SVA requires specification of a planning horizon, say, 5 or 10 years, and forecasting the cash flows and discount rates based on the underlying plans and strategies. Various strategies can then be considered to assess the implications for shareholder value.

A particular problem with SVA is specifying the terminal value at the end of the planning horizon. One approach is to try to predict the value of all cash flows beyond the planning horizon, based on that of the final year. Another is simply to take the value of the net assets predicted at the end of the horizon. Neither of these methods suggested is wholly satisfactory. It could be argued, however, that SVA does not have to be used to obtain the value of the business – rather, it can estimate the *additional* value created from implementing certain strategies. Assuming these strategies deliver competitive advantage, and therefore returns in excess of the cost of capital over the planning horizon, there may be no need to wrestle with the terminal value problem.

The real benefit of SVA is that it helps managers focus on value-creating activities. Acquisition and divestment strategies, capital structure and dividend policies, performance measures, transfer pricing and executive compensation are seen in a new light. Short-term profit-related activities may actually be counter-productive in value-creation terms.

End these short-term fudges in financial reporting

Over the past 20 years or so, executive compensation has been increasingly tied to stock prices as directors have pursued the laudable goal of aligning managers' and shareholders' interests. The unintended consequence has been executives attempting to boost their stock prices by maximising short-term results, irrespective of the long-term implications. Short-termism played a role in the corporate accounting scandals and the global financial crisis of the past decade and is setting up society for more pain.

Companies and investors fret over shortfalls of a few pennies in earnings per share even though the earnings number is incomprehensible – because it mixes realised cash flows with subjective estimates of highly uncertain future outlays

There is a better way. We need to adopt a corporate performance statement that is transparent and relevant for assessing value. This should include two separate sections: the cash flow the company realised during the reporting period and estimates of the company's future cash flow commitments. The statement begins with revenue and deducts cash outlays for operating expenses and capital investments to arrive at free cash flow.

The second section presents estimates of the cash flows that the company anticipates it will need to satisfy future

Continued

> financial commitments, such as pension liabilities. Reporting a single estimate to capture an uncertain amount leaves investors in the dark. This corporate performance statement presents a most likely, an optimistic and a pessimistic estimate for each account. Management's discussion of the factors driving the estimate, and the likelihood of each, enables investors to form their own expectations in an informed fashion.
>
> The corporate performance statement would have been useful, for instance, in informing the debate over how to value mortgage-backed securities during the sub-prime lending crisis. Critics argued that forcing banks to write down their long-duration securities to fire-sale prices under-stated their value and exacerbated the financial meltdown. Other observers maintained that the low prices fairly reflected the poor decisions that companies had made, and that investors were entitled to know the unvarnished truth.
>
> This type of controversy vanishes when there are three estimates. Fire-sale prices are appropriate for the pessimistic estimate if it is likely that creditors or regulators will force the bank to sell assets to stay afloat. The optimistic scenario reflects the present value of holding the securities until market prices recover. The most-likely estimate lies in between. This disclosure acknowledges that there is no right answer, only a range of possibilities.

FT *Source:* Mauboussin, M. and Rappaport, A. (2012) End short-term financial reporting fudges. *Financial Times*, 31 May. © The Financial Times Limited 2018. All rights reserved.

7.10 USING VALUE DRIVERS

As we have observed, in recent years, there has been much greater appreciation of the need for managers to optimise the interests of shareholders. In general terms, this can be achieved by generating a rate of return on investment which, at the very least, matches their required return on investment, i.e. the cost of equity. Remember that shareholders incur an opportunity cost when subscribing capital for firms to use, and managers are legally obliged to safeguard those funds with all due diligence.

Sometimes, managers feel that 'their' companies are not 'correctly' valued by the stock market. Moreover, share prices can swing quite violently in the short term, which tends to undermine managers' faith in market efficiency. Often nonplussed by such gyrations, both managers and shareholders may require a more objective and reliable measure of value than simply the prevailing market price.

Such a measure can be provided by the shareholder value approach, propounded by Alfred Rappaport, drawing on Michael Porter's ideas. We now use the value driver concept to analyse inherent shareholder value (SV), which may be thought of as the fundamental, or inherent, value of the firm to its owners. The SV figure also provides a cross-check on the market's current valuation of the company. This may be regarded as a more stable, and possibly more reliable, indicator of the fundamental value of the firm that is unaffected by the short-term vagaries of the market.

The example of Safa plc in Section 7.11 is the vehicle for investigating the SVA approach.

Rappaport developed a simple but powerful model to calculate the fundamental value of a business to its owners by focusing on the key factors that determine firm value. He identified seven value drivers, comprising three cash flow variables and four parameters:

- Sales, and its speed of growth
- Fixed capital investment
- Working capital investment
- Operating profit margin
- Tax rate on profits
- The planning horizon
- The required rate of return

In its simplest form, SVA takes the last four drivers as given and assumes that the first three, the cash flow variables, change at a constant rate. The key to the analysis, as with any budgeting exercise, is the level of sales and the projected rate of increase. From the sales projections, we can programme the operating profits and cash flows over the planning horizon and discount at a suitable rate to find their present value.

In the full model, the value of the firm comprises three elements: the value of the equity, the value of the debt and the value of any non-operating assets, such as marketable securities. However, to keep the analysis simple, we focus on an all-equity-financed company with no holdings of marketable assets. In addition, we need to explain the treatment of investment expenditure. To generate value, firms have to invest, i.e. to generate future cash flows requires preliminary cash outflows. These appear to reduce value in the short term but should generate a more than compensating increase in value via future cash flows.

Categories of investment

Investment in working capital, especially inventories, is required to support a planned increase in sales. Often, companies attempt to apply a roughly constant ratio of working capital to sales so that an X per cent sales increase needs an equivalent increase in working capital investment. This is called *incremental working capital investment*.

Replacement investment is undertaken to make good the wear and tear due to using equipment, or 'depreciation'. However, there are phasing issues to consider. In reality, in relation to particular items, the act of replacement is infrequent, occurring in discrete chunks, whereas depreciation in the accounts is an annual provision, so that in all but the year of replacement, depreciation will likely exceed replacement expenditure. However, taken in aggregate, and especially for larger firms, replacement may be closely related to depreciation provisions.

New investment in fixed assets. This has two dimensions. First, if the firm wants to expand sales of existing products, then, unless it has spare capacity, it will need to invest in additional capital equipment to support the planned sales increase. Second, new investment may be undertaken to accompany a major strategic venture such as the development of a new product, which will also generate an increase in sales. Taken together, these may be related to the planned sales increase, although there is likely to be a time lag before strategic investment comes fully 'on stream' and is able to deliver higher sales quantities. Notwithstanding this qualification, we can link the amount of investment in new capacity, for whatever reason, and which adds to the firm's stock of assets, to a planned increase in sales. We call the resulting sum the *incremental fixed capital investment*.

In the following demonstration example of Safa plc, replacement investment is assumed to equal depreciation provisions (which are treated as part of operating expenses in accounting statements), and both working capital investment and incremental fixed capital investment are made a percentage of any planned sales increase.

7.11 WORKED EXAMPLE: SAFA PLC

The board of Safa plc is concerned about its current stock market value of £95 million, especially as board members hold 40 per cent of the existing 100 million ordinary shares (par value £1) already issued. They are vaguely aware of the SVA concept and have assembled the following data:

Current sales	£100 million
*Operating profit margin**	20 per cent
Estimated rate of sales growth	5 per cent p.a.
Rate of Corporation Tax	30 per cent (with no delay in payment)
Long-term debt	Zero
Net book value of assets	£120 million (net fixed assets plus net current assets)

*After depreciation. On average, depreciation provisions are assumed to match ongoing investment requirements and are fully tax-deductible.

To support the increase in sales, additional investment is required as follows:

(i) Increased investment in *working capital* will be 8 per cent of any concurrent sales increase.
(ii) Increased investment in *fixed assets* will be 10 per cent of any concurrent sales increase.

The risk-free rate of interest is 7.6 per cent, Safa's Beta coefficient is 0.8 and a consensus view of analysts' expectations regarding the overall return on the market portfolio is 15.6 per cent.

Safa presently pays out 20 per cent of profit after tax as dividend. The board estimates that Safa can continue to enjoy its traditional source of competitive advantage as a low-cost provider for a further six years, at the end of which it estimates the net book value of its assets will be £140 million.

What is the inherent underlying value of this company?

The following analysis is based on discounting all the cash inflows attributable to shareholders, and may thus be described as the 'Cash Flow-to-Equity' approach, or simply Flow-to-Equity (FTE). This is used in more complex cases where there is gearing present, as will be explained in Chapter 11.

Answer and comments: Evaluating the cash flows to equity

First of all, we need to find the return required by the shareholders of Safa, using the CAPM formula. This is:

$$k_e = R_f + \beta[ER_m - R_f]$$
$$= 7.6\% + 0.8[15.6\% - 7.6\%]$$
$$= (7.6\% + 6.4\%) = 14\%$$

This becomes the appropriate rate at which to value Safa's future cash flows. There is no debt finance, so all operating profits (less tax) are attributable to shareholders. There appears to be no long-term strategic investment programme, and wear-and-tear is made good at a rate roughly corresponding to tax-allowable depreciation provisions. This means that free cash flows are equal to operating profits less tax.

The firm enjoys a temporary cost advantage for six years, beyond which cash flows are uncertain. Post-Year 6 cash flows can be handled in a number of ways:

1 The Year 6 cash flow figure can be assumed to flow indefinitely. This seems quite an optimistic assumption to make both in relation to Safa plc, and also more generally.
2 A view can be taken on the firm's efforts to restore competitive advantage, and some growth assumption can then be incorporated. Again, this can only be speculative, as there is no information on this issue.
3 Perhaps the most prudent assumption to make is that the expected Year 6 book value of assets will approximate to the value of all future cash flows, i.e. the company has no further supernormal earnings capacity. This implies that any subsequent investment has an NPV of zero (i.e. there are no abnormal returns expected).

We adopt the third approach mainly for simplicity.

Table 7.4 shows the cash flows during the 'competitive advantage period', Years 1–6 inclusive. The base year (Year 0) figures are given to establish a reference line from which future cash flows will grow.

■ Valuing Safa plc

Taking first the value created over the competitive advantage period (years 1–6):

PV of operating cash flows (line 7) = £59.7m

Table 7.4 Cash flow profile[1] for Safa plc

	£m	0	1	2	3	4	5	6, etc.
1	Sales (5% growth)	100	105	110.25	115.76	121.55	127.63	134.00
2	Operating profit margin at 20%[2]	20	2	22.05	23.15	24.31	25.53	26.80
3	Taxation at 30%	(6)	(6.30)	(6.62)	(6.95)	(7.29)	(7.66)	(8.04)
4	Incremental working capital investment at 8% of sales increase		(0.40)	(0.42)	(0.44)	(0.46)	(0.49)	(0.51)
5	Incremental fixed capital investment at 10% of sales increase		(0.50)	(0.53)	(0.55)	(0.58)	(0.61)	(0.64)
6	Free cash flow	–	13.80	14.48	15.21	15.98	16.77	17.61
7	Present value at 14%		12.11	11.14	10.27	9.46	8.71	8.02

[1] Accuracy of figures influenced by rounding errors.
[2] These can be taken as operating cash flows given the assumption that depreciation = replacement investment.

Second, we add in the estimated residual value, our proxy for all future operating cash flows:

The PV of the residual value = £140m × $PVIF_{14,6}$
= £140m × 0.4556 = £63.8

Shareholder value = £59.7m + £63.8m
= £123.5m

■ A note on taxation – two simplifications

You should appreciate how taxation is being handled in this example. All replacement investment is treated as being fully tax-deductible in the year of expenditure. This is a simplification adopted primarily for arithmetic convenience. In reality, the tax relief will be spread out over time as the firm claims the writing down allowance (WDA) each year. In addition, we have ignored the tax saving in relation to the WDA on the incremental fixed capital expenditure.

Correction for the first factor would reduce the valuation simply because delay in taking the tax relief would lower the PV of the stream of tax savings. On the other hand, inclusion of the second set of tax savings would raise the SV figure. If you calculate the 'true' valuation by allowing for these aspects, you will find a net increase in the valuation, although the calculation is a little messy.

We now turn to discuss the actual valuation obtained.

■ Commentary

Looking at the figures as calculated, we find, rather alarmingly, that a large proportion (52 per cent) of the SV is accounted for by the residual value. The SV of £125m more or less equals the current book value of £120m, both figures exceeding the market value of £95m. This seems to imply that the company might be worth more if it were broken up (although the resale value of the assets may not fetch book value).

This raises the obvious question of why the market should place such an apparently low value on Safa. We can consider some possible reasons for the apparent market undervaluation of Safa.

- The market may currently apply a higher discount rate, for example, seeking a higher reward for risk.
- The growth estimate may be regarded as optimistic.
- The flow of information provided to the market may be inadequate – for example, if it does have plans for future investment, are these generally known and understood, at least in outline?

- Board control – presumably reflecting domination by members of the founding family – may look excessive. Such enterprises rarely enjoy a good stock market rating, because there is often a suspicion that the interests of family members may be allowed to dominate those of 'outside' shareholders.
- The dividend policy may be thought ungenerous – a 20 per cent payout ratio is low by UK standards, and there appears to be little scope for worthwhile strategic investment. Retentions may simply be going into cash balances.
- There may be doubts about whether Safa can recover some form of competitive advantage.
- The market may be unimpressed with its present cost advantage-based strategy.
- Its gearing – currently, zero – may be thought to be too low. There is no tax shield to exploit (see Chapter 11).

Whatever the reason(s), there is plenty for the board to consider!

7.12 ECONOMIC VALUE ADDED (EVA)

economic value added (EVA)
Post-tax accounting profit generated by a firm reduced by a charge for using the equity (usually, cost of equity times book value of equity)

Along with SVA comes another concept, **economic value added (EVA)**, trademarked by the US consultancy house Stern Stewart (www.sternstewart.com). Whereas SVA is a forward-looking technique devised for assessing the inherent value of the equity invested in a firm, EVA is backward-looking, i.e. a measure of past performance. Like SVA, EVA relies heavily on the concept of the cost of capital. It is used as a device for assessing how much value or wealth a firm actually has created. Its roots lie in the accounting concept of Residual Income (e.g. see Horngren *et al.* 1998), which is simply the accounting profit adjusted for the cost of using the capital tied up in an activity.

However, the Stern Stewart version is rather more sophisticated as it attempts to adjust the recorded profit in various ways. The logic of these adjustments is, broadly, to avoid recording as a cost the items that are value-creating and that should perhaps be treated as capital rather than current expenditure. For example, spending on R&D and on product advertising and promotion contributes to wealth-creation in important ways. In addition, any goodwill that has been written off in relation to previous acquisitions is added back. The general impact of these adjustments – over 150 of these might be required in a full EVA calculation – is to raise the profit measure and also the capital employed figure.

Relating this, for simplicity, to an all-equity-financed firm, EVA is calculated after making a further adjustment for the opportunity cost incurred by shareholders when entrusting their capital to the firm's directors. The EVA formula can be written as:

$$EVA = NOPAT - (k_e \times \text{invested capital})$$

where:

NOPAT = the Net Operating Profit After Tax, and after adjustment for the items mentioned above

k_e = the rate of return required by shareholders

Invested capital = Net assets, or shareholders' funds.

To illustrate the concept, consider the data in Table 7.5.

Table 7.5 Calculation of EVA

	NOPAT	Equity	k_e	EVA
Firm A	£20m	£100m	15%	£20m − £15m = £5m
Firm B	£10m	£100m	15%	£10m − £15m = (£5m)

Both firms have the same equity capital employed of £100m, and both make positive accounting profits. However, after adjusting for the cost of the equity capital employed, Firm B has effectively made a loss for investors, i.e. the negative EVA indicates that it has destroyed value.

On the face of it, EVA is a simple and powerful tool for assessing performance, explaining why it has been adopted by many firms as an internal performance measurement device, e.g. for determining the performance of different operating units.

However, it is by no means problem-free:

1. Few firms have the resources required to compute EVA, division by division, with the same degree of rigour as the full Stern Stewart model with its myriad required adjustments.
2. It is based on book value, rather than market values (necessarily so for business segments).
3. It relies on a fair and reliable way of allocating shared overheads across business units, the Holy Grail of management accountants.
4. It is difficult to identify the cost of capital for individual operating units.
5. It may be dysfunctional if managers are paid according to EVA, especially short-term EVA. It is quite possible to encounter investment projects that flatter EVA in the short term by virtue of high initial cash flows but to have a negative NPV. Such projects might be favoured by managers who are paid by EVA. Similarly, some long-term projects that take time and money to develop may lower EVA in the early years but have a positive NPV. These, of course, could be rejected under an EVA regime.

The verdict is yet to be delivered on EVA, but like many other management tools, it is probably inadequate when used alone – it is one way of looking at the picture that should be supplemented by other perspectives.

Good-quality products can be made for low earners

The Godrej Group, the Indian conglomerate with interests ranging from high-tech engineering to consumer products, currently has a capitalisation of $3.8bn, employs a workforce of more than 28,000 people and has operations in more than 20 countries. It is estimated that 500m people in India alone currently use at least one Godrej product or service each day.

The current chairman, Mr Godrej, says that the key to the company's success has been in meeting the needs of the world's largest group of consumers, who also happen to be those with the lowest incomes on the planet.

By way of example, Mr Godrej talks about the hair dye market, where the Godrej group has the best-selling brands in 25 countries. 'L'Oréal is the world leader, but we have the largest-selling hair colourant,' he notes. 'Ours is a powder we sell in a sachet, and it sells for a tenth of the price of the L'Oréal cream hair product. It is not a question of competing on price. It is about innovation that meets the needs of low-income people.'

The group has around 100 manufacturing locations in India and abroad. Each generation of the Godrej family has spoken about its deep commitment to worker welfare, human development and environmental matters.

'We distinguish ourselves in a few areas,' Mr Godrej says, 'First, we use top-class business processes. We measure all our decisions, whether in marketing, advertising or acquisitions, based on economic value added. We also have a large number of our employees on variable remuneration, based on economic value added.'

Source: Moules, J. (2013) The Godrej Group: Good-quality products can be made for low earners. *Financial Times*, 11 June. © The Financial Times Limited 2018. All rights reserved.

SUMMARY

We have discussed the reasons why financial managers may wish to value their own and other enterprises, the problems likely to be encountered and the main valuation techniques available. The complexities and limitations of different valuation methods are also covered and discussed in this chapter.

Given the uncertainties involved in valuation, it seems sensible to compare the implications of several valuation models, and to obtain valuations from a number of sources. A pooled valuation is unlikely to be correct, but armed with a range of valuations, managers should be able to develop a likely consensus valuation. This consensus is, after all, what a market value represents, based upon the views of many times more market participants. There should be no stigma attached to obtaining more than one opinion – doctors do not hesitate to call for second opinions when unsure about medical diagnoses.

Key points

- An understanding of valuation is required to appreciate the likely effect of investment and financial decisions, to value other firms for acquisition, and to organise defences against takeover.
- Valuation is easier if the company's shares are quoted. The market value is 'correct' if the EMH applies, but managers may have withheld important information.
- Using published accounts is fraught with dangers, e.g. undervaluation of fixed assets.
- Some companies attempt to value the brands they control. An efficient capital market will already have valued these, but not necessarily in a fully informed manner.
- The economic theory of value tells us that the value of any asset is the sum of the discounted benefits expected to accrue from owning it.
- A company's earnings stream can be valued by applying a P:E multiple, based upon a comparable, quoted surrogate company.
- Some observers like to compare the EBITDA (Earnings Before Interest, Tax, Depreciation and Amortisation) with share price for different companies as a cross-check on valuation. Market-based EBITDA multiples can be used as valuation tools.
- Valuing a company on a DCF basis requires us to forecast all future investment capital needs, tax payments and working capital movements.
- Valuation of unquoted companies is highly subjective. It requires examination of similar quoted companies and applying discounts for lack of marketability.
- Economic Value Added (EVA) is the residual profit after allowing for the charge for the firm's use of investors' capital.
- The two main lessons of valuation are: use a variety of methods (or consult a variety of experts), and don't expect to get it exactly right.

Further reading

The theory tells us that a company is worth the total amount of cash that it is expected to generate over its lifetime, discounted at the cost of capital to present value. But the theory is the easy part – the ongoing message in valuation is that it is a mix of theory and intuition. Wise birds will remember the words of Warren Buffett, the so-called Sage of Omaha:

> It is far better to buy a wonderful company at a fair price than a fair company at a wonderful price.

Therefore, the best books on valuation are those with a practical bent that look beyond the numbers. These include books by Koller *et al.* (2015) and by Damodaran (2012). Damodaran (2015) has also written about 'hard to value' companies. Another useful and easy-to-read book is by Frykman and Tolleryd (2010). Antill and Lee (2008) offer an accounting-based approach that explains how to allow for the effect of International Financial Reporting Standards. The brand valuation issue is addressed by Salinas (2015). The text by Young and O'Byrne (2001) is a comprehensive primer on the application of EVA. Young (1997) provides a detailed practical example of the EVA concept related to a particular firm, and Klieman (1999) presents evidence on EVA generation in practice. Fernandez (2007) reviews a variety of discounted cash flow-based methods for valuing companies, and Fernandez (2013) also discusses these issues in further depth.

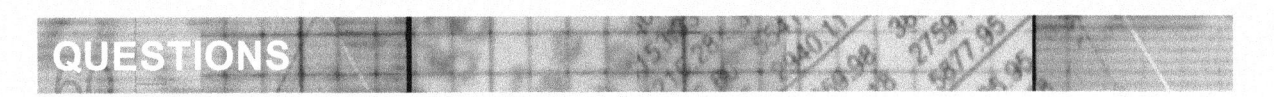

QUESTIONS

Questions with a coloured number have solutions in Appendix B on page 501.

1 Amos Ltd has operated as a private limited company for 80 years. The company is facing increased competition, and it has been decided to sell the business as a going concern.
The financial situation is as shown on the balance sheet:

Statement of financial position as at 30 June 2018

	£	£	£
Fixed (non-current) assets			
Premises			500,000
Equipment			125,000
Investments			50,000
			675,000
Current assets			
Stock	85,000		
Debtors	120,000		
Bank	25,000		
		230,000	
Creditors: amounts due within one year			
Trade creditors	(65,000)		
Dividends	(85,000)		
		(150,000)	
Net current assets			80,000
Total assets less current liabilities			755,000
Creditors: amounts due after one year			
Secured loan stock			(85,000)
Net assets			670,000
Financed by			
Ordinary shares (50p par value)			500,000
Reserves			55,000
Profit and loss account			115,000
Shareholders' funds			670,000
The current market values of the fixed (non-current) assets are estimated as:			
Premises			780,000
Equipment			50,000
Investments			90,000
Only 90 per cent of the debtors are thought likely to pay.			

Required
Prepare valuations per share of Amos Ltd using:
(i) Book value basis.
(ii) Adjusted book value.

2 The Board of Directors of Rundum plc are contemplating a takeover bid for Carbo Ltd, an unquoted company which operates in both the packaging and building materials industries. If the offer is successful, there are no plans for a radical restructuring or divestment of Carbo's assets.

Carbo's statement of financial position for the year ending 31 December 2014 shows the following:

	£m	£m
Assets employed (non-current and current)		
Freehold property		4.0
Plant and equipment		2.0
Current assets:		
stocks	1.5	
debtors	3.0	
cash	0.1	4.6
Total assets		10.6
Creditors payable within one year		(3.0)
Total assets less current liabilities		7.6
Creditors payable after one year		(1.0)
Net assets		6.6
Financed by		
Ordinary share capital (25p par value)		2.5
Revaluation reserve		0.5
Profit and loss account		3.6
Shareholders' funds		6.6

Further information:

(a) Carbo's pre-tax earnings for the year ended 31 December 2014 were £2.0 million.
(b) Corporation Tax is payable at 33 per cent.
(c) Depreciation provisions were £0.5 million. This was exactly equal to the funding required to replace worn-out equipment.
(d) Carbo has recently tried to grow sales by extending more generous trade credit terms. As a result, about a third of its debtors have only a 50 per cent likelihood of paying.
(e) About half of Carbo's stocks are probably obsolete with a resale value as scrap of only £50,000.
(f) Carbo's assets were last revalued in 2004.
(g) If the bid succeeds, Rundum will pay off the presently highly overpaid Managing Director of Carbo for £200,000 and replace him with one of its own 'high-flyers'. This will generate pre-tax annual savings of £60,000 p.a.
(h) Carbo's two divisions are roughly equal in size. The industry P:E ratio is 8:1 for packaging and 12:1 for building materials.

Required

(a) Value Carbo using a net asset valuation approach.
(b) Value Carbo using a price:earnings ratio approach.

3 Lazenby plc has been set up to exploit an opportunity to import a new product from overseas. It has issued two million ordinary shares of par value 25p, sold at a 25 per cent premium. Its projected accounts show the following annual operating figures:

Sales revenue	£500,000
Operating costs	(£300,000)
(after depreciation of £50,000)	
Operating profit	£200,000
Taxation at 30%	(£60,000)
Profit after tax	£140,000

Notes:

(i) Shareholders require a return of 10 per cent p.a.
(ii) Replacement investment is financed out of depreciation provisions and is fully tax-allowable.
(iii) 2 per cent of sales should be written off as bad debts.
(iv) Bad debt write-offs are 50 per cent tax-allowable.

Required

Value each share in Lazenby:

(a) assuming perpetual life;
(b) over a 10-year horizon.

4 The most recent statement of financial position for Vadeema plc is given in the following table. Vadeema is a stock market-quoted company that specialises in researching and developing new pharmaceutical compound. It either sells or licenses its discoveries to larger companies, although it operates a small manufacturing capability of its own, accounting for about half of its turnover:

Statement of financial position as at 30 June 2014

Assets employed	£m	£m	£m
Fixed (*non-current*) assets			
Tangible	50		
Intangible	120		170
Current assets			
Stock and work-in-progress	80		
Debtors	20		
Bank	5	105	
Current liabilities			
Trade creditors	(10)		
Bank overdraft	(20)	(30)	
Net current assets			75
10% loan stock			(40)
Net assets			205
Financed by			
Ordinary shares capital (25p par value)			100
Share premium account			50
Revenue reserves			55
Shareholders' funds			205

Further information:

1 In 2017–18, Vadeema made sales of £300 million, with a 25 per cent net operating margin (i.e. after depreciation but before tax and interest).
2 The rate of corporate tax is 33 per cent.
3 Vadeema's sales are quite volatile, having ranged between £150 million and £350 million over the previous five years.
4 The tangible fixed assets have recently been revalued (by the directors) at £65 million.
5 The intangible assets include a major patent (responsible for 20 per cent of its sales) which is due to expire in April 2015. Its book value is £20 million.
6 50 per cent of stocks and work-in-progress represents development work for which no firm contract has been signed (potential customers have paid for options to purchase the technology developed).
7 The average P:E ratio for quoted drug research companies at present is 22:1 and for pharmaceutical manufacturers is 14:1. However, Vadeema's own P:E ratio is 20:1.
8 Vadeema depreciates tangible fixed assets at the rate of £5 million p.a. and intangibles at the rate of £25 million p.a.
9 The interest charge on the overdraft was 12 per cent.
10 Annual fixed investment is £5 million, none of which qualifies for capital allowances.

Required

(a) Determine the value of Vadeema using each of the following methods:
  (i) net asset value;
  (ii) price:earnings ratio;
  (iii) discounted cash flow (using a discount rate of 20 per cent).
(b) How can you reconcile any discrepancies in your valuations?
(c) To what extent is it possible for the stock market to arrive at a 'correct' valuation of a company like Vadeema?

5 (a) The directors of Oscar plc are trying to estimate its value under its current strategy using a Shareholder Value Analysis framework. The last reported annual sales of Oscar plc were £30 million.

The key value drivers are estimated as follows:

Sales growth rate	7%
Operating profit margin (before tax)	10%
Corporation Tax	30%
Fixed capital investment	15% of sales growth
Working capital investment	9% of sales growth
Planning period	6 years
Weighted average cost of capital	13%

Depreciation is currently charged on a reducing balance basis. The most recent charge was £0.5m. This is expected to remain constant over the next few years. All depreciation is tax-allowable.

The dividend payout ratio is 20 per cent.

Assume marketable securities held are £2.5m, and debt (in the form of a bank loan) is £6m (interest payable is at the rate of 8.33 per cent p.a.).

Required

Calculate the overall company (or enterprise) value, *and* the shareholder value.
(Clearly state any assumptions that you make.)

(b) The market value of Oscar's equity is £25m (lower than the directors' estimate of value), and also below the book value of net assets of £50m.

Several directors argue that Oscar is undervalued by the stock market, and are wondering how to improve the firm's stock market rating.

Required

Suggest possible reasons for this apparent undervaluation, and evaluate suitable *financial* policies that Oscar's directors might adopt to enhance its value.

6 AB is a telecommunications consultancy based in Europe that trades globally. It was established 15 years ago. The four founding shareholders own 25 per cent of the issued share capital each and are also executive directors of the entity. The shareholders are considering a flotation of AB on a European stock exchange and have started discussing the process and a value for the entity with financial advisers. The four founding shareholders, and many of the entity's employees, are technical experts in their field, but have little idea how entities such as theirs are valued.

Assume you are one of AB's financial advisers. You have been asked to estimate a value for the entity and explain your calculations and approach to the directors. You have obtained the following information.

Summary financial data for the past three years and forecast revenue and costs for the next two years is as follows.

Income Statement for the years ended 31 March

	Actual			Forecast	
	2016 € million	2017 € million	2018 € million	2019 € million	2020 € million
Revenue	125.0	137.5	149.9	172.0	198.0
Less:					
Cash operating costs	37.5	41.3	45.0	52	59
Depreciation	20.0	22.0	48.0	48	48
Pre-tax earnings	67.5	74.2	56.9	72	91
Taxation	20.3	22.3	17.1	22	27

Other information/assumptions:

- Growth in after-tax cash flows for 2021 and beyond (assume indefinitely) is expected to be 3 per cent per annum. Cash operating costs can be assumed to remain at the same percentage of revenue as in previous years. Depreciation will fluctuate but, for purposes of evaluation, assume the 2020 charge will continue indefinitely. Tax has been payable at 30 per cent per annum for the last three years. This rate is expected to continue for the foreseeable future, and tax will be payable in the year in which the liability arises.

Statement of financial position at 31 March

	2016 € million	2017 € million	2018 € million
Assets			
Non-current assets			
Property, plant and equipment	150	175	201
Current assets	48	54	62
	198	229	263
Equity and liabilities			
Equity			
Share capital (shares of €1)	30	30	30
Retained earnings	148	179	203
	178	209	233
	20	20	30
Current liabilities	198	229	263

Note: The book valuations of non-current assets are considered to reflect current realisable values.

- The average P:E ratio for telecommunication entities' shares quoted on European stock exchanges has been 12.5 over the past 12 months. However, there is a wide variation around this average, and AB might be able to command a rating up to 30 per cent higher than this.
- An estimated cost of equity capital for the industry is 10 per cent after tax.
- The average pre-tax return on total assets for the industry over the past three years has been 15 per cent.

Required

(a) Calculate a range of values for AB, in total and per share, using methods of valuation that you consider appropriate. Where relevant, include an estimate of value for intellectual capital.
(b) Discuss the methods of valuation you have used, explaining the relevance of each method to an entity such as AB. Conclude with a recommendation of an approximate flotation value for AB, in total and per share.

(CIMA – Financial Strategy November 2006)

Practical assignment

Obtain the latest annual report and accounts of a company of your choice.* Consult the Statement of financial position and determine the company's net asset value.

- What is the composition of the assets, i.e. the relative size of fixed and current assets?
- What is the relative size of tangible fixed and intangible fixed assets?
- What proportion of current assets is accounted for by stocks and debtors?
- What is the company's policy towards asset revaluation?
- What is its depreciation policy?

Now consult the financial press to assess the market value of the equity. This is the current share price times the number of ordinary shares issued. (The notes to the accounts will indicate the latter.)

- What discrepancy do you find between the NAV and the market value?
- How can you explain this?
- What is the P:E ratio of your selected company?
- How does this compare with other companies in the same sector?
- How can you explain any discrepancies?
- Do you think your selected company's shares are undervalued or overvalued?

---

*Most large companies post their annual reports and accounts on their websites. The most common address forms of UK companies are: companyname.co.uk or companyname.com.

8

Identifying and valuing options*

The one cheap thing in financial markets today

Stock markets have entered the eighth year of their post-crisis recovery, while record-low interest rates in developed markets have driven yields on all manner of bonds into the floor. Many now believe there exists no single asset on this planet, from fine wines to Latin American junk debt, priced attractively enough to be bought today without worry.

Yet amid this angst many have overlooked something that is cheaper today than at any point since the financial crisis: the cost of hedging yourself against a market catastrophe. Thanks to the way options pricing models view the world, low levels of volatility – a key input into calculating how much an option costs – tend to beget even lower levels of volatility.

As the Financial Times reported this week it has recently been possible to put on a fairly simple options trade that would deliver a 25 times return on the premium paid if the S&P 500 index were to fall by 7 per cent in the next month. It is of course perfectly possible that the S&P 500 will not fall at all, and the options will expire worthless, but we are approaching a price point where the asymmetrical payouts of these types of hedges are starting to appear compelling.

Good hedging, as with so many things in the world of investment, is simple, but not easy. A hedge can only be as good as the price one pays for them, and many frequently pay too much.

FT *Source:* Johnson, M. (2017) The one cheap thing in financial markets today. *Financial Times*, 12 June. © The Financial Times Limited 2018. All rights reserved.

Learning objectives

By the end of this chapter, you should possess a clear understanding of the following:

- The basic types of option and how they are employed.
- The main factors determining option values.
- How options can be used to reduce risk.
- How option values can be estimated.
- The various applications of option theory in investment and corporate finance.
- Why conventional net present value analysis is not sufficient for appraising projects.

---

*The authors are grateful for the contribution to this chapter by Andrew Marshall.

8.1 INTRODUCTION

Business managers like to 'keep their options open'. Options convey the right, but not the obligation, to do something in the future. Managers should seek to create capital projects or financial instruments with valuable options embedded in them. For example, an investment proposal will be worth more if it contains the flexibility to exit relatively cheaply should things go wrong. This is because the 'downside' risk is minimised. Often it is not possible, or too costly, to build in such options. However, the financial manager can achieve much the same effect by creating options in financial markets.

Options are derivative assets. A 'derivative' is an asset which derives its value from another asset. The primary asset is referred to as the **'underlying' asset**. Option-like features occur in various areas of finance, and option theory provides a powerful tool for understanding the value of such options.

This chapter examines the nature and types of options available and how they can reduce risk or add value. It also explains why the conventional net present value approach may not tell the whole story in appraising capital projects. But, to cover the basics of option theory, we will begin by considering the options as they relate to shares.

'underlying' asset
The asset from which option value is derived

8.2 SHARE OPTIONS

In finance, *options are contractual arrangements giving the owner the right, but not the obligation, to buy or sell something, at a given price, at some time in the future*. Note the two key elements in options: (1) the right to *choose* whether or not to take up the option, and (2) at an *agreed* price. It is not a true option if I am free to buy in the future at the *prevailing* market price, or if I am *compelled* to buy at an agreed price. Many securities have option features: for example, convertible bonds and share warrants, where options to convert to, or acquire, equity are given to the owner.

■ Share options in Enigma Drugs plc

The simplest form of share option is when a company issues them as a way of rewarding employees. If the current share price of Enigma Drugs plc is £4, it might award share options to some of its employees at, say, the same price. If, over the period in which the shares can be exercised, the shares go up, employees could then purchase shares at a price below market price, either to sell at a profit or gain an equity interest.

Most options relate to assets which already exist. These are termed pure options. To begin with, we will consider pure share options, although much of our analysis could apply equally to interest rates, currency, oil and commodity markets. But first we need to go back to basics. Figure 8.1(a) depicts the payoff line for investing in ordinary shares in Enigma Drugs plc. If the shares are bought today at 400p, the payoff, or gain, from selling at the same price is zero. If, say, three months later, the share price has risen to 450p, the payoff is +50p; but if it has dropped to 350p, the payoff is −50p. The line is drawn at 45 degrees because a 50p increase in share price from its current level of 400p gives a 50p payoff.

We have all seen the warnings accompanying advertisements for financial products, reminding us that share prices can go up or down. But wouldn't it be nice if, whichever way prices moved, you ended up a winner? This can be done if you also acquire share options. With options you can create a 'no lose' option strategy providing protection from a drop in share price, as shown in Figure 8.1(b). The red arrowed line represents the payoff from the option to buy shares at a price of 400p. If share price increases above 400p, then we would exercise the option. That is, the holder of the

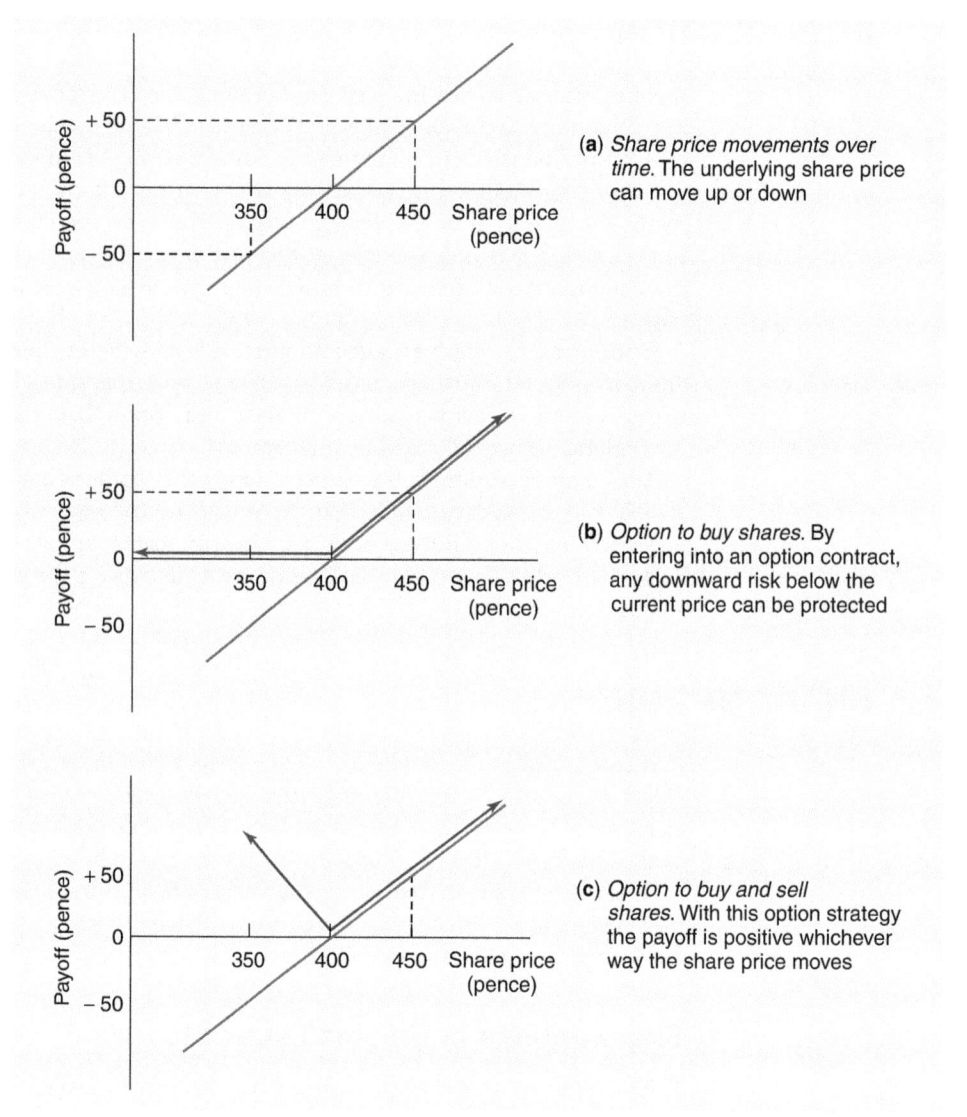

Figure 8.1 Payoff lines for shares and share options in Enigma Drugs plc
(underlying share price is blue, option contract is red)

(a) *Share price movements over time.* The underlying share price can move up or down

(b) *Option to buy shares.* By entering into an option contract, any downward risk below the current price can be protected

(c) *Option to buy and sell shares.* With this option strategy the payoff is positive whichever way the share price moves

option will exercise their right to buy the shares at 400p if the share price is above 400p. But if the share price falls below 400p, to say 350p, the option payoff remains at zero. In other words, the holder of the option will not exercise their right to buy the shares at 400p if the share price is below 400p.

By combining different types of option, you can even create a 'win–win' situation. For example, Figure 8.1(c) shows the effects of combining options to buy and sell shares at a fixed price. Here, either a rise or a fall in share price gives you a positive payoff. At this stage, however, you do not need to know how this is achieved, simply that it can be done. Of course, few things in life are free, and a share option is not one of them; there is a price for each option. Later in this chapter, we will show how to value such options.

■ Issuing options

Options on shares are issued not by the companies on whose shares they are written but by large financial institutions, such as insurance companies. The companies play no role in the issuing process. For the institutions issuing options, the primary motivation is the fee income that their sale generates, but some also use options in their portfolio of management activities to limit their risk exposure.

Considerable interest has developed in recent years in share options, and there is a highly active market on the stock exchange for traditional and traded options. **Traditional options** are available on most leading shares and last for three months. A problem with these is that they are not particularly flexible or negotiable: investors must either exercise the option (i.e. buy or sell the underlying share) or allow it to lapse; they cannot trade the option.

To overcome these difficulties, **traded options** markets were established, first in Chicago, then in Amsterdam. In Europe, options markets are now run by NYSE Euronext in London, Paris, Amsterdam, Brussels and Lisbon (see www.euronext.com). NYSE Euronext was acquired by Intercontinental Exchange Group in 2013 (www.theice.com).

An exchange-traded contract is characterised by certain standardised features, particularly the exercise date and the exercise price. This makes it far easier to develop a continuous market in options than was the case for traditional options that were developed and traded on an ad hoc basis.

> **traditional options**
> An option available on any security agreed between buyer and seller. It typically lasts for three months
>
> **traded options**
> An option traded on a market

> **European options**
> Can only be exercised at the specified maturity date
>
> **American options**
> Can be exercised at any time up to the maturity date

Options terminology

This topic has more than its fair share of esoteric jargon, some of the more essential of which are defined below.

- A **call option** gives its owner the right to *buy* specific shares at a fixed price – the **exercise price** or **strike price**.
- A **put option** gives its owner the right to *sell* (put up for sale) shares at a fixed price.
- A **European option** can be exercised only on a particular day (i.e. the end of its life), while an **American option** may be exercised at any time up to the date of expiry. These terms are a little confusing because most options traded in the United Kingdom and the rest of Europe are actually American options!
- The **premium** is the price paid for the option. Option prices are quoted for shares and traded in contracts (or units) each containing 1,000 shares.
- **'In the money'** is where the exercise price for a call option is *below* the current share price. In other words, it makes sense to take up the option.
- **'Out of the money'** is where the exercise price for a call option is *above* the current share price and it is not profitable to take up the option.
- **Long and short positions** – when an investor buys an option, the investor is 'long', and when the investor sells an option, the investor takes a 'short' position.

> **option contract**
> A contract giving one party the right, but not the obligation, to buy or sell a financial instrument or commodity at an agreed price at or before a specified date

There are two parties to an **option contract**, the buyer (or option holder) and seller (or option writer). The buyer has the right, but not the obligation, to exercise the option. One feature of an option is that, if the share price does not move as expected, it can become completely worthless, regardless of the solvency of the company to which it relates. However, if it does move in line with expectations, very considerable gains can be achieved for very little outlay. Such volatility gives share options a reputation as a highly speculative investment. But, as will be seen later, options can also be used to reduce risk.

In return for the option, the purchaser (option holder) pays a fee or **premium** (to the seller of the option). The premium is a small fraction of the share price, and offers holders the opportunity to gain significant benefits while limiting their risk to a known amount. The size of the premium depends on the **exercise price** and expected volatility

> **exercise price**
> Price at which an option can be taken up

call option
The right to buy an asset at a specified price on or before expiry date

put option
The right to sell an asset at a specified price on or before expiry date

of shares, which, in turn, is a function of the state of the market and the underlying risk of the share. The premium might range from as little as 3 per cent for a well-known share in a 'quiet' market to over 20 per cent for shares of smaller companies in a more volatile market. During past stock market collapses, or where there is substantial volatility, option premiums have shot up dramatically to reflect such uncertainty.

A **call option** gives the purchaser the right to buy a share at a given price within a set time period; a **put option** gives the right to sell. The seller of an option must meet his or her obligation to buy or sell shares if the right of the purchaser is so exercised. The reward to the seller of the option is, of course, the premium received. So, a three-month call option with an exercise price of 220p on a share currently priced at 225p gives you the right to buy the share at 220p at any time before its expiry.

Table 8.1 shows the prices (or premiums) at which options on York plc are traded on a particular day on the traded options market. Two exercise prices are given: the first, at 230p, is below the current share price of 245p and the second, at 250p, is above the share price. Notice that option prices vary both with the exercise price and the exercise date. To buy a call option on York plc shares at an exercise price of 230p costs 24.0p for expiry in June, but costs 28.5p for expiry three months later in September.

Table 8.1 Option on York plc shares (current price 245p)

Exercise price	Call option prices (p) June	Call option prices (p) Sept	Put option prices (p) June	Put option prices (p) Sept
230	24.00	28.50	11.50	20.00
250	13.00	19.50	21.50	30.50

Self-assessment activity 8.1

By now your head may be spinning with all the terms and concepts introduced. It is therefore a good time to take stock of what you should know.

1 Define a call option and a put option.
2 What is the basic difference between European and American call options?
3 Options are available on what types of asset?
4 In relation to the information on traded options in Table 8.1, explain why the following features were observed:
   (a) the lower the exercise price, the higher the value of a call;
   (b) the greater the time to maturity, the higher the price of a call; and
   (c) the price paid for calls exceeds the gross profit that could be made by immediately exercising the call.

(Answer in Appendix A)

A call option has value if the price of the underlying share is *above* the option's exercise price ('in the money'). A put option has value if the price of the underlying share is *below* the option's exercise price. This would allow you to sell shares at a higher price (the exercise price) than they are currently trading at.

Options are exercised only if they have value (i.e. if they are 'in the money'). Conversely, options that are of no value (i.e. 'out of the money') are abandoned.

For a call option:

Profit = share price − exercise price − premium paid

For a put option:

Profit = exercise price − share price − premium paid

Self-assessment activity 8.2

1. Which of the following options has intrinsic value at the start of the contract?
   (a) A three-month call option with an exercise price of 230p on a share currently priced at 240p.
   (b) A three-month put option with an exercise price of 230p on a share currently priced at 240p.
2. Which of the following options is 'out of the money'?
   (a) A three-month call option with an exercise price of 240p on a share currently trading at 230p.
   (b) A three-month put option with an exercise price of 230p on a share currently priced at 215p.

(Answer in Appendix A)

Speculative use of options: Kate Casino

Kate Casino thinks that the York plc share price will move up sharply from its current level of 245p to a level in June sufficiently above the exercise price of 230p to justify the option price of 24p. Kate instructs her broker to purchase a contract for 1,000 June call options at a cost of £240 (24p × 1,000). This is termed a *naked* option, held on its own rather than as a hedge against loss. It is a *long* call because Kate is *buying* the option.

The current share price of 245p is above the 230p exercise price, so the option is already 'in the money', since Kate could immediately exercise her option to buy shares at 230p to gain 15p, before transaction costs. Of course, she would not do this because the premium to be paid for the option is 24p.

Let us look at three possible share prices arising in June when the option expires:

Best – York plc share price will rise to 300p by June.
Likely – it will do no better than 255p.
Worst – it falls as low as 215p.

Her profit in each case would be:

Kate Casino's profit on the call option (pence)

	Best	Likely	Worst
Share price in June (pence)	300	255	215
Less exercise price (pence)	(230)	(230)	(230)
Profit on exercise (pence)	70	25	Not exercised
Less option premium paid (pence)	(24)	(24)	(24)
Profit (loss) before transaction costs	46	1	(24)
Profit on contract of 1,000 shares	£460	£10	(£240)

Kate would obviously not exercise her option if the price fell to 215p, so the loss in this case would be restricted to the 24p premium paid. The premium is the maximum loss on the contract. If York plc price on expiry is 255p, the contract profit is a modest £10. But if the share price shoots up to 300p, a large gain of £460 is made on the contract.

It is interesting to compare the option returns with those from investing directly in York plc shares. Table 8.2 shows that buying a call option has very different effects from buying the underlying share:

1. The capital outlay for the option contract for 1,000 shares is much smaller (£240 compared with £2,450 for the underlying shares).
2. The downside risk on the option contract is far greater in *relative* terms, but not in *absolute* terms. Consider if the expiry share price is 215p. Kate Casino loses all her initial investment on the option contract while the share value declines by only 8 per cent. However, in money terms, the loss is £300 if the shares had been bought or £240 if the option premium had been paid.

Table 8.2 Returns on York plc shares and options

Expiry share price	300p	215p
Buy 1,000 shares	£	£
Cost 245p each	(2,450)	(2,450)
Proceeds from sale	3,000	2,150
Profit (loss)	550	(300)
Return over three months on original cost	+22.4%	−12.2%
Call option on 1,000 shares	£	£
Cost of option	(240)	(240)
Cost of exercise at 230p	(2,300)	–
	(2,540)	
Proceeds on sale	3,000	–
Profit (loss)	460	(240)
Return over three months	+192%	−100%

3 The return achieved, if the shares reach 300p, is a phenomenal 192 per cent on the options contract compared with 22 per cent on the underlying shares (ignoring dividends).

The payoff chart in Figure 8.2 shows that, if the share price does not rise above the exercise price of 230p, the option is worthless. The option breaks even at 254p (230p + 24p premium) and the potential profit to be made thereafter is unlimited.

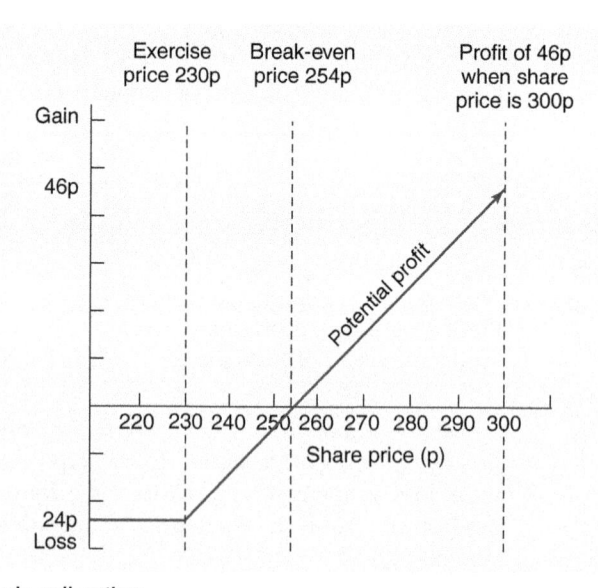

Figure 8.2 York plc call option

In general, the value of a call option at expiry (C_1) with a share price (S_1) and exercise price (E) is:

$C_1 = S_1 - E$, if $S_1 > E$

At a share price of 300p, therefore, the option value is

$C_1 = 300p - 230p$

 $= 70p$, giving a profit of 46p per share after paying the premium.

Options as a hedge: Rick Aversion

hedging
Attempting to minimise the risk of loss stemming from exposure to adverse foreign exchange rate movements

While options offer an excellent opportunity to speculate, they are equally useful as a means of risk reduction, insurance or **hedging**. Rick Aversion is concerned that the current share price on his York plc shareholding will fall over the next two months. Because he wants to keep his shares as a long-term investment, he buys a put option (see Table 8.1), giving the right to sell shares in June at the strike price of 230p. This option costs him 11.5p.

By late June, the shares have fallen to 190p, and the option has increased in value to 40p (i.e. 230p − 190p). So Rick sells the option and retains the shares, using the profit on the option to offset the loss on the shares. This is administratively cheaper and more convenient than selling his shares and then buying them back. In this way, investors can capture any profits from a rise in share price and hedge against any price fall.

Figure 8.3 shows that when share prices are above the exercise price, the option value of the put is worthless. It should be exercised when prices fall below the 230p exercise price and breaks even at 218.5p (exercise price less premium).

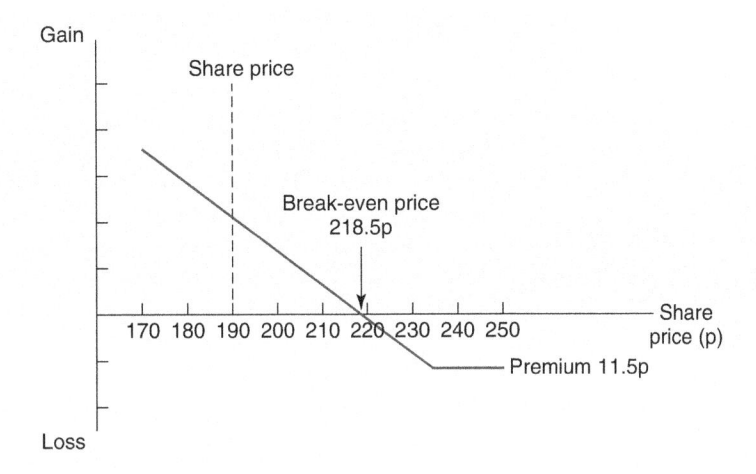

Figure 8.3 York plc put option

In general, the value of a put option (P_1) is:

$P_1 = E - S_1$, if $S_1 < E$

At a 190p share price, the value of the put option is therefore 40p:

$P_1 = 230p - 190p$
$= 40p$

This is because the holder could buy the shares in the market at 190p and exercise the option to sell at 230p. The profit on this transaction is (40p − 11.5p) = 28.5p.

Hedging pressure set to sap oil prices

With crude oil down more than 45 per cent from a year ago, no driller is thrilled to lock in a low price, but some may have no choice, particularly the smaller companies in the US shale patch emerging as the world's swing producers.

That means a wave of hedging transactions by crude producers could hit the market later this year, say bankers, analysts and industry executives. Hedging in futures, options and swaps markets allows producers to ensure a certain price for future output. If crude falls to $30 a barrel, the company that bought a put option with a strike price of $50 a barrel will capture the difference, net of fees. Hedging activity by producers puts downward pressure on prices.

Continued

> 'Producers never like to hedge on the highs. They always like to hedge on the lows,' says a Wall Street commodity derivatives executive.
>
> Today futures prices slope upwards, with prices in 2016 and 2017 higher than oil sold on the spot. If producers accelerate their forward sales, this could keep a lid on later-dated oil prices and convince traders to unload oil rather than park it in tanks for sale later, says Michael Cohen, head of energy commodities research at Barclays.
>
> 'It's going to flush more oil out of storage,' Mr Cohen says. If this happens, the spot oil price could face new pressure.

Source: Meyer, G. (2015) Hedging pressure set to sap oil prices. *Financial Times*, 13 July. © The Financial Times Limited 2018. All rights reserved.

Option strategies

Combinations of investments in options and the underlying shares are both of practical and analytical interest. From a practical standpoint, a combination can provide a means of reducing exposure to the risks associated with substantial changes in the price of the underlying asset, or, from a speculative perspective, can provide some interesting payoff patterns. The analytical interest stems from the insights provided by such portfolios for the valuation of options.

Straddles or doubles

Combining investments in a put and a call, written on a share at the same exercise price and expiry date, produces what is referred to as a **straddle** (a long straddle is where you buy both the call and put option and the opposite is true: a short straddle is where you sell both the call and put option). Why should anyone wish to invest in calls and puts simultaneously (a short straddle)? This strategy will be employed by an investor who believes that the price of the underlying share is going to change quite significantly, but is unable to predict the direction of the change. Such an expectation will arise, for example, whenever an investor knows that a company is expected to make an important announcement, but the investor has no knowledge of the content of the announcement.

This is a strategy to adopt whenever there is considerable short-term uncertainty about the price of a share, and it is anticipated that this uncertainty will be resolved before the expiry of the options. A straddle will lose an investor money if there is little change in the share price, but large price changes in either direction will produce gains.

Protective put

A protective put protects investment in the underlying asset by restricting the possible losses on the asset. Suppose an investor holds shares in Marks & Spencer. She may buy put options to help protect the value of her investment. The put options guarantee a minimum value for the shares up to the expiration date of the options. Whatever happens, the shares can be sold at the option exercise price.

> For example: buy Marks & Spencer shares at 448p
>
> Protect the investment with *out of the money* puts
>
> Exercise price = 435p Premium cost = 15p

No matter how far the share price falls, the investor can sell for 435p up to the expiration date. This is portfolio *insurance*, and the cost of the insurance is the put premium of 15p.

Alternatively, the investor might choose to protect the investment with *in the money* puts, e.g. exercise price of 465p. Obviously this guarantees a higher minimum selling price up to expiration, but the premium cost will be higher.

Covered call

The writing of calls is a risky business. One way of limiting the risk exposure is to buy the share on which the call is being written. When an investor simultaneously writes a call and purchases the underlying asset, the resulting combination is known as a covered call. The returns on the written call and the share are negatively correlated, as the liability implicit in the written call increases with rises in the value of the share. Covered calls may appeal to risk-averse investors who are mildly pessimistic about the future price performance of a share. The fee income from writing calls is attractive, and holding the share implies the risk from an unanticipated rise in the share price is neutralised. (Covered calls are of no interest to really pessimistic investors. They will not wish to purchase the share even if the writing of calls is attractive, and if they already hold the share, they will consider its sale or the purchase of puts rather than the writing of calls.) Covered calls are the combination most frequently employed by financial institutions that regularly write calls.

8.3 OPTION PRICING

We now know that the value of a call and a put option at expiry date is as follows:

Option	Share price at expiry date	Option value at expiry
Call	above exercise price	share price – exercise price
	below exercise price	Zero
Put	above exercise price	Zero
	below exercise price	exercise price – share price

Option prices comprise two elements: intrinsic value and time-value. *Intrinsic value* is what the option would be worth were it about to expire; it reflects the degree to which an option is 'in the money' – in the case of a call option, the extent to which the exercise price is below the current share price. The *time-value* element depends on the length of time the option has to run – the longer the period, the better the chance of making a gain on the contract.

Put–call parity

We showed in the previous section how the combination of buying a call option and selling a put option gave the same payoff as the underlying share price. To find a combination that yields a riskless return, we reverse the options.

When a call and a put are written on the same asset with the same exercise price and expiry date, a relationship, referred to as the put–call parity, can be expected to hold between their market values. The price of one share (S) plus the price of one put option (P) must equal the value of investing the exercise price (E) until expiry at the risk-free rate of interest (R_f) plus the price of one call option.

> **Put–call parity**
>
> Value of share + Value of put = resent value of exercise price + Value of call
>
> $$S + P = E/(1 + R_f) + C$$
>
> It follows from the above that, given four of the five factors, the fifth can be estimated.

The net cash flow expected from investing in a put and a share is equivalent to that to be expected from investing in a call and placing the present value of the sum necessary to exercise the call in a risk-free investment. In both cases, the investor will be left with a sum equivalent to the exercise price if the share price is less than the exercise price, and the value of the share if its price exceeds the exercise price.

Self-assessment activity 8.3

You take out contracts to sell a call option and buy a put option, both at the exercise price of 55p, exercisable one year hence. The cost of the put is 7p and the cost of the call is 1p. The current share price is 44p and the risk-free interest rate is 10 per cent. What is the present value of the exercise price?

(Answer in Appendix A)

Applying the put–call parity model

Melody plc has shares currently trading at 29p. Put and call options for the company are available with an exercise price of 30p expiring in one year. The price of a call option is 6p and the risk-free rate of interest is 6 per cent. What is the price of the put option?

Using the put–call parity model we know that:

$$S + P = E/(1 + R_f) + C \quad \text{(Eqn 1)}$$

or

$$P = E/(1 + R_f) + C - S \quad \text{(Eqn 2)}$$
$$= 30p/(1 + 0.06) + 6p - 29p$$
$$= 5.3p$$

The price of the put option is 5.3p. At any other price, investors would have an arbitrage opportunity to make a profit for zero risk by simultaneously buying and selling identical assets at different prices. Suppose that the actual market price of a put option for Melody plc was 6p. Looking at equation 2, we see that an arbitrage opportunity would arise from selling the put option at 6p and investing 30p in a riskless bond, for one year at 6 per cent, and at the same time acquiring a call option at 6p and selling a share priced at 29p.

■ Valuing a call

The following notation is employed with respect to valuing call options:

S_0 = Share price today
S_1 = Share price at expiry date
E = Exercise price on the option
C_0 = Value of call option today
C_1 = Value of call option on expiration date
R_f = Risk-free interest rate

A number of formal statements can be made about call options:

1. *Option prices cannot be negative.* If the share price ends up below the exercise price on the expiration date, the call option is worthless, but no further loss is created beyond that of the initial premium paid. In mathematical terms:

$$C_1 = 0 \text{ if } S_1 \leq E \quad (8.1)$$

This is the case where an option is 'out of the money' on expiry.

2. *An option is worth on expiry the difference between the share price and the exercise price.*

$$C_1 = S_1 - E \text{ if } S_1 > E \quad (8.2)$$

This is the case where an option is 'in the money' on expiry.

Thus far we have found the intrinsic values of the option – what it would be worth were it about to expire. We have previously noted that options with some time still to run will generally be worth more than the difference between current share price and exercise price because the share price may rise further.

3   *The maximum value of an option is the share price itself* – it could never sell for more than the underlying share price value.

$$C_0 \leq S_0 \tag{8.3}$$

The minimum value of a call today is equal to or greater than the current share price less the exercise price:

$$C_0 \geq S_0 - E \text{ if } S_0 > E \tag{8.4}$$

However, the exercise price is payable in the future. It was shown in the previous section that the payoffs from a share are identical to the payoffs from buying a call option, selling a put option and investing the remainder in a risk-free asset that yields the exercise price on the expiry date. In other words, we need to bring the exercise price to its present value by discounting at the risk-free rate of interest. This gives rise to the following revised statement.

4   *The minimum value of an option is the difference between the share price and the present value of the exercise price (or zero if greater).*

$$C_0 \geq S_0 - [E/(1 + R_f)^t] \tag{8.5}$$

The value of a call option can be observed in Figure 8.4. Bradford plc shares are currently priced at 700p. The diagram shows how the value of an option to buy Bradford shares at 1,100p moves with the share price. The upper limit to the option price is the share price itself, and the lower limit is zero for share prices up to 1,100p, and the share price minus exercise price when the share price moves above 1,100p. In fact, the actual option prices lie between these two extremes, on the upward-sloping curve. The curve rises slowly at first, but then accelerates rapidly.

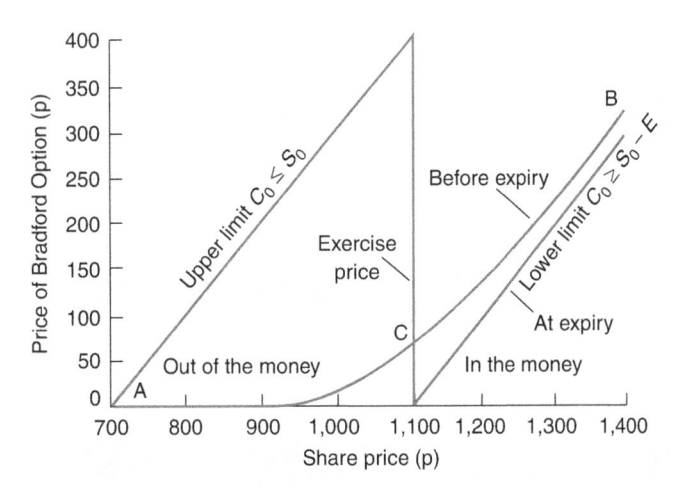

Figure 8.4 Option and share price movements for Bradford plc

At point A on the curve, at the very start, the option is worthless. If the share price for Bradford remained well below the exercise price, the option would remain worthless. At point B, when the share price has rocketed to 1,400p, the option value approximates the share price minus the present value of the exercise price. At point C, the share price exactly equals the exercise price. If exercised today, the option would be worthless. However, there may still be two months for the option to run, in which time the share price could move up or down. In an efficient market, where share prices follow a random walk, there is a 50 per cent chance that it will move higher and an equal probability that it will go lower. If the share price falls, the option will be worthless, but if it rises, the option will have some value. The value placed on the option at point C depends largely on the likelihood of substantial movements in share price. However, we can say that *the higher the share price relative to the exercise price, the safer the option* (i.e. more valuable).

5 *The value of a call option increases over time and as interest rates rise.* Equation 8.4 shows that the value of an option increases as the present value of the exercise price falls. This reduction in present value occurs over time and/or with rises in the interest rate.

6 *The more risky the underlying share, the more valuable the option.* This is because the greater the variance of the underlying share price, the greater is the possibility that prices will exceed the exercise price. But because option values cannot be negative (i.e. the holder would not exercise the option), the 'downside' risk can be ignored.

To summarise, the value of a call option is influenced by the following:

- *The share price.* The higher the price of the share, the greater will be the value of an option written on it.
- *The exercise price of the option.* The lower the exercise price, the greater the value of the call option.
- *The time to expiry of the option.* As long as investors believe that the share price has a chance of yielding a profit on the option, the option will have a positive value. So the longer the time to expiry, the higher the option price.
- *The risk-free interest rate.* As short-term interest rates rise, the value of a call option also increases.
- *The volatility in the underlying share returns.* The greater the volatility in share price, the more likely it is that the exercise price will be exceeded and, hence, the option value will rise.
- *Dividends.* The price of a call option will normally fall with the share price as a share goes ex-div (i.e. the next dividend is not received by the buyer).

A call option is therefore a **contingent claim security** that depends on the value and riskiness of the underlying share on which it is written.

contingent claim security
Claim on a security whose value depends on the value of another asset

Self-assessment activity 8.4

Explain why option value increases with the volatility of the underlying share price. List the factors that determine option value.

(Answer in Appendix A)

A simplified option-price model

Valuing options is a highly complex business, including a lot of mathematics or, for most traders, a user-friendly software package. But we can introduce the valuation of options by using a simple (if somewhat unrealistic) example. We argued earlier that it is possible to replicate the payoffs from buying a share by purchasing a call option, selling a put option and placing the balance on deposit to earn a risk-free return over the option period. This provides us with a method for valuing options.

Valuing a call option in Riskitt plc

In April, the share price of Riskitt plc is 100p. A three-month call option on the shares with a July expiry date has an exercise price of 125p. With the current price well below the exercise price, it is clear that, for the option to have value, the share price must stand a chance of increasing by at least 25p over the next quarter.

Assume that by the expiry date there is an equal chance that the share price will have either soared to 200p or plummeted to 50p. There are no other possibilities. Assume also that you can borrow at 12 per cent a year, or about 3 per cent a quarter.

What would be the payoff for a call option on one share in Riskitt?

	Best	Worst
Share price	200p	50p
Less exercise price	(125p)	(125p)
Payoff	75p	–

You stand to make 75p if the share price does well, but nothing if it slips below the exercise price. To work out how much you would be willing to pay for such an option, you must replicate an investment in call options by a combination of investing in Riskitt shares and borrowing.

Suppose you buy 200 call options. The payoffs in July will be zero if the share price is only 50p and £150 (i.e. 200 × 75p) if the share price is 200p. This is shown in Table 8.3. Note that the cash flow you are trying to determine is the April premium, represented by the question mark.

To replicate the call option cash flows, you adopt the second strategy in Table 8.3: you need to buy 100 shares and borrow sufficient cash to give identical cash flows in July as the call option strategy. This means borrowing £50. The net cash flows for the two strategies are now the same in July whatever the share price. But the £50 loan repayment in July will include three months' interest at 3 per cent for the quarter. The initial sum borrowed in April would therefore be the present value of £50, i.e. £50/1.03 = £48.54. Deducting this from the share price paid gives a net figure of £51.46, which must also be the April cash payment for 200 call options. The price for one call option is therefore about 26p.

Table 8.3 Valuing a call option in Riskitt plc

		Payoff in July if share price is	
Strategy	Cash flow in April	200p	50p
	£	£	£
1 Buy 200 call options	?	+150	–
2 Buy 100 shares	−100	+200	+50
Borrow	+48.54	−50	−50
	−51.46	+150	–

Value of call option = £51.46/200 call = 25.73p, say 26p

Risk-neutral method

In the previous Riskitt plc example we assumed that the two possible payoffs each had a 50 per cent probability. The same result is obtained even if we do not know the probabilities for the payoffs by assuming risk neutrality. Although most investors are risk-averse, requiring a risk premium for taking on greater risk, both risk-averse and risk-neutral investors place the same value on a risk-free asset and, as was shown earlier in the put–call parity model, both place the same value on a hedged portfolio of options and shares.

Recall from the Riskitt plc example that the share price is 100 pence, a three-month call option has an exercise of 125 pence, and the risk-free rate of interest is 12 per cent a year (or approximately 3 per cent a quarter). The only two possible share price outcomes after three months are 200 pence and 50 pence, but in this example the probabilities of each are not known.

Assuming no dividends are paid in the period and that investors are risk-neutral, the expected share price in three months' time is 3 per cent more than the existing price, or 103 pence. From this we can infer probabilities for the two possible outcomes. Let the probability of the high outcome be p and the probability of the low outcome will therefore be $1 - p$. The expected payoff of 103 pence will be the sum of the two outcomes multiplied by their probabilities:

$$200 \text{ pence} \times p + 50 \text{ pence} \times (1 - p) = 103 \text{ pence}$$
$$150\,p = 53 \text{ pence}$$
$$p = 0.353$$
$$1 - p = 0.647$$

We can now use these probabilities to calculate the value of the call option valued at 125 pence. It is only of value if the high outcome of 200 pence is attained, the net gain being 75 pence. Therefore, the expected cash flow is:

$$\text{Expected cash flow} = 75 \text{ pence} \times p = 75 \times 0.353$$
$$= 26.48 \text{ pence}$$

The present value of this is $26.48/(1.03) = 25.7$ pence or approximately 26 pence, as in the previous example.

■ The Black–Scholes Option Pricing Model

The Riskitt example took a highly simplified view of uncertainty, using only two possible share price outcomes. Black and Scholes (1973) combined the main determinants of option values to develop a model of option pricing. Although its mathematics are daunting, the model does have practical application. Every day, dealers in options use it in specially programmed calculators to determine option prices.

For those who like a challenge, the complex mathematics of the Black–Scholes pricing model are given in the Appendix to this chapter. However, the key message is that option pricing requires evaluation of five of the variables listed earlier: share price, exercise price, risk-free rate of interest, time and share price volatility.

Example

Acorn plc shares are currently worth 28p with a standard deviation of 30 per cent. The risk-free rate of interest is 6 per cent. What is the value of a call option on Acorn shares expiring in nine months and with an exercise price of 30p?

The fully worked solution to this problem is given in the appendix to this chapter, but we can identify here the five input variables:

Share price $(S) = 28$p

Exercise price $(E) = 30$p

Risk-free rate $(k) = 6$ per cent p.a.

Time to expiry $(t) = 9$ months

Share price volatility $(\sigma) = 30$ per cent

Application of the Black–Scholes formula to the above data (see Appendix) gives a value of the call option of 2.6p.

Black–Scholes option-pricing formula

Value of call option (C) is:

$$C = SN(d_1) - EN(d_2)e^{-tk}$$

where

$$d_1 = \frac{\ln(S/E) + tk}{\sigma t^{1/2}} + \frac{\sigma t^{1/2}}{2}$$

$$d_2 = d_1 - \sigma t^{1/2}$$

$N(d)$ is the value of the cumulative distribution function for a standardised normal random variable and e^{-tk} is the present value of the exercise price continuously discounted.

A simplified Black–Scholes formula can be used as an approximation for options of less than one year:

$$\frac{C}{S} \approx \frac{1}{\sqrt{2\pi}} \sigma \sqrt{t}$$

This formula emphasises the impact of volatility and time to expiry on the option price.

Applying the above to the previous example, we derive a slightly higher option price:

$$C \approx 0.398 \times 0.3\sqrt{0.75} \times 28 = 2.9p$$

Although the model is complex, the valuation equation derived from the model is quite straightforward to use and is widely employed in practice. Four of the five variables on which it is based are observable: the only non-observable variable, the volatility or standard deviation of the return on the underlying asset, is generally estimated from historical data.

The Black–Scholes model is based on the following assumptions:

(a) there are no transactions costs or taxes;
(b) the expected risk-free rate of interest is constant for the period of the option life;
(c) the market operates continuously;
(d) share prices change smoothly over time – there are no jumps or discontinuities in the price series;
(e) the standard deviation of the distribution of returns on the share is known;
(f) the share pays no dividends during the life of the option; and
(g) the option may only be exercised at expiry of the call (i.e. a European-type option).

The assumptions on which the model is based are clearly quite restrictive. However, as these assumptions are consistent with mainstream theorising in finance, the model integrates well into the general body of finance theory. In practice, the model appears to be quite robust, and it is feasible to relax many assumptions and incorporate more 'real-world' features into the model without changing its overall character.

Is it better to play it safe or to place bets that risk bankruptcy?

Financial options are difficult to value. It isn't really the maths that is the problem. The Black–Scholes formula, which can be used to help value some of them, may look arcane to people who struggled with school algebra but is not – as they say – rocket science. (Rocket science is not very close to the frontier of mathematical knowledge either. Nor does Black–Scholes really solve the valuation question, though it is worth knowing that many people think it does.) The problem is that the valuation of options exposes difficulties humans encounter in assessing risks and uncertainties.

While options were invented recently, their pricing and evaluation is a question as old as time. When hunter-gatherers

Continued

went out in search of prey, they were often in danger of becoming prey themselves. No doubt some prudent hunters took weapons to fend off predators, scoured the ground carefully for hostile animals or tribes and stayed at home when it was too dangerous. Others, less prudent, chose not to buy or exercise these options. They took more risks and caught more prey.

Back around the campfire, was it the meagre haul of the prudent, or the full bags of those of the imprudent who returned, that won the admiration of the tribe? Were the young women of the tribe more impressed when the cautious described their uneventful days, or when the bold recalled their heroic escape from danger?

Like all attempts to account for our behaviour by delving into our evolutionary past, this story should be taken with a large pinch of salt. But there does not have to be any historic truth in my narrative for its fundamental premise to be true. People who take foolish risks which mostly come off are likely to appear attractive mates and leaders. Our heroes are often drawn from precisely that population.

Financial regulators warn that dealing in options is for sophisticated players only and carries a risk of total loss. It is a lesson everyone should take to heart.

Source: Kay, John. (2013) Is it better to play it safe or to place bets that risk bankruptcy?. *Financial Times*, 10 December. © The Financial Times Limited 2018. All rights reserved.

8.4 APPLICATION OF OPTION THEORY TO CORPORATE FINANCE

Option theory has implications going far beyond the valuation of traded share options. It offers a powerful tool for understanding various other contractual arrangements in finance. Here are some examples:

1 *Share warrants*, giving the holder the option to buy shares directly from the company at a fixed exercise price for a given period of time.
2 **Convertible loan stock**, giving the holder a combination of a straight loan or bond and a call option. On exercising the option, the holder exchanges the loan for a fixed number of shares in the company.
3 *Loan stock* can have a call option attached, giving the company the right to repurchase the stock before maturity.
4 *Executive share option schemes* are share options issued to company executives as incentives to pursue shareholder goals.
5 *Insurance and loan guarantees* are a form of put option. An insurance claim is the exercise of an option. Government loan guarantees are a form of insurance. The government, in effect, provides a put option to the holders of risky bonds so that, if the borrowers default, the bond-holders can exercise their option by seeking reimbursement from the government. Underwriting a share issue is a similar type of option.
6 *Currency and interest rate options* are discussed in later chapters as ways of hedging or speculating on currency or interest rate movements.
7 *Underwriting* a new issue of shares when underwriters must take up any shares not subscribed for by investors.

Two further forms of option are equity options and capital investment (real) options.

convertible loan stock
A debenture that can be converted into ordinary shares, often on attractive terms, usually at the option of the holder. Some preference shares are convertible

■ Equity as a call option on a company's assets: Reckless Ltd

Option-like features are found in financially geared companies. *Equity is, in effect, a call option on the company's assets.*

Reckless Ltd has a single £1 million debenture in issue, which is due for repayment in one year. The directors, on behalf of the shareholders, can either pay off the loan at the year-end, thereby having no prior claim on the firm's assets, or default on the debenture. If they default, the debenture-holders will take charge of the assets or recover the £1 million owing to them.

In such a situation, the shareholders of Reckless have a call option on the company's assets with an exercise price of £1 million. They can exercise the option by repaying the loan, or they can allow the option to lapse by defaulting on the loan. Their choice depends on the value of the company's assets. If they are worth more than £1 million, the option is 'in the money' and the loan should be repaid. If the option is 'out of the money', because the assets are worth less than £1 million, option theory argues that shareholders would prefer the company to default or enter liquidation. This option-like feature arises because companies have limited liability status, effectively protecting shareholders from having to make good any losses.

Brussels to probe Hinkley nuclear contract

Brussels is to launch a full investigation into whether the contract for Britain's first nuclear power plant in a generation offers illegal state support, casting the project into doubt until at least next summer.

The deal under scrutiny is the contract signed in October between the UK government and French utility EDF for Hinkley Point C nuclear power station in Somerset. It will provide 7 per cent of the country's electricity. The agreement guarantees EDF a 'strike price' of £92.50 per megawatt hour – roughly double the current wholesale price – for electricity produced at the £16bn plant over 35 years.

However, it has always required approval from the European Commission, which can demand changes to any terms that distort competition through illegal state support. EDF says it cannot make a final decision on Hinkley or bring in co-investors before state aid clearance is received. A concern will be whether the government has 'overcompensated' EDF with too high a strike price.

Other elements to come under scrutiny are the rate of return on the project, the duration of the contract, arrangements for nuclear waste and decommissioning and insurance against a nuclear event, as well as the UK's infrastructure guarantee. The probe will be a crucial test case in a bitterly contested area of policy. There is huge uncertainty over how state aid rules will be applied to plans for Europe's next generation of power plants, especially any new nuclear reactors.

Some have argued a formal investigation is likely because 'many people' are questioning the deal. 'Given the challenges from anti-nuclear groups, Brussels needs to show it has followed due process,' said one person close to the discussions.

The UK has argued that the contract does not qualify as state aid and, even if the commission decides it does, it would be compatible with EU treaties. People close to the discussions said the commission was unlikely to order a reduction in the strike price, or duration of the project, but may demand closer monitoring to ensure EDF did not make 'excessive' profits.

FT *Source:* Chazan, G. and Barker, A. (2013) Brussels to probe UK nuclear power plant deal. *Financial Times*, 12 December. © The Financial Times Limited 2018. All rights reserved.

8.5 CAPITAL INVESTMENT OPTIONS (REAL OPTIONS)

real options
Options to invest in real assets such as capital projects

In Chapter 3, the principal ideas underlying **real options** were explained. The key proposal was that managers can change future activities as a project progresses and events occur that require them to re-think the project strategy. Hence, different types of real option can be identified including, for example, options to postpone, expand, contract or abandon capital projects.

Real options are closely related to financial options, as they are concerned with building flexibility into capital investment projects. For example, a firm may buy a patent from an inventor. The acquisition of this patent permits the firm to manufacture a new and innovative product if it wants to, but it does not have to manufacture the product. This is equivalent to paying a premium on a call option. Buying the patent gives the firm the right to manufacture the product, but it has no obligation to do so.

We have seen that the value of a share option will be dependent upon five main variables and, similarly, the value of a real option is dependent upon five main variables:

Share call option	Real call option
Exercise price	Investment cost
Current value of share	Value of the project
Time to expiry	Time until investment opportunity disappears
Volatility of share price	Volatility of project flows
Risk-free interest rate	Risk-free interest rate

The first four of these variables can be further understood if we consider them within the context of the firm that has bought the patent.

Exercise price

In the case of the firm that buys the patent, if it decides to manufacture the product, then capital expenditure will be needed at the outset. For example, it may need to invest in new machinery. This investment cost equates to the price incurred to exercise the option.

Current value

In making the decision whether to manufacture or not, the firm will estimate what the future cash inflows (generated from selling the product) and future cash outflows (arising from costs of manufacture and the like) will be for the capital project. The present value of the cash inflows and outflows associated with manufacturing, and then selling, the product represent the current value of the project.

Time to expiry

There will come a time after which the opportunity to manufacture the product has passed, for example, when the product is no longer considered innovative by the marketplace. Hence, the option to manufacture does not remain open indefinitely and the patent will have an expiry date after which the investment opportunity no longer exists.

Volatility

Additionally, just as share prices are uncertain then, so, too, are the future expected cash flows from any project. Therefore, some assessment of the volatility of the future cash flows will be needed if a real option valuation is to be performed.

Example: Strategic options in Harlequin plc

Harlequin plc has developed a new form of mobile phone, using the latest technology. It is considering whether to enter this market by investing in equipment costing £400,000 to assemble and then market the product in the north of England during the first four years. (Most of the product parts will be bought in.) The expected net present value from this initial project, however, is –£25,000. The strategic case for such an investment is that, by the end of the project's life, sufficient expertise would have been developed to launch an improved product on a larger scale to be distributed throughout Europe. The cost of the second project in four years' time is estimated at £1.32 million. Although there is a reasonable chance of fairly high payoffs, the expected net present value suggests this project will do little more than break even.

'Obviously, with the two projects combining to produce a negative NPV, the whole idea should be scrapped,' remarked the finance director.

Gary Owen, a recent MBA graduate, was less sure that this was the right course of action. He reckoned that the second project was a kind of call option, the initial cost being the exercise price and the present value of its future stream of benefits being equivalent to the option's underlying share price. The risks for the two projects looked to be in line with the variability of the company's share price, which had a standard deviation of 30 per cent a year.

If, by the end of Year 4, the second project did not suggest a positive NPV, the company could walk away from the decision, the option would lapse and the cost to the company would be the £25,000 negative NPV on the first project (the option premium). But it could be a winner, and only 'upside' risk is considered with call options.

Gary knew that Harlequin's discount rate for such projects was 20 per cent and the risk-free interest rate was 10 per cent. Table 8.4 shows his estimation of the main elements to be considered.

Gary then entered the five variables (asset value, exercise price, risk-free discount rate, time period and asset volatility) into the Black–Scholes option pricing formula. The outcome was that the value of the option to invest in the follow-on project was approximately £80,000. This is because there is a chance that the project could be really profitable, but the company will not know whether this is likely until the outcome of the first project is known. The high degree of risk in the second project actually increases the value of the call option. It seems, therefore, that the initial project launch, which creates an option value of £80,000 for a 'premium' of £25,000 (negative NPV) may make economic as well as strategic sense.

Table 8.4 Harlequin plc: call option valuation

	(£000)
Initial project	
Cost of investment	(400)
PV of cash inflows	375
Net present value	(25)
Follow-on-project in Year 4	
Cost of investment	(1320)
PV of cash inflows	1320
Net present value in Year 4	–
Main factors in valuing the call option:	
1 Asset value	PV of cash flows at Year 4 discounted to Year 0
	= £1.32m/(1.2)^4
	= £0.636m
2 Exercise price	= cost of follow-on project
	= £1.32m
3 Risk-free discount rate	= 10%
4 Time period	= 4 years
5 Asset volatility	= standard deviation of 30%

8.6 WHY CONVENTIONAL NPV MAY NOT TELL THE WHOLE STORY

Earlier chapters have rehearsed the theoretical argument that capital projects that offer positive net present values, when discounted at the risk-adjusted discount rate, should be accepted. A number of practical shortcomings with discounted cash flow approaches; here we introduce an important theoretical point.

We have noted that orthodox capital projects analysis adopts a 'now or never' mentality. But the timing option reminds us that a 'wait and see' approach can add value. Whenever a company makes an investment decision, it also surrenders a call option – the right to invest in the same asset at some later date. Such waiting may be passive, waiting for the right economic and market conditions, or active, where management seeks to gather project-related information to reduce uncertainty (further product trials, competitor reaction, etc.). Hence, the true NPV of a project being undertaken today should include the values of various options associated with the decision:

$$\text{True NPV} = \begin{array}{c}\text{NPV of}\\ \text{basic}\\ \text{project}\end{array} + \begin{array}{c}\text{NPV of}\\ \text{abandonment}\\ \text{option}\end{array} + \begin{array}{c}\text{NPV of}\\ \text{follow-on}\\ \text{projects}\end{array} + \begin{array}{c}\text{NPV of}\\ \text{option}\\ \text{to wait}\end{array}$$

If the total is positive, the project creates wealth. This is why firms frequently defer apparently wealth-creating projects or accept apparently uneconomic projects. Senior managers recognise that investment ideas often have wider strategic implications, are irreversible and improve with age.

Real options are particularly important in investment decisions when the conventional NPV analysis suggests that the project is 'marginal', uncertainty is high and there is value in retaining flexibility. In such cases, the conventional NPV will almost always understate the true value.

Although the ideas underlying real options are relatively new, they do appear to be of use to companies. In their survey of investment appraisal techniques, Graham and Harvey (2002) reported that more than a quarter of the companies studied used real options approaches in some form.

Icy options

Bob Dudley, BP's chief executive, likes to talk about 'optionality'. This makes the British oil major's decision to hive off onshore US operations sound like a subtle financial manoeuvre. Separate management might help the unit – still fully owned by BP – compete better with smaller shale operators. But all that's been said, really, is this: we might sell.

BP's real option play was made last year – in Russia. BP sold its stake in TNK-BP, returned some of that cash to shareholders, and put down a long-term bet on the Russian Arctic shelf (with 300bn barrels of oil equivalent recoverable resource) by accepting a fifth of Rosneft's equity as added payment.

BP will not, however, seek bids for its Rosneft stake any time soon – for good reason. Russia will contribute all of BP's production growth in the medium term. Looking out to 2017, Credit Suisse sees production volumes, on a barrel of oil equivalent basis, rising at 3 per cent annually. Remove Russian volumes and that growth almost evaporates.

BP's proven reserves are about 18bn boe (barrels of oil equivalent): Rosneft's grand plans to develop its Arctic shelf could add as much as 48bn. Note also that Rosneft and its partners have agreed to pay the first $14bn of exploration outlays. BP's option will stay in the money so long as Rosneft can eventually deliver enough of these barrels.

Geopolitical tensions amid the Ukraine crisis may make BP's Russian option appear further out of the money. But compared with the risk of Russia expropriating western energy assets, currency moves and cost overruns still weigh more on BP's future income.

FT

Source: Column, L. (2014) BP in Russia: options. Financial Times, 10 July, p. 12. © The Financial Times Limited 2018. All rights reserved.

SUMMARY

This chapter covers option pricing theory, its application and development. In particular, it explains the types of options and their role in risk management and value addition for organisations and investors. While discussing options and their application for both managers and investors, we explained share options, option pricing, the application of options theory to corporate finance, and real options. The summary of arguments raised in the existing literature on options and derivatives suggest that although, the literature has developed highly complex models for valuing options, insufficient attention has been paid to value creation through options.

Options or option-like features permeate virtually every area of financial management. A better understanding of options and the development of option pricing have made the topic an increasingly important part of financial theory. We have sought to increase your awareness of what options are, where they are to be found, and how managers can begin to value them. The topic is still in its infancy, but its study will yield important insights into financial and investment decisions.

Key points

- Option features are to be found in most areas of finance (e.g. convertibles and warrants, insurance, currency and interest rate management, and capital budgeting).
- Pure options are financial instruments created by exchanges (e.g. stock markets) rather than companies.
- The two main types of option are (1) **call options**, giving the holder the right to buy a share (or other asset) at the exercise price at some future time, and (2) **put options**, giving the holder the right to sell shares at a given price at some future time.
- The minimum value of a call option is the difference between the share price and the present value of the exercise price.
- The value of call options increases as:
  - The underlying share price increases.
  - The exercise price falls.
  - The time to expiry lengthens.
  - The risk-free interest rate rises.
  - The volatility of the underlying share price increases.
- The Black–Scholes Option Pricing Model can be applied to estimate the value of call options.
- Capital investment decisions may have options attached covering the option to (1) abandon, (2) delay or (3) invest in follow-on opportunities.
- Where the value of a company's assets falls below the value of its borrowings, shareholders may not exercise their option to repay the loan, but prefer the company to default on the debt.

Further reading

A range of books specifically focuses on derivative instruments, and within these, options are treated in detail. For example, Hull (2017) is a good book covering options, futures and other derivatives. McDonald (2012) provides a conceptual understanding of derivative instruments and their application in organisations. Similarly, Guthrie (2009) provides a detailed overview of the theory and application of real options analysis.

Dixit and Pindyck (1995) provide an easy-to-read article on the options approach to capital investment. Brennan and Trigeorgis (2000) offer a number of useful papers on real options. Those who like a mathematical challenge may want to read the Black and Scholes (1973) classic paper or Cox *et al.* (1979). Merton (1998) gives an excellent review of the application of option pricing, particularly to investment decisions. More recently, Geske, Subrahmanyam and Zhou (2016) explore the relationship between equity call options and firms' capital structure. Blanco and Wehrheim (2017) provide useful discussions on the relationship between equity options markets and firm innovation, while Hoberg and Moon (2017) investigate the use of foreign exchange derivatives by multinational corporations.

Useful websites

Futures and Options World: www.fow.com

NYSE Liffe: www.euronext.com

International Swaps and Derivatives Association: www2.isda.org

Appendix
BLACK–SCHOLES OPTION PRICING FORMULA

The Black–Scholes formula, for valuing a call option (C), with no adjustment for dividends, is given by:

$$C = SN(d_1) - EN(d_2)e^{-tk}$$

where:

$$d_1 = \frac{\ln(S/E) + tk}{\sigma t^{1/2}} + \frac{\sigma t^{1/2}}{2}$$

$$d_2 = d_1 - \sigma t^{1/2}$$

We already have described S as the underlying share price and E as the exercise price. In addition, σ is the standard deviation of the underlying asset, t is the time, in years, until the option expires, k is the risk-free rate of interest continuously compounded, $N(d)$ is the value of the cumulative distribution function for a standardised normal random variable and e^{-tk} is the present value of the exercise price continuously discounted.

■ Example

Acorn plc shares are currently worth 28p each with a standard deviation of 30 per cent. The risk-free interest rate is 6 per cent, continuously compounded. Compute the value of a call option on Acorn shares expiring in nine months and with an exercise price of 30p.

We can list the values for each parameter: $S = 28, \sigma = 0.30, E = 30, K = 0.06, t = 0.75$.

$$\sigma t^{1/2} = (0.3)(0.75)^{1/2} = 0.2598$$

$$d_1 = \frac{\ln(S/E) + tk}{\sigma t^{1/2}} + \frac{\sigma t^{1/2}}{2}$$

$$= \frac{\ln(28/30) + 0.75(0.06)}{0.2598} + \frac{0.2598}{2}$$

$$= -0.2655 + 0.1732 + 0.1299$$

$$= 0.0376, \text{ say } 0.04$$

$$d_2 = d_1 - \sigma r^{1/2} = 0.0375 - 0.2598$$

$$= -0.2223, \text{ say } -0.22$$

Using cumulative distribution function tables:

$$N(d_1) = N(0.04) = 0.5160$$
$$N(d_2) = N(-0.22) = 0.4129$$

Inserting the above into the original equation:

$$C = SN(d_1) - EN(d_2)e^{-tk}$$
$$= 28(0.5160) - 30(0.4129)e^{-0.045}$$
$$= 2.6p$$

The value of the call is 2.6p.

Strictly speaking, adjustment for dividends on shares should be made by applying the Merton formula, not dealt with in this text.

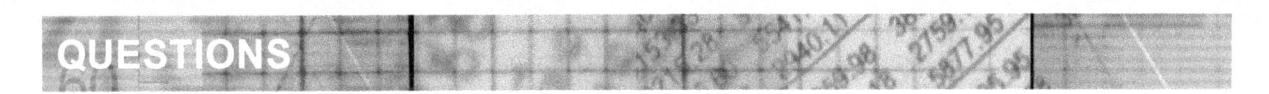

QUESTIONS

Questions with a coloured number have solutions in Appendix B on page 501.

1 Give two examples where companies can issue call options (or something similar).

2 On 1 March the ordinary shares of Gaymore plc stood at 469p. The traded options market in the shares quotes April 500p puts at 47p. If the share price falls to 450p, how much, if any, profit would an investor make? What will the option be worth if the share price moves up to 510p?

3 What is the difference between traditional and exchange traded options?

4 Explain the factors influencing the price of a traded option and whether volatility of a company's share option price is necessarily a sign of financial weakness.

5 Frank purchased a call option on 100 shares in Marmaduke plc six months ago at 10p per share. The share price at the time was 110p and the exercise price was 120p. Just prior to expiry, the share price has risen to 135p.

Required
(a) State whether the option should be exercised.
(b) Calculate the profit or loss on the option.
(c) Would Frank have done better by investing the same amount of cash six months ago in a bank offering 10 per cent p.a.?

6 Find the value of the call option given that the present value of the exercise price is 10p, the value of the put option is 15p and the current value of the share on which the option is based is 25p.

7 Find the present value of the exercise price given that the value of the call is 19p, the value of the put is 5p and the current market price of the underlying share is 30p.

8 The current price of a share is 38p, and a call option written on this share with six months to run to maturity has an exercise price of 40p. If the risk-free rate of interest is 10 per cent per annum and the volatility of the returns on the share is 20 per cent, use the Black and Scholes model to estimate the value of the call.

9 The current price of a company's shares is 420.5p and the price of a call option with a strike price of 420p with six months to maturity is 50.5p. The value of a put option with the same strike price and time to maturity is 38.5p. Determine the annualised rate of interest if put–call parity holds.

10 The following are the closing prices of options on the shares of Gilling plc on 10 March 2014.

		Calls			Puts		
Exercise Price		Apr	Jun	Sep	Apr	June	Sep
Gilling	800	36.5	53.5	62.5	9.0	20.0	31.5
(*825)	850	11.0	25.5	35.0	33.0	42.0	55.5

*Current price

Refer to the table as required when answering this question.

(a) Explain the fundamental reasons for the large difference between the price of a September 800 call and an April 800 put.
(b) Outline a strategy that combines short calls and short puts. Why would an investor adopt such a strategy? Use data from the table to illustrate some possible payoffs.

11 *Spot the options in Enigma Drugs plc.* The mini-case presented below incorporates five options. Can you identify the type of option, its length and exercise price? Recall that American options offer the holder the right to exercise at any time up to a certain date, while a European option is exercised on one particular date.

Enigma Drugs plc is an innovative pharmaceutical company. The management team is considering setting up a separate limited company to develop and produce a new drug.

The project is forecast to incur development costs and new plant expenditure totalling £50 million and to break even over the next five years (by which time its competitors are likely to have found a way round the patent rights). Enigma's management is considering deferring the whole decision by two years, when the outcome of a major court case with important implications for the drug's success will be known.

The risks on the venture are high, but should the project prove unsuccessful and have to be abandoned, the 'know-how' developed from the project can be used inside the group or sold to its competitors for a considerable sum. Enigma's management realises that there is little or no money to be made in the initial five years, but it should allow them to gain vital expertise for the development of a 'wonder drug' costing £120 million, which could be launched in four years' time.

The newly formed company would be largely funded by borrowing £40 million in the first instance, repayable in total after eight years, unless the company prefers to be 'wound up' for defaulting on the loan. Some of the debt raised will be by 9 per cent Convertible Loan Stock, giving holders the right to convert to equity at any time over the next four years at 360p compared with the current price of 297p.

12 A European call option on shares has three months to expiry. The current share price is £3 and the exercise price of the option is £2.50. The standard deviation of the share is 20 per cent, and the risk-free rate is 5 per cent. Use the Black–Scholes model to value the call option of a share.

Practical assignment

1 Choose two forms of financial contracting arrangement with option features and show how option pricing theory can help in analysing them.
2 Consider a major capital investment recently undertaken or under review (e.g. the London Olympic Games project). Does it offer an option? Could an option feature be introduced? What would the rough value of the option be?

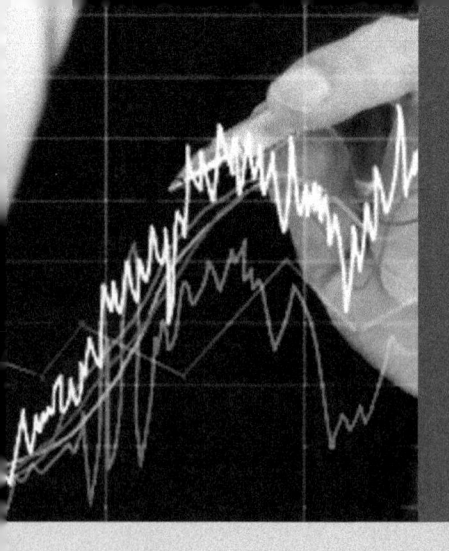

9

Returning value to shareholders: the dividend decision

RSA's Stephen Hester hits out at critics of dividend policy

Stephen Hester, RSA's chief executive, has hit back at critics of the UK insurer's dividend policy, saying the size of the payout will be based on improvements in profits. Shares in RSA closed down 0.5 per cent on Wednesday despite the company's decision to raise the first-half dividend by almost a third to 6.6p per share. The increase was below analysts' forecasts, which had pointed to a 7p per share payout.

Mr Hester said: 'We're in a slightly Alice in Wonderland world where a dividend increase of 32 per cent is not quite enough. The risk is that investors and analysts aren't looking at the quality and repeatability of earnings. Companies risk being bullied into [dividend] increases that aren't sustainable. We are going to make sure our earnings are rock solid, and the dividend will follow.'

He added that the company would not consider special dividends or share buybacks until next year.

Greig Paterson, an analyst, said the dividend increase that he expected had been 'deferred', although he added: 'In our view, management recently passed its own test to review the dividend level, namely the completion of the disposal and debt restructuring programmes, so we expect it to announce a step up in dividend policy in the future.'

RSA's pre-tax profits rose 78 per cent to £263m, while underlying earnings per share were up 31 per cent to 23.3p, helped by falling interest charges following a debt restructuring exercise. Despite the dip on Wednesday, RSA's shares are up 30 per cent over the past year, ahead of other UK-listed insurers such as Direct Line and Admiral.

FT Source: Ralph, O. (2017) RSA's Stephen Hester hits out at critics of dividend policy. *Financial Times*, 2 August. © The Financial Times Limited 2018. All rights reserved.

Learning objectives

After reading this chapter, you should:

- Understand the competing views about the role of dividend policy.
- Understand what factors a financial manager should consider when deciding to recommend a change in dividend payouts.
- Understand what is meant by signalling and the 'information content' of dividends.
- Know about alternatives to cash dividends that may be used to deliver value to owners.
- Appreciate the impact of taxation on dividend decisions.
- Understand why changes in dividend payments usually lag behind changes in company earnings.

9.1 INTRODUCTION

The introductory cameo gives a flavour of the importance of dividends to investors. This chapter will help you to appreciate the factors that drive dividend decisions.

Most quoted companies pay two types of dividends to ordinary shareholders each year: an interim dividend based on half-year results, followed by the main, or final, dividend, based on the full-year reported profits. The amount of dividend is determined by the board of directors, advised by financial managers, and presented to the Annual General Meeting of shareholders for approval. The board and their advisers thus face a twice-yearly decision about what percentage of post-tax profits to distribute to shareholders (the 'payout ratio') and hence what percentage to retain (the 'retention ratio').

Until a specified **Record Day**, the shares are traded **cum-dividend**: that is, purchasers will be entitled to receive the dividend. The approved dividends are paid to all shareholders appearing on the share register on the Record Day, after which the shares are quoted **ex-dividend**, i.e. without entitlement to the dividend. In practice, there is a time lag between the shares going ex-dividend and the Record Day to allow the company's Registrar to update the shareholders' register to reflect recent dealings. The Financial Calendar of Scottish and Southern Energy plc, the electricity supply utility, is shown in Table 9.1. People purchasing Scottish and Southern Energy plc shares whose names did not appear on the register by 18 July 2017 would not have received the final dividend payable per share (63.9p).

> **Record Day**
> The cut-off date beyond which further entrants to the shareholder register do not qualify for the next dividend
>
> **ex-dividend**
> A share trades ex-dividend (xd) when people who buy are no longer entitled to receive the upcoming dividend payment

Table 9.1 Scottish and Southern Energy plc Financial Calendar 2017

Annual general meeting	20 July 2017
Ex-dividend date	27 July 2017
Record date	18 July 2017
Final dividend payment date	22 September 2017

Source: Scottish and Southern Energy plc, *Annual Report and Accounts*, 2017 (**www.sse.com**).

When the shares first trade ex-dividend, the share price usually falls by the amount of the dividend. As dividends are usually quite a small proportion of the share price anyway, this is not a substantial fall. For example, in the case of SSE, the dividend of 63.9p compared to a share price of well over £13.50. However, sometimes, firms with a surplus of liquidity decide to pay a substantial special dividend (SD). This is good news at the time of announcement, and the shares usually rise, but it stores up the problem of a substantial fall in share price when the dividend is paid, which may alarm some investors.

It is also good news when a firm resumes dividend payments after a previous cut. For example, Anglo American has resumed dividend payments after suspending them in February 2016. Its decision was based on a strong operating performance and is in line with the market expectations.

Anglo American resumes dividend payments early on profits growth

Miner Anglo American reported a sharp rise in half year profits on Thursday and said it would resume dividend payments six months earlier than expected. Anglo chief executive Mark Cutifani said Anglo's strong operational performance and higher commodity prices allowed the company to declare an interim dividend of $0.48 cents per share.

The company had previously said it would reinstate its dividend at the end of its 2017 financial year, paying out 30 to 40 per cent of its earnings to shareholders. 'We have

Continued

nearly halved our net debt to $6.2bn over the past year to take us well below our year-end target of $7bn,' said Mr Cutifani. 'Our materially improved balance sheet strength . . . has supported the decision to resume dividend payments six months early, establishing a pay-out policy at a targeted level of 40 per cent of underlying earnings.

Anglo suspended its dividend in February 2016 as it scrambled to reduce debts during a savage downturn in commodity markets. That formed part of a wider shrink-to-survive strategy that the company had abandoned following a recovery in commodity prices.

Earnings before interest, tax, depreciation and amortisation – the figure most widely tracked by analysts – rose 68 per cent to $4.1bn in the six months to June, Anglo said, a result that was in line with market forecasts.

Shares in Anglo, the top FTSE 100 performer in 2016, have risen just 3 per cent this year, lagging some of its peers. Concerns about the political situation in South Africa, where the company has a large presence, have weighed on its stock price.

Source: Hume, N. (2017) Anglo American resumes dividend payments early on profits growth. *Financial Times*, 27 July. © The Financial Times Limited 2018. All rights reserved.

How should top management approach the dividend decision? Should it be generous and follow a high payout policy, or retain the bulk of earnings? The pure theory of dividend policy shows that, under certain conditions, it makes no difference what they do! One authority argues: 'to the management of a company acting in the best interests of its shareholders, dividend policy is a mere detail' (Miller and Modigliani, 1961). However, the conditions required to support this conclusion are highly restrictive and unlikely to apply in real-world capital markets. Indeed, many financial managers and investment analysts take the opposite view, appearing to believe that the dividend payout decision is critical to company valuation and hence a central element of corporate financial strategy. These are the extreme views – an evaluation of the case for and against dividend generosity leads to more pragmatic 'middle-of-the-road' conclusions.

In this chapter, we consider the strategic, theoretical and practical issues surrounding dividend policy, and discuss some of the alternatives to dividend payment. *The basic message for management is: define the dividend policy, make a smooth transition towards it, think very carefully before changing it, and avoid cutting dividends!*

Few people doubt that dividend levels influence share prices in some way or other. Indeed, a common method of valuation, the Dividend Valuation Model (introduced in Chapter 2) relies on discounting the future dividend stream. However, debate centres on what is the most attractive *pattern* of dividend payments, and the effects of *changes* in dividend policy.

Shareholders can receive returns in the form of dividends now and/or capital appreciation, which is the market's valuation of future expected dividend growth. But are shareholders more impressed by the higher near-in-time dividends than by the capital gain generated by a policy of low current payments, with retentions used to finance worthwhile investment? Graham *et al.* (1962) claimed that $1 of dividend was valued four times more highly by shareholders than $1 of retained earnings. Yet it is not uncommon to observe quite parsimonious (or even zero) payout ratios. Conventional wisdom warns companies subject to volatility of earnings to operate relatively high dividend covers to safeguard dividend payments in the event of depressed profitability. Similarly, smaller companies with less easy access to fresh supplies of capital are also advised to conserve cash and liquidity by operating a conservative dividend policy.

Dividend cuts are generally perceived as conveying bad news about the prospects of a company. However, it is difficult to generalise about optimal dividend policy, and Figure 9.1 demonstrates that average dividend growth rates for FT All-Share companies have fluctuated over time. For example, following the financial crisis of 2008, companies cut dividends to conserve cash as many economies went into recession and because it was difficult to obtain external finance.

In the following sections, we consider strategic and legal issues before examining the theory of dividend policy and, in particular, the 'irrelevance' hypothesis. We then consider the major qualifications to the theory, suggesting reasons why some

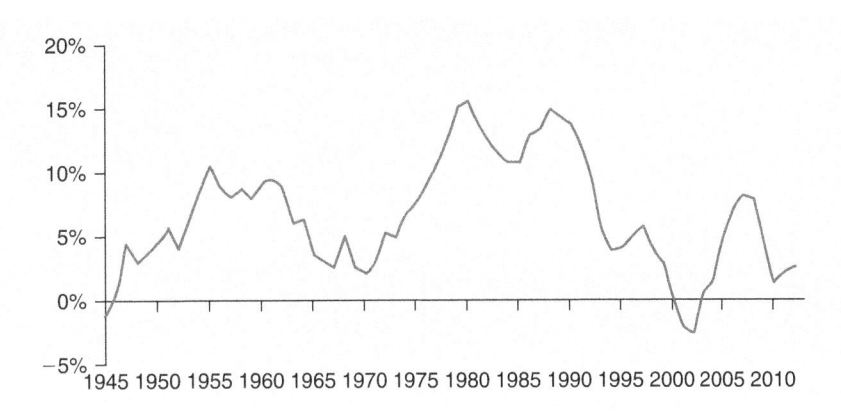

Figure 9.1 Five-year average dividend growth rates: FT All-Share companies
Source: Barclays Equity Gilt Study 2013.

shareholders may, in practice, prefer dividend income. You will see that dividend policy is an enigma with no obvious optimal strategy capable of general application. However, it will be possible to make some broad recommendations to guide the financial manager.

9.2 THE STRATEGIC DIMENSION

Formulating corporate strategy requires specification of clear objectives and delineation of the strategic options contributing to the achievement of these objectives. Although maximisation of shareholder wealth may be the paramount aim, there may be various routes to it. For example, diversifying into new industrial sectors involves a choice between internal growth and growth by acquisition. Whichever alternative is selected, the enterprise will need to consider both the level of required financing and the possible sources. The main alternatives for the listed company are short- and long-term debt capital, new share issues (normally rights issues) and internal financing (via retention of profits and depreciation provisions).

Where there are investment and growth opportunities, the amount of finance required to support the selected strategic option may exceed the borrowing capacity of the company, necessitating the use of additional equity funding. A capital-hungry firm therefore faces the choice between retention of earnings, i.e. restricting the dividend payout, or paying out high dividends but then clawing back capital via a subsequent rights issue. Neither policy is risk-free, as both may have undesirable repercussions on the ability to exploit strategic options. Retention may offend investors reliant on dividend income, resulting in share sales and lower share price, conflicting with the aim of wealth-maximisation as well as exposing the company to the threat of takeover. Alternatively, the dividend payment-plus-rights issue policy incurs administrative expenses and the risk of having to sell shares on a flat or falling market. To this extent, the dividend decision is a strategic one, since an ill-judged financial decision could subvert the overall strategic aim. Consequently, financial managers must carefully consider the likely reaction of shareholders, and of the market as a whole, to dividend proposals.

This is where we encounter the role of dividend policy, because free cash flow generating ability, investment and growth opportunities, and access to external financing are not uniform across all companies. Generally, companies based in more mature sectors produce excess cash, but such companies often have limited investment and growth opportunities and can therefore pay dividends on a consistent basis. And those firms which have more investment and growth opportunities retain earnings, and thus increase shareholders' wealth through increased future earnings and share prices. Through the payments of dividends, companies share their profits with the shareholders to encourage them to retain their shares in the company. Payment of dividend is also used as a signal to the market about companies' financial performance which helps in attracting new shareholders to the company. Understanding the strategic role of dividend policy is therefore of great importance to the corporate finance manager.

Nokia slides as it forgoes dividend

Nokia's decision to withhold a dividend payment for the first time in its history triggered a strong reaction from shareholders. After a brief rally in response to what was a better than expected end to the financial year, the shares slid 5.5 per cent to €3.30. The beleaguered mobile group said its handset business had returned to underlying profit in the fourth quarter, driven by sales of its new Lumia smartphone. The shares had rallied 20 per cent since Nokia went public with the sales data earlier.

'The market reaction looks quite irrational to me as both net cash position as well as smartphone gross margins were clearly better than expected,' said Sami Sarkamies, analyst at Nordea. 'To me those were the two key unknowns. In what way should one be more concerned with the situation at Nokia today than yesterday?' he added.

Source: Stevenson, A .(2013) Nokia slides after passing on dividend. *Financial Times*, 25 January. © The Financial Times Limited 2018. All rights reserved.

9.3 THE LEGAL DIMENSION

Legal factors impose further constraints on managers' freedom of action in deciding dividends. Although shareholders are the main risk-bearers in a company, other stakeholders, such as creditors and employees, carry a measure of risk. Accordingly, shareholders can be paid dividends only if the company has accumulated sufficient profits. They cannot be paid out of capital, except in a liquidation, as to do so would mean they would be paid ahead of prior claims on the business. The Companies Act 1985 states that, in general, companies are restricted to cumulative realised profits. However, public companies are further restricted to realised profits less unrealised losses. Furthermore, bondholders may insist on restrictive covenants being written into loan agreements to prevent large dividends being declared.

Of course, paying the maximum legally-permitted dividend is rarely likely to make strategic sense. Moreover, dividends are paid *out of profits* but *with* cash (or borrowings). It is quite common for companies to report low or negative profits, yet to maintain the previous year's dividend. This is both feasible and acceptable if the firm in question has built up sufficient reserves for previous years' retentions and has a reasonably healthy cash position. Indeed, the share prices of some struggling companies actually rise when they pay a maintained dividend out of reserves. This is because a maintained dividend is believed to be a signal to the market of expectations of better times ahead. Remember that managers have more information to hand than investors. So, in this case, some investors may believe that directors are conveying favourable information (the concept of information asymmetry again).

9.4 THE THEORY: DIVIDEND POLICY AND FIRM VALUE

The critical issue is how, if at all, does dividend policy affect the value of the firm? This section shows that the answer depends on whether or not a firm has access to external financing. In the absence of external financing, dividend payment may damage company value if the company has better investment opportunities than paying dividends to its shareholders. Payment of dividends may prevent access to worthwhile investment. With external financing, however, at least in a perfect market, dividends become totally irrelevant, since payment no longer precludes worthwhile investment, simply because the firm can recoup the required finance by selling shares.

In Chapter 2, we used the Dividend Valuation Model to show that the value of a company* ultimately depends on its dividend-paying capacity. For a company with constant and perpetual free cash flows[†] of E_t in any year t, paid wholly as dividend, D_t, the market will discount this stream at the rate of return required by shareholders, k_e, so that:

$$\text{Value of equity} = V_0 = \sum_{t=1}^{N} \frac{E_t}{(1+k_e)^t} = \frac{E_t}{k_e} \left(\text{or } V_0 = \frac{D_t}{k_e} \text{ since } E_t = D_t \right)$$

If a proportion, b, of earnings is retained each year, beginning in period 1, for example, thus reducing the next dividend payable to $E_1(1-b)$, company value is given by the forthcoming dividend divided by the cost of equity less the growth rate. The growth rate, g, is given by the retention ratio, b, times the return on re-invested funds, R (as explained in Chapter 2):

$$\text{Value of equity} = V_0 = \frac{E_1(1-b)}{(k_e - g)} = \frac{D_1}{(k_e - g)} = \frac{D_1}{(k_e - bR)}$$

Self-assessment activity 9.1

Using the following figures, remind yourself why the growth rate of earnings = (b × R)

Earnings in latest year = £1,000; b = 60%; R = 15%.

(Answer in Appendix A)

These two expressions can cause confusion. In the first case, the market appears to value the stream of earnings, while in the second, the valuation is based upon the stream of dividends. In the early stages of the debate about the importance and role of dividend policy, much attention was paid to the issue of whether the market values earnings or dividends. This apparent dichotomy can be easily resolved if we focus on the reasons for earnings retention.

In general, a firm may retain earnings for two main reasons. First, it may wish to bolster its holdings of liquid resources, because the distribution of dividends may run down current assets or perhaps increase borrowings. Thus, in order to hold a strong liquidity position, many profitable companies retain a large proportion of their earnings. Second, due to the availability of investment and growth opportunities, a firm may retain earnings to finance investment in fixed and other assets to generate higher future earnings and, hence, enhance its future dividend-paying capacity.

So, is there an optimal dividend policy that could maximise a firm's value? The answer to this question will depend on a firm's investor base. If a firm's investors are relying on the income stream generated from investments in shares, then, naturally, they would want their returns in the form of dividend yield and would prefer the payment of dividends over and above the retention of earnings. Market reaction is

---

*In this chapter, we assume no company borrowing, hence the value of the company is synonymous with the value of the equity. When referring to the present value of the whole equity, we use the symbol V_0, and when referring to the value of an individual share, P_0.

[†]In this and subsequent chapters, the letter E is used to denote a free cash flow concept of earnings, as explained in Chapter 7. Here, free cash flow is calculated *after* replacement investment but *before* strategic investment. Free cash flow is likely to deviate from accounting earnings, so when the latter accounting concept is intended, the phrases 'accounting profit' or 'reported earnings' are used.

therefore expected to the announcement of dividends and a resulting change in share prices. However, if investors are not relying on the income stream generated from investments in shares and trust the directors that retained earnings will be invested in profitable ventures, then they would be content with capital gains and retention of earnings. Therefore, by introducing retention and growth, the **Dividend Valuation Model** becomes the **Dividend Growth Model** (DGM).

It is important to remember that the DGM assumes a constant retention ratio and a constant return on new investment projects. If these assumptions hold, both earnings and dividends grow at the same rate. Whether this rate is acceptable to shareholders depends on the return they require from their investments, k_e. The relationship between k_e and R, the return on reinvested earnings, provides the key to resolving the valuation dispute.

Dividend Valuation Model
A way of assessing the value of shares by capitalising the future dividends. With growing dividend payments, it becomes the **Dividend Growth Model**

■ The 'traditional' view on dividend policy

Traditionally, dividend policy theory assumed that investors prefer consistent dividend payments in current years to receiving (perhaps higher) dividends or capital gains in the future. This preference is based on the argument that regards future dividend or capital gains as uncertain because of the risk involved, and therefore future dividends are valued less than current dividends. It is therefore argued that if a firm replaces the payment of current dividends with uncertain future dividends and capital gains, then investors will use a higher discount rate for covering the uncertainty and risk. The validity of this argument is, however, based on the assumption that considers risk as a function of time, over and above a firm's investing activities.

■ Dividend irrelevance in perfect capital markets

In 1961, Miller and Modigliani (MM) pointed out that earnings retention was simply one way of financing investment. According to the MM proposition, the market value of a company is determined by the earnings generated from its assets and that the split between dividend and retained earnings is irrelevant. Therefore, if a company's investment opportunities are a better option than paying out to its shareholders, under perfect capital market conditions, investors may benefit from the retention of earnings. MM argued that investors can make their own dividend policy by selling and buying shares in two ways. First, if there is a non-payment of dividend by firms and the investor wants a specific percentage of dividends, the investor can sell that percentage of his or her stock. Second, if companies pay more dividends than the investor wants, the investor can use the extra cash to buy additional shares. Under the MM theory, in both these cases, an investor would generate his/her own dividends policy.

When considering the MM theory, we need to bear in mind a number of assumptions on which it is based. In particular, the assumption of perfect capital markets with zero taxes, zero brokerage fees and no information asymmetry between shareholders and managers about the future investment opportunities of firms, are the most important elements on which this theory is based. If these conditions do not hold, then investors who receive dividends will be paying taxes on their returns, will pay commission to brokers on the buying and selling of securities and will also face the insider information advantage held by a firm's managers. The context and limitations of the MM theory therefore needs full understanding before applying it in real-world situations.

dividend irrelevance
The theory that, when firms have access to external finance, it is irrelevant to firm value whether they pay a dividend or not

The original MM analysis proves **dividend irrelevance** in terms of a single dividend cut to finance worthwhile investment. MM envisaged an all-equity-financed company that has previously paid out its entire annual net cash flow as dividend. To illustrate their analysis, let us examine the case of Divicut plc.

One-off dividend cuts: Divicut plc

Divicut currently generates a perpetual free cash flow of £1,000 p.a. Shareholders require a return of 10 per cent. The market will value Divicut at (£1,000/10%) = £10,000 on unchanged policies. If the management now decides to retain the whole of next year's earnings in order to invest in a project offering a single cash flow of £1,200 in the following year, the new market value of Divicut equals the present value of the revised dividend flow, assuming it reverts to 100 per cent payouts:

Year	1	2	3	4	etc.
Dividend (£)	0	2,200	1,000	1,000	⟶

This revised dividend flow is acceptable only if the resulting market value is at least equal to the pre-decision value, i.e. if the NPV of the project is at least zero. This is clearly the case, as the PV of the extra £1,200 in two years is greater than the PV of £1,000 less in one year, i.e.

$$\frac{£1,200}{(1.1)^2} > \frac{£1,000}{(1.1)}$$
or, £992 > £909

Divicut's shareholders are thus better off by £83.

Shareholder wealth is enhanced, since Divicut has used the funds released by the dividend cut to finance a worthwhile project. If these funds had been invested at only 10 per cent, the net effect would have been zero, while if investment had occurred at a rate of return of less than 10 per cent, shareholders would have been worse off. This simple example shows that the impact on company value is attributable to the investment, rather than the dividend, decision.

Self-assessment activity 9.2

Rework the Divicut example for the case where the returns on the new investment are £1,080 rather than £1,200 in year 2.

(Answer in Appendix A)

MM's dividend irrelevance conclusion was obtained in a world of certainty and then extended to the case of risk/uncertainty, where the same conclusions emerge so long as investor behaviour and attitudes conform to conditions of 'symmetric market rationality'. This requires the following:

1 All investors are maximisers of expected wealth.
2 All investors have similar expectations.
3 All investors behave rationally.
4 All investors believe both that other market participants will behave rationally and also that other investors expect rational behaviour from them.

These assumptions were spelled out by Brennan (1971) and form part of the battery of conditions required for a perfect capital market. The additional assumptions required to support the 'irrelevance' hypothesis are as follows:

1 No transaction costs or brokerage fees.
2 All investors have equal and costless access to information.
3 All investors can lend or borrow at the same rate of interest.
4 No buyer or seller of securities can influence prices.
5 No personal or corporate income or capital gains taxes.
6 Dividend decisions are not used to convey information.

The full significance of some of these assumptions will be highlighted when we examine some of the reasons why shareholders may have a definite preference for either dividends or retentions.

Rolls-Royce: first dividend cut in 24 years

Rolls-Royce is cutting its dividend for the first time in 24 years after a series of five profit warnings in two years eroded the UK engine maker's profits and share price. The engineer has cut the dividend even more deeply than anticipated, chopping it to 16.4 pence for 2015, down from 21.3 pence last year. Analysts had expected a 30 per cent cut to 17p in 2016 and to 16p in 2017. Rolls is also proposing to reduce its interim payment for 2016, by 50 per cent.

Despite the dividend cut, the engineer's shares jumped 14 per cent on the announcement day to 602 pence. It maintained the same guidance for 2016 that it provided at the end of the previous year – a £650m drop in pre-tax profit. The consistency is a welcome relief for investors who have had to endure a series of profit warnings.

'Given five warnings in the last two years, some may have feared worse,' said Jack O'Brien at Liberum Capital.

The shares are now flat for 2016, although they have more than halved over the last two years, even after the morning's jump. Underlying profit before tax fell 12 per cent last year to £1.43bn, on underlying revenue down 1 per cent to £13.4bn. Underlying profit at the marine division was almost entirely wiped out, dropping 94 per cent to £15m. 'The business is expected to be significantly loss-making in 2016,' the company said.

The civil aerospace division, which accounts for more than half of the group, suffered a 14 per cent decline in underlying profit to £812m.

The shares have dropped in recent weeks as investors became increasingly wary of the impending dividend cut. Not even a $2.7bn order from budget airline Norwegian Airshuttle could stimulate a notable bounce. The shares had dropped by more than 30 per cent since Warren East took over as chief executive in July.

Source: Lewin, J. (2016) Rolls-Royce: first divi cut in 24 years. *Financial Times*, 12 February. © The Financial Times Limited 2018. All rights reserved.

■ Permanent dividend cuts: more Divicut

This argument can also be applied to the case of permanent retentions using the Dividend Growth Model, although the analysis is a little more complex. Retention may lower the dividend payment only temporarily, resulting in a rate of growth yielding higher future dividends. This is shown in Figure 9.2. At point-in-time t_1, the company,

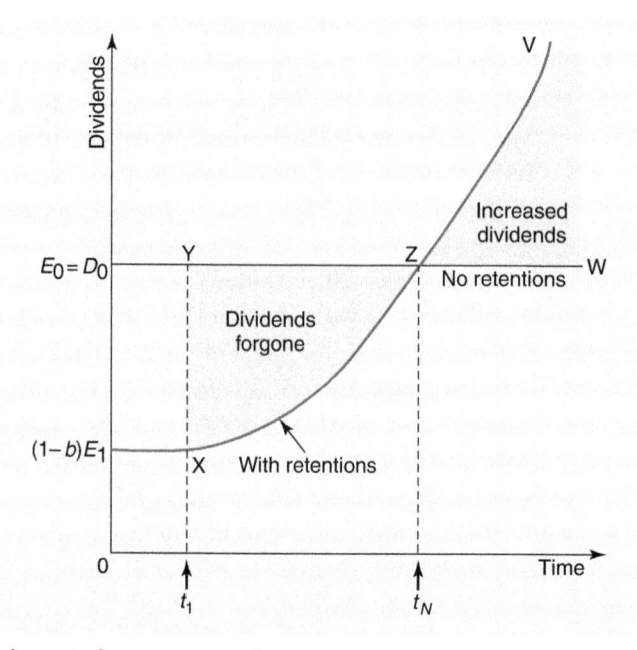

Figure 9.2 The impact of a permanent dividend cut

which currently pays out all its earnings, E_0, plans to cut dividends from D_0 to $(1 - b)E_1$, where b is the retention ratio.

Dividends do not regain their former level until time t_N, involving a cumulative loss in dividend payments equal to the area XYZ. Beyond time t_N, dividends exceed their original level as a result of continued reinvestment. Clearly, shareholders will be better off if the area of higher future dividends, VZW, exceeds XYZ (allowing for the discounting process). This holds if R, the return on retained funds, exceeds k_e. This contention can be illustrated using the example of Divicut again.

Recall that, prior to the alteration in dividend policy, the value of Divicut was £10,000, derived by discounting the perpetual earnings stream. Imagine the company announces its intention to retain 50 per cent of earnings in all future years (i.e. from and including Year 1) to finance a series of projects offering a perpetual yield of 15 per cent. Market value according to the dividend growth model is:

$$\text{Value of equity} = V_0 = \frac{E_1(1-b)}{(k_e - g)} = \frac{E_1(1-b)}{(k_e - bR)} = \frac{\pounds 1{,}000(1 - 0.5)}{0.1 - (0.5 \times 0.15)}$$
$$= \frac{\pounds 500}{0.025} = \pounds 20{,}000$$

This may seem a remarkable result. The decision to retain and reinvest doubles company value! Does this mean that dividend payments make shareholders worse off? The answer is simple.

Payment of dividends may make shareholders worse off than they otherwise might be if distribution results in failure to exploit worthwhile investment. In other words, the beneficial impact on Divicut's value is achieved because of the inherent attractions of the projected investments. Conversely, if the funds had been invested to yield only 5 per cent, market value would have fallen to £6,666.

The in-between case, where the return on reinvested funds, $R = k_e = 10$ per cent, leaves company value unchanged. This suggests that, if we strip out the effects of the investment decision, the dividend decision itself has a *neutral* effect. This can be done by assuming retentions are used to finance projects that yield an aggregate NPV of zero, i.e. yielding a return of k_e. With this assumption, dividend decisions are irrelevant to shareholder wealth. With a return on reinvested funds of 10 per cent, the company's value is:

$$\text{Value of equity} = V_0 = \frac{E_1(1-b)}{(k_e - g)} = \frac{\pounds 1{,}000(1 - 0.5)}{0.1 - (0.5 \times 0.1)} = \frac{\pounds 500}{0.05} = \pounds 10{,}000$$

Here we have valued the dividend stream, and the result is equivalent to valuing the steady stream of earnings with no retentions. This equivalence may perhaps be more readily seen by manipulating the expressions for value. If we neutralise the effect of the investment decision so that $k_e = R$, we may write:

$$\text{Value of equity} = V_0 = \frac{D_1}{(k_e - g)} = \frac{E_1(1-b)}{(k_e - g)} = \frac{E_1(1-b)}{(k_e - bR)} = \frac{E_1(1-b)}{(k_e - bk_e)} = \frac{E_1(1-b)}{k_e(1-b)} = \frac{E_1}{k_e}$$

There are clear conclusions from this analysis. In the absence of external financing:

1 *If the expected return on reinvested funds exceeds* k_e, it is beneficial to retain. A dividend cut will lead to higher value but only because funds are used to finance worthwhile projects.
2 *If the return on reinvested funds is less than* k_e, retention damages shareholder interests. A dividend cut would lower company value because shareholders have better uses for their funds.
3 *If the return on reinvested funds equals* k_e, the impact of a dividend cut to finance investment is neutral.

Self-assessment activity 9.3

How can dividend policy damage shareholder interests when no external financing is available?

(Answer in Appendix A)

■ Dividends as a residual

The dividend decision is simply the obverse of the investment decision. As observed earlier, we are examining the impact of one of the various ways in which proposed investment may be financed. Divicut is a case where the company is forced to retain funds through lack of alternative financing options. With the explicit assumption that the firm is capital-rationed having access only to internal sources of finance, we can illustrate the **residual theory of dividends**.

This theory indicates that dividends should be paid only when there are no further worthwhile investment opportunities. Having decided on the optimal set of investment projects, and determined the required amount of financing, the firm should distribute to shareholders only those funds not required for investment financing. This idea is shown graphically in Figure 9.3, using the **marginal efficiency of investment (MEI)** model, a construct borrowed from economic theory. The MEI traces out the rate of return on the last £1 invested, and thus shows investment opportunities ranked in declining order of attractiveness.

> **residual theory of dividends**
> Asserts that firms should only pay cash dividends when they have financed new investments. It assumes no access to external finance
>
> **marginal efficiency of investment (MEI)**
> A schedule listing available investments, in declining order of attractiveness

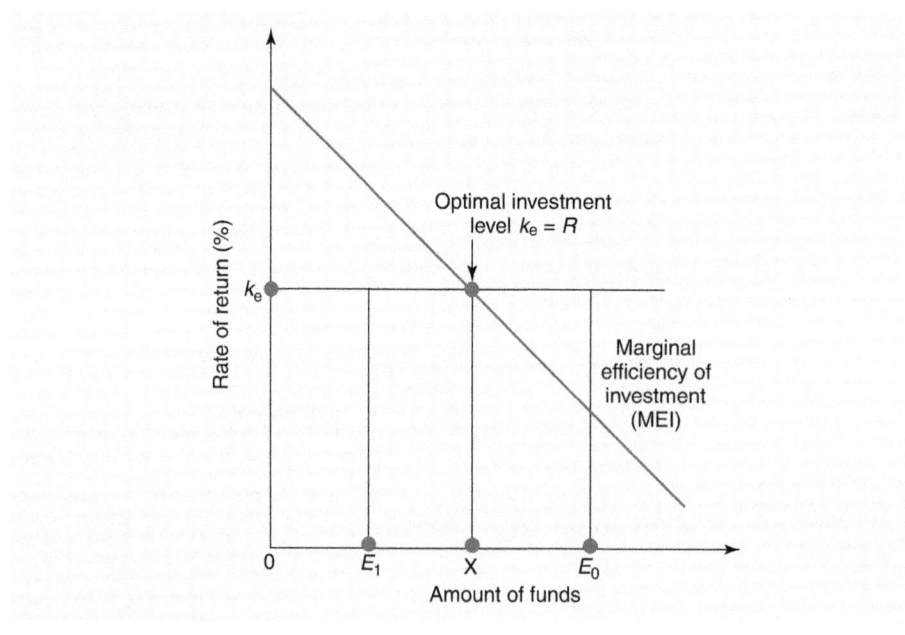

Figure 9.3 Dividends as a residual

With free cash flow of OE_0, there is scope for dividend payments. The limit of worthwhile new investment is at X, where the return on the last unit of investment is equal to the minimum required return k_e. The company can now make residual dividend payments of XE_0. However, if the free cash flow is only OE_1, distribution would impose an opportunity cost on shareholders. The whole cash flow should be reinvested, but it falls short of the finance required to support the optimal programme. The shortfall is E_1X, which could only be plugged by external financing if available.

Self-assessment activity 9.4

What dividend, if any, should the firm pay in the following situation? Earnings are £1 million, $k_e = 12$ per cent.

Project	Required outlay	IRR
A	£300,000	18%
B	£400,000	16%
C	£700,000	14%
D	£200,000	10%

(Answer in Appendix A)

External equity financing: yet more Divicut

We now consider the case where the firm has access to external financing. Rather than use earnings retention to finance investment, the firm may make a rights issue of shares, i.e. offer existing shareholders the right to buy new shares in proportion to their present holdings. If they all exercise their rights, the existing balance of control is unchanged, i.e. everyone ends up holding the same proportionate share of the firm. To sustain the irrelevance conclusion, we need to show that shareholder wealth is unaffected by choice of financing method, retention or new issues.

Consider the case where Divicut contemplates a one-off dividend cut to finance a project that requires a cash outlay of £1,000, and offers perpetual earnings of £200 p.a. The shares are not yet quoted ex-dividend. The options are to:

1. Retain the earnings.
2. Pay the dividend out of earnings and then recoup the cash via a rights issue.

The project itself is worthwhile, since its NPV is:

$$\text{NPV} = -£1,000 + \frac{£200}{0.1} = -£1,000 + £2,000 = +£1,000$$

The implications for shareholder wealth of each financing alternative are respectively:

1. If the dividend is passed, the value of shareholder wealth (W_0) is:

    W_0 = (dividend in year 0) + (PV of dividends from existing projects)
        + (PV of dividends from new projects)

    $$= 0 + \frac{£1,000}{0.1} + \frac{£200}{0.1} = (£10,000 + £2,000) = £12,000$$

    Retention therefore benefits Divicut's shareholders, since £1,000 now is exchanged for a dividend stream with present value of £2,000.

2. If a rights issue is used to recoup the required capital, the wealth of shareholders is:

    W_0 = (dividend in year 0) + (PV of dividends from existing projects)
        + (PV of dividends from new projects)
        − (amount subscribed for new shares)

    $$= £1,000 + \frac{£1,000}{0.1} + \frac{£200}{0.1} - £1,000$$

    $$= (£1,000 + £10,000 + £2,000) - £1,000 = £12,000$$

Shareholders' wealth is unaffected if they subscribe for the new shares, anticipating the higher future stream of dividends implied by the new venture. The attraction of the rights issue to some people is that it offers a choice between further investment in the company and an alternative use of capital (although this second option may be irrational if k_e accurately measures the opportunity cost of capital). Either way, in practice, companies often ensure they obtain the required funds by employing specialist financial institutions to underwrite such issues.

Summary

This section has demonstrated that dividends are relevant to company valuation in the absence of external financing, but only in the sense that, if the company has better investment opportunities than its shareholders, payment of dividends prevents worthwhile investment. With external financing, however, in a perfect capital market, dividends become totally irrelevant since dividend payment no longer precludes worthwhile investment. The firm can simply recoup the required finance via a rights issue.

In the next section, we begin to unpick some of the assumptions underpinning the irrelevance theory and consider the implications of doing so.

9.5 OBJECTIONS TO DIVIDEND IRRELEVANCE

This section examines some of the arguments advanced against the irrelevance theory. Financial managers should weigh up several important considerations before deciding upon the appropriate dividend payout policy:

- To what extent do shareholders rely on dividend income?
- Are nearer-in-time dividends less risky than future dividends?
- Do market imperfections lead companies to adopt policies that attract a particular clientèle of investors?
- Would investors accept a rights issue?
- How does taxation affect dividend policy?

Let us deal with these questions in turn.

Do shareholders rely on dividend income to support expenditure?

Shareholders who require a steady and reliable stream of income from dividends may be concerned by a sudden change in dividend policy, especially a dividend cut, albeit to finance worthwhile projects. Some groups of shareholders may well have a definite preference for current income: for example, the elderly, and institutions such as pension funds, that depend on a stable flow of income to meet their largely predictable liabilities. However, in an efficient capital market, such shareholders should be no worse off after a dividend cut, since the value of their holdings will rise on the news of the new investment. They can realise some or all of their gains, thus converting capital into income. The capital released is called a '**home-made dividend**'. (This is similar to the 'equity release schemes' whereby UK home-owners extract some of the value locked up in their homes.) A worked example of this procedure is given in the Appendix to this chapter.

home-made dividend
Cash released when an investor realises part of his or her investment in a firm in order to supplement his/her income

There are several criticisms of the validity of the home-made dividends mechanism. Even in the absence of market imperfections, the investor is forced to incur the inconvenience of making the required portfolio adjustments. Allowing for brokerage and other transactions costs, the net benefits of the project for the income-seeking investor are reduced. Also, if capital gains are taxed, the enforced share sale may trigger a tax liability. In the case of only marginally attractive projects, these effects may be sufficient to more than offset the benefits of the project, at least for some investors. Conversely, it can be argued that payment of a dividend to investors who then incur brokerage fees in reinvesting their income is equally disadvantageous.

Are future dividends seen as more risky by shareholders?

The practical limitations on the unfettered ability to home-make dividends were spelt out by Myron Gordon (1963) in a ringing attack on MM's irrelevance conclusion. However, Gordon extended his critique of MM to argue that $1 of dividend now is necessarily valued more highly than $1 of retained earnings because investors regard the (albeit higher) future stream of dividends stemming from a new project as carrying a higher level of risk. In other words, investors prefer what Gordon called an 'early resolution of uncertainty'. Gordon was, in effect, arguing that shareholders evaluate future expected dividends using a set of rising discount rates. If present dividends are reduced to allow greater investment, thus shifting the dividend pattern into the future, company value will fall.

Keane (1974) refined Gordon's position by suggesting that it is secondary whether, in fact, future dividends are more risky than near ones. If investors *perceive* them to be riskier, a policy of higher retentions, while not actually increasing risk, may unfavourably alter investor attitudes. In capital markets where full information is not released about investment projects, investors' subjective risk assessments may result in low-payout companies being valued at a discount compared to high-payout companies: that is, investors' imperfect perceptions of risk may lead them to undervalue the future dividend stream generated by retentions.

The 'bird-in-the-hand fallacy'

If the firm's dividend policy does alter the perceived riskiness of the expected dividend flow, there may be an optimal dividend policy that trades off the beneficial effects of an enhanced growth rate against the adverse impact of increased perceived risk, so as to maximise the market value. However, advocates of dividend irrelevance argue that Gordon's analysis is inherently fallacious. More distant dividends are more risky only if they stem from inherently riskier investment projects. Risk should already have been catered for by discounting cash flows at a suitably risk-adjusted rate. To deflate future dividends for risk further would involve double-counting. There is no reason why risk necessarily increases with time – a model based on this supposition incorporates the 'bird-in-the-hand fallacy'. According to MM (1961), dividend policy remains a 'mere detail' once a firm's investment policy, and its inherent business risks, is made known. This argument is examined more rigorously by Bhattacharya (1979).

bird-in-the-hand fallacy
The mistaken belief that dividends paid early in the future are worth more than dividends expected in later time periods, simply because they are nearer in time and viewed as less risky

Self-assessment activity 9.5

Why is Gordon's 'early resolution of uncertainty' argument in favour of paying early dividends logically flawed?

(Answer in Appendix A)

Market imperfections and the clientèle effect

The extent to which investors are willing and able to home-make dividends, and thus adjust the company's actual dividend pattern to suit their own personal desired consumption plans, depends on the degree of imperfection in the capital market. In practice, numerous impediments, especially when aggregated, may significantly offset the benefits of exploiting a profitable project. Some of these have already been mentioned, but the main ones are as follows:

- Brokerage costs incurred when shares are sold.
- Other transaction costs incurred, e.g. the costs of searching out the cheapest brokerage facilities.
- The loss in interest incurred in waiting for settlement.

- The problem of indivisibilities, whereby investors may be unable to sell the precise number of shares required, forcing them to deal in sub-optimal batch sizes.
- The sheer inconvenience of being forced to alter one's portfolio.
- Share sales may trigger a Capital Gains Tax liability.
- If the company is relatively small, its shares may lack marketability, requiring a significant dealing spread and hence a leakage of shareholder capital.
- If the company is unquoted, it may be difficult or impossible to find a buyer for the shares.

Under such imperfections, maximising firm value may not be the unique desire of all shareholders; the pattern of receipt of wealth may become equally or more important. Some shareholders may prefer companies that offer dividend flows which correspond to their desired consumption, perhaps being prepared to pay a premium to hold these shares. In this way, they avoid having to make their own adjustments. The vehicle for aiding such investors is to provide a stable and known dividend stream. Shareholders can then perceive the nature of the likely future dividend pattern and decide whether or not the company's policy meets their requirements. In other words, the company attracts, and attempts to cater for, a **clientèle** of shareholders.

However, such a policy has costs, including the benefits forgone from projects that might have to be passed over, the costs of borrowing if debt finance is used and/or the issue expenses of a rights issue if external financing is employed. The implications for control if rights are not fully exercised by the existing shareholders may be another problem.

The key difficulty facing the financial manager is lack of knowledge of shareholder preferences, without which it is difficult to balance the two sets of costs.

Self-assessment activity 9.6

What is meant by a shareholder clientèle? Which shareholders are most likely to prefer near-in-time dividends?

(Answer in Appendix A)

Problems with rights issues: Rawdon plc

Among the effects of a rights issue are the costs incurred. These can be substantial and will affect the required return on new investment. Among the costs are the administrative expenses, the costs of printing brochures and circulation of these to shareholders, and also the underwriters' fees. The impact of these costs is examined using the case of Rawdon plc, whose details are shown in Table 9.2.

Table 9.2 **Rawdon plc**

- $k_e = 20\%$
- Rawdon's value = £5m
- 1m shares have been issued in the past
- Market price per share is £5
- Current company earnings = £1m (EPS = £1)
- Proposed investment outlay = £950,000
- The project has a perpetual life.
- Terms of rights issue:
  One share for every five held, i.e. 200,000 new shares.
  Purchase price £5: gross proceeds = £1m
  Issue costs: 5% of gross receipts = (0.05 × £1m) = £50,000
  Net proceeds = £950,000

Although Rawdon's shareholders require a return of 20 per cent, the new project has to offer a return of *over* 20 per cent. This is because some of the finance raised by the share issue is required to meet the costs of the issue, but the holders of those shares will nevertheless demand a return. Total share capital is now £6 million, and earnings of £1.2 million are now required to generate a 20 per cent return overall. However, the required increase in earnings of £0.2 million must be generated by an investment of £950,000, necessitating a return of (£0.2m/£0.95m =) 21.1 per cent. Rawdon's required return on this project is given by:

$$\frac{\text{Normally required return}}{(1 - \% \text{ issue costs})} = \frac{k_e}{(1 - c)} = \frac{0.2}{(1 - 0.05)} = 0.211, \text{ i.e. } 21.1\%$$

However, the problem of transactions costs may operate in another direction. Some shareholders, when paid a dividend, may incur some reinvestment costs. The higher the proportion of investors who wish to reinvest, either in the same or in another company, the greater the total saving of brokerage and other fees enjoyed by shareholders when the company retains earnings. Hence, the greater is the attraction of retained earnings to finance investment.

Bearing in mind the impact on share price, the announcement of a rights issue is not always greeted with delight. The shareholder is forced either to take up or sell the rights in order to avoid losing money (even sale of rights will result in brokerage fees), and thus incur the inconvenience involved. If the market takes a dim view of the proposed use of the capital raised (for example, if the funds are required to finance a takeover whose benefits look distinctly speculative), the share price may fall. *But it is important to realise that this would be a consequence of a faulty investment decision rather than of the financing decision itself.*

The impact of taxation

In many economies, the tax treatment of dividend income and realised capital gains differs, either via differential tax rates or via different levels of exemption allowed, or both. In such regimes, the theoretical equivalence between dividends and retention becomes further distorted. Typically, tax on capital gains is lower than tax on income from dividends. In some countries, there is *no* tax on capital gains. Some shareholders might prefer 'home-made dividends' (i.e. selling shares) now or in the future when the rate of **Capital Gains Tax (CGT)** is lower than the marginal rate of income tax applied to dividends. Others may prefer dividend payments because their income tax liability (plus any reinvestment costs) is lower than CGT payments.

Capital Gains Tax (CGT)
Paid on realising an increase in share value. Capital gains are currently taxed as income in the United Kingdom depending on the investor's marginal tax rate

In addition to considerations of personal taxation, where the financial manager is often unaware of the particular tax positions of shareholders (a major exception to this is the case of institutional investors), complications may also be imposed by the corporate tax system. In an imputation tax system, shareholders receive dividend income net of basic rate tax, while the rate of tax applied to corporate profits is designed to include an element of personal tax, thus making the distribution of dividends tax-neutral.

There are so many different tax regimes operated throughout the world that it is difficult to generalise about the effect of taxation on dividend policy. However, the following simple example captures the flavour of some of the issues.

Barlow plc

Barlow plc is financed entirely by equity and its future cash flows have present value of £500 million at the start of 2017. During the whole year, it earns £100 million – for simplicity, we assume that all transactions are in cash, so it now holds cash of £100 million. Profits are taxed at 30 per cent, so Barlow must set aside £30 million for tax payments, leaving £70m (70% × £100m) available for distribution. According to the EMH, the firm will be valued at £570m (£500m + £70m).

Should Barlow distribute or retain? The answer depends on three factors:

- shareholders' marginal rates of tax;
- the relative rate of tax on dividends vs. tax on capital gains;
- the type of tax regime.

classical tax system
A system where dividends are effectively taxed twice – the firm pays profits tax and then investors pay income tax on any dividend payment

Under a **classical tax system**, profits are taxed twice if distributed, first, as profits tax, and second, as income tax paid by investors. Imagine the firm makes a full distribution. Consider two rates of investor income tax:

(i) if investors pay tax at 10%, income tax is (10% × £70m) = £7m, and the total tax charge is (£30m + £7m) = £37m (or 37 per cent of pre-tax earnings);

(ii) if investors pay tax at 50%, income tax is (50% × £70m) = £35m, and the total tax charge is (£30m + £35m) = £65m (or 65 per cent of pre-tax earnings).

It looks better to retain in the second case, but the decision also depends on the rate of Capital Gains Tax (CGT).

Assume the CGT rate is 20 per cent. If we also assume that the firm invests in zero-NPV projects (unlikely, but a necessary assumption to strip out the effect of the investment decision), the value of the firm will have risen from £500 million at start-year to £570 million at end-year. The CGT payable is thus (20% × £70m) = £14m. Along with the profits tax, the total tax payable is (£30m + £14m) = £44m.

Obviously, shareholders paying income tax at 50 per cent would prefer retention and vice versa.

Under an **imputation tax system**, the relative attractiveness of distribution and retention depends not only on the relative tax rates, but also on whether there is full or partial imputation.

With full imputation, investors get full credit for corporate profits tax already paid.

In case (i) presented earlier, the investor would face no further tax on income and may even get a tax rebate, depending on the tax regime, because the rate of corporate tax exceeds the rate of personal tax.

In case (ii), the investor obtains credit for the corporate tax already paid, and thus faces an additional income tax charge of (50% − 30%) × £70m = £14m. With these particular figures, investors would be indifferent between distribution and retention.

With partial imputation, it is less clear-cut – the relative desirability of distribution and retention depends on the degree of imputation, as well as the respective tax rates.

Current UK rates

Under the present UK system of partial imputation, income from dividends and capital gains are taxed at different rates, and different tax thresholds also apply. According to the UK Government tax reforms which have been effective from 6 April 2016, there is discrimination in favour of capital gains. Somewhat confusingly, beyond a threshold of £11,300, individuals who pay income tax at 20 per cent pay CGT at 10 per cent, and those who pay income tax at 40 per cent or more pay CGT at 20 per cent. Special rates also apply for entrepreneurs selling up a business, and for disposals of non-residential property.

In the United Kingdom, as from 6 April 2017, individuals were eligible to receive a dividend tax allowance of £5,000, but this is due to fall to £2,000 in April 2018. Beyond this allowance, any dividend income is charged tax at 7.5 per cent for the basic rate taxpayer, 32.5 per cent for higher rate taxpayers, and 38.1 per cent for additional rate taxpayers.

The tax irrelevance thesis

Some argue that, under perfect capital markets, the question of relative tax rates is irrelevant because of arbitrage. Zero/low-rate taxpayers prefer to hold shares in firms with high payouts, and those with high marginal rates of tax prefer low-payout firms. The process of tax-driven arbitrage would lead each group to bid up the share prices of the firms whose distribution policy suits their own particular tax positions, until in equilibrium, post-tax rates of return are equalised. This means there is no share price advantage to be obtained from following a particular dividend policy.

Elton and Gruber (1970) noted the importance of marginal tax brackets in determining the return required by shareholders. They defined the cost of using retained earnings as 'that rate which makes a firm's marginal shareholders indifferent between earnings being retained or paid out in the form of dividends'. Under differential tax treatments of dividend income and capital gains, the cost of using retained earnings is a function of the shareholder's marginal tax bracket. We might also expect companies whose shareholders incur high rates of income tax to exhibit low payout rates. Such a relationship between corporate dividend policy and shareholder tax brackets would support the notion of 'tax clientèles', whereby companies seek to tailor their payout policies to the tax situation of particular shareholders. Elton and Gruber's empirical work seemed to indicate that firms attract rational clientèles – *shareholders gravitate to companies whose distribution policy is compatible with their personal tax situations.*

9.6 THE INFORMATION CONTENT OF DIVIDENDS: DIVIDEND SMOOTHING

Possibly the most important consideration for corporate financial decision-makers when framing dividend policy is the information-processing capacity of the market. Any dividend declaration can be interpreted by the market in a variety of ways. In an uncertain world, information regarding a company's prospects is neither generally available nor costless to acquire. Managers possess more information about the company's trading position than is available to investors as a whole. This **information asymmetry** may mean that the announcement of a new or changed company policy may be interpreted by the market as a *signal* conveying particular information about a company's prospects, as in the Costco cameo that follows.

information asymmetry
The imbalance between managers and owners of information possessed about a firm's financial state and its prospects

For example, the decision to pay an unexpectedly high dividend may be seized upon as evidence of greater expected dividend-paying capacity in the future. It may be taken as guaranteeing an ability to sustain at least the higher declared dividend and probably more. As a result, the financial manager should consider carefully how the market is likely to decode the signals contained in the dividend decision, and the likely consequences for share price.

Costco

The stock market is bad at maths, or accounting, or possibly both. Yesterday, the discount warehouse club Costco announced a special dividend of $7 per share – a meaty payout for a stock that traded at about $97 before the announcement. Giddy buyers bid the shares up by as much as $6.

In theory, though, a dividend should not affect the value of a company. Costco's dividend will take $3bn in cash off the asset side of its balance sheet; retained earnings will drop by the same amount. Investors end up with $7 in their pockets and a share that is worth, on paper, $7 less.

There are forms of value not reflected by a balance sheet. The equity of a company is worth more if its management has a record of allocating capital wisely: deploying cash internally when high-returning opportunities are present, paying it out otherwise. A one-time dividend does not, however, demonstrate enough management skill to increase the value of a $42bn company by 6 per cent. One might argue that the special dividend signals insiders' confidence that profits are headed up. But Costco is not about to introduce an amazing new product or radical new strategy. It is a big-box retailer. The insiders can see

Continued

Costco's future only slightly better than anyone who reads its reports.

The punters bidding up Costco might suggest, finally, that $7 is worth more to investors now than it will be next year, when US Federal taxes on dividends are expected to rise. Fair enough. How much should this boost the value of a Costco share before the dividend is paid? By, at most, the difference between the payout's current and future after-tax values. Assuming the current 15 per cent tax rate goes to a draconian 38 per cent, that is about $1.61. That leaves believers in the efficient market hypothesis with, say, $4.50 of share price change to explain away.

FT *Source:* Column, L. (2012). *Financial Times*, 29 November, p. 14. © The Financial Times Limited 2018. All rights reserved.

signalling
Using financial announcements to deliver more information than is actually spelled out in detail

Company finance directors (FDs) are well aware of the **signalling** power of dividends and their capacity to influence share price.

Smoothing' of dividends can be found among many firms and has been identified empirically. Lintner (1956) showed that companies appear to raise dividends only on the basis of reported earnings increases that they expect to sustain in the long term. In a survey of 179 Finance Directors of large quoted companies conducted by 3i (1993), 43 per cent said that the single most important factor influencing dividend policy was prospective long-term profit growth, while 93 per cent agreed with the statement that 'dividend policy should follow the long-term trend in earnings'.

So do companies ever cut dividends? Obviously, in adversity, dividend cuts are forced on firms in order to preserve cash. In the 3i survey, 55 per cent of FDs agreed with the statement that 'any cut in dividend payout sends adverse signals to the market and should be avoided'. Dividend-cutting is far more common in the United States than in the United Kingdom. Empirical work by Ghosh and Woolridge (1989) suggests that even when this was motivated by the need to conserve funds for investment purposes, shareholders suffered significant capital losses, despite the merits claimed for the proposed investments. In the United Kingdom, it is almost unheard of for companies to cut dividends to finance investment – the dividend payment-plus-rights issue is invariably the preferred alternative. In the 3i survey, one FD said that 'a dividend cut is a sign of fundamental management failure – when management fails and the Board should change'. But, a dividend cut might be construed as a prudent move in sharply deteriorating market conditions as in the late 2000s. In adversity, *not* to cut a dividend may be seen as a sign of financial recklessness.

9.7 WORKED EXAMPLE

The data given below relate to three firms' dividend payouts over the last six years. None of the companies has issued, or cancelled, any shares over the period. All three firms are listed on the London Stock Exchange.

		2012	2013	2014	2015	2016	2017
Company A							
Shares issued	1,200m						
Profit after tax (£m)		600	630	580	600	640	660
Dividends declared (£m)		240	252	232	240	256	264
Company B							
Shares issued	2,000m						
Profit after tax (£m)		1,200	1,300	1,580	1,800	1,240	1,460
Dividends declared (£m)		120	132	145	160	176	194
Company C							
Shares issued	3,500m						
Profit after tax (£m)		2,200	1,400	2,100	1,950	2,200	2,560
Dividends declared (£m)		200	0	100	0	200	560

Required

Showing appropriate calculations, describe the dividend policy which each of the companies shown above appears to be following.

How would you justify each of these policies to the shareholders of each of the companies concerned?

Answers

General comments

Company A

This firm pays out a constant percentage (40 per cent) of profit after tax as dividend. It is thus prepared to tolerate fluctuations in the actual amount paid and, hence, DPS, as corporate profits, and thus EPS, oscillate. DPS fluctuates from a high of 20p in 2012 to a low of 19.3p in 2014, ending up at 22p in 2017. The range of fluctuation is thus quite narrow.

In brief: constant payout (and cover),
variable DPS

Company B

This firm increases the amount of dividend and thus the DPS by a constant 10 per cent p.a., come what may, in terms of PAT and EPS. The dividend cover thus takes the strain, although it is never less than 7 times (2016).

In brief: rising DPS,
variable payout (and cover)

Company C

This firm pays out any excess of PAT above a base level of £2 billion, accepting a zero payout if PAT undershoots this figure.

In brief: variable DPS,
variable payout (and cover)

Interpretation

The nature of the industry in which the firms operate could well be an important influence on dividend policy. Profits are relatively stable for Company A but oscillate wildly in the case of Company C. Hence, A is able to pay out a relatively high proportion in dividends reasonably safe in the knowledge that profits will soon recover after a bad year as they did in 2015, exceeding the previous peak of 2013 shortly afterwards in 2016. The maintenance of a high payout (if not the actual DPS) might be taken as an expression of confidence in the future and thus perform an important signalling function. Indeed, the fall in DPS in 2014 might be taken as a sign of financial prudence – conserving cash at a time of faltering performance.

It is likely that Company A has a clientèle that relies on a high level of dividend income, although one that is prepared to accept some belt-tightening in lean years. A fluctuating DPS does impact on liquidity; e.g. in the leaner years, despite the cut in DPS, the amount of retained earnings and, by implication, free cash flow is reduced, perhaps impacting on investment expenditure. However, it is unlikely that firms would want to push ahead with substantial investments in the lean years (although there is a strong argument in favour of this, i.e. to be primed for the fat years when they arrive). Also, if the industry is stable, and the firm has a solid record of increasing profits over time, then it may have good access to capital markets. A high payout also has agency advantages – managers have less access to discretionary spending that may not necessarily be in the best interests of the owners.

Looking at Company C, its base profits level of £2 billion before a dividend payment is made suggests that it has an ongoing investment programme to fund and is thus concerned about liquidity, or that it is highly geared and faces debt covenants that stipulate this profits threshold before a dividend can be paid. The fluctuations in profits and the dividend policy imply that the shareholder clientèle is relatively unconcerned by dividend income, but is more interested in profits and value growth. The industry is probably a high-risk one, perhaps a New Economy one, with attractive long-term prospects. Clearly, this is a residual dividend policy where other demands on cash flow take precedence over distribution of profits. Eventually, however, like the cash-rich Microsoft ultimately did, the firm will exhaust its (organic) growth potential and will have to frame a coherent dividend policy.

Finally, Company B has a highly predictable dividend policy that allows shareholders to anticipate the next year's income with great accuracy and confidence. This will suit a variety of clientéles that rely on a predictable stream of income such as institutional investors and personal investors advanced in years. However, the payout ratio is not high, so the firm is taking no risks in terms of the sustainability of its policy, i.e. there is plenty of slack to enable an increase in DPS even in bad years such as 2016. This suggests that it is using retained earnings to a significant extent to finance growth, possibly because it faces difficult access to the capital markets – perhaps it is a relatively young firm or has high gearing. Either way, it is unlikely to have to endure the ignominy of cutting the dividend in the future – profits would have to fall over 80 per cent before the dividend was uncovered.

Vodafone's special payout poised to bolster dividend payments in UK to record £100bn

Gross dividend payments from UK companies are set to exceed £100bn next year for the first time, according to research from Capita Asset Services. The record payout will be boosted by the £16.6bn special dividend from Vodafone, the study points out. Altogether, the telecoms group is handing shareholders just over £54bn – almost three-quarters of the net proceeds from the sale of its 45 per cent stake in Verizon Wireless.

Without the Vodafone payment, the Capita research suggests that the outlook for dividend growth is far gloomier than the double-digit percentage increases seen in 2011 and 2012.

Capita says that, while dividend payments in the third quarter typically outstrip those paid in the second quarter, this year, the headline payments to the end of October totalled £25.3bn – lower than the distribution in the three months to end of June. This is the first time since 2008 that the third quarter has not been the period of the largest dividend payout.

Year-on-year growth had also slowed with the 6.6 per cent increase in underlying dividends over the third quarter of 2012, lagging behind the 7.7 per cent rise in the first half of 2013 against last year.

'Profits of the UK's main companies have not yet shown strong signs of recovery. Indeed, they have been falling quite sharply over the last year across a wide variety of sectors as the sluggish economy has meant minimal pricing power, while costs of all kinds have been increasing, putting a squeeze on margins,' Capita says.

But profits are still larger than dividend payments and many companies can call on the cash piles they have built up during the past couple of years to sustain dividend increases ahead of earnings growth.

Regular dividends are a much bigger feature this year than they were in 2012, when one-off income payments of £6.8bn enabled companies to respond to shareholder calls for cash without getting locked into a progressive ordinary dividend policy that might be difficult to maintain.

Source: Alison Smith, *Financial Times*, 21 October 2013, p. 20.

9.8 ALTERNATIVES TO CASH DIVIDENDS

The motive for cutting a dividend is to save cash outflows. This suggests that liquidity considerations are another influence on the dividend decision. This section discusses how firms that wish to preserve liquidity can still offer 'dividends', and also how firms

Liquidity-saving alternatives

(i) Scrip dividends

scrip dividends
Offered to investors in lieu of the equivalent cash payment. Also called a **scrip alternative**

Most major companies offer shareholders **scrip dividends**. This is an opportunity to receive new shares instead of a cash dividend payment. It has certain advantages for both the shareholder and the company.

From the firm's point of view, the scrip alternative preserves liquidity, which may be important at a time of cash shortage and/or high borrowing costs, although it could face a higher level of cash outflows if shareholders revert to preference for cash in the future. With more shares issued, the company's reported financial gearing may fall, possibly enhancing borrowing capacity. In this respect, the scrip dividend resembles a mini-rights issue.

For shareholders wishing to expand their holdings, the scrip is a cheap way into the company as it avoids dealing fees and Stamp Duty (currently, 0.5 per cent in the United Kingdom). A scrip dividend has no tax advantages for shareholders as it is treated as income for tax purposes.

In an efficient capital market, there is no dilution effect on the share price, because it would have fallen anyway with a cash dividend due to the 'ex-dividend effect'. However, if the additional capital retained is expected to be used wisely, the share price may be maintained or may even rise, giving shareholders who elect for the scrip dividend access to higher future dividends and capital gains. As a result, there may be a longer-term tax advantage for shareholders. However, most of these effects are marginal. Perhaps the main benefit of a scrip dividend is that, by giving shareholders a choice, it makes the shares more attractive to a wider clientèle.

(ii) Enhanced scrip dividends

To overcome the low take-up rate of scrip dividends, in 1993, several companies with chronic liquidity problems began to offer 'enhanced scrip dividends' (ESDs). The first to do so was BAT Industries (www.bat.com), which announced a scrip alternative 50 per cent above the equivalent cash dividend, designed to be so generous that shareholders could not refuse. BAT declared a 22.6p final dividend, and then, later that month, offered an ESD alternative of 33.9p. Had all of BAT's shareholders taken up the ESD, the cash saving would have been £423 million.

The ESD mechanism is a rights issue in disguise. To the extent that shareholders take the scrip alternative, the company is left with as much cash as if it had paid a cash dividend and then clawed it back from the same shareholders via a rights issue. As with a rights issue, the number of shares issued will rise. Finally, because the scrip is voluntary, the control of shareholders taking cash is diluted.

Self-assessment activity 9.7

How many shares would an investor receive in lieu of cash dividends of £1,000 if offered:

(i) a pro rata scrip alternative?
(ii) an ESD of 20%?

Share price is £20.

(Answer in Appendix A)

Scrips and Drips

The effect of dividend reinvestment is often illustrated by this startling statistic from the annual Barclays Equity-Gilt study: £100 invested in the UK stock market in 1899 would have been worth £12,655 (in nominal terms) by the end of 2010 without reinvestment, and £1.7m with all dividends reinvested.

Even over shorter time-frames, dividend reinvestment makes a difference. But how do you actually go about reinvesting dividends? It depends which companies' shares you own, and how you hold them.

A few big companies – including Shell, Aviva and SSE – operate scrip dividend schemes, where the company issues shares to the value of a cash dividend. Because these are new shares, there is no stamp duty or brokerage charge to pay, so it's the most cost-effective way of reinvesting dividends.

More common is the dividend reinvestment plan (Drip). These are operated by the company's registrar, and use the cash dividend to buy existing shares in the market. There is typically a charge of about 0.5 per cent of the transaction value. Any unused cash is carried forward. Many larger companies and investment trusts operate Drips.

To participate in a scrip or a Drip, your name must appear on the company's share register, so you will need to hold share certificates or have personal membership of Crest, the UK's settlement system. If you hold your shares in a nominee account – as you must do if you have a self-select ISA – then your name will not appear on the register and you will be unable to use a Drip. However, many brokers offer a dividend reinvestment service, typically charging £1.50 per line of stock. For small shareholdings, this may be uneconomic, but will make sense for larger ones.

Source: Elay, J. (2012) Dividend reinvestment: scrips and drips. *Financial Times*, 27 October. © The Financial Times Limited 2018. All rights reserved.

■ Liquidity-reducing alternatives

The dividend decision is contorted by the case of companies with too much cash.

As an alternative to paying cash dividends, the facility to repurchase shares, subject to shareholders' approval, was introduced in the United Kingdom by the 1981 Companies Act. It resulted from pressure from the small firms lobby, concerned that low marketability of unquoted firms' equity was hampering their development. Certain conditions were stipulated, designed principally to safeguard the position of creditors, and further restrictions were imposed by the Stock Exchange and the Takeover Panel, aimed at reducing the risk of market-rigging during takeover battles. The first major company to mount such a **buy-back** was GEC in 1984, ostensibly to raise the EPS of the remaining shares. A component of British Airport Authority's (failed) defence package against a takeover bid in 2006 was a share repurchase, designed to raise the cost of the bid.

Share repurchase (or buy-back)
Where a firm offers to purchase existing shares from owners for cash

The Bank of England (1988) cited five possible reasons for repurchases:

- To return surplus cash to shareholders.
- To increase underlying share value.
- To support share price during periods of temporary weakness.
- To achieve or maintain a target capital structure.
- To prevent or inhibit unwelcome takeover bids.

The hoped-for increase in share price works through the effect on EPS. A company may attempt a buy-back when it has a cash surplus beyond what it needs to finance normal business operations. This situation is assumed in Table 9.3, which shows the before-and-after situation of a company sitting on a cash pile of £100 million earning interest at 5 per cent. It buys in 20 million shares at 180p, above the market price of 172p, the discrepancy being due to the premium required to attract enough sellers. The total buy-back cost is therefore £36 million, on which the company will lose interest income.

US evidence suggests repurchasing shares may have a strong signalling effect, whereby executives can express confidence in their firms by investing in equity. Yet

Table 9.3 Analysis of a share repurchase

	Before	After
Trading profit (£m)	200.00	200.00
Interest income at 5% (£m)	5.00	3.20
Pre-tax profit (£m)	205.00	203.20
Tax at 30% (£m)	(61.50)	(60.96)
Profits available for shareholders (£m)	143.50	142.24
Number of shares in issue	500m	480m
EPS (p)	28.70	29.63
P:E Ratio	6:1	6:1
Share price (p)	172	178
Cash balances (£m)	100.00	64.00

there remains a strong suspicion in the United Kingdom that such messages may be decoded adversely. To some critics, buy-backs are tantamount to an admission of managerial failure, signalling lack of confidence in their ability to identify and exploit wealth-creating projects.

Unclear outlook gives buy-backs a special appeal

Uncertainty about the outlook for global economic growth and corporate earnings has left equity market investors seeking fresh strategies. Could the current strength of companies' balance sheets provide inspiration? Brain Belski, chief investment strategist at BMO Capital Markets, says companies that repurchase shares consistently outperform the market.

'Repurchase strategies – often overlooked by investors – are particularly important during periods of anaemic earnings growth,' he says. 'We believe companies will struggle to deliver high rates of EPS growth in the upcoming reporting periods, given what is likely to be subdued economic growth. Unfortunately, most companies have been reluctant to part with their enormous cash piles in any significant way, despite vigorous pleas from investors to utilise cash in a more productive manner.'

'Therefore, until this scenario changes, overall market earnings growth is likely to struggle. In the meantime, companies that are in a position to repurchase shares are likely to benefit. For instance, we found that companies with the highest amount of share repurchases deliver the best average relative performance during periods of slow or negative overall EPS growth.'

'Robert Buckland, equity strategist at Citigroup, points out that, even though interest rates have increased during the last couple of months, debt financing is still cheap by historical standards, especially when compared with equity financing.'

'Given the large cash piles on company balance sheets, we think companies will continue to return capital to shareholders via buybacks,' he says. 'We find that companies doing buybacks have tended to be strong performers.'

'The percentage of S&P 500 earnings paid out as dividends – the payout ratio – has averaged 54 per cent since the early 1900s, yet stands at just 36 per cent today,' says Cheryl Rowan, portfolio strategist at Bofa ML. '[That] despite the fact that 82 per cent of securities in the index pay dividends – a level not seen since September 1999.'

Source: Shellock, D. (2013) Share buybacks could provide equity inspiration. *Financial Times*, 21 August. © The Financial Times Limited 2018. All rights reserved.

However, investment expenditure is rarely a continuous process, and small buy-backs may be a useful way of investing temporary cash surpluses, with the beneficial effects on EPS and share price providing a platform for a subsequent rights issue if development funds are needed. In addition, buy-backs may be a useful alternative to paying higher but unsustainable dividends, while preserving choice for investors.

Buy-backs: a word of warning

Share buy-back is a mechanism through which listed companies buy their own shares from secondary markets. This mechanism thus reduces the number of listed companies' outstanding shares in the marketplace. Share buy-backs are generally used by firms' management for passing a positive signal to the market as it may infer that the firm's shares are currently undervalued. This has also been regarded as a useful mechanism for those companies which possess more cash and want to make changes to their capital structure. It has been observed that those firms which use stock options as a way of compensation to their employees usually buy back shares in the stock market and use those shares to fund stock options-based compensation to their employees. In addition, share buy-backs have the advantage over dividend payments because Capital Gains Tax is paid with a delay.

However, one of the unfortunate consequences of buy-backs is that (admittedly with the benefit of hindsight) they can make directors look rather foolish. If, after the buy-back, the share price falls, it means that more money has been expended on the buy-back than would have been required at the lower price.

An example of directors looking red-faced in retrospect was the case of Next plc, the fashion retail chain. In 2007, it announced a buy-back programme at a cash cost of £513 million, some 11 per cent of the shares then in issue, for an average of £19.74 per share. In accounting terms, this pressed the right buttons, as, assisted by a modest 4 per cent profits increase, EPS rose by 15 per cent in 2008. However, amid descending gloom for the retail sector, the share price had fallen to £11.08. The amount spent acquiring 26 million shares at the old price would have bought 46 million at the new, lower price. Obviously, those shareholders who did sell benefited significantly, but the remaining 89 per cent would have been far better off had the firm distributed its surplus cash as a dividend. In 2008, Next did raise its dividend by 15 per cent.

Further consolation for shareholders was that directors missed out on performance-related bonuses amounting to around £13 million.

The following FT articles set out how Diageo decided it would commence to return cash to shareholders by way of a share buy-back. Similarly, Rio Tinto has announced the biggest interim dividends in its long history and has also launched a $1bn share buy-back.

Good cheer as Diageo announces £1.5bn share buy-back

Diageo, the world's largest producer of spirits, has announced a £1.5bn share buyback as it reported a rise in full-year profits and sales in 2016–7. The maker of Johnnie Walker scotch and Smirnoff vodka said it enjoyed growth across all its major markets last year, posting a rise in organic net sales of 4.3 per cent, while organic operating profits rose 5.6 per cent in the 12 months ending in June.

The FTSE 100 group's board has also signed off on share buyback scheme to return up to £1.5bn to shareholders in 2018.

Ivan Menezes, chief executive, said: 'We have delivered consistent strong performance improvement across all regions, and I am pleased with progress in our focus areas of US Spirits, scotch and India.'

Diageo, the world's largest distiller, said it expects to generate growth in the single digits in the coming year and has raised its margin forecast from 100 basis points (1 per cent) to 175bps.

In the coming year, Diageo said it expected exchange rate moves to hit sales by £80m but boost its overall operating profits by £70m.

Last month, Diageo announced it was buying George Clooney's tequila brand, Casamigos, for $700m. Today, Diageo said it hoped to complete the deal in the second half of the year.

The group's shares are up 7 per cent so far this year.

Source: Khan, M. (2017) Diageo announces £1.5bn share buy-back. *Financial Times*, 27 July. © The Financial Times Limited 2018. All rights reserved.

Rio Tinto delivers bumper payout for investors

Shareholders in Rio Tinto are to reap the gains of higher commodity prices as the Anglo-Australian miner declared the biggest interim dividend in its 144-year history and launched a fresh $1bn share buyback. The London-based company said it would pay out 50 per cent of first-half earnings as a dividend of $1.10 cents per share after rising prices for iron ore, Rio's key commodity, boosted profits and helped cut debt.

'The $3bn of cash returns we have announced today shows that our very simple strategy is working,' said Jean-Sébastien Jacques, chief executive. He was speaking after the miner reported half-year results that fell slightly short of market expectations.

Underlying earnings, the measure followed by analysts, rose 152 per cent to $3.9bn in the six months to June. This was lower than forecasts of $4.1bn because of a higher tax rate and a strike at Escondida, a big copper mine in Chile. Revenues rose 24 per cent to $19.3bn, while net debt fell $2bn to $7.6bn, leaving Rio with gearing of 13 per cent.

The new share buyback comes on top of a $500m programme announced earlier this year, which was more than 50 per cent complete at the end of June, Rio said.

Analysts said the bumper interim payment meant Rio's full 2017 dividend could be the largest in its history.

Rio tore up its longstanding 'progressive' policy of maintaining or increasing its dividend year by year in February 2016, moving to a payout ratio. This new policy ensures between 40 per cent and 60 per cent of underlying earnings are paid out as dividend every six months.

If commodity prices hold, analysts believe the total 2017 dividend could top the $2.15 per share it paid out under the old policy in 2015.

There could be further cash returns when the company completes the $2.6bn sale of its Australian thermal coal assets to a state-backed Chinese company. A decision on what to do with the sale proceeds will be taken later this year. But with few large projects in its pipeline, the money could be used for another buyback, said analysts.

Rio and other big mining companies are trying to regain the trust of investors after they struggled to deliver positive returns during the so-called natural resources super-cycles between 2003 and 2013.

During that period, miners ploughed billions of dollars into ambitious projects as they chased top-line growth. However, the investment unleashed by the industry created a supply glut that led to a brutal downturn in prices that ran for much of 2015 and into 2016.

With costs and spending now under control, the industry is generating large amounts of cash that is being returned to shareholders. Anglo American last week resumed dividend payments six months earlier than expected.

Shares in Rio fell 87p to £34.15, reflecting the earnings miss and disappointment that it had favoured a buyback over an even larger dividend payment.

Source: Hume, N. (2017) Rio Tinto delivers bumper payout for investors. *Financial Times*, 2 August. © The Financial Times Limited 2018. All rights reserved.

Self-assessment activity 9.8

Suggest some arguments *against* share repurchases.

(Answer in Appendix A)

9.9 THE DIVIDEND PUZZLE

So where does all this leave us at a practical level? We encounter a dilemma known as the 'dividend puzzle'. Dividend cuts are generally viewed as undesirable, yet dividend payments may not always be in the best interests of shareholders. For example, under many tax regimes, dividends are immediately taxed, while the tax on capital gains can be deferred indefinitely. Dividend distribution may force a firm subsequently to issue equity or debt instruments which incur issue costs and interfere with gearing ratios (see Chapter 10). However, markets do react favourably to news of unexpectedly high dividend increases despite the acknowledged costs of dividends. The message conveyed by firms when raising dividends seems to be:

> Despite the cash flow costs of dividend payments, we are prepared to pay higher dividends because we are confident of our ability to withstand these costs and at least to maintain these higher disbursements.

The case for a stable dividend policy

Astute financial managers appreciate that different shareholders have different needs. A financial institution reliant on a stream of income to match its stream of liabilities will prefer stable dividends, while a 'gross fund' (i.e. one exempt from tax on its income) will prefer shares that offer a high level of dividends. The private individual in the 40 per cent tax bracket will prefer capital gains, at least up to the £11,300 exemption limit (2017–18), while the old-age pensioner with a relatively short time horizon is likely to seek income rather than capital appreciation.

Given the wide diffusion of shareholdings, it is almost impossible for most financial managers to begin to assess the needs of all their shareholders. This is a powerful argument for a stable dividend policy, e.g. the application of a fairly constant rate of dividend increase, implying that dividends rise at the same rate as corporate post-tax earnings, subject perhaps to the proviso that dividends should not be allowed to fall, unless earnings suffer a serious reverse. This will enable shareholders to gravitate towards companies whose payout policies suit their particular income needs and tax positions. In this way, companies can expect to build up a clientèle of shareholders attracted by a particular dividend pattern. Hardly surprising, then, that 75 per cent of FDs in the 3i survey said that 'Companies should aim for a consistent payout ratio.'

Direct Line raises dividend as pre-tax profits beat estimates

Insurer Direct Line has raised its first-half dividend by 39 per cent and set fresh targets for future increases, as it reported growth in premiums in the first half and pre-tax profits that beat forecasts. Investors say that dividends are one of the main reasons that they invest in motor and home insurers such as Direct Line, which operate in a mature and competitive market.

The company said that its payout would grow by 2–3 per cent per year, in line with the growth it expects in profits. In the past, dividend increases were more closely linked to inflation.

Chief financial officer John Reizenstein said: 'The regular dividend may not grow as much as in the past, but it will be more anchored to the growth of the business.' He added that there would still be scope for special dividends, which Direct Line has often paid in the past. The company will consider extra payouts when its solvency ratio – a measure of capital available as a proportion of the minimum required – is more than 160 per cent. It stood at 173 per cent at the end of the first half.

The company's shares jumped 6 per cent in morning trading in response to the dividend news.

However, not everybody was pleased with the growth target. Eamonn Flanagan, analyst at Shore Capital, said: 'We are disappointed and somewhat puzzled that the group's expectations of its future growth prospects runs at just between 2 per cent and 3 per cent [per year] henceforth . . . our estimates were closer to [about] 5 per cent. This strikes us as odd.'

Direct Line said that its premiums grew by 5 per cent in the first half to £1.7bn. Pre-tax profits increased by 14 per cent to £341m, well ahead of analysts' estimates, which were closer to £250m.

Source: Ralph, O. (2017) Direct Line raises dividend as pre-tax profits beat estimates. *Financial Times*, 1 August. © The Financial Times Limited 2018. All rights reserved.

Self-assessment activity 9.9

Rehearse the arguments in favour of a stable dividend policy.

(Answer in Appendix A)

However, the notion of consistency in dividend policy took a knock during the recession years of the late 2000s. Many firms cut dividends to conserve cash and instituted a programme of cost-cutting to improve productivity, profitability and cash flow. As a result of their economy, 'blue chip' firms, in particular, found themselves sitting on substantial cash piles at the start of 2011. Given the great uncertainty in the economy following the financial crisis, it is not surprising that companies such as Direct Line (in the last cameo) have been attractive to investors. We all need motor insurance by law which is a good anchor for profits and dividends based on this. For investors, this provides some degree of certainty in an uncertain world.

9.10 CONCLUSIONS

What advice can be offered to practising financial managers? We suggest the following guidelines:

1. Remember the capacity of ill-advised dividend decisions to inflict damage. In view of the market's often savage reaction to dividend cuts, managers should operate a safe dividend cover, allowing sufficient payout flexibility should earnings decline. This suggests a commitment to a clientèle of shareholders who have come to expect a particular dividend policy from their company. This, in turn, suggests a long-term payout ratio sufficient to satisfy shareholder needs, but also generating sufficient internal funds to finance 'normal' investment requirements. Any 'abnormal' financing needs can be met by selling securities, rather than by dividend cuts. In the long term, it seems prudent to minimise reliance on external finance, but not to the extent of building up a 'cash mountain' as with certain US 'tech' firms This may merely signal to the financial world that the company has run out of acceptable investment projects. If there is no worthwhile alternative use of capital, then dividends should be paid.

2. If an alteration in dividend policy is proposed, the firm should minimise the shock effect of an unanticipated dividend cut, e.g. by explaining in advance the firm's investment programme and its financing needs.

3. In an efficient capital market, the dividend announcement, 'good' or 'bad', will be immediately impounded into share price in an unbiased fashion. News of higher dividends will lead to a higher share price because it conveys the information that management believes there is a strong likelihood of higher future earnings and dividends. In view of this, many observers argue that the primary role of dividend policy should be to communicate information to a security market otherwise starved of hard financial data about future company prospects and intrinsic value, while pursuing a year-by-year distribution rate that does not conflict with the interests of the existing clientèle of shareholders.

4. While it is impossible to be definitive in this area, the following box lists the circumstances in which shareholders are likely to prefer dividends to retention and hence, when a dividend increase may raise share price.

5. Finally, the dividend decision is 'only' a financing decision, insofar as paying a dividend may necessitate alternative arrangements for financing investment projects. There can be few companies (at least, quoted ones) for which dividends have constrained really worthwhile investment. For most companies, it is often sensible to adopt a modest target payout ratio. It is not wise to pay large dividends and then have to incur the costs of raising equity from the very same shareholders.

Where dividends fit in the financial puzzle

Dividends should not matter, and yet they evidently do. This enduring puzzle of finance is very relevant now, as low yields on bonds combine with big cash piles on balance sheets to drive ever louder calls for higher dividends. New research might just provide a resolution.

That dividends really should not matter is not an over-elaborated financial theory, but rather something closer to a mathematical identity. If a company pays out cash, that cash is no longer on its balance sheet. The book value of the company (its assets minus its liabilities) reduces by the amount it has paid out. Cash belongs to shareholders whether it is on the balance sheet or paid out in a cheque.

If shareholders want to raise cash, they can withdraw as much cash as they need – when they need it – by selling shares.

It is not always quite as simple as this. Broking commissions make a difference. If capital gains and dividend income are taxed differently, investors may have a preference for dividends, or – more often – for share buy-backs.

Some successful stocks do not pay dividends. Microsoft was the success story of the 1980s and 1990s without ever paying a dividend. Now that it pays out lots of cash, its performance is mediocre. Neither Google nor Warren Buffett's Berkshire Hathaway pay dividends – and nobody complains.

But against this, dividends do to some extent reflect the vital issue of trust. They are a fixed data point. Mess with accounting conventions and you can change a company's earnings, but not the amount written on a dividend cheque. Once money has been paid out, the company's managers can no longer misuse it.

And then there is the evidence, which shows that higher yielding stocks (which pay out a higher proportionate dividend) deliver a much greater total return over time. Research for Credit Suisse by Elroy Dimson, Paul Marsh and Roy Staunton of the London Business School rams this home.

In the long term, stock investment is all about dividends. Invest $1 in the US in 1900, and its capital value alone would have reached $217 by the end of last year – an annualised gain of 5 per cent. Take dividends and reinvest them, however, and it would have been worth $21,766, or an annualised return of 9.4 per cent. The same point holds for all markets around the world – as the professors put it, 'for the seriously long-term investor, the value of a portfolio corresponds closely to the present value of dividends'.

Over time, dividend growth has barely kept pace with inflation, and yields have fallen – maybe reflecting a growing appreciation that dividends should not matter. Since 1900, the price/dividend ratio (the inverse of the dividend yield) has risen by 0.48 per cent per year. Thus less generous payouts have not, over time, meant worse returns for shareholders.

But in general, periods of growth for stocks correlate with periods of growth for dividends. Dividend growth is a symptom of other good things for equity investors.

What is fascinating, though, is that higher-yielding companies do outperform low-yielding stocks. In the UK, a strategy of buying the higher yielding 50 of the 100 biggest stocks each year crushes a strategy of buying the lower yielding 50. £1 invested in 1900 in low-yielders would now be £5,122; it would have turned into £100,160 in high-yielders.

Since 1975, high-yielders have outperformed low-yielders in 20 of 21 countries (New Zealand, a small market, is the only exception), by an average of 4.4 percentage points per year. Since 2000, just before the dotcom crash, this excess has been 9.1 percentage points. Among nations, high-yielding countries outperformed low-yielding ones.

If dividends do not matter, how can yield possibly make such a difference? High-yielders were no riskier than other stocks, and the differences are too big to explain by chance, or by tax effects. So the best explanation is the 'value effect'. Buy stocks when they are too cheap, and they will perform better. A high dividend yield, like a low price/earnings multiple, is a sign that the market is undervaluing a stock.

Dividends, 1900–2010
Per cent

- Mean dividend yield
- Real dividend yield
- Change in price/dividend ratio

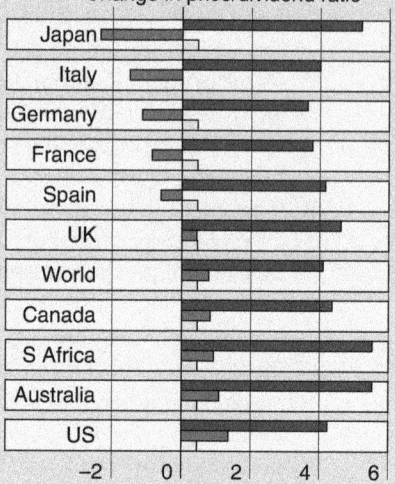

Country	
Japan	
Italy	
Germany	
France	
Spain	
UK	
World	
Canada	
S Africa	
Australia	
US	

Source: Credit Suisse Global Investment Returns Yearbook 2011. Contact London Business School at prowham@london.edu., pp 17

In conclusion, a company's dividend-paying record, as it refers to the chances that it can disburse cash to shareholders in the future, is relevant. (Thus Google, which is a great bet to disgorge a lot of cash over the decades to come, is worth buying, even though it is yet to pay out anything.) It is a good way to find value, so there is money to be made by biasing your portfolio towards high-yielding stocks. Dividends do, in this sense, matter.

But the fact remains that if you need cash, you can equally easily get it by selling shares. And if you want a company to pay out a dividend because you don't trust management to treat cash responsibly – you should ask why you invested in the first place.

Credit Suisse Global Investment Returns Yearbook 2011. Contact London Business School at prowham@london.edu.

Authers, J. (2011) Where dividends fit in the financial puzzle. *Financial Times*, 5 March. © The Financial Times Limited 2018. All rights reserved.

Dividends are likely to be higher:

- The greater the shareholders' reliance on current income.
- The more difficult it is to generate home-made dividends.
- The greater the impact of imperfections, e.g. brokerage fees.
- The lower are income taxes compared to capital gains taxes.
- The lower the costs of a rights issue.
- The greater the ease of reinvestment by shareholders.
- The more often that past dividend increases have heralded subsequent earnings and dividend increases.

SUMMARY

We have reviewed the competing arguments regarding the relative desirability of paying out dividends to shareholders and retaining funds to finance investment, resulting in capital gains.

Key points

- The market value of a company ultimately depends on its dividend-paying capacity.
- The irrelevance, or residual, theory of dividends argues that, under perfect capital market conditions, an alteration in the pattern of dividend payouts has no impact on company value, once the effect of the investment decision is removed.
- If retentions are used to finance worthwhile investment, company value increases, both for one-off retentions and for sustained retention to finance an ongoing investment programme.
- Failure to retain profits can damage shareholder interests if the company has better investment opportunities than shareholders, unless outside capital sources are available and utilised.
- Dividend irrelevance implies that shareholders are indifferent between dividends and capital gains, because the latter can be converted into income.
- In practice, various market imperfections, especially transactions costs and taxes, interfere with this conclusion, although it is difficult to be categoric about the net directional impact.
- Companies are generally unable to detect shareholder preferences, so they should follow a stable dividend policy, designed to suit a particular category, or 'clientèle', of shareholders.
- In practice, companies are reluctant to cut dividends for fear of adverse interpretation by the market of the information conveyed in the announcement.
- Similarly, companies are reluctant to increase dividends too sharply for fear of encouraging over-optimistic expectations about future performance.
- This 'information content' in dividend decisions provides a further argument for dividend stability.
- The advice regarding share re-purchases has to be 'use with care'.

Further reading

First, a couple of health warnings. Fashions change in distribution policy, so surveys that report the 'state-of-the-art' can quickly become out of date. Similarly, because of different tax regimes, the relevance of, for example, US studies in the UK context may be limited. However, some references are timeless. The best starting point is Gordon's first article (1959), followed by the original MM analysis, and Gordon's rejoinder (1963). Lintner (1956) was the first to reveal the smoothing strategy, and Brennan (1971) and Black (1976) present interesting discussions of the 'state of play' as the debate on dividend policy developed.

Bhattacharya (1979) gives a good analysis of the 'bird-in-the-hand fallacy'. Studies that analyse signalling and the information content of corporate distribution announcements are Pettit (1972), Watts (1973), Vermaelen (1981), Healy and Palepu (1988), Asquith and Mullins (1986) and Bernatzi et al. (1997). More recent contributions that examine current trends are Fama and French (2001), an article and a case study respectively by Dobbs and Rehm (2006) and Wood (2006), published in Rutterford et al. (2006), give an up-to-date perspective on alternative distribution methods in the United Kingdom.

Similarly, Benito and Young (2001) analyse reasons for dividend cuts and omissions, and Pettit (2001) gives a highly readable assessment of the advantages and dangers of share buy-backs. Copeland et al. (2013) give a thorough analysis of the competing theories while Emery, Finnerty and Stowe (2006) also contains two good chapters on this topic.

Becker et al. (2011) examine how older investors have a preference for investing in shares that pay higher dividends. Shao et al. (2010) analyse the impact of national culture on dividend policy. Similarly, Breuer, Rieger and Soypak (2014) regard behavioural and cultural patterns as determinants of corporate dividend policy. Hanlon and Hope (2014) present evidence that show a change in dividend policy in response to changes in tax rates on dividend income.

Hull (2015) examines the signalling phenomenon, while Jiang et al. (2013) and Andres et al. (2015) examine the rationale for share re-purchases, the latter in a German context. David and Ginglinger (2016) discuss the rationale for, and impact of, stock dividends.

Appendix
HOME-MADE DIVIDENDS

Kirkstall plc is financed solely by equity. Its cash flow from existing operations is expected to be £24 million p.a. in perpetuity, all of which has hitherto been paid as dividend. Shareholders require a return of 12 per cent. Kirkstall has previously issued 50 million shares. The value of the dividend stream is:

$$V_0 = \frac{£24m}{0.12} = £200m, \text{ yielding share price of } \frac{£200m}{50m} = £4 \text{(ex-div)}$$

Imagine you hold 1 per cent of Kirkstall's equity, worth £2 million. This yields an annual dividend income of £240,000, all of which you require to support your lavish lifestyle. Kirkstall proposes to pass the dividend payable in one year's time in order to invest in a project offering a single net cash flow after a further year of £40 million, when the previous 100 per cent payout policy will be resumed. Your new expected dividend flow is:

Year 1	Year 2	Year 3
0	£240,000 + (1% × £40m) = £640,000	£240,000

The market value of Kirkstall rises to:

$$V_0 = 0 = \frac{£64m}{(1.12)^2} + \left[\frac{£24m}{(0.12)} \times \frac{1}{(1.12)^2}\right]$$

$$= (£51.02m + £159.44m) = £210.46m$$

The increase in value reflects the NPV of the project. Share price rises from £4 to £4.21, thus raising the value of your holding from £2 million to £2.104 million. To support your living standards, you could either borrow on the strength of the higher expected dividend in Year 2 or sell part of your share stake in Year 1, when no dividend is proposed.

In Year 1, the value of your holding will be £2.356 million, and each share will be priced at £4.71. To provide sufficient capital to finance expenditure of £240,000, you need to sell £240,000/£4.71 = 50,955 shares, reducing your holding to (500,000 − 50,955) = 449,045 shares. In Year 2, Kirkstall will distribute a dividend of £64 million (£1.28 per share), of which your share will be £574,778. Out of this, you will require £240,000 for immediate consumption, leaving you better off by £334,778. This may be used to restore your previous shareholding, and thus your previous flow of dividends. The ex-dividend share price in Year 2 will settle back to £4, at which price, the repurchase of 50,955 shares will require an outlay of £203,820, leaving you a surplus of (£334,778 − £203,820) = £130,958. The net effect of your transactions is to yield an income flow of:

Year	1	2	3, etc.
Dividend paid by company	0	£574,778	£240,000
Market transaction	£240,000	(£203,820)	
Net income	£240,000	£370,958	£240,000

Overall, your shareholding remains the same, and you earn extra income in Year 2 of £130,958. This has a present value of £104,000, the very amount of your wealth increase when Kirkstall first announced details of the project, i.e.

$$1\% \times \text{change in market value} = 1\% \times (£210.41m - £200m) = £104,000$$

(Note that rounding errors account for minor deviations.)

QUESTIONS

Questions with a coloured number have solutions in Appendix B on page 501.

1 Tom plc follows a residual dividend policy. It has just announced earnings of £10 million and is to pay a dividend of 20p per share. Its nominal issued share capital is £5 million with par value of 50p. What value of capital expenditure is it undertaking? (You may ignore taxes.)

2 Dick plc faces the following marginal efficiency of investment profile. All projects are indivisible.

Project	IRR (%)	Required outlay (£m)
A	15	3
B	24	5
C	40	2
D	12	4
E	21	7

Dick's shareholders require a return of 20 per cent. Dick has just reported earnings of £9 million. What amount of dividend would you recommend if Dick is unable to raise external finance?

3 Harry plc prides itself on its consistent dividend policy. Past data suggest that its target dividend payout ratio is 50 per cent of earnings. However, when earnings increase, Harry invariably raises its dividend only halfway towards the level that the target dividend payout ratio would indicate. The last dividend was £1 per share and Harry has just announced earnings for the recently ended financial year of £3 per share.

What dividend per share would you expect the Board to recommend?

4 Tamas plc, which is ungeared, earned pre-tax accounting profits of £30 million in the financial year just ended. Replacement investment will match last year's depreciation of £2 million. Both are fully tax-allowable.

Corporation Tax is payable at 30 per cent. Tamas operates a 50 per cent dividend payout policy, and has previously issued 100 million shares, with par value of 25 pence each. Its shareholders require a return of 15 per cent p.a. Tamas holds £15 million cash balances.

Required
Determine the market price per ordinary share of Tamas, both cum-dividend and ex-dividend.
(N.B. Use the perpetuity formula to value Tamas' shares.)

5 Galahad plc, a quoted manufacturer of textiles, has followed a policy in recent years of paying out a steadily increasing dividend per share as shown below:

Year	EPS	Dividend (net)	Cover
2013	11.8p	5.0p	2.4
2014	12.5p	5.5p	2.3
2015	14.6p	6.0p	2.4
2016	13.5p	6.5p	2.1
2017	16.0p	7.3p	2.2

Galahad has only just made the 2017 dividend payment, so the shares are quoted ex-dividend. The main board, which is responsible for strategic planning decisions, is considering a major change in strategy whereby greater financing will be provided by internal funds, involving a cut in the 2018 dividend to 5p (net) per share. The investment projects thus funded will increase the growth rate of Galahad's earnings and dividends to 14 per cent. Some operating managers, however, feel that the new growth rate is unlikely to exceed 12 per cent. Galahad's shareholders seek an overall return of 16 per cent.

Required

(a) Calculate the market price per share for Galahad, prior to the change in policy, using the Dividend Growth Model.
(b) Assess the likely impact on Galahad's share price of the proposed policy change.
(c) Determine the break-even growth rate.
(d) Discuss the possible reaction of Galahad's shareholders and of the capital market in general to this proposed dividend cut in the light of Galahad's past dividend policy.

6 Laceby manufactures agricultural equipment and is currently all-equity-financed. In previous years, it has paid out a steady 50 per cent of available earnings as dividend and used retentions to finance investment in new projects, which have returned 16 per cent on average.

Its Beta is 0.83, and the return on the market portfolio is expected to be 17 per cent in the future, offering a risk premium of 6 per cent.

Laceby has just made earnings of £8 million before tax, and the dividend will be paid in a few weeks' time. Some managers argue in favour of retaining an extra £2 million this year in order to finance the development of a new Common Agricultural Policy (CAP) surplus crop disposal machine. This may offer the following returns under the listed possible scenarios:

	Probability	Cash flow (£m p.a.) (pre-tax)
WTO talks succeed	0.2	0.5
No reform of CAP	0.6	1.5
CAP extended to Eastern Europe	0.2	4.0

The project may be assumed to have an infinite life, and to attract an EU agricultural efficiency grant of £1 million. Corporation Tax is paid at 33 per cent (assume no tax delay).

Required

(a) What is the NPV of the proposed project?
(b) Value the equity of Laceby:
   (i) before undertaking the project;
   (ii) after announcing the acceptance of the project.
(c) Assuming you have found an increase in value in (b)(ii), explain what conditions would be required to support such a conclusion.

7 Pavlon plc has recently obtained a listing on the Stock Exchange. Ninety per cent of the company's shares were previously owned by members of one family, but, since the listing, approximately 60 per cent of the issued shares have been owned by other investors.

Pavlon's earnings and dividends for the five years prior to the listing are detailed below:

Years prior to listing	Profit after tax (£)	Dividend per share (pence)
5	1,800,000	3.60
4	2,400,000	4.80
3	3,850,000	6.16
2	4,100,000	6.56
1	4,450,000	7.12
Current year	5,500,000	(estimate)

The number of issued ordinary shares was increased by 25 per cent three years prior to the listing and by 50 per cent at the time of the listing. The company's authorised capital is currently £25,000,000 in 25p ordinary shares, of which 40,000,000 shares have been issued. The market value of the company's equity is £78,000,000.

The board of directors is discussing future dividend policy. An interim dividend of 3.16p per share was paid immediately prior to the listing and the finance director has suggested a final dividend of 2.34p per share.

The company's declared objective is to maximise shareholder wealth.

The company's profit after tax is generally expected to increase by 15 per cent p.a. for three years, and 8 per cent per year after that. Pavlon's cost of equity capital is estimated to be 12 per cent per year. Dividends may be assumed to grow at the same rate as profits.

Required

(a) Comment upon the nature of the company's dividend policy prior to the listing and discuss whether such a policy is likely to be suitable for a company listed on the Stock Exchange.
(b) Discuss whether the proposed final dividend of 2.34 pence is likely to be appropriate:
  (i)   if the majority of shares are owned by wealthy private individuals;
  (ii) if the majority of shares are owned by institutional investors.
(c) Using the Dividend Valuation Model, give calculations to indicate whether Pavlon's shares are currently undervalued or overvalued.
(d) Briefly outline the weaknesses of the Dividend Valuation Model.

(ACCA)

8 Mondrian plc is a newly formed company which aims to maximise the wealth of its shareholders. The board of directors of the company is currently trying to decide upon the most appropriate dividend policy to adopt for the company's shareholders. However, there is strong disagreement between three of the directors concerning the benefits of declaring cash dividends:

Director A argues that cash dividends would be welcomed by investors, and that as high a dividend payout ratio as possible would reflect positively on the market value of the company's shares.

Director B argues that whether a cash dividend is paid or not is irrelevant in the context of shareholder wealth maximisation.

Director C takes an opposite view to Director A and argues that dividend payments should be avoided as they would lead to a decrease in shareholder wealth.

Required

(a) Discuss the arguments for and against the position taken by each of the three directors.
(b) Assuming the board of directors decides to pay a dividend to shareholders, what factors should be taken into account when determining the level of dividend payment?

(ACCA Certified Diploma June 1996)

Practical assignment

Obtain the Annual Report and Accounts of any firm of your choice. Look at the five-year record provided, and work out the dividend cover each year and the annual rate of dividend per share increase as compared to the annual increase in EPS. Is there any obvious pattern to the dividend decisions over this period? Does the firm have a clear dividend policy?

10

Capital structure and the required return

Debt binge leaves US corporate assets exposed

A debt binge has left a quarter of US corporate assets vulnerable to a sudden increase in interest rates, the International Monetary Fund (IMF) has warned. The ability of companies to cover interest payments is at its weakest since the 2008 financial crisis, according to one measure.

The IMF's Global Financial Stability Report highlights what economists at the fund see as one of the main risks facing the US plans to boost US growth via a combination of tax cuts and infrastructure spending.

The average interest coverage ratio has fallen sharply over the past two years, the IMF said, with earnings less than six times the cost of interest, a figure 'close to the weakest multiple since the onset of the global financial crisis'.

That sort of deterioration has historically corresponded with widening credit spreads for risky corporate debt and been concentrated on smaller companies with less access to capital markets.

But, already, the IMF said, companies accounting for 10 per cent of US corporate assets appear unable to cover the cost of interest payments out of their current earnings.

FT *Source:* Donnan, S. and Tetlow, G. (2017) Debt binge endangers US corporate assets, warns IMF. *Financial Times*, 19 April. © The Financial Times Limited 2018. All rights reserved.

Learning objectives

This chapter covers firms' capital structure in general and the arguments for and against using debt as the source of finance in a company's operations. It places particular emphasis on the impact of debt capital and gearing on the overall rate of investors' actual and required returns. The chapter has a following objectives:

- To explain ways of measuring gearing.
- To provide an in-depth understanding of the advantages of debt capital.
- To explain the meaning of, and how to calculate, the Weighted Average Cost of Capital (WACC).
- To enable you to understand the likely limits on the use of debt, and the nature of 'financial distress' costs.
- To help you understand the issues involved in financing foreign operations.
- To enable you to understand the factors that a finance manager should consider when framing capital structure policy.

10.1 INTRODUCTION

Most financing decisions in practice reduce to a choice between debt and equity. The finance manager wishing to fund a new project, but reluctant to cut dividends or to make a rights issue, has to consider the borrowing option. In this chapter, we further examine the arguments for and against using debt to finance company activities and, in particular, consider the impact of gearing on the overall rate of return that the company must achieve.

The main advantages of debt capital centre on its relative cost. Debt capital is usually cheaper than equity because:

1. The pre-tax rate of interest is invariably lower than the return required by shareholders. This is due to the legal position of lenders who have a prior claim on the distribution of the company's income and who, in a liquidation, precede ordinary shareholders in the queue for the settlement of claims. Debt is usually secured on the firm's assets, which can be sold to pay off lenders in the event of **default**, i.e. failure to pay interest and capital according to the pre-agreed schedule.
2. Debt interest can be set against profit for tax purposes, reducing the effective cost.
3. The administrative and issuing costs are normally lower, e.g. underwriters are not always required, although legal fees are usually involved.

default
The failure by a borrower to adhere to a pre-agreed schedule of interest and/or capital payments on a loan

The downside of debt is that high borrowing levels can lead to the risk of inability to meet debt interest payments during poor trading conditions. This often leads to managers having to pay more attention to managing the debt position than to managing actual business operations and strategy. Shareholders are thus exposed to a second tier of risk above the inherent business risk of the trading activity. As a result, rational shareholders seek additional compensation for this extra exposure. In brief, debt is desirable because it is relatively cheap, but there may be limits to the prudent use of debt financing because, although posing relatively low risk to the lender, it can be highly risky for the borrower, i.e. the risk is two-sided.

In general, larger, well-established companies are likely to have a greater ability to borrow because they generate more reliable streams of income, enhancing their ability to service (make interest payments on) debt capital. Ironically, in practice, we often find that small developing companies that should not over-rely on debt capital are forced to do so through sheer inability to raise equity, while larger enterprises often operate with what appear to be very conservative gearing ratios compared to their borrowing capacities. Against this, we often encounter cases of over-geared enterprises that thought their borrowing levels were safe until they were caught out by adverse trading conditions.

So is there a 'correct' level of debt? Quite how much companies should borrow is another puzzle in the theory of business finance. There are cogent arguments for and against the extensive use of debt capital, and academics have developed sophisticated models which attempt to expose and analyse the key theoretical relationships.

For many years, it was thought advantageous to borrow so long as the company's capacity to service the debt was unquestioned. The result would be higher earnings per share and higher share value, provided the finance raised was invested sensibly. The dangers of excessive levels of borrowing would be forcibly articulated by the stock market by a down-rating of the shares of a highly geared company. The so-called 'traditional' view of gearing centres on the concept of an **optimal capital structure** which maximised company value. However, while the critical gearing ratio is thought to depend on factors such as the steadiness of the company's cash flow and the saleability of its assets, it has proved to be like the Holy Grail, highly desirable, but illusory and difficult to grasp. Some academics felt that a firmer theoretical underpinning was needed to facilitate the analysis of capital structure decisions and to offer more helpful guidelines to practising managers.

optimal capital structure
The financing mix that minimises the overall cost of finance and maximises market value

The Modigliani and Miller contribution

When Nobel laureates Modigliani and Miller (MM) published their seminal paper in 1958, finance academics began to examine in depth the relationship between borrowing and company value. MM's work on the pure theory of capital structure initially suggested that company value was unaffected by gearing. This conclusion prompted a furore of critical opposition, leading eventually to a coherent theory of capital structure, the current version of which looks remarkably like the traditional view.

Because this is a complex topic, we have organised the treatment of the impact of gearing into two chapters. This chapter is mainly devoted to the **'traditional' theory of capital structure** and the issue of how much a company should borrow. In Chapter 11, we deepen the analysis by discussing the 'modern' theory. However, the present chapter gives a strong flavour of the main issues involved.

> **traditional theory of capital structure**
> The theory that an optimal capital structure exists, where the WACC is minimised and market value is maximised

The two chapters together are designed to examine the following issues:

- How is gearing measured?
- Why do companies use debt capital?
- How is the cost of debt capital measured?
- What are the dangers of debt capital? How do shareholders react to 'high' levels of gearing?
- What do the competing theories of capital structure tell us about optimal financing decisions?
- How does taxation affect the analysis?
- What overall return should be achieved by a company using debt?
- What practical guidelines can we offer to financial managers?

10.2 MEASURES OF GEARING

> **capital gearing**
> The mixture of debt and equity in a firm's capital structure, which influences variations in shareholders' profits in response to sales and EBIT variations
>
> **income gearing**
> The proportion of profit before interest and tax (PBIT) absorbed by interest charges
>
> **financial gearing**
> Includes both capital gearing and income gearing

There are two basic ways to express the indebtedness of a company. **Capital gearing** indicates the proportion of debt capital in the firm's overall capital structure. **Income gearing** indicates the extent to which the company's income is pre-empted by prior interest charges. Both are indicators of **financial gearing**.

Capital gearing: alternative measures

A widely used measure of capital gearing is the ratio of all long-term liabilities (LTL), i.e. 'amounts falling due after more than one year', to shareholders' funds, as shown in the balance sheet. This purports to indicate how easily the firm can repay debts from selling assets, since shareholder funds measure net assets:

$$\text{Capital gearing} = \frac{\text{LTL}}{\text{Shareholders' funds}}$$

There are several drawbacks to this approach.

First, the market value of equity may be considerably higher than the book value, reflecting higher asset values, so this measure may seem unduly conservative. However, the notion of market value needs to be clarified. When a company is forced to sell assets hurriedly in order to repay debts, it is by no means certain that buyers can be found to pay 'acceptable' prices. The **break-up values (BUV)** of assets are often lower than those expressed in the accounts, which assume that the enterprise is a going concern. However, using book values does at least have an element of prudence. In addition, the oscillating nature of market values may emphasise the case for conservatism, even for companies with 'safe' gearing ratios.

> **break-up value (BUV)**
> The value that can be obtained by selling off the firm's assets piecemeal to the highest bidders

A second problem is the lack of an upper limit to the ratio, which hinders inter-company comparisons. This is easily remedied by expressing long-term liabilities as a fraction of all forms of long-term finance, thus setting the upper limit at 100 per cent. The gearing measure would become:

$$\frac{\text{LTL}}{\text{LTL} + \text{Shareholders' funds}}$$

A third problem is the treatment of provisions made out of previous years' income. Technically, provisions represent expected future liabilities. Companies provide for contingencies, such as claims under product guarantees, as a matter of prudence. Provisions thus result from a charge against profits and result in lower stated equity. However, some provisions turn out to be unduly pessimistic and may be written back into profits, and hence equity, in later years. A good example is the provision made for deferred taxation. This is a highly prudent device to provide for the possible tax liability if the firm were to sell its fixed assets before the end of their initially anticipated working lives.

Provisions could thus be treated as either equity or debt according to the degree of certainty of the anticipated contingency. If the liability is 'highly certain', it is reasonable to treat it as debt, but if the provision is the result of ultra-prudence, it may be treated as equity. For example, the deferred taxation provision, which is made against the possibility of incurring a Corporation Tax charge if assets are sold above their written-down value for tax purposes, is a risk that, for most firms, will diminish over time, so the provision could safely be treated as equity. In practice, company accounts carry a mixture of provisions of varying degrees of certainty, and it is tempting to delete provisions from liabilities but not to include them in equity when expressing the gearing ratio. However, the nature of provisions should be questioned when the item appears substantial. Adjusted to exclude provisions, the capital gearing ratio becomes:

$$\frac{\text{Long-term borrowings (LTB)}}{\text{Shareholders' funds}} \quad \text{or} \quad \frac{\text{LTB}}{\text{LTB} + \text{Shareholders' funds}}$$

Arguably, any borrowing figure should take into account both long-term and short-term borrowing. Many companies depend heavily on short-term borrowing, especially bank overdrafts, and having to repay these debts quickly would place a significant burden on both the cash flow and liquidity of such companies. For this reason, some firms present their gearing ratios inclusive of such liabilities. For example, BP's (www.bp.com) measure of gearing focuses on 'finance debt', i.e. borrowing via the financial markets and from financial institutions (but also including net obligations under lease contracts):

$$\frac{\text{Finance debt}}{\text{Finance debt} + \text{Shareholders' funds}}$$

There are two objections to this approach. First, since short-term borrowing can be volatile, the year-end figure in the balance sheet is not always a reliable guide to short-term debts. However, many companies effectively use their bank overdraft as a long-term form of finance. In other words, the actual bank overdraft figure may include a hard core element of long-term debt and a fluctuating component, although it is not easy to separate these two items from external examination of the accounts.

Second, it may be argued that any holdings of cash and highly liquid, marketable securities ('near cash' assets) should be offset against short-term debt, to yield a measure of '**net debt**'. For example, BP expresses it thus:

net debt
A firm's net borrowing including both long-term and also short-term debt, offset by cash holdings. Expressed either in absolute terms, or in relation to owner's equity

$$\text{Net debt} = \frac{\text{Finance debt} - (\text{cash and liquid resources})}{\text{Equity}}$$

In fact, financial commentators increasingly use this measure of gearing, which is shown in the annual reports of many companies, expressed either in absolute terms or in relation to equity.

A history of leverage and the mining industry, 2010–15

How taking on cheap debt to build fancy holes in the ground (to feed Chinese demand) blew up shareholder value in the world's biggest miners. As Investec notes:

It is the rising percentage of debt that makes this cyclical downturn so toxic for equity holders. Strangely enough, BHP Billiton, Rio Tinto and Anglo American started this century with not dissimilar gearing ratios (defined here as net debt to market capitalisation), ranging between 15% (Anglo American) and 27% (BHP Billiton).

As we progressed into the Supercycle, shareholders began to own a greater proportion of the overall enterprise value of the company, with average gearing (net debt:equity) falling to 8% in FY05/06. The adoption of debt-based growth strategies in recent years has led to profound changes within the sector. The ready availability of low-cost debt encouraged companies to take on additional gearing to finance the race to grow production, with iron ore development and expansions being the key culprits. The recent fall in commodity prices has compounded the proportion of earnings consumed by debt service – both interest and repayments. This has seen gearing ratios rise to 18% and 25% for Rio Tinto and BHP Billiton respectively, with Anglo American currently at 70% and highly geared newcomer, Glencore at over 300%, for an aggregate gearing ratio of 41%.

Investec's analysis assumes you can roughly value the equity in BHP Billiton, Rio Tinto, Glencore and Anglo at 15 times earnings through a cycle.

Its own commodity price forecasts also suggest that shareholders will wrest earnings back from paying down debt eventually. If prices remain on the floor, though, then the numbers imply that equity value would be completely wiped out at Glencore, and very nearly so at Anglo. The interesting bit is that Investec doesn't net off Glencore's trading inventory from debt.

Glencore, of course, tends to argue observers should do this with its 'readily marketable inventories' since it can liquidate them to raise cash (net debt was $47bn in its half-year results, inventories $18bn).

Source: Cotterill, J. (2015) A history of leverage and the mining industry, 2010–2015. *Financial Times*, 28 September. © The Financial Times Limited 2018. All rights reserved.

Self-assessment activity 10.1

Determine the following gearing ratios using the information supplied.

(i) debt-to-equity ratio
(ii) debt-to-debt plus equity ratio
(iii) net debt

Equity = £100m
Long-term debt = £50m
Short-term debt = £20m
Cash = £10m

(Answer in Appendix A)

All the above measures are commonly used in the United Kingdom. In some other countries, a more direct measure of gearing (or leverage) is used. The UK ratios tend to focus on the relationship between debt and equity capital, which is reasonable since equity represents net assets. However, when necessary, debts are repaid by liquidating the assets to which the capital relates. Rather than this roundabout focus on capital, a direct focus on assets available to repay debts may give a clearer picture of ability to repay. For this purpose, many US commentators use an 'American gearing' ratio, such as:

$$\frac{\text{Total liabilities (including short-term liabilities)}}{\text{Total assets}}$$

■ Interest cover and income gearing

All the above measures purport to express the ability of the company to repay loans out of capital. However, they are only really helpful if book values and market values of the assets that would have to be sold to repay creditors approximate to each other. Yet, as we have noted, the market value of assets is volatile and difficult to assess.

interest cover
The number of times the profit before interest exceeds loan interest

times interest earned
The ratio of profit before interest and tax (operating profit) to annual interest charges, i.e. how many times over the firm could meet its interest bill

income gearing
The proportion of profit before interest and tax (PBIT) absorbed by interest charges

Moreover, capital gearing only indicates the security of creditors' funds in a crisis and may be an unduly cautious way of viewing debt exposure.

The trigger for a debt crisis is usually inability to make interest payments, and the 'front line' is therefore the size and reliability of the company's income in relation to its interest commitments. Although, in reality, cash flow is the more important consideration, the ability of a company to meet its interest obligations is usually measured by the ratio of *profit* before tax and interest, to interest charges, known as **interest cover**, or 'times interest earned':

$$\text{Interest cover} = \frac{\text{Profit before interest and tax}}{\text{Interest charges}}$$

Strictly, the numerator should include any interest received and the denominator should become interest outgoings. This adjustment is rarely made in practice; net interest charges are commonly used as the denominator (as we do for the D.S. Smith plc example that follows).

The inverse of interest cover is called **income gearing**, indicating the proportion of pre-tax earnings committed to prior interest charges. If a company earns profit before interest and tax of £20 million and incurs interest charges of £2 million, then its interest cover is (£20m/£2m) = 10 times, and 10 per cent of profit before interest and tax is pre-empted by interest charges.

Arguably, cash flow-to-interest is a better guide to financial security, given that profits are expressed on the accruals basis, i.e. profit is recognised even though cash may not have been received yet for sales. Hence, the following formula is sometimes used:

$$\text{Cash flow cover} = \frac{\text{Operating cash flow}}{\text{Net interest payable}}$$

Self-assessment activity 10.2

Distinguish between capital gearing and income gearing. How is each measured?

(Answer in Appendix A)

■ Example: D.S. Smith plc's borrowings

The figures in Table 10.1 are taken from the Annual Report for D.S. Smith plc (www.dssmith.uk.com) for the year ended 30 April 2017. With these data, we can calculate various gearing indicators:

$$\frac{\text{LT borrowing}}{\text{Shareholders' funds}} = \frac{£1,144\text{m}}{£1,355\text{m}} = 84.43\%$$

$$\frac{\text{LT borrowing}}{\text{All LT funds}} = \frac{£1,144\text{m}}{(£1,144\text{m} + £1,355\text{m})} = 45.78\%$$

$$\frac{\text{All borrowing}}{\text{Shareholders' funds}} = \frac{(£1144\text{m} + £119\text{m})}{£1,355\text{m}} = 93.21\%$$

Net debt $= (£1144\text{m} + £119\text{m} - £139\text{m})$

$= £1,124\text{m}$, which is $\frac{(£1.124\text{m})}{£1,355\text{m}} = 83\%$ of equity

Interest cover $= \frac{£316\text{m}}{£55\text{m}} = 5.75$ times

Income gearing $= \frac{1}{5.75} = 17.39\%$

$$\frac{\text{Cash generated from operations}}{\text{Net interest payable}} = \frac{£629m}{£55m} = 11.444 \text{ times}$$

$$\frac{\text{Total liabilities}}{\text{Total assets}} = \frac{£3,138m}{£4,493m} = 70\%$$

Table 10.1 Financial data for D.S. Smith plc as at 30 April 2017

	£m
Shareholders' funds (total equity)	1,355
Cash and cash equivalents	139
Long-term borrowing (LTD)	1,144
Short-term borrowing	119
Operating profit before interest and tax	316
Net financing costs	55
Total assets	4,493
Total liabilities	3,138
Cash generated from operations	629

Source: D.S. Smith plc, Annual Report, 2017.

D.S. Smith net-debt-to-EBITDA ratio

A further calculation that measures the gearing of a company is the ratio of net-debt-to-EBITDA. For D.S. Smith, this figure is reported in the 2017 annual report at 1.8 times. The company notes that this is below its target ratio for this measure of 2.0 times. It is now common for bank covenants to stipulate a maximum net debt to EBITDA ratio, and currently, D.S. Smith undershoots the maximum.

Self-assessment activity 10.3

Obtain the accounts of a firm of your choice and conduct a similar exercise to the D.S. Smith plc calculations.

Why investors downplay US debt binge risks

A month after the International Monetary Fund sounded the alarm over a debt binge by US companies, investors are expressing confidence in the sector and have been eager buyers of tens of billions of new bond offerings. A quickening in global economic activity and improving earnings for companies during the first quarter has helped moderate concerns about excess leverage.

Monica Erickson, a portfolio manager with asset manager DoubleLine Capital, says for many investors 'leverage is less of a concern with earnings growth'.

Outstanding US corporate debt has swelled more than 275 per cent over the past two decades to $8.5tn, with credit ratings broadly deteriorating over that period. Interest coverage, a key metric that measures the earnings companies have to cover debt payments, hovers near its lowest level since 2010 for investment-grade US companies, according to Bank of America Merrill Lynch.

Investors have focused on net leverage, or the amount of debt companies have amassed compared with their earnings before interest, taxes, depreciation and amortisation.

Leverage measures for both high-yield and investment-grade groups have retreated from peaks touched in 2016. Excluding the energy and materials industries, US high-yield net leverage has declined from a 14-year high to 4.2 times earnings. For higher quality groups, net leverage has slipped less than two-tenths of a point to 2.37 times earnings.

FT Source: Platt, E. (2017) Why investors downplay US debt binge risks. Financial Times, May 23. © The Financial Times Limited 2018. All rights reserved.

10.3 OPERATING AND FINANCIAL GEARING

operating gearing
The proportion of fixed costs in the firm's operating cost structure

A major reason for using debt is to enhance or 'gear up' shareholder earnings. When a company is financially geared, variations in the level of earnings due to changes in trading conditions generate a more than proportional variation in earnings attributable to shareholders if the interest charges are fixed. This effect is very similar to that exerted by **operating gearing** (see Chapter 6). We will now examine these two gearing phenomena and illustrate them numerically.

Most businesses operate with a combination of variable and fixed factors of production, giving rise to variable and fixed costs, respectively. The particular combination is largely dictated by the nature of the activity and the technology involved. Operating gearing refers to the relative importance of fixed costs in the firm's cost structure, costs that have to be met regardless of output and revenue levels. In general, the higher the proportion of fixed to variable costs, the higher the firm's break-even volume of output. As sales rise above the break-even point, there will be a more than proportional upward effect on profits before interest and tax, and on shareholder earnings.

Firms with high operating gearing, mainly capital-intensive ones, are especially prone to fluctuations in the business cycle. In the downswing, as their sales volumes decrease, their earnings before interest and tax decline by a more than proportional amount, and conversely in the upswing. Hence, such companies are regarded as relatively risky. If such companies borrow, they add a second tier of fixed charges in the form of interest payments, thus increasing overall risk – the higher the interest charges, the greater the risk of inability to pay. Consequently, the risk premium required by investors in such companies is relatively high. It follows that companies that exhibit high operating gearing should use debt finance sparingly.

■ Operating and financial gearing: Burley plc

Burley plc produces and sells briefcases. It has issued 4 million 50p shares and has £2 million loan finance. Its gearing ratio, measured by the ratio of debt to equity at book values, is one-to-one (i.e. (4m × 50p)/£2m). Last year, Burley sold 60,000 units to large retailers at £30 per unit.

Its profit and loss account (income statement) is:

		£000	£000
Sales			1,800
Less:	Variable costs (VC)	(720)	
	Fixed operating costs (FC)	(480)	(1,200)
	Profit before interest and tax (PBIT)		600
Less:	Interest payable at 10%		(200)
	Profit before taxation (PBT)		400
Less:	Corporation Tax at 30%		(120)
	Profit after tax (PAT)		280

The earnings per share (EPS) are:

$$\frac{\text{Profit after tax}}{\text{No of ordinary shares}} = \frac{£280{,}000}{4\text{m}} = 7.0\text{p}$$

contribution
Revenues (turnover) less variable costs, i.e. contribution to meeting fixed costs

Notice that the profit and loss account (income statement) hides the distinction between gross and net profit. The gross profit is the sales less variable costs, i.e. (£1,800,000 − £720,000) = £1,080,000, also called **contribution** because the fixed costs are paid from this amount. Any surplus over FC is the net or operating profit (PBIT). Operating profit is thus £600,000.

Now let us consider the break-even volume, initially ignoring the debt interest obligation. Recall that breaking even means just covering fixed operating costs and variable costs. In Burley's case, this requires an output sufficient to generate a gross margin high enough to cover the fixed operating costs of £480,000. The unit variable cost is:

$$(£720,000/60,000) = £12$$

Were it financed entirely by equity, Burley's break-even output would be found by dividing fixed cost by the gross profit margin of $(£30 - £12) = £18$:

$$(£480,000/£18) = 26,667 \text{ units}$$

Allowing for the interest commitments of £200,000, Burley has to cover total fixed charges of $(£480,000 + £200,000) = £680,000$. This requires the higher output of $(£680,000/£18) = 37,778$ units to break even. Hence, using debt finance raises the break-even volume of production because fixed obligations are higher.

We can use this example to distinguish between operating and financial gearing. **Operating gearing** can be expressed in a variety of ways. Most simply, it is the proportion of total production cost accounted for by fixed costs: $(£480,000/£1,200,000) = 40$ per cent. Allowing for interest payments, Burley needs to generate a gross margin or contribution of $(£480,000 + £200,000) = £680,000$ to cover total fixed charges. At present, it is doing this fairly comfortably, since in percentage terms fixed charges account for $(£480,000 + £200,000) \div £1,080,000 = 63$ per cent of the contribution. Looking at the importance of financial gearing, out of its profit before interest and tax of £600,000, a third (£200,000) is required to cover interest payments, i.e. the interest cover is 3.3 times.

A more sophisticated way of viewing the impact of fixed charges is to calculate leverage ratios. **Operating leverage** is the number of times the contribution covers the profit before interest and tax (PBIT), i.e. a multiple of:

operating leverage
The ratio of contribution to profit before interest and tax

$$\frac{\text{Contribution}}{\text{PBIT}} = \frac{(\text{Sales} - \text{VC})}{\text{PBIT}} = \frac{£1,080,000}{£600,000} = 1.8 \text{ times}$$

This indicates the leeway between contribution and the PBIT, and hence the extent to which the fixed costs can increase without forcing the company into an operating loss. More significantly, the multiplier of 1.8 signifies the relationship between a given increase in sales and the resulting effect on PBIT. As we show later in this section, a 10 per cent increase in sales will result in an increase in PBIT of 18 per cent.

Similarly, **financial leverage** is the number of times the PBIT covers the profit before tax (PBT), i.e. a multiple of:

financial leverage
The ratio of profit before interest and tax (PBIT) to profit before tax (PBT)

$$\frac{\text{PBIT}}{\text{PBT}} = \frac{£600,000}{£400,000} = 1.5 \text{ times}$$

The difference between PBIT and PBT is the interest charge, so this multiple indicates the extent to which interest charges can rise without forcing the company into pre-tax loss. More significantly, the multiplier of 1.5 magnifies the effect of operating leverage – the effect of a sales increase on PBT is greater in a financially geared firm than in one with no borrowing. Taking the two multipliers together, we obtain a combined leverage effect. In this case, a sales increase of 10 per cent will result in an increase in PBT of $(1.8 \times 1.5) = 2.7$ times as great, i.e. 27 per cent. For a given tax rate, here 30 per cent, the profit after tax and, hence, the EPS, will also rise by the same proportion.

Aircraft manufacturing operating leverage

Textron, maker of Cessna aircraft, yesterday reduced its outlook for business jet deliveries and brought down its earnings guidance by almost a tenth. The stock fell by 13 per cent. The depth of the guidance cut, and the reaction might seem puzzling. Cessna accounted for a quarter of Textron's revenues last year, but only about 7 per cent of its segment profits (the company also makes helicopters and drones, among other things).

Part of the explanation is the high operating leverage in manufacturing aircraft: a little sales growth can mean a big jump in profit. Equally important, resurgence at Cessna has been long awaited, and is a key part of any bullish long-term view of Textron. The business jet market was historically correlated with corporate profits, but jet sales have not come back as corporate earnings have boomed since the financial crisis.

A key question is whether it can go where the growth is. Roughly 85 per cent of Cessna sales come from North America and Europe. If giddy corporate spending is going to blossom again soon, it is unlikely to happen there.

FT *Source:* Column, L. (2013). *Financial Times*, 18 April, p. 14. © The Financial Times Limited 2018. All rights reserved.

To clarify these relationships, it is helpful to demonstrate the impact of Burley experiencing a sales increase of 10 per cent. Assuming no change in unit variable costs, the profit and loss account becomes:

		£000	£000	
Sales			1,980	(10% increase)
Less:	Variable costs (VC)	(792)		
	Fixed costs (FC)	(480)	(1,272)	
	Profit before interest and tax (PBIT)		708	(18% increase)
Less:	Interest payable at 10%		(200)	
	Profit before taxation (PBT)		508	(27% increase)
Less:	Corporation Tax at 30%		(152)	
	Profit after tax (PAT)		356	(27% increase)

The new EPS is:

PAT/No. of shares = (£356,000/4m) = 8.9p (27% increase)

The increase in EPS of 27 per cent (rounded) is a far greater proportion than the sales increase, illustrating the operation of the combined gearing multiplier. It follows that the higher the proportion of fixed costs in overall costs, and the greater the commitment to interest charges, the greater will be the combined gearing effect. This may suggest that using fixed factors of production and using debt capital are both desirable things. However, as the following example demonstrates, financial gearing is double-edged. It is beneficial in favourable economic conditions, but because the gearing effect also works in reverse, it can spell trouble in adverse trading conditions.

Self-assessment activity 10.4

Show the effect on the combined gearing multiplier in the Burley example if fixed costs are £530,000 and interest charges are £240,000.

(Answer in Appendix A)

10.4 FINANCIAL GEARING AND RISK: LINDLEY PLC

Lindley plc retains no profit and its shareholders require a 20 per cent return. Issued share capital is £100 million, with par value of £1. Lindley's operating profit can vary as shown in Table 10.2, according to trading conditions characterised as bad, indifferent

Table 10.2 How gearing affects shareholder returns in Lindley plc

	Trading conditions		
	Scenario A ($p = 0.25$)	Scenario B ($p = 0.50$)	Scenario C ($p = 0.25$)
Profit before interest (PBIT)* (Net operating income)	£5m	£20m	£35m
Zero gearing (100m equity, £0m debt)			
Debt interest at 10%	—	—	—
Shareholder earnings	£5m	£20m	£35m
Return on equity (ROE)	5%	20%	35%
25% gearing (Debt/Equity = $\frac{1}{3}$) (£75m equity, £25m debt, interest 10%)			
Debt interest at 10%	£2.5m	£2.5m	£2.5m
Shareholder earnings	£2.5m	£17.5m	£32.5m
Return on equity (ROE)	3.3%	23.3%	43.3%
50% gearing (Debt/Equity = $\frac{1}{1}$) (£50m equity, £50m debt, interest 10%)			
Debt interest at 10%	£5m	£5m	£5m
Shareholder earnings	0	£15m	£30m
Return on equity (ROE)	0	30%	60%

*Taxes are ignored.

and good. These are denoted by scenarios A, B and C, which have probabilities of 0.25, 0.50 and 0.25, respectively.

After all costs, but before deducting debt interest, earnings are £5 million, £20 million and £35 million under scenarios A, B and C, respectively. This measure of earnings is termed net operating income (NOI). (For simplicity, taxation is ignored.) Let us examine shareholder returns with gearing ratios of zero, 25 per cent and 50 per cent, measured by long-term debt (interest rate 10 per cent) to total long-term finance that is held constant at £100 million.

Notice that for a given increase in income, shareholder earnings rise by a greater proportion: for example, with gearing of 25 per cent, if NOI rises by 300 per cent from £5 million to £20 million, shareholder earnings increase by 600 per cent from £2.5 million to £17.5 million. It is easy to see why adding debt to the capital structure is called gearing – the change in earnings is magnified by a factor of 2.0 in shareholders' favour. Unfortunately, this effect also applies in a downward direction – a given proportionate fall in earnings generates a more pronounced *decrease* in shareholder earnings. Indeed, with 50 per cent gearing, under scenario A, shareholder earnings are entirely wiped out by prior interest charges. The return on equity would be negative at any higher gearing level under this scenario.

Negative returns are not necessarily fatal – companies often survive losses in especially poor trading years – but the likelihood of survival when continued trading losses combine with high fixed interest charges is lowered if the company cannot pay interest charges. In these cases, the enterprise is technically insolvent, although creditors may agree to restructure the company's capital, e.g. by converting debt into equity or preference shares. There is, however, an effective upper limit of gearing for Lindley.

Beyond 50 per cent gearing, it may be unable to meet interest charges out of earnings. For practical purposes, the lower limit of earnings will dictate maximum borrowing capacity, although, in reality, this lower earnings limit is highly uncertain. This is why it is usually argued that the more reliable the company's expected cash flow stream, the greater its borrowing capacity.

Our Lindley example demonstrates that, under debt financing, although shareholders may achieve enhanced returns in good years, they stand to receive much lower returns in bad years. In other words, the residual stream of shareholder earnings exhibits greater variability. This can be examined by computing the expected value and the range, or dispersion, of the return on equity (ROE) with each of the three gearing levels.

Self-assessment activity 10.5

Calculate the expected value of Lindley's ROE under each scenario.

(Answer in Appendix A)

Table 10.3 shows that, although the expected value of the return on equity is greater at higher levels of gearing, the dispersion, or range, of possible returns is also wider, which might concern risk-averting shareholders. Notice also that we can decompose the overall risk incurred by shareholders into its underlying business and financial elements. Business risk refers to the likely variability in returns for an equivalent all-equity-financed company, i.e. the dispersion of returns is due to underlying business-related factors. Financial risk is the additional dispersion in net returns to shareholders due to the need to meet interest charges whatever the trading conditions. At every gearing ratio, the range of returns due to business risk is unchanged – nothing has happened to its product range, its customer base or any other aspect of its trading activities. Lindley would simply share out the proceeds of its operations in different ways at different gearing ratios.

Table 10.3 How gearing affects the risk of ordinary shares

Gearing (%)	Expected ROE (%)	Total dispersion (%)	Due to: Business risk (%)	Financial risk (%)
0	20	30	30	0
25	23.3	40	30	10
50	30	60	30	30

It is also helpful to show the effect on ROE graphically. Figure 10.1 shows the data for Lindley's ROE for the three different capital structures. Clearly, the higher the debt-to-equity ratio, the greater the ROE for any level of profit before interest. Figure 10.1 also shows how the break-even value of profit before interest increases as gearing rises. As gearing increases from zero to 1:3 and to 1:1, the break-even earnings increase from 0 to 0X and to 0Y, corresponding to the three interest payment levels of zero, £2.5 million and £5 million, respectively (Scenario A in Table 10.2 and Figure 10.1). Notice finally that earnings of £10 million would generate the same ROE under all three capital structures.

This discussion of the impact of gearing is incomplete in one important respect. The analysis has been based on book values, despite earlier remarks that gearing ratios may often be better measured in terms of market values. We have yet to consider the effect of gearing on the value of the firm – does gearing actually make shareholders better off?

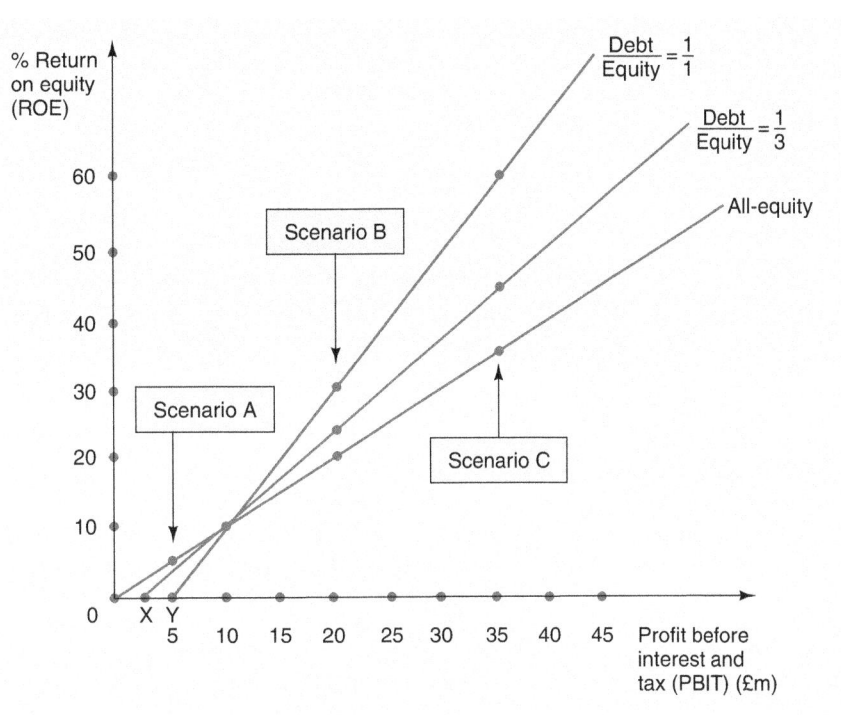

Figure 10.1 How gearing affects the ROE

To examine the effect on share price, we need to focus on the expected earnings figure and recall that the value of a share can be found by discounting its stream of earnings, in the simplest case, as a perpetuity. (No distinction is needed between earnings and dividends, as Lindley makes no retentions.) The expected values of shareholder earnings for each of the three gearing ratios are shown in Table 10.4. Recalling that Lindley's shares have a nominal value of £1, we can specify the number of shares corresponding to each gearing ratio and hence the expected value of the EPS. Share prices are found by applying the valuation formula, discounting the perpetual EPS at the 20 per cent return required by Lindley's shareholders.

It appears that, by using debt capital, financial managers can achieve significant increases in shareholder wealth. However, we ought to be suspicious of this effect. Why should shareholders' wealth increase when there have been no changes in trading activity or in expected aggregate income?

The analysis assumes that shareholders are prepared to accept a return of 20 per cent at all permissible gearing levels – they seem to be unconcerned by financial risk. Even though there may be no risk of insolvency, gearing exposes shareholder earnings to greater variability. We might therefore expect shareholders to react to gearing by demanding higher returns on their capital. If they think gearing is too risky, they may sell their holdings, thus driving down the share price.

Table 10.4 How gearing can affect share price

Gearing %	Number of shares	Expected value of shareholder earnings	EPS	Share price*
0	100m	£20m	20.0p	20.0p/0.2 = £1.00
25	75m	£17.5m	23.3p	23.3p/0.2 = £1.17
50	50m	£15m	30.0p	30.0p/0.2 = £1.50

*Share price is found by discounting the perpetual and constant EPS at 20 per cent.

We need to examine in more detail the likely reaction of shareholders to increased gearing; we will find that this is a key element in the debate about optimal capital structure. In the next section, we examine the so-called 'traditional' view of gearing, probably still the most widely supported explanation.

Self-assessment activity 10.6

What is the effect on share price in the Lindley example if shareholders require returns of 25 per cent under 25 per cent gearing, and of 35 per cent under 50 per cent gearing?

(Answer in Appendix A)

Debt's all, folks

Are you too fat? Mass is an absolute measure, but the question is vexed all the same. Whatever the doctor may say, it is not as simple as taking, say, height or cholesterol into account. It is a matter of what one wants from life, and the risks one is prepared to run. Just so with corporate debt. Petrobras, for example, clearly has a debt problem. But how the problem is measured can make the Brazilian state oil company look a little chubby or morbidly obese. Start on the income statement. Can Petrobras cover its interest payments? No worries there. Operating profits covered interest payments eight times over in the nine months that ended in September.

Now compare profits to the stock of debt on the balance sheet. Net debt at Petrobras is three times its earning before interest, tax, depreciation and amortisation (EBITDA). The global average for this measure is 1.5 according to Datastream. So, Petrobras's ratio seems high, but not wildly so. Private equity buyers are not spooked by ratios of four or more.

Or stick to the balance sheet, and compare the stock of debt to the stock of assets – judging what would be left to shareholders in case of liquidation. The average among the large US industrial companies is 60 per cent, according to S&P Dow Jones indices. Petrobras has 56 per cent of its equity covered by the debt. No red flag here.

But financial leverage must be seen in the light of operational leverage. Oil exploration and production has high fixed costs, and revenue varies with the oil price. A price drop can change all debt ratios fast. Even other nationalised emerging oil majors have less net debt, on average, of 41 per cent of equity, and just 1.6 times EBITDA.

The most important context for any measure is its trend through time. In just the first nine months of the year, Petrobras's net debt rose from $72bn to $86bn as investment overshot earnings. All its debt ratios are getting worse. Fat is a subjective matter, but objectively, Petrobras needs to go on a diet.

FT *Source:* Column, L. (2014). *Financial Times*, 18 February, p. 14. © The Financial Times Limited 2018. All rights reserved.

10.5 THE 'TRADITIONAL' VIEW OF GEARING AND THE REQUIRED RETURN

The traditional view emphasises the benefits of using relatively cheap debt capital as seen in the Lindley example: in particular, the effect on the rate of return required on investment. To analyse this approach in greater depth, we first need to make some definitions.

■ Value of an ungeared company

For an ungeared company, market value is found by discounting (or capitalising) its stream of annual earnings, E, all of which are attributable to shareholders, at the rate of return required by shareholders, k_e.

The value of an ungeared company, V_u, is simply the value of the ordinary shares, V_S. For a constant and perpetual stream of annual earnings, E:

$$V_u = V_S = \frac{E}{k_e} \quad \text{so that } k_e = \frac{E}{V_S}$$

capitalisation rate
A discount rate used to convert a series of future cash flows into a single capital sum

Much of the argument about capital structure centres on what happens to the discount rate (or **capitalisation rate**) as gearing increases and the share-out of earnings alters, due to the fixed interest charges imposed by debt. If the analysis is conducted in terms of *substituting* debt for equity, i.e. keeping size of firm constant as we did in the Lindley example, the effect of gearing can be examined while holding E constant. In this case, gearing simply rearranges the share-out of E among the company's stakeholders. We denote the book value of borrowings as B and the interest rate as i, thus involving a prior interest charge of $(i \times B)$. Gearing splits the earnings stream of the company into two components, the prior interest charge and the portion attributable to shareholders, the net income (NI) of $(E - iB)$. The overall value of the company is the value of the shares (V_S) plus the value of the debt, each capitalised at its respective rate of discount. For debt, where there is no discrepancy (as in this example) between book value (B) and market value (V_B), the capitalisation rate is simply the nominal interest rate. The overall value of the geared company, V_g, is the combined value of its shares and its debt:

$$V_g = V_S + V_B = \frac{(E - iB)}{k_e} + \frac{iB}{i} = \frac{(E - iB)}{k_e} + V_B$$

The *overall* capitalisation rate (denoted by k_0) for a company using a mixed capital structure is a weighted average, whose weights reflect the relative importance of each type of finance in the capital structure, i.e. V_S/V_g and V_B/V_g for equity and debt, respectively:

$$k_0 = \left(k_e \times \frac{V_S}{V_g}\right) + \left(i \times \frac{V_B}{V_g}\right)$$

Bearing in mind that ($k_e V_S$) and iB (or iV_B, when $V_B = B$) represent the returns to shareholders and lenders, respectively – i.e. their respective shares of corporate earnings, E – the weighted average expression simplifies to:

$$k_0 = \frac{k_e V_S + iB}{V_g} = \frac{E}{V_g}$$

weighted average cost of capital (WACC)
The overall return a firm must achieve in order to meet the requirements of all its investors

For both ungeared and geared firms alike, k_0 is found by dividing the total required earnings by the value of the whole firm. k_0 is also known as the **weighted average cost of capital (WACC)**, since it expresses the overall return required to satisfy the demands of both groups of stakeholders. The WACC may be interpreted as an average discount rate applied by the market to the company's future operating cash flows to derive the capitalised value of this stream, i.e. the value of the whole company.

It looks as if a company could lower the WACC by adding 'cheap' debt to an equity base. For instance, in the Lindley example, while the required return for the all-equity case is 20 per cent, i.e. the cost of equity, with gearing at 25 per cent, the WACC, using book value weights, becomes:

$$k_0 = (0.75 \times 20\%) + (0.25 \times 10\%) = 17.5\%$$

Apparently, gearing can lower the overall cost of capital if both k_e and i remain constant. The effect of this is highly significant. In the traditional view of gearing, shareholders are deemed unlikely to respond adversely (if at all) to minor increases in gearing so long as the prospect of default looks remote. If the cost of equity remains static, substitution of debt for equity will lower the overall cost of capital applied by the market in valuing the company's stream of earnings. This is shown in Figure 10.2 by the decline in the k_0 schedule between A and B. Corresponding to this fall in k_0 is an increase in the value of the whole geared company, V_g, in relation to that of an equivalent ungeared company, V_u.

This benign impact of gearing has already been shown in the Lindley example. Looking back to Tables 10.3 and 10.4, consider the switch from 0 to 25 per cent gearing.

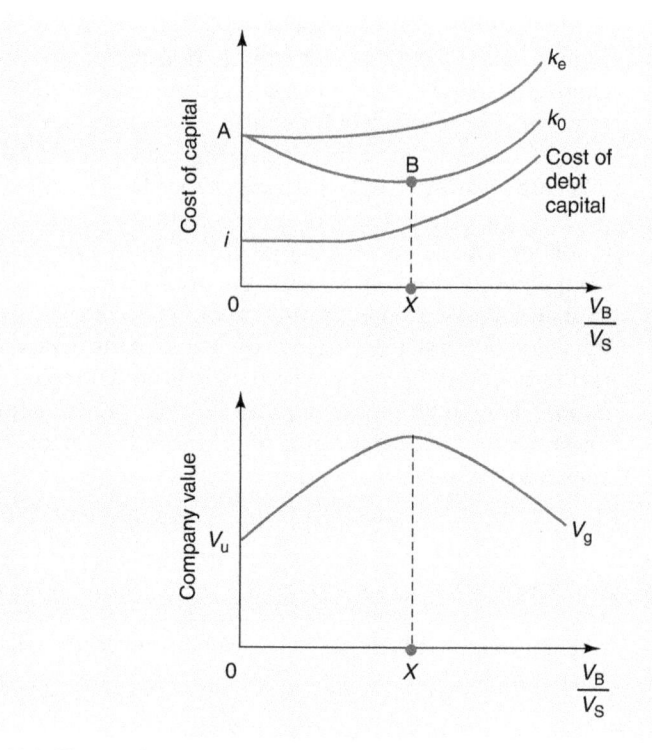

Figure 10.2 The 'traditional' view of capital structure

Assuming shareholders continue to seek a return of 20 per cent, the EPS discounted to infinity yields a share price of £1.17. The market value of equity becomes (£1.17 × 75m) = £88m, and the overall company value is:

$$V_g = V_S + V_B = (£88m + £25m) = £113m$$

Gearing up to 25 per cent raises market value by £13 million above book value, thus demonstrating the benefits of gearing to shareholders. The market value of the whole company rises because the value per unit of the residual equity increases due to the increase in EPS. Without gearing, each share would sell at £1.

However, sooner or later, shareholders will become concerned by the greater financial risk to which their earnings are exposed and begin to seek higher returns. In addition, providers of additional debt are likely to raise their requirements as they perceive the probability of default increasing. The k_e schedule will probably turn upwards before any upturn in i, given the legally preferred position of debt-holders, although the phasing of these movements is not clear in this model. Whatever the sequence of the upward revisions in required returns, the WACC profile will eventually be forced to rise, and the value of the company will fall. The model involves a clear optimal debt/equity mix, where company value is maximised and the WACC is minimised. This is gearing ratio X in Figure 10.2.

To financial managers, a major disappointment of this approach is its failure to pinpoint a specific optimal gearing ratio for all firms in all circumstances. The optimal ratio is likely to depend on the nature of the industry (e.g. whether the activity generates strong cash flows), the general marketability of the company's assets, expectations about the prospects for the industry, and the general level of interest rates. Clearly, many of these factors vary over time as well as between industries. However, a few pointers are possible.

For example, a supermarket chain, characterised by strong cash flow, can sustain a higher level of gearing than a heavy engineering enterprise, where the operating cycle is lengthy. Similarly, an airline, for whose assets there is a ready and active second-hand market, might withstand a higher gearing level (especially as flights are often paid for well in advance) than a steel company with both a high level of operating gearing and assets that are highly specific and difficult to sell.

Self-assessment activity 10.7

What is this firm's WACC? (Ignore taxation.)

- debt-to-equity ratio = 40%
- cost of equity = 18%
- cost of debt = 8%

(Answer in Appendix A)

10.6 THE COST OF DEBT

Our analysis has so far assumed that market and book values of debt coincide. This is by no means always the case. Corporate bond values behave in a similar way to the market prices of government stock (gilt-edged securities). When general market interest rates increase, the returns on previously-issued bonds may look unattractive compared with the returns available on newly-issued ones. As a result, bond dealers mark down the value of existing stocks until they offer the same yield that investors can obtain by purchasing new issues. In other words, equilibrium in the bond market is achieved when all stocks that are subject to the same degree of risk and that have the same period to redemption offer the same yield.

The simplest case is perpetual (irredeemable) stock such as the UK government's 3.5 per cent War Loan. These were issued, never to be repaid, to support the British war effort between 1939 and 1945. They offer the holder a return of 3.5 per cent (the nominal rate of interest, or '**coupon rate**') on the par value of the stock, i.e. £3.50 per £100 of stock. With higher market rates, say 7 per cent, War Loan would look unattractive, and its value would fall, e.g. a £100 unit would have to sell at £50 to generate a yield of 7 per cent. An inverse relationship applies between fixed-interest bond prices and interest rates:

coupon rate of interest
The fixed rate of interest, as printed on the debt security, which a firm must pay to lenders

$$\text{The market value of an irredeemable bond} = \left(\text{nominal value} \times \frac{\text{coupon rate}}{\text{market rate}}\right)$$

Self-assessment activity 10.8

What is the market value of the 3.5 per cent War Loan when market rates are:

(i) 11%?
(ii) 3%?

(Answer in Appendix A)

In practice, the calculation is more complex when we consider the far more common case of bonds with limited lifetimes until maturity. In assessing the value of such bonds, the market value will also include the eventual capital repayment.

For example, if the market rate is 10 per cent, a 10-year bond with a coupon rate of 10 per cent, denominated in £100 units, would have the following (present) value:

$$\begin{aligned}
\text{PV} &= \text{discounted interest payments over 10 years} + \text{discounted capital repayment in Year 10} \\
&= (10\% \times £100) \times (\text{PVIFA}_{(10,10)}) + (£100) \times (\text{PVIF}_{(10,10)}) \\
&= (£10 \times 6.1446) + (£100 \times 0.3855) \\
&= £61.45 + £38.55 = £100
\end{aligned}$$

The market value coincides with the par value because the coupon rate equals the going market rate. If, however, the market rate were to rise to 12 per cent, all future payments to the bond-holder, both capital and interest, would be more heavily discounted, i.e. at 12 per cent, reducing the market value to £88.70.

Values of corporate bonds behave in essentially the same way, although, since companies are more risky than governments, they have to offer investors a rather higher rate of interest. This allows us to identify the cost of corporate debt capital. A company can infer the appropriate rate of interest at which it could raise debt by looking at the market value of its own existing debt or that of a similar company. For example, if the market value of each £100 unit of debenture stock is £95 and has to be repaid in full in two years' time, the cost of debt can be found by solving a simple IRR expression. Someone who decided to purchase the stock in the market would anticipate two interest payments of £10 and a capital repayment of £100. The return expected is denoted by k_d in the following IRR expression:

$$£95 = \frac{£10}{(1 + k_d)} + \frac{(£10 + £100)}{(1 + k_d)^2}$$

The solution for k_d is 13 per cent. The market signals this rate as the cost of raising further debt.

There is another adjustment to make for tax relief on debt interest payments. To allow for tax, we look at the cost of debt from the company's perspective, since it is the company that enjoys the tax break. With a Corporation Tax rate of 30 per cent, each £10 interest payment will generate a tax saving of £3 for the company, reducing the effective interest cost to £10(1 − 30%) = £7.0. The IRR equation becomes:

$$£95 = \frac{£7.0}{(1 + k_d)} + \frac{(£7.0 + £100)}{(1 + k_d)^2}$$

Self-assessment activity 10.9

Verify that the solution rate in the above IRR equation is 9.9 per cent.

The tax benefits from using debt can be substantial. Take the case of a 10-year bond, issued and redeemable at a price of £100, with a coupon rate of 10 per cent. The value of the tax savings on interest payments, or the '**tax shield**', is:

$$\begin{aligned}\text{Tax shield} &= \text{interest charge} \times (\text{tax rate}) \times \text{PVIFA}_{(10,10)} \\ &= (10\% \times £100) \times (30\%) \times 6.1446 \\ &= £18.43\end{aligned}$$

In practice, this value is reduced by any delay in tax payments, which in turn delays the receipt of tax benefits. It is also assumed that the company always has sufficient taxable profits to benefit from the tax relief on interest payments.

Asian perpetual bond market fizzes to life

Companies in Asia are embracing a niche, high-risk instrument that was once at the very periphery of the region's capital markets – the perpetual bond. Perpetual bonds have characteristics of both debt and equity, often getting equity weighting from auditors and rating agencies. For borrowers, the attraction of selling such securities lies in extending the maturity of their debt over a very long horizon.

US dollar-denominated perpetual bond issuance from corporations in Asia, excluding Japan, is on course for a record year, according to Dealogic. The $8.5bn sold so far

Continued

this year has already surpassed the $7.8bn sold in 2016. Asian banks have been big drivers of the trend, selling $6.4bn in US-dollar denominated perpetual securities in the year to date. The attraction for buyers is that these bonds help investors offset long-term liabilities.

ChemChina's $600m perpetual bond sale in May drew more than $5bn in orders, and had a final yield of 3.9 per cent. The group also disclosed last month that it had sold $18bn in perpetual bonds to a handful of institutions.

Most corporate perpetual bonds are structured to incentivise borrowers to redeem the securities, with the debt's call dates paired with a jump in the coupon that is often punishing to the borrower.

A case in point is Evergrande, the Chinese property developer that made heavy use of perpetual bonds, partly to minimise the amount of total debt shown in its accounts.

This week, Evergrande announced that it would be retiring all its perpetual debt. This erased the instrument's big advantage: to present debt as equity. In turn, Evergrande shares hit an all-time high after it announced the end to its grand perpetual experiment.

However, this year several large well-known Hong Kong corporations including CK Hutchison and Sun Hung Kai have sold perpetuals without the penalising increase in yield – so-called fixed-for-life products.

The instruments are risky for the buyer in that the seller has no incentive to call the security. That means the bond can remain outstanding for a very long time, beyond the point where an investor can make a reasonable guess on the borrower's creditworthiness.

FT *Source:* Weinland, D. (2017) Asian perpetual bond market fizzes to life. *Financial Times*, 7 June. © The Financial Times Limited 2018. All rights reserved.

Self-assessment activity 10.10

What is the value of the tax shield for £10 million debt, coupon rate 6 per cent, tax rate 30 per cent:

(a) if the debt is perpetual?
(b) if it is to be repaid in 20 years?

(Answer in Appendix A)

Debt interest cost tax advantage

The basic principle of corporate taxation is that a firm's remittance to the government is linked to its net profits. Over the years, interest payments on bonds and loans have been considered an operating expense. But dividends are treated as an economic reward to shareholders. As a result, every dollar of interest paid, assuming today's 35 per cent tax rate, lowers a company's tax bill by 35 cents, but a dollar of dividends does not.

Debt capital is already cheaper than equity as it sits higher in the claim of priorities should a company go bankrupt. The tax advantage makes debt even more attractive.

Two common textbook methods for valuing companies show that executives can boost value simply by replacing their firm's equity with debt.

The Congressional Budget Office has estimated that the effective tax rate on the profits from a debt-financed capital investment at −6.4 per cent — that is to say, a tax credit.

In a widely cited paper, economist Robert Pozen noted that between 2000 and 2009, the estimated total value of the interest tax shield was $3tn, while the corporate tax collected was measured at just $2tn.

Regulators separately worry that companies which binge on borrowing become vulnerable to distress. An IMF report in 2010 concluded that 'tax distortions are likely to have contributed to the [financial] crisis by leading to levels of debt higher than would otherwise have been the case'.

The debt/equity schism has therefore attracted the interest of authorities globally. Germany, Italy, Portugal and Spain already cap interest deductions, and the EU's anti-tax avoidance directive requires members to adopt their own caps by 2018. Starting in April, the UK is set to limit interest deductions to 30 per cent of company cash flow.

FT *Source:* Indap, S. (2017) Private equity frets as Congress eyes interest cost deduction. *Financial Times*, 25 January. © The Financial Times Limited 2018. All rights reserved.

10.7 THE OVERALL COST OF CAPITAL

Section 10.5 discussed the weighted average cost of capital (WACC) concept, illustrated in Figure 10.2. This was interpreted as the overall rate of return required in order to satisfy all stakeholders in the company. It described a U-shaped profile as the firm's level of gearing increased. It fell initially, as cheap debt was added to the capital structure, reached a minimum at the optimal gearing ratio, then rose as gearing came to be regarded as 'excessive'. The behaviour of this schedule provides a clue to the appropriate rate of return required on the company's activities, and, by implication, on new investment projects. We will examine this issue using the Lindley example (covered in Section 10.4).

Lindley plc and the cut-off rate for new investment

Lindley's shareholders require a 20 per cent return and its pre-tax cost of debt is 10 per cent. Let us make the simplifying assumptions that Lindley's debt is perpetual and sells at par. Adjusting for tax at 30 per cent, as explained above, this corresponds to an after-tax cost of 7 per cent. What return on investment should Lindley achieve when issuing debt to finance a new project?

It is tempting to argue that the cut-off rate on this new project should be the cost of servicing the finance raised specifically to undertake the project. However, this is probably erroneous because using debt has an opportunity cost. The use of 'cheap' debt now may erode the company's ability to undertake worthwhile projects in the future by the depletion of credit lines. For example, assume that in 2017 Lindley uses debt costing 7.0 per cent after tax to finance a project offering a post-tax return of 12 per cent, but this exhausts its credit-raising capacity. As a result, it becomes unable to exploit a project available in 2018 that offers 14 per cent. This suggests that the 'true' cost of the finance used in 2017 exceeds 7.0 per cent. Hence, to assess the 'correct' cost of capital really requires forecasting all future investment opportunities and capital supplies.

In addition, our previous analysis leads us to expect, at some level of gearing, an adverse reaction by shareholders, who may demand higher returns to compensate for higher financial risk. Consider two possible cases, denoted by points A and B, respectively, on the WACC profile in Figure 10.2. Note that A corresponds to zero gearing and B to the critical ratio.

Case A

Lindley has no debt at present and shareholder capital is £100 million. A new project with perpetual life is to be financed by the issue of £10 million debt at an after-tax cost of 7 per cent. No impact on the cost of equity is expected. In this case, the company will have to generate additional post-tax annual returns of (7% × £10m) = £0.70 million in order to meet the extra financing costs associated with the new project, so that the hurdle rate for the new project is 7 per cent. Here, with the explicit assumption that shareholders will not react adversely, it may be reasonable to use the cost of debt as the cut-off rate. In this case, the required return would be simply the interest cost divided by the debt financing provided, i.e. the interest rate:

Required return = $iB/B = i$

However, this position is unlikely to be tenable, except for very small projects, and hence small borrowings, since significant changes in gearing (in either direction) are likely to provoke a market reaction.

Case B

We will assume that the optimal gearing ratio involves a capital structure with £50 million of each type of capital. Any further debt financing, even at a constant debt cost, will cause the cost of equity to increase. Assume that the extra £10 million debt financing will provoke shareholders to demand a return of 24 per cent. This would be expressed by downward pressure on share price until the return on holding Lindley's shares became 24 per cent. Now, the project has to meet not only the debt financing costs, but also the additional returns required by shareholders. The total additional required income is:

Required extra income = debt financing costs + extra return required on equity
= (7% × £10m) + (4% × £50m)
= £0.70m + £2m
= £2.70m

Instead of an apparent cost of just 7 per cent, the true cost of using debt to finance this project is actually (£2.70m/£10m) = 27 per cent. This figure of 27 per cent is the **marginal cost of capital (MCC)**.

In the next section, we pinpoint the conditions under which it is acceptable to use the WACC as the cut-off rate for evaluating new investment.

marginal cost of capital (MCC)
The extra returns required to satisfy all investors as a proportion of new capital raised

Required conditions for using the WACC

Some major requirements have to be satisfied before use of the WACC can be justified:

1. The project is a marginal, scalar addition to the company's existing activities, with no overspill or synergistic impact likely to disturb the current valuation relationships.
2. Project financing involves no deviation from the current capital structure (otherwise the MCC should be used).
3. Any new project has the same systematic risk as the company's existing operations. This may be a reasonable assumption for minor projects in existing areas and perhaps for replacements, but hardly for major new product developments.
4. All cash flow streams are level perpetuities (as in the theoretical models).

In the short term, at least, firms are almost certain to deviate from the target structure, especially as market values fluctuate and financial managers perceive and exploit ephemeral financing bargains, e.g. an arbitrage opportunity in an overseas capital market. It is thus unrealistic to expect the hurdle rate for new investment to be adjusted for every minor deviation from the target gearing ratio. To all intents and purposes, the capital structure is given – only for major divergences from the target gearing ratio should the discount rate be altered. Similarly, even where a project is wholly financed by debt or equity, so long as the project is a minor one with no appreciable impact on the overall gearing ratio, then it is appropriate to use the WACC as the cut-off rate.

The preceding discussions suggest that the marginal cost of capital (MCC), rather than the cost of debt or the WACC, should be used as the cut-off rate for new investment. However, the MCC does have operational limitations. In particular, we are required to anticipate *how* the capital market is likely to react to the issue of additional debt. Given that we seem unable to define the WACC profile or pinpoint the optimal gearing ratio at any one time, this presents a problem. We could assume that the present gearing ratio is optimal, but this prompts the question of why different firms in the same industry have different gearing ratios.

The target capital structure: a solution?

target capital structure
What the firm regards as its optimal long-term ratio of debt to equity (or debt to total capital)

A solution commonly adopted in practice is to specify a **target capital structure**. For example, RWE, one of Europe's largest electricity and gas companies, has set a target for gearing at 3.0 (gearing defined as the ratio of net debt to EBITDA = 22,709/5,403). In 2016–17, the ratio achieved was higher than this at 4.20, and the company was working to move to the target ratio (www.rwe.com).

The firm defines what it regards as the optimal long-term gearing range or ratio, and then attempts to adhere to this ratio in financing future operations. If the optimal ratio is deemed to involve, say, 50 per cent debt and 50 per cent equity (i.e. a debt-to-equity ratio of 100 per cent), any future activities should be financed in these proportions. For example, a £10 million project would be financed by £5 million debt and £5 million equity, via retained earnings or a rights issue. The corollary is to use the WACC as the cut-off rate for new investment. When shareholders require 20 per cent and debt costs 7 per cent post-tax, the WACC is:

(cost of equity × equity weighting) + (post-tax cost of debt × debt weighting)
= (20% × 50%) + (7% × 50%) = (10% + 3.5%) = 13.5%

The WACC is recommended because it is difficult to anticipate with any precision how shareholders are likely to react to a change in gearing. The somewhat pragmatic solution proposed assumes that the new project will have no appreciable impact on gearing: in other words, that the company already operates at or close to the optimal gearing ratio and does not significantly deviate from it. Obviously, the WACC and the MCC will coincide in this case.

The panel explains how E.ON, the German utility group, calculates its WACC.

The WACC in practice

The cost of capital is determined by calculating the weighted average cost of equity and debt. This average represents the market-rate returns expected by stockholders and creditors. The cost of equity is the return expected by an investor in E.ON stock. The cost of debt equals the long-term financing terms that apply in the E.ON Group. The parameters of the cost-of-capital determination are reviewed on an annual basis.

Our review of the parameters in 2016 led us to adjust our after-tax cost of capital from 4.9 percent to 4 percent, mainly because of a lower risk-free interest rate resulting from the persistently low interest-rate environment. The table shows the derivation of cost of capital before and after taxes.

Cost of Capital

	2016	2015
Risk-free interest rate	0.5%	1.25%
Market premium[1]	6.75%	6.75%
Debt-free beta factor	0.50	0.52
Indebted beta factor[2]	0.92	0.90
Cost of equity after taxes	**6.70%**	**7.30%**
Average tax rate	31%	27%
Cost of equity before taxes	9.7%	10.0%
Cost of debt before taxes	2.6%	3.4%
Marginal tax rate	31%	27%
Cost of debt after taxes	**1.80%**	**2.40%**
Share of equity	45%	50%
Share of debt	55%	50%
Cost of capital after taxes	**4.00%**	**4.90%**
Cost of capital before taxes	**5.80%**	**6.70%**

[1] The market premium reflects the higher long-term returns of the stock market compared with German treasury notes.
[2] The beta factor is used as an indicator of a stock's relative risk. A beta of more than one signals a higher risk than the risk level of the overall market; a beta factor of less than one signals a lower risk.

Source: E.ON Annual Report 2016.

10.8 WORKED EXAMPLE: DAMSTAR PLC

Damstar plc produces and sells computer modems. The company obtained a stock market quotation four years ago, since when it has achieved a steady annual return for its shareholders of 14 per cent after tax. It has an issued share capital of 2 million 50p ordinary shares. The ordinary shares sell at a P:E ratio of 11:1. In the year ended 31 March 2017, the company sold 20,000 units.

The annual profit and loss account (income statement) as at 31 March 2017 is given here:

	£000	£000
Sales		1,600
Less: Variable expenses	(880)	
Fixed expenses	(350)	(1,230)
Profit before interest and taxation		370
Less: interest payable (10% loan stock)		(150)
Profit before taxation		220
Less: Corporation Tax (at 30%)		(66)
Profit after taxation		154
Dividend		(120)
Retained profit		34

In recent months, the company has been experiencing labour problems. As a result, it has decided to introduce a new highly automated production process in order to improve efficiency. The production process is expected to increase fixed costs by £140,000 (including depreciation), but will reduce variable costs by £19 per unit.

The new production process will be financed by additional debt in the form of a secured £1,000,000 debenture issue at an interest rate of 12 per cent. If the new production process is introduced immediately, the directors believe that sales for the forthcoming year will be unchanged.

Required
(a) Determine how the proposal affects Damstar's break-even volume.
(b) Assuming no change in P:E ratio, calculate the change in EPS and share price if Damstar introduces its new production process immediately.
(c) What is the effect of the new process on Damstar's weighted average cost of capital using market value weights?

Answer to Damstar example
(a) First, we establish the revenue and cost parameters. Currently, the price is (£1.6m/20,000 = £80) per unit. The average variable cost (AVC) = (£0.88m/20,000) = £44. Hence, the gross profit margin (GPM) = (£80 − £44) = £36.

The break-even volume (BEV) can be expressed in operating terms, i.e. before fixed financing charges, and also after allowing for interest. Ignoring interest, the BEV is:

(Fixed costs of £0.35m/£36) = 9,722 units

Allowing for interest of £0.15 million, the BEV is:

(£0.35m + £0.15m/£36) = 13,889 units.

With the new process, the AVC becomes (£44 − £19) = £25, and the GPM becomes (£80 − £25) = £55.

The new level of fixed operating costs is £0.49 million.
The BEV ignoring interest = (£0.49m/£55) = 8,909 units. Allowing for the interest, increased by (12% × £0.12m) to (£0.15 + £0.12m) = £0.27m, the BEV is:

(£0.49m + £0.27m)/£55 = 13,818 units.

Notice that despite the increase in interest charges and the increase in fixed operating costs, the BEV has actually fallen due to the substantial fall in AVC. This warns that higher fixed costs does not always raise the BEV – it depends on what other changes are occurring at the same time.

(b) Currently, the EPS = (£154,00/2m) = 7.7p. With the 11:1 P:E ratio, the share price is (7.7p × 11) = 85p.

Predicted profit and loss account for the year ending 31 March 2018

	£(000)	£(000)
Sales		1,600
Variable Costs (20,000 × £25)	(500)	
Fixed Costs (£0.35m + £0.14m)	(490)	(990)
PBIT		610
Interest (£0.15m + £0.12m)		(270)
PBT		340
Taxation at 30%		(102)
PAT		238

EPS now becomes (£238,000/2m) = 11.9p, and with the same P:E ratio, the new share price would be (11.9p × 11) = £1.31.

(c) Based on market value weights, where available the WACC is:

	£	Weight
Value of equity = (£0.85 × 2m) =	1.7m	53
Value of debt = (£150,000/0.1) =	1.5m	47
(unknown market value, so book value used)		
Total	3.2m	100

WACC = (cost of equity × % of equity) + (post-tax debt cost × % of debt)
= (14% × 53%) + (10% [1 − 30%] × 47%)
= (7.4% + 3.3%) = 10.7%

After the issue of £1 million debt at 12 per cent interest, there are now two categories of debt, senior and junior.

	£	Weight
Value of equity = (£1.31 × 2m) =	2.62m	54
Value of senior debt = (10/12 × £1.5m) =	1.25m	26
Value of junior debt =	1.00m	20
Total	4.87m	100

WACC = (14% × 54%) + (10% [1 − 30%] × 26%) + (12% [1 − 30%] × 20%)
= (7.6% + 1.8% + 1.7%) = 11.1%

Comment: In this example, the increase in borrowing hardly affects the WACC, as the equity value increases to compensate. This result, of course, depends on the P:E ratio remaining at 11:1. Note also that the market value of the existing debt falls if interest rates rise. If the market rate of interest becomes 12 per cent, existing debt with a coupon of 10 per cent must sell at a discount.

Analysing the true cost of capital aids valuations

The key determinant to the estimate of weighted average cost of capital is the cost of equity, which to most firms and investors remains a sketchy financial concept, a residual of financial theory rather than its real foundation, the risk to the free cash flows.

We concluded long ago that the cost of equity must account for any and all events, quantitative and qualitative, that could serve to impact prospective free cash flows. This would include everything from sales and input cost variability to tax holidays, self-insurance risk, patent expirations, sovereign and litigation risk, and so on, down the line. Unfortunately, business schools and investment bankers utilise a naive approach to the calculus of return on equity, that of the capital asset pricing model, which often results in

Continued

a value not properly reflective of a company's real economic risks.

It is no wonder why analysts and investment pundits, as well as firms like Shire, prefer to speak of generally accepted accounting principles (GAAP) estimates. Yet without the use of an appropriate discount rate, the cost of equity, such estimates are often for naught, as a 1 percentage point change to cost of equity capital often results in changes to fair market value on the order of 20–30 per cent. A properly defined WACC is remarkably stable over time.

Source: Based on Kenneth S. Hackel, *Financial Times*, 14 January 2015.

10.9 MORE ON ECONOMIC VALUE ADDED (EVA)

In Chapter 7, we explained the concept of EVA, a popular tool for assessing the amount of value created by a firm. In that chapter, we confined the analysis to all-equity-financed firms. In that form, the resulting EVA measured the wealth created for the owners of the business. EVA can also be calculated in a broader sense. Instead of focusing on wealth-creation for the owners, one can focus on total economic value added for distribution to all the investors in the business. As such, for a geared firm, the EVA is arguably a better way of assessing managers' performance, i.e. the efficiency with which they utilise financial resources, because it is not distorted by the particular method of financing the business.

The adjustment is simple. Instead of applying the cost of equity to the net assets, we apply the WACC to the total capital employed to measure the capital cost, and deduct this from the NOPAT. For consistency, since the cost of debt appears in the WACC, the returns to debt should appear in the NOPAT, i.e. in this case the NOPAT is before charging interest, and thus includes returns to all types of investor.

The EVA formula thus becomes:

$$\text{EVA} = \text{NOPAT} - (\text{WACC} \times \text{Capital employed}).$$

It is usual to apply the WACC to long-term capital, given the relative volatility of short-term assets and liabilities.

Example

EVA plc's assets have a total book value of £900 million. It is financed by 60 per cent equity and 40 per cent debt. The costs of equity and debt are 12 per cent and 7 per cent (pre-tax), respectively. Operating profits are £100 million, and the tax rate is 30 per cent.

$$\text{NOPAT} = (\text{Operating profit-tax}) = £100\text{m}(1 - 30\%) = £70\text{m}$$
$$\text{WACC} = (60\% \times 12\%) + (40\% \times 7\%[1 - 30\%])$$
$$= 7.2\% + 1.96\% = 9.16\%$$
$$\text{EVA} = £70\text{m} - (9.16\% \times £900\text{m}) = (£70\text{m} - £82.44\text{m}) = -£12.44\text{m}$$

As this result is negative, EVA plc appears to have destroyed value.

Readers may notice that under the traditional view of gearing, as a firm raises the debt/equity ratio, the EVA is likely to increase, so long as the WACC declines.

10.10 FINANCIAL DISTRESS

This is an appropriate stage to clarify our terminology. Up to this point, we have implied that the reason for the upturn in the WACC profile is the threat of 'bankruptcy' resulting in 'liquidation', i.e. a company that fails to meet its debts will be forced by its creditors to liquidate. The term 'bankruptcy' in the UK strictly applies to personal insolvency. Individuals go bankrupt, and firms become insolvent. But what happens to a firm in severe financial distress? Broadly speaking, there are two main forms of treatment. The first is called 'receivership'.

Creditors – and it only takes one of many – may apply to a court to appoint a 'receiver' to recover the debt if the firm defaults on interest or capital repayments.

The order of priority for creditor payment

Creditors qualify for payment in the following order:

- *Secured creditors* These have a fixed legal charge over company assets such as land and buildings, plant and machinery, patents and other intellectual property such as trademarks. Factoring companies may also hold a fixed charge against specified debtors. Where there exist multiple fixed charge creditors, they rank in chronological order of registering the charge, hence the distinction between 'Senior' and 'Junior' debt.

- *Preferential creditors* These comprise employees' wages and other monetary entitlements, e.g. bonus payments.

- *Floating charge creditors* Floating charge assets are those that a firm uses in day-to-day operations including inventories, work-in-progress and non-factored debtors.

- *Unsecured creditors* These include trade creditors, VAT and PAYE debts payable to the tax authorities, loans that are not secured such as a bank overdraft, or a loan made by a director.

Shareholders are last in line, and rarely receive anything.

Source: Based on a listing provided by Wilson Field & Co. Ltd (**www.wilsonfield.co.uk**).

The receiver may sell the business, or parts of it, as a going concern, which continues to trade in a different guise, often involving a reduced scale of operation. However, the receiver's primary duty is to the appointing bank, and once sufficient funds have been realised to repay the loan, the receiver is under no obligation to maximise the proceeds of the sale of the remaining assets, or even to keep them operating. The receiver may choose to liquidate them *in toto* and disburse the net proceeds to remaining creditors and then any residue to shareholders.

The Insolvency Act 1986 introduced a new procedure, **administration**, as an attempt to rescue ailing companies and to protect employment, a procedure that became all too common during the recession years following the financial crisis. The company is allowed to continue trading under the overall control of an administrator, who will attempt to reorganise the company's finances and its operating structure. The administrator is appointed by a court at the request of the directors and has an equal duty to all creditors. In effect, administration, rather like filing for Chapter 7 bankruptcy under the US Bankruptcy Code, is an attempt to protect the company from its creditors, thus giving the administrator a breathing space during which it can attempt to secure the company's survival as a reorganised going concern. The main difference compared with the US equivalent is that Chapter 7 bankruptcy allows the incumbent managers and owners to retain control. In addition, Chapter 7 enables the firm to impose a moratorium on interest payments on existing debts for a specified period and also to borrow more funds as money lent after the filing has a prior claim on assets.

administration
An attempt to reorganise an insolvent firm under an administrator, rather than liquidate it

■ Distress costs

Any visitor to an auction of bankrupt stock will have no difficulty in appreciating the importance of postponing the break-up decision. Similarly, when repossessed assets, such as consumer durables and houses, are sold by creditors, they rarely fetch 'market values'. This is partly because the vendor often does not need to recover the full market value, having deliberately set the loan itself at less than the market value of the asset upon which it is secured. The vendor is interested in a quick sale to minimise depreciation, interest and other carrying costs. Moreover, when it is generally known that the assets are offered under distressed conditions, asset values usually head south! In January 2002, Britain's BG Group plc announced it would pay distressed US energy firm Enron $350 million for its stake in oil and gas fields off the coast of India. The 30 per cent stake in the Tapti and Panna-Mukta fields plus 63 per cent of a further untapped field was valued by Dutch bank ABN AMRO at $450 million, 30 per cent above the agreed price.

The costs incurred at and during liquidation are called the 'direct' costs of financial distress. Empirical studies (e.g. van Horne, 1975; Sharpe, 1981) have suggested that liquidation costs, including legal and administrative charges, may lower the resale value of distressed companies by 50 per cent or more.

However, a more recent US study suggests that distress costs of this magnitude may be an overestimate. In a study of 31 Highly Leveraged Transactions (HLTs) occurring between 1980 and 1989, Andrade and Kaplan (1998) tried to differentiate between the costs of dealing with economic distress, e.g. reacting to loss of contracts, and direct costs of financial distress. Comparing enterprise values at the date of the HLT and at the date of resolution of the distress, they estimated an average loss in firm value of 38 per cent, of which 26 per cent was due to economic distress and 12 per cent due to financial distress.

A more insidious form of financial distress is the impact of increasing gearing on managerial decision-making and the performance of the firm – the so-called 'indirect' costs. As a firm's indebtedness begins to look excessive, it may develop an overriding concern for short-term liquidity. This may be manifested in reduced investment in training and R&D, thus damaging long-term growth capability, and reducing credit periods and stock levels, which may hamper marketing efforts. Supplier power triggered the collapse of US discount retailer K-Mart in January 2002. Its sole supplier of grocery products suspended payments after K-Mart failed to make a regular weekly payment.

More obviously, a distressed firm may sell established operations at bargain prices, sell or abandon promising new product developments, and, to the extent that it does continue to invest, may express a preference for short-payback projects, cash-generating projects, rather than strategic activities. Troubled companies often cut their dividends to preserve liquidity, but this often signals to the market the extent of their difficulties. Finally, there may be a pervasive 'corporate gloom effect', which saps morale internally and damages public image externally.

Such costs are likely to be encountered well before the trigger point of cash flow crisis, and, of course, many firms have successfully surmounted them, but not without an often prolonged dip in the value of the company. In other words, both actual and anticipated liquidation costs detract from company value, lowering the effective limit to debt capacity.

The practical importance of the facility to appoint an Administrator before creditors can appoint receivers may now be seen. Administration enhances the probability of survival of a company unable to meet its immediate liabilities and may thus lead to lower costs of financial distress. However, there may be an element of '**moral hazard**' to the extent that financial managers might undertake more dangerous levels of debt, knowing that there is a more relaxed legal procedure in the event of insolvency.

Two other procedures for managing distress situations are company voluntary arrangements, and so-called pre-pack insolvency. These are discussed in turn.

■ Company Voluntary Arrangements (CVAs)

A CVA is a device whereby an essentially profitable, but temporarily illiquid, firm can buy time to stave off its creditors in order to restructure its debts. The negotiations may involve repayment of a lesser sum than that owed, or payment over a longer period of time or both. As well as obtaining court protection from creditors, the main benefits are that deferral of payment will ease pressure on cash flow, and that the firm continues to trade under the control of the directors. A CVA may be accepted by creditors such as suppliers, who agree that the firm is inherently profitable, expecting to receive future orders. Moreover, they may feel that they will receive more money via a CVA than through more complex and therefore more expensive procedures such as outright liquidation. In recent years, several well-known retailers have signed a CVA, especially regarding rentals owed to landlords. Examples include Oddbins, the vintners, and JJB Sports.

Seadrill warns on 'substantial' losses as bankruptcy fears mount

Seadrill's shares plunged on Tuesday after the oil rig owner warned investors to brace for 'substantial' losses in the face of potential bankruptcy proceedings. Shares in the heavily-indebted Norwegian and US-listed group fell as much as 46 per cent in Oslo as concerns mounted over its attempts to refinance its $8.5bn debt burden.

Seadrill has been trying to reach an agreement with its bank lenders, bondholders and others that might be prepared to inject cash into the company, including Mr Fredriksen's private vehicle Hemen Holdings, over its debts, which stood at $8.48bn at the end of 2016.

Mr Fredriksen, who has previously described Seadrill's efforts to restructure its debts as the most complicated transaction in his five-decade career in shipping, said that Seadrill had become too reliant on short-term bank lending. 'The capital structure was wrong. It was too short loans, too much guarantees, things like that.'

FT *Source:* Thomas, N. (2017) Seadrill warns on 'substantial' losses as bankruptcy fears mount. *Financial Times*, 4 April. © The Financial Times Limited 2018. All rights reserved.

■ Pre-pack insolvency

A pre-pack insolvency deal is where an insolvent firm's business is sold before entering a formal insolvency process. The deal is usually agreed before the insolvency practitioner is appointed and then swiftly completed once the appointment is made. This procedure has been available for many years but has increased substantially since the Enterprise Act of 2002, and particularly during the recession of the late 2000s, when it attracted considerable adverse publicity. A pre-pack is often used for owner-managed firms or for those whose main value lies off balance sheet in the form of key staff who might leave, or in assets that may fall in value sharply once a formal insolvency is announced. Hence, the distressed firm is usually sold with a minimum of, or no, open marketing. Unsecured creditors are often informed only after the event, although secured creditors are normally made aware of the situation ahead of the finalised deal as they are required to release their security.

The main advantages of the pre-pack deal are that the debts of the business remain with the old company, and the new firm, often called a 'phoenix company', can start afresh unencumbered by debt. The old firm will move into administration and the new entity will start trading immediately. This speed of the process minimises the danger of 'drift' while an orthodox process of administration is conducted, and the consequent danger of loss of business and staff at a time of great uncertainty. The main problem with a pre-pack is the compromising of the interests of the unsecured creditors – it is always possible that a better deal might have been struck if the firm was put on the block for general sale, especially in cases where the outgoing directors were able to buy the business at a 'bargain price'. The UK government announced it would be undertaking a review of the pre-pack procedure to assess whether it provides value for creditors in 2014. The outcome of this review has been a set of recommendations designed primarily to improve the success rate of businesses that are sold to connected parties.

An explanation of modern insolvency procedures can be found in Bailey and Groves (2014).

Self-assessment activity 10.11

Identify examples of distressed behaviour by highly geared firms from your reading of the financial press.

10.11 TWO MORE ISSUES: SIGNALLING AND AGENCY COSTS

An unexpected reduction in indebtedness is usually greeted with pleasure by the market, whereas a debt increase can be regarded in a favourable or unfavourable light depending on the accompanying arguments. According to Ross (1977), managers naturally have a vested interest in not busting the company, so an increase in gearing might be construed by the market as signalling a greater degree of managerial confidence in the ability of the company to service a higher level of debt. This argument relies on asymmetric information between managers and shareholders, and reflects the pervasive principal/agent problem.

Financial managers, as appointees of the shareholders, are expected to maximise the value of the enterprise, but it is difficult for the owners to devise an effective, but not excessively costly, service contract to constrain managerial behaviour to this goal. In the context of capital structure theory, the financial manager acts as an agent for both shareholders and debt-holders. Although the latter do not offer remuneration, they do attempt to limit managers' freedom of action by including restrictive covenants in the debt contract, such as restrictions on dividend payouts, to protect the asset base of the company.

Such restraints on managerial decision-making may adversely affect the development of the firm and, together with the monitoring costs incurred by the shareholders themselves, may detract from company value. Conversely, it is possible that the close monitoring by a small group of creditors, aiming to protect their capital, may induce managers to pursue more responsible policies likely to enhance the wealth of a widely diffused group of shareholders.

10.12 CONCLUSIONS

What conclusions does this body of analysis lead to, and how does it help financial managers?

1. Gearing can lower the overall or weighted average cost of capital that the company is required to achieve on its operations, and can raise the market value of the enterprise. However, this benign effect can be relied upon only at relatively safe gearing levels. Companies can expect the market to react adversely to 'excessive' gearing ratios. The implications for project appraisal are reasonably clear. Strictly, the appropriate cut-off rate for new investment is the marginal cost of capital, but if no change in gearing is caused by the new activity, the WACC can be used.

2. Considerable care should be taken when prescribing the appropriate use of debt that will enhance shareholder wealth without ever threatening corporate collapse. Levels of gearing that look quite innocuous in calm trading conditions may suddenly appear ominous when conditions worsen. Corporate difficulties do not usually occur singly, and highly geared companies are relatively less well placed to surmount them.

3. The capital structure decision, like the dividend decision, is a secondary decision – secondary, that is, to the company's primary concern of finding and developing wealth-creating projects. Many people argue that the beneficial impact of debt is largely an illusion. Clever financing cannot create wealth (although it may enable

exploitation of projects that would not otherwise have proceeded). It may, however, transfer wealth if some stakeholders are prepared, perhaps due to information asymmetry, to accept too low a return for the risks they incur, or if the government offers a tax subsidy on debt interest.

4 The decision to borrow should not be over-influenced by tax considerations. There are other ways of obtaining tax subsidies, such as investing in fixed assets, which qualify for tax allowances. A highly geared company could find itself unable to exploit the other tax-breaks offered by governments when a favourable opportunity is uncovered.

5 Remember that interest rates fluctuate over time. If interest rates move from what seems a 'high' level, financial managers should take advantage of the reduction. For example, if 10 per cent seems like the 'normal' long-term level of interest rates, when rates next fall below 10 per cent, and bankers are offering variable rate loans at, say, 9 per cent, one should not be afraid to take a fixed rate loan at, say, 9.5 per cent. Readiness to work with a slightly higher than minimum rate in the short term could have significant payoffs in the longer term. Anyone who thinks that rates will continue to fall should reserve some borrowing capacity to retain flexibility.

6 Firms should avoid relying on too many bankers, as with syndicated loans, despite the benefits of access to a variety of banking facilities. If the company hits trading and liquidity problems, it is hard enough to convince one banker that the company should be saved. But if it has to persuade 10 or 20, and their decision has to be unanimous, it is virtually impossible to reach a satisfactory conclusion about capital restructuring. The ill-fated Eurotunnel venture (now called Groupe Eurotunnel SE) had to deal with 225 banks at one stage of its troubled existence, later reduced to a mere 200. It was reported that Nissan had 170 banking relationships before implementing its recovery plan after the merger with Renault.

7 The finance manager should question whether debt is the most suitable form of funding in the circumstances. For example, there should be a clear rationale to support the case for debt rather than retentions (i.e. lower dividends) or a rights issue. He or she should recognise the value of retaining reserve borrowing capacity to draw upon under adverse circumstances or when favourable opportunities, like falling interest rates, arise.

8 These considerations are reflected in two popular theories that attempt to explain how firms address long-term financing decisions. These are:

- **The Trade-off Theory.** This recognises that firms seek to exploit the lower-cost benefits of borrowing, especially the tax shield, but at the same time, they are reluctant to increase the financial risk entailed in entering contractual commitments to make ongoing interest and capital repayments. In other words, they trade off the returns (the cost benefits) against the risks. We might thus expect to find that firms enjoying higher and more stable profit levels, which offer greater scope to shelter profits from tax, should operate at higher borrowing levels.

- **The Pecking Order Theory.** This suggests that firms have an order of priorities in selecting among alternative forms of finance:

    – First, they prefer to use the internal finance generated by operating cash flow.
    – Second, they prefer to borrow when internal sources are drained.
    – Third, they regard selling new shares almost as a last resort.

information asymmetry
The imbalance between managers and owners of information possessed about a firm's financial state and its prospects

The reason for this order of preference lies yet again in **information asymmetry** – managers know far more about the firm's performance and prospects than outsiders. They are unlikely to issue shares when they believe shares are 'undervalued', but more inclined to issue shares when they believe they are 'overvalued'. Naturally, shareholders are aware of this likely managerial behaviour and thus regard equity issues with suspicion. For example, they may interpret a share issue as a signal that management thinks the shares are overvalued and mark them down accordingly – a very common occurrence – thereby increasing the cost of equity. Investors would expect managers to finance investment programmes, first, using internal resources, second, via borrowing up to an appropriate debt/equity combination, and finally through equity issues. Yet again, signalling considerations are crucial.

SUMMARY

This chapter has explained firms' capital structure decisions and the effect on shareholders' returns. It covered the meaning of gearing, its likely benefits to shareholders, its dangers and its possible impact on the overall required return on investment. The cost of capital and gearing was further explained with real-life examples. Due to its tax advantage, debt is a cheaper source of finance than equity, and it is therefore commonly argued that up to a certain level, at least, inclusion of debt in capital structure increases shareholders' wealth. However, excessive debt in firms' capital structure increases both the operational and financial risk and thus negatively affects the financial health of organisations.

Key points

- Borrowing often looks more attractive than equity due to its lower cost of servicing, tax-deductibility of interest and low issue costs.
- A company's indebtedness is revealed by its capital gearing and by its income gearing.
- The sum of discounted tax savings conferred by the tax-deductibility of debt interest is called the tax shield.
- In a geared company, variations in earnings before interest and tax generate a magnified impact on shareholder earnings.
- The downside of gearing is the creation of a prior charge against profits, which results in the risk of possible default as well as greater variability of shareholder earnings.
- Default risk is likely to impose further costs on the geared company's shareholders, referred to as the 'costs of financial distress'.
- An insolvent company, i.e. one unable to meet its immediate commitments, is unlikely to achieve full market value in a sale of assets.
- For companies using a mixture of debt and equity, there may be an optimal capital structure at which the overall cost of capital (WACC) is minimised.
- The WACC is found by weighting the cost of each type of finance by its proportionate contribution to overall financing, and may fall as gearing increases.
- The increased risks imposed by gearing are likely to cause lenders and shareholders eventually to demand a higher rate of return, raising the WACC.
- The WACC is the appropriate cut-off rate for new investment so long as the company adheres to the optimal capital proportions.
- When companies deviate from the optimal capital structure, the marginal cost of capital becomes the correct cut-off rate.
- Because the optimal gearing ratio is difficult to identify in practice, many firms aim for a target gearing ratio, which they regard as 'acceptable'.
- In view of the risks of gearing, an increase in borrowing may be a way of signalling to the market greater confidence in the future.

Further reading

Because Chapters 10 and 11 are 'paired', the reading guides have been amalgamated. A composite guide is given at the end of Chapter 11.

Appendix
CREDIT RATINGS

Standard & Poor's credit rating system is shown below, together with that of the other main credit rating agency, Moody's.

Credit risk	S & P	Moody's
Prime	AAA	Aaa
Excellent	AA	Aa
Upper Medium	A	A
Lower Medium	BBB	Baa
Speculative	BB	Ba
Very Speculative	B, CCC, CC	B, Caa
Default	C, D	Ca, C

Source: www.moodys.com, www.standardandpoors.com.

Both agencies make further differentiation on the quality of bonds within each category. Moody's uses a numerical system (1, 2, 3) and S & P uses a plus or minus. For example, a rating of Aa1 from Moody's is a superior rating than Aa3, and an A+ from S & P is a better rating than *A−*.

Both rating systems are based on 'default risk and an assessment of the likelihood of recovery'. In each case, the cut-off between investment grade bonds and speculative ones is critical – anything of a speculative nature ('significant speculative characteristics' according to Moody's, and having 'speculative elements whose future cannot be considered as well-assured', according to Standard & Poor) is critical. Anything speculative attracts the unattractive label 'junk bonds', which, of course, incur higher rates of interest.

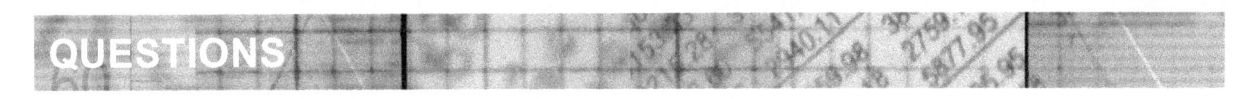

QUESTIONS

Questions with a coloured number have solutions in Appendix B on page 501.

1. Using the accounting information provided below, calculate the following measures of gearing:
   - long-term debt (LTD) to equity
   - LTD to LTD plus equity
   - total debt to equity
   - net debt in absolute terms
   - net debt to equity
   - total debt to total assets
   - interest cover
   - income gearing
   - total liabilities to total assets

Shareholders' funds	£500m
Cash	£20m
Short-term deposits	£40m
Short-term bank borrowing	£50m
Debentures and other long-term debts	£200m
Total assets	£800m
Total liabilities	£300m
Profit before interest and tax	£120m
Net interest payable	£25m

2. Calculate the cost of debt facing a firm that issued £50 million in debentures in £100 units two years ago at a nominal interest rate of 8 per cent p.a., in each of the following cases:
   (i) market value of debt is £45 million; perpetual life;
   (ii) as for (i), but allowing for Corporation Tax at 30 per cent;
   (iii) as for (i), but lifespan of debt is 8 years;
   (iv) as for (iii), but with tax payable at 30 per cent.

3. Darnol plc is currently ungeared and is considering a buy-back of ordinary shares via an open market purchase, borrowing in order to do so. You have been commissioned to report on the likely impact of two alternative policies, depending on the level of sales and operating profit for its products. You are given the following information:

Level of sales	PBIT	Probability
Weak	£5m	0.3
Average	£50m	0.5
Strong	£150m	0.2

Equity is currently £200 million at book value. Corporate tax is paid at 30 per cent. Two alternative share buy-back programmes are under consideration:
(i) Borrowing £40 million at 8 per cent.
(ii) Borrowing £80 million at 8.5 per cent.

Required
(a) Calculate the current, and potential, expected annual return on equity (ROE) under each programme.
(b) Calculate the standard deviation of the ROE in each case.
(c) Using the figures you have obtained, explain and illustrate the distinction between business and financial risk.

4 (a) Calculate the value of the tax shield in each of the following cases, all based on borrowing of £100 million at 10 per cent interest p.a., pre-tax.
   (i) Perpetual life debt, tax rate is 30 per cent.
   (ii) Debt repayable in full after five years.
   (iii) Debt repayable in equal tranches over five years, interest paid on the declining balance.
   (b) Specify the factors that determine the value of the tax shield that a firm can exploit.

5 Calculate the weighted average cost of capital for the following company, using both book value and market value weightings.

	Statement of financial position (Balance sheet) values	Cost of finance
Ordinary shares: (par value 50p)	£10m	20%
Reserves:	£20m	20%
Long-term debt:	£15m	10%

The debt is permanent and its market value is equal to book value.
The rate of corporate tax is 30%.
The ordinary shares are currently trading at £4.50.

6 The directors of Zeus plc are considering opening a new manufacturing facility. The finance director has provided the following information:
Initial capital investment: £2,500,000.
Dividends for the last five years have been:

Year	2013	2014	2015	2016	2017
Net dividend per share (pence)	10.0	10.8	11.4	13.2	13.7

The following is an extract from the statement of financial position of Zeus plc for the year ended 31 December 2017.

Creditors due in more than one year

8% Debenture	£700,000
Long-term loan (variable rate)	£800,000
Capital and reserves	
2,000,000 shares of 25p each	£500,000

The authorised share capital is 4 million shares, and the current market price per share at 31 December 2017 is 136p ex-dividend.
The current market price of debentures is £60 (ex-interest), and interest is payable each year on 31 December.
The interest rate on the long-term loan is 1 per cent above LIBOR, which at present stands at 16 per cent.
The debentures are irredeemable.
Ignore taxation.

Required
Calculate the weighted average cost of capital (WACC) for Zeus plc at 31 December 2017.

7 RH plc manufactures machine tools. It has issued two million ordinary shares, quoted at 168 pence each, and £1 million 10 per cent secured debentures quoted at par. To finance expansion, the directors of the company want to raise £1 million for additional working capital.
Cash flow from trading before interest and tax is currently £1 million per annum. It is expected to rise to £1.3 million per annum if the expansion programme goes ahead. To simplify placing a value on the company's equity, you should assume that:

- The forecast level of cash flow, and a tax rate of 33 per cent, will continue indefinitely.

- The required rate of return on the market value of equity, 18 per cent post-tax, will be unaffected by the new financing.
- There is no difference between taxable profits and cash flow.

The company's directors are considering two forms of finance – equity via a rights issue at 15 per cent discount to current share price, or 12 per cent unsecured loan stock at par.

Required

(a) Calculate for both financing options, the expected
  - **(i)** increase in the market value of equity;
  - **(ii)** debt/(debt + equity) ratio;
  - **(iii)** weighted average cost of capital.
(b) Assume you are the financial manager for RH plc. Write a brief report to the board advising which of the two types of financing is to be preferred. Include in your report brief comments on non-financial factors which should be considered by the directors before deciding how to raise the £1 million finance.

(CIMA)

8 Celtor plc is a property development company operating in the London area. The company has the following capital structure as at 30 November 2017.

	£000
£1 ordinary shares	10,000
Retained profit	20,000
9% debentures	12,000
	42,000

The equity shares have a current market value of £3.90 per share and the current level of dividend is 20 pence per share. The dividend has been growing at a compound rate of 4 per cent per annum in recent years. The debentures of the company are irredeemable and have a current market value of £80 per £100 nominal. Interest due on the debentures at the year-end has recently been paid.

The company has obtained planning permission to build a new office block in a redevelopment area. The company wishes to raise the whole of the finance necessary for the project by the issue of more irredeemable 9 per cent debentures at £80 per £100 nominal. This is in line with a target capital structure set by the company where the amount of debt capital will increase to 70 per cent of equity within the next two years.

The rate of corporation tax is 25 per cent.

Required

(a) Explain what is meant by the term 'cost of capital'. Why is it important for a company to calculate its cost of capital correctly?
(b) What are the main factors which determine the cost of capital of a company?
(c) Calculate the weighted average cost of capital of Celtor plc which should be used for future investment decisions.

9 Redley plc, which manufactures building products, experienced a sharp increase in operating profit (i.e. profits before interest and tax) from £27 million in 2015–16 to £42 million in 2016–17 as the company emerged from recession and demand for new houses increased. The increase in profits has been entirely due to volume expansion, with margins remaining static. It still has substantial excess capacity and therefore no pressing need to invest, apart from routine replacements.

In the past, Redley has followed a conservative financial policy, with restricted dividend payouts and relatively low borrowing levels. It now faces the issue of how to utilise an unexpectedly sizeable cash surplus. Directors have made two main suggestions. One is to redeem the £10 million of the secured loan stock issued to finance investment several years previously; the other is to increase the dividend payment by the same amount.

Redley's present capital structure is shown below:

	£m
Issued share capital (par value 50p)	90
Reserves	110
Creditors due after more than one year:	
9% secured loan stock 2004	30

Further information
- **(i)** Redley has no overdraft.
- **(ii)** Redley pays corporate tax at a rate of 33%.
- **(iii)** The last dividend paid by Redley was 1.45 pence per share.
- **(iv)** Sector averages currently stand as follows:

dividend cover	2.5 times
gearing (long-term debt/equity)	48%
interest cover	5.9 times

- **(v)** Redley's P:E ratio is 17:1.

Required

(a) Calculate (i) the dividend cover and (ii) the dividend yield for both 2015–16 and for the reporting year 2016–17, if the dividend is raised as proposed.

(b) You have been hired to work as a financial strategist for Redley, reporting to the Finance Director. Using the information provided, write a report to your superior, which identifies and discusses the issues to be addressed when assessing the relative merits of the two proposals for reducing the cash surplus.

(ACCA)

Practical assignment

For a company of your choice, undertake an analysis of gearing similar to that conducted in the text for D.S. Smith plc. Pay particular attention to the treatment of provisions and other components of long-term liabilities. If you decide to include short-term indebtedness in your capital gearing measure, would you include trade and other creditors as well?

Try to form a view as to whether your company is operating with high or low gearing.

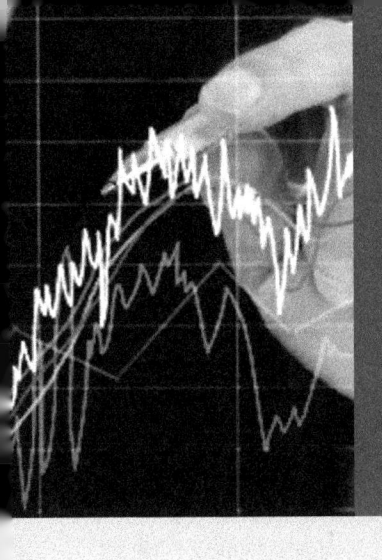

11

Does capital structure really matter?

A theorem fit to terrify bankers

Looking down the list of winners of the Nobel memorial prize in Economics, two names are causing bankers across the world to break into a cold sweat. They are Franco Modigliani (laureate in 1985) and Merton H. Miller (laureate in 1990). Both men have been dead for years, but their most important idea lives on with the undignified label of M&M.

M&M refers to an important-seeming decision for any company: how much should it be funded by borrowing, and how much through raising money by issuing shares or retaining profits? Some companies, famously Apple, have no debt to speak of. Others, including any bank you can name, raise most of their resources by borrowing rather than issuing shares.

Regulators want banks to fund themselves more through equity and less through debt. Bankers are reluctant. Bankers have tended to argue that equity is scarce and expensive and too much equity means that banks will make fewer loans at higher rates. M&M shows us that this argument is wrong in theory. In practice, M&M roughly holds: as leverage falls, equity becomes substantially cheaper.

Source: Harford, T. (2013) A theorem fit to terrify bankers. *Financial Times*, 9 March. © The Financial Times Limited 2018. All rights reserved.

Learning objectives

This chapter offers a more rigorous analysis of capital structure decisions. After reading, it, you should be able to:

- Understand the theoretical underpinnings of 'modern' capital structure theory.
- Appreciate the differences between the 'traditional' view of gearing and the Modigliani–Miller versions of optimal capital structure and gearing.
- Appreciate how the CAPM is integrated into capital structure analysis.
- Identify the extent to which a Beta coefficient incorporates financial risk.
- Apply the Modigliani-Miller theory to firms suffering financial distress.
- Explain the use of the adjusted present value method in valuation and capital budgeting decisions.

11.1 INTRODUCTION

The title of this chapter poses a question. In the last chapter, we warned that excessive debt could be lethal to the survival of firms. Yet such debt-burdened firms can, and often do, 'rise from the dead'.

Insolvency does not necessarily mean total loss of *enterprise value*. Insolvency is the formal acceptance that the business entity cannot meet its financial obligations, whether payment to creditors for supplies, or payments to lenders. Yet it is possible for insolvent firms to retain value as operating entities even though their owners' equity may have been wiped out. A few figures may help.

XYZ owes £10 million to lenders and its assets are only £8 million, so it is technically insolvent, unable to cover its debts with its assets, i.e. its net assets are negative – minus £2 million. However, if its operating activities generate more cash inflows than outflows, then as a debt-free entity, it would be viable and have value. Hence, it might look attractive as a restructured going concern to other investors prepared to take responsibility for the debts. Creditors might be prepared to exchange debt for equity (or preference shares), or take a discount on their principal, accepting, say, 30p in the pound, just to salvage something from the mess. The equity value has disappeared, but the enterprise still has value as a going concern if investors can be found to refinance it and reorganise it into a viable operation.

Even the heavily indebted Eurotunnel (now Groupe Eurotunnel SE), whose financial liabilities have reached €3.786 billion in 2016, was able to deliver a positive EBITDA of €514 million in 2016 (http://www.eurotunnelgroup.com). On this basis, it has an enterprise value even though the original equity has been all but wiped out.

One might then conclude that indebtedness does not really matter – a firm that cannot pay its way can be restructured and the jobs of the workers, if not the management, can be preserved.

In 2014, Readers Digest, the magazine publisher, was sold for $1. This might seem to be a small price to pay for a long-established company. However, the company had been struggling and filed for bankruptcy with liabilities of $1.2 billion and assets of $1.1 billion. Therefore, the price paid reflects the state of the company and the high level of indebtedness.

So long as assets can be sold at their full economic value, i.e. reflecting operating cash flows, then debt is of most consequence to the hapless owners whose equity is usually all but obliterated. Meanwhile, the business can proceed, often in a slimmed-down form and usually under different management, with a new set of backers hoping to do better next time round. This suggests that the sting of insolvency can be drawn.

The traditional theory of gearing says that debt should be handled with great caution but there is a body of analysis that proves that, under certain conditions, debt is truly irrelevant in determining company value and the cost of capital. This is the famous theory developed by Franco Modigliani and Merton Miller (MM), both Nobel prizewinners for Economics. Our next task is to explain this theory.

11.2 THE MODIGLIANI–MILLER MESSAGE

Modigliani and Miller's (MM) Capital Structure Theories
(i) MM-no tax, which 'proves' that no optimal capital structure exists, and that the WACC is invariant to debt/equity ratios
(ii) MM-with tax which suggests that the tax shield should be exploited up to the point of almost 100 per cent debt financing

To **Modigliani and Miller (MM)**, the traditional perception of the impact and desirability of gearing seemed unsupported by a theoretical framework. In particular, there seemed little reason, apart from some form of market imperfection such as information deficiency, why merely altering the capital structure of a firm should be expected to alter its value. *After all, neither its earnings stream nor its inherent business risk would alter* – it would remain essentially the same enterprise, operating under the same managers and in the same industry.

MM contended that, in a perfect capital market, the value of a company depended simply on its income stream and the degree of business risk attaching to this, regardless of the way in which its income was split between owners and lenders, i.e. its capital structure. Therefore, any imbalance between the value of a geared company and an otherwise identical ungeared company could only be a temporary aberration and would be quickly unwound by market forces. The mechanism for equalising the values of companies, identical except for their respective gearing, was the process of 'arbitrage', a feature of all developed financial markets which ensures that assets with the same risk–return characteristics sell at the same prices.

To support these contentions, some algebraic analysis is required, although readers will find that it is much less complex than may appear at first sight.

MM's analytical framework

No distinction is made between short- and long-term debt, and we assume that all borrowing is perpetual. The company is expected to deliver constant and perpetual estimated annual earnings, described by a normally-distributed range of possible outcomes. Investors are assumed to have homogeneous expectations, i.e. they all formulate similar estimates of company earnings, E, the net operating income (NOI) before interest and tax, or, more simply, revenues less variable costs less fixed operating costs. It is important to note that we are using a **free cash flow (FCF)** concept of earnings as explained in Chapter 7, i.e. income net of any investment required to rectify wear-and-tear on capital equipment and hence maintain annual earnings at E.

free cash flow (FCF)
A firm's cash flow free of obligatory payments. Strictly, it is cash flow after interest, tax and replacement investment, although it is measured in many other ways in practice, e.g. after all investment

The discount rate applied to the stream of expected earnings depends on the degree of business risk incurred by the enterprise. MM used the concept of 'equivalent risk classes', each one containing firms whose earnings depend on the same risk factors and from which the market expects the same return. In terms of the Capital Asset Pricing Model, this means that the earnings streams from firms in the same risk category are perfectly correlated and that member companies have identical activity Betas.

For consistency, we use the same definitions and notation as in Chapter 10. The key definitions are reproduced in Table 11.1.

The overall rate of return that the company must achieve to satisfy all its investors is the weighted average cost of capital (WACC), denoted by k_0. This can be expressed as:

$$k_0 = \left(k_e \times \frac{V_S}{V_0}\right) + \left(k_d \times \frac{V_B}{V_0}\right) = \frac{E}{V_0}$$

The WACC equals E/V_0, since net operating income is composed of earnings attributable to shareholders, $k_e V_S$, plus payments to lenders, iB.

Using this set of definitions, we now examine the impact of variations in capital structure on V_0 and k_0. Using debt-for-equity substitution rather than adding debt to equity has the major advantage of enabling us to hold constant both the book values of assets and capital employed and also the PBIT (a device used in the Lindley example in Chapter 10). Any gearing change alters only the company's capital structure, with no effect on company size or the level and riskiness of operating earnings. As a result, we can focus directly on the relationship between V_0 and k_0.

MM's assumptions

The MM thesis did not go unchallenged. Much criticism of MM's analysis stemmed from failure to understand positive scientific methodology. Their analysis attempted to isolate the critical variables affecting firm value under the restrictive conditions of a perfect capital market. This provided a systematic basis for examining how imperfections in real-world markets could influence the links between value and risk. The key assumptions are:

- All investors are price-takers, i.e. no individual can influence market prices by the scale of their transactions.

> **Table 11.1 Key definitions in capital structure analysis**
>
> V_0 = the overall market value of the whole company
> V_S = the value of the shareholders' stake in the company
> V_B = the market value of the company's outstanding borrowings
> B = the book value of borrowings (generally assumed equal to its market value)
> k_e = the rate of return required by shareholders
> k_d = the rate of return required by providers of debt capital
> k_0 = the overall (weighted average) cost of capital
> i = the coupon rate on debt
> iB = annual interest charges (i.e. payments to lenders, based on book value)
> $k_e V_S$ = payments to shareholders = $(E - iB)$, so that
> E = annual net operating income (NOI) = $(iB + k_e V_S)$
>
> It should be stressed that we are assuming no retention of earnings, i.e. D (dividends) = E, and hence no growth, and, for the moment, no taxes on corporate profits.
>
> The value of equity in an all-equity firm is:
>
> $$V_S = \frac{D}{k_e} = \frac{E}{k_e}$$
>
> The value of a geared firm making interest payments of iB is:
>
> $$V_S = \frac{(E - iB)}{k_e}$$
>
> The value of the whole firm in either case is:
> $V_0 = V_S + V_B$

- All market participants, firms and investors, can lend or borrow at the same risk-free rate.
- There are neither personal nor corporate income taxes.
- There are no brokerage or other transactions charges.
- Investors are all rational wealth-seekers.
- Firms can be grouped into 'homogeneous risk classes', such that the market seeks the same return from all member firms in each group.
- Investors formulate similar expectations about future company earnings. These are described by a normal probability distribution.
- The assets of an insolvent firm can be sold at full market values (i.e. no distress costs).

11.3 MM'S PROPOSITIONS

MM's analysis was presented as three propositions, the first being the crucial one.

Proposition I

The central proposition is that *a firm's WACC is independent of its debt/equity ratio, and equal to the cost of capital that the firm would have with no gearing in its capital structure.* In other words, the appropriate capitalisation rate for a firm is the rate applied by the market to an ungeared company in the relevant risk category, i.e. that company's cost of equity. The arbitrage mechanism will operate to equalise the values of any two companies whose values are temporarily out of line with each other. The example of Nogear plc and Higear plc will illustrate this.

Nogear plc and Higear plc

Nogear plc is ungeared, financed by 5 million £1 shares, while Higear plc's balance sheet shows £1 million debt, interest payable at 10 per cent, and 4 million £1 shares. Higear's debt/equity ratio is thus (£1m/£4m) = 25 per cent, at book values. The two firms are identical in every other respect, including their business risks and levels of annual expected earnings (E) of £1 million. The market requires a return of 20 per cent for ungeared streams of equity income of this risk.

Imagine that, temporarily, the market value of Nogear is £4 million and that of Higear is £6 million. Higear's equity is thus valued by the market at (£6m − £1m) = £5m. (Its debt/equity ratio expressed in terms of *market* values is thus £1m/£5m) = 20 per cent.) These market values correspond to respective share prices of (£4m/5m shares) = 80p for Nogear and (£5m/4m shares) = £1.25 for Higear.

The different share values conform to the traditional relationship at relatively low gearing ratios. Higear has a greater value presumably due to its gearing. Also, it appears that Nogear is undervalued by the market since, at a required return of 20 per cent, its value should be (£1m/0.2) = £5m.

MM argue that such imbalances can only be temporary, and the benefit obtained by Higear for its shareholders is largely illusory. It will pay investors to sell their holdings in the overvalued company and buy stakes in the undervalued one. Specifically, shareholders can achieve a higher return by selling holdings in Higear, and simultaneously replicate its gearing (MM call this **'home-made gearing'**) and achieve a higher overall return. This process of arbitrage will force up the value of Nogear and lower Higear's value, until their values are equalised. There is thus little point in a firm borrowing to gear-up its capital structure when investors can achieve the same benefits by acting independently.

'home-made gearing'
Where an investor borrows to arbitrage between two identical but differently valued assets

Home-made gearing

Consider the case of an investor with a 1 per cent equity stake in Higear. At present, this stake is worth (1 per cent of £5m) = £50,000, attracting an income of 1 per cent of (£1 million less interest payments of 10% × £1m), i.e. (1% × £900,000) = £9,000. This investor could realise his or her holdings for £50,000 and duplicate Higear's debt/equity ratio of 20 per cent by borrowing £10,000 at 10 per cent and investing the total stake of £60,000 in Nogear shares. This would buy (£60,000/£4m) = 1.5% of Nogear's equity, to yield a dividend of (1.5% × £1m) = £15,000. Personal interest commitments amount to (10% × borrowings of £10,000) = £1,000 for a net return of (£15,000 − £1,000) = £14,000, well in excess of the income formerly obtained from their holding in Higear, i.e. £9,000. Clearly, it would pay all investors to undertake this arbitrage exercise, thus pushing down the value of Higear and pushing up the value of Nogear until there was no further scope to exploit such gains. This point would be reached when the market values of the two companies were equal and when each offered the appropriate 20 per cent return required by the market:

$$\text{Value of Nogear} = \text{Value of Higear} = \frac{E}{k_e} = \frac{£1m}{0.2} = £5m$$

At this equilibrium relationship, the price of each company's shares is £1. For Nogear, the calculation is (£5m/5m shares) = £1, while for Higear, the relevant figures are (£5m − £1m debt) divided by 4m shares = £1. *In an MM world, there are no prolonged benefits from gearing, and any short-term discrepancies between geared and otherwise identical ungeared companies quickly evaporate.* As a result, MM concluded that both company value and the overall required return, k_0, are independent of capital structure.

In reality, not all the conditions required to support the arbitrage process may apply, suggesting that any *observed* benefits may derive from imperfections in the capital market. Moreover, if gearing does result in higher company value, there must have been a wealth transfer, since nothing has occurred to alter the fundamental wealth-creating properties of the company.

Proposition II: the behaviour of the cost of equity

Underpinning Proposition I is a statement about the behaviour of the relevant cost of capital concepts – in particular, the rate of return required by shareholders. This is expressed in MM's second proposition which states 'the expected yield of a share of equity is equal to the appropriate capitalisation rate, k_e, for a pure equity stream in the class, plus a premium related to the financial risk equal to the debt/equity ratio times the spread between k_e and k_d'. This proposition can be expressed as:

$$k_{eg} = k_{eu} + (k_{eu} - k_d)\frac{V_B}{V_S}$$

where k_{eg} and k_{eu} denote the returns required by the shareholders of a geared company and an equivalent ungeared company, respectively. The expression is easily obtained from Proposition I. (See Appendix I to this chapter.) It simply tells us that *the rate of return required by shareholders increases linearly as the debt/equity ratio is increased*, i.e. the cost of equity rises exactly in line with any increase in gearing to offset precisely any benefits conferred by the use of apparently cheap debt. The relevant relationships are shown in Figure 11.1.

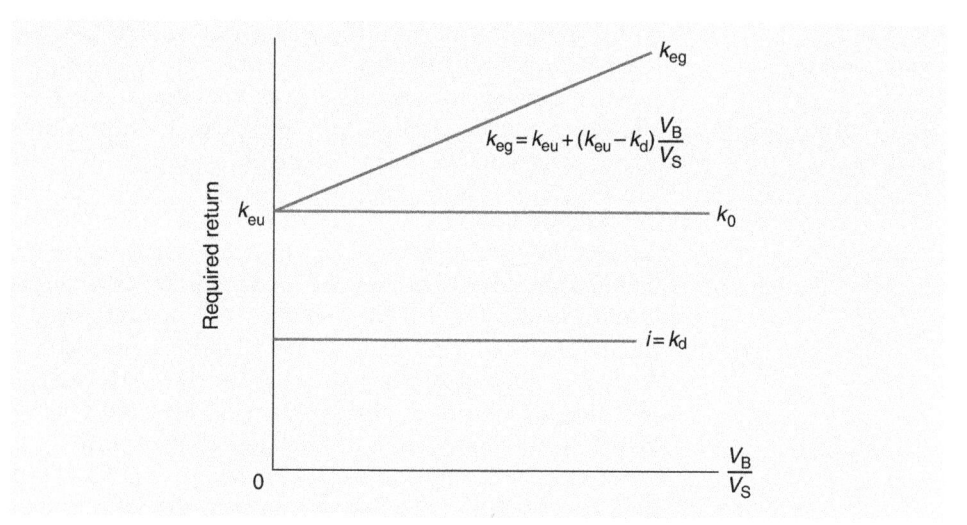

Figure 11.1 MM's Propositions I and II

If you check back to Chapter 10, which covered the traditional view of gearing, and to Figure 18.2 in particular, you will find that the behaviour of k_e is the critical difference between the MM version and the traditional theory. In the latter, there is little or no reaction by shareholders to an increase in debt-to-equity ratio over 'modest' levels of gearing. They presumably are not alarmed by the 'judicious' use of debt. By contrast, shareholders, in the MM view, respond immediately when any gearing is undertaken, i.e. to them, *any* use of debt introduces an element of financial risk.

It should now be appreciated that in the Nogear/Higear example, Higear shareholders were seeking too low a rate of return, i.e. Higear was overvalued, and the market was temporarily offering Nogear's shareholders too high a return, i.e. Nogear was undervalued. Via the process of arbitrage, their values were brought back into line, and appropriate rates of return on equity were established, reflecting their respective levels of gearing. The correct rate of return for Higear's equity, for its particular debt/equity ratio of 25 per cent (at equilibrium market values) is:

$$k_{eg} = k_{eu} + (k_{eu} - k_d)\frac{V_B}{V_S} = 20\% + (20\% - 10\%)\frac{£1m}{£4m} = 22.5\%$$

Proposition III: the cut-off rate for new investment

MM's third proposition asserts that *'the cut-off rate for new investment will in all cases be k_0 and will be unaffected by the type of security used to finance the investment'*.

A proof of this proposition is given in Appendix II to this chapter, but it is quite easy to justify intuitively. Proposition I states that the WACC, k_0, is constant and equal to the cost of equity in an equivalent ungeared company. Since k_0 is invariant to capital structure, it follows that, however a project is financed, it must yield a return of at least k_0, the overall minimum return required to satisfy stakeholders as a whole.

It is worth illustrating this contention for the case where a company invests to yield a return *above* the cost of the debt used to finance the project, but *below* the cost of equity in an ungeared company.

Nogear: right and wrong investment cut-off rates

Nogear decides to raise £2 million via a debt issue at 10 per cent to finance a new project expected to yield an annual return of 15 per cent for many years into the future. Is this an acceptable project? Proposition I tells us that the initial value of the company, V_0, and hence the equity, V_{S0}, prior to the issue is:

$$V_0 = V_{S0} = \frac{E}{k_e} = \frac{£1m}{0.2} = £5m$$

Incorporating the new project's earnings, the post-issue value of the whole company, V_1, is:

$$V_1 = \frac{£1m + (15\% \times £2m)}{20\%} = \frac{£1.30m}{0.2} = £6.50m$$

Denoting R as the return on the new investment, I, and V_B as the value of the debt issued, the new value of the equity, V_{S1}, is:

$$V_{S1} = V_0 + \frac{RI}{k_0} - V_{B0} - I = £5m + \frac{£0.30m}{0.2} - 0 - £2m = (£6.50m - £2m)$$
$$= £4.50m$$

The value of the equity falls because the new project's return, although above the interest rate on the debt used to finance it, is less than the capitalisation rate applicable to companies in this risk category.

Self-assessment activity 11.1

Why does a geared company have the same value (allowing for size) as an ungeared company of equivalent risk in the 'basic' MM model?

(Answer in Appendix A)

11.4 DOES IT WORK? IMPEDIMENTS TO ARBITRAGE

The operation of the arbitrage process requires that corporate and personal gearing are perfect substitutes in a perfect capital market. The Nogear/Higear example showed how individual investors could replicate corporate gearing to unwind any transitory premium in the share price of a geared company. Much criticism of MM centres on the perfect capital market assumptions and hence the extent to which the arbitrage process can be expected to operate in practice.

In reality, brokerage fees discriminate against small investors, and other transaction costs limit the gains from arbitrage. Moreover, if companies can borrow at lower rates than individuals, investors may prefer the equity of geared companies as vehicles for obtaining benefits otherwise denied to them. It is well known that, for reasons of size, security and convenience, large firms can borrow at lower rates than small firms and individuals. In addition, some major UK investors (e.g. pension funds) face restrictions on their borrowing powers, limiting their scope for home-made gearing. Finally, whereas the shareholders in a geared firm have the protection of limited liability, personal borrowers enjoy no such protection in the event of bankruptcy.

Some authors suggest that such imperfections may foster investor demand for the equity of geared companies. However, to sustain this argument, we would need to produce evidence that relatively (but safely) geared companies are more attractively rated by the market. There is little evidence that such firms sell at relatively high P:E ratios. Indeed, UK investment trust companies, which invest in equities, often using substantial borrowed capital, typically sell at significant *discounts* to their net asset values – discounts far higher than can be plausibly explained by the transactions costs that would be incurred in liquidating their portfolios.

Self-assessment activity 11.2

What factors restrict the ability of investors to arbitrage in the way envisaged by MM?

(Answer in Appendix A)

11.5 MM WITH CORPORATE INCOME TAX

The analysis of MM's three propositions in Section 11.3 is a theoretical exercise, designed to isolate the key variables relating company value and gearing. This only becomes operational when 'real-world' complications are introduced. Perhaps the most important of these is corporate taxation. In most economies, corporate interest charges are tax-allowable, providing an incentive for companies to gear their capital structures. In a taxed world, the MM conclusions change significantly.

Because Corporation Tax is applied to earnings after deducting interest charges, the value of a geared company's shares is the capitalised value of the after-tax earnings stream (net income), i.e. $(E - iB)(1 - T)$:

$$V_S = \frac{(E - iB)(1 - T)}{k_{eg}}$$

where k_{eg} is the return required by shareholders, allowing for financial risk, and T is the rate of tax on corporate profits.

Assuming that the book and market values of debt capital coincide ($B = V_B$), so that the cost of debt, k_d, equates to the coupon rate, i, the value of debt is the discounted interest stream, i.e. $V_B = iB/i$. The value of the whole company is thus:

$$V_0 = V_S + V_B = \frac{(E - iB)(1 - T)}{k_{eg}} + \frac{iB}{i}$$

It can be shown that geared companies will sell at a premium over equivalent ungeared companies because of the benefits of tax-allowable debt interest. The post-tax annual expected earnings stream, E_T, comprises the earnings attributable to shareholders plus the debt interest:

$$E_T = (E - iB)(1 - T) + iB$$

This simplifies to:

$$E_T = E(1 - T) + TiB$$

This second expression is very useful: the first element is the net income that the shareholders in an equivalent ungeared company would receive, while the second element is the annual tax benefit afforded by debt interest relief. The total value of the geared company, V_g, is found by capitalising the first element at the cost of equity capital applicable to an ungeared company (k_{eu}), while the second is capitalised at the cost of debt, which we have assumed equals the nominal rate of interest, i:

$$V_g = \frac{E(1-T)}{k_{eu}} + \frac{TiB}{i} = \frac{E(1-T)}{k_{eu}} + TB = V_u + TB$$

This is a highly significant result. The expression for the value of the geared company comprises the value of an equivalent ungeared company, V_u, plus a premium derived by discounting to perpetuity the stream of tax savings that can be claimed so long as the company has sufficient taxable capacity, i.e. if $E > iB$. The introduction of this second term, TB, the discounted value of future tax savings, or the **tax shield**, is a major modification of MM's Proposition I, as shown in Figure 11.2.

tax shield
The tax savings achieved by setting tax-allowable expenses such as interest payments against profits

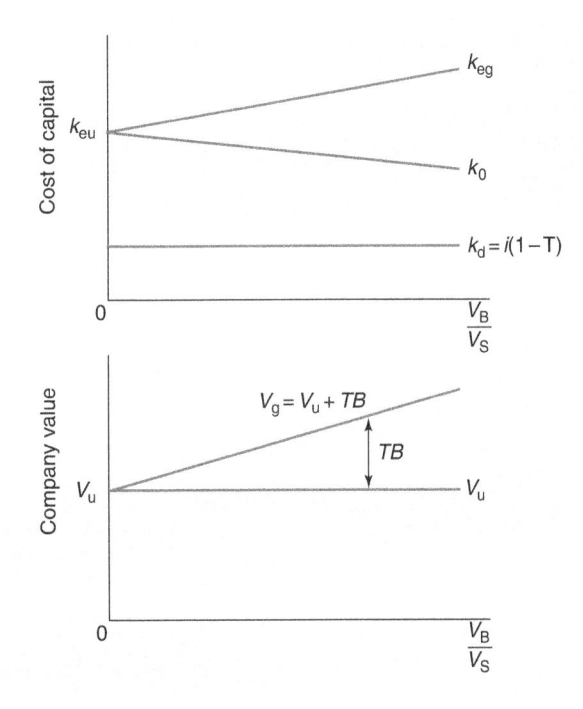

Figure 11.2 The MM thesis with corporate income tax

Self-assessment activity 11.3

Determine the respective values of geared and ungeared firms if:

- Earnings = £100m before tax
- Tax rate = 30%
- k_{eu} = 15%
- The geared firm borrows £200m.

(Answer in Appendix A)

Impact on the required return

The company value profile now rises continuously with gearing. Proposition II also needs modification. With no corporate tax, this stated that the shareholders in a geared company require a return, k_{eg}, of:

$$k_{eg} = k_{eu} + (k_{eu} - k_d)\frac{V_B}{V_S}$$

However, in a taxed world, the return required by shareholders becomes:

$$k_{eg} = k_{eu} + (k_{eu} - k_d)(1 - T)\frac{V_B}{V_S}$$

The return required by the geared company's shareholders is now the cost of equity in an identical ungeared company plus a financial risk premium related to the corporate tax rate and the debt/equity ratio.

The premium for financial risk required by shareholders is lower in this version owing to the tax deductibility of debt interest, making the debt interest burden less onerous. This relationship is also shown in Figure 11.2. It follows that if, at every level of gearing, the cost of equity is lower and also the cost of debt itself is reduced by interest deductibility, the WACC (k_0) is lower at all gearing ratios, and declines as gearing increases. Figure 11.2 shows the effect on the WACC.

The tax advantage of debt financing is incorporated in the revised equation for the WACC:

$$k_0 = \left[k_{eg} \times \frac{V_S}{V_S + V_B}\right] + \left[i(1 - T) \times \frac{V_S}{V_S + V_B}\right]$$

This can also be written as:

$$k_0 = k_{eu}\left[1 - \frac{T \times V_B}{V_S + V_B}\right]$$

Clearly, there are significant advantages from gearing, with the implication that companies should gear up until debt provides almost 100 per cent of its financing. However, this does not seem plausible. Surely there are practical, 'sensible' limits to company gearing, given the risks involved? More of this later!

Self-assessment activity 11.4

Compare the overall required return in geared and ungeared firms if:

- k_{eu} = 15%
- Tax rate = 30%
- The geared firm has borrowed £200m at 7% interest, and has issued equity of £400m.

(Answer in Appendix A)

Example of the impact of corporate taxation

It is now helpful to demonstrate 'with-tax' relationships using the examples of Nogear and Higear. Recall that both companies had E of £1 million and their equilibrium market values were £5 million under the 'no-tax' version of the MM thesis. After taxation, shareholder earnings in Nogear fall to £1m(1 − T). With 30 per cent corporate tax, this is £1m(1 − 30%) = £0.70m. Capitalised at 20 per cent, the value of the ungeared company is:

$$V_u = \frac{£1m(1 - 30\%)}{k_{eu}} = \frac{£0.70m}{0.2} = £3.50m$$

In the case of Higear, net income for shareholders is given by taxable earnings of $(E - iB)$ less the tax charge of $T(E - iB)$ to yield net income of:

$$NI = (E - iB)(1 - T) = [£1m - (10\% \times £1m)](1 - 30\%)$$
$$= (£0.9m \times 0.7) = £0.63m$$

This might be capitalised at the geared cost of equity and added to the value of debt to yield the overall company value. However, there is a circular problem here, since the calculation of the market value of the shares, V_S, derives from the calculation of k_{eg}, which itself depends on V_S. A remedy for this problem is to use the expression $V_g = V_u + TB$ encountered in Figure 11.2. This yields:

$$V_g = V_u + TB = £3.50m + (30\% \times £1m) = (£3.50m + £0.30m) = £3.80m$$

It is useful also to cross-check on the components of V_g and the return required by Higear's shareholders. If $V_g = £3.80m$, and the value of debt is £1 million, the value of Higear's equity must be $(£3.80m - £1m) = £2.80m$. Using the revised expression for the return required by the shareholders of a geared company, we find:

$$k_{eg} = k_{eu} + (k_{eu} - i)(1 - T)\frac{V_B}{V_S}$$
$$= 20\% + (20\% - 10)(1 - 30\%)\frac{£1m}{£2.8m}$$
$$= (20\% + 2.5\%) = 22.5\%$$

The geared company clearly has a greater market value – it is worth more due to the value of the tax shield. The size of this tax shield depends on the gearing ratio, the rate of taxation and the taxable capacity of the enterprise. Since gearing has raised company value, the earlier conclusion, that the benefits of gearing are illusory, must be modified. The reason is that the stakeholders of Higear benefit at the expense of the taxpayer due to the tax deductibility of debt interest. (Whether this is desirable or not in a wider context depends on the value of the forgone tax revenues in their alternative use, which is an issue for welfare economists.)

In its tax-adjusted form, the MM thesis looks rather more like the traditional version, in so far as the WACC declines over some range of gearing. However, the benefits from gearing clearly derive from the tax system, rather than from the apparent failure of the shareholders to respond fully to financial risk by seeking higher returns. We will discover that the similarity becomes even closer when we allow for financial distress. Before doing this, we will show how the MM approach can be integrated with the CAPM.

11.6 CAPITAL STRUCTURE THEORY AND THE CAPM

A feature of MM's initial model was the classification of firms into 'homogeneous risk classes' as a way of controlling for inherent operating or business risk. The modern distinction between systematic and specific risk makes this device unnecessary, as relevant business risk is expressed by the Beta. The key point is that gearing introduces additional risk so that shareholders require additional compensation. Whereas in an ungeared firm, the cost of equity is:

$$k_{eu} = R_f + \beta_u(ER_m - R_f)$$

where k_{eu} and β_u represent the required return and Beta values, respectively, that are applicable to an ungeared firm. In a geared firm, this becomes

$$k_{eg} = R_f + \beta_g(ER_m - R_f)$$

with

$$\beta_g > \beta_u$$

and

$$k_{eg} > k_{eu}$$

Clearly, gearing increases the equity Beta. It is a relatively simple task to integrate the MM analysis with the CAPM. This was first performed by Hamada (1969), who demonstrated that the required return on the equity of a geared firm in a CAPM framework is:

$$k_{eg} = R_f + (ER_m - R_f) \times \beta_u \times \left[1 + \frac{V_B(1-T)}{V_S}\right]$$

where β_u is the Beta applicable to the earnings of an ungeared company, or the pure equity Beta. Multiplying out, we derive:

$$k_{eg} = R_f + \beta_u(ER_n - R_f) + (ER_m - R_f) \times \beta_u \times \left[\frac{V_B(1-T)}{V_S}\right]$$

This looks unwieldy, but is a useful vehicle for making the distinction between business and financial risk. The Betas, recorded by the London Business School, are geared equity Betas, incorporating elements of both types of risk. Given that, and using Hamada's revised CAPM expression, the geared Beta, β_g, is:

$$k_{eg} = R_f + \beta_g(ER_m - R_f)$$

$$\beta_g = \beta_u \left[1 + \frac{V_B(1-T)}{V_S}\right]$$

The ungeared equity Beta is therefore:

$$\beta_u = \frac{\beta_g}{\left[1 + \frac{V_B(1-T)}{V_S}\right]}$$

This can also be written as:

$$\beta_u = \beta_g \times \left[\frac{V_S}{V_S + V_B(1-T)}\right]$$

The shareholders of a geared company seek compensation for two separate types of risk – the underlying or basic risk of the business activity, and also for financial risk. The rewards for bearing these two forms of risk are the respective premiums for business risk and for gearing.

■ Higear and Nogear: separating the risk premiums

To explore this distinction, consider again the example of Nogear and Higear. Assume that the ungeared Beta applicable to this risk class is 1.11, the risk-free return is 10 per cent, the return expected on the market portfolio is 19 per cent and the corporate tax rate is 30 per cent. Recall that when we last encountered these companies (see Section 11.5), their respective values were:

Nogear: $V_u = V_S = £3.50m$
Higear: $V_g = V_u + TB = (£3.50m + £0.30m) = £3.80m$
$V_B = £1m$
$V_S = (£3.80m - £1m) = £2.80m$

First, we can verify the return required by Nogear's shareholders. This is:

$$k_{eu} = R_f + \beta_u[ER_m - R_f]$$
$$= 10\% + 1.11[19\% - 10\%] = (10\% + 10\%) = 20\%$$

Second, we can analyse the composition of the return required by Higear's shareholders. To find the overall return they seek, we need to know the geared Beta. This is given by:

$$\beta_g = \beta_u\left[1 + \frac{V_B(1-T)}{V_S}\right] = 1.11 \times \left[1 + \frac{£1m(1-30\%)}{£2.80m}\right] = 1.3875$$

For $\beta_g = 1.3875$, the return required by Higear's shareholders is:

$$k_{eg} = R_f + \beta_g[ER_m - R_f] = 10\% + 1.3875[19\% - 10\%]$$
$$= (10\% + 12.5\%) = 22.5\%$$

Analysing the cost of equity for Higear into its components, we find:

$$k_{eg} = \text{Risk-free rate} + \text{Business risk premium} + \text{Financial risk premium}$$

$$= R_f + \beta_u[ER_m - R_f] + [ER_m - R_f]\beta_u \times \frac{V_B(1-T)}{V_S}$$

$$= 10\% + 1.11[19\% - 10\%] + [19\% - 10\%]1.11 \times \frac{£1m(1-30\%)}{£2.80m}$$

$$= (10\% + 10\% + 2.5\%) = 22.5\%$$

This corresponds to the result obtained more directly with the CAPM formula. The two separate components of the geared Beta are shown in Figure 11.3. The increase in the geared Beta, as the debt/equity ratio increases, drives up the additional required premium *pro rata*.

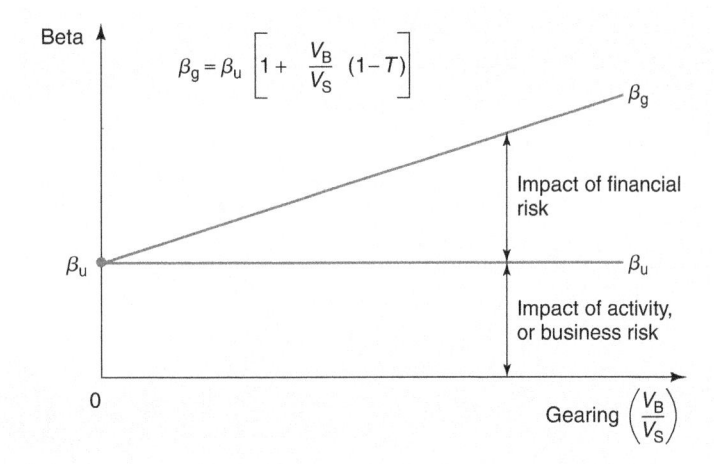

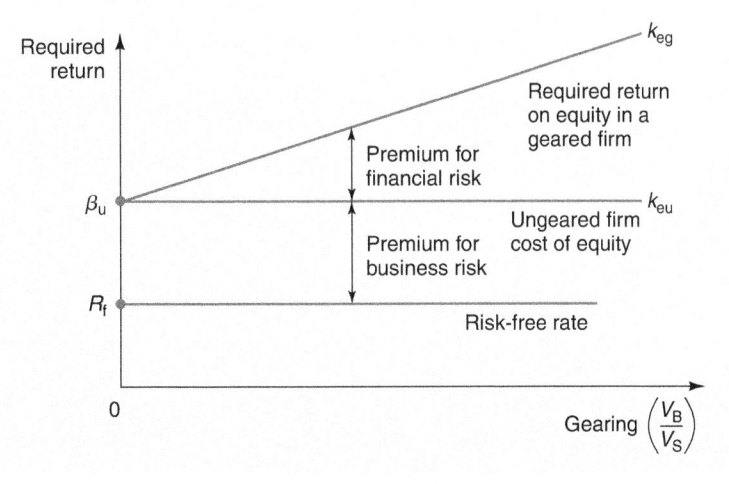

Figure 11.3 Business and financial risk premia and the required return

11.7 LINKING THE BETAS: UNGEARING AND RE-GEARING

There is a useful expression available to show how the various Betas are linked together. It is important to recall the MM message that the underlying business or activity risk is unaffected by the method of financing. If a firm chooses to borrow, thus introducing financial risk, the shareholders will respond by looking for a higher return as they perceive greater financial risk affecting their future income, but the risk attaching to the firm's actual operating activities is untouched – it is the same firm operating in the same business environment and operated by the same managers. All that has happened is a repackaging of the firm's flow of operating income resulting in lenders now having a prior claim. The size of the operating income itself is unaffected, only its distribution changes.

Given that the activity risk is unaffected by gearing, we can use the accounting equation to show the linkages. The accounting equation tells us that the assets are equal to the methods of financing them. Translating this into CAPM terms, the asset Beta (i.e. the activity Beta) equals the Beta of the methods of finance used to acquire those assets. In other words, the asset Beta equates to a weighted average of the Betas of the various methods of financing, according to the importance of each source of finance in the capital structure.

Algebraically, this is given by:

Beta of assets

= (Equtiy Beta × proportion of equity) + (Debt Beta × proportion of debt)

$$\text{Beta}_A = \left(\text{Beta}_S \times \frac{V_S}{V_S + V_B(1-T)}\right) + \left(\text{Beta}_B \times \frac{V_B(1-T)}{V_S + V_B(1-T)}\right)$$

Notice that the tax shield is reflected in applying the term $(1 - T)$ to the debt component. Notice also that, as the debt proportion increases, the equity Beta must increase to preserve the constant asset Beta. It is usual to assume that the debt Beta is zero, although there is some evidence that corporate debt has a very low Beta, around 0.1 to 0.2.

However, if we do assume a debt Beta of zero, this becomes a very versatile expression, e.g. when moving into a new activity we can take a firm's equity Beta and ungear it to reveal the underlying activity Beta. This is particularly useful when diversifying into a new activity – we might borrow a Beta from another firm (a so-called 'surrogate'), whose gearing may differ from our own. In this case, we might ungear the borrowed Beta to strip out that firm's financial risk, and then re-gear to incorporate our own firm's gearing ratio.

To illustrate this, assume we have the following data:

Equity Beta of surrogate firm operating in new activity = 1.35

Gearing ratio (debt/equity) of this firm = 40:60

(i.e. debt proportion = 40:100)
Tax rate = 30%
Own gearing ratio = 10% (debt/equity)

Ungearing the other firm's equity Beta, assuming the debt Beta is zero, we have:

$$\beta_A = \beta_S \times \left(\frac{V_S}{V_S + V_B(1-T)}\right) = 1.35 \times \left(\frac{60}{60 + 40(1-T)}\right)$$

$$= 1.35 \times 60/88 = 0.92$$

Re-gearing to incorporate our own gearing, the equity β^* is given by:

$$0.92 = \beta_S \times \frac{100}{100 + 10(1 - T)} = \beta_S \times 100/107$$

Whence, equity Beta $= 0.92 \times 107/100 = 0.98$

Self-assessment activity 11.5

Ungear a β of 1.45 if:

- Tax rate = 30%
- The debt/equity ratio = 1:2

(Answer in Appendix A)

11.8 MM WITH FINANCIAL DISTRESS

In Section 11.5, we saw how including corporate taxation in the MM model implied that companies should rely on debt for nearly 100 per cent of their financing. This implication is clearly at odds with observed practice – few companies gear up to extreme levels, through both their own and lenders' fear of insolvency, and its associated costs. MM's omission of liquidation costs from their analysis was a logical consequence of their perfect capital market assumptions. In such a market, where investors are numerous and rational, and have homogeneous expectations and plentiful access to information, the resale value of assets, even those being sold in a liquidation, will reflect their true economic values. Investors will recognise the worth of such assets as measured by the present values of their future income flows, and be prepared to bid up to this value, so that the price realised by a liquidator should not involve any discount.

costs of financial distress
The costs incurred as a firm approaches, and ultimately reaches, the point of insolvency

In effect, liquidation costs and the other **costs of financial distress** introduce a new imperfection into the analysis of capital structure decisions: namely the actual or expected inability to realise 'full value' for assets in a distress sale and the costs of actions taken to forestall this contingency.

Incorporating financial distress

Denoting the 'costs of financial distress' by *FD*, the value of a geared company becomes:

$$V_g = V_u + [TB - FD]$$

From this, we may conclude that the *financial manager should attempt to maximise the gap between tax benefits and financial distress costs, i.e. (TB − FD), and that there exists an optimal capital structure where company value is maximised.* This occurs where the marginal benefit of further tax savings equals the marginal cost of anticipated financial distress. This occurs with debt of X^* in Figure 11.4.

The costs of financial distress rise with gearing once the market starts to perceive a substantially increased risk of financial failure. The likelihood of *FD* being non-zero depends on the probability distribution of the firm's earnings profile. For example, in the Lindley example in Chapter 10, for gearing ratios up to 50 per cent, the probability of inability to meet interest payments is zero, but it would be 0.25 for any higher gearing ratio. For most companies, the probability, p, of financial distress will increase with the book values of debt, B, so that the *FD* function increases with gearing. If d denotes

---

*A note on terminology and notation: the Beta of the shares, or the equity Beta, β_S, is the same here as β_g, since the latter denotes the Beta of the equity in a geared firm. Of course, β_S becomes equal to β_g in the case of the ungeared firm.

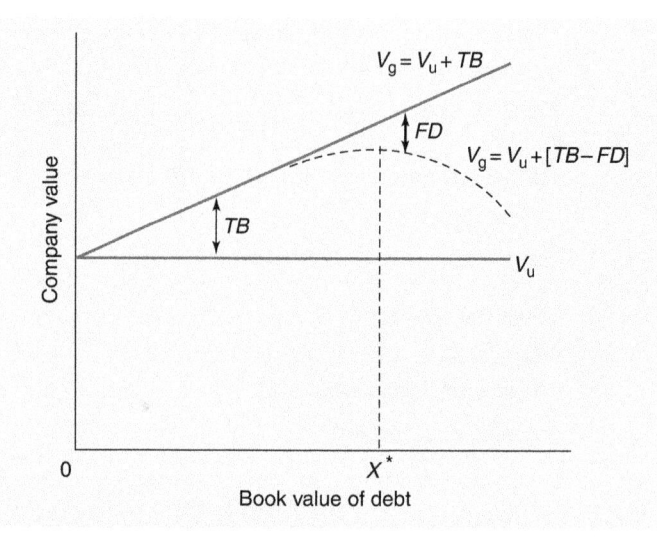

Figure 11.4 Optimal gearing with liquidation costs

the expected percentage discount on the pre-liquidation value in the event of a forced sale, the expected costs of financial distress are:

$$FD = (p \times d \times V_g)$$

and the value of the geared firm is:

$$V_g = V_u + (TB - p \times d \times V_g)$$

This suggests that market imperfections can be exploited to raise company value so long as TB exceeds $(p \times d \times V_g)$. Notice that the inverted U-shaped value profile now appears remarkably similar to the traditional version and, of course, is associated with a mirror-image WACC schedule.

You may recall our earlier comment that, after introducing market imperfections such as tax, the MM model begins to look more like the traditional version. With the inclusion of financial distress costs, this resemblance is closer still. The Noble Group cameo that follows illustrates the contortions of a firm in financial distress.

However, the discussion of the impact of personal taxation in Appendix III at the end of this chapter shows that the debate is not yet dead.

Noble Group investors brace for heavy losses as bond prices fall

Noble Group's bond prices fell heavily on Monday as investors braced themselves for heavy losses should the Asian commodities trader be unable to get to grips with its debt pile.

Noble's $750m 8.75 per cent 2022 bond plumbed a new low of 42 cents on the dollar having been issued at par less than three months ago. A credit-rating downgrade from S&P added pressure, with the agency slashing its rating three notches to triple C plus on Monday. The rating remains on a negative outlook. 'The negative outlook on Noble reflects the potential that the company will face distress and a non-payment of its debt obligations over the next 12 months,' S&P said in its downgrade statement.

Traders said the collapse in bond prices reflects increasing pessimism about the recovery value of the debt, given the company's lack of hard assets and the difficulty in independently valuing its portfolio of contracts to source and supply commodities.

One bond investor said it was very difficult to accurately model the recovery value for the commodity trader's assets. 'You have to make all these assumptions about the nature of their swap book, and that's very difficult unless you can see the book itself and know how it's marked,' he said. 'And some of the assets are joint ventures – in a distressed situation those are hard to monetise at book value.' Noble needs to roll over a $2bn credit facility with banks that help finance its trading activities in the next month.

Over the next year, Noble must then find $1.5bn to repay a $379m bond and a $1.14bn loan. Analysts estimate that

Continued

the company has about $700m in cash and $400m of unused credit lines, though some of its money is tied up with derivative brokers.

In its statement, S&P also said, 'we believe the company's capital structure is not sustainable. This is due to continuing weak cash flows and profitability.'

Noble has raised $3bn through asset sales and bond and share issuances in the past two years to try to buttress its balance sheet, but weak trading results have kept the focus on its debt load.

Industry sources say Noble's weakened position may see rival trading houses try to cherry pick individual supply deals from the company rather than investing in, or buying, the commodities trader.

Noble, once Asia's largest independent commodities trader, has seen its share price collapse by more than 90 per cent since early 2015.

Source: Smith, R.; Hume, N. and Sheppard, D. (2017) Noble Group investors brace for heavy losses as bond prices fall. *Financial Times*, 22 May. © The Financial Times Limited 2018. All rights reserved.

11.9 CALCULATING THE WACC

Before progressing, you may find it useful to reread Chapter 6, where we discussed the hierarchy of discount rates and required rates of return but deferred consideration of the problems posed by mixed capital structures until Chapter 10.

The WACC is the overall required return needed to satisfy all stakeholders. It is also the required return on the assumption that new projects are financed in exactly the same way as existing ones. If the company is all-equity-financed, then the WACC is simply the return required by shareholders.

Gearing does not affect the underlying risk of the company's business activities. If a company uses debt capital, it is merely repackaging its operating income into different proportions of debt interest and equity income, but not influencing the size or the riskiness of this income before appropriation. What does change is the riskiness of the stream of residual equity income, which is why the equity Beta rises, pulling up with it the return required by shareholders.

We can explore this proposition with the case of Higear. The relevant figures for Higear were:

Value of debt	$= V_B =$	£1m
Value of equity	$= V_S =$	£2.80m
Shareholders' required return	$= k_{eg} =$	22.5%
Interest cost of debt	$= i =$	10%
Rate of corporate tax	$= T =$	30%

The expression for the WACC in the MM case with corporate tax is:

$$k_0 = \left(k_{eg} \times \frac{V_S}{V_S + V_B}\right) + \left[i(1 - T) \times \frac{V_B}{V_S + V_B}\right]$$

Using the data for Higear, this expression yields:

$$k_0 = \left(22.5\% \times \frac{£2.80m}{£2.80m + £1m}\right) + \left[10\%(1 - 30\%) \times \frac{£1m}{£2.80m + £1m}\right]$$

$$= (22.5\% \times 0.74) + (7\% \times 0.26)$$

$$= 16.6\% + 1.8\% = 18.4\%$$

Alternatively, we can obtain the same result by using the expression:

$$k_0 = k_{eu}\left[1 - T \times \frac{V_B}{V_S + V_B}\right]$$

$$= 20\%\left[1 - 30\% \frac{£1m}{£3.80m}\right]$$

$$= 20\% \times 0.92$$

$$= 18.4\%$$

Relaxing critical assumptions

Two important questions now arise. First, what happens to the discount rate if a company diversifies into an activity with a risk profile different from existing operations? Second, what happens if the gearing ratio is altered? The first issue is easier to handle.

Allowing for different risks

Imagine Higear proposes to diversify into a higher-risk business. Because the discount rate applicable to evaluating this project should reflect the systematic risk involved, the required return previously calculated is no longer appropriate. To cope with this problem, the following procedure is suggested:

1. Select a company already operating in the target activity, ideally, one with operating characteristics very similar to those exhibited by the project, and identify its Beta coefficient, e.g. by using the RMS.
2. If the surrogate company's gearing differs from that of Higear, the Beta must be adjusted by removing the effect of the surrogate's own gearing, and then superimposing Higear's gearing on the resulting ungeared Beta.
3. Calculate the WACC incorporating the surrogate activity Beta, adjusted for Higear's own gearing.

Assume Higear plans to enter an activity already served by Supergear, whose equity Beta is 1.8, and which has a debt/equity ratio of 1:2. Supergear's Beta is ungeared as follows:

$$\beta_u = \frac{\beta_g}{1 + \frac{V_B}{V_S}(1-T)} = \frac{1.8}{1 + \frac{1}{2}(1-30\%)} = \frac{1.8}{1.35} = 1.33$$

The geared Beta applicable to Higear's capital structure (i.e. £1 million debt and £2.80 million equity) is:

$$\beta_g = \beta_u \left[1 + \frac{V_B}{V_S} \times (1-T) \right]$$

$$= 1.33 \left[1 + \frac{£1m}{£2.80m} \times (1-30\%) \right]$$

$$= 1.33[1.25] = 1.663$$

For this risk, and with a 9 per cent market risk premium, Higear's shareholders require a return of:

$$ER_j = R_f + \beta_g[ER_m - R_f] = 10\% + 1.663[9\%] = 25\%$$

Finally, the WACC applicable to this activity risk and Higear's own gearing is:

$$(25.0\% \times 0.74) + (10\%[1-30\%] \times 0.26) = 18.5\% + 1.8\% = 20.3\%$$

The second issue, the effect of a change in gearing, poses more of a conundrum.

Allowing for a change of gearing

In the Higear example, no change in gearing was envisaged when financing new projects. However, as we have repeatedly warned, a significant change in gearing affects the market values of both debt and equity capital: for example, shareholders may respond adversely to higher gearing and the higher financial risk. Also, the value of debt may be marked down in the market. To compute the WACC, we would have to assess the new return required by shareholders, k_{eg}, given by:

$$k_{eg} = k_{eu} + (k_{eu} - i)(1-T)\frac{V_B}{V_S} = R_f + \beta_g(ER_m - R_f)$$

where

$$k_{eu} = R_f + \beta_u(ER_m - R_f)$$

β_u = the ungeared Beta Coefficient

To value the equity, i.e. to derive a measure for V_S, we would need to apply the (perpetuity) expression for valuing a stream of post-tax geared equity income:

$$V_S = \frac{(E - iB)(1 - T)}{k_{eg}}$$

We now encounter a circular problem, since the market value depends on k_{eg}, and to find k_{eg}, we need to know the market value!

A possible solution is to work in terms of a 'tailor-made' WACC based on the project's characteristics (i.e. its systematic risk, allowing for any divergence from existing operations) and on the project's own financing. For example, imagine the project in the previous example were to be financed 20 per cent by debt and 80 per cent by equity. You should verify that with $\beta_u = 1.33, \beta_g = 1.56$, that shareholders would seek a return of 24 per cent and that the WACC is:

$$(24\% \times 4/5) + (10\%[1 - T] \times 1/5) = (19.2\% + 1.4\%) = 20.6\%$$

As it happens, use of the WACC in this situation may be inappropriate anyway, since unless the firm is at, and adheres to, the target ratio, the WACC and the marginal cost of capital (MCC) will diverge. If the firm is below the optimal capital structure, the MCC is less than WACC, and the MCC exceeds the WACC when it overshoots the optimal gearing ratio. We found, in Chapter 10, that when the firm departs from the optimal gearing ratio, the appropriate required return is the MCC:

$$\text{MCC} = \frac{\text{Change in total returns required by shareholders and lenders}}{\text{Amount available to invest}}$$

However, to calculate the MCC, we again need to know the market values of both equity and debt at the higher level of gearing, i.e. we encounter the circular problem described earlier. It is clear that the WACC is suitable only for small-scale projects that do not materially disturb the gearing ratio, and that the theoretically more correct MCC is also problematic.

An 'off-the-cuff' solution is to work in terms of book values. This pragmatic approach has the merit of simplicity, as book values do not vary with gearing, and it might be appropriate for unlisted firms, which, by definition, have no market values. Nevertheless, it is desirable to work, whenever possible, in terms of market values, given that most investors are more concerned with the current values of their investments, and the returns thereon, than with historic balance sheet values. Fortunately, as we shall see in the next section, help is at hand.

Meanwhile, the following Jawbone cameo highlights several of the issues surrounding the MM theory.

Jawbone debunks Modigliani–Miller

A privately-held tech company is desperate for cash. In this age of 'decacorns', you might think it would raise equity from over-eager venture investors. But Jawbone, which competes with, among others, Apple, decided to borrow $300 million from Blackrock. Analyst Dan Primack thinks this financing choice creates value:

'Structuring this deal as debt instead of as equity allows the company to maintain a $3 billion valuation it reportedly received last fall. That means it needn't reprice existing employee stock options, and gives it upside flexibility when recruiting new employees.'

This flies in the face of standard corporate finance theory. Franco Modigliani and Merton Miller both won Nobel prizes in economics for arguing that the underlying value of a company doesn't depend on its capital structure.

After all, a factory produces the same amount of product irrespective of how you financed it. You could have borrowed to build it, issued common equity, or had fun with a weird hybrid security like a contingent convertible bond, but the real output of the factory would be the same. That should mean that the all-in cost of financing the factory is not affected by the financing mix chosen. In theory, more debt just means paying creditors higher interest rates, while more equity means shareholders demand higher expected returns, but the weighted average cost of capital is the same.

There are already some well-known exceptions to the universal application of Modigliani–Miller, but none of them explain what Jawbone is up to. The ability to deduct interest payments from your corporate tax bill, but not dividends, affects the relative appeal of debt vs equity. That doesn't matter in the case of Jawbone, though, since it's bleeding money and therefore has no corporate tax liability.

Another big issue with Modigliani–Miller is that it doesn't account for financial distress costs. High levels of debt to equity increase the odds of bankruptcy, which ought to lower the value of the underlying business. Equity is also valuable for its flexibility. The upfront 'cost' may appear high, but it doesn't come with any contractual obligations to pay investors cash at fixed times. That is a better fit for firms that need to make big bets on research and capital investment in order to grow, which explains why tech and pharma companies overwhelmingly prefer to fund themselves with equity rather than debt.

Jawbone is going in the opposite direction, though, issuing debt when equity is a more natural fit with its business model.

Primack's analysis provides us with a new violation of Modigliani–Miller that can be explained by the peculiarity of the private equity markets:

VCs typically value portfolio companies based on the most recent financing round and, in this case, that would still be around $3 billion. The longer that number remains, the easier it is for the VCs to raise new funds from institutional investors who might not look too hard under the hood . . . The can just got kicked a bit further down the road, meaning that everyone gets to keep playing the game. At least, for as long as $300 million lasts.

The benefit of the public equity markets is that you can always see how much the market values a company at any point in time. This is a useful signal for corporate managers trying to figure out whether they should boost investment, return capital to shareholders, make acquisitions, or make cuts in an effort to boost margins. (It also has implications for how much you should pay your employees in cash vs shares.)

The private equity markets don't provide this signal, which encourages companies to game the system to keep valuations high by borrowing when they run into trouble. Sadly, the biggest losers of this charade are probably Jawbone's employees, who will still get paid in illiquid shares with made-up values.

FT *Source:* Klein, Matthew C. (2015) Jawbone debunks Modigliani-Miller. When's the crash?. Financial Times, 21 May. © The Financial Times Limited 2018. All rights reserved.

11.10 THE ADJUSTED PRESENT VALUE METHOD (APV)

adjusted present value (APV)
The inherent value of a project adjusted for any financial benefits and costs stemming from the particular method(s) of financing

The **adjusted present value (APV)** of a project is simply the 'essential' worth of the project, adjusted for any financing benefits (or costs) attributable to the particular method of financing it. The rationale for the APV method was provided by Myers (1974), using MM's gearing model with corporate tax, but is valid only so long as the WACC profile is declining due to the value of the tax shield. In Section 11.5, we saw that the value of a geared firm, V_g, is the value of an equivalent all-equity-financed company, V_g, plus a tax shield, TB, which is the discounted tax savings resulting from the tax-deductibility of debt interest:

$$V_g = V_u + TB$$

This can be translated from the value of a whole firm to the value of an individual project. However, different projects can probably support different levels of debt. For example, they may involve different inputs of easily resaleable fixed assets and may also differ in their operational gearing. As a result, it may be more appropriate to evaluate the effects of the financing of each project separately.

The APV is calculated in three steps:

Step 1 Evaluate the 'base case' NPV, discounting at the rate of return that shareholders would require if the project were financed wholly by equity. This rate is derived by ungearing the company's equity Beta.

Step 2 Evaluate separately the cash flows attributable to the financing decision, discounting at the appropriate risk-adjusted rate.

Step 3 Add the present values derived from the two previous stages to obtain the APV. The project is acceptable if the APV is greater than zero.

A simple example will illustrate the use of the APV.

11.11 WORKED EXAMPLE: RIGTON PLC

Rigton plc has a debt/equity ratio of 20 per cent. The equity Beta is 1.30. The risk-free rate is 10 per cent and a return of 16 per cent is expected from the market portfolio. The rate of corporate tax is 30 per cent. Rigton proposes to undertake a project requiring an outlay of £10 million, financed partly by equity and partly by debt. The project, a perpetuity, is thought to be able to support borrowings of £3 million at an interest rate of 12 per cent, thus imposing interest charges of £0.36 million. It is expected to generate pre-tax cash flows of £2.3 million p.a.

Required
Using the APV method, determine whether this project is worthwhile.

Answer
Using the formula developed earlier for the ungeared Beta:

$$\beta_u = \frac{\beta_g}{\left[1 + \frac{V_B}{V_S} \times (1 - T)\right]} = \frac{1.30}{1 + 0.20(1 - 0.30)} = \frac{1.30}{1.14} = 1.14$$

This yields a required return on ungeared equity of:

$$ER_j = R_f + \beta_u(ER_m - R_f) = 0.10 + 1.14(0.16 - 0.10) = (0.10 + 0.068)$$
$$= 0.168, \text{ i.e. } 16.8\%$$

The base case NPV is:

$$\text{NPV} = -£10\text{m} + \frac{£2.3\text{m}(1 - 0.30)}{0.168} = -£10\text{m} + \frac{£1.61\text{m}}{0.168}$$
$$= -£10\text{m} + £9.58\text{m}$$
$$= -£0.42\text{m}$$

The present value of the tax savings, i.e. the tax shield, *TB*, is given by:

$$\frac{TiB}{i} = \frac{(0.30)(0.12)(£3\text{m})}{0.12} = \frac{(0.30)(£0.36\text{m})}{0.12} = \frac{£0.108\text{m}}{0.12} = £0.9\text{m}$$

The adjusted present value is thus:

$$\text{APV} = -£0.42\text{m} + £0.90\text{m} = +£0.48\text{m}$$

and the project appears worthwhile. The significance of this result is that, although the base case NPV is negative, the project is rescued by the tax shield of £0.90 million. An essentially unattractive project is rendered worthwhile by the taxation system.

In the Rigton example, the project creates wealth only for Rigton's shareholders. From the perspective of the overall economy, it is wealth-reducing and, unless there are compelling 'social' reasons to justify it, should not be undertaken. This sort of reasoning led the UK government in 1984 to reduce the rate of Corporation Tax specifically, it was claimed, in order to lower the tax advantage of debt financing, and hence reduce the extent to which investment decisions were likely to be distorted by the system of tax breaks.

Self-assessment activity 11.6

What is the APV and how is it calculated?

(Answer in Appendix A)

11.12 FURTHER ISSUES WITH THE APV

Before leaving the APV, several related issues are worth examining.

1. The APV in practice is affected by the terms and conditions of a pre-arranged schedule for debt interest and capital repayment. Sometimes, the calculations can be exceptionally tedious. Rather than using the convenient assumption of perpetual debt financing, let us assume that the debt plus interest must be repaid over two years, with interest and two equal capital payments occurring at year-end. Table 11.2 shows the repayment schedule and the resulting tax savings.

Table 11.2 The tax shield with finite-life debt

Balance of loan at start of year	Interest at 12%	Tax saving (T = 30%)	Repayment	Balance of loan at end of year
£3.0m	£0.36m	(30% × £0.36m) = £0.108m	£1.5m	£1.5m
£1.5m	£0.18m	(30% × £0.18m) = £0.054m	£1.5m	0

With no tax delay assumed, the present value of the tax savings is:

$$\frac{£0.108m}{(1.12)} + \frac{£0.054m}{(1.12)^2} = (£0.096m + £0.043m) = £0.139m$$

Obviously, the value of the tax shield is much lower with the shorter payment profile.

2. Although our example focused on the side-effects of debt financing, the APV routine can be easily applied to any other financing costs and benefits, many of which are awkward to handle with the simple WACC. For example, if equity capital is externally raised, normally, there are various issuing and underwriting costs to bear. Including these would alter the APV formula as follows:

   APV = Base case NPV + Tax shield − PV of issue costs

   A similar treatment would be applied to subsidised borrowing costs, investment grants and tax savings from exploiting investment allowances.

3. Tax savings are not certain because they depend on the inherent profitability of the company. As this is a random variable, the company's ability to set off interest payments (and other tax reliefs) against income is also random. Our examples assume continuous profitability, but if there are periods during which the company is expected to be tax-exhausted, this should be allowed for in the computation of the APV. If the future pattern of liability to tax is uncertain, then it is not appropriate to use a risk-free rate to discount the tax savings.

4. Finally, we have glossed over the issues that impact on the debt-supporting capacity of particular projects. In principle, the debt capacity of a project is given by the present value of future expected earnings from the firm as a whole, taking into account any existing borrowings. It might seem obvious that more profitable companies are able to borrow relatively more than unprofitable companies. However, this assumes that there are no costs of financial distress. Enhanced borrowing ability for more

profitable companies is not universal, since a would-be lender would still look at the break-up value of the enterprise. In the final analysis, the crucial factor which governs debt capacity is how much can be raised by a distress sale of assets.

Self-assessment activity 11.7

How would you identify the point beyond which a firm would be unable to borrow?

(Answer in Appendix A)

11.13 WHICH DISCOUNT RATE SHOULD WE USE?

Specifying the correct discount rate to use when a new project involves financing and other differences from parent company activities is something of a puzzle. Now that we have examined the main variations on the discount rate theme, this checklist should help.

If the new project has:

Case 1 *Similar business risk and capital structure as the parent company.*
Use the parent's WACC.

Case 2 *Higher/lower business risk than the parent but similar financing mix.*
Adjust the Beta, using a surrogate firm's Beta as a basis but adjust for relative gearing, i.e. ungear the surrogate Beta and gear up the residual equity Beta. Then use the parent's capital structure weights to calculate the WACC.

Case 3 *Similar business risk, but capital structure different from that of the parent.*
Use the parent's equity Beta, gear it for the project financing mix and then use the project's financing mix to find the project WACC.

Case 4 *Higher/lower business risk, and a different capital structure.*
Use the project Beta, and, as in Case 2, gear it for the project financing, and calculate the WACC using the project financing mix.

Case 5 *Complex mixture of risk, financial structure and side-effects.*
Use the APV method.

11.14 VALUATION OF A GEARED FIRM

Having explained how to evaluate an investment project using the APV in Sections 11.11 and 11.12, it is a short step to reminding readers that this approach also provides a method for valuing a geared firm, and that is equivalent to two other approaches.

If the NPV of a geared project is found by following these steps:

- Forecast the future operating cash flows.
- Adjust for expected taxation liabilities.
- Discount future net-of-tax cash flows at the ungeared equity cost of capital.
- Add in the PV of any financing benefits.

The result is the value of a geared enterprise, V_g, which is based on the expected income accruing to all investors before division into the respective equity and lenders' payments. The value of the equity, V_S, is then found by deducting the market value of the firm's debt, V_B:

$$V_S = V_g - V_B$$

The only difference from the APV of a new investment project is that when valuing a firm as a whole, the capital outlay term drops out of the equation, as it is a sunk cost, i.e. the firm is being valued as a set of existing investment projects that are already up-and-running. However, capital spending would come into play if the valuer were attempting to include in the calculation any **additional** cash flows stemming from new investment projects envisaged. Failing this, the APV thus values the firm as it stands.

In principle, this approach should yield exactly the same answer as the standard Weighted Average Cost of Capital approach to valuing a geared enterprise. This also discounts the stream of ungeared after-tax net income, i.e. before deducting interest, but after subtracting corporate taxation. As with the APV, this yields the enterprise value, as it is based on the expected stream of income accruing to all investors before dividing the spoils into the respective equity and lenders' payments. The value of the equity is found in the same way. Before making this split, the only adjustment for debt that is required is in calculating the geared cost of equity for insertion into the WACC formula.

Alternatively, it may be useful to focus directly on the value of the equity, V_S. This can be done by the 'Cash Flow-to-Equity', or 'Flow-to-Equity (FTE)' approach, noted in Chapter 6. The steps in the FTE approach are:

- Forecast the operating cash flows.
- Deduct debt interest.
- Apply the relevant rate of tax to obtain residual equity income (in cash flow terms).
- Discount at the geared cost of equity.

The value of the whole geared enterprise, V_g, is then found by adding the market value of the firm's debt, V_B:

$$V_g = V_S + V_B$$

All three approaches should yield the same answer, but whichever approach is adopted, it is essential to be consistent. The valuer should always compare like with like, either by discounting the ungeared stream of cash flows at the WACC to arrive at the enterprise value, or by discounting the geared flow of income to equity holders at the geared cost of equity.

The three methods are displayed schematically in Table 11.3.

Table 11.3 Valuing a geared firm: the three approaches

Approach	Focus	Method	Formulae*
APV (Adjusted Present Value)	Value of Geared firm, V_g whence $V_S = V_g - V_B$	■ Discount ungeared cash flows, using ungeared equity cost ■ Add in PV of financing benefits	$V_g = \dfrac{\overline{X}(1-T)}{k_{eu}} + TB$ whence $V_S = V_g - V_B$
WACC (Weighted Average Cost of Capital)	Value of Geared firm, V_g whence $V_S = V_g - V_B$	■ Discount ungeared cash flows, using the WACC	$V_g = \dfrac{(\overline{X} - iB)(1-T) + iB}{k_0}$ whence $V_S = V_g - V_B$
FTE (Flow-to-Equity)	Value of Equity, V_S whence $V_g = V_S + V_B$	■ Discount geared stream of equity income using geared equity cost	$V_S = \dfrac{(\overline{X} - iB)(1-T)}{k_{eg}}$ whence $V_g = V_S + V_B$

* Where: V_g = value of geared firm; V_S = value of equity; V_B = market value of debt; $\overline{X}$ = expected future operating cash flows; T = rate of corporate tax; k_{eu} = ungeared cost of equity; k_0 = Weighted Average of Capital; B = book value of debt; i = interest rate on debt; k_{eg} = geared cost of equity

11.15 PERFORMANCE EVALUATION IN A GEARED FIRM: THE EVA REVISITED

In Chapter 7, we briefly explained the notion of EVA and how it can be calculated in an ungeared firm. The EVA purports to measure the increase in wealth generated by a firm, after taking into account the cost of using scarce capital. In the ungeared firm, the relevant cost to consider is the cost of equity. The EVA can be expressed before or after tax, although from a shareholder perspective, the post-tax measure is probably more informative. However, the before-tax measure is the most relevant measure of basic wealth creation before the tax authorities carve out their share. As such, it offers an insight into managerial efficiency while the post-tax measure assesses contribution to the owners' disposable assets, or wealth.

In some firms, EVA is used as an internal performance measuring rod to assess the relative efficiencies of managers in the various operating divisions. As such, it can assist in the allocation of capital to new projects, or inform divestment decisions. For this purpose, the pre-tax measure of EVA is most suitable as it is an indicator of basic wealth or value creation. One firm that uses EVA to monitor the performance of individual business segments is the German utility group, E.ON. Its annual report shows how it assesses the EVA (E.ON refers to this as its 'value added' approach) at the aggregate level, i.e. in terms of the whole enterprise, based on the pre-tax cost of capital of 5.8 per cent in 2016. This percentage is relevant for this purpose as the focus is on pre-tax EVA. (The Annual Report can be found on E.ON website.)

SUMMARY

Chapters 10 and 11 have covered extensive ground, attempting to isolate the critical variables relating company value to capital structure. In this process, we have moved from the somewhat crude 'traditional' version to the pure and less pure MM analyses, before arriving at the model displayed in Figure 11.4. This closely resembles the traditional theory itself, with its U-shaped cost of capital schedule and optimal capital structure. We have established that *the benefits of debt stem mainly from market imperfections, especially the tax relief on debt interest, but that a different type of imperfection, distress costs, can offset these tax breaks at higher levels of gearing.* In addition, even the tax benefits of gearing may be overstated as they depend on the particular mix of personal and corporate tax rates faced by the company and its stakeholders (see Appendix III at the end of this chapter).

So in response to the question posed in the title of the chapter, 'Does capital structure really matter?' the answer seems to be 'yes', but in a number of complex ways. Debt – or rather, excessive debt – certainly matters to the owners, but it may not destroy value. Distressed, but operationally viable, companies can still survive. For non-distressed companies, debt can offer significant tax advantages. While searching for their optimal capital structure, firms should bear in mind that the costs of financial distress may outweigh the benefits of the tax shield from debt financing. The extended theory suggests that an optimal capital structure is a debt-to-equity combination where the marginal benefit of tax savings equals the marginal cost of financial distress. The last two chapters should have also helped the reader understand why many firms have a target capital structure in mind, which may change over the course of their business operations and financial requirements.

Key points

- MM argue that, as the method of financing a company does not affect its fundamental wealth-creating capacity, the use of debt capital, under perfect market conditions, has no effect on company value.
- Shareholders respond to an increase in the likely variability of earnings, i.e. financial risk, by seeking higher returns to offset exactly the apparent benefits of 'cheap' debt.
- The appropriate cut-off rate for new investment is the rate of return required by shareholders in an equivalent ungeared company.
- When corporate taxation is introduced, the tax-deductibility of debt interest creates value for shareholders via the tax shield, but this is a wealth transfer from taxpayers.
- The value of a geared company equals the value of an equivalent ungeared company plus the tax shield:

   $V_g = V_u + TB$
- With corporate taxation, the rate of return required by the geared company's shareholders is less than that in the all-equity company, reflecting the tax benefits.
- A further effect of corporation taxation is to lower the overall cost of capital, which appears to fall continuously as gearing increases.
- However, this result relies on the absence of default risk and the consequent costs of financial distress incurred as a company reaches or approaches the point of insolvency.
- For geared companies, the required return can be derived by combining k_e with the after-tax debt cost to obtain the WACC.
- However, the WACC is acceptable only under restrictive conditions: in particular, when project financing replicates existing gearing, and when project risk is identical to that of existing activities.
- To resolve the problems of the WACC, the adjusted present value (APV) can be used. This is the 'basic' worth of the project, i.e. the NPV assuming all-equity financing, adjusted for any financing benefits such as tax savings on debt interest, or costs such as issue expenses.
- Eventually, the costs of financial distress may begin to outweigh the benefits of the tax shield. A major cost of financial distress is the inability to achieve 'full market value' in a 'distress sale'.
- There is, in theory, an optimal capital structure where the marginal benefit of tax savings equals the marginal cost of financial distress.
- In reality, while companies should balance the benefits of the tax shield against the likelihood of financial stress costs, most finance directors will restrain gearing levels, especially as tax savings are uncertain, depending on fluctuations in corporate earnings.
- There are three ways to value a geared enterprise, all of which generate the same answer if used consistently: the APV, the WACC approach and the Flow-to-Equity (FTE) approach.
- The Economic Value Added concept can be applied in the geared firm at either the pre-tax level to assess managerial operational effectiveness, or at the post-tax level to assess contribution to shareholder wealth.

Further reading

Similar health warnings apply here as with dividend policy, i.e. the fashion aspect, and the different taxation and institutional regimes that apply in different countries. But, as with dividend policy, the relevance of key papers is timeless and universal.

Look at the original articles by Modigliani and Miller (1958, 1963). Other important articles are those by Myers (1974, 1984), which analyse the interactions between financing and investment decisions, and Miller's attempt to resurrect the capital structure irrelevance thesis (Miller, 1977) and his subsequent Nobel lecture (Miller, 1991). As ever, Copeland *et al.* (2013) offer a more rigorous, mathematical development. Resumés of current thinking on capital structure theory can be found in Barclay *et al.* (1995) and Barclay and Smith (2006). Luehrman (1997a, 1997b) offers two articles on the present state of valuation theory and analysis, with strong emphasis on APV, and also on strategic options.

Good textbook treatments can be found in Baker and Martin (2011), Berk and Demarzo (2013), Miglo (2016) and Ehrhardt and Brigham (2017).

Important articles include: DeAngelo and Masulis (1980) and Schepens (2016) on taxation and capital structure, Bradley, Jarrell and Kim (1984) and Rajan and Zingales (1995) for empirical evidence, Ross (1977) on signalling, Warner (1977) on bankruptcy costs, Marsh (1982) on target debt ratios, Harris and Raviv (1990) on debt signalling and Harris and Raviv (1991) for an overview of the debate, Myers and Majluf (1984) on information asymmetry and Danis, Rettl and Whited (2014) on the relationship between profitability and capital structure of firms.

Appendix I
DERIVATION OF MM'S PROPOSITION II

Given that:

$$\frac{E}{V_S + V_B} = \frac{E}{V_0} = k_0$$

and

$$k_e = \frac{(E - iB)}{V_S}$$

we may write

$$E = k_0 V_0 = k_0(V_S + V_B)$$

Substituting for E,

$$k_e = \frac{k_0(V_S + V_B) - iB}{V_S} = \frac{k_0 V_S + k_0 V_B - iB}{V_S} = k_0 + (k_0 - i) \times \frac{V_B}{V_S}$$

Since Proposition I argues that k_0 equals the return required by shareholders in an equivalent ungeared company, k_{eu}, and so long as the book and market values of debt capital coincide, thus ensuring that $i = k_d$, then this expression may be written as:

$$k_{eg} = k_{eu} + (k_{eu} - k_d)\frac{V_B}{V_S}$$

as in the text. In other words, the return required by shareholders is a linear function of the company's debt/equity ratio.

Appendix II
MM'S PROPOSITION III: THE CUT-OFF RATE FOR NEW INVESTMENT

MM's third proposition asserts that 'the cut-off rate for investment will in all cases be k_0 and will be unaffected by the type of security used to finance the investment'.

To show this, consider a firm whose initial value, V_0, is:

$$V_0 = V_{S0} + V_{B0} = \frac{E_0}{k_0} \qquad (A)$$

It contemplates an investment project, with outlay £I, involving a perpetual return of R per £ invested. After the investment is accepted, the new value of the firm, V_1, is:

$$V_1 = \frac{E_1}{k_0} = \frac{E_0 + RI}{k_0} = V_0 + \frac{RI}{k_0}$$

Assuming the project is debt-financed, the post-project acceptance value of the shares is:

$$V_{S1} = (V_1 - V_{B1}) = V_1 - (V_{B0} + I) \qquad (B)$$

Substituting Equation A into Equation B yields:

$$V_{S1} = V_0 + \frac{RI}{k_0} - V_{B0} - I$$

and since

$$V_{S0} = (V_0 - V_{B0})$$

the change in V_S equals

$$(V_{S1} - V_{S0}) = \frac{RI}{k_0} - I$$

This exceeds zero only if $R > k_0$. Hence, *a firm acting in the best interests of its shareholders should only undertake investments whose returns at least equal k_0, the weighted average cost of capital, which itself is invariant to gearing according to Proposition I.*

Appendix III
ALLOWING FOR PERSONAL TAXATION: MILLER'S REVISION

The MM analysis including corporate earnings taxation still leaves something of a 'puzzle'. The expression for the value of a geared company indicates that the tax shield is equal to the corporate tax rate (T) times the book value of corporate debt (B), i.e. TB. With Corporation Tax of 30 per cent, for every £1 of corporate debt, the value of the company would be increased by £0.30. If such tax benefits can stem from corporate gearing, why do we find widely dispersed gearing ratios even in the same industry? And why are some of these so much lower than the MM theory (even allowing for the costs of financial distress) might suggest? According to Miller (1977), the answers to such questions lie in the interaction of the corporate taxation system with the personal taxation system, an issue omitted from the MM analysis.

Miller's agenda was to re-establish the irrelevance of gearing for company value, thus explaining why US firms did not appear to exploit apparently highly valuable tax shields. Miller argued that if individuals and corporations can borrow at the same rate, and if individuals invest in corporate debt as well as equity, there are no advantages to corporate borrowing because corporations that borrow are simply doing what personal investors can do for themselves. Any temporary premium in the market valuation of a geared company will be quickly unwound by the usual arbitrage process. However, this presupposes that individuals also can obtain tax relief on their personal borrowing (as applies in the United States, but not generally in the United Kingdom). Intuitively, we may expect to find some benefit to corporate borrowing in the United Kingdom because tax breaks on personal borrowing are not available.

Greatly simplifying, the Miller position can be expressed by the simple expression:

Post-tax cost of debt = pre-tax cost$[1 - (T_c - T_p)]$

where T_c is the tax rate at which corporations enjoy relief on debt interest, and T_p is the tax rate at which individuals enjoy relief on debt interest.

If $T_c = T_p$, then there is no tax advantage of corporate debt and hence no tax shield to exploit.

Only if T_c and T_p differ is there a tax shield. Note that for $T_c > T_p$, the tax shield is positive, and for $T_c > T_p$, the tax shield appears to be negative, as might apply for shareholders subject to very high rates of tax.

Miller introduced a further mechanism to support the irrelevance of gearing for company value. He argued that if there is a (temporary) tax advantage relating to debt financing, this will lead firms to increase their demand for debt (i.e. increase the supply of debt instruments), thus exerting upward pressure on interest rates until the advantage of issuing further debt disappears. If the effective tax rate on equity income were zero, and personal investors paid tax on debt interest income, companies would have to compensate investors for switching from untaxed equity to taxed debt investments by a higher interest rate. This would stop when the net-of-tax cost of debt to companies equalled the cost of equity. Miller concludes that movement to capital market equilibrium would eliminate any tax advantage of debt, so that $V_g = V_u$.

Ashton and Acker (2003) undertook an assessment of the average tax advantage of debt in a UK context, and concluded it is 'likely to be no more than 13% of the value of debt'.

QUESTIONS

Questions with a coloured number have solutions in Appendix B on page 501.

1. With the following information about Rushden plc, determine its cost of equity according to the MM no-tax model.

$$k_{eu} = 20\%; \quad k_d = 8\%; \quad \frac{V_B}{V_B + V_S} = 20\%$$

2. Diamonds plc estimates its costs of debt and equity for different capital structures as follows:

% Debt	% Equity	k_d	k_e	WACC
–	100	–	20%	?
25	75	8%	24%	?
50	50	8%	32%	?
75	25	8%	56%	?

Required

(i) What theory of capital structure is portrayed? (Complete the WACC column.)

(ii) Restate the table allowing for taxation of corporate profits (hence, tax relief on debt) at 30 per cent. Assume Diamonds plc always has sufficient taxable capacity to exploit the tax shield.
Identify the relevant theory of capital structure.

3. Demonstrate how the process of home-made gearing-cum-arbitrage would operate in an MM world so as to equalise the values of the following two firms. The companies are identical in every respect except their capital structures.

	Geared	Ungeared
Expected earnings	£100	£100
Debt finance (nominal)	£200	–
Interest rate	5%	–
Market value of equity	£900	£950
Market value of company	£1,100	£950

Assume that the market value of geared debt is equal to the nominal value, and the investor holds 10 per cent of Geared's equity.

4. Kipling plc is a food manufacturer which has the following long-term capital structure:

	£
£1 ordinary shares (fully paid)	2,500,000
Share premium account	1,000,000
Retained profit	1,400,000
8% preference shares	1,200,000
10% debentures (secured)	2,600,000
	8,700,000

The directors of the company wish to raise further long-term finance by the issue of either preference shares or debentures. One director, who supports the issue of debentures, believes that, although a debenture issue will increase the company's gearing, it will reduce the overall cost of capital.

Required

(a) Discuss the arguments for and against the view that the company's overall cost of capital can be reduced in this way. The views of Modigliani and Miller should be discussed in answering this part of the question.

(b) Discuss the major factors which the directors should consider when deciding between preference shares and debentures as a means of raising further long-term finance.

(c) Identify and discuss the major factors which will influence the amount of additional debenture finance that Kipling plc will be able to raise.

(ACCA Certified Diploma)

5 (a) Berlan plc has annual earnings before interest and tax of £15 million. These earnings are expected to remain constant. The market price of the company's ordinary shares is 86 pence per share cum div and of debentures £105.50 per debenture ex-interest. An interim dividend of six pence per share has been declared. Corporate tax is at the rate of 35 per cent and all available earnings are distributed as dividends. Berlan's long-term capital structure is shown below:

	£000
Ordinary shares (25 pence par value)	12,500
Reserves	24,300
16% debenture 31 December 2017 (£100 par value)	36,800
	23,697
	60,497

Required

Calculate the cost of capital of Berlan plc according to the traditional theory of capital structure. Assume that it is now 31 December 2014.

(b) Canalot plc is an all-equity company with an equilibrium market value of £32.5 million and a cost of capital of 18 per cent per year. The company proposes to repurchase £5 million of equity and to replace it with 13 per cent irredeemable loan stock.

Canalot's earnings before interest and tax are expected to be constant for the foreseeable future. Corporate tax is at the rate of 35 per cent. All profits are paid out as dividends.

Required

Using the assumptions of Modigliani and Miller, explain and demonstrate how this change in capital structure will affect Canalot's:

(i) market value;
(ii) cost of equity;
(iii) cost of capital.

(c) Explain any weaknesses of both the traditional and Modigliani and Miller theories and discuss how useful they might be in the determination of the appropriate capital structure for a company.

(ACCA)

6 The ordinary shares of Stanley plc are quoted on the London Stock Exchange. The directors, who are also major shareholders, have been evaluating some new investment opportunities. If they go ahead with these, new capital of £38 million will be required. The directors expect the new projects to earn 15 per cent per annum before tax.

Financial information about the company for 2017 is as follows:

| EBIT (existing operations) | £79.50 million |
| Number of shares in issue (par value £1) | 50 million |

The company is at present all-equity-financed. It has the choice of raising the £38 million new capital by an issue of equity or debt. Equity would be issued by a new issue at a 15 per cent discount to current market price. Debt will be raised by an issue at par of 12 per cent unsecured loan stock.

If the finance is raised via equity, the company's P:E ratio is likely to rise from its current level of 9 to 9.5. However, if debt is introduced into the capital structure, the company's financial advisers have warned the two directors that the market is likely to lower the P:E ratio of the company to 8.5.

The company's marginal tax rate is 33 per cent.

Issue costs should be ignored.

(a) Determine the expected share price, total value of equity and value of the firm under the two financing options and comment briefly on which financing option appears the most advantageous.

(b) Assume the company's average cost of equity as an ungeared firm is 14 per cent and it expects to continue to pay tax at 33 per cent. The estimated cost of bankruptcy or financial distress is estimated at £5 million. According to Modigliani and Miller, what would be the value of equity and the firm if the company finances the expansion by (i) equity or (ii) debt?

(c) Explain the basic assumptions underlying MM's theories of capital structure and why, in an efficient market with no taxes, capital structure can have no effect on the value of the firm.

7 You are given the following information about Electronics plc. It has a payout ratio of 0.6, a return on equity of 20 per cent, an equity Beta of 1.33 and is expected to pay a dividend next year of £2.00. There are one million shares outstanding and it is fairly valued. It also has nominal debt of £20 million issued at 10 per cent and maturing in five years. Yields on similar debt have since dropped to 8 per cent. The risk-free rate is 6 per cent and the expected market return is 13.5 per cent.

(a) Find Electronics' cost of capital and cost of equity.
(b) The company decides to retire half its debt at current prices. Find the company's cost of capital and equity and explain your results.
(c) The company decides to diversify into a completely different business area and decides to look at Betas of firms currently trading in the new business area. The information is given below.

Company	Beta	Debt/Equity	Market capitalisation
A	1.5	1:2	£20 million
B	1.8	1:1	£30 million
C	1.2	No debt	£50 million

What discount rate should the company use for the new business?

8 Claxby is an undiversified company operating in light engineering. It is all-equity-financed with a Beta of 0.6. Total risk is 40 (standard deviation of annual return). Management want to diversify by acquiring Sloothby Ltd, which operates in an industrial sector where the average equity Beta is 1.2 and the average gearing (debt to total capital) ratio is 1:3. The standard deviation of the return on equity (on a book value basis) for Sloothby is 25 per cent. The acquisition would increase Claxby's asset base by 40 per cent. The overall return on the market portfolio is expected to be 18 per cent and the current return on risk-free assets is 11 per cent. The standard deviation of the return on the market portfolio is 10 per cent. The rate of corporate tax is 33 per cent.

(a) What is the asset Beta for Sloothby?
(b) Analyse both Sloothby's and Claxby's total risk into their respective specific and market risk components.
(c) What would be the Beta for the expanded company?
(d) Using the new Beta, calculate the required return on the expanded firm's equity.
Under what conditions could this be taken as the cut-off rate for new investment projects?
(e) In the light of the figures in this example, discuss whether the acquisition of Sloothby may be expected to operate in the best interests of Claxby's shareholders.

9 The managing director of Wemere, a medium-sized private company, wishes to improve the company's investment decision-making process by using discounted cash flow techniques. He is disappointed to learn that estimates of a company's cost of equity usually require information on share prices which, for a private company, are not available. His deputy suggests that the cost of equity can be estimated by using data for Folten plc, a similar-sized company in the same industry whose shares are listed on the AIM, and he has produced two suggested discount rates for use in Wemere's future investment appraisal. Both of these estimates are in excess of 17 per cent

p.a., which the managing director believes to be very high, especially as the company has just agreed a fixed rate bank loan at 13 per cent p.a. to finance a small expansion of existing operations. He has checked the calculations, which are numerically correct, but wonders if there are any errors of principle.

Estimate 1: Capital Asset Pricing Model
Data have been purchased from a leading business school
Equity Beta of Folten: 1.4
Market return: 18%
Treasury Bill yield: 12%

The cost of capital is 18% + (18% − 12%)1.4 = 26.4%. This rate must be adjusted to include inflation at the current level of 6 per cent. The recommended discount rate is 32.4 per cent.

Estimate 2: Dividend Growth Model

Folten plc

Year	Average share price (pence)	Dividend per share (pence)
2010	193	9.23
2011	109	10.06
2012	96	10.97
2013	116	11.95
2014	130	13.03

The cost of capital is: $D_1/(P - g)$, where D_1 is the expected dividend, P is the market price and g is the growth rate of dividends (= 14.20p/(138p − 9) = 11.01%)
When inflation is included, the discount rate is 17.01 per cent.
Other financial information on the two companies is presented here:

	Wemere £000	Folten £000
Fixed assets	7,200	7,600
Current assets	7,600	7,800
Less: Current liabilities	(3,900)	(3,700)
	10,900	11,700
Financed by:		
Ordinary shares (25 pence)	2,000	1,800
Reserves	6,500	5,500
Term loans	2,400	4,400
	10,900	11,700

Notes
1 The current ex div share price of Folten plc is 138 pence.
2 Wemere's board of directors has recently rejected a takeover bid of £10.6 million.
3 Corporate tax is paid at the rate of 35 per cent.

Required
(a) Explain any errors of principle that have been made in the two estimates of the cost of capital and produce revised estimates using both of the methods.
State clearly any assumptions that you make.
(b) Discuss which of your revised estimates Wemere should use as the discount rate for capital investment appraisal.

(ACCA)

Practical assignment

Reread the exposition in Chapter 6 of how we obtained tailored discount rates for the Whitbread plc divisions. How close do you think our surrogates were?

For another divisionalised company of your choice (try to find a two- or three-division company):

1. Consult the Risk Measurement Service for an up-to-date estimate of the equity Beta, and use the CAPM to assess the shareholders' required rate of return.
2. Estimate discount rates for each division. You will need to select surrogate companies, record their Betas, and obtain an indication of their own asset Betas by ungearing their equity Betas.
3. Determine whether the weighted average Beta for the company corresponds to its ungeared Beta. You will probably have to use weights based on earnings or sales as very few companies report book values (let alone market values!) of their segments.

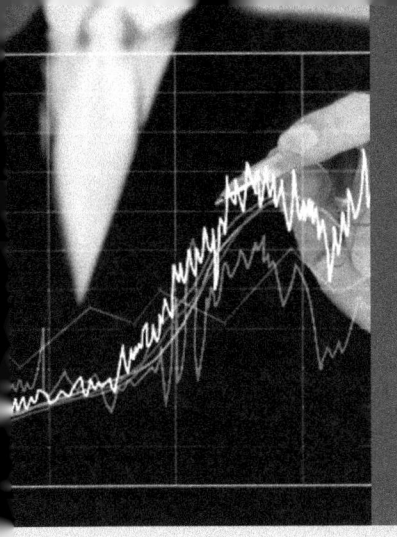

12

Acquisitions and re-structuring

Glencore chief sees synergies of $44bn deal

By outlining $2bn of synergies after taking over Xstrata and promising more to come, Ivan Glasenberg showed what he described as the 'Glencore way' of bearing down on costs – and repudiated many practices of the mining group with which he once intended to merge.

Glencore Xstrata's chief executive said that it expected synergies from the $44bn takeover to grow when it completes an operating review. 'There is still more to come,' said Mr Glasenberg. 'We have not really gone deep into the asset side.' Mr Glasenberg said that he had been surprised by how much 'fat' was to be cut at Xstrata.

Glencore said it found $1.4bn of extra savings from rationalising Xstrata's divisional offices, on top of marketing synergies identified when the commodities house planned to merge with the miner. Glencore has closed 33 offices since it took control of Xstrata.

Xstrata tended to 'gold-plate operations', had multiple offices in the same cities and was 'five plcs within a plc', said Steven Kalmin, Glencore Xstrata's chief financial officer. Mr Glasenberg said: 'We don't need a whole bunch of people analysing every asset purchase or whatever . . . we want mining engineers to run mines.'

Consistent with the hard-driving, trading mentality Glencore likes to portray, Mr Kalmin said that mine managers in coal – where the efficiency drive is most advanced – were now getting called 'every two days' in a vigilant approach to costs. 'There is pressure from us all at the top,' said Mr Kalmin.

FT *Source:* Wilson, J. and Hume, N. (2013) Ivan Glasenberg shows the 'Glencore way' to cut Xstrata 'fat'. *Financial Times*, 10 September. © The Financial Times Limited 2018. All rights reserved.

Learning objectives

A major aim of this chapter is to emphasise the interaction between the financial and strategic dimensions of corporate acquisitions and mergers. Having read it, you should understand the following:

- Why firms select acquisitions rather than other strategic options.
- How acquisitions can be financed.
- How acquisitions should be integrated.
- How the degree of success of a takeover can be evaluated.
- How corporate re-structuring can enhance shareholder value.
- How private equity-based investment houses operate in the acquisition and re-structuring process

12.1 INTRODUCTION

Acquisitions of other companies are investment decisions and should be evaluated as (if not more) thoroughly and on essentially the same criteria as, say, the purchase of new items of machinery. However, there are two important differences between takeovers and many 'standard' investments.

First, because takeovers are frequently resisted by the target's managers, bidders often have little or no access to intelligence about their targets beyond published financial and market data, and any inside information they may glean. (As and when takeover is accepted as inevitable, the defending board is obliged to provide key information to enable the bidder to conduct 'due diligence' examinations. This is essentially a search for 'skeletons in the cupboard'. See Sudarsanam (2010) for due diligence procedures.)

Second, many takeovers are undertaken for longer-term strategic motives, and the benefits are often difficult to quantify. It is common to hear the chairmen of acquiring companies talk about an acquisition opening up a 'strategic window'; what they often do not add is that the window is usually not only shut, but also has thick curtains drawn across it! To a large extent, a takeover is a shot in the dark, partly explaining why so many firms that launch giant takeovers come to grief.

But there are other reasons. Targets are often too large in relation to bidders, so that excessive borrowings or unexpected integration problems throttle the parent.

There are important lessons to be learned from risk analysis and portfolio theory. When acquisitions have highly uncertain outcomes, the larger they are, the more catastrophic the impact of any adverse outcomes. As a result, it may be rational and less risky to confine takeover activity to small, uncontested bids. Alternatively, a spread of large acquisitions might confer significant portfolio diversification benefits, so long as the components have low cash flow correlation. However, the greater the scale of takeover activity, the greater the resulting financing burden placed on the parent, and the greater the impact of diverting managerial capacity into solving integration problems. As the following cameo suggests, some people and firms can surmount these pitfalls.

asset-stripping
Selling off the assets of a taken-over firm, often in order to recoup the initial outlay

The acquisition decision is thus a complex one. It involves significant uncertainties (except in purely **asset-stripping** takeovers), it often requires substantial funding and it may pose awkward problems of integration. Yet, as some takeover 'kings' like

---

Buffett buys Texas utility to transform US energy group

Warren Buffett has scooped up Oncor, the crown jewel of bankrupt Texas utility Energy Future Holdings, in a deal that will nearly double the number of customers of Berkshire's US energy group.

Berkshire Hathaway agreed to acquire the re-structured EFH for $9bn in cash, implying an equity value of $11.25bn and an enterprise value of just over $18bn for Oncor, the regulated transmission and distribution business of which EFH owns 80 per cent.

EFH's creditors will also be looking closely at how they will be compensated as part of the deal. Elliott Management, a New York hedge fund and the largest creditor, would consider launching a rival bid if it was unsatisfied with the offer it receives, according to people familiar with its thinking. It is not currently planning to make a bid.

NextEra Energy had agreed 12 months ago to buy Oncor for $18.4bn but the deal was later blocked by Texas regulators, a decision that gave Berkshire the opportunity to secure the asset at a slightly lower price. In contrast to NextEra, Berkshire plans to keep Oncor ringfenced so any financial problems in other parts of its business would not affect service to its 10m customers across the state.

Berkshire's latest deal will bolster its 86-year-old chairman's reputation for seizing on other companies' failures to add new assets at attractive valuations. He has built a conglomerate with a market value of $416bn, whose operations range from insurers to consumer goods companies.

'Oncor is an excellent fit for Berkshire Hathaway, and we are pleased to make another long-term investment in Texas – when we invest in Texas, we invest big!' said Mr Buffett. 'Oncor is a great company with similar values and outstanding assets.'

Source: Fontanella-Khan, J. (2017) Buffett buys Texas utility to transform US energy group. *Financial Times*, 7 July. © The Financial Times Limited 2018. All rights reserved.

12.2 TAKEOVER ACTIVITY

Warren Buffett have shown, spectacular payoffs can be achieved. These are some of the themes of this chapter – how to evaluate a takeover, how to finance it and how to integrate it. But first, we examine the phenomenon of takeover surges.

takeover
Acquisition of the share capital of another firm, resulting in its identity being absorbed into that of the acquirer

mergers
Pooling by firms of their separate interests into newly-constituted business, each party participating on roughly equal terms

Although the terms 'takeover' and 'merger' are used as synonyms, there is a technical difference. A **takeover** is the acquisition by one company of the share capital of another in exchange for cash, ordinary shares, loan stock or some mixture of these. This results in the identity of the acquired company being absorbed into that of the acquirer (although, of course, the expanded company may continue to use the acquired company's brand names and trademarks). A **merger** is a pooling of the interests of two companies into a new enterprise, requiring the agreement of both sets of shareholders. For example, in June 2017, Amazon announced the acquisition of Whole Foods Market for $13.7 billion. Acquisition of the biggest premium grocer in the United States will help Amazon in fulfilling its ambition to compete within the $800 billion US grocery market. Similarly, in 2014, a US merger was announced between Safeway and Albertson. The merger of the two grocery store chains created a company with 2,400 stores and nearly 250,000 employees. By definition, mergers involve the friendly (initially, at least) re-structuring of assets into a new organisation, whereas many takeovers are hotly resisted. In practice, the vast majority of business amalgamations are takeovers rather than mergers. However, mergers are quite common in some sectors, e.g. aviation. Air France merged with KLM in 2004, United Airlines and Continental merged in 2010, while British Airways and Iberia combined to form International Airlines Group in 2011 and, in 2013, American Airlines merged with US Airways. This is undoubtedly due to the twin drivers of deregulation and chronic overcapacity.

Table 12.1 shows takeovers of UK firms over the past decade undertaken by other UK firms. It can be seen that the majority involve acquisitions of independent companies rather than trade sales, whether one looks at number, or value of, deals.

Table 12.1 Summary of mergers and acquisitions in the United Kingdom by UK companies

£ million

	Total all mergers and acquisitions		Mergers and acquisitions of independent companies		Sales of subsidiaries between company groups	
	Number	Value	Number	Value	Number	Value
2001	492	28,994	319	21,029	173	7,965
2002	430	25,236	323	16,998	107	8,238
2003	558	18,679	392	10,954	166	7,725
2004	741	31,408	577	22,882	164	8,526
2005	769	25,134	604	16,276	165	8,858
2006	779	28,511	628	20,180	151	8,331
2007	869	26,778	698	19,779	171	6,999
2008	558	36,469	445	33,469	113	3,000
2009	286	12,196	198	11,455	88	740
2010	325	12,605	243	7,775	82	4,830
2011	373	8,089	276	5,265	97	2,824
2012	266	3,413	216	2,536	50	877
2013	240	7,658	173	4,129	67	3,529
2014	189	8,032	150	5,968	39	2,063
2015	245	6,920	194	4,640	51	2,280
2016	428	24,688	383	11,038	45	13,650

Source: Office for National Statistics, August 2017 (**https://www.ons.gov.uk**). Crown copyright material is reproduced under the terms and conditions of the Open Government Licence (OGL).

If one examines the UK data for longer periods, there are clear examples of waves in motion, for example, in terms of number of firms, that of the early 1970s, the late 1980s and the mid-2000s. The significant rise in mergers and acquisitions in the mid-2000s was driven by factors such as globalisation. This wave ended abruptly in mid-2007 when the financial crisis began to emerge. When share prices are high and rising, it becomes easier to conduct a takeover bid by exchange of shares. Accordingly, the proportion of acquisitions completed in this way rose to historically high levels at this time. So, here we have one reason for takeover waves – takeover booms tend to reflect general stock market activity, so when the stock market booms, listed firms tend to become more acquisitive. Post-2008, following the financial crisis, there has been a noticeable drop in merger and acquisition activity. However, a significant increase was recorded in 2016, with 428 mergers and acquisitions, the total value of which was recorded as £24,688 million.

There may be a 'chicken-and-egg' argument here. It has been argued that takeover activity often provides the trigger for a stock market recovery. When share prices fall, and the market value of firms looks low in relation to the replacement cost of their assets (i.e. the cost of setting up an equivalent operating facility), acquisition may seem the cheaper way for a firm wishing to expand compared to internal (or 'organic') growth.

According to the late Peter Doyle, the eminent marketing academic (1994), the motives for mergers are changing from those of the 1980s. In earlier waves, companies like Hanson and BTR were looking to exploit financial economies by re-structuring badly-run companies and giving managers incentives to deliver strong cash flows to create value. By contrast, Doyle suggested that, increasingly, mergers are more likely to be driven by strategic factors. Prominent among these are the increased globalisation of markets, with greater exposure to more aggressive international competition.

According to Doyle, this process was fuelled by deregulation and privatisation in many countries, which have freed companies in the telecommunications and airline industries, in particular, to seek out global strategic alliances. In addition, technological change raised the investment expenditures required to research and market new products, so that size of firm conferred a major advantage in industries like pharmaceuticals. Moreover, distance is no longer a barrier, given the improvements in transportation and information technology; hence, the wave of banking mergers in North America and Europe in the late 1990s, and the flurry of mergers in the US telecommunications industry in 2005, as well as persistent high levels of M&A activity in the pharmaceutical sector (see the 'Cost of pharma M&A deals doubles since 2015' cameo later in this section).

The importance of cross-border acquisitions involving UK firms can be seen in Table 12.2, which shows data on both acquisitions and disposals abroad by UK companies, and also by foreign companies in the United Kingdom.

The international data clearly show the fall-back in activity following the 2007–8 financial crisis. Over the period, foreign companies have conducted a high level of net acquisitions of UK firms, accelerated by the fall in sterling following the referendum vote to exit the European Union. In value terms, this easily outweighs the acquisition of UK firms by other UK firms. In this sense, internal merger activity by UK firms has become a relative sideshow, although UK firms continue to spend large amounts on foreign firms as they increasingly globalise their activities.

The surge in foreign acquisitions has involved several high-profile, very large deals such as Tata Steel (India)/Corus, Telefonica (Spain)/O_2, Ferrovial (Spain)/British Airports Authority, and Dubai Ports World (United Arab Emirates)/P&O. In some of these cases, the acquirer was a 'sovereign wealth fund (SWF)' set up by the foreign government to invest income from oil or other sources. The increased ownership and involvement of such investors has raised issues of potential foreign influence in UK economic affairs (and those of other countries), and appears to contradict the UK government's desire to reduce state ownership of industry. Following further foreign takeovers during 2010, e.g. Kraft's acquisition of Cadbury and train company Arriva's acquisition by Deutsche Bahn, a new set of concerns arose about dubious practices.

Table 12.2 Summary of cross-border mergers, acquisitions and disposals

£ million

| | Transactions abroad by UK companies ||||Transactions in the UK by foreign companies ||||
| | Acquisitions || Disposals || Acquisitions || Disposals ||
	Number	Value	Number	Value	Number	Value	Number	Value
2001	371	41,473	139	28,494	162	24,382	62	4,464
2002	262	26,626	128	7,074	117	16,798	60	7,912
2003	243	20,756	136	8,643	129	9,309	55	3,620
2004	305	18,709	118	5,485	178	29,928	54	5,514
2005	365	32,732	110	12,668	242	50,280	61	8,387
2006	405	37,412	89	21,214	259	77,750	55	14,208
2007	441	57,814	104	10,221	269	82,121	66	7,524
2008	298	29,670	71	12,062	252	52,552	49	5,139
2009	118	10,148	37	5,101	112	31,984	38	7,820
2010	199	12,414	73	11,411	212	36,643	58	9,891
2011	286	50,234	80	14,111	237	32,967	69	11,748
2012	122	17,933	40	*	161	17,414	27	*
2013	58	*	*	*	135	31,144	25	1,586
2014	113	20,647	36	5,288	110	15,041	23	2,794
2015	170	25,561	42	16,852	145	33,335	35	7,451
2016	141	17,292	42	15,420	262	189,968	35	6,143

* Data not disclosed
Source: Office for National Statistics, August 2017 (https://www.ons.gov.uk). Crown copyright material is reproduced under the terms and conditions of the Open Government Licence (OGL).

Kraft was roundly reprimanded for promising to keep open a Cadbury plant at Summerdale, near Bristol, only to close it down seven days after the deal was closed and then move production to Poland. Following this, the Takeover Panel introduced rules whereby it could act against companies that have not adhered to undertakings made as a part of a bid. This concern about post-bid practices was a feature of the (failed) Pfizer bid for AstraZeneca in 2014.

Cost of pharma M&A deals doubles since 2015

Pharmaceutical companies paid twice as much for acquisitions in 2016 than a year earlier as cheap credit and the need to secure a pipeline of new drugs inflated the value of deals.

Not only has the value of deals increased, but buyers are having to pay much more for companies to build sales and take on greater risk.

The median value of an acquisition in 2016 was 39 times the revenue of the acquired company, compared with 19 times a year earlier and eight times in 2014. While the number of deals fell from 86 in 2015 to 78, the median value almost doubled to $1.97bn.

The analysis of 316 deals conducted in the past three years comes as the saga over the acquisition of Actelion, Europe's largest biotech group, continues to unfold. Actelion has been in discussions with Johnson & Johnson of the US and Sanofi of France over a deal that could value the company at as much as $30bn.

Industry insiders believe the search for new drugs will intensify in 2017. Political uncertainty in 2016 held back acquisitions by large companies, which also face pricing pressures from pharmacy benefit managers in the US and from generic drug manufacturers.

Mr Rountree, partner at Novasecta, said that 'the companies that are being acquired cannot, on average, be now worth twice as much as they were only five years ago. The pressure for companies to overpay for acquisitions that give short-term growth is intense, and the era of cheap capital has exacerbated this phenomenon.'

Source: Vina, G. (2017) Cost of pharma M&A deals doubles since 2015. Financial Times, 4 January. © The Financial Times Limited 2018. All rights reserved.

The regulation of takeovers

UK takeovers are regulated in three ways. The first mode of regulation is under the competition policy of the European Union, set out in the EC Merger Regulation 139/2004 (ECMR). The ECMR provides that a merger that creates a dominant position, as a result of which competition would be significantly impeded, shall be declared incompatible with the common market. The Regulation applies to all mergers with a 'Community Dimension', defined in terms of turnover levels. The ECMR was designed to provide 'one-stop' merger control to avoid the risk of mergers being investigated under two or more jurisdictions. National authorities may not normally apply their own competition laws to mergers falling within the ECMR, which are investigated by the Competition Commission. The bid by Kraft for Cadbury's was referred to the European Commission and was not dealt with by UK authorities.

Mergers falling outside the ambit of the ECMR are the responsibility of the Department for Business, Innovation and Skills. Mergers qualify for investigation if UK turnover of the target enterprise exceeds £70 million, or if the merger creates or increases a 25 per cent share in a market for goods or services in the United Kingdom, or in a substantial part of it (i.e. local monopolies can qualify).

Qualifying mergers are investigated by the Competition and Markets Authority (CMA) (www.gov.uk/government/organisations/competition-and-markets-authority). The CMA was established under regulations created by the Enterprise and Regulatory Reform Act 2013. This Act merged together the Competition Commission and the Office of Fair Trading, and the CMA began operating in April 2014. The overall mission of the CMA is to ensure 'markets work well in the interests of consumers, businesses and the economy'. Consequently, in respect of mergers, the CMA has a statutory duty to investigate any merger 'that could potentially give rise to a substantial lessening of competition, and require the merging parties to take steps to protect competition while the investigation takes place'. Mergers may come to the attention of the CMA either because a business notifies the CMA of the merger or through the CMA acting on its own initiative. Companies may opt to inform the CMA of an impending merger to reduce uncertainty.

The first phase of the CMA review must be completed within 40 working days, and this review phase is to assess whether the merger will result in 'a realistic prospect of a substantial lessening of competition'. If there is a prospect of a substantial lessening of competition, a more detailed second review phase will take place and is normally completed with 24 weeks. The CMA will then set out any actions the two companies undertaking the merger would need to take to remedy any competition issues. For example, the CMA may stipulate that parts of the business must be sold prior to the merger. The two companies also have the option to suggest appropriate remedial actions at the end of the first review phase and, thereby, avoid the second review phase.

The CMA considers that substantial lessening of competition occurs 'when rivalry [between businesses] is substantially less intense after the merger than would otherwise have been the case, resulting in a worse outcome for customers [through, for example, higher prices, reduced quality or reduced choice]'. There is a need for the use of judgement in determining whether this is the case, and a panel of independent members carries out the phase two review process.

The third control on takeovers is operated by **The Panel on Takeovers and Mergers** (www.thetakeoverpanel.org.uk), formed in 1968 to counter the perceived inadequacy of the statutory mechanisms for regulating the conduct of both parties in the takeover process. It states that 'its central objective is to ensure fair treatment for all shareholders in takeover bids'. The Panel consists of representatives from City and other leading business institutions, such as the CBI, the Stock Exchange and the ICAEW accounting body, thus representing the main associations whose members are involved in takeovers, whether as advisers, shareholders or regulators. The Panel promulgates and administers the **Takeover Code**, a set of rules originally with no force of law, reflecting

Takeover Code
The non-statutory rules laid down by the Takeover Panel to guide the conduct of participants in the takeover process

what those most closely involved with takeovers regard as best practice. It did, however, have some sanctions to enforce its authority, such as public reprimands, thereby damaging the reputation of violators of the Code, risking the collapse of the bid and, for financial advisers, jeopardising long-term business. Originally, the Panel's ultimate sanction was to request its members to withdraw the facilities of the City from offenders, although this was extremely rare.

In 2006, the EU Takeover Directive (2004/5/EC) came into force. This is very largely based on the UK Takeover Code, but with one important difference in that it is has statutory backing. The Panel can now order compensation to be paid in certain cases, and it can pursue miscreants in the UK courts. It can also ask the Financial Services Authority to take enforcement action in cases of market abuse for which penalties include unlimited fines.

■ The chronology of a hostile bid

The following schedule details the necessary timing of bids and provision of information as required by the Takeover Code.

Day 1: Bid announced. Bidder has 28 days in which to post a formal offer to target's shareholders.

Day 14 after formal offer: Deadline for target company to publish its 'defence document'.

Day 21 after formal offer: First date at which the offer can be ended. Bidder must disclose how many of target's shares have been voted in its favour. If over 50 per cent, the bidder has won; if less, it may choose to walk away.

Day 39 after formal offer: Last day for defender to produce new arguments ('material new information') to encourage shareholder loyalty.

Day 46 after formal offer: Last day for offer or to revise its offer.

Day 60 after formal offer: Last day for offer to be declared unconditional as to acceptances.

Normally, the maximum time span allowed for the whole process is thus 89 days, although the Takeover Panel may 'stop the clock' pending clarification of key points. In the event of a reference to the CMA, the process is halted *sine die* to await its report. This can take upwards of six months, during which the initial 'urge to merge' has been known to evaporate.

The key requirements of the Takeover Code, now into its 12th edition (issued September 2016), are summarised by the Takeover Panel as:

- When a person or group acquires interests in shares carrying 30 per cent or more of the voting rights of a company, they must make a cash offer to all other shareholders at the highest price paid in the 12 months before the offer was announced.
- When interests in shares carrying 10 per cent or more of the voting rights of a class have been acquired by an offeror (i.e. a bidder) in the offer period and the previous 12 months, the offer must include a cash alternative for all shareholders of that class at the highest price paid by the offeror in that period.
- If the offeror acquires an interest in shares in an offeree company (i.e. a target) at a price higher than the value of the offer, the offer must be increased accordingly.
- The offeree company must appoint a competent independent adviser whose advice on the offer must be made known to all the shareholders, together with the opinion of the board.
- Favourable deals for selected shareholders are banned.
- All shareholders must be given the same information.
- Those issuing takeover circulars must include statements taking responsibility for the contents.
- Profit forecasts and asset valuations must be made to specified standards and must be reported on by professional advisers.

- Misleading, inaccurate or unsubstantiated statements made in documents or to the media must be publicly corrected immediately.
- Actions during the course of an offer by the offeree company which might frustrate the offer are generally prohibited unless shareholders approve these plans.
- Stringent requirements are laid down for the disclosure of dealings in relevant securities during an offer.
- Employees of both the offeror and the offeree company and the trustees of the offeree company's pension scheme must be informed about an offer. In addition, the offeree company's employee representatives and pension scheme trustees have the right to have a separate opinion on the effects of the offer on employment appended to the offeree board's circular, or published on a website.

12.3 MOTIVES FOR TAKEOVER

Managers seeking to maximise the wealth of shareholders should continually seek to exploit value-creating opportunities. There are two situations when managers feel able to enrich shareholders via takeovers:

1. *When managers believe that the target company can be acquired at less than its 'true value'.* This implies disbelief in the ability of the capital market consistently to value companies correctly. If a company is thought to be undervalued on the market, there may well be opportunities for 'asset-stripping', i.e. selling off the components of the taken-over company for a combined sum greater than the purchase price.
2. *When managers believe that two enterprises will be worth more if merged than if operated as two separate entities.* Thus, for two companies, A and B:

$$V_{A+B} > V_A + V_B$$

value additivity
The notion that, other things being equal, the combined present value of two entities is their separate present values added together

The principle of **value additivity** would refute this unless the amalgamation resulted in some form of synergy or more effective utilisation of the assets of the combined companies.

In practice, it is very difficult to differentiate between these two explanations for merger, especially as many mergers result in only partial disposals, when activities that appear to fit more neatly into existing operations are retained. Companies are valued by the market on the basis of information that their managements release regarding market prospects, value of assets, R&D activity and so on. Market participants may suspect that an under-performing company could be operated more efficiently by an alternative management team, but until a credible bidder emerges, poor results may simply be reflected in a poor stock market rating.

How different types of acquisition create value

Acquisitions can be split into three types:

horizontal integration
The acquisition of a competitor in pursuit of market power and/or scale economies

1. **Horizontal integration** – where a company takes over another from the same industry and at the same stage of the production process: for example, a brewery acquiring a competitor, e.g. Greene King's acquisition of Cloverleaf, the pubs-and-eateries chain, in January 2011. The motivation is usually enhancement of market power and/or to obtain production economies.

vertical integration
Extension of a firm's activities further back, or forward, along the supply chain from existing activities

2. **Vertical integration** – where the target is in the same industry as the acquirer, but operating at a different stage of the production chain, either nearer the source of materials (backward integration) or nearer to the final consumer (forward integration), e.g. Ford's takeover of Kwikfit, the car spares firm (since divested by MBO).

conglomerate takeover
The acquisition of a target firm in a field apparently unrelated to the acquirer's existing activities

3 **Conglomerate takeover or unrelated diversification** – where the target is in an activity apparently dissimilar to the acquirer although some activities such as marketing may overlap (known as concentric diversification). These takeovers are often said to lack 'industrial logic', but they can lead to economies in the provision of company-wide services such as Head Office administration and access to capital markets on improved terms, i.e. financial economies.

In reality, most mergers are difficult to classify into such neat categories, as they are motivated by a complex interplay of factors, which it is hoped will enhance the value of the bidder's equity. The more specific reasons cited for launching takeover bids usually reflect the anticipated benefits that a merger is expected to generate:

scale economies
Cost efficiencies, e.g. bulk-buying, due to increasing a firm's size of operation

1 *To exploit* **scale economies**. Larger size is usually expected to yield production economies if manufacturing operations can be amalgamated, marketing economies if similar distribution channels can be utilised, and financial economies if size confers access to capital markets on more favourable terms.

synergies
Gains in revenues or cost savings resulting from takeovers and mergers, not resulting from firm size, i.e. stemming from a 'natural match' between two sets of assets

2 *To obtain synergy*. The term **synergies** is often used to include any gains from merger, but, strictly, it refers to benefits unrelated to scale. Gains may emerge from a particular way of combining resources. One company's managers may be especially suited to operating another company's distribution systems, or the sales staff of one company may be able to sell another company's, perhaps closely related, product as part of a package.

3 *To enter new markets*. For firms that lack the expertise to develop different products, or do not possess the outlets required to access different market segments, takeover may be a simpler, and certainly a quicker, way of expanding, as with EADS' acquisition of Vector Aerospace, and Pepsico's acquisition of Wimm-Bill-Dann, Russia's biggest food company, for about $5.5 billion in 2010.

4 *To fill in gaps in the product line*. The Swatch Group acquisition of Harry Winston Diamond Corporation in 2013 was to fill a product gap. Swatch needed to add to its watch business a further business that would give it a position in the very 'high end' of the jewellery and watch market, and Harry Winston has filled this (see cameo).

5 *To provide 'critical mass'*. As many product markets have become more global and the lifespan of products has tended to diminish, greater emphasis has to be placed on R&D activities. In some industries, such as aerospace, telecommunications and pharmaceuticals, small enterprises are simply unable to generate the cash flows required to finance R&D and brand investment. This factor was largely responsible for the sale by Fisons and Boots of their drug-development activities in 1994 to much larger German companies. There is also a credibility effect. For example, companies may be unwilling to use small firms as a source of components when their future survival, and hence ability to supply, is suspect.

Swatch fills gap in portfolio with purchase of Harry Winston

For all its other successes, the ventures of Swatch Group into the world of high-end jewellery watches have not always ended in smiles. Its most recent foray collapsed in acrimony in 2011 when the Swiss watchmaker abruptly terminated a partnership with Tiffany, the US luxury jeweller, with accusations from both sides that the other had failed to honour the terms of their deal.

As well as sparking bitter legal tit-for-tat, the imbroglio left a gap in Swatch's portfolio in an area of the jewellery and watchmaking business that many observers think could see decent growth in coming years, and which is currently dominated by brands such as Cartier – owned by Swatch's Swiss rival, Richemont – and Chopard.

Continued

On 14 January, Swatch moved to fill the gap, disclosing that it had struck a deal to buy the watches and jewellery division of Harry Winston Diamond Corporation, a swanky brand immortalised by Marilyn Monroe in the song *Diamonds are a Girl's Best Friend*, and which remains a red carpet staple, counting the likes of Gwyneth Paltrow and Halle Berry among its Hollywood admirers.

Analysts were quick to approve the rationale of the deal, which accompanies a flurry of corporate activity in the luxury sector. 'Strategically it make sense,' says John Guy, an analyst at Berenberg Bank, pointing out that as well as filling a gap in Swatch's brand portfolio, the acquisition will also bulk up the watchmaker's hitherto slender presence in the Americas, which accounted for just 8 per cent of Swatch's sales in 2011, but which has been a traditional area of strength of Harry Winston.

The potential co-operation on diamond polishing also has significant strategic implications, Mr Guy says. 'Vertical integration is the holy grail in the luxury goods sector. This is particularly true where diamonds are concerned – if you can trace a diamond from the mine to the shelf in the boutique, then that is a big plus, given all the concerns around blood diamonds,' he says. 'It eliminates any ethical risk. But it is also important because the diamond market can be a volatile and capacity-constrained business. The greater your control over supply, the better,' he says.

FT *Source:* Shotter, J. (2013) Corporate strategy: Swatch fills gap in portfolio with purchase of Harry Winston. *Financial Times*, 21 January. © The Financial Times Limited 2018. All rights reserved.

Southampton FC acquired by China's Gao family

Southampton has become the latest European football club to come under Chinese ownership, after real estate magnate Jisheng Gao sidestepped a mainland crackdown on overseas acquisitions to finalise a deal worth about £200m.

Katharina Liebherr, the Premier League club's Swiss owner, confirmed that a deal with Mr Gao had been completed and welcomed the new 'partners' to the club.

The Gao family acquired an 80 per cent stake in a transaction that valued the south coast club at about £200m.

In recent years, Chinese groups and individuals had spent more than $2bn on European football clubs, and Southampton becomes the third Premier League club to gain major Chinese investment.

FT *Source:* Ahmed, M. and Massoudi, A. (2017) Southampton FC acquired by China's Gao family. *Financial Times*, 14 August. © The Financial Times Limited 2018. All rights reserved.

Prudential merger of UK businesses opens way to a sale

Prudential is to merge its two big UK businesses in a move seen as paving the way for a dramatic break-up of the £47bn insurer as it shifts its focus to fast-growing Asian markets. The move comes amid a shake-up in financial services, with many of the industry's top names combining in an effort to cut costs.

Until now, Prudential has had two separate businesses in its domestic market: a life assurance business and M&G, an asset manager. The company said that it would merge them to create 'a leading savings and investments business'. The combination will also generate £145m per year of cost savings.

Analysts say that the UK merger will ease the path to a split. 'M&G was on the outside of the UK fold. This brings it into the fold very neatly,' said Eamonn Flanagan at Shore Capital. 'Having M&G as part of the UK business makes [a break-up] easier and tidier.'

Mike Wells, Prudential chief executive, would not comment on whether the decision to merge the two businesses was the first step on the road to a break-up. However, he added: 'Any time you improve efficiency and effectiveness, that increases value and increases optionality.'

Abid Hussain, analyst at Credit Suisse, said: 'Arguably you would get a better valuation for the combined business than you would for the insurance business alone. When you combine the two, there is some growth there. It could be worth £12–13bn, or possibly higher.'

Jason Hollands of Tilney Investment Management said the merger was the latest evidence that 'the tectonic plates are shifting in UK financial services'. 'The market is developing towards the creation of a small cluster of supergroups that have both broad manufacturing capabilities across asset classes and significant distribution,' he added.

FT *Source:* Ralph, O. (2017) Prudential merger of UK businesses opens way to a sale. *Financial Times*, 10 August. © The Financial Times Limited 2018. All rights reserved.

6 *To impart or restore growth impetus.* Maturing firms whose growth rate is weakening may look to younger, more dynamic companies both to obtain a quick, short-term growth 'fix', and also for entrepreneurial ideas to achieve higher rates of growth in the longer term. For some years, British American Tobacco has been using its substantial cash flows to push into markets such as Serbia and Turkey where the health lobby is weaker than in Western Europe.

7 *To acquire market power.* Obtaining higher earnings is easier if there are fewer competitors. Competition-reducing takeovers are likely to be investigated by the regulatory authorities, but are often justified by the need to enhance ability to compete internationally on the basis of a more secure home market. In addition, backward vertical integration, mergers undertaken to capture sources of raw materials (e.g. Shell's acquisition of British Gas in 2016 to increase its exploration and production capability), and forward vertical integration to secure new outlets for the company's products have the effect of increasing the firm's grasp over the whole supply chain, and are thus competition-reducing in a wider sense. Many past brewery takeovers were mounted not to obtain production capacity, but to secure access to the target's estate of tied public houses, and to acquire brands.

8 *To reduce dependence on existing, perhaps volatile, activities.* In Chapter 5, we concluded that risk reduction *per se* as a motive for diversification may be misguided. There is no reason why two enterprises owned by one company should have greater value unless the amalgamation produces scale economies or some other synergies. If shareholder portfolio formation is a substitute for corporate diversification, there is no point in acquiring other companies to reduce risk – rational shareholders will already have diversified away specific risk, and market risk is undiversifiable. There are two major qualifications to this argument. First, diversification into overseas securities may lower market risk, given that different economies, and hence stock markets, are not perfectly correlated (Madura and Fox, 2017). Second, it is possible that achieving greater size via conglomerate diversification may lower the costs of financial distress.

9 *To obtain a stock market listing.* This is achieved via a 'reverse takeover' in which an unlisted firm acquires a smaller listed firm. This 'back-door' method of achieving a listing is conducted by the listed firm issuing new shares in order to acquire the unlisted firm. Because of the difference in size, the bidder has to issue so many shares that the shareholders in the unlisted company emerge with a majority stake in the expanded firm.

Janus Henderson's transformational merger

On October 3 2016, Janus Capital and Henderson Group, announced a 'transformational' deal to merge into a $6.4bn investment house with $331bn under management, called Janus Henderson Investors. The money management industry had long been swirling with chatter of mergers and acquisitions, but the audacity of the Janus-Henderson marriage still struck like a thunderbolt.

For some analysts and rivals, it looked like a defensive, even desperate, move by two respectable but mid-sized asset managers settling for each other after treading water in an unforgiving environment. The punchy target of saving $110m annually within three years – heavily tilted towards the first 12 months – also made it look like it was mostly about cost-cutting.

The deal finally closed this month, and Henderson has been delisted from the London Stock Exchange to make New York the merged company's primary listing. But the merger process continues. 'Scale benefits and synergies can drive earnings accretion and help firms better insulate against intensifying disruptive threats. But there's no guarantee of value creation in a sector in which the assets can walk out the door; deal execution is critical, and so is the importance of culture and relationships,' the bank's analysts said.

Source: Wigglesworth, R. (2017) Janus Henderson Investors: when Andrew met Dick. *Financial Times*, 12 June. © The Financial Times Limited 2018. All rights reserved.

The 'market for management control'

Several of the motives for merger mentioned earlier suggest that some companies can be more efficiently operated by alternative managers. A more general motive for merger is thus to weed out inefficient personnel. There are three ways in which the market mechanism can penalise managerial inefficiency:

1 Insolvency, which usually involves significant costs.
2 Shareholder revolt, which is difficult to organise given the diffusion of ownership and the general reluctance of institutional investors to interfere in operational management.
3 The takeover process, which may be regarded as a 'market for managerial control'. The threat of takeover provides a spur to inefficient managers; while removing inefficient managers lowers costs and removes barriers to more effective utilisation of assets. Theory suggests that incompetently-managed firms will be acquired at prices that ensure the owners of the acquirer suffer no loss in value. If a bid premium over the market price is payable, this should be recoverable from the higher cash flows generated from more efficient asset utilisation. To this extent, takeover activity is seen by authors such as Jensen (1984) as a perfectly healthy expression of the workings of the market system, potentially benefiting all parties.

Managerial motives for takeover

The motive of diversification to reduce risk suggests a second possible explanation for takeover activity. With the divorce of ownership and control, and the consequent high level of managerial autonomy, managers are relatively free to follow activities and policies, including acquisition of other firms, which enhance their own objectives, both in monetary and non-pecuniary forms.

Managerial salaries and perquisites are usually higher in large and growing firms, and since growth by acquisition is usually easier and swifter than organic growth, managers may view acquisition with some eagerness. If acquisitions are 'managerial' in this sense, then acquirers may be prepared to expend 'excessive' amounts to gain ownership of target companies simply to secure deals that promote managerial well-being, but at the expense of shareholder value. If this explanation is correct, acquisitions may result in a transfer of wealth from shareholders of acquiring firms to shareholders of acquired companies, even when presented as promoting the best interests of the former.

Takeovers may also be related to the way managers are remunerated. In the 1980s, UK managers increasingly came to be paid by results, with the commonest criterion of performance being growth in EPS. This is a notoriously unreliable measure of performance, as it is not only dependent on accounting conventions, but also relatively easy to manipulate and easy to increase by takeover. For example, shutting down a loss-making activity can raise reported EPS.

Self-assessment activity 12.1

Suggest some 'managerial' motives for growth by takeover.

(Answer in Appendix A)

How to increase EPS by takeover: Hawk takes over Vole

A common means of increasing EPS has been to acquire other companies with lower P:E ratios than one's own, these being companies out of favour with the market, either through poor performance or because too little was known about them. The acquisition of such companies, in certain conditions, can raise both EPS and share price. Consider the example in Table 12.3. Hawk, with a P:E ratio of 20, reflecting strong

Table 12.3 Hawk and Vole

	Pre-bid		Post-bid
	Hawk	Vole	Hawk + Vole
Number of shares	100m	20m	100m + 5m = 105m
Earnings after tax	£20m	£2m	£20m + £2m = £22m
EPS	20p	10p	£22m ÷ 105m = 21p
P:E ratio	20:1	10:1	20:1
Share price	£4	£1	20 × 21p = £4.20
Capitalisation (market value)	£400m	£20m	105m × £4.20 = £441m

growth expectations, contemplates the takeover of Vole, whose P:E ratio is only 10. Hawk proposes to make an all-share offer. If it were able to obtain Vole at the current market price, it would have to issue 5 million shares to Vole's shareholders in exchange for their 20 million shares, i.e. (5 million × £4) = (20 million × £1) = £20 million.

Table 12.3 shows the impact of the exchange if the P:E ratio of the expanded company were to remain at 20. The new EPS is (£22m/105m) = 21p, resulting in a post-bid share price of £4.20 and an overall market value of £441 million. This apparently magical effect seems to have generated wealth of £21 million. If it works out this way, the beneficiaries are the two sets of shareholders: Hawk's existing shareholders find their 100 million shares valued at a price higher by 20p, i.e. £20 million in total, and Vole's former shareholders find they now hold shares valued at £21 million, rather than the value of £20 million placed on Vole prior to the bid, i.e.:

Gains to Hawk's shareholders = £20m
Gains to Vole's shareholders = £1m
Total gain = £21m

This so-called **'boot-strapping'** effect may simply be 'financial illusion' because it is unlikely to occur quite like this in reality. First, it assumes the absence of a bid premium. In practice, Hawk would have to offer above the market price to tempt Vole's shareholders into selling, thus altering the balance of gain. Second, it assumes that the market applies the same P:E ratio to the expanded group as the pre-bid ratio for Hawk. If no synergies were expected, then the likely post-bid P:E ratio is the total pre-bid value of the two firms relative to their total pre-bid earnings, i.e.:

$$\frac{(£400m + £20m)}{(£20m + £2m)} = \frac{£420m}{£22m} = 19.09$$

However, if Hawk is expected to re-organise Vole and impart the same growth impetus expected from Hawk itself, the P:E ratio post-bid could exceed this figure and approach Hawk's pre-bid P:E value of 20. If this occurs, then both groups of shareholders can enjoy the value created by the expectation of more efficient operation of Vole's assets and higher cash flows thereafter. Conversely, expectations of integration difficulties might offset such gains.

It does not follow that a higher EPS will lead to a higher share price. If the acquisition moved Hawk into riskier areas of operation, its activity Beta should rise accordingly, and the higher expected cash flows will be discounted at a higher required return. Similarly, if instead of financing the bid by a share exchange, Hawk had borrowed the required £20 million, then the share price might not rise if the greater gearing and accompanying financial risk resulted in a higher equity Beta. The suspicion remains that many acquisitions, ostensibly undertaken to raise the acquirer's share price, are really undertaken for 'managerial' reasons (see Gregory, 1997).

Certainly, the subsequent difficulties commonly experienced in post-merger integration and operation do not support the view that mergers are always in the best interests of the bidders' shareholders.

Self-assessment activity 12.2

Suggest how managerial pay schemes might encourage takeovers against the interests of shareholders.

(Answer in Appendix A)

12.4 ALTERNATIVE BID TERMS

Table 12.4 shows UK data on the three main ways of financing takeovers: cash, issue of ordinary shares and fixed-interest securities (loan stock, convertibles and preference shares). Clearly, the first two methods predominate, although their relative importance varies over time. As a rule of thumb, share exchange is favoured when the stock market is high and rising, while cash offers are used more when interest rates are relatively low or falling, given that many cash offers are themselves financed by the acquirer's borrowing. This pattern is illustrated clearly by the figures for the early 2000s, when the stock market was depressed and interest rates low and falling. Increasingly, however, bidders offer their targets a choice of cash or shares, or even a three-way choice between straight cash, cash with shares, or shares alone.

Table 12.4 Mergers and acquisitions in the United Kingdom by UK companies: category of expenditure

£ million

	Expenditure Cash					Percentage of expenditure		
	Total	Independent companies	Subsidiaries	Issues of ordinary shares	Issues of fixed interest securities	Cash	Issues of ordinary shares	Issues of fixed interest securities
2001	28,994	8,489	6,704	12,356	1,445	52	43	5
2002	25,236	9,574	7,991	6,780	891	69	27	4
2003	18,679	8,956	7,183	1,667	873	86	9	5
2004	31,408	12,080	7,822	10,338	1,168	63	33	4
2005	25,134	13,425	8,510	2,768	431	87	11	2
2006	28,511	N/A	8,131	N/A	335	N/A	N/A	2
2007	26,778	13,671	6,507	4,909	1,691	76	18	6
2008	36,469	31,333	2,851	1,910	375	94	5	1
2009	12,195	2,937	709	8,435	114	30	69	1
2010	12,605	6,175	4,523	1,560	350	85	12	3
2011	8,089	4,432	2,667	719	271	87	10	4
2012	3,413	1,937	789	419	268	82	10	8
2013	7,658	3,683	3,475	353	147	92	6	2
2014	8,032	3,249	1,947	2,782	51	65	35	–
2015	6,920	3,365	1,871	1,418	265	74	22	4
2016	24,688	5,493	5,308	13,471	418	43	55	2

Source: Office for National Statistics, August 2017 (**https://www.ons.gov.uk**). Crown copyright material is reproduced under the terms and conditions of the Open Government Licence (OGL).

For example, when bidding for a smaller property company, City North plc, a former BES company, in 2005, the considerably larger Grainger Trust plc offered two alternatives. Shareholders of City North could either opt for a full cash consideration of 270 pence per share, or accept 180 pence in cash plus 0.2423 of a Grainger share, worth 95 pence on the last dealing day prior to the bid announcement. The cash plus paper offer was thus worth 275 pence, a little higher than the straight cash offer, which is typically the case, as the target shareholder bears the twin risks of exposure to share price falls and the danger of projected synergies not materialising.

Such complex offers are designed to appeal to the widest possible body of shareholders. The chosen package depends on the balance of relative advantages and disadvantages of the different methods, from both the bidder's and the target shareholders' viewpoints.

Cash

Everyone understands a cash offer. The amount is certain, there being no exposure to the risk of adverse movement in share price during the course of the bid. The targeted shareholders are more easily able to adjust their portfolios than if they received shares, which involve dealing costs when sold. Because no new shares are issued, there is no dilution of earnings or change in the balance of control of the bidder (unless, in the case of borrowed capital, creditors insist on restrictive covenants). Moreover, if the return expected on the assets of the target exceeds the cost of borrowing, the EPS of the bidder may increase, although perceptions of increased financial risk may mitigate this apparent benefit. A disadvantage from the recipient's viewpoint is possible liability to capital gains tax (CGT). However, in the case of cross-border takeovers, there are major advantages in receiving cash rather than the shares of the bidder, traded only on a foreign stock exchange, one reason why Akzo Nobel offered cash to ICI shareholders. Nevertheless, the cash has to be found from somewhere.

Share exchanges

Any liability to CGT is delayed with a share offer, and the cash flow cost to the bidder is zero, apart from the administration costs involved. However, equity is more costly to service than debt, especially for a company with taxable capacity, and an issue of new shares may interfere with the firm's gearing ratio. There could be an adverse impact on the balance of control if a major slice of the equity of the bidder came to be held by institutions looking for an opportunity to sell their holdings. The overhanging threat of a substantial share sale may depress the share price of the bidder.

A disadvantage with a share offer is that it involves yielding a share of the ownership of the expanded firm, and thus a share of the benefits, to the owners of the target firm. Conversely, some part of the risk involved in exploiting synergies is also transferred. A further disadvantage of a share exchange is that the bid terms may be undermined by adverse stock market movements before the deal is agreed and completed, possibly necessitating a higher bid. For these reasons, a share offer is usually pitched higher in value than a corresponding cash offer when target shareholders are offered a choice.

Other methods

The use of other instruments is comparatively rare. When fixed-interest securities are used, they are usually offered as alternatives to cash and/or ordinary shares. Convertibles have some appeal because any diluting effect is delayed and the interest cost on the security, which qualifies for tax relief, can usually be pitched below the going market rate on loan stock, due to the expectation of capital gain on conversion. Preference share financing in general is comparatively rare, owing to the lack of tax-deductibility of preferred dividends and to limited voting rights.

Some takeover considerations are quite ingenious. In Sanofi's acquisition of Genzyme, the latter's shareholders were offered tradable 'Contingent Value Rights (CVRs)' to run until 2020, worth an extra $4 billion on paper, but only valid dependent on the success of new drugs in the Genzyme pipeline.

The Westar and Great Plains utilities cameo is an example of share exchange in a merger bid.

Self-assessment activity 12.3

Why might the shareholders of a target company prefer to be paid in cash rather than shares?

(Answer in Appendix A)

Westar and Great Plains utilities agree revised merger

Westar Energy and Great Plains Energy, two big US electricity utilities that scrapped a deal last year due to regulatory concerns, have agreed a new all-shares merger that will create a company with a combined equity value of $14bn. Under the new deal structure, Westar shareholders will lose the 36 per cent premium that Great Plains had offered to pay last year as part of a $60 cash-and-stock deal worth $12.2bn, including $3.6bn in debt.

Under the new terms, Westar shareholders will receive a share in the new merged entity for each of their shares, while Great Plains stock holders will receive 0.5981 shares of common stock in the new holding company for each of their shares.

Once the transaction is completed, Westar shareholders will own approximately 52.5 per cent of the new combined group, while Great Plains shareholders will own about 47.5 per cent.

Source: Fontanella-Khan, J. (2017) Westar and Great Plains utilities agree revised merger. *Financial Times*, 10 July. © The Financial Times Limited 2018. All rights reserved.

12.5 EVALUATING A BID: THE EXPECTED GAINS FROM TAKEOVERS

Evaluating an acquisition is little different from other investments, assuming the motive of the bid is economic rather than managerial, i.e. designed to maximise the post-bid value of the expanded enterprise. It would be worthwhile Company A taking over Company B as long as the present value of the cash flows of the enlarged company exceeds the present value of the two companies as separate entities:

$$V_{A+B} > V_A + V_B$$

Thus, $[V_{A+B} - (V_A + V_B)]$ measures the increase in value. The net cost to the bidder is the value of the amount expended less the value of the target as it stands:

$$\text{Net cost} = [\text{Outlay} - V_B]$$

so that the net present value of the takeover decision is the gain less the cost, i.e.:

$$\begin{aligned} \text{NPV} &= V_{A+B} - (V_A + V_B) - [\text{Outlay} - V_B] \\ &= V_{A+B} - V_A - \text{Outlay} \end{aligned}$$

The NPV will depend on the method of financing and, of course, the terms of the transaction. Essentially, the bidder is hoping to extract the maximum value of any expected cost savings and synergies from the takeover for its own shareholders. Conversely, the offer must be made attractive to the owners of the target to induce them to sell.

■ Fewston plc and Dacre plc

An example will illustrate the way in which the division of the spoils can depend on the method of financing. Fewston plc is launching a cash bid for Dacre plc, both are quoted companies, and both are ungeared. The market value of Fewston is £200 million (100 million 50p shares, market price £2) and that of Dacre is £40 million (10 million 50p shares, market price £4). Fewston hopes to exploit synergies, etc., worth £20 million after the takeover. It offers the shareholders of Dacre £50 million in cash. The NPV of the bid to Fewston is thus:

$$\begin{aligned} \text{NPV} &= V_{A+B} - V_A - \text{Outlay} \\ &= (£200\text{m} + £40\text{m} + £20\text{m}) - £200\text{m} - £50\text{m} = £10\text{m} \end{aligned}$$

The overall gain from the takeover (i.e. the synergies of £20 million) is split equally between the two sets of shareholders. The need to make a higher bid, or the appearance of another bidder, would probably tilt the balance of gain towards Dacre's shareholders.

If the bid is made in the form of a share-for-share offer to the same value, the arithmetic alters. In this case, Fewston is giving up part of the expanded firm and hence a further share of the gains to Dacre's shareholders. Assuming a bid of the same value, Fewston must offer them (£50/£2) = 25 million shares. This would increase the shares in issue to 125 million shares, i.e. Fewston is handing over 20 per cent of the expanded company to Dacre's shareholders. In this case, the gain enjoyed by Fewston's shareholders will be lower. The NPV of the takeover is still the gain less the cost; but the cost is greater, i.e. the proportion of the expanded company handed over less the value of Dacre as it stands:

$$\text{Cost} = \left(\frac{25m}{100m + 25m} \times £260m\right) - £40m$$

$$= (£52m - £40m) = £12m$$

Hence, the NPV of the takeover from Fewston's perspective is:

$$\text{NPV} = (\text{gain in value} - \text{cost}) = (£20m - £12m) = £8m$$

Fewston's shareholders are thus left with only £8 million of the net gains from the takeover, 20 per cent lower than in the cash offer case, which is the same proportion as the share of the expanded company handed to Dacre's shareholders.

A share exchange of equivalent value to a cash bid generally leaves the bidder's shareholders worse off compared to a cash deal because their share of both the company and the gains from the takeover are diluted among the larger number of shares. The post-bid share prices in these two cases are as follows:

Cash bid: (£260m/100m) = £2.60
Share exchange: (£260/125m) = £2.08

Against this, given that takeovers carry risks, for example, the risk of inability to capture the anticipated synergies, a share-based deal has the merit of transferring a portion of these risks to the target's former owners.

However, if Fewston has to borrow in order to make the cash bid, the increase in gearing may result in shareholders seeking a higher return, thus lowering the market price. In addition, the analysis hinges on the existence of an efficient capital market whose assessment of the gains from takeover corresponds with that of the two parties.

Self-assessment activity 12.4

Predator is valued on the market at £1,000 million, and Prey at £200 million. Predator values the expected post-merger synergies at £50 million. If it bids £230 million for Prey, what is the NPV of the bid? What is the share of the gains for each firm?

(Answer in Appendix A)

12.6 WORKED EXAMPLE: ML PLC AND CO PLC

The following part-question appeared on the CIMA Strategic Financial Management examination paper, May 1999. (It carried 15 of the total 20 marks available for the whole question.)

350 Introduction to Finance

■ **Question**

ML plc is an expanding clothing retailer. It is all-equity-financed by ordinary share capital of £10 million in shares of 50p nominal. The company's results to the end of March 1999 have just been announced. Pre-tax profits were £4.6 million. The Chairman's statement included a forecast that earnings might be expected to rise by 5 per cent per annum in the coming year and for the foreseeable future.

CO plc, a children's clothing group, has an issued share capital of £33 million in £1 shares. Pre-tax profits for the year to 31 March were £5.2 million. Because of a recent programme of re-organisation and rationalisation, no growth is forecast for the current year but, subsequently, constant growth in earnings of approximately 6 per cent per annum is predicted. CO plc has had an erratic growth and earnings record in the past and has not always achieved its often ambitious forecasts.

ML plc has approached the shareholders of CO plc with a bid of two new shares in ML plc for every three CO plc shares. There is a cash alternative of 135 pence per share.

Following the announcement of the bid, the market price of ML plc shares fell while the price of shares in CO plc rose. Statistics for ML plc and two other listed companies in the same industry immediately prior to the bid announcement are shown below. All share prices are in pence.

1998				
High	Low	Company	Dividend % Yield	PER
225	185	ML plc	3.4	15
145	115	CO plc	3.6	13
187	122	HR plc	6.0	12
230	159	SZ plc	2.4	17

Both ML plc and CO plc pay tax at 33 per cent.

ML plc's cost of capital is 12 per cent per annum and CO plc's is 11 per cent per annum.

Required

Assume you are a financial analyst with a major fund manager. You have funds invested in both ML plc and CO plc.

■ Assess whether the proposed share-for-share offer is likely to be beneficial to the shareholders in ML plc and CO plc, and recommend an investment strategy based on your calculations.
■ Comment on other information that would be useful in your assessment of the bid. Assume that the estimates of growth given above are achieved and that the new company plans no further issues of equity.

State any assumptions that you make.

Answer

First of all, some introductory calculations are needed before we can analyse the impact of the bid.

Basic information

	ML	CO	Combined
Profit after tax (PAT) for each firm is			
ML: (0.67 × £4.6m) CO: (0.67 × £5.2m)	£3.082m	£3.484m	£6.566m
Given respective P:Es, market values are:			
ML: (15 × £3.082m) CO: (13 × £3.484m)	£46.230m	£45.292m	£91.520m
Given the number of shares, share price is:			
ML: (£46.230m/20,000) CO: (£45.292m/33,000)	£2.31	£1.37	
EPS:			
ML: (£3.082m/20,000) CO: (£3.484m/33,000)	15.41p	10.56p	

Analysis

No. of shares post-bid: 20,000 + (2/3 × 33,000) = 42,000

Expected market price post-bid = Total market value/No of shares
= (£91.520m/42,000) = £2.18

Value of bid at post-issue price = (2 shares × £2.18) = £4.36

Cash value of bid per 3 shares offered: (£1.35 × 3) = £4.05

Assessment

Assuming no changes in the level of market prices, and no re-rating of the sector, ML's share price would fall post-acquisition to £2.18. At this price, the value of the 2-for-3 share offer should attract CO shareholders. They would get shares worth (2 × £2.18) = £4.36 in exchange for shares currently worth (3 × £1.37) = £4.11

The share-for-share offer is also worth more than the cash alternative: £4.36 vs £4.05.

This is a 'reverse takeover', where the shareholders of the target end up holding a majority stake in the expanded company – but who gains from this?

Former CO shareholders would hold (22,000/42,000) × £91.520m = £47.939m of the value of the expanded firm, a gain of (£47.939m − £45.292m pre-bid value of CO) = £2.649m.

ML shareholders would lose £2.649m, making the share-financed deal distinctly unattractive to them.

Conversely, the cash offer would create wealth for ML shareholders, i.e. they give £4.05 for something worth £4.11 post-bid.

The advice to the fund manager is: 'accept the bid in respect of CO shares and sell ML shares in the market if you can achieve a price above £2.18'.

Commentary on other information required

The advice given above hinges on the behaviour of ML's share price – it has already fallen on the announcement, but by how much? It may already be too late if the market is efficient, as it would already have digested the information contained in the announcement.

Also:

- What benefits are expected from the merger, i.e. cost savings and synergies? To make sense of the bid, ML must be setting the PV of these benefits above £2.649m to yield a positive NPV for the acquisition.
- How quickly are these benefits likely to show through? Any delay in exploiting these lowers the NPV.
- It is feasible that the market might apply a higher PER to the expanded company – maybe not as high as ML's but possibly at the market average, currently 14.25, compared to the weighted average PER for ML/CO of 14.
- Is ML likely to sell part of CO's operations? And to whom? If ML has already lined up a buyer, it must expect to turn a profit on the deal.
- Is the bid likely to be defended by the target's managers, fearful for their jobs? If so, a higher bid might be expected.
- Is a White Knight likely to appear with a higher bid on more favourable terms?
- Are there competition implications likely to attract the interest of the authorities?

12.7 THE IMPORTANCE OF STRATEGY

Considerable evidence has emerged that acquisitions have less than an even chance of success. Although definitions of 'success' may vary, any activity that fails to enhance shareholder interests is unlikely to be regarded favourably by the stock market. While it is often difficult to assess what would have happened had a company not embarked on the takeover trail, it is difficult to argue that the acquisition has not been a failure if post-acquisition performance is inferior to pre-acquisition performance, or if the acquisition actually leads to a fall in shareholder wealth.

The McKinsey firm of management consultants studied the 'value-creation performance' of the acquisition programmes of 116 large US and UK companies, using financial measures of performance. The criterion of success used was whether the company earned at least its cost of capital on funds invested in the acquisition process. On this basis, a remarkable 60 per cent of all acquisitions failed, with large unrelated takeovers achieving a failure rate of 86 per cent.

Acquisitions fail for numerous reasons:

1 Acquirers often pay too much for their targets, either as a result of a flawed evaluation process that overestimates the likely benefits or as a result of getting caught up in a competitive bidding situation, where to yield is regarded as a sign of corporate weakness.
2 'Skeletons' appear in cupboards with alarming frequency. The infamous and disastrous takeover by defence contractor Ferranti of International Signal Corporation was a good example of a badly researched acquisition that ultimately destroyed the acquirer.
3 Acquirers often fail to plan and execute properly the integration of their targets, frequently neglecting the organisational and internal cultural factors. Inadequate knowledge about the target's business should be corrected in the process of due diligence. Lees (1992) explains how all too often this aspect is overlooked.

Yet many companies have sound acquisition records. Reckitt Benckizer, the Anglo-Dutch producer of household products, is often held up as a prime example. Firms like Reckitt have several things in common. Their targets are carefully selected, they rarely get involved in competitive auctions, they often have the sense to walk away from deals when they realise the gravity of the likely integration problems, and they seem able quickly and successfully to integrate acquisitions once deals are completed. What these companies have in common is a coherent strategic approach to acquisitions.

12.8 THE STRATEGIC APPROACH

Most successful acquirers see their acquisitions as part of a long-term strategic process, designed to contribute towards overall corporate development. This requires acquirers to approach acquisitions only after a careful analysis of their own underlying strengths, and to identify candidates that satisfy chosen criteria and, most importantly, provide 'strategic fit' with the company's existing activities.

Figure 12.1 displays a simple strategic framework within which a thoroughgoing acquisition programme might be conducted. It begins with a full strategic review of the company as it stands, and its strategic options, followed by a detailed consideration of the role of acquisitions (i.e. the reasons why an acquisition target may be selected), leading to the process of selecting and bidding for the chosen prey, and culminating in the often-neglected activities of post-merger integration and post-audit.

The takeover of Banco Popular by Santander in June 2017 was part of its overall strategy to become a dominant bank in Spain, as outlined in the following cameo.

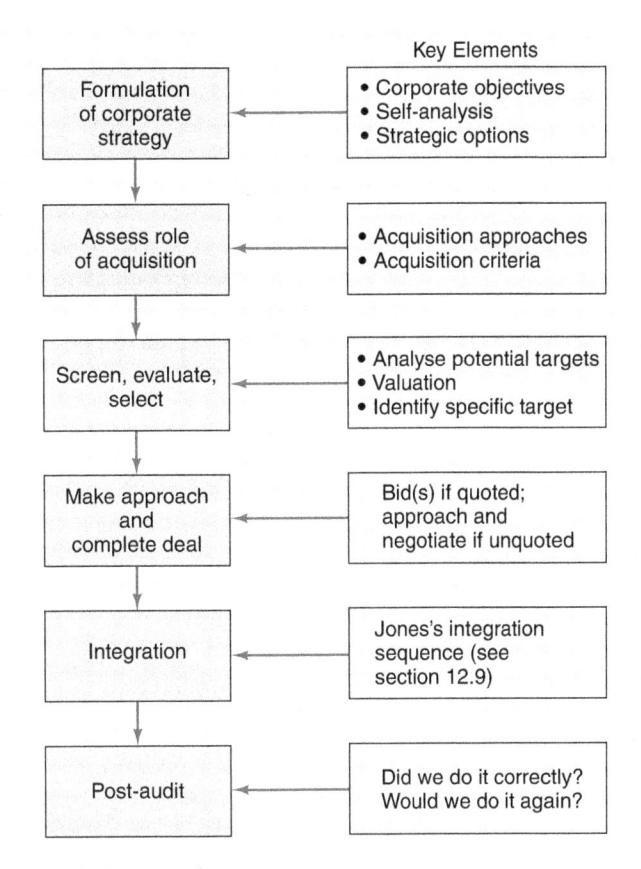

```
                           Key Elements
  ┌──────────────┐      ┌──────────────────────┐
  │ Formulation  │      │ • Corporate objectives│
  │ of corporate │◄─────│ • Self-analysis      │
  │  strategy    │      │ • Strategic options  │
  └──────┬───────┘      └──────────────────────┘
         ▼
  ┌──────────────┐      ┌──────────────────────┐
  │ Assess role  │◄─────│ • Acquisition approaches│
  │of acquisition│      │ • Acquisition criteria │
  └──────┬───────┘      └──────────────────────┘
         ▼
  ┌──────────────┐      ┌──────────────────────┐
  │Screen, evaluate,│◄──│ • Analyse potential targets│
  │   select     │      │ • Valuation          │
  │              │      │ • Identify specific target│
  └──────┬───────┘      └──────────────────────┘
         ▼
  ┌──────────────┐      ┌──────────────────────┐
  │Make approach │      │ Bid(s) if quoted;    │
  │     and      │◄─────│ approach and         │
  │complete deal │      │ negotiate if unquoted│
  └──────┬───────┘      └──────────────────────┘
         ▼
  ┌──────────────┐      ┌──────────────────────┐
  │              │      │ Jones's integration  │
  │ Integration  │◄─────│ sequence (see        │
  │              │      │ section 12.9)        │
  └──────┬───────┘      └──────────────────────┘
         ▼
  ┌──────────────┐      ┌──────────────────────┐
  │  Post-audit  │◄─────│ Did we do it correctly?│
  │              │      │ Would we do it again?│
  └──────────────┘      └──────────────────────┘
```

Figure 12.1 A strategic framework
Source: (Based on Payne, 1987)

Santander/Popular: marriage of convenience

Santander has taken over rival Banco Popular for a nominal value of €1.

Arranged marriages have traditionally involved a dowry. The lower the eligibility of the bride compared with the groom, the higher the price.

If there was ever any doubt European bank regulators would flex their muscles to prevent wider financial contagion, there is none now. On paper, Popular looked safe enough: its core equity tier one ratio was in excess of minimum requirements. And yet shareholders, and some creditors, were cleaned out after the European Central Bank forced through Popular's sale for a nominal €1 to Santander, citing concerns about deteriorating liquidity. A partnership has its attractions. The combination will make Santander the dominant bank in Spain, with one-fifth of the credit market and a one-quarter share of SME lending, double the nearest competitor.

Santander, which one suspects was nudged into the match, argues the deal is 'at the right point of the cycle' – meaning interest rates are likely to go up and falling domestic credit demand has bottomed out.

Cost cuts offer a firmer excuse: Santander targets €500m in pre-tax savings over three years, mainly through IT integration and stripping out Popular's head office expenses. However, it is hard to see how the deal will be earnings 'accretive' by 2019, taking into account re-structuring costs of €1.3bn.

A fall in Santander's share price implies shareholders are not yet supportive of a marriage in which Popular has practically given itself away. Achieving synergy targets will ensure a more lasting union.

FT *Source:* Santander/Popular: marriage of convenience. *Financial Times*, 7 June. © The Financial Times Limited 2018. All rights reserved.

■ Objectives

Formulating strategy should begin with an expression of corporate objectives, concentrating on maximising shareholder wealth. Many firms now publish mission statements, but these are usually somewhat vague expressions of the image that the company would like to portray, often largely for internal consumption in order to motivate staff (Klemm *et al.*, 1991). If, in building the desired image, the company's managers fail to earn at least the cost of equity, they will themselves invite the risk of takeover. Strategy concerns the examination of alternative routes to achieving the ultimate aim, and then the optimal way of executing the chosen path. Achieving long-term goals usually involves expansion of the enterprise, a route often preferred by managers for personal motives.

■ Internal or external growth?

There are two main ways of achieving growth: (1) by self-development of new products, markets and processes (internal growth) and (2) by acquisition (external growth). Although both of these routes are usually expensive in executive time and resources, external growth has the advantage of securing quick access to new markets or productive capacity. However, firms should not overlook intermediate strategies, such as **licensing**, whereby a royalty is paid to the developer of new technology in exchange for rights to exploit it, or **joint ventures**, where an existing company could be partially acquired, or a totally new one set up in partnership with another firm.

The decision to grow internally or externally will depend partly on an analysis of the strengths, weaknesses, opportunities and threats (SWOTs) of the firm. This self-analysis should make the potential acquirer aware of any competitive advantages it enjoys over rival companies. Competitive advantage stems from two sources: cost advantage, where products are virtually similar, and product differentiation. Exploitation of each of these creates value for shareholders. When areas of competitive advantage have been identified, the company can decide whether to build upon existing strengths or to attempt to develop distinctive competence in areas of perceived weakness. This evaluation may also result in a decision to divest certain activities where no obvious advantage is possessed, or where too many resources would be required to sustain an advantage.

Porter (1987) examined the acquisition record of 33 large diversified US companies. The criterion for judging 'success' was the subsequent divestment rate of earlier acquisitions. The main finding was that successful acquirers almost invariably diversify into related fields, and vice versa. In other words, diversifications into activities unrelated to the core business of the acquirer carry much greater risks of failure. Even companies with successful 'related diversification' records achieved poor results when they wandered into unrelated fields. Porter concluded that the corporate portfolio strategy of many diversifying companies had failed because most diversifiers fail 'to think in terms of how they really add value'.

External growth is often the result of a decision to move into a different sector. By acquiring other firms, the strategic aim of reconfiguring the firm's portfolio of activities can be more rapidly achieved. General Electric made several acquisitions in the oil services industry – for example, in 2011, the firm acquired the Aberdeen-based John Wood Group's well support division, famed for its electric submersible pumps, for $2.8 billion. This brought GE's spending on the drilling and production support business to about $10 billion since 2007.

---

licensing
Involves the assignment of production and selling rights to producers based in foreign locations in return for royalty payments

joint venture
A strategic alliance involving the formal establishment of a new marketing and/or production operation involving two or more partners

■ Acquisition criteria

The bidder should next assess what specific role it hopes the acquisition will perform. There often exist a variety of strategic routes for achieving the aims that underpin the proposed merger.

At an early stage, the bidder should reassess the various alternatives to merger, in view of the many difficulties involved. Taking over another company is rather like moving to a larger, more expensive house. Mergers involve considerable disruptions during the planning and bidding phase; costs, such as legal advice and the printing and publishing of documents; possible exposure to increased financial risk; and the upheavals of integration. Just as some marriages do not survive the strains of house-moving, some companies often fail to recover after the stress of merger. Having identified the specific role of the acquisition, the company can now consider whether it can be achieved in other, perhaps more cost-effective ways.

Harrison (1987) suggests that, for every merger motive, there are several alternative ways of achieving the same end. For example, if the aim is sales growth, this can be achieved by internal expansion or by a joint venture. If the aim is to improve earnings per share, a loss-making subsidiary can be shut down or efficiency-enhancing measures can be implemented. If it is wished to use spare cash, this can be invested in marketable securities and trade investments, or even returned to shareholders as special dividends, or in the form of share repurchases. If an improvement in management skills is sought, appropriately skilled personnel can be bought in to replace existing managers, outside consultants can be used for advice or incentive and bonus schemes can be introduced. In short, if the decision to grow by acquisition is made, the potential acquirer must be very sure that the stipulated aims are unattainable by alternative measures.

Most firms with corporate planning departments exercise a continuous review of the key members of the industry in which they operate and also of related and, often, unrelated areas. Some firms are known to 'track' potential takeover candidates, assessing their various strengths and weaknesses, and estimating the likely net value obtainable if they were acquired. Such target companies are continually cross-checked against a set of possible acquisition criteria.

When the decision to expand by acquisition is taken, the corporate planning staff should be able rapidly to provide a short-list of candidates, expressing the SWOTs of each, especially its vulnerability to takeover at that time. It is common for defending managements to dismiss takeover bids as 'opportunistic' in a pejorative way. For an acquisitive company that adopts the strategic approach, this means 'well-timed', as such companies are continually seeking opportune moments to launch a bid, especially when the stock market rating of the target appears low. The joint takeover by the former GEC and Siemens of Plessey in 1989 was opportunistic, in the sense that the target's return on capital was relatively low due to a recent substantial investment programme. Whether the market had correctly valued Plessey is arguable, but the bidders undoubtedly spotted a favourable opportunity to acquire Plessey at a time when its performance looked weak in relation to the market, thus eliminating a major competitor for lucrative British Telecom contracts.

There has been a resurgence in M&A activity recently following a slowdown after the financial crisis of 2008. However, as the following cameo explains, in an era of historically low interest rates, companies are taking advantage of the low financing cost and use debt as the source of funding for their merger and acquisition activities. The issue of debt was therefore at a record high level as a source of finance for merger and acquisition activity in 2015. However, as debt financing is riskier than equity, this may have implications for the future of these companies which may not be all good news.

Better ways to play the merger mania

Mega-mergers are back. This week, advertising groups Omnicom and Publicis announced a $35bn tie-up. Just a day or two earlier, Irish pharmaceuticals group Elan ended a long courtship by recommending a takeover by Perrigo. Closer to home, engineering group Invensys has recommended an offer from France's Schneider Electric.

The re-emergence of M&A has been long predicted, and there have been several false starts. Companies are sitting on big cash piles, having restructured and refinanced in the wake of the credit crunch, and that money is earning only trivial returns in cash and other short-term instruments. The global economic recovery might still be slow and uneven, but there are now at least some tangible signs that it is heading in the right direction, giving chief executives the confidence to deploy some of that cash.

Is this good news for investors? There's a mountain of academic evidence that takeovers destroy value for shareholders in the bidding company, and that the hubris of senior managers leads them to overestimate the benefits of combining one company with another. If you want a practical example, look no further than Rio Tinto's disastrous $38bn takeover of Alcan in 2007, which was followed by a dividend cut, a $15bn rights issue, a $10–11bn write-off – and a change of chief executive.

On the other hand, takeovers are a sign of growing confidence, and institutions generally have to reinvest whatever cash takeovers generate in other shares, which boosts the broader market. And for a private investor, a conventional cash takeover offer should be manna from heaven. You wake up one morning to find you've been offered a fat premium and no dealing costs to sell your shares. The only downside is that you might incur a capital gains tax liability on the profits, or face a conundrum when it comes to reinvesting them. Both are nice problems to have.

Source: Eley, J. (2013) Better ways to play the merger mania. *Financial Times*, 2 August. © The Financial Times Limited 2018. All rights reserved.

■ Bidding (and defending)

Bidding is an exercise in applied psychology. Readiness to bid implies an assessment that the target is either undervalued as it stands or would be worth more under alternative management. In such cases, the bid itself provides new information about prospective value, and the bidder should expect to have to pay above the market price to secure control. However, it is often unclear before the event how much of a bid premium, if any, is already built into the market price as the market attempts to assess the probability of a bidder emerging and succeeding with its offer. The trick in mounting profitable takeover bids is to promise to use assets more effectively in order to entice existing shareholders to sell, without making such extravagant claims that the target's market price moves up too sharply before the acquisition is completed. Conversely, to accentuate the difficulties of reorganising the target could be regarded as disingenuous or even call into question the wisdom of the bid itself, leading to a fall in the bidder's own share price. The following box summarises some of the defence tactics which a bidder may encounter.

Choose your weapons! Takeover defence tactics

Takeover strategy is not a one-sided affair. Very few takeovers are recommended at once by the directors of target companies. Even if they expect to lose the fight, the incumbents usually reject the initial bid in the hope of attracting better terms. The first line of defence, therefore, is rejection because the bid is too low, or because the proposed union 'lacks industrial logic'.

Once defenders have had time to marshal their resources and get their public relations act together, more effective defences can be adopted. Some are more credible than others, and some are illegal in the United Kingdom but common in the United States. Typical defence ploys by UK firms are:

- Revalue assets – this is often a waste of time, as the market should already have assessed the market value.
- Denigrate the profit and share price record of the bidder, and hence the quality of its management. This invites retaliation in kind.
- Promise a dividend increase – this calls past dividend policy into question, and bidders usually offer this anyway.
- Publish improved profit forecasts – a dangerous ploy, since the forecast has to be plausible yet attractive, and once made, the company has to deliver. Companies that repel raiders but fail to meet profit forecasts are susceptible to further bids.
- Seek a **White Knight** – an alternative suitor that will acquire the target on more favourable terms (mainly for the management?).
- Lobby the competition authorities.

White Knight
A takeover bidder emerging after a hostile bid has been made, usually offering alternative bid terms that are more favourable to the defending management

The following defences mostly originated in the United States, and some are difficult to reconcile with the Takeover Code:

- The Crown Jewels defence – selling off the company's most attractive assets.
- Issuing new shares into friendly hands – this, of course, requires shareholder agreement.
- The Pacman defence – launching a counter-bid for the raider.
- Golden Parachutes – writing such attractive severance terms for managers that the bidder will recoil at the prospective expense.
- Tin Parachutes – offering excessively attractive severance terms for blue-collar workers.
- Launching a bid for another company – if successful, this will increase the size of the firm, making it less digestible for the bidder.
- Leveraged buy-out – the purchase of the company by its own management using large amounts of borrowed funds.
- Poison pills – undertaking methods of finance that the bidder will find unattractive to unwind, e.g. large issues of convertibles that the bidder will have to honour.
- Repurchasing of shares to drive up the share price and increase the cost of the takeover (common now in the United Kingdom), although not allowed once an informal approach has been made (although it can be promised if the bid fails).

Examples of poison pills are mechanisms to trigger deeply discounted rights issues if predator holdings rise above a certain level. Both Newscorp and Yahoo have implemented such arrangements. In the case of Yahoo's 'stockholder rights plan', a rights issue can be made if another firm builds a stake in Yahoo above 15 per cent. In Germany, the so-called 'VW law' of 1960 limits any investor's voting rights in the carmaker to 20 per cent, and confers a blocking vote on the minority stake held by the state of Lower Saxony (this has been declared illegal by the European Court of Justice).

12.9 POST-MERGER ACTIVITIES

Probably the most difficult part of takeover strategy and execution is the integration of the newly-acquired company into the parent. In the case of contested bids, the acquirer will normally have only a limited amount of information to guide its integration plans and should not be too shocked to encounter unforeseen problems regarding the quality of the target's assets and personnel. The difficulty of integration depends on the extent to which the acquirer wants to control the operations of the target. If only limited control is required, as in the case of unrelated acquisitions, integration will probably be restricted to meshing the financial reporting systems of the component companies. Conversely, if full integration of common manufacturing activities is required, integration assumes a different order of complexity.

Jones (1982, 1986) points out that the degree of complexity of integration depends on the type of acquisition: for example, whether it is a horizontal takeover of a very similar company, requiring a detailed plan for integrating supply, production and distribution; or, at the other extreme, a purely conglomerate acquisition where there is little or no overlap of functions. Because we believe that integration is perhaps the most important part of the acquisition process, we devote most of this section to further analysis of this issue.

Finally, the acquisition should be post-audited. The post-audit team should review the evaluation phase to assess whether, and to what extent, the appraisal was under- or over-optimistic, and whether appropriate plans were formulated and executed. The review should centre on what lessons can be learned to guide any subsequent acquisition exercise.

Poor planning and poorly-executed integration are two of the commonest reasons for takeover failure. All too often, acquisitive companies focus senior management attention on the next adventure rather than devoting adequate resources to absorbing the newly acquired firm carefully. It is rash to lay down optimal integration procedures in advance, because the appropriate integration procedures are largely situation-specific. The 'right' way to approach integration depends on the nature of the company acquired, its internal culture and its strengths and weaknesses (Lees, 1992). However, Drucker (1981) contends that there are Five Golden Rules to follow in the integration process:

1 Ensure that acquired companies have a 'common core of unity' with the parent. In his view, mere financial ties between companies are insufficient to obtain a bond. The companies should have significant overlapping characteristics like shared technology or markets in order to exploit synergies.
2 The acquirer should think through what potential skill contribution it can make to the acquired company. In other words, the takeover should be approached not solely with the attitude of 'what's in it for the parent?' but also with the view 'what can we offer them?'
3 The acquirer must respect the products, markets and customers of the acquired company. Disparaging the record and performance of less senior management is likely to sap morale.
4 Within a year, the acquirer should provide appropriately skilled top management for the acquired company.
5 Again, within a year, the acquirer should make several cross-company promotions.

These are largely common-sense guidelines, with a heavy emphasis on behavioural factors, but many studies have shown that acquirers fail to follow them. A study undertaken by Hunt and Lees of the London Business School with Egon Zehnder Associates (Hunt *et al.*, 1987) commented that 'unless the human element is managed carefully, there is a serious risk of losing the financial and business advantages that the acquisition could bring to the parent company'.

■ Jones's integration sequence

Jones (1986) explains that integration of a new company is a complex mix of corporate strategy, management accounting and applied psychology. Acquirers should follow an 'integration sequence', based on five key steps, the relative weight attaching to each step depending on the type of acquisition. The sequence is as follows:

1 Decide upon, and communicate, initial reporting relationships.
2 Achieve rapid control of key factors.

3 Review the resource base of the acquired company via a 'resource audit'.
4 Clarify and revise corporate objectives and develop strategic plans.
5 Revise the organisational structure.

Each of these is now examined.

Reporting relationships
Clear reporting relationships have to be established in order to avoid uncertainty. An important issue is whether to impose reporting lines at the outset or whether to await the new organisational structure. In resolving this issue, it is desirable to avoid managers establishing their own informal relationships, and to stress that some changes may only be temporary.

Control of key factors
Control requires access to plentiful and accurate information. To control key factors, acquirers should rapidly gain control of the information channels that export control messages and import key data about resource deployment. It may sometimes be desirable not to introduce controls identical to those of the parent, first, because group controls may not be appropriate for the acquired company, and second, because those group controls may no longer be appropriate for the revised organisation. If the acquired company's existing control systems are thought to be adequate, it may be worth retaining them. Two important financial controls are the setting of clear borrowing limits and an early review of capital expenditure limits and appraisal procedures.

Jones notes that poor financial controls are often found within newly-acquired companies, and, indeed, have often contributed to their acquisition. Examples are over-reliance on financial rather than management accounting systems (MAS), a MAS that provides inappropriate information in an inappropriate format, poor use of the MAS, and distortions in the overhead allocation mechanism, making it difficult to pinpoint unprofitable products and customers. The net result is often poor budgetary control, inadequate costing systems and inability to monitor and control cash movements.

Resource audit
The resource audit should examine both physical and human assets to obtain a clear picture of the quality of management at all levels. The extent of the audit required will depend on how much information is made available prior to the acquisition, but auditors should not be surprised if 'skeletons' are found in cupboards, requiring a reappraisal of the value of the acquired firm and possibly a different way of integrating it into the parent's future strategy and plans. For example, a business that was meant to be absorbed into the parent's operations may be divested if its capital equipment is unexpectedly dilapidated.

Corporate objectives and plans
These should be harmonised with those of the parent, but should also reflect any differences due to industrial sector, such as different 'normal' rates of return or profit margins in different industrial sectors. Managers of acquired firms should have some freedom to formulate their plans to meet the stated aims, but the degree of freedom should depend on the complexity of the merger. For example, in a conglomerate acquisition, where the primary aim is to secure financial control, it may be appropriate to allow executives to develop a system of management control suitable for their own operating patterns, so long as these are consistent with the aims of the takeover. In cases where cash generation is the main spur, all that may be needed is centralised cash management plus control over capital allocations.

Revising the organisational structure

A discussion of organisational design is beyond our scope, but obviously a demoralised labour force is unlikely to offer optimal performance.

Two important factors enhancing the success of a takeover are the thoroughness of the resource audit and the degree of senior management contact in the very early stages of the takeover. Employees of acquired companies seek a rapid resolution of uncertainty, especially regarding how they and their company fit into the future structure and strategy of the acquirer, and how soon the new management team will assume control. Particularly important for morale are the lifting of any previous embargo on capital expenditure and the provision of improved performance incentives, pension schemes and career prospects.

However, in the case of Apollo Tyres' acquisition of Cooper Tire and Rubber in 2014, a key concern was that the post-merger strategy and integration would not work effectively (see the following cameo).

Apollo Tyres skids on fears over $2.5bn Cooper Tire deal

Shares in Apollo Tyres, India's largest tyre company by sales, plunged by a quarter yesterday amid investor concerns about higher debt related to the group's planned $2.5bn acquisition of US-based Cooper Tire and Rubber. The all-cash deal, which would be the largest-ever Indian acquisition of a US company, is also set to increase Apollo's consolidated net debt-to-equity ratio from 0.8 to around 3.8, according to Angel Broking, a Mumbai-based brokerage.

'The deal will leave the company with a huge debt and that is the biggest concern,' said Yaresh Kothari, an automotive analyst at the broker. The two companies say they expect a measure of profitability, of up to $120m a year for three years.

The duo have also said they expect to see benefits in operating scale, as well as greater efficiencies in sourcing, technology and manufacturing operations. Around two-thirds of Apollo's revenues come in India, but the company has long held global ambitions.

The acquisition of Ohio-based Cooper Tire, the world's 11th largest tyre company by revenue, will give the company a presence in the US and Chinese markets. Post-merger strategy has been cited as a potential concern of the deal, expected to be completed in the second half of the year.

'I'm not worried about the deal size; it's more about integration of the companies and how you use the opportunities in the marketplace,' said Abdul Majeed, head of automotive at consultants PwC in India. The two companies have said the incumbent management team will remain in place at Cooper and its manufacturing operations will continue at the company's existing facilities.

Source: Chilkoti, A. (2013) Apollo Tyres skids 24% on Cooper deal fears. *Financial Times*, 13 June. © The Financial Times Limited 2018. All rights reserved.

Self-assessment activity 12.5

What are the key elements of an acquisition strategy?

(Answer in Appendix A)

12.10 ASSESSING THE IMPACT OF MERGERS

The impact of mergers can be assessed at various levels. At the macroeconomic level, if takeover activity is performing its function of weeding out inefficient managements, we might expect to find takeovers resulting in superior economic performance. However, over the long haul, the two economies where takeover activity is most prevalent – the United States and the United Kingdom – have underperformed economies where growth by takeover is less common (e.g. until the mould-breaking takeover of Mannesmann by Britain's Vodafone in 2000, there had been only four completed hostile takeovers in Germany since 1945, and not one completed by a foreign bidder). Measures of economic performance such as growth in gross domestic product (GDP) per head and capital formation as a percentage of GDP were, certainly until the 1990s, considerably lower in the United Kingdom than in Japan and Germany, as were figures for 'growth drivers' like R&D expenditure as a percentage of GDP.

Although such associations do not prove causation, the presumed link is via the impact of horizontal mergers reducing competition and through the pressures for short-term performance. It is often argued that managers in the 'Anglo-Saxon' economies are forced to pay out higher dividends to bolster share price in order to deter prospective raiders. Ever higher payouts represent cash that could have been used to finance investment and growth. However, it seems implausible to argue that the institutions would withhold funds from companies that showed a willingness to perform according to short-termist rules. Nevertheless, after reviewing the evidence, Peacock and Bannock (1991) concluded that mergers and takeovers did not create wealth but merely transferred ownership of assets. The full explanation of why merger-active economies underperform is probably less simple, as Porter (1992) explains, involving a complex interplay of economic, social and political factors.

Another level of analysis is that of the performance of individual companies. If takeovers are beneficial, we should expect to see merger-active firms improving their performance post-merger.

Investigating the effects of merger activity is one of the busiest areas of contemporary applied finance research. There are two main ways of attempting to assess the impact of mergers.

The first, **the financial characteristics approach**, is based on examining the key financial characteristics of both acquiring and acquired firms before the takeover, to study whether they are more or less profitable (taking profitability as an indicator of efficiency) than firms not involved in acquisitions, and whether their profitability improves after the acquisition. The second, '**the capital markets approach**', is based on examining the impact of the takeover on the share prices of both acquired and acquiring firms, to assess the extent to which expected benefits from merger are impounded in share prices and how these are shared between the two sets of shareholders.

The first method, the financial characteristics approach, suffers from severe limitations:

1 Different accounting conventions used by different firms (e.g. treatment of R&D) often make comparisons misleading.
2 Measures of profitability may have been distorted due to the application of acquisition accounting procedures. Prior to the issue of FRS 10 in 1997, UK firms were allowed to write off goodwill (the excess of purchase price over 'fair value') against reserves. This lowered their equity bases and raised their recorded return on investment. Goodwill now has to be shown on the balance sheet as an asset and amortised over its useful life up to 20 years. This abrupt change in the rules of accounting for goodwill means that pre- and post-takeover measurement of performance of firms active in takeovers before and after 1997 could be seriously distorted.
3 To assess properly the impact of the takeover requires an extended analysis ranging over, say, 5 to 10 years. Many acquisitions are undertaken for 'strategic' purposes, the benefits of which may emerge only after several accounting periods, perhaps following lengthy and costly reorganisation. Very frequently, when 'efficient' companies take over sizeable 'inefficient' companies, the group's return on net assets and fixed asset turnover ratios automatically fall.
4 Accounting studies are not capable of assessing what the performance of the expanded group would have been in the absence of the merger, and are thus unable to assess what improvement in performance (if any) was due to factors beyond the merger. This problem increases with the time period used for the post-merger investigation.

5 Any improvement in profitability may simply be due to a restriction of competition, rather than more efficient use of resources.
6 The approach does not allow for risk. If the aim of many mergers is to lower total risk (possibly for managerial reasons), or to shift the company into a lower Beta activity, a lower return post-merger is not especially surprising, since according to the EMH/CAPM, relatively low-risk investments offer relatively low returns.

The second method, **the capital markets approach**, caters for many of these difficulties and is thus the most frequently used mode of analysis. By adopting a CAPM framework, it enables the returns on shares of acquiring firms to be examined prior to, and following, the merger. As noted in Chapter 5, the market model indicates that the expected return on any security, j, in any time period t, ER_{jt}, is a linear function of the expected return on the market portfolio:

$$ER_{jt} = \alpha_{jt} + \beta_j ER_{mt}$$

However, the actual return in any time period, R_{jt}, results from a compound of market-related and company-specific factors:

$$R_{jt} = \alpha_{jt} + \beta_j R_{mt} + u_{jt}$$

u_{jt} is an error term with zero expected value, indicating that random company-specific factors are expected to cancel out over several time periods.

If, over a suitable period, and allowing for overall movements in the market, we examine the differences between the expected returns and the actual returns, the 'residuals' or 'abnormal returns' should sum to zero, i.e. the expected value of the cumulated differences between ER_{jt} and R_{jt} is zero.

A takeover bid is a company-specific event likely to raise the share price, and hence, the return on holding the shares. When a bid occurs, the increase in returns can be attributed to the market's assessment of the impact of the bid, i.e. the evaluation of its likelihood of success, and if successful, its appraisal of the benefits likely to ensue. Therefore, both in the period leading up to the bid, as the potential bidder builds a stake, and also on the day of announcement of the bid, we might expect the residuals to be non-negative. For example, if the market thinks the takeover is a mistake, we may find negative residuals for the bidder but positive residuals for the target, if, as usually happens, the share price of the target rises sharply. Hence, the cumulated residual returns may be taken as the stock market's assessment of the value of the takeover to the shareholders of the acquirer and acquired companies, respectively.

To illustrate this use of the market model, consider the data in Table 12.5. This relates to the successful takeover bid for the Kennings Motor Group by the conglomerate Tozer Kemsley Milbourn (TKM) in 1986. There was a degree of industrial logic in this bid, as both TKM and Kennings retailed motor cars and Kennings operated a substantial car hire business. Kennings had attempted in previous years to diversify, but owing to the haphazard selection of targets and poorly-executed integration, its core business was suffering, reflected in declining profitability and weakening cash flow. The data show the residual returns for both companies in the three months prior to, and also following, the bid; month 0 is the day of the bid, eventually completed at a price of £3.10 per share.

The data clearly show positive residuals for Kennings, before the bid, on the day of the bid itself and also in the following periods as TKM raised its bid. In this case, both sets of shareholders enjoyed substantial returns. After allowing for the movement in the market as a whole, the returns on the shares of both companies were substantially positive, indicating market expectations that this merger would be wealth-creating. This proved to be the case, following very swift and effective reorganisation of Kennings by TKM.

Table 12.5 Pre- and post-bid returns

Kennings Motor Group

Time period (months)	Share price (p)	Actual return (%)	Expected return (%)	Residual	Cumulated residuals
−3	140	−3.45	−0.29	−3.16	−3.16
−2	160	14.29	1.67	12.61	9.45
−1	158	1.25	−6.64	−7.89	1.56
0	212	34.18	7.63	26.54	28.10
1	268	26.42	−0.19	26.60	54.70
2	310	15.67	−3.04	18.71	73.41
3	310	0	3.08	−3.08	70.33

Tozer Kemsley Milbourn

Time period (months)	Share price (p)	Actual return (%)	Expected return (%)	Residual	Cumulated residuals
−3	66	−2.94	−0.32	−2.62	−2.62
−2	81	22.73	1.87	20.86	18.24
−1	108	33.33	7.42	25.91	44.15
0	136	25.93	8.53	17.39	61.54
1	177	30.15	−0.21	30.36	91.90
2	172	−2.82	−3.40	0.58	92.48
3	180	4.65	3.44	1.21	93.69

Source: Data collected by Krista Bromley.

Until quite recently, the bulk of the empirical evidence (e.g. see surveys by Jensen and Ruback (1983), Department of Trade and Industry (1988) and Mathur and De (1989)) suggested that positive gains from takeovers accrue almost entirely to the shareholders of target firms. While the average abnormal returns (the cumulated residuals for all firms divided by the number of firms examined in the study) recorded in these studies are invariably positive and statistically significant, returns to the shareholders of bidding firms are negative for mergers, and not significantly different from zero for takeovers. In other words, on average, takeovers and mergers are not wealth-creating, but the acquisition process transfers wealth from the shareholders of acquirers to those of the acquired. These are very important results as they seem to question the judgement or the motives, or both, of the instigators of takeover bids.

However, a very significant study by Franks and Harris (1989), based on both UK and US data, contradicted much earlier work in an important respect. The study is especially important for two reasons. First, the authors took mergers and takeovers over a much longer period (1955–85) than most other studies; and second, they examined a considerably larger sample than any previous study. For the UK sample, 1,900 acquisitions involving 1,058 bidders were studied, and the US sample was 1,555 acquisitions involving 850 bidders. The targets were all publicly traded, facilitating a capital markets approach. In sympathy with previous research findings, this study shows a substantial increase in wealth for the shareholders of target firms, but unlike the findings of earlier studies, the results indicate a relatively smaller, but statistically significant, increase in wealth for the shareholders of acquirers over the whole period leading up to, and just after, the bid.

A subsequent study by Limmack (1991), using only UK data for the period 1977–86, suggested that 'the gains made by target company shareholders are at the expense of shareholders of bidder companies'. He also suggested that the average wealth decreases suffered by the shareholders of bidding companies were mainly confined to the period 1977–80, and that bids made in the years 1981–6 produced no significant wealth decrease for shareholders of bidding firms.

Limmack's study seemed to imply that bidding firms and the capital market in general might have learned from earlier mistakes, and that some of the gains from merger might be retained by the bidder.

However, Sudarsanam *et al.* (1996), in a study of returns around bid announcement dates over the period 1980–90, found significant negative CARs (Cumulative Abnormal Returns) of around 4 per cent for the announcement period minus 20 days to plus 40 days. In a subsequent study of 398 takeovers during 1984–92 involving bid values of over £10 million, Gregory (1997) found 'the post-takeover performance of UK companies undertaking large domestic acquisitions is unambiguously negative on average, in the longer term'. The results were clearly 'not compatible with shareholder wealth maximisation on the part of acquiring firms' management'. Gregory found that acquiring firms underperformed the stock market by 18 per cent on average for two years following a bid. The method of financing the takeover was also discovered to be significant, with share exchanges being especially poor for shareholders. Agreed bids were less successful for acquiring companies than hostile takeovers, and companies making their first takeovers were likely to be poorer performers than more experienced bidders. Finally, companies bidding to diversify their interests were less likely to succeed than takeovers in related business areas (which echoes many previous analyses).

US studies, by both academics and firms of consultants, have found parallel results. Research in 1995 by the Mercer consultancy and *Business Week* of 150 deals valued at $500 million or above during 1990–5 showed that about half destroyed shareholder wealth and only 17 per cent created results that were more than 'marginal'. These and similar studies appear to confirm the view that bidders overpay for their targets (Gregory found an average bid premium of around 30 per cent) and that managers underestimate the work required to make a takeover succeed. Moreover, many managers seem determined to ignore the warning signs.

Some researchers in both the United States and the United Kingdom have studied the post-merger behaviour of corporate cash flows. This has the merit of avoiding the problems of accounting measurement and policy when profitability data are used, and also avoids relying on the efficiency of the capital market if share price data are used. For example, Manson *et al.* (1994) studied 38 UK mergers over 1985–7, and found that, on average, takeovers produced significant improvements in operating performance, reflected in higher cash flow. This supports the view that the market for corporate control provides a discipline for managers, and is consistent with US studies using similar methods.

Franks and Mayer (1996a, 1996b) undertook an explicit test of the disciplinary role of hostile takeovers. They hypothesised that hostile takeovers would have a disciplinary impact, shown by association with, first, a high rate of managerial turnover, second, with substantial internal re-structuring (asset sales exceeding 10 per cent of the value of post-acquisition fixed assets) and third, with weak firm performance post-acquisition.

Their study of hostile UK takeovers completed in 1985–6 found:

- Fifty per cent of directors resign soon after a friendly bid as compared to 90 per cent after a hostile bid.
- Asset sales exceeded 10 per cent of the total fixed asset value in 26 per cent of friendly bids compared to 53 per cent of hostile bids.
- Bid premiums averaged 30 per cent of firm value for hostile bids compared to 18 per cent for friendly bids.

- Bid premiums on hostile bids were not correlated with rate of management turnover.
- Using four measures of performance – abnormal share price performance, dividend payments, pre-bid cash flow rates of return and Tobin's Q (the ratio of market value to replacement cost of assets) – they found little significant evidence that recipients of hostile bids were poor performers prior to the bid.

Overall, the evidence was not consistent with hostile takeovers exerting a form of natural selection in which underperforming managements are supplanted by alternative teams offering improved results.

Finally, what about international mergers? The accounting firm KPMG (1999) reported a study of 700 of the largest cross-border takeovers occurring between 1996 and 1998, in which it attempted to assess the value created. KPMG measured companies' share price performance before and after the deal, and compared the post-deal performance with trends in each of the firm's industries.

The results were:

- 17 per cent of takeovers added value to the combined company;
- 30 per cent produced no significant difference;
- 53 per cent actually destroyed value.

Commenting on why 83 per cent of mergers apparently fail to generate net benefits for shareholders, it was suggested that many firms concentrate too heavily on the business and financial mechanics and overlook the personnel-related issues, echoing the earlier study by Lees (1992).

KPMG identified six factors that merit close attention:

- evaluation of synergies;
- integrated project planning;
- due diligence;
- selection of the right management team;
- dealing with culture clashes;
- communication with staff.

Not much new here, readers may think, but it is remarkable how often over-ambitious managers have to be reminded of the ingredients of a successful merger.

In a further survey released in 2002, KPMG claimed that over a third of giant international takeovers completed at the peak of the bull market were being unwound, that 32 per cent of chief executives or Finance Directors responsible for planning the original deals had moved on and that two-thirds of firms acquired during 1996–8 still needed to be properly integrated. The lesson appears to be that, like Chris Gent of Vodafone, following the acquisition of Mannesmann, top managers should negotiate their bonuses after completion of the mega-deal, but before the problems begin to appear.

The KPMG study suggests the importance of internal cultural issues. One might be forgiven for thinking that acquisitions by British firms of US enterprises would have a greater chance of success given the similarity in language and corporate cultures. Yet research by Gregory and McCorriston (2004), based on a study of 197 major British takeovers in the United States (excluding banking – itself a disaster area), suggests exactly the opposite.

Failure to address cultural issues was also highlighted by a report by the Hay Group (Dion *et al.*, 2007). Its study of European mergers concluded that only 9 per cent of mergers achieve their pre-stated aims. The researchers found that only 29 per cent of acquirers had conducted a cultural audit of the target, suggesting that firms had over-prioritised the 'hard keys' like financial and IT due diligence.

However, although echoing many earlier findings, a slightly less gloomy picture was obtained in more recent KPMG surveys (KPMG, 2007, 2010). Using a telephone interview approach, this covered a sample of global companies that had conducted deals worth over US$100 million between 2002 and 2003. The KPMG team came to six broad conclusions.

1 More deals enhanced value (31 per cent), in terms of shareholder value relative to the relevant industry average, than in its earlier study, and more deals enhanced value than reduced value (26 per cent). Yet, still over two-thirds of deals failed to increase value. By contrast, executives from 93 per cent of firms claimed that their deals did enhance value. The 'perception gap' suggested that firms were not yet prepared to make an honest assessment of their deals.
2 There was strong correlation between firms that enhanced value and those that met or exceeded their synergy and performance improvement targets. This suggests that firms that set out to outperform their targets achieved the targets. KPMG surmised that synergies arrive from unexpected areas, and that narrow pursuit of cost savings may fail to capture the full benefit of revenue synergies.
3 Almost two-thirds of acquirers failed to meet their synergy targets, 43 per cent of which was included in the purchase price. This suggests that firms typically overpay for synergies.
4 Firms found they did not start post-deal planning early enough. Although 59 per cent of firms had started planning for the integration process, the most commonly cited actions that firms said they would adopt on their next deal was earlier planning. Stated advantages of early planning were limiting the risk of losing customers, bringing forward synergy delivery, and avoiding a communication vacuum, in which rumour and speculation are rife.
5 Despite citing differences in organisational culture as the second greatest post-deal challenge, 80 per cent of firms said they had not been well prepared to handle this. The top three post-deal challenges were stated as: complex integration of two businesses, dealing with different organisational cultures and difficulty in integrating IT and reporting systems. About half said they had been well-prepared for challenges one and three, but over two-thirds had placed low emphasis on addressing people and cultural issues. Only 20 per cent said these issues were less important than expected. The top three actions that executives said they would adopt in their next deal were: to plan earlier, to perform additional cultural due diligence and to set up a dedicated team to handle the post-deal tasks.
6 It required on average nine months for companies to feel they had obtained control of the key issues facing the business post-deal. A third said it had taken longer than expected, and over 10 per cent took more than two years before being able to feel in control. More than two-thirds of firms stated that the two critical activities were gaining understanding of the target's finances and reporting systems, and understanding and overcoming the cultural difficulties between the two companies.

KPMG (2007, 2010) has undertaken a series of studies examining the association between M&A success and characteristics of deal transactions. In the first study, it analysed 510 worldwide deals by listed companies (thus excluding acquisitions by private equity houses) covering the period calendar 2000 to calendar 2004. In contrast to the earlier KPMG studies that focused on share price changes, the success of a deal was measured using the normalised share return (share price returns relative to share price returns in the same industry) at one and two years after the deal was announced. Only deals that involved a purchase price in excess of US$100 million were included (thus imparting a large-firm bias to the results). In addition to focusing on share returns, the impact on EBITDA margins was examined to assess whether acquisitions had delivered improved accounting results.

The research showed that:

- For the acquirers, there was an average gain in normalised share return of 3.7 per cent after one year and 10.8 per cent after two years, i.e. acquiring firms that performed better than their industry peers.
- Cash deals had significantly higher returns than deals financed with shares or a combination of cash and shares, being associated with a return of 15 per cent after one year, and 27 per cent after two years. All-share-financed deals delivered negative returns after one year (minus 2 per cent), but positive (4 per cent) after two years. Mixed-finance deals (shares plus cash) performed in between −4 per cent returns after one year and 10 per cent after two years. This is probably due to the fact that companies that use shares to finance a deal may perceive their shares to be a 'cheaper' currency than cash and may judge their stock prices to be around their peaks. Also, failures are 'easier' to write off when using shares (through impairment on the balance sheet) than when using cash, although this is not of benefit to the shareholders. In addition, cash deals are often (at least, partly) financed with debt, thus exerting more pressure to perform, as well as offering benefits to equity returns from gearing.
- Deals by acquirers with relatively low P:E ratios were most successful – 22 per cent returns after one year and 42 per cent after two years for acquirers in the lowest quartile P:E ratios. Acquirers that were able to purchase firms with below-average P:E ratios also outperformed. These findings probably reflect the fact that it is difficult for companies with high P:E ratios, whose shares may be 'fully' valued, to further increase their value, and that acquirers already with low P:E ratios may be less tempted to engage in riskier deals.
- Deals by smaller firms were more successful, with returns of 6 per cent after one year and 16 per cent after two years, compared to larger firms (minus 4 per cent and minus 8 per cent, respectively). The reasons for this discrepancy may be connected with other factors – large companies tended to conduct more deals and to have targets with higher P:E ratios. However, it could be that smaller companies are better prepared and are less willing to take risks. Also, such a deal will have a bigger impact on a smaller firm than it would have on a larger firm.
- Companies with above-average deal activity were less successful than companies with below-average deal activities. Negative returns were found for companies with more than ten deals a year, 7 per cent after one year and minus 8 per cent after two years, compared to positive returns for less active firms (one or two deals) – an 8 per cent increase after one year, and 18 per cent after two years Apparently, more deals, despite the experience obtained, does not necessarily mean more success, presumably due to the increased complexity of controlling the integration of several targets.
- Different rationales for an acquisition lead to different results. When companies stated that their main reason for an acquisition was to increase financial strength or to improve distribution channels, this resulted in an increase in normalised share price after one year. Vertical integration as a motivation, however, led to a significant decrease in share return. Deals driven by intellectual property and technology acquisition were significantly less successful than those driven by more mundane motives, possibly because the target firms had higher P:E ratios and key staff were more difficult to retain post-merger.
- Regarding the impact on EBITDA margins, it was found that these were 4 per cent higher for firms that made acquisitions. Results were broadly in line with those using share returns measures – firms that outperformed were those with lower deal activity, and deals motivated by financial strength tended to lead to an improved EBITDA margin.
- Geographical location was insignificant as a discriminating variable – it seemed not to matter if the acquirer and target were in the same or in different countries.

In 2010, KPMG updated the research when it examined 460 worldwide deals undertaken between 2002 and 2006 (KPMG, 2010), investigating the same variables as in 2007. The study showed largely the same results:

- Deals that were financed by cash, and acquirers with a relatively low P:E ratio were most successful.
- Too many deals lessen success: acquirers that made between six and ten deals were less successful than acquirers making between three and five deals.
- Again, this study showed that deals motivated by increasing financial strength were most successful, while deals motivated by a desire to purchase intellectual property or technology and to increase revenues were least successful.
- The main difference in findings was in the capitalisation area. Firms able to acquire targets with P:E ratios below the industry median suffered a negative return after one year (6 per cent) and also after two years (again, 6 per cent).
- In addition, size of acquiring firm was not a significant factor.
- Again, geographic location was insignificant.
- No results for the impact on EBITDA were reported.

In the next section, we return to a recurrent theme in this text: the meaning and reliability of the values placed on companies by the stock market.

Self-assessment activity 12.6

What are the main causes of 'failure' of takeovers?

(Answer in Appendix A)

12.11 VALUE GAPS*

Evidence from *some* studies indicates that there may be net gains from merger, while *most* surveys indicate that the shareholders of target companies experience a beneficial wealth effect. The near certainty that shareholders of targets will benefit suggests that market values typically fall short of the value that potential or actual bidders would place on them. These disparities in value are called value gaps, and there are four main explanations of how they arise.

■ Poor corporate parenting

Value gaps may arise because some business segments do not make their maximum possible cash or profit contributions to the parent. Ultimately, this is a reflection of poor central management, which is thus failing to add value to the group or actually reducing value. The following are some examples of management deficiencies:

1. Some assets, such as land and premises, may not be fully utilised by either the parent or its subsidiaries.
2. The parent pursues too many ventures of dubious value, perhaps intending to gain entry into other areas of business, but in which it does not possess appropriate expertise.
3. HQ may fail to take sufficiently decisive action to prevent or correct poor profitability in business segments.
4. HQ may indulge in costly central activities or services that are a net burden rather than of benefit to business units.

---

*This section relies on ideas presented in Young and Sutcliffe (1990).

5 Poor group structure may leave business units at a disadvantage compared with competitors. For example, a business unit may be too small to compete effectively in its main markets, or it may be denied sufficient capital resources to develop its activities. As a result, it may have a greater value under alternative, more perceptive, management.

Poor financial management

The HQ corporate finance department might have followed a gearing policy that fails fully to exploit its ability to borrow and gear up returns to equity; or alternatively, it may be severely over-borrowed. Similarly, its past dividend policy may have been over- or under-generous.

Over-enthusiastic bidding

It has been said that takeover bidders' greatest victims are themselves. Many bids are undoubtedly successful, such as the acquisition of Arcelor by Mittal. Lakshmi Mittal, CEO of the new entity, was able to report cost savings of US$973 million after just a year of operation, around two-thirds of the synergies of $1.6 billion promised at the time of the takeover. Reported earnings rose 42 per cent in 2006–7. However, many others are outright failures; and some, such as Morrisons' purchase of Safeway, are totally disastrous. Perhaps, at the time of the bid, the assessment of the bidding management was correct, but they were caught out by changed circumstances. A more likely explanation is that they were buoyed up with excessive enthusiasm about the bid. Although some bidders have the sense to walk away from a bid (e.g. Comcast's aborted bid for Disney in 2004), in too many cases, bidders delude themselves that the proposed takeover is vital to the development of the group.

Referring to such cases, cynics use the term 'winners' curse', for obvious reasons.

Stock market inefficiency

Does the stock market fail to assess the full value of a business, perhaps because it belongs to a sector that is 'out of favour', or because the market adopts too short-term a view of the prospects of the company?

Assessing the relative weights of these arguments is a major challenge for finance and business researchers.

Marrying in haste

Merger and acquisitions continue apace in spite of an alarming failure rate and evidence that they often fail to benefit shareholders. Last week's collapse of the planned Deutsche–Dresdner Bank merger tarnished the reputation of both parties. Deutsche Bank's management was exposed as divided and confused. Dresdner Bank lost its chairman, who resigned. Senior members of Dresdner Kleinwort Benson, its investment banking unit, walked out.

Deutsche–Dresdner was a fiasco that damaged both parties. But even if the takeover had gone ahead, it would probably still have claimed its victims. A long list of studies have all reached the same conclusion: the majority of takeovers damage the interests of the shareholders of the acquiring company. They do, however, often reward the shareholders of the acquired company, who receive more for their shares than they were worth before the takeover was announced. Mark Sirower, visiting professor at New York University, claims that 65 per cent of mergers fail to benefit acquiring companies, whose shares subsequently underperform their sector. Yet the evidence of failure has done nothing to dim senior managers' enthusiasm for takeovers.

Why do so many mergers and acquisitions fail to benefit shareholders? Colin Price, a partner at McKinsey, the management consultants, who specialises in mergers and acquisitions, says the majority of failed mergers suffer from poor implementation. And in about half of those, senior management failed to take account of the different cultures of the companies involved.

Melding corporate cultures takes time, which senior management does not have after a merger. 'Most mergers are based on the idea of "let's increase revenues", but you have to have a functioning management team to manage that process. The nature of the problem is not so much that there's open warfare between the two sides, it's that the cultures don't meld quickly enough to take advantage of the opportunities. In the meantime, the marketplace has moved on.'

Many consultants refer to how little time companies spend before a merger thinking about whether their organisations are compatible. The benefits of mergers are usually couched in financial or commercial terms: cost-savings can be made or the two sides have complementary businesses that will allow them to increase revenues.

Mergers are about compatibility, which means agreeing whose values will prevail and who will be the dominant partner. So, it is no accident that managers as well as journalists reach for marriage metaphors in describing them. Merging companies are said to 'tie the knot'. When mergers are called off, as with Deutsche Bank and Dresdner Bank, the two companies fail to 'make it up the aisle' or their relationship remains 'unconsummated'. Yet the metaphors fail to convey the scale of risk companies run when they launch acquisitions or mergers. Even in countries with high divorce rates, marriages have a better success rate than mergers. And in an age of frequent pre-marital cohabitation, the bridal couple usually know one another better than the merging companies do.

Mr Sirower rejects the view that the principal problem is 'post-merger implementation'. 'Many large acquisitions are dead on arrival, no matter how well they are managed after the deal is done,' he says. He asks why managers should pay a premium to make an acquisition when their shareholders could invest in the target company themselves. How sure are managers that they can extract cost savings or revenue improvements from their acquisition that match the size of the takeover premium?

Perhaps it would help if senior managers abandoned the marriage metaphor in favour of the story of the princess and the toad. Warren Buffett, the US investor, said nearly 20 years ago that many acquisitive managers appeared to see themselves as princesses whose kisses could turn toads into handsome princes. Investors, he observed, could always buy toads at the going price for toads. 'If investors instead bankroll princesses who wish to pay double for the right to kiss the toad, those kisses better pack some real dynamite. We've observed many kisses, but very few miracles. Many managerial princesses remain serenely confident about the future potency of their kisses, even after their corporate backyards are knee-deep in unresponsive toads.'

Source: Michael Skapinker, *Financial Times*, 12 April 2000. © The Financial Times Limited 2018. All rights reserved.

M&A deal failure at highest since 2008

The value of deals that fail to complete has reached its highest level since 2008, in the latest sign that the best year for mergers and acquisitions since the financial crisis will also feature a number of high-profile failures.

Roy Kabla, head of technology, media and telecoms for Europe, Middle East and Africa at Nomura, said: 'The companies getting hit on M&A right now are those doing heavily structured transactions, including tax-driven ones, or large-cap corporates seeking deals on the back of stable, high stock prices.'

He said: 'A decline in valuations will give private equity or entrepreneurs using the leveraged finance markets a chance to be very competitive again in the M&A market or vis-à-vis the IPO alternative.'

A total of $573bn worth of deals have been withdrawn, setting this year up to surpass the $640bn in deals that went uncompleted in 2008, according to Dealogic.

Luis Vaz Pinto, deputy head of corporate finance at Société Générale, said the market conditions meant IPO markets were going to cool but that M&A activity should continue. 'I don't think M&A will be that impacted as large corporates are still flush with cash and financial sponsors can take advantage of lower valuations.'

Source: Massoudi, A. (2014) M&A deal failure at highest since 2008. *Financial Times*, 19 October. © The Financial Times Limited 2018. All rights reserved.

12.12 CORPORATE RE-STRUCTURING

Corporate re-structuring is an important vehicle by which managements can enhance shareholder value by changing the ownership structure of the organisation. It involves three key elements:

1. Concentration of equity ownership in the hands of managers or 'inside' investors well-placed to monitor managers' efforts.
2. Substitution of debt for equity.
3. Redefinition of organisational boundaries through mergers, divestment, management buy-outs, etc.

In the dynamic environment within which companies operate, financial managers should be ever-alert to new and better ways of structuring and financing their businesses. The value-creation process will involve the following:

- Review the corporate financial structure from the shareholders' viewpoint. Consider whether changes in capital structure, business mix or ownership would enhance value.
- Increase efficiency and reduce the after-tax cost of capital through the judicious use of borrowing.
- Improve operating cash flows through focusing on wealth-creating investment opportunities (i.e. those having positive net present values), profit improvement and overhead reduction programmes and divestiture.
- Pursue financially-driven value creation using various new financing instruments and arrangements (i.e. financial engineering).

Types of re-structuring

Recent years have seen the development of new and elaborate methods of corporate re-structuring. Re-structuring can occur at three different levels:

1. *Corporate re-structuring* refers to changing the ownership structure of the parent company to enhance shareholder value. Such changes can arise through diversification, forming strategic alliances, leveraged buy-outs and even liquidation.
2. *Business re-structuring* considers changing the ownership structure at the strategic business unit level. Examples include acquisitions, joint ventures, divestments and management buy-outs.
3. *Asset re-structuring* refers to changing the ownership of assets. This can be achieved through sale and leaseback arrangements, offering assets as security, factoring debts and asset disposals.

The levels of re-structuring are summarised as follows:

Corporate	Business unit	Asset
Diversification/demerger	Acquisitions	Pledging assets as security
Share issues	Joint ventures	Factoring debts
Share repurchase	Management buy-outs	Leasing and HP
Strategic alliances	Sell-offs	Sale and leaseback
Leveraged buy-outs	Franchising	Divestment
Liquidation	Spin-offs	

Most of these devices have been covered elsewhere in this text. We devote the next two sections to a brief discussion of divestments and management buy-outs (MBOs), which have so far received only passing mention.

Divestment

A divestment is the opposite of an investment or acquisition; it is the sale of part of a company (e.g. assets, product lines, divisions, brands) to a third party. The heavy use of divestment as a means of re-structuring reflects the continuing efforts of corporate management to adjust to changing economic and political environments.

One of the motives for acquisition, identified earlier, is the managerial belief that the two businesses are worth more when combined than separate. A form of reverse synergy is a major reason for divestment: the two elements of an existing business are worth more separated than combined. Whereas the arithmetic of synergy for acquisitions argues that $(2 + 2) = 5$, the arithmetic behind divestment, or reverse synergy, argues that $(5 - 1)$ can be worth more than 4. In other words, part of the business can be sold off at a greater value than its current worth to the company. The management team may not relish the prospect of divesting itself of certain business activities, but it is often necessary as the strategic focus changes.

Self-assessment activity 12.7

Suggest reasons why a firm may choose to divest part of its business.

(Answer in Appendix A)

Two particular forms of divestment are sell-offs and spin-offs. Sell-offs involve selling part of a business to a third party, usually for cash. The most common reason for sell-offs is to divest less profitable, non-core business units to ease cash flow problems. In spin-offs, there is no change in ownership. A new company is created with assets transferred to it, as in BT's spin-off of MMO_2 in 2002, but the shareholders now have holdings in two companies rather than one.

In theory, the value of the two companies should be no different from that of the single company prior to spin-off. But numerous US studies suggest that spin-offs usually result in strong positive abnormal returns to shareholders. Why should this be so?

1 It enables investors to value the two parts of the business more easily. Poor-performing business units are more exposed to the stock market, necessitating appropriate managerial action. For example, some high-street retailers have spun off their properties into separate companies, so that investors can judge performance on retailing and property activities more easily.
2 The creation of a clearer management structure and strategic vision of the two companies should result in greater efficiency and effectiveness.
3 Spin-offs reduce the likelihood of a predatory takeover bid where the bidder recognises underperforming assets in a single company. They also make it easier for the group to sell a clearly defined part of its business at a price better reflecting its true worth.

Divestments enable companies to move their resources to higher-value investment opportunities. They should be evaluated along exactly the same lines as investment decisions, based on the net present value resulting from the divestment.

The motives for a demerger are broadly the same as for divestment discussed earlier. However, with the current vogue to focus on core businesses, it is easy to forget the drawbacks of demerger or divestment:

- Loss of economies of scale where the demerged business shared certain activities, including central overheads.
- A smaller firm may find it harder to raise finance or may incur a higher cost of capital.
- Greater vulnerability to takeover.

Qinetiq to offload struggling US arm

Qinetiq is to sell its US services division, closing a chapter on the defence technology company's aggressive expansion into the country. The London-listed group has agreed to offload its loss-making US business – one of the largest contractors to NASA – for as much as $215m in a deal with the SI Organization, the private US defence company. Qinetiq also announced that it would return £150m to shareholders – equivalent to a tenth of the company's market capitalisation – by way of a share buyback.

The US services operation was the product of what chief executive Leo Quinn called a 'flawed' strategy of buying up assets in US defence services, which pushed up debt levels at the former research arm of the Ministry of Defence. 'David [Mellors, finance director] and I have spent four years systematically unbundling what had been created, and this divestment is really the final piece in the jigsaw for creating a more focused strategy,' said Mr Quinn.

JPMorgan Cazenove analysts said: 'Given . . . that US services will no longer be a drain on management time, and that Qinetiq is now a "cleaner" company . . . in our view makes it more likely Qinetiq could be acquired over time'.

Source: Sharman, A. (2014) Qinetiq agrees to offload US services division. *Financial Times*, 22 April. © The Financial Times Limited 2018. All rights reserved.

Management buy-outs

management buy-out (MBO)
Acquisition of an existing firm by its existing management usually involving substantial amounts of straight debt and mezzanine finance

Management buy-outs (MBOs) occur when the management of a company 'buys out' a distinct part of the business that the company is seeking to divest. MBOs usually arise because a parent company decides to divest a subsidiary for strategic reasons. For example, it may decide to exit a certain activity; to sell off an unwanted subsidiary acquired by a takeover of the parent company; to improve the strategic fit of its various business units; or simply to concentrate on its core activities. MBOs can also be purchaser-driven, where the local management recognises that the business has greater potential than the parent company management realises, or where the alternative is closure, with high redundancy and closure costs.

Once a company decides to divest itself of part of its activities, it will usually seek to sell it as an ongoing business rather than selling assets separately. With an MBO, the firm sells the operation to its managers, who put in some of their own capital and obtain the remainder from venture capitalists.

The growth of MBO activity has been fuelled by venture capital firms enabling managers to raise large sums of capital through borrowings (leveraged buy-outs), particularly mezzanine finance, a cross between debt and equity, offering lenders a high coupon rate and, frequently, the right to convert to equity should the company achieve a quotation. The Finance Act 1981 gave considerable help by allowing finance raised to be secured on the acquired assets.

An MBO typically has three parties: the directors of the group looking to divest, the management team looking to make the buy-out and the financial backers for the buy-out team. A private company may agree to an MBO because the directors wish to retire or because it needs cash for the remaining operations.

It is quite common for the new management team to obtain a better return on the business than the old company. Reasons for this include:

- the greater personal motivation of management;
- flexibility in decision-making;
- lower overheads;
- negotiating a favourable buy-out price.

Checklist for a successful buy-out

The venture capitalist will ask a number of penetrating questions in evaluating whether the MBO is worth backing.

1. Has the management team got the right blend of skill, experience and commitment? The financial backers may require changes in personnel, frequently the introduction of a finance director.
2. What are the motives for the group selling and the management team buying? If the business is currently a loss-maker, how will the new company turn it round? A convincing business plan with detailed profit and cash flow projections will be required.
3. Is it the assets or the shares of the company that are to be purchased?
4. Will assets require replacement? What are the investment and financing needs?
5. What is an appropriate price?
6. Is there an exit strategy?

Buy-out failure is often the result of a wrongly priced bid, lack of expertise in key areas, loss of key staff or lack of finance.

Once the financial backers are satisfied that the MBO is worth backing, a financial package will be agreed. The management team will typically have a minority shareholding, with the financial backers (often more than one) taking the majority stake. While the venture capitalist company views the investment as long term, it will look for a potential exit route, frequently through a stock market flotation.

The management team will usually be expected to demonstrate commitment by investing personal borrowings in the business. Redeemable convertible preference shares often form part of the financial arrangements. These shares give voting rights should the preference dividend fall into arrears and enable the holder to redeem shares should the investment fail, or to convert to equity if the business performs well.

Venture capitalists often make handsome returns from MBOs and similar deals – much higher than the returns on the stock market investments. The question must be asked as to whether large companies are acting in their shareholders' best interests in permitting buy-outs on such favourable terms. It is all very well to say that a particular division is a non-core activity; but firms are constantly changing their definitions as to what exactly is core. Re-structuring, whether through MBOs or other forms, is wasteful and non-value-adding if the group selling the business could have achieved the same efficiency and other gains as the new company.

From wheels to deals for software sales chief

Not many people have beaten Sir Chris Hoy in a competitive cycling race. Very few have undertaken a management buyout – twice – before the age of 35. Jon Jorgensen has. Despite this, the co-owner and group sales director of software services company Access does not come across as a man in a hurry. Laid-back and affable, he is happy to recount his successes from the age of seven, when he was the national BMX champion, but you get the feeling he does not dine out on it.

Access today is a software developer that sells its own range of business applications (also known as ERP or enterprise resource planning) for finance, HR and payroll, supply chain and procurement, and provides associated consultancy to clients ranging from Marks and Spencer to the Bank of England.

Aged just 24, Mr Jorgensen was asked if he wanted to be part of a management buyout team. 'After I looked up "MBO" on the internet, I said: "So I get to own the company? Yeah, I'm in."' Forming a three-person debt-leveraged MBO team for a £2.8m turnover business was 'a massive learning curve', he says. 'The challenge comes with the way you leverage an MBO. Suddenly, you have a company that's doing very well trying to service a level of debt that needs to be paid before you stump up the

> salaries.' The MBO was ultimately successful and the debt paid off.
>
> Then came his second MBO. 'When one person owns the majority of a company they are fearful of risk,' he says. 'We weren't able to do what we wanted to.' An MBO was mooted among the executive team as a way to 'unleash the shackles'. Unlike the First debt-financed MBO, this was better suited to private equity. 'This was a whole new ballgame . . . The fees that were racked up were the size of a small company. You learn these terminologies of "below the line" "ebitda" . . . We have more classes of shares now than there are Smarties in a tube.'
>
> The eventual £50m deal with Lyceum Capital in 2011 gave Mr Jorgensen and his fellow MBO team the freedom they craved. 'Without private equity, we'd probably still be turning over about £25m–26m. As it is, we've gone from 230 people employed to 580 and a £50m turnover. 'More importantly, we got a lot of skills from them. Two really good non-exec directors came on board. The equity house is also very involved . . . They've never said "do this and do that" but they do help us look at the business in a slightly different way.' The company has had an impressive record for growth ever since.

Source: Tim Smedley, *Financial Times*, 20 March 2014, p. 3 © The Financial Times Limited 2018. All rights reserved.

management buy-in (MBI)
Acquisition of an equity stake in an existing firm by new management that injects expertise as well as capital into the enterprise

Management buy-ins (MBI) are the opposite of buy-outs. A group of business managers with the necessary expertise and skills to run a particular type of business search for a business to acquire. The ideal candidate is a business, or part of a business, with strong potential, but which has been underperforming or is in financial difficulty, perhaps because of poor management. The new team rarely has the necessary capital to buy in and often requires the backing of a venture capitalist.

Joint ventures and strategic alliances

Unlike mergers or acquisitions, **joint ventures** and other strategic alliances enable both sides to retain their separate identities. They have been employed to good effect to achieve a variety of objectives, but they have become a particularly popular way of developing new products and entering new markets, especially overseas. One of the financial benefits is that the strength of two organisations coming together for some specific strategic purpose can often lower capital costs associated with the new investment.

There are two main types of joint venture. An *industrial cooperation* joint venture is for a fixed period of time, where the responsibilities of each of the parties are clearly defined. These have been particularly popular in the emerging mixed economies of Central and Eastern Europe and in China. A *joint-equity* venture is where two companies make significant investments in a long-term joint activity. These are more common as a means of investing in countries where foreign ownership is discouraged, such as in Japan and parts of the Middle East.

Like any other investment, the potential partners need to assess the costs and benefits of the joint venture and identify and manage the activities critical to success. One problem can be the inability of the joint venture management team to make decisions without the approval of parent companies. This can be overcome by structuring the alliance with its own board of directors and financial reporting system.

How does re-structuring enhance shareholder value? We suggest four ways in which value can be created.

1 Business fit and focus

As we saw with divestments, a business unit may 'fit' one company better than another. Management should review their strategic business units and ask whether they operate best under the present ownership or whether they would create more value under some other ownership through an external acquisition or management buy-out. When unrelated activities have been divested, management has a much better focus on its core businesses and can concentrate on pursuing wealth-creating investment opportunities and improving efficiencies.

2 Eliminate sub-standard investment

Managers commonly enter into investments that do not enhance shareholder value:

1. A decision to reduce reliance on a single business may lead to diversification. Quite apart from the additional overheads that may be created from diversification and the lack of managerial expertise, such diversification may have no real benefit for shareholders. As we saw in Chapters 4 and 5, shareholders can often achieve the same, or better, risk-reduction effects by creating diversified portfolios.
2. Pursuit of growth in sales and earnings brings power and, possibly, protection from takeover, but does little for shareholders. Rather than pay out larger dividends, management may be tempted to reinvest in projects or acquisitions that do not add value.
3. While a strategic business unit may be profitable, it is often an amalgamation of profitable and unprofitable projects, the former subsidising the latter. Re-structuring the business creates a leaner operation with no room for cross-subsidisation.

3 Judicious use of debt

Cautious managers argue that borrowing should be minimised, as it increases financial risk and leaves little room for errors. Aggressive managers take a very different view.

Debt provides a powerful incentive to improve performance and minimise errors. The consequences of management's successes and mistakes are magnified through gearing, leaving little room for error. Managerial mediocrity is no longer acceptable. Cash flow – not profit – becomes the all-important yardstick, for it is cash flow that must be generated to service the debt and meet repayment schedules. In this respect, incurring debt obligations may provide an important signal to the market concerning the resolve of the management team.

Furthermore, debt is a cheaper source of finance because interest is tax-deductible, while dividends on equity are not. Re-structuring the balance sheet by substituting debt for equity, within acceptable gearing limits, creates a tax shield and increases the company's market value.

4 Incentives

Raising debt to realise equity can be a powerful incentive to both shareholders and managers. Equity is concentrated in the hands of fewer shareholders, providing a greater incentive to monitor managerial actions. This often leads to the creation of managerial incentives to enhance shareholder value, through executive share options or profit-sharing schemes. Remuneration packages may increase profit-related pay at the expense of salaries and wages. This will also benefit loan stockholders, who have priority ahead of profit-sharing, but after employees' wages and salaries.

12.13 PRIVATE EQUITY

One of the most important mechanisms for industrial re-structuring is the investment activity of private equity houses. Private equity investment is conducted by private equity fund management firms, usually in the form of a Limited Liability Partnership. The partners consist of syndicates of financial institutions, such as pension funds. They specialise in buying majority stakes in high-growth businesses or firms where greater efficiencies can be achieved by re-structuring activities. In principle, private equity covers all investment activities in unquoted firms including development and venture capital, management buy-outs and buy-ins.

However, in recent years, the term has become associated, often in a pejorative context, with the practice of private equity firms buying out quoted companies, thus taking them off the Stock Exchange into private hands. These deals are usually associated with high levels of borrowing to gear up the capital structure while re-structuring the firm, and paying the interest out of both existing cash flow and the proceeds of more efficient operations. In most cases, the ultimate aim is to refloat the firm on the Stock Exchange and make a capital gain. Until the enterprise is refloated, the private equity firm is the only shareholder in the business and has total control over strategy and operations.

Despite achieving some notable successes, private equity has received considerable bad publicity for various reasons. A flavour of the opprobrium can be gleaned from the Boots case.

In July 2006, Boots, the chain of chemists, and Alliance, a firm of drug distributors, completed a £7 billion 'nil-premium' merger. Less than a year later, in March 2007, a private equity firm, Kohlberg Kravis Roberts (KKR), and Stefano Pessina, the former CEO of Alliance, made an indicative offer of £10 per share for Alliance Boots, as it was known. This was rejected, the offer was increased to £10.40, and accepted. Meanwhile, Terra Firma, another private equity firm, and the Wellcome Trust, a privately-owned charitable organisation, made a counter-bid of £10.85 per share. KKR/Pessina responded with a bid of £10.90 that was accepted. Terra Firma then responded with a higher offer worth £11.15 per share, only to be trumped by KKR/Pessina with a winning bid of £11.39 per share. The equity was valued at £11 billion, making this Europe's biggest private equity deal, and the first time a FTSE 100 firm had been taken out by a private equity firm. The bid raised several ethical issues.

No details were given until after the battle was over as to how the bid would be financed, or what the winning consortium planned to do with its prize. It was suggested that Pessina could well double his money in just five years if the venture paid off. As one observer put it: 'There remains a strong feeling among fund managers [other than private equity firms] that they may have been mugged by an inside job.' The books had been opened to KKR/Pessina at £10.40 per share, almost £1.00 below the final bid, suggesting the Board of Alliance Boots (many of whom were former colleagues of Pessina) had been far too ready to capitulate to Pessina and his partners. The following box gives a 'back-of-the-envelope' evaluation of the possible arithmetic underlying the bid.

Filling your Boots – did the numbers stack up?

- At the final bid price of £11.39 per share, making the equity worth £11 billion, and with net debt of £1.2 billion, the enterprise value was £12.2 billion.
- The projected re-structuring thus appeared to involve £7.6 billion of debt plus £4.6 billion of direct equity investment (KKR £3.6 billion plus Pessina's £1.0 billion).
- At an interest rate of, say, 7.5 per cent (2 per cent above LIBOR), the interest bill would be about £500 million p.a.
- It could sell off property assets (100 freehold stores plus the Nottingham HQ) to pay down debt. The property portfolio value was estimated at over £1 billion but valued in the books at £400 million. This might lower debt to, say, £6.5 billion.
- After property disposals, the interest bill could fall by about (7 per cent × £1 billion =) £70 million to £430 million, compared to pre-tax profit estimated for 2007 of £600 million, a comfortable enough cushion, ignoring the rent that now became payable.

■ Criticisms of private equity

Against this background, it may be easier to appreciate some of the criticisms of private equity firms, or at least in the buy-out arena:

- They are only interested in 'quick flips', stripping out company assets, and cutting jobs before selling firms on, or closing them down.
- They increase unemployment.
- They may curtail the pension benefits of existing members.
- Returns paid out to investors and managers are 'excessive'.
- They pay little tax. Until 2008, UK private equity firms and their partners could pay Capital Gains Tax on disposal at a concessionary rate applicable to business sales of 10 per cent, that often fell to as low as 5 per cent after allowances. CGT was raised to 18 per cent in 2008, but was still below the new threshold rate of income tax of 20 per cent.
- They lower government tax revenues – £130 million in Corporation Tax being at stake in the case of Alliance Boots. As equity is replaced by debt, so pre-tax profits reduce, thus reducing the firm's tax bill, given the tax shield.
- As they do not have to report to anyone other than their small number of shareholders, their activities are not transparent, allegedly unacceptable for a sector that accounts for such a high proportion of the economy.

■ Rejoinders

Such criticisms have not gone unchallenged. For example, using US data, Lerner (2008) has shown that the private equity investment period is much longer than popularly imagined – in the United States, this averages over five years and is increasing. There is a lower insolvency rate among private equity-owned firms than for orthodox firms, suggesting superior management. Against this, private equity-owned firms did cut more jobs in the two years after takeover – possibly because many taken-over firms were already distressed. However, private equity-owned firms tend to grow faster, and may create more employment as they recover in the longer term, as well as saving jobs in firms that might otherwise have failed.

In the United Kingdom, the trade association for the industry, the British Private Equity and Venture Capital Association (BVCA: www.bvca.co.uk) produces an annual report to chart the contribution of the industry, which boasted over 650 members in 2017. The BVCA reckons that firms with private equity involvement now account for about a fifth of the whole private-sector workforce, and 8 per cent of the national workforce, having grown considerably faster than their listed peers, and the overall economy in terms of sales, employment and exports in the early-to-mid 2000s, although its growth has slackened sharply in the recession years. However, the BVCA does acknowledge that the industry has an 'image problem', and, partly at the urging of the Financial Services Authority, commissioned a report on the industry, published in November 2007. The committee, chaired by City 'grandee' Sir David Walker, was briefed to make recommendations about higher standards of transparency, and disclosure of operations and results, by private equity-backed firms, which it duly did, but was generally criticised for the anodyne nature of its conclusions.

This is doubtless an ongoing debate, although the recession of the late 2000s had taken the spotlight away from private equity. Time will tell whether private equity-inspired re-structuring is on balance good or bad. For the moment, it may be useful to peruse Table 12.6 that shows the claimed advantages of private equity-backed firms over orthodox public companies.

Table 12.6 Public vs private equity

Public companies	Private equity-backed firms
▪ Large number of shareholders, many of them very small.	▪ Small number of large shareholders.
▪ Most shareholders have no say in strategy or operations, except at the AGM.	▪ All private equity shareholders intimately involved in strategy and operations.
▪ Shareholders may have conflicting personal investment aims and views on company strategy.	▪ Shareholders usually have common interests.
▪ Incentives of managers could lead to conflict with owners' interests.	▪ Management highly incentivised; incentives closely aligned with investors' aims.
▪ Public companies often over-focused on short-term earnings; may take decisions that damage long-term prospects to safeguard short-term earnings.	▪ Freedom from stock-market pressures may encourage a more long-term focus.
▪ Need shareholder approval for major decisions, e.g. mergers and divestments; may slow decision-making and execution.	▪ Decision-making and implementation can be quicker; more likely to capture market opportunities.
▪ Tend to be relatively low geared; WACC may be sub-optimal.	▪ Able to employ much higher levels of gearing, so long as cash flow 'comfortably' exceeds interest commitments.
▪ Difficult for shareholders to remove under-performing management.	▪ Management changes can be quickly and easily made.
▪ Possible that talented managers may seek higher rewards attainable in private equity.	▪ Prospect of higher rewards can lure talented personnel.
▪ Increasing burden of regulation and disclosure requirements, e.g. to meet corporate governance standards.	▪ Less regulation and fewer disclosure requirements.
▪ Pressure to increase, or at least to maintain, dividends.	▪ No external pressure to pay dividends thus preserving cash flow for other uses.

Source: Based on JPMorgan/Cazenove Ltd (2008).

A 3-eyed venture capitalist (www.3i.com)

3i Group is way out in front as the UK's leading venture capital investment company, with assets under management of almost £13 billion in value in 2013. Its roots go back to 1929, when a report under the chairmanship of Lord Macmillan identified the 'Macmillan gap' – a shortage in the financing of small and medium-sized companies. Little was done, however, until 1945, when the Industrial and Commercial Finance Corporation, backed by the Bank of England, was created to bridge this gap with just £10 million of capital to invest. In 1973, it united with the Finance Corporation for Industry to form Investors in Industry, which later became simply 3i. It was floated on the stock market in 1994 in a £1.6 billion IPO making it a FTSE Top 100 company.

During its long history, spanning nearly 70 years, it has played a major role in helping to bridge the finance gap experienced by small companies and bringing many firms to their IPOs. Among its major successes were the sale in 2005 of foreign exchange specialist Travelex for a tenfold return on investment, and the sale of Go Fly, the low-cost airline in 2002 to easyJet for £374 million. But venture capital is a risky business, and 3i has had its share of failures, the largest of which was its investment in Isosceles, the company set up to mount a contested £2.4 billion management buy-in of the Gateway supermarket chain. The deal backfired, leaving 3i with £83 million debt and equity to write off. Many well-known businesses, like Waterstones, Geest and Laura Ashley, have benefited from its financial backing.

Guy Hands seeks $3.4bn for fresh buyout fund

Guy Hands, the British private equity investor behind the disastrous takeover of music label EMI, is raising his first buyout fund since 2007. Mr Hands, chairman and founder of Terra Firma, is asking investors, including some of the world's largest pension funds, for $3.4bn as he seeks to benefit from a buoyant fundraising environment. While Terra Firma has so far failed to raise money from US investors, the company will also look to raise funds from European investors.

Mr Hands, regarded as one of the 'big beasts' of private equity, nearly went bust after his firm bought EMI in 2007 when the financial crisis hit.

The new Terra Firma fund comes at a time when private equity groups with strong records are raising capital in record time as investors desperately seek yield.

Earlier this year, CVC Capital Partners raised €16bn, a record in Europe, and in the US, Apollo raised nearly $25bn, the largest buyout fund ever.

'If you can't raise money now, you never will,' the seasoned fundraiser said.

FT *Source:* Espinoza, J. (2017) Guy Hands seeks $3.4bn for fresh buyout fund. *Financial Times*, 8 August. © The Financial Times Limited 2018. All rights reserved.

SUMMARY

This chapter explored various motives for merger and takeover activity. We have argued about the importance of a coherently structured strategic approach to acquisitions, including planned integration that emphasises human and organisational factors. Poor management motivation, and effort in evaluation, excessive debt-based outlays and a poorly-planned integration process, have been regarded as the most important determinants of the failure of a corporate merger and acquisition activity. We have also discussed other forms of corporate re-structuring and argued that a focused and well-planned corporate re-structuring process, that recognizes the interests of all the stakeholders, enhances shareholder value. In discussing the role of private equity houses, we noted that, although these play an important role in the organisational re-structuring process, there is a mixed reaction to their role in the marketplace.

Key points

- The decision to acquire another company is an investment decision and requires evaluation on similar criteria to the purchase of other assets.
- Added complications are the resistance of incumbent managers to hostile bids and the presence of long-term strategic factors.
- The takeovers most likely to succeed are those approached with a strategic focus, incorporating detailed analysis of the objectives of the takeover, the possible alternatives and how the acquired company can be integrated into the new parent.
- If the takeover mechanism works well, it is an effective and valuable way of clearing out managerial deadwood.
- Many takeovers appear to be launched for 'managerial' motives, such as personal and financial aggrandisement.
- The main reasons for failure of takeovers are poor motivation and evaluation, excessive outlays (often with borrowed capital) and poorly planned and executed integration.
- The complexity of takeover integration is related to the motive for the takeover itself, ranging from cash generation, requiring only a loose control over operations, to economies of scale, requiring highly detailed integration.
- The impact of mergers can be studied by comparing the financial characteristics of merger-active and merger-inactive firms to assess any performance differentials, but this approach suffers from many problems.

- The main alternative is a capital market-based approach to assess how the market judges a merger in terms of share price movements.
- The available evidence suggests that the bulk of the gains from merger accrue to shareholders of acquired companies, although some evidence suggests that shareholders of acquirers can also share in the benefits, presumably if the takeover is well-considered.
- Corporate re-structuring enhances shareholder value through (i) improving the business fit and focus, (ii) judicious use of debt and (iii) providing incentives for management.
- Private equity houses are increasingly important agents for re-structuring, but their activities have prompted mixed reactions.

Further reading

There has been an explosion in books on M&A in recent years echoing the high levels of M&A activity, its increasingly cross-border nature and the amount of academic research resources devoted to understanding the whole process. The most comprehensive UK text is Sudarsanam (2010), while a more international flavour can be gleaned from de Pamphilis (2017). Neither book is especially strong on valuation for takeover, but Arzac (2010), Damodaran (2012), Koller *et al.* (2015), and Grabowski *et al.* (2017), fill this gap. Rankine and Howson (2014) provide a clear guide to acquisitions. As ever, Grant (2011) gives an excellent analysis of the strategic factors underpinning M&A.

An important article that explains the market for corporate control is Jensen (1984). As evidence accumulates about the disappointing results of M&A, more attention is being given to post-merger integration. Books that concentrate on this aspect are those by Gaughan (2015), Whitaker (2012) and Galpin and Herndon (2014).

A collection of leading papers in the M&A field is Gregoriu and Neuhauser (2007). Two other useful papers that focus on post-merger integration are by Angwin (2004) and Quah and Young (2005). Alexandridis *et al.* (2013) examine the relationship between the premiums paid in acquisitions and deal size. Schmidt (2015) explores the association between acquisitions' returns and friendly (less independent) corporate boards.

KPMG is undertaking an ongoing survey of determinants of takeover success, the latest published in 2010. Zenner *et al.* (2008) provide a recent discussion of cross-border merger and acquisitions from both a European and a US perspective. Ahammad *et al.* (2016) examine the impact of knowledge transfer on cross-border mergers and acquisitions' performance. Similarly, Ahammad *et al.* (2017) investigate the influence of those factors affecting the share of equity ownership in UK cross-border mergers and acquisitions.

QUESTIONS

Questions with a coloured number have solutions in Appendix B on page 501.

1. As treasurer of Holiday Ltd, you are investigating the possible acquisition of Leisure Ltd. You have the following basic data:

	Holiday	Leisure
Earnings per share (expected next year)	£5	£1.50
Dividends per share (expected next year)	£3	£0.80
Number of shares	1 million	0.6 million
Share price	£90	£20

You estimate that investors currently expect a steady growth of about 6 per cent in Leisure's earnings and dividends. Under new management, this growth rate would be increased to 8 per cent per year, without any additional capital investment required.

Required
(a) What is the gain from the acquisition?
(b) What is the cost of the acquisition if Holiday pays £25 in cash for each Leisure share? Should it go ahead?
(c) What is the cost of the acquisition if Holiday offers one of its own shares for every three shares of Leisure? Should it go ahead?
(d) How would the cost of the cash offer and the share offer alter if the expected growth rate of Leisure were not changed by the takeover? Does it affect the decision?

2. The directors of Pochettino plc have made an 850p-per-share cash bid for Kain plc, a company that is in a similar line of business. The summarised accounts of these two companies are as follows:

	Pochettino £m		Kain £m	
Sales (all credit)		216		110
Operating costs		(111)		(69)
Operating profit		105		41
Interest		(8)		(10)
Earnings before tax		97		31
Tax		(25)		(10)
Earnings for shareholders		72		21
Fixed assets		76		50
Current assets				
Stock	20		25	
Debtors	40		24	
Cash	8		1	
	68		50	
Current liabilities				
Creditors	(28)		(12)	
Bank overdraft	–		(8)	
	(28)		(20)	
Net current assets		40		30
Total assets less current liabilities		116		80
Long-term liabilities		(60)		(50)
Net assets		56		30

Included in the operating costs for each company are the purchases made during this year – £100 million for Gross and £70 million for Klinsmann.

The number and market value of each company's shares are:

	Pochettino	Kain
No. of shares issued	100m	20m
Share price	600p	700p

Required

Analyse this bid to include:
(a) Possible ways in which Pochettino may hope to recoup the bid premium when operating Kain.
(b) The final and strategic effects on Pochettino if the bid is accepted by Kain's shareholders.

3 Dangara plc is contemplating a takeover bid for another quoted company, Tefor plc. Both companies are in the leisure sector, operating a string of hotels, restaurants and motorway service stations. Tefor's most recent statement of financial position shows the following:

	£m	£m
Fixed assets (net)	800	
Current assets *less*		
Current liabilities	50	
Long-term debt		
(12% debenture 2020)	(200)	
		650
Issued share capital (25p units)	80	
Revenue reserves	420	
Revaluation reserve	150	
		650

Tefor has just reported full-year profits of £200 million after tax.

You are provided with the following further information:

(a) Dangara's shareholders require a return of 14 per cent.
(b) Dangara would have to divest certain of Tefor's assets, mainly motorway service stations, to satisfy the competition authorities. These assets have a book value of £100 million, but Dangara thinks they could be sold on to Lucky Break plc for £200 million.
(c) Tefor's assets were last revalued in 2008, at the bottom of the property market slump.
(d) Dangara's P:E ratio is 14:1, Tefor's is 10:1.
(e) Tefor's earnings have risen by only 2 per cent p.a. on average over the previous five years, while Dangara's have risen by 7 per cent p.a. on average.
(f) Takeover premiums (i.e. amount paid in excess of pre-bid market values) have recently averaged 20 per cent across all market sectors.
(g) Many 'experts' believe that a stock market 'correction' is imminent, due to the likelihood of a new government, led by Jerry Carbine, being elected. The new government would possibly adopt a more stringent policy on competition issues.
(h) If a bid is made, there is a possibility that the Chairman of Tefor will make a counter-offer to its shareholders to attempt to take the company off the Stock Exchange.
(i) If the bid succeeds, Tefor's ex-chairman is expected to offer to repurchase a major part of the hotel portfolio.
(j) Much of Tefor's hotel asset portfolio is rather shabby and requires refurbishments, estimated to cost some £50 million p.a. for the next five years.

Required

As strategic planning analyst, you are instructed to prepare a briefing report for the main board, which:
(i) assesses the appropriate value to place on Tefor, using suitable valuation techniques. (State clearly any assumptions you make.)
(ii) examines the issues to be addressed in deciding whether to bid for Tefor at this juncture.

4 Larkin Conglomerates plc owns a subsidiary company, Hughes Ltd, which sells office equipment. Recently, Larkin Conglomerates plc has been reconsidering its future strategy and has decided that Hughes Ltd should be sold off. The proposed divestment of Hughes Ltd has attracted considerable interest from other companies wishing to acquire this type of business.

The most recent accounts of Hughes Ltd are as follows:

Statement of financial position as at 31 May 20XX

	£000	£000	£000
Fixed assets			
Freehold premises at cost		240	
Less Accumulated depreciation		(40)	200
Motor vans at cost		32	
Less Accumulated depreciation		(21)	11
Fixtures and fittings at cost		10	
Less Accumulated depreciation		(2)	8
			219
Current assets			
Stock at cost		34	
Debtors		22	
Cash at bank		20	
		76	
Creditors: amounts falling due within one year			
Trade creditors	(52)		
Accrued expenses	(14)	(66)	10
			229
Creditors: amounts falling due beyond one year			
12% loan – Cirencester Bank			(100)
			129
Capital and reserves			
£1 ordinary shares			60
General reserve			14
Retained profit			55
			129

Income statement for the year ended 31 May 20XX

	£000
Sales turnover	352.0
Profit before interest and taxation	34.8
Interest charges	(12.0)
Profit before taxation	22.8
Corporation Tax	(6.4)
Profit after taxation	16.4
Dividend proposed and paid	(4.0)
	12.4
Transfer to general reserve	(3.0)
Retained profit for the year	9.4

The subsidiary has shown a stable level of sales and profits over the past three years. An independent valuer has estimated the current realisable values of the assets of the company as follows:

	£000
Freehold premises	235
Motor vans	8
Fixtures and fittings	5
Stock	36

For the remaining assets, the values on the statement of financial position were considered to reflect their current realisable values.

Another company in the same line of business, which is listed on the Stock Exchange, has a gross dividend yield of 5 per cent and a price:earnings ratio of 12.

Assume a standard rate of income tax of 25 per cent.

Required

(a) Calculate the value of an ordinary share in Hughes Ltd using the following methods:
   (i) net assets (liquidation) basis;
   (ii) dividend yield;
   (iii) price:earnings ratio.
(b) Briefly evaluate each of the share valuation methods used above.
(c) Identify and discuss four reasons why a company may undertake divestment of part of its business.
(d) Briefly state what other information, besides that provided above, would be useful to prospective buyers in deciding on a suitable value to place on the shares of Hughes Ltd.

5 The directors of Fama Industries plc are currently considering the acquisition of Beaver plc as part of its expansion programme. Fama Industries plc has interests in machine tools and light engineering while Beaver plc is involved in magazine publishing. The following financial data concerning each company are available:

Income Statements for the year ended 30 November 20XX

	Fama Industries £m	Beaver £m
Sales turnover	465	289
Profit before interest and taxation	114	43
Interest payable	(5)	(9)
Profit before taxation	109	34
Taxation	(26)	9
Net profit after taxation	83	25
Dividends	(8)	(12)
Retained profit for the year	75	13

Statements of financial position as at 30 November 20XX

	Fama Industries £m	Beaver £m
Fixed assets	105	84
Net current assets	86	38
	191	122
Less creditors due beyond one year	(38)	(58)
	153	64
Capital and reserves		
Ordinary shares	50	30
Retained profit	103	34
	153	64
Price:earnings ratio prior to bid	16	12

The ordinary share capital of Fama Industries plc consists of 50p shares and the share capital of Beaver plc consists of £1 shares. The directors of Fama Industries plc have made an offer of four shares for every five shares held in Beaver plc.

The directors of Fama Industries plc believe that combining the two businesses will lead to after-tax savings in overheads of £4 million per year.

Required

(a) Calculate:
   (i) the total value of the proposed bid
   (ii) the earnings per share for Fama Industries plc following the successful takeover of Beaver plc

(iii) the share price of Fama Industries plc following the takeover, assuming that the price:earnings ratio is maintained and the savings are achieved.

(b) Comment on the value of the bid from the viewpoint of shareholders of both Fama Industries plc and Beaver plc.

(c) Identify, and briefly discuss, two reasons why the managers of a company may wish to take over another company. The reasons identified should not be related to the objective of maximising shareholder wealth.

6 Europium plc is a large conglomerate which is seeking to acquire other companies. The Business Development division of Europium plc has recently identified an engineering company – Promithium plc – as a possible acquisition target.

Financial information relating to each company is given below:

Income Statement for the year ended 30 November 20XX

	Europium plc	Promithium plc
Turnover	820	260
Profit on ordinary activities before tax	87	33
Taxation on profit on ordinary activities	(27)	(9)
Profit on ordinary activities after tax	60	24
Dividends	(15)	(5)
Retained profit for the year	45	19
Price:earnings ratio	16	10
Capital and reserves		
£1 ordinary shares	80	30
Retained profits	195	124
	275	154

The Business Development division of Europium plc believes that shares of Promithium plc can be acquired by offering its shareholders a premium of 25 per cent above the existing share price. The purchase consideration will be in the form of shares in Europium plc.

Required

(a) Calculate the rate of exchange for the shares and the number of shares of Europium plc which must be issued at the anticipated price in order to acquire all the shares of Promithium plc.

(b) Suggest reasons why Europium plc may be prepared to pay a premium above the current market value to acquire the shares of Promithium plc.

(c) Calculate the market value per share of Europium plc following the successful takeover and assuming the P:E ratio of Europium plc stays at the pre-takeover level. Would you expect the P:E ratio of Europium plc to stay the same?

(d) State what investigations Europium plc should undertake before considering a takeover of Promithium plc.

7 As a defence against a possible takeover bid, the managing director proposes that Woppit make a bid for Grapper plc, in order to increase Woppit's size and, hence, make a bid for Woppit more difficult. The companies are in the same industry.

Woppit's equity Beta is 1.2 and Grapper's is 1.05. The risk-free rate and market return are estimated to be 10 and 16 per cent p.a., respectively. The growth rate of after-tax earnings of Woppit in recent years has been 15 per cent p.a. and of Grapper 12 per cent p.a. Both companies maintain an approximately constant dividend payout ratio.

Woppit's directors require information about how much premium above the current market price to offer for Grapper's shares. Two suggestions are:

(i) The price should be based upon the net worth on the statement of financial position of the company, adjusted for the current value of land and buildings, plus estimated after-tax profits for the next five years.

(ii) The price should be based upon a valuation using the Dividend Valuation Model, using existing growth rate estimates.

Summarised financial data for the two companies are shown below:

Most recent statements of financial position (£m)

		Woppit		Grapper
Land and buildings (net)[a]		560		150
Plant and machinery (net)		720		280
Stock	340		240	
Debtors	300		210	
Bank	20	660	40	490
Less: Trade creditors	(200)		(110)	
Overdraft	(30)		(10)	
Tax payable	(120)		(40)	
Dividends payable	(50)	(400)	(40)	(200)
Total assets less current liabilities		1,540		720
Financed by:				
Ordinary shares[b]		200		100
Share premium		420		220
Other reserves		400		300
		1,020		620
Loans due after one year		520		100
		1,540		720

[a] Woppit's land and buildings have been recently revalued. Grapper's have not been revalued for four years, during which time the average value of industrial land and buildings has increased by 25 per cent p.a.
[b] Woppit 10p par value, Grapper 25p par value

Most recent income statements (£m)

	Woppit	Grapper
Turnover	3,500	1,540
Operating profit	700	255
Net interest	(120)	(22)
Taxable profit	580	233
Taxation	(203)	(82)
Profit attributable to shareholders	377	151
Dividends	(113)	(76)
Retained profit	264	75

The current share price of Woppit is 310 pence and of Grapper 470 pence.

Required
(a) Calculate the premium per share above Grapper's current share price that would result from the two suggested valuation methods. Discuss which, if either, of these values should be the bid price. State clearly any assumptions that you make.
(b) Assess the managing director's strategy of seeking growth by acquisition in order to make a bid for Woppit more difficult.
(c) Illustrate how Woppit might achieve benefits through improvements in operational efficiency if it acquires Grapper.

(ACCA)

Practical assignment

Select one of the merger/takeover situations that has been given prominence recently in the media. Analyse your selected case under the following headings (indicative guidelines are provided).

1 *Strategy* – How does the 'victim' appear to fit into the acquirer's long-term strategy?
2 *Valuation and bid tactics* – Has the acquirer bid or paid 'over the odds'? What were the pros and cons of the financing package?
3 *Defence tactics* – Were the tactics employed sensible ones? Were the managers of the target company genuinely resisting or simply seeking to squeeze out a higher offer?
4 *Impact* – Will the acquired company be difficult to integrate? Are any sell-offs likely?

13

Managing currency risk

Hedging your bets

The perceived haven properties of sterling on international currency markets generate a clear problem for British business: a strong pound makes exports more expensive. At a time when domestic demand is also under pressure from faltering consumer confidence, the impact of adverse currency movements on competitiveness abroad adds a fresh layer of difficulty. For companies, this makes mitigating the impact of a strengthening pound all the more important.

Sarah French, finance manager at IT4Automation, started using currency hedging four years ago, after becoming aware that the business, which distributes networking products, was paying more than it needed to in euros for products bought from Taiwan. 'We brought in specialist help to reduce the frequency with which we had to revise prices, as well as to keep down our euro-costs. We were not getting a great exchange rate through the banks, and we also had to pay transaction costs. The services offered by our hedging provider have been more flexible and offer us greater clarity. For us, it definitely has worked, and has also been cost-effective.'

FT *Source:* Hunter, M. (2012) Currencies: Hedging your bets. *Financial Times*, 31 May. © The Financial Times Limited 2018. All rights reserved.

Learning objectives

This chapter explains the nature of the special risks incurred by companies that engage in international operations. It:

- Explains the economic theory underlying the operation of international financial markets.
- Examines the three forms of currency risk: translation risk, transaction risk and economic risk.
- Explains how firms can manage these risks by adopting hedging techniques internal to the firm's operations.
- Discusses how firms can use the financial markets to hedge these risks externally, including more complex external hedging techniques such as futures and swaps.

13.1 INTRODUCTION

With the huge growth in world trade over the last few decades, companies increasingly deal, as buyer, seller or investor, in foreign currency, making it a key factor in financial management. For competitive reasons, exporters are commonly obliged to invoice in the customer's currency – the greater the strength of competition from exporters based in other countries, the greater the likelihood of a UK exporter having to accept the foreign exchange risk and the associated exposure to the risk of loss.

Foreign currency can change in value relative to the home currency to significant degrees over a short time. Such changes can seriously undermine the often wafer-thin profit margin of a trader, say, a Japanese car exporter awaiting payment in foreign currency. If the yen appreciates, the yen value of the deal can evaporate before its eyes, while the likelihood of repeat business diminishes unless it lowers price, i.e. takes a smaller profit margin in yen terms. It is easy to understand the concern of a major exporter like Toyota, a great proportion of whose export trade is priced in dollars.

In this chapter, we explain both the theory of foreign exchange markets, and also how they work in practice, and how exporters and importers can protect themselves against the risks of foreign exchange rate variations. There are two key issues for the treasurer of a company with significant foreign trading links to address:

1 *Whether* to seek protection against these variations, i.e. to '*hedge*', or to ride the risks, on the basis that in the long term they will even out. Most companies do seek hedges, being risk-averters. Yet some actively seek out foreign exchange risk, and use dealing opportunities as a source of profit by deliberately taking 'positions' in particular currencies. A multinational with a substantial two-way flow in several currencies can exploit its position (usually with quite strict dealing and exposure limits) to operate its currency dealing activity as a separate profit centre. Such companies are called '*speculators*'.

2 The second issue concerns the *extent* to which the firm wants to **hedge** – whether totally to avoid exposure to exchange rate risk or to control the degree of exposure to risk.

hedge
A hedge is an arrangement effected by a person or firm attempting to eliminate or reduce exposure to risk – hence to hedge and hedger

Some firms attempt to eliminate their exposures by matching their operating inflows in a foreign currency with operating outflows in that currency to achieve a perfect hedge. However, it is difficult to keep these two flows perfectly in unison due to timing differences in receipt and disbursement of cash.

A variation on this policy is to match operating cash flows with borrowings in the same currency. Such an approach is adopted by Compass Group plc. Its 2016 Annual Report stated that:

> The Group's policy is to match as far as possible its principal projected cash flows by currency to actual or effective borrowings in the same currency. As currency cash flows are generated, they are used to service and repay debt in the same currency.

Some firms actively court foreign exchange risks. In October 2003, Nintendo, the Japanese videogame producer, reported its first-ever loss of £16 million, largely as a result of the strength of the yen. Nintendo kept much of its foreign earnings in local currencies to take advantage of better interest rates outside Japan. This policy resulted in losses of some £215 million on foreign currency transactions as the yen rose strongly against the US dollar. Understandably, Nintendo now has policies in place to reduce currency risk, as the extract from its Annual Report (which follows) illustrates.

The primary task of this chapter is to explain the various types of exchange risk and the various ways they can be managed.

Risks around economic environment

Nintendo distributes its products globally with overseas sales accounting for about 70% of its total sales. The majority of monetary transactions are made in local currencies. In order to reduce the influence of fluctuations in foreign exchange rates, we have implemented measures such as increasing purchases in US dollars; however, it is difficult to eliminate the risks completely. In addition, the Company holds a substantial amount of assets in foreign currencies. Thus, fluctuations in foreign exchange rates have a strong influence not only when accounts in foreign currencies are converted to Japanese yen, but also when they are re-evaluated for financial reporting purposes.

Source: Nintendo *Annual Report*, 2017.

To hedge or not to hedge – it all depends . . .

To hedge or not to hedge foreign currency investment exposure? That is a question posed repeatedly by investors, and answered by their advisers and investment managers. Some will advise to hedge fully. Some will advise to hedge partially. Some will advise that investors embrace the naked foreign exposure in full, enjoy it as much as possible and eventually profit from it. A central recurring phrase heard throughout the discussions that formed the research for this article was 'it all depends'.

Solutions should always be tailored to the needs and wants of the individual investor, however large or small. Every investor has a different location, a different risk/return profile and different views. For John Normand, head of foreign exchange strategy at JP Morgan, the issue is a no-brainer. 'You should hedge if you think the currency in question is going down, any loss would be large relative to the value of the asset and the cost of hedging is low,' he recommends. He lists four principal reasons why investors might not hedge. One, they might not know the risk exists. Two, they know it exists but think it is trivial. Three, they perceive that it costs too much. Four, they think that any fall in the value of the currency will eventually be reversed.

In the end, it is clear, everything depends on the investors' understanding and tolerance of foreign currency risk. There is no single right answer to the question of whether to hedge or not to hedge. Consideration of the question does, however, prompt the posing of at least one other. If an investor has zero tolerance of foreign-currency risk, should that investor even be considering investing in a foreign-currency asset?

FT *Source:* Bollen, B. (2013) To hedge or not to hedge. *Financial Times*, 31 March. © The Financial Times Limited 2018. All rights reserved.

Self-assessment activity 13.1

What is the distinction between a foreign exchange 'speculator' and a 'hedger'? How would you describe Nintendo?

(Answer in Appendix A)

13.2 THE STRUCTURE OF EXCHANGE RATES: SPOT AND FORWARD RATES[*]

Most currency transactions are conducted between firms and individuals on one hand, and banks which make a market (i.e. quote an exchange rate in a variety of currencies) on the other. As in any other market, the two parties set a price – in this case, the exchange rate is the price of one currency in terms of another. There are two ways of quoting the resulting price, which is often a source of confusion:

- **The direct quote** gives the exchange rate in terms of the number of units of the home currency required to purchase one unit of the foreign currency.

---

[*]Throughout the following sections, we use standard international abbreviations for currencies (based on SWIFT money transmission codes), e.g. pound sterling = GBP, US dollar = USD, etc. We also frequently use the abbreviation FX to denote foreign exchange (rates).

- **The indirect quote** gives the price in terms of how many units of the foreign currency can be bought with one unit of the home currency.

In London, dealers usually use the indirect quote (although this is changing). When we hear that the sterling/US dollar exchange rate (the so-called 'cable rate') is $2.00, this means that each pound can buy two units of the 'greenback', the US dollar. The corresponding direct quote would be £0.50 which indicates how many units of sterling that one US dollar can purchase. The direct quotation is simply the reciprocal of the indirect quotation.

In continental Europe, the direct quotation is used. In the United States, dealers generally use the indirect quotation when dealing with European banks, except for ones in London.

It is also misleading to talk of '*the* exchange rate' between currencies because there always exists a spectrum of rates according to when delivery of the currency traded is required.

The simplest rate to understand is the **spot market rate** that the bank quotes for 'immediate' (in practice, within two days) delivery. For example, assume on a particular day in August 2017, the closing quotation for the spot rate for Swiss francs (CHF) against sterling (GBP) was

1.2253–1.2255

spread
The difference between the exchange rates (interest rates) at which banks buy and sell foreign exchange (lend and borrow)

The first figure is the rate at which the currency can be purchased from the bank, and the higher one is the rate at which the bank sells CHF. The difference (0.02 centimes), or **spread**, provides the bank's profit margin on transactions. At times of great volatility in currency markets, the spread usually widens to reflect the greater risk in currency trading.

It is also possible to buy and sell currency for delivery and settlement at specified future dates. This can be done via the **forward market**, which sets the rate applicable for advance transactions. On the above day, assume the following terms were quoted for CHF delivery in three months:

−24   −23

The numbers are referred to as 'points', with each point representing 1 per cent of a centime, or 0.0001 of a CHF. The negative sign in front of each number indicates that the CHF is selling at a *premium*, i.e. it is 'predicted' to appreciate versus sterling. Had the numbers been positive, this would indicate CHF is selling at a *discount*. The terms forward premium and forward discount are typically abbreviated to 'pm' and 'ds', respectively.

The quotation given is not an exchange rate as such, but a 'prediction' of how the CHF spot exchange rate will change over the relevant period: in this case, depreciate against sterling. The rate itself (called an *outright*) is found by deducting the expected premium from the spot rate (or adding a discount to it). In this case, deduction is required because the market expects that one unit of sterling will purchase less CHF in the future, i.e.

Spot	1.2253	1.2255
1F/w premium	(0.0024)	(0.0023)
F/w outright	1.2229	1.2232

Notice that the spread widens from 0.02 centimes (or 2 points) to 0.03 centimes (3 points). This reflects the greater risk associated with more distant transactions. An important point to note is that, when a forward transaction is entered into, there exists a contractual obligation to deliver the currency that is legally binding on both parties. The rate of exchange incorporated in the deal is thus fixed. Hence, a forward contract is a way of locking in a specific exchange rate, and is appealing when there is great uncertainty about the future course of exchange rates.

From spot to forward

Spot and **forward rates** for other currencies against GBP are thus connected as follows:

$$\text{Forward rate} = \text{spot rate} \begin{cases} \textit{plus} \text{ forward discount} \\ \qquad \text{OR} \\ \textit{minus} \text{ forward premium} \end{cases}$$

spot rate
The rate of exchange quoted for transactions involving immediate settlement. Hence, **spot market**

forward rate of exchange
The rate fixed for transactions that involve delivery and settlement at some specified future date

Forward rates, therefore, appear to be an assessment of how the currency market expects two currencies to move in relation to each other over a specified time period, and are sometimes regarded as a prediction of the future spot rate at the end of that period. As we shall see, this is not entirely a correct interpretation.

The reader may wish to visit the website (www.bis.org) of the Bank of International Settlements (BIS) for statistics on the volume of trading on these markets. The BIS conducts a triennial survey of foreign currency trading activity on a specified trading day. In April 2016, 52 banks and other dealers participated using data provided by some 1,300 dealers. The average *daily* turnover in April 2016 totalled US$5.1 trillion (2013, US$2.0 trillion) of which $1.7 trillion was in spot transactions, $2.4 trillion in foreign exchange swaps, and $0.7 trillion in outright forward transactions (BIS, 2016).

By currency, 88 per cent of all trades involved the US dollar, 31 per cent the euro, 22 per cent the Japanese yen, and 13 per cent sterling. The most frequently traded pair was US$/euro (23 per cent), while by location, 37 per cent of activity was conducted via London, 19 per cent New York, 15 per cent in Tokyo and other Asian centres. The share of the euro zone fell to 8 per cent.

Self-assessment activity 13.2

The spot rates and forward quotations for GBP versus two other currencies are as shown below. Calculate the forward outrights.

	Spot closing rates	Forward quotation (3 months)
Swedish krona	10.5895 – 10.6045	1 16 [i.e. a discount]
Singapore dollar	2.0499 – 2.0510	–18 –3 [i.e. a premium]

Source: www.investing.com.

(Answer in Appendix A)

13.3 FOREIGN EXCHANGE EXPOSURE

foreign exchange exposure
The risk of loss stemming from exposure to adverse foreign exchange rate movements

Foreign exchange exposures occur in three forms:

1. Transaction exposure
2. Translation exposure
3. Economic exposure

Transaction exposure

transaction exposure
The risk of loss due to adverse foreign exchange rate movements that affect the home currency value of import and export contracts denominated in a foreign currency

Transaction exposure is concerned with the exchange risk involved in sending money over a currency frontier. It occurs when cash, denominated in a foreign currency, is contracted to be paid or received at some future date.

For example, a UK company might contract to buy US$45 million worth of computer chips from a US company over a three-year period. When the contract is set up, the rate of exchange between the dollar and the pound is US$2.00 to £1, but what will happen in a year or two's time? What if the rate of exchange alters to US$1.75 to £1 in a year's time?

The US$45 million was equivalent to $45m/2.00 = £22.50m at the beginning of Year 1, but after the fall in the value of the pound against USD, the cost of the contract in GBP rises to $45m/1.75 = £25.71m. Such a substantial rise in costs could easily eliminate the UK company's profit margin.

Similar risks apply to expected cash inflows. If the UK company was due to receive 50 million Canadian dollars (CAD) and the CAD actually rose from C$2.2 to £1 to C$2.0 to £1, the UK company would gain £2.28 million on the contract (i.e. the difference between the expected income of £22.72m (C$50/2.2) and the actual income of £25m (C$50/2.0)).

Thus, unexpected changes in exchange rates can inflict substantial losses (and provide unexpected gains) unless action is taken to control the risk.

■ Translation exposure

translation exposure
Exposure to the risk of adverse currency movements affecting the domestic currency value of the firm's consolidated financial statements

Translation exposure is the exposure of a multinational's consolidated financial accounts to exchange rate fluctuations. If the assets and liabilities of, say, the Australian subsidiary of a UK parent firm are translated into sterling at year-end at a rate different from the start-year rate, exchange losses or gains will be reflected in the new balance sheet and will also affect the profit and loss account. Similarly, the earnings of the subsidiary when translated into sterling are also affected by exchange rate changes.

Whereas transaction exposure is concerned with the effect on *cash flows* into the parent company's currency, translation exposure affects *balance sheet values*, and to a lesser extent (because assets typically exceed profits or cash flow in magnitude) the profit and loss account.

Examples of items that a treasurer might consider to be subject to translation exposure if denominated in foreign currency are debts, loans, inventory, shares in foreign companies, land and buildings, plant and equipment, as well as the subsidiary's retained profits.

Not everyone accepts that this risk is important. If the CAD falls in value by 3 per cent between the date an export contract is signed and the date the dollars are received in the UK, this represents a real loss to the UK company if no action is taken to hedge the exchange risk. But is a real loss sustained by a UK company with a Canadian subsidiary if C$30 million of its capital stock or C$10 million of its inventory are being held in Toronto at the time of a devaluation of the CAD against GBP? Or is this just a paper loss? This question has been much debated over the years.

It is often argued that translation risk is a purely accounting issue, i.e. it relates to past transactions, so it has no impact on the economic value of the firm and thus there is no need to hedge, i.e. people already know about it in an efficient market. However, it may become a problem if there are plans to realise assets held overseas and/or if earnings cannot be profitably reinvested in the location where they arise, and the parent wishes to repatriate them. (Arguably, these upcoming cash movements essentially reflect a transaction exposure rather than a translation exposure.) Moreover, a policy of 'benign neglect' tends to overlook possible effects on key performance measures and ratios, especially EPS, in relation to reporting overseas earnings, and gearing, via reported asset and liability values.

A multinational company may have significant borrowings in several currencies. If foreign currencies have been used to acquire assets located overseas, then, should the GBP decline in value, any adverse effect on the GBP value of borrowing will be offset by a beneficial effect on the sterling value of overseas assets. In this respect, the overseas borrowing is 'naturally' hedged, and no further action is required.

However, the UK company may face limits on its total borrowing which could be violated by adverse foreign exchange rate movements. For example, a weaker domestic currency, relative to currencies in which debt is denominated, could adversely affect borrowing capacity and the cost of capital.

Say a company has debt expressed in both GBP and USD, as in the following capital structure:

	£m
Equity	350
Loan stock: sterling	50
Loan stock: (US$80m)	40
Total	440

The valuation of the USD loan is translated at the exchange rate of $2.00:£1, the rate ruling at the end of the financial year. At this juncture, the gearing ratio (debt/equity) is (£90m/£350m) = 25.7%. Imagine there is a covenant attaching to the sterling loan which limits the gearing ratio to 30 per cent. If GBP falls to, say, $1.50:£1, the company has a problem. Its USD-denominated debt now represents a liability of $80m/1.50 = £53.33m, and the debt/equity ratio rises to:

$$(£50m + £53.33m) \div £350m = \frac{£103.33m}{£350m} = 29.5\%$$

The firm is now on the verge of violating the covenant. To avoid this situation occurring, the company could borrow in a range of currencies that might move in different directions relative to GBP, with adverse movements offset by favourable ones. For example, Bunzl plc (www.bunzl.com), the multinational distribution group, mixes a so-called currency cocktail that reflects its main operating currencies, as shown in Table 13.1.

Table 13.1 Net debt of Bunzl plc as at 31 December 2016

Currency	Amount (£m)	%
USD	538.4	43.82
GBP	414.4	33.73
EUR	221.6	18.04
Other	54.2	04.41
Total	1,228.6	100%

Source: Bunzl plc, Annual Report 2016.

Bunzl, whose stated policy is not to hedge translation risk, reckons that a 10 per cent strengthening/weakening in sterling will result in a fall/rise in equity of around £142/£116 million, a relatively small proportion of its balance sheet equity (well over £1.3 billion).

English Premier League faces loss after currency own goal

The Premier League is set to announce a record loss after new accounting rules and the declining value of sterling forced it to declare the cost of protecting itself from the currency risk attached to its lucrative TV contracts.

The organisation behind the top tier of English football will reveal a pre-tax loss of £312m when it releases annual results, according to documents seen by the *Financial Times*.

For many years, the TV contracts that have fuelled the league's boom have been paid in sterling, dollars and euros with the company paying the league clubs in sterling and using derivatives to manage the exchange rate risk.

Last summer was the first time the Premier League was required to present its results under new UK accounting standards that changed the reporting for derivatives.

Continued

Companies using hedges to insure against unexpected or adverse moves in the currencies market had to value their contracts annually at market prices, instead of making a final record once any deals had matured.

On the last day of the Premier League's financial year, July 31, the pound stood at $1.32, a 12 per cent decline since the EU referendum.

That turned what would have been a gain of £638,000 under the old standards into a paper loss of £250m, the Premier League said. It insisted that the figure had no impact on its real income or operations, or on its ability to pay the clubs.

The Premier League has a number of hedging contracts lasting for periods up to three years and maturing at different times. Some of these remain open. If exchange rates remain stable, then the Premier League may crystallise its losses when they run out.

Like the Premier League, the biggest football clubs in the league hedge against currency, earning euros from playing in European competition and dollars from international sponsorship deals. But smaller clubs looking to acquire foreign players are most likely to be stretched by the drop in the pound.

FT *Source:* Ahmed, M.; Blitz, R. and Stafford, P. (2017) English Premier League faces loss after currency own goal. *Financial Times*, 14 April. © The Financial Times Limited 2018. All rights reserved.

■ Economic exposure

Economic exposure is also known as long-term cash flow or operating exposure. Imagine a UK company which buys goods and services from abroad and sells its goods or services into foreign markets. If the exchange rate between sterling and foreign currencies shifts over time, then the value of the stream of foreign cash flows in sterling will alter through time, thus affecting the sterling value of the whole operation.

In general, a UK company should try to buy goods in currencies falling in value against GBP and sell in currencies rising in value against GBP.

Of course, the transaction exposure could be eliminated by denominating all its contracts in GBP, which shifts the risk to the trading partner. However, this tactic cannot remove economic exposure. The foreign company will convert the GBP cost of purchases and sales into its own currency for comparison with purchases or sales from companies in other countries using other currencies. Management of economic exposure involves looking at long-term movements in exchange rates and attempting to hedge long-term exchange risk by shifting out of currencies that are moving, to the detriment of the long-term profitability of the company. It is worth noting that many economic exposures are driven by political factors, e.g. changes in overseas governments resulting in different economic policies such as taxation.

Self-assessment activity 13.3

Distinguish between translation, transaction and economic exposure.

(Answer in Appendix A)

13.4 SHOULD FIRMS WORRY ABOUT EXCHANGE RATE CHANGES?

Purchasing Power Parity (PPP)
The theory that foreign exchange rates are in equilibrium when a currency can purchase the same amount of goods at the prevailing exchange rate anywhere in the world

Law of One Price
The proposition that any good or service will sell for the same price, adjusting for the relevant exchange rate, throughout the world

According to the theory of **Purchasing Power Parity (PPP)**, the answer to this question is a resounding 'No!'.

PPP says that the purchasing power of any currency should be equivalent in any location. It is based on the **Law of One Price**, which asserts that identical goods must sell at the same price in different markets, after adjusting for the exchange rate. For example, if the market rate of exchange between USD and GBP is $2.00:£1, a microcomputer could not sell for very long at simultaneous prices of, say, £1,500 in London and $2,000 (i.e. £1,000) in New York. People would buy in the 'cheap' market (New York) and ship the goods to London, thus tending to equalise the two prices at, say, a London price of £1,200 and a New York price of $2,400 (£1,200). (In reality, transport and other transaction costs may prevent the precise operation of PPP.)

The Law of One Price states that, for tradeable goods and services, the

(£ price of a good × $/£ exchange rate) = USD price of a good

However, part of the adjustment will occur via the effect on the exchange rate itself.

Absolute and relative PPP

In fact, the Law of One Price only applies under a rarified form of PPP called **absolute PPP (APPP)**. For the law to apply (i.e. for prices of similar products to be equal after adjusting for currency values), resources would have to be perfectly mobile so that the levels of supply and demand should equalise at just the appropriate level. In reality, the existence of transport costs, different local taxes such as VAT, barriers to trade such as tariffs, quotas and other government restrictions, not to mention sheer inertia, prevent APPP from operating, and price discrepancies will persist. One only has to think about land and property to appreciate that some resources are quite difficult to move (although titles to land can be traded).

In practice, market theorists put their faith in a more limited theory, the **relative PPP theory (RPPP)**, which allows for all the market imperfections listed above. RPPP theorists accept that the Law of One Price will probably not hold in its purest form, but it suggests that rates of change of prices will be similar when expressed in common currency terms, for a given set of trade restrictions. Take the previous example, with the computer selling at two different prices in New York and London ($2,000 and £1,500, respectively, or in terms of GBP, at the ruling exchange rate of $2.00 = £1, £1,000 and £1,500). It may be that this pair of prices reflects the market equilibria after all scope for price equalisation is exhausted. It should be noted that the prices infer a 'correct' exchange rate of:

US price/UKprice = $2,000/£1,500 = US$1.33 per £1

This compares to the market rate of US$2.00 = £1. This implies the USD is undervalued or, to say the same thing, that the GBP is overvalued.

Obviously, the Law of One Price does not apply here, as the purchasing power of sterling is lower in London (where £1,000 buys only 2/3 of a computer) than in New York (where £1,000 buys a whole computer).

RPP focuses on the differential in inflation through time – if prices rise faster in one location, say London, the local currency would decline in relation to others such as the USD. If, say, prices rose by 10 per cent in London and only 5 per cent in the United States, the local prices for the computer would be £1,500(1.1) = £1,650 and $2,000(1.05) = $2,100, respectively. To preserve the purchasing power of both currencies, the exchange rate would have to alter to:

2.00 × US inflation/UK inflation = 2.00 × (1.05)/(1.10) = 1.91

This reflects a sterling depreciation of about 5 per cent, the inflation differential. Thus RPPP involves the assertion that a currency will fall (or is expected to fall) in relation to another according to the difference in actual (or expected) inflation rates between the two countries.

Exchange rate changes

If foreign exchange markets operate freely without government intervention, goods that can be easily traded on international markets, such as oil, are highly likely to obey the Law of One Price, although transport costs between markets may explain a continued price discrepancy. However, not all goods can be easily transported. Most notably, with land and property, which are physically impossible to shift, a sustained price discrepancy may apply between markets. In the longer term, however, even these differentials may close as investors and property speculators perceive that one market is cheap relative to the other.

PPP may be expected to operate broadly in the longer term for most goods and services, although it can be distorted by government intervention in the foreign exchange markets and the formation of currency blocs. The monetary authorities often attempt to smooth out currency fluctuations to minimise the dislocation to business activity that sudden sharp swings in currency values might cause. However, while exchange controls and official intervention can delay any adjustment necessary to reflect differential rates of inflation, the required change will eventually take place.

Accepting PPP and the Law of One Price, we arrive at a remarkable conclusion regarding the need to hedge FX risks – there is no need to worry! The Stonewall plc example explains the mechanics.

Example: Stonewall plc

A British-based firm, Stonewall plc has a factory in Baltimore, USA. It plans to produce and sell goods to generate a net cash inflow of $180 million at today's prices over the coming trading year. For simplicity, we assume all transactions are completed at year-end, and that any price adjustments resulting from inflation also occur at year-end.

At the current exchange rate of US$2.00 vs. £1, the sterling value of its planned sales = ($180m/2.00) = £90m. Stonewall is worried about the USD falling due to the annual rate of inflation in the United States of 6 per cent compared to 3 per cent in the United Kingdom.

Concern about exposure to foreign exchange risk seems justified – with these inflation rates, PPP predicts the USD will decline to:

$2.00 \times (1.06/1.03) = \$2.058$ after one year.

At this exchange rate, the sterling value of the USD cash flow is ($180m/2.058) = £87.46m, a fall of about 3 per cent on the start-year valuation. But should sleep be lost over this?

The answer is 'yes' if selling prices within the United States remained static. However, prices within the United States are *not* static – the reason why the FX rate will change is due to inflation at a higher rate in the United States relative to the United Kingdom.

With US prices rising at 6 per cent, the USD cash flow *ought* to rise to $180m (1.06) = $190.8m. Converted to sterling at the year-end rate, this is worth ($190.8/2.058) = £92.70m. This is precisely equal to its sterling-denominated value at the end of one year with UK price inflation at 3 per cent (£90m $\times$ 1.03 = £92.70).

So what has been lost from inflation affecting the relative value of sterling and USD? The answer is nothing if PPP operates! Should the firm take precautions against FX exposure? The answer is 'no' – why should it bother when it is automatically protected by market adjustments? Should the firm try to forecast future rates of exchange, e.g. by comparing the respective inflation rates? It could, but again, it is a waste of time, at least in theory, as the rate of $2.058 should already be quoted in the market for one-year forward deals.

However, it is not always this simple. In reality, prices rise in a continuous process rather than in a series of year-end adjustments. The policy of benign neglect only works if prices of the traded goods are adjusted *pari passu* as prices in general alter and the exchange rate 'crawls' in the appropriate direction, by the appropriate amount, and if the movement is synchronised.

In reality, FX rates adjust in response to relative inflation rates at the national level, as measured by a basket of goods. The basket may well inflate at a different rate from the goods traded. Indeed, competitive conditions (i.e. strategic considerations) may be so powerful that firms may be unable to raise prices even to compensate for inflation. For these reasons, most firms seek protection against FX movements.

13.5 ECONOMIC THEORY AND EXPOSURE MANAGEMENT

The first step in currency management is to identify the transaction, translation and economic exposure to which the company is subject. The second step is to decide how the exposure should be managed. Should the risk be totally hedged, or should some degree of risk be accepted by the company?

The international treasurer must devise a hedging strategy to control exposure to exchange rate changes. The precise strategy adopted is likely to be influenced by several economic theories that have evolved over the last century, and the extent to which they are considered valid. These theories are as follows:

1. The Purchasing Power Parity (PPP) Theory.
2. The Expectations Theory.
3. The Interest Rate Parity (IRP) Theory.
4. The Open, or International, Fisher Theory.
5. The international version of the efficient markets hypothesis (EMH).

We will provide brief sketches of these important contributions to the literature of international economics.

Purchasing Power Parity (PPP) Theory

In the last section, we encountered the Law of One Price and Purchasing Power Parity. PPP and the Law of One Price have important implications for the relationship between spot and forward rates of exchange. If people possessed perfect predictive ability, and the rates of inflation were certain, the market could specify with total precision the appropriate exchange rate between USD and GBP for delivery in the future (i.e. the *forward rate* of exchange).

More specifically, PPP states that foreign exchange rates will adjust in response to international differences in inflation rates and so maintain the Law of One Price. Thus, the forward rate should be:

$$\text{Forward rate} = \text{Spot rate} \times \frac{(1 + \text{US inflation rate})}{(1 + \text{UK inflation rate})}$$

If the spot rate between sterling and the USD is $2.00 vs. £1, and people expect UK inflation at 10 per cent and only 3 per cent in the United States, this implies a one-year *forward rate* of:

$2.00:£1 spot rate $\times$ (1.03)/(1.10) = $1.87:£1

Self-assessment activity 13.4

Use the Law of One Price and PPP to predict the relative local prices of a cup of coffee and the future sterling/dollar spot rate under the following conditions:

- Price now in New York = $2.00
- Price now in London = £1.00
- Exchange rate for USD vs. GBP = $2.00:£1
- UK inflation is 4 per cent; US inflation is 2 per cent

(Answer in Appendix A)

Expectations Theory

In the previous example, the forward rate is predicting the spot rate that *should* apply in the future. If buyers and sellers of foreign exchange can rely on the currency markets to operate in this way, the risks presented by differential inflation rates could be removed by using the forward market. Forecasting future spot rates would then be a trivial exercise.

Unfortunately, the forward rate has been shown to be a poor predictor of the future spot rate. Yet it has also been shown to be an **unbiased predictor** in that, although the forward rate often underestimates and often overestimates the future spot rate, it does not consistently do either. In the long run, the differences between the forward rate's 'prediction' for a given date in the future and the actual spot rate on that date in the future should sum to zero. If the forward market operates in this way, firms can regard today's forward rate as a reasonable expectation of the future spot rate. This is the **Expectations Theory**.

> **Expectations or unbiased forward predictor theory**
> The postulate that the expected change in the spot rate of exchange is equal to the difference between the current spot rate and the current forward rate for the relevant period

■ Interest Rate Parity (IRP) Theory

The **Interest Rate Parity (IRP)** Theory is concerned with the difference between the spot exchange rate (the rate applicable for transactions involving immediate delivery) and the forward exchange rate (the rate applicable for transactions involving delivery at some future specified time) between two currencies. Suppose the spot rate for USD to GBP is $2.00:£1, and the one-year forward rate is $1.85:£1. Here, the USD is selling at a 15 cent premium – it is more expensive in terms of GBP for forward deals. The currency market thus expects the USD to rise in value against GBP during the year by about 7.5 per cent.

> **Interest Rate Parity (IRP)**
> Asserts that the difference between the spot and forward exchanges is equal to the differential between interest rates prevailing in the money markets for lending/borrowing in the respective currencies

IRP converts this expected rise in the value of the USD against GBP into a difference in the rate of interest in the two countries. The rate of interest on one-year bonds denominated in USD will be lower than bonds otherwise identical in risk, but denominated in GBP. The difference will be determined by the premium on the forward exchange rate. If depreciation of GBP against USD is expected, this should be reflected in a comparable interest rate disparity as borrowers in London seek to compensate lenders for exposure to the risk of currency losses. In other words, interest rates offered in different locations tend to become equal, to compensate for expected exchange rate movements.

The equilibrium relationship that operates under IRP is given by:

$$\text{Forward rate} = \text{Spot rate} \times \frac{(1 + \text{US interest rate})}{(1 + \text{UK interest rate})}$$

For example, if the interest rate available in London is 12 per cent p.a., the figures in our example will indicate a US interest rate as follows:

$$(1 + \text{US interest rate}) = 1.12 \times \frac{1.85}{2.00} = 1.036$$

So, the US interest rate is $(1.036 - 1) = 0.036$, i.e. 3.6% p.a.

This is an interesting result. A New Yorker attracted by high UK interest, who is tempted to place money on deposit for a year in London, will find that what is gained on the interest rate differential will be lost on the adverse movement of GBP against USD over the year. To appreciate this 'swings and roundabouts' argument, consider the following figures, which relate to the two investment options faced by a US investor wanting to deposit $1,000:

1 *Invest in GBP:*

    January   Convert $1,000 into GBP at 2.00 = £500.
                    Invest for one year in London at 12%: £500(1.12) = £560.
    December Convert back to USD at 1.85 = $1,036.

vs.

2 *Invest in USD:*

    January   Invest $1,000 in New York at 3.6% = $1,036 in December.

Clearly, the rational investor should be indifferent between these two alternatives, unless interest rates are expected to fall in New York relative to those in London, or the forward rate is not a good predictor of the spot rate in one year's time.

One reason why this predictive ability is weakened in practice is intervention in foreign exchange markets by governments. In the absence of such intervention, exchange rates seem to operate so as to smooth out interest rate disparities, but with the creation of artificial market inefficiencies, there often exist opportunities to arbitrage: for example, borrowing money at low interest rates in one market, hoping to repay it before IRP fully exerts itself. However, in the past, many corporate treasurers were wrong-footed by borrowing apparently cheap money overseas but having to repay at exchange rates quite different from those envisaged when raising the loan, because market forces have eventually asserted themselves to remove the interest rate discrepancy.

This equalising process is effected by financial operators called **arbitrageurs**, who act upon any short-term disparities. For example, if in the previous example, the interest rate disparity were 3 per cent, it would pay to borrow in GBP and purchase US bonds in London.

arbitrageurs
Arbitrageurs attempt to exploit differences in the values of financial variables in different markets, e.g. borrowing in a low-cost location and investing where interest rates are relatively high (interest arbitrage)

interest agio
The percentage difference between interest rates prevailing in the money markets for lending/borrowing in two currencies

exchange agio
The percentage difference between the spot and forward rates of exchange between two currencies

covered interest arbitrage
Using the forward market to lock in the future domestic currency value of a transaction undertaken to exploit an interest arbitrage opportunity

Checking the agios: the scope for arbitrage

When currency and money markets are in equilibrium, any difference in interest rates available through investment in two separate locations should correspond to the differential between the spot and forward rates of exchange. The interest rate differential is called the **interest agio**, and the spot/forward differential is called the **exchange agio**. If these are not equal, arbitrageurs have scope to earn profits.

Consider this example. An investor has £1 million to invest for a year. The interest rate is 5 per cent in London and 8 per cent in New York. The current spot rate of exchange (ignoring the spread) is $2.00:£1 and the dollar sells at a one-year-forward discount of 5 cents, i.e. the forward outright is $2.05:£1. What is the best home for the investor's money?

The investor could invest the £1 million on deposit in London to earn £50,000 interest over one year, thus increasing that person's cash holding to £1.05 million. Alternatively, the investor could engage in **covered interest arbitrage**. This works as follows:

1 Convert £1m at spot into USD, i.e.

  £1m × 2.00 = $2.00m

2 Invest $2.00m at 8 per cent for one year in the United States, i.e.

  $2.00m × 1.08 = $2.16m

3 Meanwhile, sell this forward over one year, i.e. for delivery in one year:

  $2.16m/2.05 = £1,053,658

The guaranteed proceeds from arbitrage are greater by £3,658. However, this so-called 'carry trade' cannot last for very long. As other investors spot the scope for risk-free profits and rush into the market, their actions will quickly eliminate the opportunity. This is why spot/forward relationships almost always reflect prevailing interest rate differentials.

For this reason, the forward rate is the product of a technical relationship linking the spot rate to relative interest rates, rather than a prediction in the true sense.

Equilibrium requires equality between the exchange agio and the interest agio, i.e. the spot/forward differential should equal the interest rate differential:

$$\frac{F_0 - S_0}{S_0} = \frac{i_\$ - i_£}{1 + i_£}$$

where F_0 is today's forward quotation, S_0 is today's spot quotation, $i_\$$ is the interest rate available by investment in USD, and $i_£$ is the interest rate available by investment in GBP.

Note that the interest agio is found by discounting the interest differential over one year at the UK interest rate. If the period concerned were less than a year – say, three months – the equivalent three-monthly interest rate would be used.

In the above example, the two agios are:

$$\frac{2.05 - 2.00}{2.00} \quad \text{vs.} \quad \frac{0.08 - 0.05}{1.05}$$

i.e.:

2.5%   vs.   2.86%

uncovered arbitrage
Interest arbitrage without the use of the forward market to lock in future values of proceeds

This inequality signifies the scope for risk-free profit via covered interest arbitrage. **Uncovered arbitrage** is where the arbitrageur does not sell forward but takes a gamble on how the spot rate changes over the year. This is the essence of **the carry trade**. In the example, he or she would earn bigger profits if the spot rate in one year turned out to be lower than $2.05:£1 (e.g. $2.02). This distinction highlights the difference between hedging and speculation. However, although differences in agios can persist for a while, transactions costs may preclude profitable arbitrage.

Self-assessment activity 13.5

If interest rates are higher in London than New York by 2.5 per cent p.a. and today's spot rate is $2.0250 vs. £1, what would you expect the three-month forward quotation to be if IRP applied?

(Answer in Appendix A)

Rebound in pound prompts revival in hedging

UK companies have responded to the pound's recent rebound to close to $1.30 by taking out new sterling hedges.

The pound fell as much as 22 per cent after the Brexit vote in June, dipping below $1.20 in January. That had been weighing on importers, particularly retailers, who regularly need to sell sterling to pay for materials from overseas.

Companies were reluctant to take out hedges when sterling was so low, while those whose hedges were expiring were faced with passing costs on to customers, absorbing them or renegotiating supply terms.

But forex hedging advisers are reporting a pick-up in activity as finance directors reassess budgets in light of the rise in the pound, which climbed 3.2 per cent in the two weeks since April 18.

Payments provider World First recorded a 120 per cent increase in clients hedging their sterling liabilities in the week after the general election was called, and said hedging durations, which had fallen to seven weeks in March, were now averaging three months.

Barclays reported that some UK retailers were putting in hedges for 2018 for the first time since the Brexit vote.

FT *Source:* Blitz, R. (2017) Rebound in pound prompts revival in hedging. *Financial Times*, 14 May. © The Financial Times Limited 2018. All rights reserved.

■ The Open Fisher Theory

The 'Open Fisher Theory', sometimes called the 'International Fisher Theory', claims that the difference between the interest rates offered on identical bonds in different currencies represents the market's estimate of the future changes in the exchange rates over the period of the bond. The theory is particularly important in the case of fixed-rate bonds having a long life to maturity, say, 5 to 15 years' duration.

Suppose that a firm wishes to raise £50 million for a one-year period. It approaches a bond broker and is offered the following loan alternatives:

1 A loan in GBP at 12 per cent p.a.
2 A USD loan at 5 per cent p.a.

The Open Fisher Theory asserts that the interest rate difference represents the market's 'best estimate' of the likely future change in the exchange rates between the currencies over the next year. In other words, the market expects GBP to depreciate by around 7 per cent against USD over the next year.

The Fisher Effect concerns the relationship between expectations regarding future rates of inflation and domestic interest rates – investors' expectations about future price level changes will be translated directly into nominal market interest rates. In other words, rational lenders will expect compensation not only for waiting for their money, but also for the likely erosion in real purchasing power. For example, if in the United Kingdom, the real rate of interest that balances the demand and supply for capital is 5 per cent, and people expect inflation of 10 per cent p.a., then the nominal rate of interest will be about 15 per cent (actually 15.5 per cent). Recall that real and nominal interest rates are connected by the Fisher formula:

$$(1 + P)(1 + I) = (1 + M)$$

where P is the real interest rate, I is the expected general inflation rate and M is the market interest rate.

The Open Fisher Theory asserts that all countries will have the same real interest rate, i.e. in real terms, all securities of a given risk will offer the same yield, although nominal or market interest rates may differ due to differences in expected inflation rates. It can be more precisely expressed by amalgamating the PPP and IRP theories:

$$\frac{(1 + \text{US interest rate})}{(1 + \text{UK interest rate})} \times \text{Spot rate} = \text{Forward rate}$$

$$= \frac{(1 + \text{US inflation rate})}{(1 + \text{UK inflation rate})} \times \text{Spot rate}$$

For example, suppose the London and New York interest rates are 12 per cent and 5 per cent, respectively, as quoted by our bond brokers, and the respective expected rates of inflation are 10 per cent and 3 per cent. If the spot rate is $2.00:£1, then the Open Fisher Theory predicts a depreciation in the pound as expressed by the forward rate thus:

$$\frac{1.05}{1.12} \times 2.00 = \mathbf{1.87} = \frac{1.03}{1.10} \times 2.00$$

In other words, when the spot rate is $2.00:£1, this combination of inflation rates and interest rates is consistent with a forward rate of $1.87:£1, as calculated earlier.

These economic theories are interlocking or mutually reinforcing, as shown by the 'equilibrium grid' in Figure 13.1. Several other factors, such as the timing of the change,

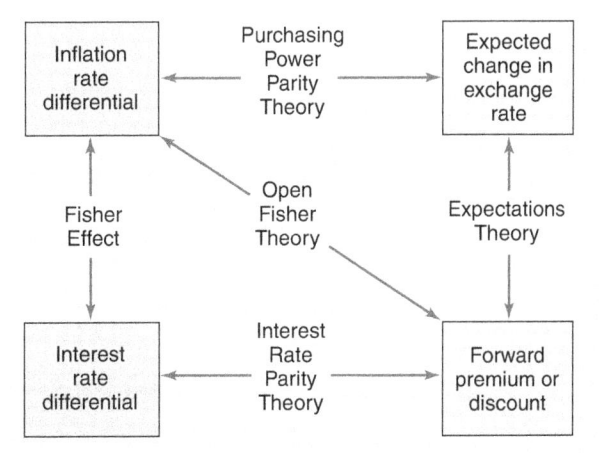

Figure 13.1 **Interlocking theories in international economics**

tax and exchange controls can also affect the relative movement of currencies, but the major factor influencing the movements in exchange rates is claimed to be the expected future movement in inflation rates, which is signalled by current differentials in interest rates.

The international efficient markets hypothesis (EMH)

The EMH claims that, in an efficient market, all publicly-available information is very quickly incorporated into the value of any financial instrument. In other words, past information is of no use in valuation. Any change in value is due to future events, which are, by definition, unknowable at the present time. Past trends in exchange rates cannot provide any useful information to assist in predicting future rates.

This theory applies only to information-efficient markets. Currencies operating within a system of fixed average rates (or maximum permitted bands of fluctuation), such as the former European exchange rate mechanism (ERM), are operating within a controlled market, so the EMH will not apply fully. *Where markets are information-efficient, the EMH casts doubt on the ability of treasurers to make profits out of using exchange rate forecasts.*

This section of the chapter has provided a brief sketch of some economic theories relevant to devising a foreign exchange management strategy. We will shortly try to design such a strategy by applying these theories to the various types of foreign exchange exposure outlined earlier. But because these theories may not always apply (and some people think they rarely, if ever, apply), it is helpful to examine approaches to forecasting FX rates.

13.6 EXCHANGE RATE FORECASTING

First of all, consider why firms may want to forecast future exchange rates. There are both short-term and long-term reasons for this:

- To help decide whether to protect outstanding current assets and liabilities from potential foreign exchange losses.
- To assist in quoting prices in foreign currency when constructing an international price list.
- To aid working capital management, e.g. accurate exchange rate forecasts may assist the decision regarding the most efficient timing of transmitting currency in situations where the firm is able to lead and lag payments.
- To evaluate foreign investment projects requiring exchange rate forecasts over several years.

Because FX forecasts are required for both short- and long-term purposes, they may require continuous revision. In addition, long-term forecasts for investment appraisal purposes often require more intensive analysis of a range of different scenarios. In general, the firm's FX forecasting needs hinge on:

- The pattern of its trading and investment activities, i.e. its degree of globalisation.
- The required frequency of forecast revision.
- The internal resources and expertise available for forecasting analysis.

fundamental analysis
Estimation of the 'true' value of a share based on expected future returns

technical analysis
The intensive scrutiny of charts of foreign exchange rate movements attempting to identify persistent patterns

Approaches to FX forecasting

There are two broad approaches to FX prediction: **(a) fundamental analysis**, which bases forecasts on the financial and economic theories outlined earlier, and **(b) technical analysis**, which is based on analysis and projection of time series trends.

(a) Fundamental analysis
This approach is sub-divided into two analytical perspectives:

(i) The balance of payments (BOP) perspective
This regards a country's BOP (more accurately, its balance of payments on current account) as an indicator of likely pressure on its exchange rate. When a country, say, the United Kingdom, spends more on foreign-produced goods and services than its export earnings, the resulting deficit on current account increases the probability of depreciation of its currency. Overseas residents accumulate monetary claims on sterling – when they convert into their own currencies, this will exert downward pressure on the GBP (and vice versa for a surplus of exports over imports).

Analysts who focus on the BOP try to evaluate not only the country's ongoing BOP performance but also the determinants of international competitiveness, such as prospects for inflation, e.g. a government budget deficit and how it is financed, and underlying productivity movements.

(ii) The asset market approach
This examines the willingness of foreign residents to hold claims on the domestic currency in monetary form. Their willingness depends on relative real interest rates and on a country's prospects for economic growth and the profitability of its industry and commerce. The asset market perspective could explain the continuing strength of the USD during the 'Greenspan Boom' of the 1990s, during which the United States received a massive inflow of overseas funds seeking a home in the stock markets, helping to offset the continuing gaping US current account deficit.

Any factor expected to increase real returns on investment, e.g. technological progress such as the rise of e-commerce, promising higher corporate profitability is thus likely to lead to relative exchange rate appreciation (and vice versa).

In practice, it is difficult to disentangle the various fundamental pressures on exchange rates to *identify* the true reasons for their movements. Some argue that short-term movements are largely determined by the relative attractiveness of international asset markets, interest rates and the expectations of market players plus a dose of speculation, while in the long term, equilibrium exchange rates depend on PPP.

(b) Technical analysis
Technical analysts conduct intensive scrutiny of charts to identify trends in foreign exchange rate movements. These **chartists** focus on both price and volume data to ascertain whether past trends are likely to persist into the future. The underlying premise behind "chartism" is that future FX rates are based on past rates. Chartists assert that FX movements can be split into three temporal categories:

chartist
Analyst who relies on charts of past share movements to predict future movements

(i) day-to-day movements, mainly random 'noise';
(ii) short-term movements, which extend from a few days to periods lasting several months;
(iii) long-term movements, characterised by persistent upward and/or downward trends.

The longer the forecasting time horizon, the less accurate the prediction is likely to be. However, for most firms, a major part of their forecasting needs are short-to-medium term, so 'expert' forecasting may have some role to play. Forecasting for the long term, however, depends on the economic fundamentals of exchange rate determination, although some people believe in the existence of long-term waves in currency movements (at least, when they float!). A major flaw of technical analysis is that it is purely mechanical, with no attempt to provide supporting theory regarding explanation of causation.

Forecasting in practice

Most leading banks offer FX forecasting services, and many MNCs employ in-house forecasting staff. The value of these activities is open to question, but this really depends on the motivation for forecasting. A long-term forecast may be needed to underpin an investment decision in a foreign country. A forecast based on long-term fundamentals may not need to be perfectly accurate but may help in analysing more fully the risks surrounding the decision and its implementation.

Conversely, short-term forecasts may be needed to hedge debtors or creditors for settlement in a month or so. In such cases, long-term fundamentals may be less important than market-related technical factors, e.g. closing of positions, political factors or 'sentiment' in the market. The required degree of accuracy increases as the prospect of loss is more immediate and less remedial action is possible. In general, long-term forecasts are based on economic models reflecting fundamentals, while short-term forecasts tend to rely on technical analysis. Chartists often attempt to correlate exchange rate changes with various other factors regardless of the economic rationale for the co-movement.

UK companies use pound strength to hedge forex risk

The pound may not yet have risen beyond $1.30, but for Norfolk-based picture frames maker Nielsen Bainbridge there is no time to lose.

Last week, it purchased sterling hedges worth €950,000 and $650,000 against the euro and the dollar, which mature at the end of the year, capitalising on the recent recovery in the pound. 'We took advantage of the rise in exchange rates,' says finance director Sarah Burdett.

Sterling's newfound strength is a relief for UK importers such as Nielsen Bainbridge, enabling them to pick up the phone to forex specialists for the first time in months to discuss sterling hedges – a trend now being widely reported by currency hedging advisers.

Yet the pound's post-Brexit decline from $1.50 has been a test of nerve for Nielsen Bainbridge and many other importers. The company's suppliers are located in Europe or China. 'Currency therefore has a big impact on our business and the margins we can obtain,' says Ms Burdett.

When the pound was stronger, Nielsen Bainbridge could hedge sterling over three months to cover short-term currency needs. Currency hedges enable institutions, businesses and individuals to lock in an exchange rate over a certain period regardless of how the rate moves during that time.

Then came the UK's Brexit vote, which Ms Burdett says delivered an 'unexpected shock', driving up costs that forced the company to raise prices.

Hedging activity may be on the rise again, and the UK corporate mood is a bit brighter. 'A good percentage of clients is considering or has locked in either short or longer-term hedges,' says Michael McGowan of Bibby Financial Services. Some of its clients even ask why, if sterling is rising, they would want to be locked into a hedge.

They should take heed. 'Sterling is still some 15 to 20 per cent from where we were pre-Brexit, so companies have the same sort of issues,' says Danny Goldblum of HSBC.

Source: Blitz, R. (2017) UK companies use pound strength to hedge forex risk. *Financial Times*, 16 May. © The Financial Times Limited 2018. All rights reserved.

FX forecasting and market efficiency

The likelihood of forecasts being consistently useful or profitable depends on whether the FX markets are efficient. The more efficient the market, the more likely that FX rates are random walks, with past behaviour having no bearing on future movements. The less efficient the market, the more likely that forecasters will 'get lucky' and stumble on a key relationship that happens to hold for a while. Yet, if such a relationship really exists, others will soon discover and exploit it, and the market will regain its efficiency regarding that item of information.

The role of central banks

A key requirement of market efficiency is that all market players are rational wealth seekers. This is often not the case with a major market participant, the central bank that tries to raise or lower its currency by buying or selling in the open market, often in defiance of market trends and sentiment. Evidence exists that at times when central banks intervene, markets become less efficient, and it is possible to make money by betting against them. This happened most notably on 'Black Wednesday' in 1992, when sterling was evicted from the ERM despite the Bank of England spending billions of GBP-worth of foreign exchange and raising bank base rate from 10 per cent to 15 per cent. However, these opportunities are likely to be only very short-term phenomena.

Forecasting in practice

The jury is still out on FX forecasting – it should not be possible to outguess the market, but sometimes it works: the question is 'when?' Meanwhile, some businesspeople derive comfort from having 'expert' forecasts available, possibly as a focus of blame! The implications for hedging are hazy – if one believes in PPP in the short term, then hedging is pointless, but PPP seems only to operate in the longer term and with unclear time lags. So, for peace of mind, most firms try to devise a hedging strategy.

Morgan analysts boost euro forecast

Morgan Stanley analysts have turned decidedly bullish on the common currency, ditching their call for euro-dollar parity and instead forecasting an almost 5 per cent rally through the end of 2017 amid a strengthening economy and dimming political risk.

The New York investment bank said on Monday that it expects the euro to jump to $1.18 by the end of this year, and rise further to $1.19 in the first three months of 2018. That compares with forecasts as recently as June 1 of $0.97 and $1, respectively. It traded at $1.1248 in early US action.

Morgan's currencies strategists said 'political stability and growth-related equity market inflows should boost' the currency.

Wall Street's sentiment on the currency bloc has shifted dramatically over the past few months. Its economy has outpaced developed-market rivals, like the US, this year, surprising many economists who were expecting weaker growth. Political headwinds have also eased, after last month's election of Emmanuel Macron as French president and as German chancellor Angela Merkel has polled well ahead of an election there this autumn.

Source: Samson, A. (2017) Morgan analysts boost euro forecast; see currency at $1.18 by year-end. *Financial Times*, 5 June. © The Financial Times Limited 2018. All rights reserved.

The Economist magazine publishes an annual survey on PPP. This is based on the global price of a Big Mac (The Big Mac Index), and purports to identify – in a tongue-in-cheek fashion – cases where PPP does not apply between currencies. This has recently been extended to cover the worldwide price of Starbucks coffee, to widen the range of goods examined. Results are broadly similar although, of course, a more rigorous approach (as *The Economist* concedes) would scrutinise the prices of a standard 'basket' of goods, as in national price indices.

13.7 DEVISING A FOREIGN EXCHANGE MANAGEMENT (FEM) STRATEGY

■ Hedging translation exposure: balance sheet items

Total exchange exposure is made up of cash flowing across a national frontier plus the assets and liabilities of the company that are denominated in a foreign currency.

An international treasurer who does not believe the theories outlined earlier might decide to hedge all foreign currency transactions plus the total net worth of all foreign subsidiaries. This strategy is over-elaborate and very expensive but is adopted by many companies, particularly those dealing in currencies that fluctuate widely in value over short periods.

Figure 13.2 illustrates a more systematic approach. The basic strategy is to remove from consideration all items that are self-hedging so far as exchange rate risk is concerned, and to concentrate attention on those cash flows, assets and liabilities that are subject to exchange rate risk in the short term.

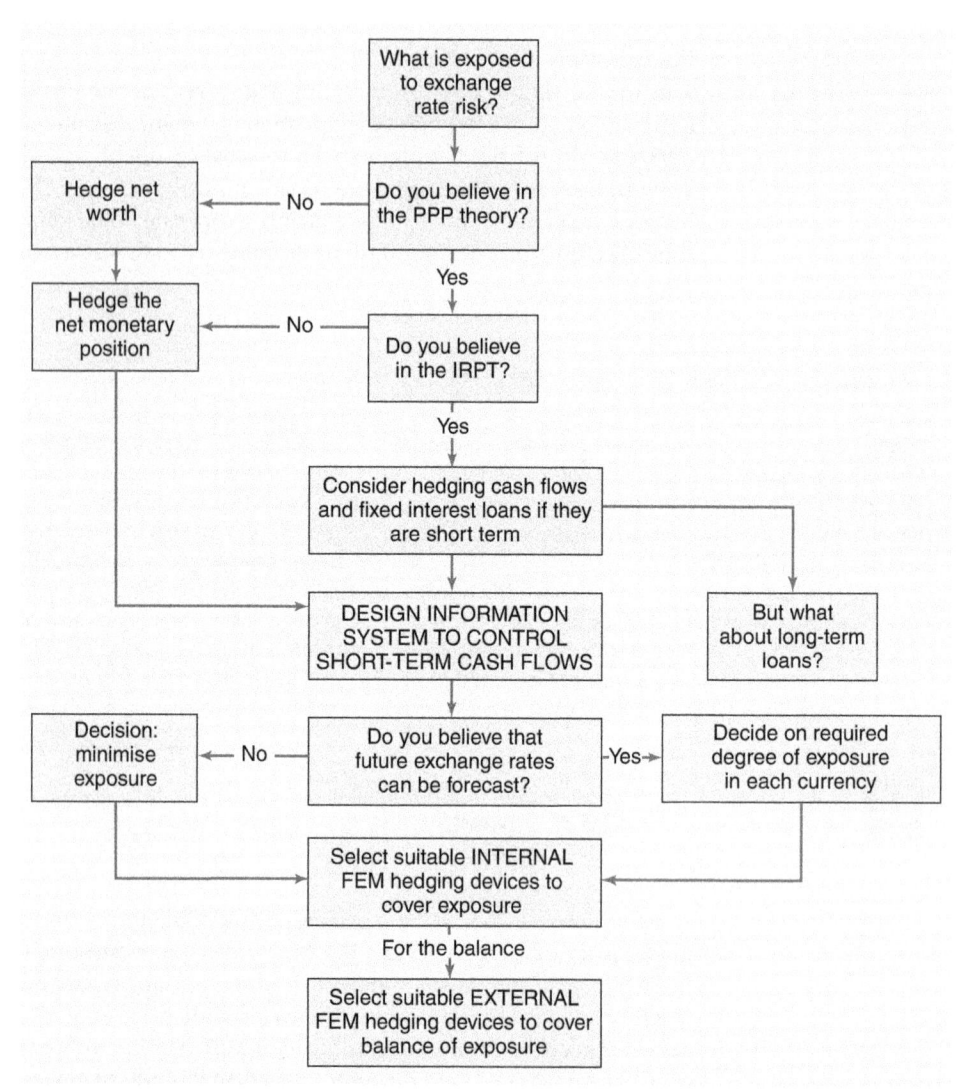

Figure 13.2 Flow chart demonstrating a logical approach towards devising a foreign exchange management strategy

(Based on McRae, 1996)

We start with a position where all cash flows, assets and liabilities denominated in foreign currency values are assumed to be subject to exposure. Let us now try to eliminate some of these items from the exposure equation. First, we eliminate all non-monetary assets such as land, buildings and inventory. These should float in value with internal inflation. The rate of adjustment in value will vary, and internationally traded goods will jump in local value faster than the value of land, but eventually, the prices of all of these non-monetary assets should rise to compensate for the fall in value of the local currency. PPP relates inflation differences to changes in exchange rates. In time, the asset or liability denominated in the foreign currency will rise in value sufficiently to compensate for the fall in the foreign currency value. In other words, the owner of the asset could sell it for more foreign currency units, each commanding a lesser external value than before. The total in terms of home currency will remain unchanged.

Self-assessment activity 13.6

Langer plc, a UK firm, is worried about a fall in the Australian dollar by 5 per cent, compared to the present A$1.75 per £1, that might inflict translation losses regarding its A$100 million assets located in Adelaide. Why should it not worry?

(UK inflation is 2 per cent. Australian inflation is 7 per cent.)

(Answer in Appendix A)

Non-monetary assets are thus self-hedging at least in the long term. If the asset has to be sold in the short term and the foreign cash exchanged into local currency, the amount then becomes a part of transaction exposure because a real loss might be involved.

Short-term loans can, for the most part, also be considered self-hedged. The higher or lower interest rate on the foreign currency loan is a kind of insurance policy against the future fall or rise of the 'away' currency in terms of the 'home' currency. A forward contract could be taken out to cover the risk, but this would be a needless expense (given that spreads are wider on forward transactions), since the forward rate is an unbiased predictor of the future spot rate. On average, the forward contracts would make neither a profit nor a loss.

Long-term loans are more problematic. A fervent believer in the Open Fisher Theory would claim that the long-term loan, like the short, is also self-hedged. The interest rate difference is the market's best guess as to the future changes in the value of the currency. A lower-rate loan suggests a higher capital sum to repay in the home currency. A higher-rate loan suggests a smaller capital sum.

If in doubt about monetary assets or liabilities being self-hedging, one solution is to calculate the 'net monetary asset position' in each currency and make sure it is either in balance or in the 'right' direction. *In other words, if it is predicted that a currency will fall in value against GBP, the firm should owe money in that currency. If it is predicted that a currency will rise in value against GBP, then it should be owed money in that currency.* This might require some juggling with the financing mix of the firm via 'currency swaps', which we discuss later in the chapter.

The key problem in currency risk management is thus to identify the various types of exposure facing the company and then to hedge any unwanted exposure risks. Non-monetary assets and short-term loans in foreign currency are for the most part self-hedged. The exchange risk involved in financing with foreign loans and bonds is less clear. With regard to transaction exposure, a currency information system needs to be designed and installed to identify estimated short-term cash flow exposure in each currency.

■ Transaction exposure: hedging the cash flows

currency information system
An information system set up to identify values that are exposed to currency risk, e.g. cash in- and outflows and asset and liability values

The first step in identifying and hedging cash flow exposure in foreign currency is thus to set up a **currency information system**. The control of currency risk is much simplified if this information system is centralised, but this is not a necessary condition of efficient currency management.

Once this system is in place, the company must decide whether it (1) believes that future exchange rates can be forecast and (2) will permit speculation in currency. If the answer to either question is 'no', then the company must seek to minimise the exposure position in all currencies. If a profit-maximising strategy is adopted, the company will use currency forecasts to decide on an optimal position in each foreign currency. If

risk-minimising policy
A foreign exchange policy designed to eliminate, as far as possible, the firm's exposure to currency risk

the company believes that currency forecasting is impossible, or not profitable, then it has to adopt a **risk-minimising policy**. The aim will be to reduce exposure in all currencies to a minimum unless the cost of this policy is prohibitive.

Once the estimated cash flows in each currency have been identified, the next step is to consolidate the data. The individual flows are netted to arrive at the estimated net balance in each currency for each future period. Monthly estimates for six months ahead are the most common requirement, but large companies holding, or trading in, many currencies may require weekly or even daily reports (especially if speculative positions are opened).

If the company believes that currency forecasting is both possible and profitable, it must decide, in the light of current currency forecasts, the degree of imbalance desirable in each currency in which it trades. Even if forecasting is thought to be possible and profitable, the company might decide to prohibit currency speculation as a matter of principle. Many UK multinationals take this position. In the past, US multinationals have been more willing than similar UK companies to speculate in currency.

The next step is to convert the 'natural' exposure position arising from normal trading into the 'desired' exposure position. This is done by using various currency hedging devices, some of which are internal to the firm and others external. Prindl (1978), who introduced the distinction between internal and external hedging, also pointed out that internal hedging is almost invariably cheaper than external hedging. The international treasurer should first adjust the 'natural' exposure position using internal techniques and use the more expensive external techniques only after the internal hedging possibilities have been exhausted.

Volvo to build krona hedges

Volvo Cars is considering exporting vehicles from China to the US and even building an American factory as it seeks to counter the currency effects from a strong Swedish krona. Stefan Jacoby, chief executive, said the strength of the krona – the best-performing significant currency over the summer – was a 'disadvantage' in Volvo's fight with German premium car makers such as BMW, Audi and Mercedes. 'We need natural hedging in US dollars. That could be production [a factory] or sourcing or exports out of China,' he told the *Financial Times*.

Volvo, based in Gothenburg but owned by Chinese car maker Geely, is preparing to open two car plants and an engine factory in the coming years in China. The first is set to open next year in Chengdu, the capital of Sichuan province in central China, while a second is planned for Daqing in the north-west of the country. An engine plant in Zhangjiakou, near Beijing, will follow.

Any natural hedging in the US would have to cover about 10–15 per cent of Volvo's production, he added. Volvo produced 450,000 cars last year, generating SKr125bn ($19bn) in sales. However, Mr Jacoby hinted that importing cars from China and boosting local purchasing in the US might not be enough over time. 'It could be an interim solution but maybe not a sustainable solution'.

Mr Jacoby has scotched any suggestion that Volvo could cut back on investments in the next few years as it looks to almost double the number of cars it sells to 800,000 by 2020, including a fourfold increase in China to 200,000. He acknowledged the risk he was taking: 'We have worsened our break-even point, obviously. This is a big risk that we are taking in a period of unpredictability. When the markets are going south, it is an even bigger exposure.'

The Volvo car manufacturing factory in South Carolina will start manufacturing US-made Volvo cars by the end of 2018.

Source: Milne, R. (2012) Volvo aims to mitigate strong krona. *Financial Times*, 10 September. © The Financial Times Limited 2018. All rights reserved.

13.8 INTERNAL HEDGING TECHNIQUES

Internal hedging techniques exploit characteristics of the company's trading relationships without recourse to the external currency or money markets. Most are simple in concept and operation.

Managing Currency Risk

netting
Offsetting a firm's internal currency inflows and outflows in the same currency to minimise the net flow in either direction

Netting applies where the head office and its foreign subsidiaries net off intra-organisational currency flows at the end of each period, leaving only the balance exposed to risk and hence in need of hedging. Netting is illustrated in the following simple example.

A UK-based multinational has a German operating subsidiary. In a particular month, it transfers components worth €20 million to Germany. In the same month, the subsidiary transfers finished goods worth €40 million to the United Kingdom. With netting, the company need only make a net currency transfer of €20 million rather than making two separate transactions totalling €60 million As well as reducing exposure, netting saves transfer and commission costs, but it requires a two-way flow in the same currency.

bilateral netting
Operated by pairs of firms in the same group netting off their respective positions regarding payables and receivables

multilateral netting
A central treasury department operation to minimise net flows of currency throughout an organisation

Bilateral netting applies where pairs of companies in the same group net off their own positions regarding payables and receivables, often without the involvement of the central treasury. If the previous company also had a Swiss subsidiary, a bilateral netting arrangement could operate between the German and the Swiss subsidiaries. **Multilateral netting** is performed by the central treasury where several subsidiaries interact with the head office. Subsidiaries are required to notify the treasury of the intra-organisational flows of receivables and payments. Again, a common currency is required. To illustrate this, Oilex is a UK-based oil company with an exploration division based in Norway, major interests in the United States and chemical plants in the United Kingdom. The group treasury 'holds the ring' at the centre of this nexus, as shown in Figure 13.3. All intra-group transactions are conducted in USD, which is the operating currency of the oil industry.

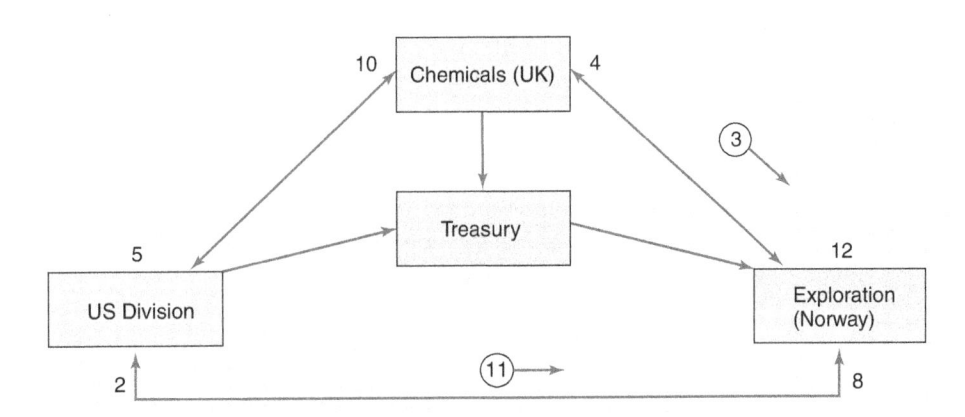

Figure 13.3 Illustration of multi-lateral netting

Table 13.2 shows transactions expected for one particular month. In total, currency flows of $41 million would be required with no treasury intervention. By multilateral netting, the treasury can reduce the exposed flows by $27 million. Such a system produces greatest benefits when the inter-subsidiary positions are most similar, and where payments are made directly to the relevant subsidiaries, thus avoiding cash transfers into and then out of the treasury. In this case, chemicals would transfer $3 million direct to exploration and the US operation would transfer $11 million likewise, resulting in total flows of only $14 million.

Some experts dispute whether netting is a true hedging technique, rather than a cost-saving device, especially where the netted currency differs from the parent's

Table 13.2 Oilex's internal currency flows

		Paying subsidiary ($m)				
		UK	US	Norway	Total	Net
Receiving	UK	–	10	4	+14	–3
subsidiary	US	5	–	2	+7	–11
($m)	Norway	12	8	–	+20	+14
	Total	–17	–18	–6	41	
	Net	–3	–11	+14		

Source: The Times, 29/08/2007, © The Times/NI Syndication.

reporting currency. However, if it does result in lower values of currency being shipped across the exchanges, then it is undeniable that it is capable of saving considerable banking and money-transmission costs.

Matching is similar in concept to netting, but involves third parties as well as intra-group affiliates. A company tries to match its currency inflows by amount and timing with its expected outflows. For example, a company exporting to the United States and thus anticipating USD receipts could match this payable by arranging a USD outflow, perhaps by contracting to import from the same country. Clearly, as with netting, a two-way flow of currency is desirable – '**natural matching**'. 'Parallel matching' can be achieved by matching in terms of currencies that tend to move closely together over time, e.g. matching USD outflows to Canadian dollar inflows. Matching can also be achieved by offsetting balance sheet items against profit and loss account items. For example, a company with a long-term cash inflow stream in USD may also borrow in USD, to create an offsetting outflow of interest and capital payments. Earlier in the chapter, we observed Compass Group plc doing exactly this.

Leading and lagging currency payments is done to speed up or delay payments when a change in the value of a currency is expected. This involves forecasting future exchange rate movements and therefore carries an element of speculation. Where payables are involved, the transfer is speeded up if the foreign currency is expected to appreciate against the domestic currency and slowed down if the overseas currency is expected to depreciate. A UK company importing from the United States at a time when the USD was falling against sterling may well have tried to lag payments. Leading and lagging within a group of companies is relatively easy to arrange, but when dealing with other firms, this can be problematic. A customer buying on credit will advance payment only if offered an inducement such as a discount for early payment. The same applies to delaying payment to an external supplier – the danger is loss of goodwill. Even for intra-firm transactions, there may still be local regulations and currency controls that limit flexibility.

Currency transfers by companies into and out of less-developed countries, whose currencies tend to be weak, are closely scrutinised by the governments of those countries because of the de-stabilising effect they may have on their currency. In some cases, they are illegal, both for their ability to exacerbate currency weakness and also because of the effect on local minority shareholders of an overseas subsidiary. Leading a payment from the overseas subsidiary to the UK parent will raise the GBP profits of the parent, but lower the overseas currency profits of the subsidiary, thus damaging local shareholders' interests, which risks alienating local opinion and antagonising the host government. This is one reason why repatriation of profits from overseas subsidiaries is often closely controlled by foreign governments.

---

matching
Offsetting a currency inflow in one currency, e.g. a stream of revenues, by a corresponding stream of costs, thus leaving only the profit element unmatched. Firms may also match operating cash flows against financial flows, e.g. a stream of interest and capital payments resulting from overseas borrowing in the same currency

natural matching
A natural match is achieved where the firm has a two-way cash flow in the same currency due to the structure of its operations, e.g. selling in a currency in which it sources supplies

leading
Advancing before the due date a payable denominated in a foreign currency that is expected to strengthen, or advancing a receivable in a currency expected to weaken

Chocolate maker cuts euro exposure

Until recently, Malachy McReynolds, managing director of Bristol-based chocolate maker Elizabeth Shaw, traded in euros, even outside the eurozone. But, in the past six weeks, the company, which exports about 10 per cent of its £10m sales, has insisted on being paid in sterling, or even the buyer's local currency rather than the euro. 'We took a policy decision to reduce our currency risk,' he said.

The company is reluctant to take out forward cover from the bank because it is too costly. Instead it uses a 'natural hedge'. The company not only sells into the EU but also sources part of its product range from euro area manufacturers on a contract basis. 'So we always look at our net euro exposure. If necessary we ask our euro area suppliers to invoice us in sterling,' said Mr McReynolds.

It is not just diversifying export markets that reduces euro exposure – companies can also switch suppliers. BSA Machine Tools in Birmingham used to buy parts from the Luxembourg branch of Fanuc, the Japanese manufacturer, paying in euros, but now buys from its UK branch.

FT *Source:* Bounds, A.; Murray, J. and Tighe, C. (2012) Businesses look beyond EU for growth. *Financial Times*, 29 July. © The Financial Times Limited 2018. All rights reserved.

Self-assessment activity 13.7

Delete as appropriate.

Leading is advancing outflows in a *strong/weak* currency and advancing inflows in a *strong/weak* currency. Lagging is delaying inflows in a *strong/weak* currency and delaying outflows in a *strong/weak* currency.

(Answer in Appendix A)

---

price variation
Adjustment of a firm's pricing policy to take into account expected foreign exchange rate movements

The UK exporter might also consider a pre-emptive **price variation**. If it expects GBP to strengthen against the currency of an overseas customer, it may raise the contract price. However, this may have adverse consequences for sales, especially if competitors are prepared to shoulder currency risk by accepting payment in the overseas currency. Conversely, the acceptability of this ploy may be greater if the exporter quotes a price based on the forward rate rather than the spot rate when setting the value of the contract. Generally, however, such price variations require a strong competitive position in overseas markets. For this reason, another such device, switching the currency in which the contract is denominated to a third currency, say USD, also has to be used with caution. However, traders in basic commodities (most notably, oil) have no such flexibility, since most of these are priced in USD.

risk-sharing
An arrangement where the two parties to an import/export deal agree to share the risk, and thus the impact of unexpected exchange rate movements

Risk-sharing is a contractual arrangement whereby the buyer and seller agree in advance to share between them the impact of currency movements. This is recommended when the two parties want to build a long-term relationship. However, if exchange rate variations exceed tolerable limits, the arrangement may have to be renegotiated.

It might work like this. Firm X supplies Firm B in another country. They may agree that all transactions will be made at the ruling spot rate between the two parties' respective currencies. If, however, the rate at settlement varies by up to, say, 5 per cent either side of the original spot rate, X may accept the transaction exposure. If the rate varies by, say, 5–10 per cent of the original spot, they may share the difference equally, but for variations in excess of 10 per cent, the agreement may become void. Harley Davidson is known to operate this policy with foreign importers.

re-invoicing centre
A corporate subsidiary set up usually in an off-shore location to manage transaction exposure arising from trade between separate divisions of the parent firm

A **Re-invoicing centres**. A re-invoicing centre (RIC) is a separate corporate subsidiary that manages from one location, often off-shore, all the transaction exposure arising from intra-company trading.

For example, a manufacturing unit may sell goods to distribution subsidiaries of its parent firm indirectly by selling first to the re-invoicing centre, which then re-sells the goods to the distribution subsidiary. Title to the goods passes to the RIC but the goods are shipped directly from the manufacturing subsidiary to the distributor. The RIC thus manages the transactions on paper but keeps no physical stocks. All transactions exposure resides with the RIC.

A problem may arise due to allegations of profit-shifting via transfer pricing. To avoid such allegations, the RIC may sell at cost plus a commission for its services. The resale price is commonly the manufacturer's price times the forward exchange rate for the date when settlement by the distributor is expected.

RICs offer the major benefit of concentrating the management of all FX transactions in one location. As a result, the multinational corporation (MNC) can develop specialist expertise in judging which hedging technique is optimal at any one time. However, it should avoid conducting business with other firms in its country of location in order to establish non-resident status.

13.9 SIMPLE EXTERNAL HEDGING TECHNIQUES

forward contract
An agreement to sell or buy at a fixed price at some time in the future

credit risk
The risk that a foreign customer might not pay up as agreed on time or at all

counterparty risk
The risk that the bank which is party to a hedging transaction such as a forward contract may not deliver the agreed amount of currency at the agreed time

The best known external hedging technique is the **forward contract**. It involves pre-selling/buying a specific amount of currency at a rate specified now for delivery at a specified time in the future. It is a way of totally removing risk of currency variation by locking in the rate quoted today by the forward market. However, there remain the risks of the trading partner defaulting (**credit risk**) and that of failure of the bank that arranges the deal (**counterparty risk**).

Consider the case of a UK exporter entering an export contract in February for $10 million with a company in Denver. The companies agree on payment in three months' time, i.e. in May. The current spot rate is $2.00:£1, valuing the contract at $10m/2.00 = £5m. If the exporter is concerned by the possibility of a decline in the USD versus GBP, it will look carefully at the rate quoted for three-month delivery of USD. Assume the forward market quotes '2c discount'. The forward outright is thus:

Spot $2.00 plus 2.0c = $2.02:£1

If the exporter believes in the predictive accuracy of the forward market, it may decide to sell forward the anticipated $10 million receipt for $10m/2.02 = £4.95m. This involves taking a discount on the current spot value of the deal. Hedging costs the exporter £50,000, 1 per cent of the original value of the deal (although a higher proportion of his profits), but this may look trivial beside the losses that could materialise if GBP strengthens further than this. Conversely, the exporter is excluded from any gains if the USD appreciates in value.

forward option
A forward currency contract that incorporates a flexible settlement date between two fixed dates

If the exporter is unsure about the precise payment date by its customer, it may enter a **forward option**. In this case, the bank leaves the currency settlement date open but books the deal at the worst forward rate ruling over the period concerned. Say the two companies had agreed on payment 'sometime over the next three months', but the exporter knows that the customer may delay payment for six months. The relevant forward quotations are:

1 month:	0.5c dis	Outright:	2.005
2 months:	1.0c dis	Outright:	2.010
3 months:	2.0c dis	Outright:	2.020
6 months:	3.0c dis	Outright:	2.030

The worst rate for the exporter is the six-month rate, so the deal will be booked for $10m/2.03 = £4.93m, again, a minor increase in cost. If the customer pays up at any other time, the bank is committed to paying the exporter the amount agreed in the forward contract when the $10 million is handed over.

foreign currency swap
A way of using the forward markets to adjust the maturity date of an initially-agreed contract with a bank

Another way of covering uncertainty over settlement dates is to undertake a **foreign currency swap**. The Bank of International Settlements (BIS, www.bis.org) defines a swap as follows:

> Foreign exchange swaps commit two counterparties to the exchange of two cash flows and involve the sale of one currency for another in the spot market with the simultaneous repurchase of the first currency in the forward market.

An exporter can take forward cover to a specified date, but if a later settlement date than this is agreed, it can extend the contract to the newly-agreed date. For example, a **forward–forward swap** is needed if our exporter covers ahead from February until May, but if, in March, a firm settlement date is agreed for June. Contractually, it has to meet the first contract maturing in May, and then take cover for a further month. This is done in March by buying $10 million two months forward, i.e. for delivery in May to meet the existing contract, and by selling $10 million three months forward for delivery in June. In this case, the exporter swaps the maturity date and ends up holding three separate contracts. Instead, it could adopt the riskier alternative of a **spot–forward swap**, fulfilling the May contract by buying the $10 million on the spot market, and also arranging to sell $10 million one month forward, i.e. in June. The BIS estimated average daily foreign exchange swap transactions at US$2,228 billion in its 2013 survey, 42 per cent of all foreign exchange-related transactions.

forward–forward swap
Where the original forward contract is supplemented by new contracts that have the effect of extending the maturity date of the original one

spot–forward swap
A less comprehensive forward swap that involves speculation on the future spot market

money market cover
Involves an exporter borrowing on the money market (i.e. creating a liability) in the same currency in which it expects to receive a payment

Money market cover involves the exporter creating a liability in the form of a short-term loan in the same currency that it expects to receive. The amount to borrow will be sufficient to make the amount receivable coincide with the principal of the loan plus interest. Assume the Eurodollar rate of interest, the annual rate payable on loans denominated in USD, is 8 per cent, i.e. 2.00 per cent over three months. The UK exporter would borrow ($10m/1.02 = $9.80m). This would be converted into GBP at the spot rate – in our example, $2.00:£1 – to realise ($9.80m/2.00) = £4.90m. This looks like a considerable discount on the spot value of the export deal (£5.00m), but the GBP proceeds of this operation can be invested for three months to defray the cost. Obviously, if the exporter could invest at a rate in excess of 8 per cent p.a., it would profit from this, but IRP should make this impossible, i.e. if USD sells at a forward discount, interest rates in New York should exceed those in London. If USD should unexpectedly fall in value against GBP, lower-than-expected receipts from the US contract are offset by the lower GBP payment required to repay the Eurodollar loan.

An alternative to a one-off loan to cover a specific contract is for the exporter to operate an overdraft denominated in one or a set of overseas currencies. The trader will aim to maintain the balance of the overdraft as sales are made, and use the sales proceeds as and when received to reduce the overdraft. This is a convenient technique where a company makes a series of small overseas sales, many with uncertain payment dates. A converse arrangement, i.e. a currency bank deposit account, may be arranged by a company with receivables in excess of payables.

Export invoice finance is a fast-expanding business among UK traders. Data published by the UK-based Asset Based Finance Association (ABFA) for the year-ended 31 December 2016, estimated export factoring at £1.27 billion, an increase of 4 per cent on 2015, but put export invoice discounting at £22.44 billion, a huge increase of 30 per cent on 2015. (www.abfa.org.uk). The international factor can provide many services to the small company, including absorbing the exchange rate risk. Once a foreign contract is signed, the factor pays, say, 80 per cent of the foreign value to the UK exporter in GBP. If the exchange rate moves against the UK company before receipt of the foreign currency, the factor absorbs the loss. In compensation, the factor also takes any gain arising from a change in rates. Factors make use of overseas 'correspondent' factors, enabling clients to benefit from expert local knowledge of overseas buyers' creditworthiness. Overseas factoring is usually expensive but offers the benefits of lower administration and credit collection costs.

Export receivables that involve settlement via **Bills of Exchange** can also be discounted with a bank in the customer's country and the foreign currency proceeds repatriated at the relevant spot rate. Alternatively, the bill can be discounted in the exporter's home country, enabling the exporter to receive settlement directly in home currency.

The most sophisticated external hedging facilities involve derivatives such as options, futures and swaps. These are treated in more detail in the next section.

Farmers embrace hedging to minimise currency risk

The recent rally in sterling may reflect an upswing in the fortunes of the UK economy, but it comes at an unfortunate time for one sector: farming. The exchange rate at which EU subsidies totalling more than €3bn are paid to about 200,000 British farmers is fixed on the last day of September each year, adding currency risk to the vagaries of drought, floods and commodity prices they already contend with.

Almost all opt to receive the single farm payment [SFP], as the subsidy is termed, in sterling. Most do nothing to mitigate the risk. 'We like to keep things simple,' said a spokesman for the Royal Society for the Protection of Birds, one of the biggest recipients, which receives a single payment of more than £1m.

But a sizeable minority now take out forward contracts to fix an acceptable exchange rate, with some following forex markets as closely as they do the weather. 'In the daytime, if I come in for lunch, I'll watch [the exchange rate] and when I'm happy with what I see and what I'm going to get, I hedge it,' said Llyr Hughes, who breeds Limousin cattle and early-lambing ewes on a 450-acre farm. Their single farm payment of about £30,000 represents roughly 40 per cent of profits.

Source: Strauss, D. (2013) Farmers embrace hedging to minimise currency risks. *Financial Times*, 29 September. © The Financial Times Limited 2018. All rights reserved.

13.10 MORE COMPLEX TECHNIQUES

■ Currency options

A currency option confers the right, but (unlike the forward contract) not the obligation, to buy or sell a fixed amount of a particular currency at or between two specified future dates at an agreed exchange rate (the **strike price**).

call option
A financial derivative that gives the buyer the right but not the obligation to buy a particular commodity or currency at a specific future date

A **call option** gives the purchaser of the option the right to buy, while a put option gives the right to sell. In each case, the buyer of the option pays the 'writer' of the option a premium. Options traded through exchanges are written in specified contract sizes: for example, on the Philadelphia Stock Exchange (PHLX – now owned by NASDAQ OMX), the contract size is 10,000 units of foreign currency except for Japanese yen (1,000,000 units). Most exchanges offer a limited number of alternative exercise prices and maturity dates. PHLX trades USD options against the British pound, the Australian dollar, the Canadian dollar, the Japanese yen and the Swiss franc, as well as euro contracts. Delivery dates are for the quarter months of March, June, September and December plus the two immediately upcoming months. For non-standard options, the would-be purchaser may have to shop around for a customised quotation on the **over-the-counter** (OTC) market. This may be necessary for unusual or 'exotic' currencies.

over-the-counter
An over-the-counter transaction, e.g. the purchase of an option, where the terms are tailor-made to suit the requirements of the purchaser

A '**European option**' can be exercised only at the specified maturity date, while an '**American option**' can be exercised at any time up to the specified expiry date. If an option is not exercised, it lapses and the premium is lost. However, the appeal of an option is that the maximum loss is limited to the cost of the premium, while the purchaser retains the upside potential. The size of the premium depends on the difference between the current exchange rate and the strike price (for an unlikely strike price, premiums will be very low), the volatility of the two currencies, the period to maturity and, for OTC contracts, the size of the contract.

Here is an example of how a trader could use a currency option for hedging purposes. A UK exporter sells goods for $5.95 million to a customer in Baltimore in June 2014 for settlement in September. The contract is worth £3.5 million when valued at spot of $1.70:£1, but the exporter is concerned that sterling might appreciate before settlement, thus eroding the profit margin. In this case, it might purchase a call option on GBP, i.e. an option to sell USD in exchange for GBP.

Imagine that a leading exchange sells contracts in £10,000 units and quotes a strike price of 1.73 cents for call contracts in June for settlement in September (The quotation convention followed is that one point = $100, so a premium quotation of, say, 2.11 would correspond to $211.

Choosing the $1.70 strike price gives the exporter insurance against the value of sterling going higher than $1.70. The cost of purchasing September options is:

$$\text{Number of contracts} = \frac{\$5.95m}{\$1.70} \div £10,000 = 350$$

$$\text{Cost of option} = \$100 \times 1.73 \times 350 = \$60,550$$

i.e. £35,617 at spot.

If the spot rate in September is less than $1.70, the option is not worth exercising, and is said to be 'out of the money', while if the spot is over $1.70, say $1.75, the option is 'in the money'. In the last case, export earnings of $5.95 million can be sold at $1.70 to realise £3.5 million, compared with a spot value of:

$$\frac{\$5.95m}{\$1.75} = £3.4m$$

Although the option has cost £35,617, it has prevented the exporter from losing (£3.5m − £3.4m) = £100,000. In this case, there is a net gain, allowing for the premium, of (£100,000 − £35,617) = £64,383.

It is important to appreciate that options are 'zero-sum games' – what the holder wins, the writer loses, and vice versa. It is relatively unusual to use currency options to hedge ongoing trading exposures – options are complex, they are often expensive compared to using the forward market and it is time-consuming to monitor an American option to judge whether it is worth closing out the position prematurely. Options tend to be used to cover major isolated expenditures, e.g. the cost of completing the acquisition of an overseas company or the phased payments in a major overseas construction project.

The Nasdaq trader website (www.nasdaqtrader.com) gives trading information on options.

■ Example: Hogan plc

Hogan plc exports computer components valued at 18 million Australian dollars (AUD) to Dundee Proprietary in Australia on three months' credit. The current spot exchange rate is A$1.80 vs. £1. Because of recent volatility in the foreign exchange markets, Hogan's directors are worried that a fall in the AUD could wipe out their profits on the deal. Three alternative hedging strategies have been suggested:

(i) using a forward market hedge;
(ii) using a money market hedge;
(iii) using an option hedge.

Hogan's treasurer discovers the following information:

- The three-month forward rate is A$1.805 vs. £1.
- Hogan could borrow in AUD at 9 per cent interest (annual rate), and could deposit in London at 4 per cent p.a.
- A three-month American put option to sell A$18 million at an exercise rate of A$1.81 vs. £1 could be purchased at a premium of £200,000 on the London OTC option market.

Required

Show how each hedge would work out, assuming the following spot rates apply in three months' time:

(a) A$1.78 vs. £1;
(b) A$1.82 vs. £1.

In your answer, consider whether interest rate parity applies as between these two currencies.

Answer

(i) The forward hedge

The bank contracts to buy A$18m for GBP in three months' time. The sterling value = (A$18m/1.805 = £9.97m).

(a) At future spot of A$1.78, Hogan could have received (A$18m/1.78 = £10.11m), involving an opportunity cost of:

(£10.11m − £9.97m) = £0.14m (1.4% of contract value)

(b) With future spot at A$1.82, Hogan would receive (A$18m/1.82 = £9.89m). The hedge offers a gain of:

(£9.97m − £9.89m) = £0.08m

(ii) The money market hedge

The three-month interest rate is (9%/4) = 2.25%. Hogan will borrow in AUD sufficient to accumulate at 2.25% to the AUD value of its receipts, i.e.:

(A$18m/1.0225) = A$17.60m

Exchanged for GBP at today's spot rate, this is worth:

(A$17.60m/1.80) = £9.78m

This can be invested at 4% p.a., i.e. (4%/4) = 1% over three months, accumulating to £9.78m(1.01) = £9.88m.

(a) At future spot of A$1.78 vs. £1, the unhedged income = £10.11m. The loss using the money market hedge is:

(£10.11m − £9.88m) = £0.23m (2.3% of the original contract value)

(b) At future spot of A$1.82 vs. £1, the unhedged income = £9.89m. Hence, the hedge still just loses, viz:

(£9.89m − £9.88m) = −£0.01m

Apparently, IRP does not apply! With a difference in interest rates of 5% p.a., the forward rate should show the AUD trading at a greater discount than just half a cent, i.e. the AUD is overvalued on the forward market. If these interest rates prevail, and IRP does reassert itself, we might conclude that the forward market is overstating the future spot rate (from an AUD perspective).

(iii) The OTC option hedge

(a) At future spot of A$1.78 vs. £1, the option is 'out of the money', i.e. it is better to sell AUD at spot rather than exercise the options at A$1.81 = £1. Hogan's unhedged income is £10.11m. Net of the option premium, the proceeds are:

(£10.11m − £0.20m) = £9.91m

Hogan's loss through the option hedge is simply the option premium.

(b) At future spot of A$1.82 vs. £1, the option is 'in the money', i.e. it is better to exercise it than sell GBP at spot to yield (A$18m/1.81 = £9.94m). This nets:

(£9.94m − £0.20m) = £9.74m

Self-assessment activity 13.8

What is the net cost/benefit of an option that is 'at the money'?

(Answer in Appendix A)

13.11 MORE COMPLEX TECHNIQUES: FUTURES AND SWAPS

Currency futures

In principle, a futures contract can be arranged for any product or commodity, including financial instruments and currencies. A currency futures contract is a commitment to deliver a specific amount of a specified currency at a specified future date for an agreed price incorporated in the contract. It performs a similar function to a forward contract but has some major differences.

Currency futures contracts have the following characteristics:

1 They are marketable instruments traded on organised futures markets.
2 They can be completed (liquidated) before the contracted date, whereas a forward contract has to run to maturity.
3 They are relatively inflexible, being available for a limited range of currencies and for standard maturity dates. The world's largest market for currency futures is the Chicago Mercantile Exchange (CME). It trades futures in 11 different currencies for delivery four times each year: March, June, September and December.
4 They are dealt in standard lot sizes, or contracts.
5 The CME requires a down-payment called a 'performance bond' or 'margin' of about 1.5 per cent of the contract value, whereas forward contracts involve a single payment at maturity.
6 They also involve 'variation payments', essentially the ongoing losses on the contract to be paid to the exchange on which the contract is dealt.
7 They are usually cheaper than forward contracts, requiring a small commission payment rather than a buy/sell spread.

It is difficult to 'tailor make' a currency future to the precise needs of the parties involved, which explains why some exchanges have now stopped currency futures trading.

How a currency future works

This is best shown with an example. In June, a UK importer agrees to buy goods worth $10 million from a firm in Detroit. The sterling/dollar spot rate is $1.50:£1, valuing the deal at $10m/1.50 = £6,666,666. Settlement is agreed for 15 August, but the importer is concerned that appreciation of USD will undermine its profitability (it will have to find more GBP to meet the import cost). On the CME, the market price (i.e. the exchange rate) for September GBP futures is $1.48, suggesting that the market expects the USD to appreciate.

The importer needs eventually to acquire GBP to pay for its imports, so it should sell (i.e. go short of) GBP by selling GBP futures contracts at $1.48. With the standard contract size of £62,500, the number of whole contracts required is:

[$10m/(£62,500 × 1.48)] = 108 approx.

Note the indivisibility problem – 108 contracts cover exposure of only (108 × £62,500 × 1.48) = $9,990,000. This makes hedging by futures unattractive to small exporters. There is also a timing problem, as the importer has to supply USD before the expiry of the contract in August. When payment is due, the importer will close out the contract by arranging a reverse trade, i.e. one with exactly opposite features, which means buying 108 September GBP futures at the ruling market price. If USD has strengthened against GBP between June and August, the importer will make a profit on the futures contract.

Imagine this does happen and the spot rate on 15 August is $1.49 and the September futures price is $1.475. As payment for the goods is required, the importer converts GBP for USD on the spot market at a cost of ($10m/1.49) = $6,711,409. Compared with the cost of the deal at the June spot rate, it has made a loss of £44,743, owing to the feared USD appreciation. However, the importer holds 108 futures contracts, enabling it to sell GBP at $1.48. To close its position, the importer can buy the same number of contracts at an exchange rate of $1.475. It will thus make a profit on the futures market of:

Sells	108 × £62,500 × 1.480 =	$9,990,000
Buys	108 × £62,500 × 1.475 =	$9,956,250
Profit		$33,750

Valued at spot of $1.49, this is worth ($33,750/1.49) = £22,651, leaving a net loss of (£44,743 − £22,651) = £22,092. This demonstrates the difficulty of achieving a perfectly hedged position with currency futures. Moreover, the futures market may not always move to the same degree as the spot market, owing to expectations about future exchange rate movements.

The CME website (www.cmegroup.com) provides a beginner's guide to using the futures markets.

■ Currency swaps

The BIS defines currency swaps as follows:

> A currency swap (or cross-currency swap) commits two counterparties to several cash flows, which in most cases involve an initial exchange of principal and a final re-exchange of principal upon maturity of the contract, and, in all cases, several streams of interest payments.

currency swaps
Where two or more parties swap the capital value and associated interest streams of their borrowing in different currencies

back-to-back loans
A simple form of a swap where firms lend directly to each other to satisfy their mutual currency requirements

Currency swaps originated from controls applied by the Bank of England over foreign exchange movements prior to 1979. Firms wishing to obtain foreign currency to invest overseas, say in the United States, found they could avoid these controls by entering an agreement with a US company that operated a UK subsidiary. In return for receiving a loan from the US company to finance its own activity in the United States, the UK company would lend to the UK-based subsidiary of the US company. The two firms would agree to repay the loans in the local currency after an agreed period, thereby locking in a particular exchange rate. The interest rate would be based on prevailing local rates. Such arrangements were called '**back-to-back loans**' – from the UK company's perspective, they involved agreeing to make a series of future USD payments in exchange for receiving a flow of GBP income.

After exchange controls were removed in 1979, such loans were replaced by currency swaps. These need not involve two companies directly. In general terms, a currency swap is a contract between two parties (e.g. between a bank and an overseas investor) to exchange payments denominated in one currency for payments denominated in another. A simple example will illustrate this.

How currency swaps work

Currency swaps are complex. In particular, they require matching up two companies' mutual requirements in terms of type and amount of currency required and term of financing. The final agreement will reflect the bargaining power of the parties involved and is most viable when each party has a differential borrowing advantage in one currency which it can transfer to the other. This point is important – a currency swap almost invariably involves an interest rate swap.

To illustrate the process, consider the example of two companies, ABC and XYZ. ABC, which can borrow in Swiss francs (CHF) at 5.5 per cent, is seeking USD financing of $40 million for three years. The Dutch subsidiary of a US bank is prepared to act as intermediary, which involves finding a suitable matching company which has a borrowing advantage in USD and is seeking CHF finance. Until the match is found, the bank will be exposed to currency and interest rate risk, which it may cover by entering the spot market, or possibly using the options market. Company XYZ emerges as a suitable swap candidate. (More complex swaps might involve several participant companies if a directly corresponding currency requirement cannot be identified.)

XYZ has a borrowing advantage in USD, being able to borrow at 7 per cent, compared to ABC's borrowing rate of 7.75 per cent. Conversely, XYZ would have to borrow in CHF at 6 per cent. XYZ is seeking CHF finance of 52 million. At the ruling exchange rate of 1.3 CHF per USD, this is an exact match. With the bank's intermediation, the two companies now agree to swap currencies and assume each other's interest rate obligations over a three-year term, with transactions conducted via the bank. Figure 13.4 shows the structure of the swap and the sequence of transactions. In reality, the two companies would have to pay rather higher interest rates than those shown in order to yield a profit margin for the bank, sufficient to compensate it for assuming the risks of either company defaulting on interest payments or re-exchange of principal.

There are three legs to such deals:

1 Exchange of principal at spot (either notional or a physical transfer) in order to provide a basis for computing interest.
2 Exchange of interest streams.
3 Re-exchange of principal on terms agreed at the outset.

The principal is fully hedged, unlike the interest rate payments, which may require hedging perhaps via the forward market.

In the example, the company benefits from lower interest rates and effectively uses the superior credit rating of the swap specialist to access cheaper finance. Most currency swaps are undertaken to exploit such interest rate disparities, whereby one party can pass on to another the benefit of superior creditworthiness. There are two main forms of currency swap. In a **fixed/fixed swap**, one party swaps a stream of fixed interest payments for a corresponding stream of fixed interest payments in another currency (as in the example of companies ABC and XYZ). In a **fixed/floating swap**, or **cross-currency interest swap**, one or both payment streams are on a variable basis, e.g. linked to LIBOR.

fixed/fixed swap
A swap agreement where the parties agree to swap fixed interest rate commitments

cross-currency interest swap
A swap agreement where the parties agree to swap a fixed interest rate commitment for a floating interest rate

The sequence of transactions

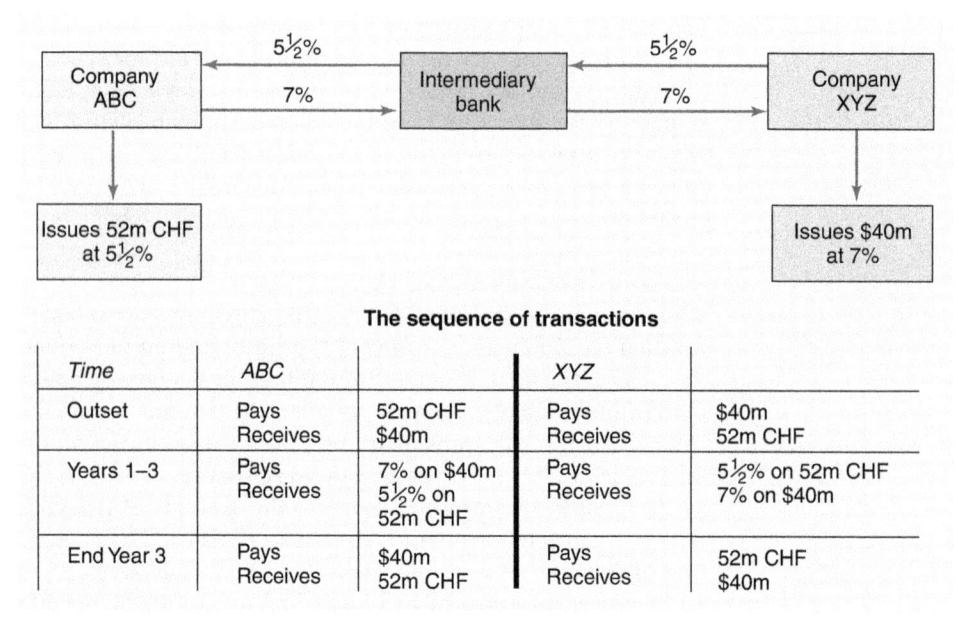

Time	ABC		XYZ	
Outset	Pays Receives	52m CHF $40m	Pays Receives	$40m 52m CHF
Years 1–3	Pays Receives	7% on $40m 5½% on 52m CHF	Pays Receives	5½% on 52m CHF 7% on $40m
End Year 3	Pays Receives	$40m 52m CHF	Pays Receives	52m CHF $40m

Figure 13.4 Achieving the swap

US producers build up sales hedges as oil falls

US independent oil companies have used derivatives to protect much more of their expected revenues against a fall in crude prices than they had a year ago, helping them sustain capital spending and production even if the market continues to weaken.

Filings from the leading US exploration and production companies show they have hedged the revenues from about 27 per cent of their expected 2017 oil production.

The hedges, which include swaps and collars using options, typically have strike prices of $50–$60 per barrel of benchmark Brent crude, and an average price of $54. That compares with an average strike price of $42 per barrel for new contracts in the first quarter of last year.

Anadarko Petroleum and Apache, two of the larger independent oil producers that have assets offshore as well as in US shale reserves, were the most active in the fourth quarter, accounting for about 28 per cent of the oil hedges taken on in the quarter.

Source: Crooks, E. (2017) US producers build up sales hedges as oil falls. *Financial Times*, 27 March. © The Financial Times Limited 2018. All rights reserved.

13.12 CONCLUSIONS

The globalisation of world trade has forced financial managers to take a keener interest in managing foreign exchange exposure. There are three types of exposure: transaction exposure, affecting the flow of cash across a currency frontier; translation exposure, affecting the value of assets and liabilities denominated in a foreign currency in consolidated financial statements; and economic exposure, which is the impact on long-term cash flows of possible changes in exchange rates.

Not all transactions, assets and liabilities denominated in foreign currencies are necessarily exposed to exchange rate risk. The essential skills in currency management are to identify the assets and cash flows which are at risk and to devise suitable means of hedging the risks. It is important to differentiate between hedging techniques internal and external to the firm. Several financial markets have been developed that allow the international treasurer to hedge foreign exchange risk, and financial instruments such as swaps, options, futures and forwards can be used for this purpose.

The international treasurer must decide whether or not exchange rates can be forecast with any degree of reliability. With exchange rates floating freely, research suggests that forecasting is not profitable. However, when governments begin to interfere with the free market, forecasting has proved to be a profitable activity. The dogged, but ultimately doomed, commitment by international monetary authorities to support artificially high or low exchange rates may make forecasting worthwhile.

SUMMARY

This chapter examined the nature and sources of a company's exposure to the risk of adverse foreign exchange rate movements. We explained that due to the nature of a company's business, its profitability can be adversely affected by unfavourable exchange rate movements. In line with this, companies either translate foreign currency for immediate payment on the spot market or use the forward market for future payments. This chapter, therefore, explained a number of widely-used strategies to hedge or safeguard against foreign exchange risks. Applying techniques which are either internal to the firm or those available from external financial markets will help in protecting companies from foreign exchange risks.

Key points

- Corporate profitability can be seriously affected by adverse movements in foreign exchange rates.
- Currency can be transacted for immediate payment on the spot market or for future delivery via the forward market.
- The international treasurer is faced with three kinds of foreign exchange exposure: transaction exposure, translation exposure and economic exposure.
- Transaction exposure relates to the likely variability in short-term operating cash flows: for example, the cost of specific imported raw materials and the income from specific exported goods.
- Translation exposure relates to the risk of exchange rate movements altering the sterling value of assets located overseas or the sterling value of liabilities due to be settled overseas.
- Economic exposure refers to the ongoing risks incurred by the company in its choice of long-term contractual arrangements, such as licensing deals or decisions to invest overseas. These risks are the long-term equivalent of transaction exposure.
- Companies that trade internationally should devise a foreign exchange strategy.
- The strategy might depend on the treasurer's belief in the validity of various international trade theories: Purchasing Power Parity (PPP), Interest Rate Parity (IRP), the Expectations Theory and the Open Fisher Theory.
- PPP states that, allowing for the prevailing exchange rate, identical goods must sell for a common price in different locations. If inflation rates differ between locations, exchange rates will adjust to preserve the Law of One Price.
- IRP asserts that any differences in international interest rates are a reflection of expected exchange rate movements, so that the interest rate offered in a location whose currency is expected to depreciate will exceed that in an appreciating currency location by the amount of the expected exchange rate movement.
- The forward premium or discount should equal the expected rate of appreciation or depreciation of a currency.

- The Open Fisher Theory asserts that investment in different countries will offer the same expected real interest rate, so that differences in nominal rates of interest can be explained by expected differences in rates of inflation.
- Once the exposure position of the company is identified and measured, the treasurer must devise a hedging strategy to control the foreign exchange risk faced by the firm.
- Many apparent exposures are often self-hedging: for example, holdings of plant and machinery that can be traded internationally.
- Generally, internal hedging techniques are cheaper to apply than using the external markets, which offer various financial instruments for hedging currency risks.

Further reading

There has been an upsurge in texts on international financial management, but the leading book in the field is generally reckoned to be that by Shapiro (2013), which also contains excellent bibliographies. The texts by Madura and Fox (2017) and Eiteman *et al.* (2015) are also highly regarded. The leading British text is Buckley (2012), while Pilbeam (2013) is also recommended.

Books on hedging include Chisholm (2010) and Taylor (2010).

Hedging is often considered to be useful as a means for reducing volatility and increasing shareholder value. Aretz and Bartram (2010) review the evidence for this claim and provide a sound analysis of the various theoretical arguments used to support it. For an article examining what factors affect financial derivative usage, see Bartram *et al.* (2009). Baldeaux *et al.* (2015) present a derivative contracts-based model for foreign exchange options. Carroll *et al.* (2017) is an interesting paper on currency and interest rates derivatives.

To keep abreast of trends and emerging issues in the field, regular reading of *Euromoney* and *The Economist* magazines is recommended.

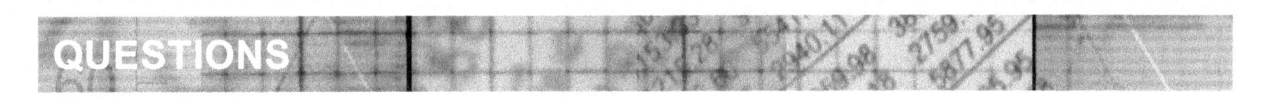

QUESTIONS

Questions with a coloured number have solutions in Appendix B on page 501.

1 The Local Bank plc quotes the following rates for the euro versus sterling:

   1.6296–1.6320

   (a) How many euros would a firm receive when selling £10 million?
   (b) How much sterling would it receive when selling €12 million?

2 On 30 November, a UK exporter sells goods worth £10 million to a French importer on three months' credit. The customer is billed in euros, for which the spot rate versus sterling is €1.6 vs. £1. The three-month forward rate is €1.62 per £1.
   (a) What is the amount invoiced?
   (b) If the spot rate is €1.7 vs. £1 at the settlement date, what is the exporter's gain or loss, assuming it does not hedge?
   (c) If the spot rate is €1.5 vs. £1 at the settlement date, what is the exporter's gain or loss, assuming it does not hedge?
   (d) If the exporter takes forward cover, what is the cost of the hedge
       (i) compared to the current spot rate?
       (ii) compared to case **(b)**?
       (iii) compared to case **(c)**?

3 Work out the forward outrights from the exchange rates versus sterling given in the table below.

Country/Currency	Closing market rates	One-month forward rates
Denmark/krona	10.960–10.967	−25–11 (pm)
Japan/yen	230.11–230.16	−110–97 (pm)
Norway/kronor	11.717–11.723	−21–4 (pm)

Source: The Times, 29 August 2007. © The Times/NI Syndication.

4 A selected bundle of goods costs £100 in the United Kingdom, and a similar bundle costs 1,200 krona (DKR) in Denmark. People generally expect the rate of inflation to be 5 per cent in the United Kingdom and 3 per cent in Denmark.

   (a) Assuming that PPP applies, what is the current exchange between GBP and DKR?
   (b) Assuming that PPP will continue to hold, what spot exchange rate would you predict for 12 months hence?
   (c) Again, assuming PPP, what exchange rate should be quoted for three-month forward transactions?

5 The respective interest rates in the United States and the United Kingdom are 9 per cent and 10 per cent, respectively, in annual terms. If the spot exchange rate is US$1.6000 to £1, what is the forward rate if IRP applies?

6 Assume you are the treasurer of a multinational company based in Switzerland. Your company trades extensively with the United States. You have just received US$1 million from a customer in the United States. As the company has no immediate need of capital, you decide to invest the money in either US$ or Swiss francs for 12 months. The following information is relevant:

   - The spot rate of exchange is CHF1.3125 to US$1.
   - The 12-month forward rate is CHF1.275 to US$1.
   - The interest rate on a 1-year Swiss franc bond is $4\tfrac{9}{16}$ per cent.
   - The interest rate on a 1-year US$ bond is $7\tfrac{5}{8}$ per cent.

   Assume investment in either currency is risk-free and ignore transaction costs.

Required

Calculate the returns under both options (investing in US$ or Swiss francs) and explain why there is so little difference between the two figures.

Your answer may be expressed either in US$ or in Swiss francs.

(CIMA May 1998)

7 The following situation is observed in the money markets.

Sterling: US dollar exchange rates:

	Spot	$1.6550–1.6600
	Forward (1 Year)	$1.6300–1.6450
Interest rates (fixed):	New York	5½%–5¼%
	London	5¾%–5⅝%

(a) Calculate *both* the interest and the exchange agios.

(b) Using the figures provided, investigate whether an arbitrageur operating in London could profit from covered interest arbitrage.

Notes:

(a) Assume he borrows £100,000.

(b) You may ignore commission and transaction costs other than the spreads.

8 Europa plc is a UK-based import–export company. It is now 15 May and the following transaction has been agreed:

The sale of pine furniture worth $1,250,000 to the United States receivable on 15 August.

$/£ FX rates

Spot	1.6480–1.6490
Two months' forward	−88–76 (premium)
Three months' forward	−130–124 (premium)
Three-month money market interest rates	
	£10%–8%
	$8%–6%

Required

(a) Hedge Europa's risk exposure on the forward market.

(b) Hedge Europa's risk exposure on the money market.

(c) Which is the more favourable hedge from Europa's point of view?

9 Slade plc is a medium-sized UK company with export and import trade links with US companies. The following transactions are due within the next six months. Transactions will be in the currency specified.

Purchase of components, cash payment due in 3 months:	$116,000
Sale of finished goods, cash receipt due in 3 months:	$197,000
Purchase of finished goods for resale, cash payment due in 6 months:	$447,000
Sale of finished goods, cash receipt due in 6 months:	$154,000
Exchange rates quoted on London market	$/£
Spot	1.4106–1.4140
3 months' forward	0.82–0.77
6 months' forward	1.39–1.34

Interest rates (annual)

3 months or 6 months	Borrowing	Lending
Sterling	7.5%	4.5%
Dollars	6.0%	3.0%

Required

Calculate the *net* sterling receipts which Slade might expect for both its three- and six-month transactions if it hedges foreign exchange risk on:

(a) the forward foreign exchange market;
(b) the money market.

10 Exchange-traded foreign currency option prices for dollar/sterling contracts are shown below:

	Sterling (£12,500) contracts			
	Calls		Puts	
Exercise price ($)	December	September	December	September
1.90	5.55	7.95	0.42	1.95
1.95	2.75	3.85	4.15	3.80
2.00	0.25	1.00	9.40	–
2.05	–	0.20	–	–

Option prices are in cents per £. The current spot exchange rate is $1.9405–$1.9425/£.

Required

Assume that you work for a US company that has exported goods to the United Kingdom and is due to receive a payment of £1,625,000 in three months' time. It is now the end of June.

Calculate and explain whether your company should hedge its sterling exposure on the foreign currency option market if the company's treasurer believes the spot rate in three months' time will be:

(a) $1.8950–1.8970/£
(b) $2.0240–2.0260/£

(ACCA)

11 Ashton plc, a UK-based firm, imports computer components from the Far East. The trading currency is Singapore dollars and the value of the deal is 28m Singapore dollars (S$). Three months' credit is given. The current spot exchange rate is S$2.80 vs. £1. Because of recent volatility in the foreign exchange markets, Ashton's directors are worried that a rise in the S$ could wipe out the profits on the deal. Three alternative hedging methods have been suggested:

- a forward market hedge;
- a money market hedge;
- an option hedge.

Ashton's treasurer discovers the following information:

- The three-month forward rate is S$2.79 vs. £1
- Ashton can borrow in S$ at 2% interest (annual rate), and in London at 5 per cent p.a.
- Deposit rates are 1 per cent p.a. in Singapore and 3 per cent p.a. in London
- A three-month American call option to buy S$28m at an exercise rate of S$2.785 vs. £1 could be purchased at a premium of £200,000 on the London OTC option market

Required

Show how *each* hedge would operate for *each* of the following spot rates in three months' time:

(a) S$2.78 vs. £1
(b) S$2.82 vs. £1

12 TLC Inc manufactures pharmaceutical products. The organisation exports through a worldwide network of affiliated organisations. Its headquarters are in the United States, but there is a large volume of inter-organisation sales, dividend flows and fee and royalty payments. These inter-organisational payments are made in US$. An example of payment flows among four affiliates for the past six months is shown in the diagram below:

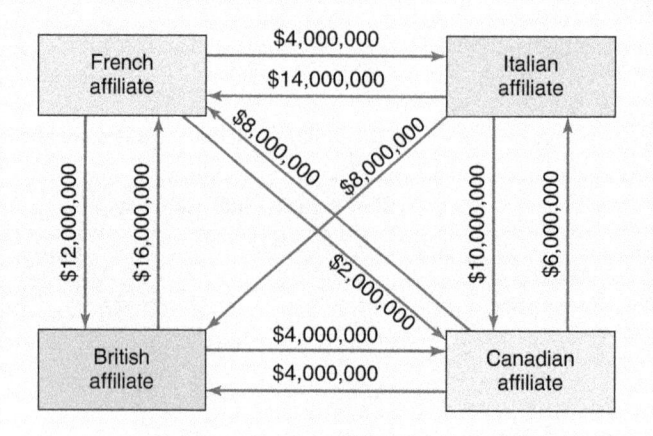

```
                    $4,000,000
    French    ───────────────────►   Italian
   affiliate  ◄───────────────────  affiliate
                   $14,000,000
         ▲   ▲    $8,000,000  $8,000,000   ▲   ▲
         │   │         ╲     ╱              │   │
    $12,000,000  $16,000,000              $10,000,000  $6,000,000
         │   │         ╱     ╲              │   │
         ▼   ▼    $2,000,000                ▼   ▼
                    $4,000,000
    British   ───────────────────►  Canadian
   affiliate  ◄───────────────────  affiliate
                    $4,000,000
```

At present, each affiliate has control over its own cash management and foreign currency hedging decisions. The Corporate Treasurer is considering centralising cash and foreign currency management.

Required

(a) Explain, briefly, the characteristics of a bi- or multilateral netting system and, using the information in the diagram, advise the Corporate Treasurer of the pattern of cash flows that would have been evident if such a system had been in operation in TLC Inc.
(b) Discuss the advantages TLC Inc might obtain from centralising international cash management and foreign exchange management and advise on the potential disadvantages of such a change in policy.

(CIMA 2004)

Practical assignment

Many companies experience accounting problems in recording overseas transactions and in translating foreign currency values into their accounts. Select a company involved in international trade. Examine its report and accounts to determine its policy with regard to foreign exchange, and the extent of foreign currency losses or gains for the year concerned. Do you think these were 'real money' losses or gains, or merely accounting entries?

14

Foreign investment decisions

Taste remains for the big cross-border deal

Less than a month into his role as head of German conglomerate Bayer, Werner Baumann decided to launch the biggest takeover in the company's 153-year history. Four months later, he successfully convinced US agribusiness giant Monsanto to accept a $66bn offer that would position the combined group as the world's most powerful supplier of crop chemicals and seeds. The calculations made by Mr Baumann help explain why large cross-border transactions remain a major feature of global markets. First, it was a sector that had accepted a need for massive consolidation. Second, it was an opportunity to gain scale in new markets. And finally, debt financing remained abundant at historically low rates – with central banks even stepping in to purchase corporate debt to stimulate activity.

In the UK, ARM was taken over by Japanese Softbank for £24bn, Micro Focus agreed a $8.8bn deal to merge with a set of software assets spun off from Hewlett Packard Enterprise, and Liberty Media reached a deal to take control of Formula One in a deal valuing the sport at $8bn.

FT *Source:* Massoudi, A.; Weinland, D. and Fontanella-Khan, J. (2016) Taste remains for the big cross-border deal. *Financial Times*, 29 September. © The Financial Times Limited 2018. All rights reserved.

Learning objectives

This chapter focuses on foreign investment decisions by multinational corporations (MNCs). In particular, it covers different entry strategies of multinational corporations and pinpoints the complexities they face in setting up and managing their operations. It also discusses foreign exchange issues, political and country-specific risks and various risk management methods used by multinational corporations. After reading this chapter, you should be able to:

- Understand the advantages of MNCs.
- Evaluate different ways of entering foreign markets.
- Appreciate the particular complexities of foreign direct investment (FDI).
- Analyse and explain the appraisal of FDI projects.
- Gauge the impact of foreign exchange variations on foreign projects.
- Assess different ways of insulating projects against foreign exchange risk.
- Identify political and country risk, and appreciate how to manage these.

14.1 INTRODUCTION

portfolio investment
Investment in financial securities such as bonds and equities, with no stake in management

direct investment
Investment in tangible and intangible assets for business operating purposes

Foreign direct investment (FDI)
Investment in fixed assets located abroad for operating distribution and/or production facilities

Foreign investment may be divided into **portfolio** (or financial) and **direct** (or strategic) **investment**. Portfolio investment involves the purchase of shares or loan stock in an overseas organisation, usually without control over the running of the business. **Foreign direct investment (FDI)** is a lasting interest in an enterprise in another economy where the investor's purpose is to have an effective voice in the management of the enterprise. Such direct investment may arise from the acquisition of a controlling interest in an existing overseas business, as applies to the cases cited in the introductory cameo, or from setting up an overseas branch or subsidiary from scratch. The former is called 'brownfield investment' and the latter 'greenfield investment'.

■ The strategic significance of FDI

Firms that engage in FDI are called multinational corporations (MNCs). For such firms, FDI almost always has a strategic dimension because:

- **The outlay is often substantial**
  FDI thus places large amounts of capital at risk.
- **The investment is often not easily reversed.**
  One of the risks involved is the inability to exit quickly or cheaply. Because the firm is often lured to the country in question by tax breaks and other incentives, there is usually a lock-in time period before the firm can terminate the investment, or if it can exit, penalties may become payable. Finding a buyer for a failed overseas investment is difficult. Moreover, there is reputational damage in having to exit prematurely.
- **FDI is important for at least two parties:**
  (a) *The investing firm*
      FDI makes a difference in several financial areas. By accessing local cost advantages, such as lower labour costs, by exploiting scale economies such as bulk-buying or by tapping into more extensive overseas market, the FDI can provide a major boost to the parent firm's cash flows.
  (b) *The host country*
      The host country stands to benefit from greater employment (assuming no displacement of local firms), greater tax revenues and greater inflows of foreign currency, both initially, due to the up-front outlay, and during the project's lifetime, if the facility is used as an exporting platform.
- **Risks are different from those in domestic investment**
  This aspect is explored in more detail later in this chapter, but one should note the exposure to foreign exchange fluctuations, the operational risks involved in working in a different business and cultural context, and the danger of politically-inspired interference by the host government (especially if it changes). Intuitively, one may conclude that FDI is more risky than domestic investment, which may be accurate regarding total risk, but due to the sort of favourable correlation effects discussed in earlier chapters, there may be useful portfolio effects. In other words, FDI may be a vehicle for diversifying risk across a wider range of global operating arenas.
- **FDI often opens up new opportunities.**
  The experience obtained in investing and operating abroad may reveal further opportunities to exploit the initial market, for example, by extending the product line or by taking over other firms, or by providing a springboard for expanding into other nearby territories, whereby the initial investment becomes a regional 'hub'. Thus, FDI may offer follow-on options, of which the firm may only be dimly aware at the outset.
- **FDI is a vehicle of competition**
  FDI is sometimes undertaken as an aggressive move to 'steal a march' over competing firms in a new market, or as a defensive move to exploit one particular market

after a rival has already secured an important presence elsewhere, and it would be too costly to challenge that established presence. Such moves are a reflection of the struggle among MNCs for market-leadership in a global context.

Battle for Lidl and Aldi in the US grocery market

A red and white flag of the Statue of Liberty, emblazoned with '100% made in the USA', greets shoppers at the entrance to a new grocery store in Hackensack, New Jersey. The store's debut is one of hundreds that Aldi, the German discount grocer, has planned as part of a $3.4bn expansion drive across the US.

The price of food eaten at home in the US has fallen for 18 straight months, the longest stretch since the 1950s, which has in turn triggered a price war among supermarket operators.

The battle is only set to intensify as Lidl and Aldi, the German grocers that have ravaged European rivals with a no-frills, low-price strategy, set their sights on the US. Aldi last month said it would increase the number of its US stores to 2,500 in the next five years, while Lidl opened its first US shop on June 15. The next day, Amazon unveiled plans to buy upmarket grocer Whole Foods for $13bn, in a deal expected to upend US food retail.

Amazon's bid fired a shot at already beleaguered grocers, with competitors swiftly losing $30bn in market capitalisation as investors contemplated how the e-commerce group might redefine their trade.

In this environment, more consolidation is likely, says Mr Roberts. Walmart is large enough to compete on prices, he argues, and premium chains like Whole Foods will not be chasing the same customers, but for those 'stuck in the middle, it's like death by a thousand cuts'.

FT *Source:* Nicolaou, A. (2017) Aldi and Lidl step up battle with US grocers. *Financial Times*, 3 July. © The Financial Times Limited 2018. All rights reserved.

The multinational corporation

multinational company (MNC)
One that conducts a significant proportion of its operations abroad

A working definition of a **multinational company (MNC)** is: a firm that owns production, sales and other revenue-generating assets in a number of countries (although a wider definition would include firms that simply sell home-produced goods overseas). Foreign direct investment by MNCs includes establishment and acquisition of overseas raw material and component operations, production plants and sales subsidiaries. This occurs because of potentially greater cost-effectiveness and profitability in sourcing inputs and servicing markets through a direct presence in a number of locations, rather than relying solely on a single 'home' base and on imports and exports to support operations. A global firm is one that trades *and* invests abroad.

It is tempting to think of MNCs as 'Western' firms that invest in developing countries. The acquisition of firms in developed countries by firms in developing countries is increasingly common. According to the United Nations Conference on Trade and Development [UNCTAD]'s World Investment Report (2017), for the year 2016, FDI inflows to developed economies totalled $1.03 trillion, whereas, FDI outflows from these countries totalled about $1.00 trillion. Overall totals were as follows: FDI inflows to developing economies, $646 billion; FDI outflows from developing economies, $383 billion; and FDI outflows from transition economies, about $25 billion. The UNCTAD Report notes that the so-called BRICS countries – Brazil, Russia, India, China, South Africa – received 11 per cent of the global inward FDI. The United States is ranked as the top host country for inward FDI, with a total inflow of FDI of $391 billion, followed by the United Kingdom with $254 billion. In third position is China, with an overall FDI inflow of $134 billion. With outward FDI, the United States is again ranked as the top nation with an overall outward investment of $299 billion, followed by China at $183 billion.

Self-assessment activity 14.1

What is meant by a multinational corporation?

(Answer in Appendix A)

The next cameo highlights examples of FDI from various sources, especially, from China entering Italy.

> ### Record high merger and acquisition deals in Italy
>
> The value of cross-border merger and acquisition deals in Italy reached a new high in 2015 at over $50bn. Italian companies were the most targeted by foreign acquisitions in the European Union after the UK, along with France. Some big deals, including the $9bn acquisition in March of the tyremaker Pirelli by the Chinese company ChemChina contributed to the rise in capital invested last year, but the number of deals – at 248 – also pointed to an exceptional year.
>
> Marco Simoni, a top economic adviser to the Prime Minister, Matteo Renzi, in an interview with the FT, described a large part of the growth due to the radical changes in the political climate for foreign investors.
>
> Greenfield investments – a form of direct investment where a parent company starts a new venture in a foreign country by constructing new operational facilities from the ground up – are also rising, but not as fast as acquisitions.
>
> One third of cross-border greenfield investments in Italy since 2014 was in manufacturing production, traditionally a strong sector in the country.
>
> 'Take the example of Philip Morris International,' continues Dr Simoni, 'they opted to open their most modern plant in Italy rather than pursuing any other option because of the availability of machinery and packaging firms in the area of Bologna (central Italy) and because, they said, problem-solving capacity of Italian workers is a global best practice'.
>
> Italy has been lagging behind in terms of attractiveness of FDI for more than a decade. 'I am glad of the news of the rise in mergers and acquisitions,' concludes Dr Simoni, 'a greater internationalization will help the firms to grow'.

Source: Romei, V. (2016) Record high merger and acquisition deals in Italy. *Financial Times*, 23 March. © The Financial Times Limited 2018. All rights reserved.

14.2 ADVANTAGES OF MNCS OVER NATIONAL FIRMS

The MNC may be in a position to enhance its competitive position and profitability in four main ways:

1. It can take advantage of differences in country-specific circumstances. In a world where countries are at different stages of economic evolution (some industrially advanced, others mainly primary producers), certain advantages in a country may have knock-on effects that the MNC can exploit on a global basis. For example, the MNC may locate its R&D establishments in a technologically advanced country in order to draw on local scientific and technological infrastructure and skills. Similarly, it may locate its production plants in a less-developed country in order to take advantage of lower input costs, especially cheap labour. JCB, the UK firm famous for its yellow diggers, operates plants in Brazil, India and China. Alternatively, the MNC may continue to produce its outputs in its 'home' country but seek to remain competitive by sourcing key components from subsidiary plants based abroad.

2. MNCs can choose the appropriate mode of serving a particular market. For example, exporting may provide an entry route into a low-price, commodity-type market, with the MNC taking advantage of marginal pricing and the absence of set-up costs; licensing may be an appropriate mode if market size is limited or market niches are being targeted; direct investment in production and sales subsidiaries may be a more effective way of capturing a large market share where proximity to customers is important, or where market access via exporting is limited by tariffs. These various routes enable an MNC to pursue a complex global market-servicing strategy. For example, Ford operates assembly plants in 19 different countries (e.g. Argentina and China), and engine plants in 14 (e.g. Australia and Brazil). It ships engines from the latter to the former for final assembly according to the level of demand for the various models in different markets, including the export market. As a result, engine and car may be produced in two different locations and sold in a third one. The following box reproduces Ford's manufacturing policy with an emphasis on flexibility.

> We are committed to maintaining an appropriate manufacturing footprint in markets around the world, both in the more mature markets in which we have an established presence, and in fast-growing newly-developed and emerging markets. We are making substantial investments in newly-developed and emerging markets, including in China, India, and Thailand, to increase our production capacity with flexible new manufacturing plants. We and our unconsolidated affiliates in Asia Pacific Africa have launched four new plants in the past two years, and have announced that we expect to complete six more plants in the region by mid-decade.
>
> *Source:* Ford Motor Company 2013 *Annual Report.*

3 'Internalisation' of the MNC's operations by foreign direct investment provides a unique opportunity for the firm to maximise its global profits by using transfer pricing policies. The transfer price is 'the price at which one affiliate in a group of companies sells goods and services to another affiliated unit' (Buckley, 2004). While a national, vertically-integrated firm needs to establish transfer prices for components and finished products that are transferred between component and assembly plants, and between assembly plants and sales subsidiaries, the greater scale of cross-frontier transactions by MNCs makes these transfer prices more significant because of the impact on relative profitability and tax charges in different locations.

4 An international network of production plants and sales subsidiaries enables an MNC to protect component supplies. The Swedish/Swiss engineering conglomerate Asea Brown Boveri (ABB) has built up a network of component-manufacturing subsidiaries in the Baltic region, including the former Soviet bloc, in order to diversify sources of supply. Networks also help in the simultaneous introduction of new products in several markets. This is important (where products have a relatively short life cycle and/or patent protection) in order to maximise sales potential. Equally importantly, it spreads the risk of consumer rejection across a diversified portfolio of overseas markets, so that failure in one market may be offset (or perhaps more than compensated by) rapid acceptance in another. Additionally, it enables the MNC to develop a 'global brand' identity (e.g. Coca-Cola, Levi's and Subway) or to 'customise' a product more effectively to suit local demand preferences.

Nissan gears up to build cars in Nigeria

Nissan will become the first global carmaker to build cars in Nigeria since west Africa's largest economy rolled out a policy to tempt investors to its nascent automotive industry. The Japanese car maker, which has aggressively identified growth in emerging markets as the centrepiece of its global strategy, plans to build 45,000 cars a year in the country, probably starting with an SUV early next year.

Nissan, which last month announced it would be the first international car maker to build vehicles in Myanmar, wants to double sales in Africa to 220,000 a year by 2016. Nigeria, which imports millions of dollars' worth of new and used cars every year, has embarked on a drive to attract industrial and manufacturing investment into the country since former Goldman Sachs banker Olusegun Aganga was made Minister of Trade and Investment this year.

While Nigeria is sub-Saharan Africa's biggest recipient of foreign investment with about $7bn last year, or 14 per cent of the region's total, investors complain that the country remains a challenging destination for industrial ventures due to power shortages, poor transport infrastructure and an unskilled labour force.

'Nissan is preparing to make Nigeria a significant manufacturing hub in Africa,' said chief executive Carlos Ghosn, the global car industry's most prominent believer in emerging market potential. 'As the first-mover in Nigeria, we are positioned for the long-term growth of this market and across the broader continent.'

Source: Foy, H. and Blas, J. (2013) Nissan to build cars in Nigeria. *Financial Times*, 9 October. © The Financial Times Limited 2018. All rights reserved.

14.3 FOREIGN MARKET ENTRY STRATEGIES

Firms enter foreign markets in pursuit of incremental profits and cash flows by exploiting advantages over local producers and other MNCs. The two basic vehicles for foreign market entry are, first, via transactions, and second, via direct investment. Each mode can be pursued in a number of ways. Figure 14.1 shows the spectrum of entry modes arranged by degree of commitment.

Grant (2011) provides an in-depth explanation of 'Transactions' and 'Direct Entry' as the two alternative modes of overseas market entry. The overall findings of this study are summarised as follows:

Exporting (one-off or 'spot' transactions) involves least commitment, as it is relatively inexpensive and withdrawal is easy, whereas, establishing a wholly owned foreign operating subsidiary involves managing a range of complex functions including production, marketing and distribution which is relatively expensive and requires substantial long-term commitment. Exporting includes both indirect export of products from the home country via independent agents or distributors, and direct export of products through the firm's own export division to foreign markets. With exporting, most value-adding activity takes place in the home country, while **FDI** transfers many of these activities to the foreign location. Both exporting and FDI involve **internalisation**, i.e. retaining value-adding activities within the firm (although to different degrees). **Licensing** is often a halfway house that results in **externalising** most of these activities. It involves transferring to a licensee the right to use corporate assets, such as a brand name, and often the sale of intermediate goods for the licensee to use in production. Licensing enables a firm to gain rapid overseas market penetration when it lacks the resources to set up overseas operations.

exporting
Sale of goods and services to foreign customers

internalisation
The retention by the MNC of key management functions and technology

externalisation
The transfer of key functions and expertise to an overseas strategic partner

■ Choosing between entry modes: the determinants

The choice of entry mode hinges on several factors:

1. Whether the firm's source of competitive advantage is based on location-specific factors, e.g. low labour costs. If so, the firm is more likely to export. If managerial skills are transferable to other locations, FDI is more likely.
2. Whether the product is tradable, and whether barriers to trade exist. If import restrictions such as tariff barriers and government-imposed regulations make trade infeasible, licensing or FDI becomes more likely.
3. Whether the firm possesses the required skills and resources to build and exploit competitive advantage abroad. Marketing and distribution capabilities are essential for foreign operation, which argues in favour of appointing a distributor or agent when these skills are lacking. If a wider range of manufacturing and/or marketing skills is needed, the firm may license its product and/or technology to a local operator.

    In marketing-intensive industries, MNCs may offer their brands to local firms by trademark **licensing**. Licensing involves assigning production and selling rights to producers based in foreign locations in return for royalty payments. If tighter control over operations is required, a joint venture with a local firm may be set up.
4. Whether the resources are 'appropriable' – can the technology be stolen? In some industries, technology can be closely guarded via **patents**, but in more service-oriented activities such as computer software, ownership rights are far more difficult to enforce. In the former case, FDI involves less risk, while in the latter case, exporting may be preferred. When licensing a foreign partner, the firm must consider any potential damage to the reputation of its brand resulting from poor quality or service provided by a local operator.

licensing
Involves the assignment of production and selling rights to producers based in foreign locations in return for royalty payments

patent
A legal device giving the holder the exclusive right to exploit the technology described therein

Where a firm wants to exert close control over the use of its trademarks, technologies or trade secrets, **franchising** may be chosen as a way of licensing a fully-packaged business system, as in the international fast food business.

franchising
Licensing out of a fully packaged business system, including technology and supply of materials, to an entrepreneur operating a separate legally constituted business

5 What transactions costs are involved? These are the costs of negotiating, monitoring and enforcing the terms of such agreements as compared with internationalisation via a fully-owned subsidiary. With low or no transactions costs, exporting would usually be preferred.

US and Mexico boost re-shoring credentials

The US and Mexico have become attractive as manufacturing locations relative to other large economies over the past 10 years, thanks to slow labour cost growth and falling natural gas prices. The analysis of the world's largest manufacturing economies from Boston Consulting Group shows that costs have been rising fastest in resource-rich countries such as Brazil, Australia and Russia, while China and some European countries such as France and Italy have also experienced significant increases.

The trends are expected to drive long-term movements in manufacturing activity towards the US and Mexico. The evidence of 're-shoring' in the US – the relocation of production away from previously low-cost centres such as China – is still only tentative. However, the international cost comparisons are an encouragement for expectations that American manufacturing will gather strength in the coming years.

The widening cost disadvantage of some western European countries is ominous for the outlook for their industries. Hal Sirkin of BCG said: 'Unless things change, you're going to see significant falls in manufacturers opening factories in higher-cost countries, and more manufacturing plants shutting down.' Average cost indices calculated by the consultancy show the advantage enjoyed by China has been eroded rapidly over the past decade.

For the US, the most important factor behind the relative improvement in its costs has been the slow growth in manufacturing wages, which have risen much less than the average for large economies. Mexico has had wage rises in line with the global average, but has had much faster growth in labour productivity.

The impact of cost differences on location decisions will vary across industries. Sectors where transport costs are relatively high or being close to the customer is important offer the most attractive prospects for re-shoring to the US.

FT *Source:* Crooks, E. (2014) US and Mexico boost manufacturing credentials. *Financial Times*, 25 April. © The Financial Times Limited 2018. All rights reserved.

■ Factors favouring foreign direct investment (FDI)

International expansion through FDI is an alternative to growth focused on the firm's domestic market. A firm may choose to expand horizontally on a global basis by replicating its existing business operations in a number of countries, or via international vertical integration, backwards by establishing raw material/components sources, or forwards into final production and distribution. Firms may also choose product diversification to develop their international business interests. Firms may expand internationally by greenfield (new 'start-up') investments in component and manufacturing plants, etc.; takeover of, and merger with, established suppliers; or forming joint ventures with overseas partners. In the case of foreign market servicing, the MNC may also choose to complement direct investment with some exporting and licensing.

FDI also provides opportunities for exploiting competitive advantages over rival suppliers. A firm may possess advantages in the form of patented process technology, know-how and skills, or a unique branded product that it can better exploit and protect by establishing overseas production or sales subsidiaries. A production facility in an overseas market may enable a firm to reduce its distribution costs and keep it in closer touch with local market conditions – customer tastes, competitors' actions, etc. Moreover, direct investment enables a firm to avoid government restrictions on market access, such as tariffs and quotas, and the problems of currency variation. For example, growing protectionism by the European Union and the rising value of the yen were important factors behind increased Japanese investment in the EU, especially in the UK motor and electronics sectors.

Firms may benefit from grants and other subsidies by 'host' governments to encourage inward investment. Much Japanese investment (e.g. Nissan's plant near Sunderland) was attracted into the United Kingdom by regional selective assistance. In the case of sourcing, direct investment allows the MNC to take advantage of some countries' lower labour costs or provides them with access to superior technological know-how, thereby enhancing their international competitiveness.

Moreover, direct investment, by internalising input sourcing and market servicing within one organisation, enables the MNC to avoid various transaction costs: the costs of finding suppliers and distributors and negotiating contracts with them; and the costs associated with imperfect market situations, such as monopoly surcharges imposed by input suppliers, unreliable sources of supply and restrictions on access to distribution channels. It also allows the MNC to take advantage of the internal transfer of resources at prices that enable it to minimise its tax bill ('transfer pricing') or practise price discrimination between markets.

Finally, for some products (e.g. flat glass, metal cans, cement), decentralised local production rather than exporting is the only viable way an MNC can supply an overseas market because of the prohibitive costs of transporting a bulky product or one which, for competitive reasons, has to be marketed at a low price.

The following cameo illustrates an example of direct investment undertaken by the supermarket group, Walmart. Initially, it had entered the Indian market via a joint venture, and this had resulted in problems regarding regulation in India. Walmart dissolved the joint venture and adopted a new FDI strategy to overcome the regulatory problems.

Walmart shops for stake in Indian e-commerce leader Flipkart

Walmart is in talks to buy a stake in Indian e-commerce leader Flipkart as the world's largest retailer by sales tries a new tack in a country where its ambitions have been hamstrung by strict regulation. The talks are at a preliminary stage and come just three months after Walmart sold its Chinese e-commerce operation to local rival JD.com and completed its $3bn purchase of Jet.com at home.

Any deal would see Walmart square off against US rival Amazon, which is locked in a battle for supremacy with Flipkart in an Indian e-commerce market that Morgan Stanley analysts predict will hit turnover of $119bn by 2020.

Flipkart was founded in 2007 by two former Amazon employees, who emulated their former employer's strategy by starting with book sales before diversifying into other products. Last week, it claimed to have become the first Indian e-commerce company to register 100m users, but analysts believe it has been steadily losing market share to Amazon.

Walmart has had a troubled decade in India. In 2007, it formed a joint venture with Bharti Enterprises to run wholesale stores, in what was seen as a pre-cursor to the opening of retail outlets, in the light of regulations requiring foreign retailers to partner with local companies.

That partnership was dissolved in 2013 with Walmart taking sole control of the wholesale outlets.

The New Delhi government opened a potential route for Walmart into the retail sector this June, however, when it legalised 100 per cent foreign ownership of food retailers selling Indian produce.

FT *Source:* Mundy, S. and Fontanella-Khan, J. (2016) Walmart shops for stake in Indian ecommerce leader Flipkart. *Financial Times*, 27 September. © The Financial Times Limited 2018. All rights reserved.

US opens arms to foreign investors

Indian conglomerate Tata has placed a big bet on the US. It generates $8bn of annual revenues in the world's biggest economy and employs more than 18,000 people in IT centres, gourmet coffee production, and steel plants across the country. President Barack Obama would like many more global companies to follow suit, but the recent US record in attracting foreign investment has been worrying.

In 2000, the US gobbled up 37 per cent of the worldwide stock of inward foreign investment, but by 2012, that had shrivelled to 17 per cent. And annual inflows have almost halved from their 2008 peak. To boost those figures, the US president is donning his salesman cap for 'Brand USA' at an international conference starting today. 'This is the beginning of a sustained commitment to attracting FDI in the US,' said Penny Pritzker, commerce secretary, who is hosting the two-day affair. 'We have so many great assets that should be celebrated and promoted at a time when the world is a very competitive place,' Ms Pritzker adds.

The US's need for inward investment is clear. 'The policy challenge isn't just that we need to create 20m jobs in the next 10 years, but we need to create 20m high-productivity, high-wage jobs,' said Matthew Slaughter, Associate Dean at the Tuck School of Business at Dartmouth University. 'Companies connected to the global economy tend to generate those types of jobs.'

According to the United Nations Conference on Trade and Development's World Investment Report (2017), the United States had become the top host country for inward FDI with a total inflow of $391 billion in 2016.

Source: Politi, J. (2013) US courts foreign investment for economic boost. *Financial Times*, 30 October. © The Financial Times Limited 2018. All rights reserved.

14.4 ADDITIONAL COMPLEXITIES OF FOREIGN INVESTMENT

Evaluation of foreign direct investment decisions is not fundamentally different from the evaluation of domestic investment projects, although the political structures, economic policies and value systems of the host country may cause certain analytical problems. There is evidence (Robbins and Stobaugh, 1973; Wilson, 1990; Neale and Buckley, 1992) that the majority of MNCs use essentially similar methods for evaluation and control of capital investment projects for overseas subsidiaries and for domestic operations, although they may well apply different discount rates.

Appraising foreign investment involves financial complexities not encountered in evaluating domestic projects. The main ones are:

1 Fluctuations in exchange rates over lengthy time periods are largely unpredictable. On the one hand, these may enhance the domestic currency value of project cash flows, but depreciation of the currency of the host country will reduce the domestic currency proceeds.
2 A foreign investment project may involve levels of operating risk quite different from those of the equivalent project undertaken in the domestic economy. This poses the problem of how to estimate a suitable required rate of return for discounting purposes.
3 Once up and running, the foreign investment is exposed to variations in economic policy by the host government (e.g. tax changes), which may reduce net cash flows.
4 Investment incentives provided by the host country government. Several countries in the 'New Europe' have been able to attract new investment from MNC firms, especially in the motor industry. Slovakia, with a tax rate of 21 per cent, can offer definite advantages over established EU members such as Germany (30–3 per cent) and France (33⅓ per cent), among the alleged losers in this process, but some other EU countries can offer even lower tax rates (as at July 2017). These include Bulgaria (10 per cent), Ireland and Cyprus (12.5 per cent) as well as Rumania (16.6 per cent). Several developed countries have recently announced reductions in their rates of corporate tax in order to combat 'tax competition'. For example, in the United Kingdom, the corporate tax rate is falling, to 23 per cent in 2013, 21 per cent in 2014, 20 per cent in 2015 and 2016, and 19 per cent in 2017. (For updates, see **www.dits.deloitte.com**).
5 Overspill effects on the firm's existing operations; e.g. goods produced overseas may displace some existing sales (referred to as 'cannibalisation').

6 The host government may block the repatriation of profits to the home country. A project that is inherently profitable may not be worth undertaking if the earnings cannot be remitted. This raises the issue of whether the evaluation should be conducted from the standpoint of the subsidiary (i.e. the project itself), or from that of the parent company. But for a company pursuing shareholder value, the relevant evaluation is from the parent's standpoint. Some companies have adopted ingenious ways of repatriating profits. PepsiCo, which invested in a bottling plant in Hungary, found it difficult to repatriate profits from this operation. To overcome this problem, it financed the local shooting of a motion picture (*The Ninth Configuration*), which was then exported to the West. It was not a box-office hit.

Usually, only remittable cash flows (whether or not they are actually repatriated) should be considered, and the project accepted, only if the NPV of the cash flows available for investors exceeds zero. Thus, items like management fees, royalties, interest on parent company loans, dividend remittances, and loan and interest payments to the parent should all be included. In effect, a two-stage analysis is applied:

(i) specify the project's own cash flows;
(ii) isolate the cash flows remittable to the parent.

Due allowance should be made for taxation in the foreign location.

■ Overcoming exchange controls

Possible ways of minimising the impact of controls over cash repatriation include:

(i) Paying interest on loans or dividends on equity. Maximising dividend flows may involve 'creative accounting' to inflate the local profits, although this may be counter-productive if local tax rates exceed those in the home country. It may also antagonise local interests.
(ii) Paying royalty fees where the foreign project utilises any process over which the parent claims proprietary rights, e.g. control of a patent or trademark, such as Levi's.
(iii) **Transfer pricing** policies that involve charging the overseas subsidiary high prices for components and other supplies.
(iv) Applying a management charge if the senior managers are seconded from the parent. Similar charges can be used to make the foreign subsidiary pay for other services provided by the parent, e.g. IT and treasury costs. However, this may provoke close scrutiny by the host authorities.

transfer price
The cost applied to goods transferred between operating units owned by the same firm

Self-assessment activity 14.2

How does FDI differ from domestic investment?
(Answer in Appendix A)

14.5 THE DISCOUNT RATE FOR FOREIGN DIRECT INVESTMENT (FDI)

Opinions differ as to the appropriate discount rate to apply when discounting net cash flows from foreign investment. 'Gut feelings' may suggest that FDI should be evaluated at a higher discount rate than domestic investment 'simply because it involves more risk'. But is this valid?

Assuming all-equity finance, two commonly suggested possibilities are:

- Use a required return based on the risk of similar activities in the home country. This would be the equity cost for projects in activities similar to existing ones, or a 'tailored' project-specific rate for ventures into new spheres.
- Use a required return comparable to that of local firms.

Before deciding which approach is preferable, there are several issues to consider:

1 Foreign projects generally involve higher levels of risk than domestic ones. However, much of this risk can be dealt with in better ways than simply 'hiking' the discount rate. For example, currency risk can be handled by the sort of hedging techniques mentioned in Chapter 13 (if thought necessary), and political risk can be handled in the ways discussed later.
2 Although the total risk of FDI is often very high, the relevant risk is generally much lower, and sometimes lower than for comparable investment at home. FDI involves diversifying into overseas markets in the same way as an investor might diversify shareholdings across international markets. Solnik (1974) showed that the correlation between national stock markets is generally much less than one (although it may have increased in recent years). If investors can lower relevant risk by cross-border portfolio diversification, why should firms not do so? This is especially relevant for firms whose investors cannot diversify internationally, due to exchange controls or transactions costs, or into countries where no organised stock exchange operates' or, if one does exist, its efficiency may be in doubt.

The relevant Beta value for, say, a UK firm operating abroad may not be the Beta calculated by reference to the UK market portfolio, but the Beta in relation to the local market (if there is one). Consider the following example.

Example: Malaku Mining

Malaku Mining is the newly formed Indonesian subsidiary of Mowmack plc, an all-equity-financed UK firm, whose shares have a Beta value of 0.9 relative to the UK market portfolio. The total risk (standard deviation) of the Malaku project is 30 per cent and the risk of the Jakarta Stock Exchange is 20 per cent. The UK stock market has a 50 per cent correlation with the Jakarta market.

Here, the parent Beta of 0.9 is inappropriate. Instead of using this value, it is more appropriate to consider the risk of the proposed activity in relation to the local market and allow for the low correlation between the London and Jakarta exchanges. We can do this by using a variation of the formula found in Section 5.5:

Project Beta = correlation coefficient × (risk of the activity/local market risk)

This yields a project-specific Beta of:

$(0.5 \times 30\%/20\%) = (0.5 \times 1.5) = 0.75$

The cost of equity would be calculated using the UK risk-free rate of, say, 5 per cent and the UK equity market risk premium of, say, 5 per cent, as the firm has a UK investor base. Hence, the required rate of return for all-equity funding would be found from the usual CAPM formula:

$k_e = R_f + \text{Beta}[ER_m - R_f] = 5\% + 0.75[5\%] = 8.75\%$

Self-assessment activity 14.3

An ungeared UK firm, with a Beta of 1.4, plans to invest in an emerging country that has no stock exchange. Its economy has a weak correlation (0.4) with the United Kingdom. Due to operating gearing, the foreign project is 25 per cent more risky than the UK parent. The risk-free rate is 5 per cent and the expected overall return on the UK stock market is 11 per cent p.a. What return should the UK firm seek on this project?

(Answer in Appendix A)

14.6 EVALUATING FDI

Under certain conditions, analysing foreign project cash flows will yield the same result as analysing the cash flows to the parent. The key conditions are:

(i) Exchange rates adjust to reflect inflation differences between the parent country and the foreign location, i.e. PPP applies.
(ii) Project cash inflows and outflows move in line with prices in general in both locations.
(iii) No tax differentials exist between the two countries.
(iv) No exchange controls.

Because one or more of these conditions probably will not apply in practice, the following steps are generally recommended:

1. Predict local cash flows in money terms, i.e. including local inflation.
2. Allow for any 'overspill' effects like the 'cannibalisation' of existing exports. The opportunity cost is neither the sales revenue nor indeed the profit lost, but the gross margin or contribution.
3. Calculate the project's NPV using a discount rate reflecting the cost of finance in host country terms.
4. Allow for any management charges and royalties.
5. Estimate parent company cash flows by applying the expected future exchange rate to host country cash flows if there are no blocks on remittances, or to net remittable cash flows if exchange controls operate.
6. Allow for both local and parent country taxation.
7. Calculate the project's NPV.

Differences between host and parent country taxation

Quite apart from different tax rates, taxation issues can complicate FDI in several ways, most notably if there are different systems of investment incentives in the two countries, and whether or not a **Double Taxation Agreement (DTA)** operates. Under a DTA, tax paid in the host country is credited in calculating tax in the parent country. The generally recommended procedure is to:

double tax agreements (DTAs)
Reciprocal arrangements between countries whereby tax paid in one location is credited in the second, thus avoiding doubling up the firm's tax bill. Hence, Double Tax Relief (DTR)

1. Allow for host country investment incentives before applying the local tax rate to local cash flows.
2. Apply the relevant UK rate of tax to remitted cash flows only.
3. Adjust stage 2 for any double tax rules. For example, with a DTA and host country tax payable at 15 per cent and where the UK rate of tax applicable is 30 per cent, the relevant tax rate to apply to remittances is (30% − 15%) = 15%.

Self-assessment activity 14.4

A UK MNC earns cash flow (all taxable) of $100 million in the United States. What is its overall tax bill if the rate of tax on profits in both the United States and the United Kingdom is 30 per cent and a DTA applies?

(Answer in Appendix A)

A full examination of the complexities of FDI is beyond our scope. However, several of these features are brought out in the example in the next section.

14.7 WORKED EXAMPLE: SPARKES PLC AND ZOLTAN KFT

A UK company, Sparkes plc, is planning to invest £5 million in the Zoltan consumer electronics factory in Hungary. The project will generate a stream of cash flows in the local currency, Forints, which have to be converted into sterling as in Table 14.1. Should Sparkes invest?

Table 14.1 Sparkes and Zoltan: project details

- Expected net cash flows from Zoltan in millions of Hungarian Forints (HUF) (at current prices):

Year	0	1	2	3	4
	−1,000	+400	+400	+400	+400

- The project may operate for a further six years, but the local government has expressed its desire to purchase a 50 per cent stake at the end of Year 4. The purchase price will be based on the net book value of assets.
- The spot exchange rate between sterling and Forints is 200 per £1. The present rates of inflation are 25 per cent in Hungary and 5 per cent for the United Kingdom. These rates are expected to persist for the next few years.
- For this level of risk, Sparkes requires a return of 10 per cent in real terms.

First, we must consider the time dimension. The project is capable of operating for 10 years, but the host government has expressed its desire to buy into the project after four years. This may signal to Sparkes the possibility of more overt intervention, possibly extending to outright nationalisation, perhaps by a successor government. It seems prudent to confine the analysis to a four-year period and to include a terminal value for the project based on net book values. If we assume a 10-year life, straight-line depreciation and ignore investment in working capital, the Net Book Value (NBV) after four years will be 60 per cent of Ft1,000m = Ft600m. Half of this can be treated as a cash inflow paid by the host government and half as a (perhaps conservative) assessment of the value of Sparkes' continuing stake in the enterprise.

In practice, we often encounter complications in assessing terminal values. For example, the assets may include land, which may appreciate in value at a rate faster than general price inflation. If so, there may be holding gains to consider, gains which may well be taxable by the host government. However, it is unwise to rely overmuch on terminal values – if project acceptance hinges on the terminal value, it is probably unwise to proceed with this sort of project.

Second, how should we specify the cash flows? Here, we have two problems: first, divergence between UK and Hungarian rates of inflation; and second, the need to convert locally-denominated cash flows into sterling. To be consistent, we should discount nominal cash flows at the nominal cost of capital or real cash flows at the real cost. Each will give the same answer, but we conduct the analysis in nominal cash flows, thus incorporating the effect of inflation. Hence, all cash flows are inflated at the anticipated Hungarian rate of inflation of 25 per cent.

As it is assumed that we are evaluating this project from the standpoint of Sparkes' owners, we need to obtain a sterling NPV figure. There are two ways of doing this.

The inflated cash flows in HUF are shown in Table 14.2. These are converted into sterling using forecast future spot rates. According to PPP, sterling will appreciate by the ratio of the respective inflation rates, i.e. (1.25)/(1.05) = 19% p.a. The predicted future spot rates are also shown in Table 14.2. The sterling cash flows are discounted at 15.5% ([1.10] × [1.05] − 1 = [1.155 − 1]) to reflect the Fisher Formula.

Alternatively, we could proceed by discounting the inflated cash flows at a discount rate applicable to a comparable firm in Hungary, thus arriving at an NPV figure in local currency, and then convert to sterling. The local discount rate using the Fisher formula ((I_H) = Hungarian inflation) is:

$$(1 + P)(1 + I_H) - 1 = (1.10)(1.25) - 1 = (1.375 - 1) = 0.375, \text{ i.e. } 37.5\%$$

Table 14.2 Evaluation of the Zoltan project

Year	Un-inflated cash flow in HUFm	Inflated at 25% (HUFm)	Forecast future spot rates: HUF vs. £1	Cash flows in sterling (£m)	PV in £m at 15.5%
0	(1,000)	(1,000)	200	(5.00)	−(5.00)
1	400	500	238	2.10	1.82
2	400	625	283	2.21	1.74
3	400	781	337	2.32	1.51
4	400	977	401	2.44	1.37
4	600*	600	401	1.50	0.73
				NPV=	+2.17
				i.e.	+£2.17m

*not inflated

To obtain a sterling NPV, we adjust the NPV in HUF terms at *today's* spot rate of 200HUF vs. £1. Table 14.3 shows the result of this operation. Allowing for rounding, the NPVs are identical, i.e. the project is worth £2.18 million to Sparkes' shareholders.

Table 14.3 Alternative evaluation of the Zoltan project

Year	Inflated cash flows (HUFm)	PV in HUFm at 37.5%
0	(1,000)	(1,000)
1	500	364
2	625	331
3	781	300
4	977	273
4	600	168
	NPV=	436
	In sterling, at spot of 200HUF vs. £1 = 436/200	= £2.18m

■ The two equivalent approaches: which is best?

Consider the following example. Say a UK firm is investing in Canada. The two approaches are:

A The predicted C$ cash flows are converted to sterling cash flows, using expected future spot rates. These sterling cash flows are discounted at the sterling discount rate to yield a sterling NPV, numerically the same as in Approach B.

B The cash flows denominated in C$ are discounted at the local Canadian discount rate to generate a C$ NPV. This is then converted at the current spot rate for C$ against sterling to yield a sterling NPV.

Each approach has the same departure point, i.e. the C$ cash flows, and ends up at the same place, i.e. the sterling NPV. Which approach is 'better'? This depends on what information is available. Both approaches require forecasting cash flows in C$, so forecasts of Canadian inflation are required. Beyond this, it depends whether the financial manager is happier in forecasting future FX rates than in forecasting the required return in local currency terms. Approach B requires merely a one-year forecast of FX rates to derive the required return in C$ terms, whereas Approach A requires forecasts of FX rates over all future years of the project.

Remember that the equivalence of each approach depends on several factors, in particular, the operation of PPP and the existence of project inflation rates similar to those experienced at the national economy level. PPP ensures that if, say, the Canadian inflation rate exceeds the UK rate, the exchange rate of C$ vs sterling will deteriorate, i.e. sterling will strengthen to ensure the parity of purchasing power of each currency in each country.

Either approach is acceptable, although the first is preferable as it has the advantage of allowing cash flows to be adjusted at inflation rates specific to the project where these may differ from the national rate, although this does require more detailed forecasting.

■ Using Interest Rate Parity as an alternative

In both of the previous examples, the calculation has relied on the validity of PPP. As an alternative, Interest Rate Parity might be used. Bear in mind that, in theory at least, the difference in interest rates at any one time should reflect expected differences in inflation rates. Taking the Zoltan example, where the difference in inflation rates is (25% − 5%) = 20%, this would be consistent with a similar difference in interest rates.

Imagine that instead of being given information about expected inflation rates, we were told that the risk-free rate of interest in the United Kingdom was 7 per cent and that in Hungary it was 27 per cent: this would imply that the markets were expecting an inflation differential of 20 per cent, and thus, depreciation in the Forint versus Sterling. Future spot rates would be calculated as follows:

Year 1 spot rate = 200 × (1.27)/(1.07) = 237.4
Year 2 spot rate = 200 × (1.27)^2/(1.07)^2 = 281.8

Notice that the rates are slightly different from those mentioned earlier due to simplifying assumptions about converting from the real interest rate to the nominal interest rates, but the principle is identical. Obviously, one would only want to trust the first year's prediction as IRP is a technical relationship, but in later years, unless there is a forward market between these two currencies, predictions become far less reliable. A rate of exchange implied from interest rate differentials is called a **synthetic forward rate**.

14.8 EXPOSURE TO FOREIGN EXCHANGE RISK

You may appreciate now that FX variations are not always disastrous. The extent of FX exposure, and thus the urgency of dealing with it, depends on the structure of the firm's net cash flows in terms of its FX denomination. Firms with naturally-hedged cash flows may be relatively unconcerned by FX variations. However, firms differ in the extent to which they are naturally hedged.

■ The four-way classification

Figure 14.1 shows a schema for classifying the extent of a firm's exposure to FX variations. Essentially, this depends on the sensitivity of their domestic currency cash flows to FX movements. Net cash inflows are broken down into their revenue and operating cost components, in order to focus on firms' net exposure. Classified by corresponding sensitivity, the four types of firm are:

- *Domestics* generate little or no income from abroad and source mainly from local suppliers. Their net exposure is indirect and usually low, stemming from the exposure suffered by their competitors on the UK markets, and by their local suppliers.

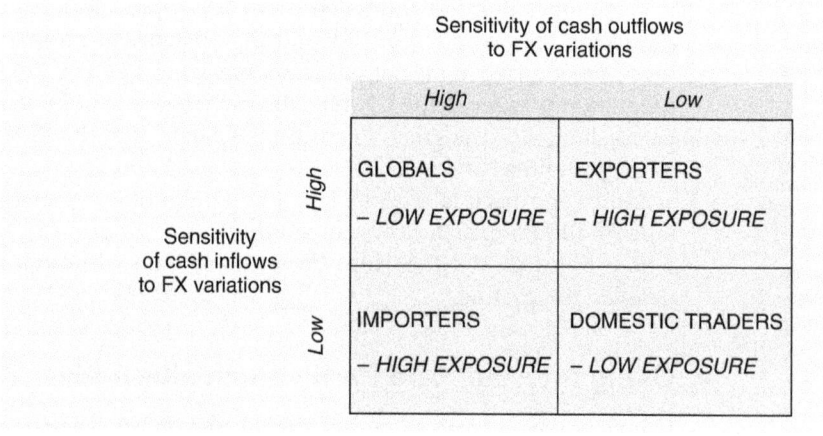

	Sensitivity of cash outflows to FX variations	
	High	**Low**
High (Sensitivity of cash inflows to FX variations)	GLOBALS – LOW EXPOSURE	EXPORTERS – HIGH EXPOSURE
Low	IMPORTERS – HIGH EXPOSURE	DOMESTIC TRADERS – LOW EXPOSURE

Figure 14.1 **Classification of firms by extent of operating exposure**

- *Exporters* source mainly from their own country, have high direct net exposures as their cash inflows and outflows are not naturally hedged, being in different currencies. They might consider adjusting their operating and/or financial strategies to achieve more insulated positions.
- *Importers* are in a similar position to exporters but in reverse – their net exposure is high because they source from abroad and sell on domestic markets.
- *Globals* have the lowest, and often minimal, net exposure. They have structured their operations so as to match as far as possible the currencies in which their inflows are denominated with those in which they incur costs. The match may not be perfect, given the indivisibility of some types of operation, e.g. production facilities, but regarding the overall profile of activities, their portfolios of cash inflow currencies should correlate highly with their portfolios of outflow currencies. At the group level, global firms should have little concern about FX exposures.

This is a powerful set of distinctions but is counter-intuitive to many people. Firms heavily engaged in foreign operations may actually have low net exposures while many domestics, blissfully thinking they are insulated from overseas-generated exposures may, in reality, be more highly exposed. A high indirect exposure could conceivably outweigh a low direct exposure.

The BMW case that follows explains how moving production outside Germany reduced the company's exposure to foreign exchange risk. The case also illustrates that FDI strategies can have more than one benefit as BMW also gained from diversifying supply chains.

Managing foreign exchange risk – BMW moves production overseas

The BMW Group, owner of the BMW, Mini and Rolls-Royce brands, has been based in Munich since its founding in 1916. But by 2011, only 17 per cent of the cars it sold were bought in Germany. In recent years, China has become BMW's fastest-growing market, accounting for 14 per cent of BMW's global sales volume in 2011. India, Russia and Eastern Europe have also become key markets.

The challenge. Despite rising sales revenues, BMW was conscious that its profits were often severely eroded by changes in exchange rates. BMW did not want to pass on its exchange rate costs to consumers through price increases. Its rival Porsche had done this at the end of the 1980s in the US and sales had plunged.

BMW took a two-pronged approach to managing its foreign exchange exposure. One strategy was to use a

Continued

'natural hedge' – meaning it would develop ways to spend money in the same currency as where sales were taking place, meaning revenues would also be in the local currency. However, not all exposure could be offset in this way, so BMW decided it would also use formal financial hedges. To achieve this, BMW set up regional treasury centres in the US, the UK and Singapore.

The natural hedge strategy was implemented in two ways. The first involved establishing factories in the markets where it sold its products; the second involved making more purchases denominated in the currencies of its main markets.

The overseas regional treasury centres were instructed to review the exchange rate exposure in their regions on a weekly basis and report it to a group treasurer, part of the group finance operation, in Munich. The group treasurer team then consolidates risk figures globally and recommends actions to mitigate foreign exchange risk.

The lessons. By moving production to foreign markets, the company not only reduces its foreign exchange exposure but also benefits from being close to its customers. In addition, sourcing parts overseas, and closer to its foreign markets, also helps to diversify supply chain risks.

Source: Bin, X. and Ying, L. (2012) The case study: How BMW dealt with exchange rate risk. *Financial Times*, 29 October. © The Financial Times Limited 2018. All rights reserved.

Operating/economic/strategic exposure

If PPP always worked, forecasting FX rates would be very simple – in practice, prolonged uncertainty over future exchange rates and thus the effect on the firm's future cash flows in domestic currency terms greatly concerns many financial managers. The longer the time horizon that the firm works to, the greater is its concern. Continuing exposure over a period of years is called **economic exposure**. This refers to the effect of changing FX rates on the value of a firm's operations, generally the result of changing economic and political factors, hence the alternative label **operating exposure**. Because these variations will also affect the firm's competitive position, and because protecting or enhancing that position often provokes a change in strategy, it is also called **strategic exposure**.

These three terms are often used as synonyms. Whatever we call it, the impact is felt on the present value of the firm's operating cash flows over time, and thus the value of the whole enterprise. To prevent or mitigate damage, the firm can adopt various strategies to protect its inherent value. Measurement of exposure is the first step.

Measuring operating exposure

Operating exposure is both direct and indirect. Firms are concerned not only about how FX changes affect their own cash flows, but also how their competitors are affected by these changes. If the Chinese yuan declines against the US dollar, this may seem of no great consequence to a UK firm that sources in the United States. However, it becomes important if, for example, US competitors that import from China see their import costs fall. These indirect effects are part of a firm's overall exposure.

Measurement of operating exposure thus involves identification and analysis of all future exposures both for the individual firm and also its main competitors, actual and even potential ones, bearing in mind that FX changes may even entice new entrants into existing markets.

It is worth repeating that operating exposure is concerned less with *expected* changes in FX rates, because, in efficient financial markets, both managers and investors will have already incorporated these into their anticipation of parent company currency cash flows. If the markets expect sterling to decline vs the US dollar, the likely higher future sterling cash inflows of UK firms that export to the United States will have been factored into company valuations. In this situation, it is generally advisable to incorporate the forward rate of exchange into projections for future planning purposes. The damage is done when expectations are not fulfilled and/or when changes result from totally unexpected factors.

Example: Pitt plc

Pitt plc produces half its output in the United States, valued at today's exchange rate (US$1.50 vs. £1) at £100 million. The other half is sold in the United Kingdom. About 25 per cent of Pitt's supplies are sourced from the United States, valued at £15 million. Labour costs are £10 million per annum, and cash overheads are £5 million per annum. Shareholders require a return of 12 per cent per annum.

Required
(a) Determine the present value of Pitt's operating cash flows in sterling terms over a 10-year time horizon.
(b) Identify Pitt's direct and indirect operating exposures.
(c) What is the effect on Pitt's PV if the sterling/dollar exchange rate changes to US$1.40 vs. £1?

Solution
(a) At the present exchange rate, Pitt's cash flows are:
- Cash inflows: 2 × £100m p.a.   = £200m
- Cash outflows:
    - Supplies (4 × £15m p.a.)   = (£60m)
    - Labour   = (£10m)
    - Overheads   = (£5m)
    - Net cash flow   = £125m

Present value = (£125m × 10-year annuity factor at 12%)
              = (£125m × 5.650) = £706m

(b) Direct exposures:
- 50 per cent of cash inflows are exposed.
- 25 per cent of payments to suppliers are exposed.
- Any USD content of labour input and cash overheads would also be exposed.

Indirect exposures stem from the extent to which:
- US competitors are exposed to currency fluctuations.
- US suppliers are exposed.
- UK competitors are exposed.
- UK suppliers are exposed.

As discussed, it is important to realise that overall exposures transcend variations in the USD/£ rate. If, for example, suppliers in the United Kingdom import from India, they face exposure from the exchange rate of the rupee vs sterling. Adverse variations are likely to spur them to recoup cost increases from their customers. Obviously, the extent to which they can achieve this depends on their own market power, e.g. the number and relative size of their own competitors and the importance of the components to customers like Pitt plc.

(c) Sterling depreciation to US$1.40 vs. £1 will increase the sterling value of the net cash inflows, because, at present, annual USD cash inflows exceed USD cash outflows. At the current exchange rate of US$1.50 vs. £1, the annual difference is (£100m − £15m) = £85m p.a.

Revised valuation:
- Inflows: [£100m + (£100m × 1.50/1.40)]   = £207m p.a.
- Outflows:
    - Supplies: (3 × £15m) + (£15m × 1.50/1.40)   = (£61m)
    - Labour   = (£10m)
    - Overheads   = (£5m)
    - Net Cash Inflow   = £131m
- PV at 12% = (£131m × 5.650) = £740m

Continued

In this example, depreciation of sterling by $(1-1.40/1.50) = 7\%$ has resulted in an increase in firm value of about 5 per cent. The sensitivity of a firm's value will depend on the structure of the firm's cash inflows and outflows – the greater the net foreign currency component, the greater the sensitivity of firm value.

Comment

The result is somewhat oversimplified for several reasons:

It assumes no change in the volumes of US-generated business in response to sterling depreciation. In reality, Pitt may lower the USD price to stimulate sales as it can now afford a price cut of up to 7 per cent and still achieve the same sterling cash inflow, after converting USD into sterling at the more favourable rate.

The effect will depend on:

(i) the extent of the price cut, i.e. whether Pitt matches the 7 per cent fall in sterling or takes some or all of this as windfall profit;
(ii) the elasticity of US demand for the product, i.e. the extent to which demand is stimulated by a price cut;
(iii) whether Pitt can produce enough to satisfy the demand increase;
(iv) the extent to which both US competitors and also other foreign firms supplying the US market follow a price cut.

Consequently, a full answer would depend on more rigorous strategic evaluation of the various consequences of the sterling depreciation. Similar comments apply to the increased sterling costs of supplies. Will Pitt try to absorb these costs? Will it try to pass them on wholly or partly? Will it seek alternative UK suppliers? In addition, there may be wider effects – will Pitt win sales from US competitors in the United Kingdom and elsewhere? How will fellow UK rivals respond to the sterling depreciation? How will non-exporting UK firms that import from the United States respond?

Having to grapple with these issues provides a powerful stimulus for seeking ways of trying to negate the effects of FX exposure.

Self-assessment activity 14.5

A UK-owned MNC produces in the United States and also exports to South American countries directly from the United Kingdom where it is paid in USD. Its US revenue is $50 million and its operating costs are $30 million. Export sales to South America are $100 million. What is its exposure to the USD/sterling exchange rate?

(Answer in Appendix A)

14.9 HOW MNCS MANAGE OPERATING EXPOSURE

Managing operating exposure involves taking steps to insulate the firm's operating cash flows as far as possible from the effect of unexpected FX changes, so as to minimise the effect on the value of the whole firm.

In Chapter 13, we explained a number of theories of the operation of FX markets. The upshot of these is that, if they are valid, firms need not worry about FX variations. However, because foreign exchange markets cannot always be relied upon to move quickly to new equilibria, it is often considered prudent to safeguard against the impact of future contingencies. Moreover, given the strongly competitive nature of many international markets, it is sensible to anticipate how competitors are likely to behave when operating conditions change.

There are two broad ways in which operating exposure can be minimised. The first involves structuring the firm's operations to insulate it from damage, and the second, structuring its financial policy to this end.

natural hedge
Where the adverse impact of FX rate variations on cash inflows are offset by the effect on cash outflows, or vice versa

The general aim is to construct a **natural hedge**. This occurs when there is little or no exposure because the adverse impact on cash inflows is exactly offset by the beneficial impact on cash outflows. A British firm producing and selling in the United States has a high degree of protection against sterling/dollar variations. If sterling appreciates, thus reducing the sterling value of dollar inflows, the adverse effect is largely counterbalanced by the corresponding fall in the sterling value of its USD-denominated inputs. Only the profit element is unhedged.

Firms that operate in the aerospace sector are particularly exposed to movements in the USD, the currency in which planes and engines are priced. Two firms that have tried to moderate their exposures are Rolls-Royce and Airbus. The former is constructing manufacturing and assembly plants in the United States and in Singapore, having already located the Head Office of its marine business on the island.

The following box shows details of how Airbus has attempted to moderate some of its operating exposure.

Airbus operations

The first Airbus final assembly line to operate outside of Europe, located in Tianjin, officially opened on 28 September 2008. This production site for A320 Family aircraft is a joint venture between Airbus and a Chinese consortium of Tianjin Free Trade Zone (TJFTZ) and China Aviation Industry Corporation (AVIC).

On 18 May 2009, the facility marked a milestone when the Chinese final assembly line's first jetliner – an A320 – completed its maiden flight, taking off from Tianjin International Airport for a 4-hour 14-minute airborne evaluation. This same A320 was delivered on 23 June 2009 to Dragon Aviation Leasing for operation by Chengu-based carrier Sichuan Airlines, marking the first customer handover of an Airbus jetliner produced outside Europe.

From 1 January to 26 May 2010, Airbus delivered a total of ten A320 Family jetliners assembled in Tianjin – demonstrating that this facility's production ramp-up was on track at the rate of two aircraft per month. In 2014, the joint venture was extended to cover the period 2016–25.

Source: Airbus website: **www.airbus.com**.

Firms that service overseas locations can achieve this 'self-hedging' effect in various ways:

- Source components and other inputs in the countries where sales are made.
- Open an operating subsidiary there to manufacture or assemble the product.
- Borrow in the same currency as that of cash inflows. The stream of outflows (interest and capital repayments) will help to match the series of inflows.
- The firm may pay suppliers in other countries with the currency received from sales. If it sells in USD, and sources from Poland, it can pay the Polish suppliers in USD rather than zlotys. This is called **currency switching**.

currency switching
Where an exporter pays for imported supplies in the currency of the export deal

The hedge constructed may not be a match in the same currency. As some currencies tend to move together due to the interdependence of the associated economies, e.g. Canada and the United States, the MNC could offset, say, a USD revenue stream with a C$ cost stream. This is termed **parallel matching**.

parallel matching
Applies where a firm offsets inflows in one currency with outflows denominated in a closely correlated currency

Where several locations are serviced, the key is diversification of operations. A diversified firm is better placed both to recognise disequilibrium situations in foreign exchange markets and also to adapt accordingly. For example:

- If relative costs in sterling terms alter as between different locations, a diversified MNC can arrange to reschedule production between locations.
- If product prices change in different markets, the MNC may strengthen its marketing efforts to exploit greater profit opportunities where prices are higher.

- If raw material prices alter as between different locations, the MNC can alter its sourcing policy.

Admittedly, such adjustments are likely to trigger various conversion or switch-over costs, but the MNC may still benefit from favourable 'portfolio effects'. The variability of cash flows in domestic currency terms is likely to fall if the firm receives income in a variety of currencies – foreign exchange rate variations may increase competitiveness in some markets to offset lower competitiveness in others. This, of course, underpins the diversification motive for foreign investment, mentioned earlier in the chapter. Portfolio diversification was considered more fully in Chapter 4.

Self-assessment activity 14.6

Revisit Self-assessment exercise 14.6. Suggest three ways for the firm to lower its exposure.
(Answer in Appendix A)

14.10 HEDGING THE RISK OF FOREIGN PROJECTS

This issue has already been addressed. Operating a foreign investment involves both translation exposure and economic exposure. The translation risk stems from exposure to unexpected exchange rate movements: for example, a fall in the value of the Australian dollar (AUD) against GBP will reduce the GBP value of assets appearing in the Australian subsidiary's balance sheet. When consolidated into the parent's accounts, this will require a write-down of the value of assets in GBP terms. This problem can be avoided if the exposed assets are matched by a corresponding liability. For example, if the initial investment is financed by a loan denominated in AUD, the diminution in the sterling value of assets will be matched by the diminution in the GBP value of the loan.

Perfect matching of assets and liabilities is not always possible. Many overseas capital markets are not equipped to supply the required capital. Besides, it is probably politic to provide an input of parent company equity to signal commitment to the project, the government and the country. However, perfect matching is probably unnecessary, since some assets such as machinery can be traded internationally. The cause of the exchange rate depreciation (i.e. higher internal prices) will lead to a rise in prices, and if the Law of One Price holds, this appreciation in the value of locally-held assets will compensate for the reduced GBP value of the currency. As a result, the need to match probably applies only to property assets and items of working capital such as debtors, which cannot readily be traded on international markets. (Note the obvious attraction of operating with a sizeable volume of short-term creditors if sterling is strengthening, especially at the financial year-end.)

Economic exposure is the long-term counterpart of transaction exposure – it applies to a stream of cash inflows and outflows. In theory, the problem of variations in the prices of inputs and outputs should also be solved by the operation of the Law of One Price. For example, local price inflation at a rate above that prevailing in the parent company's country will be exactly offset by depreciation in the local currency, thus maintaining intact the GBP value of locally-produced goods.

However, in practice, problems arise when PPP does not apply in the short term and when *project* prices alter at different rates from *prices in general*. The movement in the local price index is only an average price change, hiding a wide spread of higher and lower price variations. In principle, the firm could use the forward market to remove this element of unpredictability in the value of cash flows, but in practice, the forward market has a very limited time horizon, or is non-existent for many currencies.

Nevertheless, the parent company with widely-spread overseas operations can adopt a number of devices. It can mix the project's expected cash flows and outflows with those of other transactions to take advantage of netting and matching opportunities. It can lead and lag payments when it expects adverse currency movements, although host governments usually object to this. It can also use third-party currencies. For example, if it invests in oil extraction, its output will be priced in USD and the otherwise exposed cost of inputs may be sourced or invoiced in USD or in a currency expected to move in line with USD. A more aggressive policy might involve invoicing sales in currencies expected to be strong and sourcing in currencies expected to be weak, perhaps including the local one.

Another tactic is to use the foreign project's net cash flows to purchase goods produced in the host country that are exportable, or can be used as inputs for the parent's own production requirements. This converts the foreign currency exposure of the project's cash flow into a world price exposure of the goods traded. This may be desirable if the degree of uncertainty surrounding the relevant exchange rate is greater than that attaching to the relevant product price.

Much world trade is conducted on the stipulation that the exporter accepts payment in goods supplied by the trading partner, or otherwise undertakes to purchase goods and services in the country concerned. This linking of export contracts with reciprocal agreements to import is known as **counter-trade**. It is usually found where the importer suffers from a severe shortage of foreign currency or limited access to bank credits.

counter-trade
A form of trade involving reciprocal obligations with a trading partner, or counterparty, e.g. a commitment to buy from a firm or country that the firm sells to

buy-back
A method of obtaining payment for building a manufacturing unit overseas by taking the future physical product of the plant in return

One form of counter-trade is **buy-back**, which is a way of financing and operating foreign investment projects. In a buy-back, suppliers of plant, equipment or technical know-how agree to accept payment in the form of the future output of the investment concerned. This long-term supply contract with the overseas partner raises some interesting principal/agent issues, concerning, in particular, the quality of the output and the management of the operation. Ideally, the output should be a product for which a ready market is available or that the exporter can use as an input to its own production process. In recent years, Iran has signed buy-back deals with European energy majors Shell, TotalFinaElf and ENI to finance the development of oil and gas projects.

The advantage of buy-backs for a Western company is that they secure long-term supplies and obviate any need to worry about exchange rate movements. The effective cost is the cost incurred in financing the original construction, and perhaps an opportunity cost if world prices of the goods received fall. Buy-backs thus offer a way of locking into the present world price for the goods transferred, which has some appeal in markets where prices fluctuate widely, for example, oil.

14.11 POLITICAL AND COUNTRY RISK

According to *Euromoney*, which conducts a regular analysis of political risk: 'Political Risk is the risk of non-payment or non-servicing of payment for goods and services, or trade-related finance and dividends, and the non-repatriation of capital.'

The definition and the above discussion imply a distinction between economic and **political risk**, the latter resulting from governmental interference and the former from general economic turbulence. But because these are usually intertwined, the two risks are often grouped under the heading of **country risk**.

political risk
The risk of politically-motivated interference by a foreign government in the affairs of a MNC, that adversely affects its net cash flows

country risk
The risk of adverse effects on the net cash flows of a MNC due to political and economic factors peculiar to the country of location of FDI

It is not surprising that FDI by MNCs involves strong elements of political risk. Their very size and strength in relation to host countries creates the possibility of politically-inspired action, whether favourable, e.g. granting generous incentives, or adverse, e.g. expropriation of oil company assets as in Venezuela in 2006. Where the goals of the host government and the MNC conflict, the political risk escalates. Political risk is heightened where political and social instability prevails, and host government objectives are unclear.

The task of the MNC's planners is to define, identify and predict these sources of instability. Instability results from internal pressures or civil strife that may be caused by factors such as inequities, actual or perceived, between internal factions (whether racial, religious, tribal, etc.), extremist political programmes, forthcoming independence or impending elections.

Any MNC that is considering FDI may observe the signals of political instability, but to measure its extent is a complex task. A major cause of political and social instability is due to economic influences. Factors such as oscillating oil prices, banking crises, foreign exchange crises and rampant inflation all promote instability.

As in Argentina, Turkey and Egypt in the early 2000s, economic instability often necessitates heavy overseas borrowing to finance reconstruction. Because reforms take time to implement, risk of default is ever-present. Default risk can be gauged by factors such as a country's debt service ratio (debt service payments relative to exports) and the debt age profile. The political risks of such pressures can provoke actions such as:

- exchange controls;
- restrictions on registration of foreign companies;
- restrictions on local borrowing;
- expropriation or nationalisation;
- tax discrimination;
- import controls;
- limitation on access to strategic sectors of the economy;
- asset freezing.

Expropriation (confiscation of corporate assets with or without compensation), asset freezing (loss of control over asset management) and outright nationalisation represent the greatest political threat to foreign investors. The main risk is less that of expropriation *per se*, but the risk that compensation will be inadequate or delayed.

'Creeping' expropriation may also occur where mounting restrictions on prices, issue of work permits, transfer of shares, imports and dividends become likely when a nation feels threatened by the size and influence of MNCs. Hence, prior to deciding whether to operate in a new country, a pertinent question to consider is whether the MNC, either individually, or collectively with other MNCs, will dominate the industry, as occurs when oligopolistic rivals follow the strategic entry of a leader. If this is a strong probability, the political risk is greater than when penetration is low.

Assessing political and country risk (PCR)

There are several ways of assessing PCR:

1 Scoring systems

The magazine *Euromoney* produces country risk ratings on a regular basis. Its ratings are based on a weighted average method, using the following scoring system, based on percentages:

- Political risk – 30 per cent
- Economic performance – 30 per cent
- Structural assessment – 10 per cent
- Debt indicators – 10 per cent
- Credit ratings – 10 per cent
- Access to bank finance and capital markets – 10 per cent

The Euromoney 2016 Global Risk Trends guide explains how the world has become a riskier place. For example, the 2008 crisis has affected relative levels of risk in European countries. The Euromoney Country Risk Survey for 2016 rates Singapore as the least risky country, closely followed by Norway and Switzerland (see https://www.euromoneycountryrisk.com).

2 Delphi technique

Also known as 'consulting the oracle', this involves canvassing a panel of experts for their opinions, via questionnaires or direct personal or telephone contact, and then aggregating the replies. The *Euromoney* analysis is essentially a combination of check-listing and the Delphi technique.

3 Inspection visits

Key staff from the MNC's Head Office make a 'Grand Tour' to the prospective host country, often accompanied by local embassy officials.

4 Using local intelligence

Consulting local experts, e.g. official insiders and credit analysts from banks, to advise on prevailing local trends.

Corruption

A major issue in dealing with foreign officials is often corruption. Several agencies attempt to assess the extent to which local officials misuse their positions for personal gain when dealing with MNCs. For example, Transparency International (www.transparency.org) publishes a regular league table, based on a scale of 0–100 (100 = minimum perceived levels of public/sector corruption). In its table published in 2016 covering 176 countries, Denmark (1), New Zealand (2) and Finland (3) were reckoned to be the least corrupt countries in the world. Other European countries ranked as follows: Germany (10=), Britain (10=), France (23), Italy (68 – lower than many 'less developed' countries), while North Korea (174), South Sudan (175) and Somalia (176) were reckoned to be the most corrupt.

14.12 MANAGING POLITICAL AND COUNTRY RISK (PCR)

Protection against the adverse consequences of changes in the political or economic complexion of a host country can be achieved in four ways:

- Pre-investment negotiation
- Laying down operating strategies
- Preparation of a contingency crisis plan
- Insurance

These aspects are now considered in turn.

Pre-investment negotiation

The best approach to PCR management is to anticipate problems and negotiate an understanding beforehand. Different countries apply different codes of ethics regarding the honouring of prior contracts, especially if concluded under a previous regime. Nevertheless, pre-negotiation does provide a better basis for subsequent wrangling.

An investment agreement sets out respective rights and obligations on both the MNC and the host government. It could cover aspects such as:

- The basis whereby financial flows, such as dividends, management fees, royalties, patent fees and loan repayments may be remitted back to the home country.
- The basis for setting transfer prices used for costing inputs delivered from the home country.
- Rights relating to third-country markets, i.e. who can serve them.

- Obligations to build or fund social infrastructure like schools and hospitals.
- Methods of taxation – rates and calculation procedures.
- Requirements for **offset**, i.e. local sourcing.
- Access to host country financial markets.
- Employment practices, especially regarding openings for nationals. This is very common in the Middle East, e.g. Oman has an 'Omanisation' policy, and the United Arab Emirates operates an 'Emiratisation' policy.

offset
The requirement for an MNC to undertake a proportion of local sourcing as a condition of the award of an export deal (very common in the armaments industry)

Operating strategies

Flexible, risk-averting strategies that enhance the MNC's bargaining position can be devised in several areas.

Production and logistics

- Local sourcing increases local employment and may head off trouble if local interests would be damaged thereby.
- Siting production facilities to minimise risk, e.g. siting oil refineries in low-risk locations.
- Retaining control of transportation facilities like oil tankers and pipelines.
- Control of technology embodied in patents and the appointment of home country staff to manage complex technological processes. Coca-Cola has never divulged its magic formula, reputedly locked in a bank vault in Atlanta, Georgia.

Marketing

- Controlling markets by eliminating competition – locals are often happy to sell out.
- Controlling brand names and trademarks. McDonald's only franchises operations to local entrepreneurs.

Financial

- Issuing equity on the local stock market to extend ownership to locals. A Joint Venture is also an effective way to promote local participation.
- Restricting parental equity input – local debt financing is preferable to equity funding as it creates a hedge to offset local inflation and exchange rate depreciation, and also exerts leverage on local politicians if local banks stand to suffer from political intervention.
- Multi-source borrowing – raising loans from banks in several countries, and perhaps international development agencies, will build a wide nexus of vested interests in keeping the MNC healthy.

Preparation of a contingency crisis plan

Contingency planning helps in two ways, first, by providing an action plan to implement if things do go wrong, and second, it forces managers to think about the contingencies to which their foreign operation is most vulnerable.

Investment insurance

MNCs may be able to shift risk to a home country agency that specialises in accepting international risks. In the United Kingdom, the Export Credits Guarantee Department (ECGD) offers confiscation cover for new overseas investments, and Lloyds offers insurance facilities for existing and new investments in a comprehensive and non-selective form. In the United States, the government-owned Overseas Private Investment Corporation (OPIC) will cover risks relating to inability to convert overseas earnings into dollars, expropriation, war and revolution, and loss of business income arising from events of political violence that damage MNC assets.

■ A loaded dice?

In some countries, an apparently independent business partner may prove to have very strong links with the state, as BP has discovered with its joint ventures in Russia. In such countries, when difficulties arise, the local officials are more likely to side against the MNC as several firms have found in dealing with India, as well as Russia.

The following cameo illustrates the difficulties faced by companies when governments make policy changes. Too much official interference can also be counterproductive, as Thailand discovered in 2007 when IKEA pulled out of a new store development, as it faced increasingly restrictive laws on foreign ownership.

When a haven harbours unseen risk

If you had asked board directors which of two situations – the stand-off between Russia and Ukraine in Crimea, and the forthcoming British Budget – was politically riskier, they would have chosen the first. But for a few insurers involved in the lucrative business of offering annuities to pensioners, Britain turned out to be the more perilous place after the UK Chancellor astounded them by announcing reforms that could cut the size of that market by 90 per cent.

The Crimean crisis, for all its unpredictability, fits into the category of political risk that risk analysts love to analyse, risk managers to manage and insurers to insure against. If a capricious commander-in-chief orders men in fatigues in faraway places to do something that disrupts your supply chain or shuts down your factory, you may not like it, but the chances are you have braced yourselves for it. But if a minister in an industrialised country marches in and annexes your company's profit forecasts overnight, it may come as a shock. It should not. 'Safe' countries are riskier than they look.

Much recent economic growth has been concentrated in places where political and regulatory risk is high.

Geopolitical threats include terrorism, civil war, guerrilla activities, military repression, civil disorder, crime, workforce instability, change in government policy or the ruling party, economic or other sanctions imposed by other countries, extreme fluctuations in currency exchange rates or high inflation.

Source: Hill, A. (2014) When a haven harbours unseen risk. *Financial Times*, 24 March. © The Financial Times Limited 2018. All rights reserved.

14.13 FINANCING FDI

A multinational company (MNC) may have more opportunities to lower the overall cost of capital than a 'domestic'. This is often due to its larger size, and partly due to greater access to international financial markets, allowing it to exploit any temporary disequilibria as well as receive host government concessions.

The international financing decision has three elements:

1 *Whether* to borrow?
2 *How much* to borrow?
3 *Where* to borrow?

■ Key issues

The issues that determine these decisions are:

- **Gearing ratio.** The debt–equity mix selected for overseas activities is influenced by the gearing of the parent, or by the debt/equity ratios of comparable, competing firms in the location of the FDI. If the parent guarantees the subsidiary's borrowing, so long as the existing gearing of the parent is 'reasonable', the subsidiary's borrowing may be a separate issue, especially if a joint venture is formed and the borrowing of the overseas affiliate can be kept off-balance sheet. This enables fuller exploitation of subsidised loans and lower tax rates.

- **Taxation.** MNCs need to examine differences between the treatment of withholding taxes, losses, interest and dividend payments. Tax-deductibility of interest provides an incentive to borrow locally.
- **Currency risk.** Local borrowing can also reduce foreign exchange exposure by enabling a match of interest and capital repayments against locally-generated cash inflows denominated in local currency.
- **Political risk.** Expropriation of assets or other interference is less likely if the MNC borrows from local banks or from the international markets. The host government is unlikely to want to offend the international financial community as it would damage its own credit standing. If the MNC borrows via the World Bank, it can include a **cross-default clause**, so that a default to any creditor automatically triggers default on a World Bank loan.

The case for borrowing

- Less risky than using equity which puts owners' capital at risk.
- Debt service is based on a strict schedule, helping cash flow planning and currency hedging. Dividends are more erratic.
- Debt service payments are less likely to antagonise host governments. Erratic dividend flows may interfere with a host government's attempts to manage the external value of its currency, especially if the MNC is a major contributor to local GDP.
- Tax relief on interest.
- Opportunity to hedge foreign exchange risk by matching.
- Protection against political risk.
- Access to concessionary local finance.
- Overseas equity markets (if they exist) can be highly inefficient.

The case against borrowing

- The parent's debt/equity ratio may already be high.
- There may be only limited local borrowing facilities.
- Local borrowing may entail more intensive credit risk investigation fees, and higher interest rates if the MNC has no local credit rating.
- The host government may place an upper limit on local borrowing to restrict tax avoidance.

$4bn CNOOC international debt issue breaks Chinese records

CNOOC, the Chinese state-run oil company, has joined the global rush to raise cheap corporate credit, with a $4bn bond, the biggest international issue in Asia in a decade. The offering consists of $750m of 1.125 per cent guaranteed notes due 2016; $750m of 1.75 per cent guaranteed notes due 2018; $2,000m of 3.0 per cent guaranteed notes due 2023; and $500m of 4.250 per cent guaranteed notes due 2043.

The net proceeds of $3.94tn will be used mainly to repay part of a $6bn short-term credit taken out to finance its $18bn acquisition of Nexen, the Canadian energy group. A string of banks backed the deal which was five times subscribed, with investors offering about $24bn.

Source: Wagstyl, S. (2013) Cnooc: the bonds bandwagon rolls on ... but for how long?. Financial Times, 3 May. © The Financial Times Limited 2018. All rights reserved.

Assessment

The balance of argument usually points to borrowing to finance foreign subsidiaries; indeed, braver corporate treasurers may try to exploit perceived disequilibria in global financial markets to access 'cheap' finance. However, the International Fisher Effect (explained in Chapter 13) should caution against this. The benefit of borrowing at 'low' interest rates should always (eventually at least) be offset by the appreciation in currency in which debts are to be repaid.

Special Purpose Vehicles (SPV)
An entity set up specifically for managing a firm's financial requirements and obligations

Larger MNCs may set up their own financial subsidiaries as **Special Purpose Vehicles (SPV)**, established largely for the purpose of obtaining the funds required to finance the entire firm's ongoing growth needs. This avoids problems over costs and access to capital in the host country. The SPV simply borrows on world markets using the credit rating of the parent. Firms that use SPVs include General Electric Corporation, BMW and Ford.

The currency cocktail

There is a strong argument for borrowing in a range or 'cocktail' of currencies to spread the risk over a diversified portfolio of borrowed currencies. By diversifying sources of finance, the MNC may take advantage of what it perceives as unusually low rates in certain financial centres. This requires the MNC to be well-known in international financial markets and to have established, sound banking relationships. Thus, a firm needing to refinance a medium-term loan maturing in London where interest rates are 7 per cent may decide to borrow in Japan where interest rates for corporate borrowing are, say, 2–3 per cent.

To illustrate a currency cocktail, consider Table 14.4 which shows the long-term indebtedness of International Airlines Group by currency and by type of borrowing instrument.

Table 14.4 International Airlines Group borrowings at 31 December 2016

	Millions 2016	Millions 2015
Loans		
Bank:		
US dollar	$176	$246
Euro	€498	€536
Pound sterling	£47	£119
Chinese yuan	CNY623	CNY716
	€809	€1,027
Fixed rate bonds:		
Euro	€1,104	€1,381
Pound sterling	–	£250
	€1,104	€1,725
Finance leases		
US dollar	$3,246	$3,464
Euro	€2,343	€1,458
Japanese yen	¥63,614	¥44,599
Pound sterling	£527	£656
	€6,602	€5,878
	€8,515	€8,630

Source: International Airlines Group *Annual Report*, 2016.

14.14 THE WACC FOR FDI

In Section 14.6, we explained how a project-specific discount rate could be obtained for a foreign investment. At that point, we were assuming all-equity funding. But what if the project is partly debt-financed? This issue is often highly relevant where foreign governments offer concessionary interest rates, often prompting a level of local debt financing well above the parent's own gearing. The most appropriate solution is to use a tailor-made WACC calculated to reflect the particular financing mix of the project.

To illustrate this, let us revisit the case of Malaku Mining from earlier in this chapter. Recall that it was decided that a local Beta value of 0.75 was appropriate to use, resulting in a project-specific equity cost of 8.75 per cent.

Now assume that Malaku can borrow in Indonesia at the concessionary rate of 3 per cent and that local regulations allow it to offset interest charges against local taxation, paid at 40 per cent. The WACC for the Indonesian mining project is found in the usual way by weighting the cost of each form of finance by its contribution to financial structure, in this case, project financing. Now assume that the project is financed 25 per cent by parental equity and 75 per cent by local borrowing. The WACC is thus:

$$(8.75\% \times \text{equity weight}) + (3\%[1 - 40\%] \times \text{debt weight})$$
$$= (8.75\% \times 25\%) + (1.8\% \times 75\%) = (2.2\% + 1.4\%) = 3.6\%$$

This is an interesting result indeed. The combination of low interest rate and high debt proportion results in a remarkably low required return. These sorts of calculation, although based on sound CAPM logic, can often generate much lower project cut-off rates than for comparable UK investment. To many executives, it is inconceivable that high-risk foreign projects should be evaluated at lower discount rates than UK projects.

Financial managers often have some difficulty in explaining and justifying lower WACCs to sceptical executives whose natural inclination is to use *higher* rates for foreign projects. The response is that, although foreign projects often have higher total risks, additional risks are usually project- and country-specific, and are thus very different from those affecting UK projects. These risks are best handled in more effective ways, e.g. by hedging foreign exchange risk, than by simply hiking the discount rate. Raising the hurdle rate, and possibly excluding an attractive, albeit risky, project is inferior to a considered policy of risk management.

14.15 APPLYING THE APV TO FDI

Discounting at the WACC implies that all the complex interactions involved in the investment can be factored into a single discount rate. In no case is this more difficult than for foreign investment projects that differ from domestic activities in aspects such as taxation, foreign exchange rate variability, concessionary financing and numerous additional dimensions of risk. This makes FDI a prime candidate for evaluation by the APV method.

For FDI, the evaluation procedure is:

1. Evaluate the core project assuming it is financed entirely by owners' equity to find the base case, as if the project were undertaken in the home country.
2. Separately evaluate the 'extras' such as the tax breaks and subsidies offered by the host government, and any spill-over effects on other activities, e.g. lost export trade.
3. Calculate APV = [base case NPV − PV of 'extras'].
4. Accept the project if the APV is positive.

A simple APV model is shown in Figure 14.2. The APV is defined as the inherent value of the foreign-located project to the firm's owners, adjusted for all positive and negative side-effects. For foreign projects, the APV is particularly useful when project financing differs from the parent firm's capital structure, but suffers the limitation that calculation of these side-effects and their associated degrees of risk is difficult in practice. Inevitably, a high degree of judgement is required.

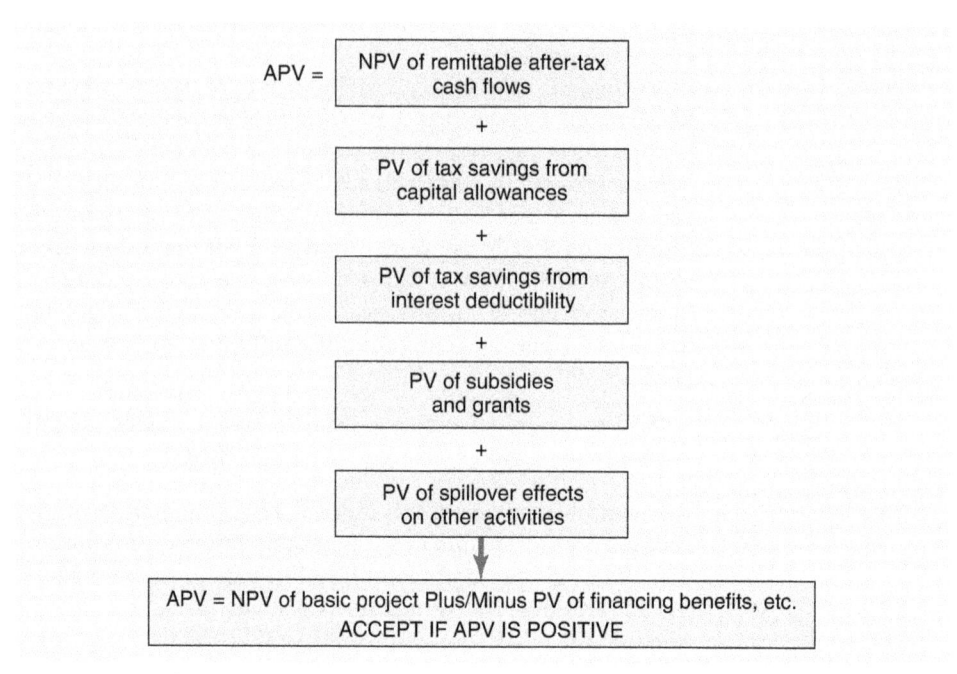

```
APV = NPV of remittable after-tax cash flows
      +
      PV of tax savings from capital allowances
      +
      PV of tax savings from interest deductibility
      +
      PV of subsidies and grants
      +
      PV of spillover effects on other activities
      ↓
APV = NPV of basic project Plus/Minus PV of financing benefits, etc.
ACCEPT IF APV IS POSITIVE
```

Figure 14.2 A simple APV model

14.16 WORKED EXAMPLE: APPLYING THE APV

(This question was part of a CIMA question in the May 2006 P9 Financial Strategy exam paper, in which it carried 15 of the available 25 marks.)

Question

GHI is a mobile phone manufacturer based in France with a wide customer base in France and Germany, with all costs and revenues based in the euro (€). GHI is considering expanding into the Benelux countries and has begun investigating how to break into this market.

After careful investigation, the following project cash flows have been identified:

Year	€million
0	(20)
1	5
2	5
3	4
4	3
5	3

The project is to be funded by a loan of €12 million at an annual interest rate of 5 per cent and repayable at the end of five years. Loan issue costs amount to 2 per cent and are tax-deductible.

GHI has a debt/equity ratio of 40:60 (at market values), a pre-tax cost of debt of 5.0 per cent and a cost of equity of 10.7 per cent.

Under the terms of a Double Tax Treaty, tax is payable at 25 per cent wherever the earnings of a project are made, and not taxed again when cash is repatriated. The initial investment of €12 million will qualify for full tax relief.

Required

Advise GHI on whether or not to accept the project, based on a calculation of its Adjusted Present Value (APV), and comment on the limitations of an APV approach in this context.

Answer

The first step is to obtain an ungeared, equity discount rate. Substituting into the formula:

$$k_{eg} = k_{eu} + [k_{eu} - k_d]\frac{V_B(100 - t)\%}{V_S}$$

$$10.7\% = k_{eu} + [k_{eu} - 5\%] \times \frac{4 \times (100 - 35)\%}{6}$$

$$10.7\% = k_{eu} + 0.433 k_{eu} - 2.167\%$$

Hence, the cost of equity is:

$$k_{eu} = 12.867\%/1.433 = 8.98\% \text{ or, approximately, } 9\%$$

Year	0	1	2	3	4	5
Project cash flows	−12	5	5	4	3	3
Local tax on cash flows at 25%		−1.25	−1.25	−1	−0.75	−0.75
Net cash flows	−12	3.75	3.75	3	2.25	2.25
Discount factor at 9%	1	0.917	0.842	0.772	0.708	0.650
Present Value	−12	3.43	3.15	2.32	1.59	1.46

NPV of basic project at 9% = −£12 million + £8.95 million = −£3.05 million

The next step is to find the PV of the 'extras'. Beginning with the tax shield on investment expenditure (assumed offsettable against earnings from other activities)

= 25% × £12 million = £3 million

The tax shield on debt is:

Tax relief on debt interest = €150,000 each year for five years (= €12 × 5% × 25%)
PV of tax relief on debt interest = €0.67 million (= €150,000 × 4.452)

Finally, the issue costs:

Issue costs = €240,000 (= €12 million × 2)
PV of tax relief on issue costs = €0.06 million (= €240,000 × 0.25 × 0.952)

The full APV calculation is thus:

Adjusted present value	€000
Base case NPV	(3.05)
Tax relief on initial outlay	3.00
PV of tax relief on debt interest	0.67
Issue costs	(0.24)
PV of tax relief on issue costs	0.06
Adjusted present value	0.44

Hence, although the basic project is not worthwhile, adding in the present value of the financing costs and benefits and the investment tax break, the APV is positive. The project should thus be accepted.

Limitations of the APV
- Determining the costs and benefits involved in the financing method to be used can be difficult (especially where they are based on an estimate of the enhanced debt capacity provided by the project, as in this case).
- Finding a suitable cost of equity for the base NPV calculation is subjective and may not truly reflect the risk associated with the new project, especially if the project is based abroad (as here – although there are no currency complications).
- Whether the tax rate will remain at this level, and the tax treaty will stay in force.
- Whether to discount the tax savings from the debt at the post-tax rate of interest or at the cost of equity.

Self-assessment activity 14.7

List eight ways in which MNCs can lower political risk.
(Answer in Appendix A)

SUMMARY

This chapter has examined the strategic motivations that drive firms to enter foreign markets, and methods of effecting entry, in particular, direct investment. Evaluating FDI is a complex process that differs in several important respects from evaluation of home country investment, not least the exposure to FX rate variations. As a result, FDI evaluation is more art than science, especially as it involves so many unquantifiable aspects such as the prevailing political mood of the host country, assessing political and other country risks and devising appropriate safeguards. Clearly, this topic transcends purely *financial* strategy for multinational organisations.

Key points

- Foreign direct investment (FDI) may be undertaken for a variety of strategic reasons: for example, globalisation of component sources or meeting the threat of a competitor already based overseas.
- FDI is generally undertaken when exporting (with relatively high variable costs, but low fixed costs) becomes more expensive than overseas production (with relatively high fixed costs but low variable costs).
- In principle, the evaluation of FDI is similar to appraisal of domestic investment, but there are important additional complications that may cloud the analysis.
- Among such complications are exchange rate complications, political risk, such as the risk of expropriation, exceptional inducements to invest in a particular location, and cannibalisation of existing export sales.
- Most of these complexities can be alleviated by (i) evaluating the project from the perspective of the parent company's shareholders, and (ii) as a first approximation at least, relying on the four-way parity relationships.
- If the parity relationships hold, then there are two equivalent ways of evaluating FDI: (i) predicting all future cash flows in the foreign currency, and discounting these at the local (i.e. overseas) cost of capital, and then converting to domestic

- currency at spot; and (ii) converting all the predicted foreign currency cash flows to the domestic currency using estimates of the future spot exchange rates, and discounting these at the domestic cost of capital.
- A tailor-made discount rate can be found by using the cost of capital of a comparable overseas firm, but allowing for the likely less-than-perfect correlation between the foreign economy and the domestic one.
- Foreign investment risk is mainly economic risk. This can be alleviated by strategic decisions, e.g. location of production facilities in a range of countries, and hence, operating in a variety of currencies.
- Similarly, diversification of markets can produce the same sort of currency cocktail.
- The extent to which a firm needs to hedge investment project risk depends on its international profile of activities, and thus the extent to which operating risks net off against each other in natural hedges. For example, a firm producing in Italy and selling in France has no direct operating exposure as all transactions are conducted in euros.
- Counter-trade, i.e. making reciprocal dealing arrangements with firms and governments in other countries, can be used to mitigate foreign exchange risk. Available methods extend from crude barter to buy-back facilities.
- Political risk can be moderated in various ways, e.g. borrowing from local banks, but the guiding principle is to make the MNC indispensable to the local economy and society.
- Corruption is endemic in some foreign countries, so a sad fact of life is that failure to play the local game can lead to loss of business.
- If the complexities of evaluating FDI make the conventional DCF model too cumbersome, a short-cut approach is offered by the adjusted present value (APV) approach which separates out the cash flows from basic operations from those attributable to financing and other complexities.

Further reading and website

Books on international/multinational financial management (see Chapter 13) invariably carry chapters on evaluation of FDI – Shapiro (2013) has excellent coverage on this topic. Similarly, Eun (2012) is a challenging book containing detailed materials on international finance with several real-life examples.

More general texts on international business such as those by Daniels *et al.* (2009) and Rugman and Collinson (2012) include extensive treatments of international strategy and operations, and usually cover appraisal of foreign projects also, but to a lesser depth. Buckley (2012) gives probably the most comprehensive coverage of overseas capital budgeting. Excellent analyses of operating exposure can be found in Lessard and Lightstone (2006) and in Grant and Soenen (2004). Rossi and Volpin (2004) investigate the determinants of cross-border mergers and acquisitions activity in different countries. Similarly, Xie *et al.* (2017) review 250 studies on the determinants of cross-border mergers and acquisitions and provide a good summary and critique on their findings.

Dunning and Lundan (2008) is perhaps the most authoritative text on the role of the MNC in the global economy. Butler (2016) also contains detailed information on the concepts and operations of international finance and financial management.

The World Investment Report, published each autumn (usually September) by UNCTAD (**www.unctad.org**), is a mine of information on trends in FDI.

QUESTIONS

Questions with a coloured number have solutions in Appendix B on page 501.

1. The USD vs. GBP exchange rate is $1.50 vs. £1. A UK MNC operating in the United States plans to sell goods worth $100 million at today's prices to US customers. Show that its GBP revenue *in real terms* will not be affected if PPP applies under each of the following conditions:
   - (i) UK and US inflation at 5% p.a.
   - (ii) UK inflation 5%, US inflation 2%.
   - (iii) UK inflation 2%, US inflation 5%.

2. OJ Limited is a supplier of leather goods to retailers in the United Kingdom and other Western European countries. The company is considering entering into a joint venture with a manufacturer in South America. The two companies will each own 50 per cent of the limited liability company JV (SA) and will share profits equally. Of the initial capital, £450,000 is being provided by OJ Limited, and the equivalent in South American dollars (SA$) is being provided by the foreign partner. The managers of the joint venture expect the following net operating cash flows which are in nominal terms:

	SA$ 000	Predicted future rates of exchange to £ sterling
Year 1	4,250	10
Year 2	6,500	15
Year 3	8,350	21

   For tax reasons, JV (SA), the company to be formed specifically for the joint venture, will be registered in South America.

   Ignore taxation in your calculations.

   Assume you are a financial adviser retained by OJ Limited to advise on the proposed joint venture.

   Required

   (a) Calculate the NPV of the project under the two assumptions explained below. Use a discount rate of 16 per cent for both assumptions, and express your answer in sterling.

   Assumption 1: The South American country has exchange controls which prohibit the payment of dividends above 50 per cent of the annual cash flows for the first three years of the project. The accumulated balance can be repatriated at the end of the third year.

   Assumption 2: The government of the South American country is considering removing exchange controls and restrictions on repatriation of profits. If this happens, all cash flows will be distributed as dividends to the partner companies at the end of each year.

   (b) Comment briefly on whether or not the joint venture should proceed based solely on these calculations.

   (CIMA)

3. PG plc is considering investing in a new project in Canada that will have a life of four years. Initial investment is C$150,000, including working capital. The net cash flows that the project will generate are C$60,000 per annum for Years 1, 2 and 3 and C$45,000 in Year 4. The terminal value of the project is estimated at C$50,000, net of tax.

   The current spot rate for C$ against the pound sterling is 1.70. Economic forecasters expect the pound to strengthen against the Canadian dollar by 5 per cent per annum over the next four years. The company evaluates UK projects of similar risk at 14 per cent per annum.

   Required

   Calculate the NPV of the Canadian project using the following two methods:

   (i) Convert the foreign currency cash flows into sterling and discount at a sterling discount rate.

   (ii) Discount the cash flows in C$ using an adjusted discount rate that incorporates the 12-month forecast spot rate.

   (CIMA)

4 Kay plc, a UK-based chemical firm but with plants in Germany and the Netherlands, manufactures man-made fibres. It would like to expand its exports to Latin America and the country of Copacabana, in particular. However, Copacabana is unable to pay in Western currency and its own currency, the poncho, is subject to rapid depreciation, due to high local inflation. One solution to this problem is an arrangement whereby Kay manages and pays for the construction of a fibres plant and accepts payment in the form of the finished product of fibres (a so-called buy-back).

Construction will take two years and expenditures can be treated as four equal half-yearly payments of 10 million ponchos at today's prices, beginning in six months' time. The plant will have a 15-year life, but will attract no local investment incentives. The inflation rate in Copacabana is expected to average 20 per cent p.a. over the construction period. The current exchange rate of the poncho vs. sterling is 1:4 and inflation in the United Kingdom has recently averaged 5 per cent.

The fibres produced and taken as payment can be traded on world markets, probably in Europe, where the present price is €500 per tonne. Kay is not prepared to accept payment in this way for more than five years. The expected production rate of the plant is 20,000 tonnes per annum, and Kay would take 40 per cent of this in payment.

The current euro vs sterling rate is €1.60 per £1, and sterling is expected to depreciate by 5 per cent per annum prior to joining the euro bloc.

Further information

- The project will be financed by equity only.
- Kay is at present debt-free. Its shareholders seek a return of 20 per cent p.a. for projects of this degree of risk.
- Profits from the operation will be taxed at 30 per cent when repatriated to the United Kingdom. Assume no delay in tax payment. All development costs will qualify for UK tax relief.
- Any losses will be carried forward to qualify for tax relief.
- There will be no tax liability in Copacabana.

Required

Determine whether Kay should undertake this project.

5 Brighteyes plc manufactures medical and optical equipment for both domestic and export sale. It is investigating the construction of a manufacturing plant in Lastonia, a country in the former Soviet bloc. Initial discussions with the Ministry of Economic Development in Lastonia have met with favourable response, providing the project can generate a 10 per cent pre-tax return. Shareholders look for a return of 15 per cent in real terms.

The investment will be partly import-substituting and partly export-based, selling to neighbouring countries. The project has been offered a local tax holiday, exempting it from all taxes for the first 10 years, except for cash remittances, for which a 20 per cent withholding tax will apply. Modern factory premises on an industrial estate with convenient road and rail links have been offered at a reasonable rent.

The initial investment will be £10 million in plant, machinery and set-up costs, all payable in sterling by the parent company. Additional funds will come from a bank loan of 20 million latts, the local currency (4 latts = £1), negotiated with a local bank, at a concessionary rate of interest of 10 per cent p.a. This will be used to finance working capital. Operating cash flows, the basis for calculating tax, are estimated at L10 million in Year 1 and L22 million thereafter until Year 5.

The whole of the parent's earnings after payment of local interest and taxation will be repatriated to the United Kingdom. The Lastonia withholding tax is to be allowed as a deduction before calculating the UK Corporation Tax, currently at the rate of 30 per cent. All transfers can be treated as occurring on the final day of each accounting period, when all taxes become due.

The new venture is expected to 'cannibalise' exports that Brighteyes would otherwise have made to neighbouring countries, resulting in post-tax cash flow losses of £0.5 million in each of Years 2 to 5. For planning purposes, Year 5 is the cut-off year, when the realisable value of the plant and equipment is estimated at L24 million. The working capital will be realised, subject to losses of L2 million on stocks and L2 million on debtors. Funds realised will be used to repay the local borrowing, and the balance transferred to the United Kingdom without further tax penalty or restriction.

The exchange rate is forecast to remain at L4 vs. £1 until Year 2, when the latt is expected to fall to L5 vs. £1.

Required

(i) Is the project acceptable from the Lastonian Ministry's point of view?
(ii) Is it worthwhile from the viewpoint of the foreign subsidiary?
(iii) Does it create wealth for Brighteyes' shareholders?

6 Palmerston plc operates in both the United Kingdom and Germany. In attempting to assess its economic exposure, it compiles the following data:

- UK sales are influenced by the euro's value as it faces competition from German suppliers. It forecasts annual UK sales based on three possible scenarios:

Euro: sterling exchange rate	Revenue from UK business
1.65:1	£200m
1.60:1	£215m
1.55:1	£220m

- Revenues from sales made in Germany are expected to be £120m p.a.
- Expected cost of goods sold is £120m p.a. from UK materials purchases, and €200m from purchases in Germany.
- Estimated cash fixed operating expenses are £50m p.a.
- Variable operating expenses are estimated at 20 per cent of total sales value (including German sales translated into sterling).
- Palmerston is financed entirely by equity and shareholders require a return of 15 per cent p.a.

Required
(i) Construct a forecast cash flow statement for Palmerston under each scenario.
(ii) Value Palmerston's equity under each scenario, assuming a 10-year operating time horizon. Ignore terminal values.
(iii) Suggest how Palmerston might restructure its operations to lower its sensitivity to exchange rate movements.

Ignore taxation.

7 A professional accountancy institute in the United Kingdom is evaluating an investment project overseas in Eastasia, a politically stable country. The project involves the establishment of a training school to offer courses on international accounting and management topics. It will cost an initial 2.5 million Eastasian dollars (EA$) and it is expected to earn post-tax cash flows as follows:

Year	1	2	3	4
Cashflow (EA$000)	750	950	1,250	1,350

The following information is available:

- The expected inflation rate in Eastasia is 3 per cent a year.
- Real interest rates in the two countries are the same. They are expected to remain the same for the period of the project.
- The current spot rate is EA$2 per £1 sterling.
- The risk-free rate of interest in Eastasia is 7 per cent and in the UK 9 per cent.
- The company requires a sterling return from this project of 16 per cent.

(CIMA)

Required
Calculate the sterling net present value of the project using *both* the following methods:
(i) by discounting annual cash flows in sterling,
(ii) by discounting annual cash flows in Eastasian $.

Practical assignment

Inspect the Annual Report for a company of your choice, to examine how its international profile of activities has changed over the years. You may find difficulty in obtaining a full set of accounts reaching very far back in time, but examination of a sample should give you a flavour of the company's policy regarding internationalisation.

Look also at the chairman's statements to glean an indication of the importance attached to overseas operations in the company's strategy.

15

Key issues in modern finance: a review

What is a fund manager?

What I do: pension funds entrust us money to invest in the stock market, hoping that my team can achieve better returns than the market. We are so-called value investors, with a 'horizon' of about three to five years. After a lot of homework, we buy shares in companies we hope to sell half a decade later for a good profit. We are like marathon runners, where traders are more like sprinters – they close their positions [sell all their stocks] at the end of each day.

Ultimately what you are after as a fund manager is what we call the underlying reality, the fundamentals of a particular company. What kind of returns can a company make? What kind of investment and growth opportunities are there? To what extent is management willing and able to take advantage of these opportunities? These key drivers determine the company's value. We then build a model that we can feed new developments into, to keep our assessment of the company's value and prospects up-to-date.

Finally, we have to follow the psychology of the markets, because not everyone invests like we do, with a five-year perspective. There's a lot of herd behaviour. Successful investors are contrarians, they go where others are not.

Source: Copyright Guardian News & Media Ltd 2018

15.1 INTRODUCTION

This final chapter summarises the main principles of finance underpinning the text, and it also provides the opportunity to extend the discussion to review key ideas relating to behavioural finance. This extension of the discussion is especially important as it reminds us that finance is not merely a technical subject. In finance, it is commonly assumed that we are rational beings seeking to maximise wealth. However, as the introductory article shows, this is not always the case; there is also the 'psychology of the markets' to contend with. Behavioural finance sets out to understand how our behaviour affects financial decision-making. It alleges that individuals do not always act entirely rationally. This is not to suggest that we act randomly; rather, that there are observable patterns to individuals' behaviours arising from psychological biases. Behavioural finance has gained more followers in recent years, and one reason for this is the 2007–8 financial crisis. The crisis caused many to observe that certain behaviours had played a role in the crisis. The topic of behavioural finance is considered later in this chapter.

A good finance theory is one that offers useful explanations of present behaviour and provides a guide to future behaviour. We frequently find that rather restrictive assumptions are made in developing financial models. For example:

1 All markets – not just capital markets – are perfectly competitive.
2 Information is perfect and costless.
3 Transaction costs are zero.
4 No taxes exist.

These assumptions lead naturally to certain propositions that can be questioned. First, only shareholders really matter. A perfect labour market implies that managers and workers have sufficient mobility and can always find other equally attractive alternative employment. Second, shareholders are only interested in maximising the market value of their shareholdings. Given perfect, costless information, managers are tightly controlled by the shareholders to implement and pursue value-maximising strategies. Third, the pursuit of shareholder wealth is achieved by instructing managers to invest only in those projects that are worth more than they cost. Financing strategies, whether concerning dividends, capital structure or leasing, are largely irrelevant as they do little to increase shareholders' wealth.

The assumptions underlying the theory of finance appear to be at odds with reality. Information is imperfect; transaction costs and information costs may be sizeable. Markets are frequently highly imperfect; management will usually have a good deal of interest in the firm – an interest that may well conflict with that of shareholders. Managers have far from complete knowledge of the set of feasible financing strategies available, their cash flow patterns and impact on market values. Shareholders are even less well informed. Taxation policy, bankruptcy costs and other factors can have a major influence on financial strategies.

Whether we talk about markets, firms or managers, we are essentially looking at behaviour – the behaviour of individual managers, investors or groups.

Most readers will be familiar with the popular board game Monopoly. There is more than a passing resemblance between this game and corporate finance. Both are about maximising investors' wealth in risky environments, making investment decisions with uncertain payoffs, raising finance and managing cash flow. Players and managers must stick to the rules of governance and seek to devise appropriate investment, financing and trading strategies to gain competitive advantage. While rational analysis and sound judgement are essential, there remains room for sentiment, psychology, fun, and, to make the game interesting, a generous portion of luck!

Some aspects of finance, particularly routine finance decisions, can be operationalised through clear rules and procedures. But good finance managers look for something more than rules and procedures. They seek to understand the behaviour of markets and companies. Theories of finance seek to provide explanations for such behaviour – the better the theory, the better we understand how to make financing and investment decisions and set appropriate policies. Throughout this text, we have sought to combine the 'why' with the 'how' in the theory and practice of corporate finance. This final chapter reminds the reader of the main pillars on which much of finance theory rests, many of which have been recognised as significant economic developments through the award of the Nobel Prize in Economic Sciences, and reflects on their practical relevance.

More respect for behavioural studies

The growing field of behavioural finance is attempting to explore the bounds of rationality in decision-making, working out whether our irrationality is systematic (it is) and whether a better understanding of it can improve investments (the jury's still out). Even more important for asset managers, it looks at how individuals value outcomes – not symmetrically. Losing something hurts more than gaining something of the notional equivalent value pleases us.

At the moment, behavioural finance as a discipline is still very largely based on the experiments done in controlled conditions, usually on college students. Critics like to point out that this is a far cry from financial markets, where billions of decisions are made, mostly by professionals, in distinctly uncontrolled conditions. But since the pure mathematical approach appears to have let down its proponents badly, whether because of a fundamental wrongness or because it was incorrectly applied, perhaps the behaviouralists should be allowed more respect (and possibly more funding for their research).

This is important, because in spite of the Nobel Memorial prize for Economics awarded in 2002 to Daniel Kahneman (a psychologist), behavioural finance is still not sufficiently developed for it to be properly integrated with market theory. It is true the turbulence of the past couple of years can be used to learn more about the risks of financial markets. It is even likely that complex mathematical models will have useful insights to offer chief risk officers, responsible for making sure asset management companies know what risks they are taking. But unless they somehow incorporate the discoveries of behavioural finance, they will be no better at understanding either how markets are likely to behave or how investors are likely to react to them.

Source: Grene, S. (2010) More respect for behavioural studies. *Financial Times*, 3 January. © The Financial Times Limited 2018. All rights reserved.

15.2 UNDERSTANDING INDIVIDUAL BEHAVIOUR

To understand how organisations function, we must first understand individual behaviour. There are many models of human behaviour (e.g. sociological, psychological and political); we shall restrict our examination to two models of most relevance to finance.

The first is the traditional economic model of human behaviour. Here the manager is seen as a short-run wealth maximiser. The model is a useful starting point in studying finance because it offers a simple approach to model-building, using only the pursuit of wealth as a goal. Much of the argument underlying the theories discussed in this text is based on this model. But we all know that this is a poor explanation of many aspects of human behaviour. For many people, and in many situations, money may not come before morality, honesty, love, altruism or having fun. As the song said, 'Money can't buy me love'.

This leads us to develop a more realistic model of human behaviour which Jensen and Meckling (1994) term the resourceful, evaluative, maximising model (or REMM).

This model assumes that people are resourceful, self-interested maximisers but rejects the notion that they are only interested in making money. They also care about respect, power, quality of life, love and the welfare of others. Individuals respond creatively to opportunities presented, seeking out opportunities, evaluating their likely outcomes, and working to loosen constraints on their actions.

Neither of the above models places much emphasis on psychological factors in human information-processing and decision-making. This growing area of finance, termed behavioural finance, is discussed in Section 15.5.

To sum up the foregoing discussion, money is not the only, or even the most important, thing in life. But when all else is equal, we act in a rational economic manner, choosing the course of action that **most** benefits us financially. In the field of managing corporate finance, two fundamental conclusions naturally follow.

■ Managers should only consider present and future costs and benefits in making decisions

This is the principle of incrementalism – only the additional costs or benefits resulting from a choice of action should be considered. For example, expenditures already incurred are not relevant to the decision in hand; they are **sunk costs**.

Choices often involve trade-offs, denying the possibility of other alternatives. The **opportunity cost** of making one decision is the difference between that choice and the next best alternative.

■ Managers are risk-averse

Most managers are risk-averse; given two investments offering the same return, they would choose the one with lesser risk. Unlike the risk-seeker or gambler, most managers try to avoid unnecessary risks. Risk-aversion is a measure of a manager's willingness to pay to reduce exposure to risk. This could be in the form of insurance or other 'hedging' devices. Alternatively, it could be by preferring a lower-return investment because it also has a lower risk.

In business, risk and the expected return are usually related. Rational managers do not look for more risk unless the likely benefits are commensurately greater. This is the principle of **risk-aversion**. One way in which investors can reduce risk is by spreading their capital across a range (portfolio) of investments. This is the principle of **diversification**, or not putting all your eggs in one basket. However, the key to risk management should not simply be to reduce it, but to take decisions in a risky business environment that also create value i.e. to trade off risk against return.

15.3 UNDERSTANDING CORPORATE BEHAVIOUR

■ Managers are agents for shareholders

A firm may be viewed as a collection of individuals and resources. More precisely, it is a set of contracts that bind individuals together, each with their own interests and goals. Agency theory explores the relationship between the shareholders (the principals) and the agents (e.g. board of directors) responsible for taking actions on their behalf.

Shareholders want managers to maximise firm value. It follows that to understand how firms behave, and whether managers pursue this goal, we must first understand the nature of the contracts, monitoring procedures and reward mechanisms employed.

Information is not available to all parties in equal measure. For example, the board of directors will know more about the future prospects of the business than the shareholders, who have to rely heavily on published information. This information

information content
The extra, unstated intelligence that investors deduce from the formal announcement by a firm of any financial news, i.e. what people read 'between the lines', or 'financial body language'

asymmetry means that investors not only listen to the board's rhetoric and confident projections but also examine the information content in its corporate actions. This **signalling effect** is most commonly seen in the reaction to dividend declarations and share dealings by the board. An increase in dividends signals that the company is expected to be able to sustain the level of cash distribution in the future, because it is usually regarded as the height of financial incompetence to be forced to cut a dividend.

■ Apply the NPV rule

A company will have perhaps thousands of shareholders, all with different levels of wealth and different risk attitudes. How can a firm make decisions that satisfy all of them? **The NPV rule states that decisions should be taken which maximise wealth, and this can be achieved by accepting all positive net present value projects.** A firm's value is largely determined by two things: the cash generated over the life of the company and the risk of those cash flows. **Shareholder value analysis** advocates that firms should seek to maximise cash flows and manage risks. They should invest in those areas in which their firms have some competitive advantage, giving rise to superior return or positive net present value when discounted at the rate commensurate with the perceived level of risk. This rate reflects the return on risk-free investments plus a risk premium to compensate for the additional risk in the company's cash flow stream.

When properly applied, the NPV approach is the best method for evaluating forms of investment, where cash flows are fairly predictable and there are few investment options. However, two points are worth mentioning:

1 In long-run equilibrium, all projects have a zero NPV. In other words, it may be possible for a firm to achieve positive NPVs because they are the first to spot a market opportunity, or have built entry barriers, but, ultimately, these will be overcome and competitors will continue to enter the market until the benefits no longer exist.
2 The DCF approach is most useful when evaluating bonds and financial leases, where cash flows are highly predictable. They become less relevant as risk and growth opportunities increase. Table 15.1 illustrates this.

Table 15.1 Usefulness of DCF methods

Usefulness of DCF methods	Financial investment	Capital investment projects
Very	Bonds and fixed-income securities	Financial leases
Moderate	Shares paying regular dividends	1 Replacement decisions 2 Businesses where there are no strategic options ('Cash Cows')
Limited	Shares where there are significant growth opportunities	Business with significant growth opportunities
Very low	Derivatives, e.g. share options	Pure research and development expenditure

■ Options have value

The DCF framework has come under increasing criticism in recent years for failing to consider the options embedded in investment opportunities. **An option allows an**

investor to buy or sell an asset at a fixed price during a given period. A firm should exercise its option only if it adds value to the business. Unlike the conventional NPV approach, however, the more volatile the option, the more valuable it is, because the 'good news' is taken up. With capital projects, selecting projects offering the highest NPV at a specific point in time, conventional investment appraisal ignores the possibility that projects may have valuable options (called real options). Such options include greater flexibility for management in terms of growth, delay or abandonment options. The traditional approach of selecting the project with the highest NPV at a particular point in time disadvantages those projects offering greater flexibility to management and the benefits of possible add-on investments in the future. The price paid for an acquired company may look too high based on conventional NPV calculations. But this ignores any valuable strategic options embedded in the decision which may well justify the price paid. As a minimum, management should look to identify and evaluate subjectively any options linked to projects, particularly when projects with known options cannot be financially justified on conventional NPV grounds.

The increasing recognition of the importance of options means that investors need to understand how they are valued. Black and Scholes (1973) first developed a formula for option pricing. In summary, it argues that **option value is based on the current market value of the underlying share, the strike price, the time to contract maturity, and the risk-free rate of interest**.

Options and other derivative instruments offer considerable scope for corporate treasurers in managing risk, such as foreign exchange and interest rate risk, by developing appropriate hedging strategies.

Look for an optimal capital structure and dividend policy

Managers need to know the cost of capital, or cut-off rate, for capital projects. Traditionally, it was argued that the cost of capital depended, in part at least, on the mix of equity and debt in the company. The Modigliani–Miller propositions offer an elegant theory demonstrating that how the firm finances its investment schedule is irrelevant. The cost of capital for determining the cut-off rate for capital projects depends only on the risk class of the projects. In other words, financing decisions do not increase a firm's overall value. Value is therefore independent of capital structure.

For any company operating below the capital structure deemed 'appropriate', the private equity industry, with huge amounts of capital at its disposal, is ready to take over the business, introduce far higher gearing levels and return cash to shareholders. This is well illustrated by the car manufacturer Volvo. The company is known as a well-managed company maintaining prudent cash balances and relatively low gearing levels. In 2006, a venture capitalist, that had built up a 5 per cent stake in Volvo, began pressing the company to return to shareholders part of its sizeable cash balance of over £1 billion. The Volvo board responded by setting higher targets for profits, cash flow and gearing, the latter being an increase in the debt/equity ratio from 30 per cent to 40 per cent, and it stated that it would look favourably on opportunities to return cash to investors while also looking for suitable acquisitions.

Although the underlying assumptions are far removed from the world of everyday finance, even in practice, it is generally agreed that, in a no-tax world, issuing low-cost debt does not automatically reduce the overall cost of capital because the cost of equity will rise to compensate for the increased financial risk. However, in practice, we see that having to service higher borrowing levels is a powerful driver for managers to work harder and smarter, and offers tax advantages for firms through the tax relief on interest payments. On the other hand, excessive levels of debt threaten the firm's very existence and could lead to costly financial distress.

Related to the above is the need to identify the **optimal working capital** to be employed in the firm. This involves striking the right balance between minimising the cash conversion cycle and maintaining good supplier/customer relations. Many of the improvements in working capital management come through supply chain efficiencies and sound management of cash and accounts receivables/payables.

Much the same argument as for capital structure was made by Modigliani and Miller for the **irrelevance of dividends.** Under given assumptions, dividend policy does nothing to improve the value of the firm.

In a perfect capital market, rational investors are indifferent between a cash dividend and retention, once the impact of the investment decision is stripped out. If there is an increase in value when a firm retains, it is because investors expect the project to be wealth-creating. If a dividend increase raises value in such a market, it must be because investors have an extremely powerful desire for dividends rather than capital gains (i.e. an overwhelming preference for current dividends).

Compass Group unveils £1bn special dividend

Compass Group, the world's biggest contract catering company, is to pay a £1bn special dividend after being unable to identify suitable large-scale deals in a first half in which profits and free cash flow jumped.

Richard Cousins, chief executive, said the company had 'examined all the opportunities for acquisitions and decided we could not see value, we could only see risk'. The £1bn special dividend equates to 61p a share and the group will take on some debt to help finance it.

Revenues for the six months rose 20 per cent compared with last year, to £11.5bn, boosted by favourable currency moves. Pre-tax profit rose 25 per cent year on year to £831m, bolstered by currency moves. Operating profit rose 5.2 per cent at constant currencies to £894m. The group also posted a 20 basis point increase in operating profit margins on the back of efficiency savings.

Compass said its net debt was £2.87bn and that its policy was for this to be 1.5 times earnings before interest, tax, depreciation and amortisation. It also said it was raising its interim dividend by 5.7 per cent to 11.2p per share.

Investec analysts said the results were 'slightly ahead of our expectations' while Deutsche Bank described the performance as 'solid'.

Source: Sullivan, C. and Megaw, N. (2017) Compass Group unveils £1bn special dividend. *Financial Times*, 10 May. © The Financial Times Limited 2018. All rights reserved.

In imperfect markets, different conclusions apply. For example, dividends are said to be tax-disadvantaged compared to retention-plus-capital gains, as taxes on gains are delayed and often levied at a rate lower than the rate most investors face on their dividend income. Moreover, **dividends have a powerful signalling effect**. In a world where managers possess more information than investors, a dividend increase conveys the information that directors are confident about the future, while a dividend cut signals pessimism about the future. However, one should not exaggerate the signalling effect. When dividend changes are made, they are usually well-telegraphed – the market is usually aware that the firm is struggling and that a dividend cut is both sensible and likely. When the crunch comes, it is usually confirmation of what people generally expect. Indeed, failure to cut a dividend is often taken more seriously than a dividend cut in such circumstances. Converse arguments apply to the case of a dividend increase. It is unexpected changes that have the most impact on price.

So, as dividend cuts are to be avoided, and most shareholders like dividends, for most firms, the sensible policy is to follow a 'progressive' dividend policy, steadily increasing payment but only if supported by earnings increases that are regarded as sustainable. 'Declare a policy and stick to it' seems to be the message in order to attract and retain a clientèle of shareholders who find the policy in question suits their needs. However, as ever, there are exceptions. Firms with turbulent operating environments will be forgiven if dividend payouts fluctuate, while firms with highly stable environments, e.g. water and tobacco, had better tell a good story if they retain a high proportion of their earnings. Effective and clear communication, as in most walks of life, is essential.

■ Hedging adds value

Derivative instruments – like options, forward and futures contracts and swaps – can be used for speculation or for hedging. The main difference is that speculation is effectively a bet on a price move over time, whereas **hedging is used in combination with the underlying security; any gain or loss in the cash position is offset by an equivalent loss or gain in the derivatives position**.

At first sight, it may seem questionable whether hedging is an appropriate tool for increasing the value of the firm. After all, if investors can eliminate all specific risk by holding a well-diversified investment portfolio, does incurring costs to hedge financial risks do anything for the shareholder? It seems that it does in the following ways:

1. Hedging reduces the probability of corporate failure. The greater security thereby extended to managers, suppliers and employees enables them to take a longer-term view in their decision-making. This is consistent with a net present value approach.
2. Hedging reduces the probability of financial distress which, in turn, reduces the firm's cost of capital.
3. Investors prefer a steady stream of corporate cash flows above the more volatile pattern likely without managing risk exposure.
4. Management may be reluctant to disclose to investors the full picture on risk exposure, making it difficult for investors to make an accurate assessment of the risk on their portfolios.

15.4 UNDERSTANDING HOW MARKETS BEHAVE

To make sound financial decisions consistently, managers need to have a good understanding of how financial markets operate and behave. This involves understanding the time-value of money, how risk affects value, and the efficiency of markets.

■ Money has a time-value

To make sound financial decisions consistently, we need to understand how financial markets deal with the transfer of wealth between individuals or firms. This may take the form of investors lending money to borrowers in exchange for future interest and capital repayment, or purchasing a share of a company and participating in its future profits. This inevitably involves the transfer of wealth from one time period to another, based on the **time-value of money**. Put simply, we cannot add current and future money together in a meaningful way without first converting it into a common currency. This currency can be expressed in future value terms, but far more relevant to decisions being considered today is to express all future cash flows in **present value** terms. The value of money changes with time because it has an alternative use (opportunity cost): it can be invested in financial markets or elsewhere to earn a rate of return.

The present value of a cash flow is the amount of money today that is equivalent to the given future amount after considering the rate of return that can be earned. The higher the discount rate and the further the cash flow is from today, the lower its present value. In well-functioning financial markets, all assets of equivalent risk offer the same expected return. An asset's positive net present value implies that, after considering the time-value of money, its benefits outweigh the costs. This important concept allows investors and corporate managers alike – regardless of their attitudes to risk – to advocate a simple decision rule: accept investment opportunities that maximise net present value.

■ Non-diversifiable risk matters

In 1952, Harry Markowitz published a paper that provided a more accurate definition of risk and return for shares. The expected return on an investment is the weighted average of the returns of its possible outcomes, while the risk is the variance of those outcomes around the mean. These days, we simply talk of the share's expected return and its variance (squared deviations around the expected mean). The significance of this is that risk is no longer seen as purely 'downside' risk but also includes the likelihood of exceeding the expected value.

From this, Markowitz was able to calculate the risk and return for a portfolio which, in turn, could be used to select efficient portfolios which offered the best combinations of risk and return for investors. **Portfolio risk** is the weighted sum of the variance plus twice the weighted sum of the covariance. The implication of such a model is that investors should focus on portfolio risk rather than the risk of the individual shares within that portfolio. This diversification effect is not simply a matter of how many different shares are included in the portfolio, but the covariance between such shares.

While the mean–variance model offered insights into portfolio risk and return, it was less successful in practice in portfolio selection. However, it formed the basis for William Sharpe to develop his **Capital Asset Pricing Model (CAPM)**. Risk can be categorised into that which can diversify away and that which remains (non-diversifiable or market risk). The theory argues that investors should really be concerned only about the latter type of risk and the required return on an asset is commensurate to the amount of non-diversifiable risk. Sharpe's argument went as follows. Suppose every investor holds portfolios that are mean–variance efficient, and that they all have the same risk–return expectation. In such a world, all investors will hold the same portfolio of risky assets, termed the **market portfolio**. However, these investors may have very different risk attitudes – some may be more risk-averse than others.

Different risk profiles can be accommodated by holding different combinations of riskless investments (such as Treasury Bonds) and the market portfolio. It is even possible to further leverage risk and return by borrowing riskless assets and investing in the market portfolio. The investment strategy of investing in the market portfolio is followed by many institutions who invest in index (or tracker) funds employing passive investment strategies.

The attraction of the CAPM lies in its simplicity; the relationship between market (non-diversifiable) risk and the expected return on risky assets is reflected in the **security market line**, which is linear. The only risk that really matters is that which cannot be diversified away. The risk inherent in the market (the sensitivity of each share's returns to the market portfolio) is the only thing that changes with each investment. The expected return, ER_i, is a function of the risk-free rate of interest, R_f, and the risk premium on the market portfolio, $[ER_m - R_f]$, adjusted by the investment's Beta value, β_i.

$$ER_i = R_f + [ER_m - R_f] \times \beta_i$$

Everyone recognises that many of the assumptions behind the CAPM are far removed from the real world. But the issue is whether it is useful as a predictive model. Forty years of empirical observation suggests that while the model is fairly robust, it does not tell the whole story. Academics and practitioners may dispute just how deficient the model is, but most agree that it fails to capture the full effects of differences in:

- *Size* – why do smaller firms seem to offer higher returns than large firms after adjusting for risk?
- *Market-to-book ratio* – why do firms with high market-to-book ratios tend to exhibit higher returns than others?

Various models have been suggested that move away from a single factor pricing model (for example, Arbitrage Pricing Theory), but these too have their own problems.

From looking at financial markets over a lengthy period of time, we observe that there is a reward for bearing risk, and that the greater the potential reward, the greater is the risk.

■ Capital markets are efficient

Many of the theories in finance assume that capital markets are reasonably efficient in reflecting all available information. An efficient market is one where there are large numbers of rational profit-maximisers actively competing, with each trying to predict future market values of individual securities, and where important current information is almost freely available to all participants. The efficient markets hypothesis (EMH) argues that in such markets, new information on the intrinsic value of shares will be reflected instantaneously in actual prices.

The exact form of market efficiency in financial markets, in developed and developing countries, has been the subject of much debate and research. For major European stock markets, however, the consensus is that they exhibit efficiency in both the weak form (i.e. share prices contain all past data and superior returns cannot consistently be achieved from trading rules based on past stock market data) and the semi-strong form (i.e. share prices contain all publicly-available information, and superior returns cannot consistently be achieved from trading rules based on such information).

Prize-winning work on asset prices goes to heart of financial crisis debate

The Nobel Prize for Economics has been awarded to a trio of American academics for their work on what drives asset prices, a question that goes to the heart of the macroeconomic debate over the crisis. Eugene Fama, Lars Peter Hansen and Robert Shiller have all spent their careers analysing how the value of assets, such as stocks and bonds, vary over time. However, mirroring the broad disagreements that typically characterise the economics profession, the three scholars have come to radically different conclusions.

Prof Fama is one of the fathers of the so-called 'efficient market hypothesis'. This theory, which underlies his seminal 1965 paper 'Random Walks in Stock Market Prices', formulates that markets are 'informationally efficient', as investors immediately incorporate any new available information in the price of an asset.

In contrast, Prof Shiller, from Yale University, believes that any explanation of investors' behaviour cannot be fully based on rationality and must acknowledge the role played by psychology. In the 1980s, he showed that stock prices tended to fluctuate more than corporate dividends. This should not happen if investors were fully rational, since stock prices forecast future dividends. In the 2000s, Prof Shiller applied his insights on investors' 'irrational exuberance' to the US housing market, which he believed was overvalued. Prof Hansen, a co-founder of the Becker Friedman Institute also at the University of Chicago, designed methods to explore the drivers of stock market volatility. His statistical brainchild, the 'Generalized Method of Moments', confirmed Prof Shiller's finding that swings in asset prices could not be explained via standard models based on rationality. Subsequent work has shown that at least some of this volatility can be explained by investors' different attitude towards risk.

At different stages over the past decade, the three academics have all individually been considered as possible favourites for the $1.23m prize. However, yesterday, the economics community buzzed with astonishment at the joint award.

Source: Giugliano, F. and Aglionby, J. (2013) Fama, Hansen and Shiller win Nobel Prize for economics. *Financial Times*, 14 October.
© The Financial Times Limited 2018. All rights reserved.

Is it true that stock prices are essentially random walks? While the study of past stock prices may well produce interesting patterns, if they arise randomly, they cannot, by definition, have predictive power when it comes to share prices or returns. This implies that, based on available information, there is no simple rule to generate above-average returns.

However, empirical studies suggest that share price movements are not truly random and the EMH moved its position to one where no gain can be made after allowance for transaction costs in buying/selling and changes in risk over time. The undeniable economic logic of the EMH is that if anyone finds a trading rule that consistently 'beats the market' by giving above-normal returns after all costs, it will quickly be imitated by others until the benefits from such a rule evaporate.

This does not mean that the market share price is perfectly 'correct' at any point in time. It does, however, imply that the market share price is an unbiased estimate of the true value of the share. While actual market prices may fluctuate in a random fashion around the 'true' value, investors cannot consistently outperform the market.

Criticisms of the EMH

Michael Jensen, a leading financial economist, argued that 'the efficient markets hypothesis is the best-established fact in all of social science' (Jensen, 1978). Why, then, is the EMH debate still hotly disputed? The main issue is whether investors react correctly to new information or whether they make systematic errors by over- or under-reacting. The **overreaction hypothesis** argues that share prices tend to overshoot the true value due to excessive optimism or pessimism by investors in their initial reactions to new information. There is some evidence for this in UK financial markets (Dissanaike, 1997).

Much criticism of the EMH is misplaced because it is based on a misconception of what the hypothesis actually says. For example, it does not mean that financial expertise is of no value in stock markets and that a share portfolio might as well be selected by sticking a pin in the financial pages. This is clearly not the case. It does suggest, however, that in an efficient market, after adjusting for portfolio risk, fund managers will not, on average, achieve returns higher than that of a randomly selected portfolio. Roll (see Ross *et al.*, 2002) makes the point that all publicly-available information need not be reflected in share prices. Instead, the link 'between unreflected information and prices is too subtle and tenuous to be easily or costlessly detected'.

Inefficient markets

It's a tricky one for the efficient market theory. Last Wednesday, the *Wall Street Journal* reported that BlackBerry was cutting 40 per cent of its staff. The company couldn't even manage a denial. This looked like final confirmation of the Canadian company's demise. Yet news of the layoffs did not move the shares. Perhaps, at $10.25, the stock was already trading on the assumption that BlackBerry would be sold for scrap. But then the group said on Friday it would report a terrible second quarter, with revenue falling by half from the first. The shares then tumbled by a fifth – stopped only by a conditional $9 buyout offer yesterday. Had Friday's sellers thought everybody was getting fired because things were going *well*?

The best explanation of the bizarre trading may be the same one that behavioural economists use to explain the allure of lottery tickets. Small probabilities of big gains do strange things to people's risk appetites. If the chance of a gain moves from, say, 51 per cent to 52 per cent, most people will pay just a bit more to invest. But if you move the probability from 0–1 per cent, some investors will stump up big. This is the 'possibility effect' and it is ugly when it goes into reverse. Those who held on to BlackBerry until Friday were emotionally attached to the big gain they could make if BlackBerry fixed things. This sort of hope cannot be extinguished by strong evidence –only ironclad proof. The lesson is to be careful about buying a beat-up stock because 'the worst is priced in'. You may be co-investing with dangerous optimists.

Source: Inefficient markets: dangerous hopes. *Financial Times*, 24 September. © The Financial Times Limited 2018. All rights reserved.

Market efficiency also suggests that share prices are 'fair' in the sense that they reflect the value of that stock given the available information. So, shareholders need not be unduly concerned with whether they are paying too much for a particular share.

The fact that many investors have done very well through investing on the stock market should not surprise us. For much of the last century, the market generated positive returns. Most investment advice, if followed over a long period of time, is likely to have done well; the point is that, in efficient markets, investors cannot consistently achieve above-average returns except by chance (or persistent inside trading).

■ A few apparent anomalies in the EMH

There appear to be three main anomalies in the EMH: the effects of size and timing, and the periodic emergence of 'bubbles'.

Size effects

Market efficiency seems to be less in evidence among smaller firms. Shares of smaller companies tend to yield higher average returns than those of larger companies of comparable risk. Dimson and Marsh (1986) found that in the United Kingdom, on average, smaller firms outperformed larger firms by around 6 per cent per annum. Some of the difference can be accounted for by the higher risk and trading costs involved in dealing with smaller companies. Another explanation is institutional neglect. Financial institutions dominating the stock market often neglect small firms offering what appear to be high returns because the maximum investment is relatively small (if they are not to exceed their normal 5 per cent maximum stake). The costs of monitoring and trading may not warrant the sums involved.

Timing effects

In the longer term, disparities in share returns seem to correct themselves. A share performing poorly in one year is likely to do well the following year. Seasonal effects have also been observed. At the other extreme, it has been observed that share performance is related to the day of the week or time of the day. Prices tend to rise during the last 15 minutes of the day's trading, but the first hour of Monday trading is generally characterised by heavy selling. Investors may evaluate their portfolios over the weekend and decide what to sell first thing on Monday, but are more cautious in their buying decisions, preferring to take their broker's advice.

Stock market surges and bubbles

An investor holding a wide portfolio of shares (e.g. the FTA All-Share Index) for, say, 25 years would have been rewarded handsomely. But the capital growth was not a steady monthly appreciation; the bulk of it came in just a fraction of the investment period through stock market surges. In an efficient market, few – if any – are clever enough to be able to predict short-term stock market surges.

The famous South Sea Bubble of 1722 was one of the early speculative stock market 'bubbles' where investors adopt the 'herd' instinct and drive up prices well above any rational valuation based on economic fundamentals. The economist J.M. Keynes described this in terms of a 'beauty contest' where investors are not following their own judgements but trying to guess how other investors are going to behave. The Internet Bubble of 1999 and the House Price Bubble of the 2000s show that speculative bubbles are still with us and the cost of following the trend can be considerable.

A physicist argues that time is the only constant

The world of money is a frustratingly unpredictable place. So when some economists decided in the middle of the last century that they could apply mathematics and physics to explain the movement of markets, it seemed like a thrilling development. Today, we need few reminders that their optimism was misplaced. But could it be that the effort to apply scientific laws to economics was itself wrong? Indeed, could it be foolhardy to think that universal, timeless laws of *any* type exist, be that in physics or elsewhere? These are some of the questions raised by Lee Smolin, an American theoretical physicist and writer, in his book *Time Reborn*.

Smolin argues that it is a mistake to view scientific laws as universal. The lay reader may find it difficult to work out exactly why Smolin feels so confident in making such claims. Nevertheless, the implication is clear: if he is correct, we need to drop our assumption that we will ever find a single formula that explains what makes the universe 'tick'.

This has serious implications for economics. For if there are no timeless truths, then the premise of orthodox economics – or, at least, the efficient market hypothesis – is also wrong. Economies do not have a 'natural balance'; nor do they operate according to timeless 'rules'. Rather, they too are 'path-dependent', in the sense that humans always react to each other and to what has happened before.

This assertion will come as no surprise to behavioural economists, who have been vociferous in their criticism of classical economics since the 2007 crisis; nor will it shock many Western policymakers, who often argue that it is wrong to presume that there is any single 'rule' to how economies should work. But to hear a physicist attacking the concept of timeless truth is nevertheless unnerving.

Source: Tett, G. (2013) No more rules. *Financial Times*, 24 May. © The Financial Times Limited 2018. All rights reserved.

Self-assessment activity 15.1

If the stock market is efficient, can no one beat the market average return?

(Answer in Appendix A)

A modern perspective – chaos theory

The EMH is based on the assertion that rational investors rapidly absorb new information about a company's prospects, which is then impounded into the share price. Any other price variations are attributable to random 'noise'. This implies that the market has no memory – it simply reacts to the advent of each new information snippet, registers it accordingly and settles back into equilibrium; in other words, all price-sensitive events occur randomly and independently of each other.

The crash of 1987, possibly attributed to the market's realisation that shares were overvalued and triggered by the collapse of a relatively minor management buy-out deal, has provoked more detailed scrutiny of the pattern of past share prices. This has uncovered evidence that share price movements do not always conform to a 'random walk'. For example, significant downturns happen more frequently than significant upturns.

A new branch of mathematics, chaos theory, has been harnessed to help explain such features. Observations of natural systems such as weather patterns and river systems often give a chaotic appearance – they seem to lurch wildly from one extreme to another. However, chaos theorists suggest that apparently random, unpredictable patterns are governed by sets of complex sub-systems that react interdependently. These systems can be modelled, and their behaviour forecast, but predictions of the behaviour of chaotic systems are very sensitive to the precise conditions specified at the start of the estimation period. An apparently small error in the specification of the model can lead to major errors in the forecast.

Edgar Peters (1991) has suggested that stock markets are chaotic in this sense. Markets have memories, are prone to major price swings and do not behave entirely randomly. For example, in the United Kingdom, Peters found that today's price movement is affected by price changes that occurred several years previously. The most recent changes, however, have the biggest impact. In addition, he found that price moves were persistent, i.e. if previous moves in price were upwards, the subsequent price move was more likely to be up than down. Yet chaos theory also suggests that persistent uptrends are also more likely ultimately to result in major reversals!

Peters's work suggests that world stock markets exhibit patterns that are overlaid with substantial random noise. The more noise, the less efficient the market. In this respect, the US markets appear to be more efficient than those in the United Kingdom and Japan. Other observers suggest that markets are essentially rational and efficient, but succumb to chaos on occasions, with bursts of chaotic frenzy being attributed to speculative activity. This suggests some scope for informed insiders to outperform the market during such periods.

Wanted: new model for markets

Modern portfolio theory, developed over the past 50 years in academia, has all been based on the common premise that market prices at all times attempt rationally to incorporate all known information.

From this emerged the ideas that drove countless investment decisions: that the pattern of returns in financial markets follows the normal 'bell curve' distribution often observed in natural sciences, that risk can be defined by the extent to which securities prices vary around their mean, and that observing how they have moved in relation to each other in the past allows a precise and measurable trade-off between risk and return.

In spite of the weight that was put on the theory, it has long been known to have problems. First, market returns do not follow a 'bell curve'. Instead, extreme events happen far more often than a 'normal' distribution would imply

Another obvious weakness in efficient markets is the assumption that investors always make their decisions rationally. Virtually everyone knows this is not true. Indeed, over the past two decades, a new discipline of behavioural economics had started to substitute findings from psychology for the assumption of rationality.

According to modern portfolio theory, there is an 'efficient frontier' in which different assets can be mixed to maximise return for a given level of risk. This rests on the correlation among the assets – the extent to which they tend to move in line with each other – and their risk, which is defined as the amount they tend to vary or move away from their long-term average. This is common sense – add an asset to a portfolio that will move up when the others move down, and you have made the overall portfolio less risky.

But this relies on these correlations being static. Investing using this formula – and borrowing money to do so – can be a recipe for disaster if the correlations change. According to Jeremy Siegel, whose book *Stocks for the Long Run* was influential in persuading asset allocators to put a big weighting towards equities: 'The most serious attack on efficient markets is the change in correlation of asset classes under extreme conditions.'

Source: Authers, J. (2009) Wanted: new model for markets. *Financial Times*, 29 September. © The Financial Times Limited 2018. All rights reserved.

Which view is right? Are stock markets efficient, chaotic or somewhere in between? Pending the results of further research, it seems that corporate financial managers cannot necessarily regard today's market price as a fair assessment of company value, but that the market may well correctly value a company over a period of years. Examination of long-term trends gives more insight than consideration of short-term oscillations. For example, if a company's share price persistently underperforms the market, then perhaps its profitability really is low, or its management poor, or it has failed to release the right amount of information. To conclude, it seems that the efficient markets hypothesis does not hold, except perhaps in its very weakest form, in today's capital markets. Evolving from both the EMH and chaos theory is a possible successor termed the coherent market hypothesis (CMH) based on a combination of fundamental factors and market sentiment or technical factors (see Vaga, 1990). The CMH argues that capital markets are, at any point in time, in one of the following states, depending on a combination of economic fundamentals and 'crowd behaviour' in the market:

- *Random walks* – market efficiency with neutral fundamentals.
- *Unstable transition* – market inefficiency with neutral fundamentals.
- *Coherence* – crowd behaviour with bullish fundamentals.
- *Chaos* – crowd behaviour with bearish fundamentals.

We will have to wait to see how well it helps explain stock market behaviour.

Baillie Gifford plans to use AI to improve fund performance

Baillie Gifford has launched a project exploring how to harness artificial intelligence to improve the performance of its funds, becoming one of the first traditional investment companies to push into an area traditionally dominated by hedge funds.

The goal is to assess whether AI can eliminate mundane tasks that take up fund managers' time, enabling them to investigate a wider range of potentially market-beating investment ideas.

The Edinburgh-based fund house, which tends to hold stocks for a minimum of five years, plans to assess whether AI has a discernible impact on fund performance before hiring more specialists in this area.

Kyle McEnery, an investment analyst at the fund house and a former physicist who is closely involved in the project, said the company felt compelled to explore the potential benefits of AI, given the 'explosion of data and the increase in processing power' in recent years. 'Considering we always look at things in the long term, understanding where things could go is something we should be doing,' he said. 'Our approach is helping our investors to do what they do better.

We are breaking down the investment process and seeing if there are any areas where a computer would be helpful.'

The fund house, which oversees £145bn of assets, is testing algorithms that can scan for stocks that might suit a particular investment style. The global equity team might want to search for companies that generate a certain level of sales revenue or gross profits, have significant insider ownership and meet several other criteria. 'The power of machine learning is you can put in much more than five criteria, and allow [a computer] the freedom to place different weights on the data you put in,' Mr McEnery said.

A growing number of mainstream asset managers are looking to adopt AI to shore up their performance, according to Aldous Birchall, AI lead at PwC, the professional services firm.

'Specialised quant funds have been using this for a long time. What we are seeing now is a broader acceptance [of AI] across the traditional asset management industry,' he said. 'It will enable them to do a lot more with the same resources: cover more companies and assess more opportunities.'

Source: Marriage, M. (2017) Baillie Gifford plans to use AI to improve fund performance. *Financial Times*, 14 August. © The Financial Times Limited 2018. All rights reserved.

15.5 BEHAVIOURAL FINANCE

Behavioural finance is the study of how psychological and sociological factors influence financial decision-making and financial markets. Financial economics traditionally assumes that people behave rationally. We have focused in this text on market efficiency and predictive models based on rational economic choices. This assumes that people have the same preferences, perfect knowledge of all alternatives and understanding of the consequences of their decisions. The reality is frequently somewhat different. Behavioural finance relaxes the tight assumptions of financial economics to incorporate models based on observable, systematic and human departures from rationality. Behavioural finance thus challenges the efficient markets hypothesis and explains how investors use the available information in their investment decisions, and it is useful in enhancing our understanding of investors' behaviours and stock market operations. It is regarded as a new paradigm of finance which adds psychological, economic and sociological factors into research frameworks and provides a platform for analysing the methods which market participants use in their investment decisions. By predicting and explaining systematised market implications of human psychology, it helps in enhancing the market participants' decision-making process and associated market effects.

Its adherents claim that it helps understand stock market anomalies, including stock market overreaction, underreaction, bubbles and irrational pessimism. Some of the most successful investors have long held the view that to understand the stock market, you must first understand the psychology of investors. There are some common objections to the psychological approach to understanding market behaviour. Hirshleifer (2001) however argues that there are equivalent objections to both the psychological and rational approaches.

Behavioural finance has attracted the attention of significant numbers of people who work in finance, including the financial regulator in the United Kingdom (see the following cameo), and draws on the work of psychologists such as Kahneman and Tversky. Their considerations of how we make decisions when there is uncertainty led to the development of prospect theory (Kahneman and Tversky, 1979) which has been hugely influential. Kahneman and Tversky have further developed their initial version of prospect theory (Figure 15.1) but fundamentally, it encompasses a number of important propositions including:

- *We frame losses and gains relative to a subjective reference point.*
  This means that we are concerned not so much about absolute wealth, but about our relative wealth. For example, if I have bought a house for £150,000, then this is likely to become my reference point, and it is against this value that I measure any gains or losses. If I sell the house for more than £150,000, then I view this as a gain; if I sell the house for less than £150,000, then I view this as a loss. But note that my reference point may not remain static over time. If I hear that, on average, house prices have increased by 10 per cent in the period since I purchased the property, then I may shift my reference point and judge whether I have made a gain or loss relative to a reference value of £165,000. A parallel situation can occur in stock markets where I set the initial reference value according to the purchase price I paid for the shares; but I may shift the reference value in the future according to how the stock market has performed overall.
- *Twice the gain does not give twice the pleasure.*
  Therefore, a gain of £200 does not give twice the pleasure of a gain of £100. This suggests that people become less willing to take risks as they make more gains.

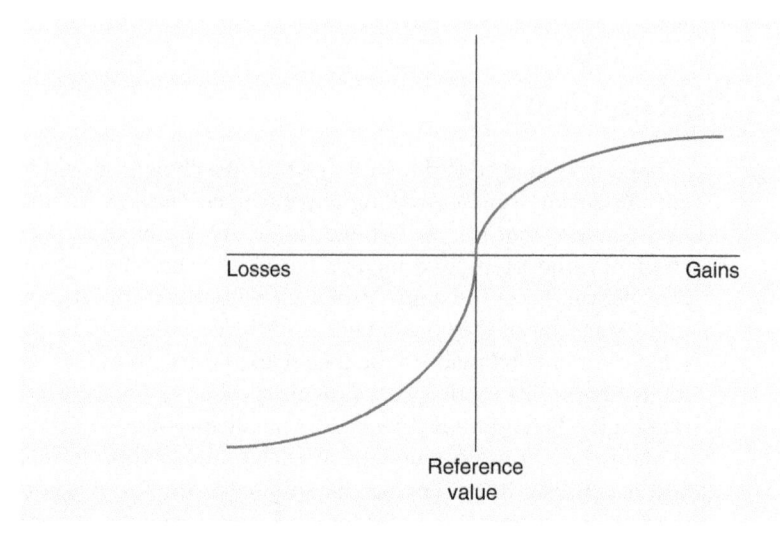

Figure 15.1 Prospect theory

Source: Kahneman and Tversky (1979).

- *Twice the loss does not give twice the pain.*
  Therefore, a loss of £200 does not give twice the pain of a loss of £100. This suggests people become more willing to take risks as losses mount up.
- *But, we are loss-averse.*
  Therefore, losing £100 hurts more than gaining £100. Losses and gains are felt asymmetrically.

Shefrin and Statman (1985) provide support for prospect theory in the context of stock markets by demonstrating that investors are inclined to sell 'winners' (i.e. shares that have gained value) too early but hold on to 'losers' (i.e. shares that have lost value) for too long. Investors are unwilling to risk forfeiting gains and, hence, sell these shares early; but they hold on to losing shares in the hope the price may turn and rise. This is referred to as the 'disposition effect'. Similarly, Barberis *et al.* (2016) test prospect theory by examining whether investors use the past image of stocks in their investment decisions. They assume that some investors evaluate future stock returns by keeping the distribution of past returns and risks of those stocks in mind. Their findings provide support for prospect theory-based predictions in relation to understanding the cross-section of returns as well as application of past image of stocks in investors' decision-making. They argue that their predictions of prospect theory are valid for both US and international stocks, and that not only is prospect theory able to explain the cross-section of stock returns, but investors may commonly use the past image and future prospects of stocks in their investment decisions.

Success with money is in the mind

You cannot ignore how people think about money – and the methods by which they psychologically separate their cash into different 'buckets'. One bucket for retirement, one for vacations, a couple for kids and education, and so on. Advisers are taking a greater interest in these thought processes in order to understand how they affect investor decision-making.

Drew McMorrow, chief executive of Massachusetts-based Ballentine Partners, is one of a growing number of wealth advisers who believe in behavioural finance. He applies a method to help clients better understand their mental accounting decisions to fit their aspirations into an investment strategy, because different portfolios will have different goals and varying degrees of risk. He says this method helps his clients understand and confront their behavioural biases when investing.

The concept, says Nicholas Barberis of Yale University, has been used to understand why many people are uncomfortable investing in risky asset classes. At the other end of the spectrum is overconfidence, when people overestimate their ability relative to others and overestimate the precision of their forecasts. Using modelling and big data analysis, researchers have found that people often attach too much importance to outcomes they have personally experienced. 'This is called the "experience effect", and it isn't optimal. We should pay attention to all past data, not just the data we have lived through,' says Prof Barberis. He adds that we still do not know for certain which are the most important psychological principles that affect our investment decision-making processes.

Michael Liersch, head of behavioural finance at Merrill Lynch, says he thinks that investors should approach concepts of behavioural finance with a healthy degree of scepticism. Acknowledging that investors have preferences and biases can help them better understand their own trading and asset allocation decisions.

FT *Source:* Love, B. (2016) Success with money is in the mind. *Financial Times*, 16 June. © The Financial Times Limited 2018. All rights reserved.

■ Heuristics and biases

Researchers have found that when decisions have to be made that involve risk or uncertainty, we unknowingly use strategies to aid us in the decision-making process. These strategies help us to take mental short-cuts in processing information for decision-making and are termed 'heuristics'. The heuristic devices we use to assist us have patterns, and, therefore, they lead to systematic biases in our decision-making. Important heuristics identified include:

Anchoring

When asked to form a judgement about prices or values, we are apt to do so by reference to prior information. For example, when Northcraft and Neale (1987) asked people to estimate the value of a house, they found that the estimates were significantly influenced by the asking price that was listed within the house details provided by the researchers to the study participants. The asking price became the anchor price for forming the estimate. A parallel situation in corporate finance might be if a board of directors is asked to place a valuation on an unlisted company prior to a takeover. In this situation the directors may be strongly influenced by the suggested price of the vendor, using this as the anchor for their estimate. Traditional budgeting is a further example of this phenomenon, where the current year's budget forms the basis for the next year's budget.

Hindsight bias

Once an event has occurred, we find it difficult to recall what our initial prediction was prior to the event, and we often believe that we correctly predicted the eventual outcome. Therefore, our memories are not wholly reliable, and we come to see the outcome that occurred as having been inevitable. In part, hindsight bias may be a process that helps us to 'impose' order upon the world. Hindsight bias can help explain why we come to view the stock market crash of 1987 or the global financial crisis of the late 2000s as events that were obviously going to occur. We believe that we really did see the signs of the crash or the crisis in advance of their happening. In an investment context, adjusting our view of the world in this way is potentially risky as it leads us to become overconfident about our abilities to spot good investment opportunities and we are less likely to learn from prior mistakes.

Sample size neglect

When we make decisions, we are disposed to draw conclusions based upon very limited evidence. This is the idea of a 'belief in the law of small numbers' (Tversky and Kahneman, 1971). This bias, which results in our arriving at unfounded conclusions, occurs in different parts of our lives. For example, Gilovich *et al.* (1985) have observed that we attribute 'hot hands' (when a player is on a real winning streak) to basketball players when, in fact, their prior performance in scoring baskets does not justify this. In the context of finance, this can be important as we may create stock market investment strategies based on an inadequate evidence base. For example, we act on the advice of an investment analyst we believe is on a 'winning streak', but if there is insufficient evidence to back this assumption, then the advice may be flawed.

This idea is closely linked to the 'gambler's fallacy', whereby we are inclined to assume (incorrectly) that if the ball on the roulette wheel has just landed on red, then it is more likely it will land on black on the next spin of the wheel. But each spin of the wheel is an independent event and, therefore, it is as likely that the ball will land on red on the next spin.

Availability bias

Information which is easier to recall causes us to be biased in our estimation of the likelihood of an event occurring. For example, we commonly overestimate the likelihood of a plane crash occurring, because when plane crashes do occur, they are particularly dramatic and receive considerable publicity. Additionally, if the information is relatively recent, it has an even greater effect upon us. This can occur with investing, where investors can overreact to bad news, causing the price of shares to fall to a greater extent than the bad news really justifies, and vice versa when the news is good (DeBondt and Thaler, 1985).

Overconfidence

We have a predisposition to overestimate our abilities. For example, it has been shown that the overwhelming majority of motorists are convinced that they are a better-than-average driver. Similarly, when individuals set up a new business, they believe they have twice as much chance of making a success of the new venture as other individuals setting up a new business. This inclination to overconfidence is related to self-attribution bias, whereby we attribute success to our own actions whilst attributing failure to external factors beyond our control. Hence, if I am a trader, then when a trade goes well and I make substantial profits on the deal, it must be due to my great trading skills. However, when a trade makes a loss, it is due to the market turning in the wrong direction unexpectedly because of some unforeseen event such as a movement in interest rates or commodity prices. Heaton (2002) considers the problem of overconfidence in a corporate finance setting and discusses how overconfidence leads managers to believe that the marketplace undervalues the company's shares whilst the managers overvalue their own endeavours.

One reason why we are overconfident is that we attend more closely to evidence that will support our viewpoint than to evidence that challenges our viewpoint. This confirmation bias also implies that when we come across new information, we misconstrue it so that our established viewpoint remains supported.

This propensity to be overconfident has also been noted in respect of illusions of control where we overestimate our ability to control and influence events. For example, traders have been observed to overestimate how much control they really have over events, and the relationship between illusion of control and performance has been found to be inverse (Fenton-O'Creevy et al., 2003).

Behavioural finance raises some important issues.

1 Is it possible to exploit irrational behaviour when it arises? If any investor can identify that the market is acting irrationally, giving rise to a gap between market share price and underlying value, that investor has the potential to exploit this profitable opportunity.
2 How can investors avoid making irrational decisions, and so achieve returns superior to other investors?

We consider these as they relate to market efficiency and corporate managers.

■ Mental accounting

In addition to using heuristics to make short-cuts in our decision-making, it has been suggested that our thinking is also influenced by what has been described as mental accounting. Ideas associated with mental accounting are particularly associated with the work of Richard Thaler. The basic idea is that the way we think is based upon having mental filing cabinets, and this affects our decision-making. Consider an individual who is saving money to buy a second home and is earning interest at (say) 4 per cent, whilst, at the same time, this person is borrowing money to pay for a car purchase at an interest cost of (say) 11 per cent. Thaler, in his research, has observed that individuals in this position are unwilling to use their savings to pay off their borrowings even though they would be better off financially by doing so. The reason for this reluctance is that two mental accounts have been created. One account is for 'second home savings' and the other for 'car loan payments', and we will not merge the two accounts.

This idea of mental accounts has been developed in different ways. For example, Prelec and Loewenstein (1998) found that a majority of people prefer to pay for a holiday in advance than in arrears, even though the concept of time-value of money tells us that it is better to pay later than earlier. The reasoning behind this seeming 'irrationality' is that we look to match costs to benefits within our mental accounts. If we pay for a holiday in arrears, then the cost is incurred after we have received the benefit, and we just don't like this. We are happy to incur the 'pain' of paying in advance for the holiday because we know we will then derive a *future* benefit. This kind of reasoning can also explain why, if we buy a pair of shoes that we subsequently find don't fit properly, we either continue to wear them even though they cause blisters, or refuse to throw them out. In the mental account for this shoe purchase, we have incurred the cost of buying the shoes, and we also want to have a benefit to match the cost. Throwing the shoes out means we are closing the mental account with the cost unmatched by a benefit. It is only over time that we find it easier to close this mental account, and this is why it is less emotionally painful to get rid of the shoes after 12 months than after one month.

This idea of mental accounting can be applied to investing. If we place each of our investments into a different mental account, then there is a danger that we do not look at our investments as a portfolio, in which case, we may ignore the diversification benefits that arise from having a portfolio of shares. This can lead investors to make simplistic decisions about which shares to hold in a portfolio, as they do not take full account of the risk of the shares, or of how the share returns are correlated.

If we also add to mental accounting the ideas associated with prospect theory, then we can begin to understand some other investment behaviours that appear to be irrational. It has been found that investors are inclined to sell 'bundles' of loss-making shares at the same time. That is, they prefer to close a number of mental accounts (for each of the loss-making shares) all at once. Lim (2006) notes this is because investors prefer to take one overall hit of pain by closing these mental accounts simultaneously. On the other hand, investors prefer to separate out gains by selling such shares on different days. The irrationality in this is that investors should be selling shares at what they judge to be the right time, and they should not be timing sales to either minimise the pain of selling loss-making shares or maximise the happiness associated with selling shares that have made gains.

Richard Thaler, in conjunction with Cass Sunstein, has developed these initial ideas regarding mental accounting to suggest how we can 'nudge' people into making better decisions about, for example, investing in pension funds. These ideas have been influential with governments that want to find ways to persuade people to make better decisions. For example, the UK government now has a Behavioural Insights Team (often referred to as the 'Nudge Unit') which uses insights from behavioural finance to aid in making policy (www.gov.uk).

■ Behavioural finance and market efficiency

Behavioural finance has examined how investors react to new information. As explained earlier, share prices appear to underreact to financial news such as earnings announcements, but overreact to a series of good or bad news. Adherents of the efficient markets hypothesis argue that:

- Investors, in the main, value securities rationally.
- Even if some investors do not act rationally, their irrational behaviour is random and therefore, cancels out.
- But even if most investors act irrationally, the market will be rectified by rational arbitrageurs who profit from the irrationality of others. Fama (1998) examined the impact of stock market anomalies on market efficiency. He concluded that 'market efficiency survives the challenge from the literature on long-run return anomalies. Consistent with the market efficiency hypothesis that the anomalies are chance results, apparent overreaction to information is about as common as underreaction, and post-event continuation of pre-event returns is about as frequent as post-event reversal.'

The psychology literature shows that people are irrational in a systematic manner.

Collective behaviour relates to the irrational behaviour of groups. Typically, this gives rise to excessive market swings. Two examples of such are 'herding' and 'price bubbles'. These arise when a large group of investors make the same choice based on the actions of others, which cannot be explained by fundamentals. The 'dotcom' price bubble of the 1990s is a clear example of this type of behaviour, as is the house price bubble of the 2000s. Most individuals find comfort in being part of a crowd, rather than acting independently. Of course, more often than not, the crowd can be right for a while, at least, until an overvalued market lurches downwards into its long-overdue correction phase.

Most financial practitioners are subject to bias. Bias, and emotion, cloud their judgement and misguide their actions. The question is whether they recognise this behaviour and take steps to minimise this bias. Practical steps that can be taken to reduce such bias include:

1 Recognise the circumstances leading to bias.
2 Have a written plan for each position, especially exit strategies.
3 Review actions.

Adaptive Markets – emotional investment theory

It takes a theory to beat a theory. That line returns like a leitmotif throughout Andrew Lo's remarkable new book 'Adaptive Markets'. It is the challenge he has been attempting to meet throughout his academic career; if the efficient markets hypothesis does not work, as many now regard as evident, can we come up with anything better?

Lo, an economics professor at MIT, is one of the most cogent critics of the efficient markets hypothesis, the doctrine that holds in its purest form that share prices incorporate all known information, meaning that they move in a 'random walk' and that beating the market in the long term is impossible other than by luck. That hypothesis, formulated more than half a century ago, remains a staple of business school curricula.

Many, including Lo himself, have made clear that the efficient markets hypothesis in its strongest form is ridiculous. Empirical work has shown anomalies in market behaviour (so that the 'walk' is not 'random'); neuroscience shows the human mind is incapable of the rational thought presupposed by efficient markets; and behavioural psychologists have shown biases in decision-making that will distort markets.

But efficient markets ideas still dominate in academia and in practical finance. The reason is that at least efficient markets is a complete theory that allows precise mathematical calculations. Critics have not come up with an alternative and certainly nothing that can help make money.

Meanwhile, study of the brain shows that the ability to think rationally depends on having emotions, and that we think in terms of stories. Constructing a narrative, Lo says, is central to what we mean by intelligence; we are not rational beings so much as rationalising beings.

This richer version of human rationality destroys the rational utility-optimising '*homo economicus*' on which efficient markets theory is based. The theories that Lo produces to buttress these ideas are of interest far beyond financial economics. But can this subtler emotional thinker, with thinking apparatus geared to surviving in a cruel Darwinian world, be modelled quantitatively, so as to allow us to put a price on securities?

Lo believes it can, and sketches out how the mathematics might work. But he admits: 'We are still beginners at the quantitative understanding of human behaviour.'

Source: Authers, J. (2017) Adaptive Markets, by Andrew Lo — emotional investment theory. *Financial Times*, 24 April. © The Financial Times Limited 2018. All rights reserved.

■ Behavioural finance and corporate managers

While much of the behavioural finance literature considers the psychological aspects of stock market trading, it also applies to investment and financing decisions within firms, which is the main focus of this text. If finance managers are able to recognise the biases in their judgements, they will be better prepared to avoid or manage such bias in future.

Behavioural finance helps us understand:

- Why most boards believe the market undervalues 'their' firm's shares.
- Why, more often than not, acquisitions fail to deliver the hoped-for financial benefits.

- Why financial projections in capital investment proposals are usually over-optimistic.
- Why boards find it difficult to terminate (or even decide to escalate) unprofitable projects or strategies.

Share valuation

Good financial public relations and communication with shareholders is vital for any listed company, not least because the market should reflect all relevant information in the company's share price. Typically, we find that senior executives believe that the market tends to underprice 'their' shares and fails to recognise the true worth of the company. But in efficient markets, the market price is an unbiased estimate of the true value of the investment. Corporate managers may be prone to biases of overconfidence, over-optimism and the illusion of control, resulting in the self-deception that they are better judges of share price than the market, and that they can control outcomes.

In recent years, there has been a flurry of firms exiting the stock market, whereby managers use finance provided by private equity–capital specialists. Although the motivation for this is diverse, it is common to hear directors complaining that the market does not correctly value their firm, and/or analysts are insufficiently interested to generate much research about their prospects (Evans, 2005).

Acquisitions

The bias of over-optimism and overconfidence may also lead boards to believe that they can acquire a firm and produce greater returns than the previous management. As discussed in Chapter 12, there may be sound strategic and economic motives for mounting a takeover bid, but the evidence suggests that, on average, acquisitions are bad news for the shareholders of the acquiring firm.

When takeover bids are contested, the bidding company may end up paying far more for the target firm than was originally intended. In the language of behavioural finance, this may be seen as the loss aversion bias – the strong desire to have something because it looks like it is being taken away from you – and the associated desire to avoid regret from takeover failure.

Investors psyched by the endowment effect

Whenever you are trying to value your own investments, beware of the 'endowment effect'. It is one of the most pervasive errors we make, and one of the most costly. It vitiates portfolio returns and it also has profound consequences in more important areas of human endeavour.

The endowment effect is the phrase used by behavioural psychologists to describe an almost universal tendency to overvalue those things that we own.

According to Michael Ervolini of Cabot Research, the endowment effect is by far the most widespread psychological flaw in investors. Based on research of global equity portfolios worth more than $1tn in total, some 25 per cent suffer from the endowment effect.

In investment, the endowment effect revolves around fear and it afflicts successful stockpickers. In a typical example, the manager buys a stock at $20, expecting it to go to $50. It reaches $43 or $44 swiftly, and then stalls. But the manager cannot bear to sell until they have gained their full expected value. 'Fear of not getting their due makes managers far too forgiving with their old winners.'

The fear of embarrassment, of not getting full value for a good investment, fools talented stockpickers into tying up too much capital in what has become 'dead money', when their skills would be far better put to work finding new stocks to buy.

As for portfolio managers, Rick Di Mascio, another behavioural investing consultancy, suggests the endowment effect could almost be helpful. He suggests overvaluing what you own can be good, as it concentrates your mind on the limited number of stocks that you own. Skilful managers will place a high value on the stocks they hold – but they need to be manically focused on knowing everything they can about those stocks, and be prepared to sell if it becomes clear they are not living up to high hopes.

Source: Authers, J. (2015) Investors psyched by the endowment effect. *Financial Times*, 25 November. © The Financial Times Limited 2018. All rights reserved.

Unprofitable projects and strategies

Many companies continue to operate projects or strategies long after they cease to be profitable or value-creating. Similarly, firms may continue to invest heavily in a corporate turnaround even though there is little likelihood of it ever recovering such investment. Overconfidence in management's ability to improve performance is one explanation. Another is termed **entrapment**; managers become entrapped in a strategy or project to which they have committed not just corporate capital, but also personal capital. Against all economic logic, they postpone decisions to terminate such projects or strategies in the hope that they will eventually come good. Sometimes, the only way to change direction is to remove the managers entrapped in this mindset.

There is considerable evidence (e.g. Staw, 1976, 1981) that managers are often reluctant to 'pull the plug' on failing projects, or may even decide, in the teeth of adversity, to escalate their commitment, hoping for an eventual turnaround, when the 'rational' thing to do is to abandon (Staw and Ross, 1987). However, for managers, blessed with information advantages, the rational course of action is to prolong their employment. Indeed, because they often have a reputation to protect or at least not to sully, prolongation is the lesser evil (Kanodia *et al.*, 1989).

Firms need to have in place clear guidelines preventing the above arising, through such mechanisms as regular post-audit reviews (Neale and Holmes, 1990). These mechanisms should specifically look for over-optimistic forecasts, irrational escalation of commitment, entrapment and other systematic biases in behavioural finance.

SUMMARY

In this final chapter, we have reviewed the main theories behind the corporate finance principles and practices outlined in previous chapters. The key material introduced was on the contribution that the emerging area of behavioural finance makes to our understanding of the subject.

This extension of the discussion is important as fundamental ideas in finance, such as the efficient markets hypothesis, have come under greater and greater scrutiny. It is always right to question the basic tenets of any discipline, and this is as true in finance as in any other discipline. The re-evaluation of major aspects of financial theory has occurred as practitioners and academics have tried to reconcile these theories with the behaviour of markets in practice. The comparison of theory and practice takes place all the time, but there can also be periods when major episodes seem to demonstrate that the practice–theory divide needs to be examined even more closely than ever. The global credit crisis that commenced in the late 2000s has been just such an episode. The crisis has been persistent and has been well documented in newspapers, in journals and on websites, and coming out of the crisis, many government, industry and professional body reports have been researched and written. These crisis-related documents do different things; some aim to understand the origins of the crisis, some try to apportion blame and some offer solutions for future crisis-avoidance. The outcomes of the crisis include an increased interest in topics such as behavioural finance and risk management. It has also demonstrated that finance is a complex and dynamic subject, and that there is considerable scope for the refinement of existing theories and for the development of new theories. Recognising that much of finance theory is related to economics then it is understandable why students are looking to their universities to give room in their teaching for ideas that help the students understand practice as well as theory.

Key points

- Financial management is more than applying rules and procedures. It explores the behaviour of markets, firms and individuals.
- Various theories explaining such behaviour include those of agency, risk-aversion, present value, portfolio, information asymmetry, options, capital structure and market efficiency.
- Behavioural finance is the study of psychological traits that investors and managers display that prevent them from acting in a purely rational manner.
- Examples of behavioural finance bias include regret, overconfidence, over-optimism, the illusion of control, herd behaviour, anchoring and adjustment.
- Behavioural finance is particularly in evidence in stock market anomalies, share valuation, acquisitions and loss-making projects.

Further reading

A number of texts have been written in the area of behavioural finance. These include books by Forbes (2009), Baker and Nofsinger (2010), Redhead (2008), Wilkinson and Klaes (2012), and Burton and Shah (2013). The work of Kahneman and Tversky has been of immense importance in establishing and developing ideas in behavioural finance, and their 1979 prospect theory article is an important foundation. Kahneman's *Thinking Fast and Slow* (2012) is an excellent and accessible summary of how our judgement is biased when making decisions. The idea of mental accounting as developed by Thaler is also important, and his paper (Thaler, 1999) provides a good summary of various key facets of this area. There are many other recent, interesting studies that also extend the ideas in behavioural finance: for example, Barber and Odean (2001) demonstrate how overconfidence affects the investment decisions of males. The textbooks listed above all refer to key studies. Barberis *et al.* (2016) test prospect theory and examine whether investors keep the past image of stock returns performance in their current investment decisions.

The French academic Thomas Piketty (2014) has produced a best-selling book that examines whether the current economic system creates vast inequalities. Thaler and Sunstein's ideas on 'nudging' people into making better decision are discussed in their book *Nudge: Improving Decisions about Health, Wealth and Happiness* (Thaler and Sunstein, 2009).

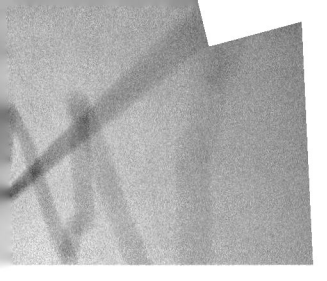

Solutions to self-assessment activities

CHAPTER 1

1.1 Financial intermediaries are the various financial institutions, such as pension funds, insurance companies, banks, building societies, unit trusts and specialist investment institutions. Their role is to accept deposits from personal and corporate savers to lend to customers (e.g. companies) via the capital and money markets.

Financial intermediaries perform a vital economic service:

(a) Re-packaging finance: collecting small amounts of finance and re-packaging into larger bundles for specific lending requirements (e.g. banks).
(b) Risk reduction: investing sums, on behalf of individuals and companies, into large, well-diversified investment portfolios (e.g. pension funds and unit trusts).
(c) Liquidity transformation: bringing together short-term lenders and long-term borrowers (e.g. building societies).
(d) Cost reduction and advice: minimising transaction costs and providing low-cost services to lenders and borrowers.

1.2 (a) Companies using the main market are generally those with a lengthy track record (i.e. a history of stable/growing sales and profits), seeking large amounts of capital, where the board is prepared to release a sizeable proportion of its controlling interest.
(b) The AIM is designed to appeal to smaller and growing companies which seek access to risk capital or where the board wishes to sell some of its holding, but cannot meet all the requirements for a full listing and prefers less regulation.
(c) The OTC market is for the remaining, smaller companies where shareholders occasionally wish to dispose of shares. This is performed on a 'matched bargain' basis, using facilities offered by authorised securities dealers.

1.3 A major function of an active capital market is to provide a mechanism whereby investors can realise their holdings by selling securities, and, obviously, for every seller, there has to be a buyer. Investors will be reluctant to commit their funds to the capital market by subscribing to new share issues if they doubt their ability to find a willing buyer as and when they decide to sell their holdings. The more liquid the market, the greater its ability to entice firms to make new share issues and investors to subscribe to them. Where market liquidity is poor, companies will have to offer much higher returns, making share issues uneconomic.

1.4 If these rules ever applied, investors would have soon realised the potential, and would have bought in November rather in advance of the expected price increase in December, thus creating a 'November effect', and so on.

Try the same argument on the old stock market advice 'Sell in May, and go away, and come back on St Leger Day' (the date of a horse race in the United Kingdom).

Many statistical tests have shown that all such dealing rules are usually inferior, and never superior, to a simple 'buy and hold' strategy.

1.5 (a) On the face of it, this represents insider dealing, by people in the know.
(b) It could represent speculation and rumour. If the company is known to be weak, then it is a candidate for takeover, and people begin to speculate about how much the company may be worth in the hands of an alternative owner.
(c) Most bidders build up a 'strategic stake' in a takeover target prior to formal announcement. The present UK rules (*The City Code*) allow a holding of up to 3 per cent without declaration of beneficial ownership. The upward movement could simply be due to this buying pressure. In reality, 'abnormal' buying also promotes speculation.

1.6 The reader is referred to Section 2.7.

CHAPTER 2

2.1 Most likely, the banker would wish to reflect on the rate of interest required:

(a) the rate of interest available from a risk-free investment,
(b) the expected changes in purchasing power over the five years, and
(c) the risk that you may not be able to repay.

We consider other factors a banker will consider in a later chapter.

2.2 $PV = \dfrac{£623}{(1.07)^8} + \dfrac{£1,092}{(1.07)^{16}} = £732$

2.3 Discounting at 15 per cent, a pound halves in value every five years. The present value of the purchase cost is therefore £750,000 (£500,000 today and £250,000 in year 5).

2.4 $PV = \dfrac{£1,000}{(1.12)^{12}} = £257$

2.5 Using the tables:

$PV = (£250 \times 8.0751) + (£1,200 \times 0.10067) = £2,140$

2.6 Price per share $= \dfrac{D_1}{k_e - g} = \dfrac{D_0(1 + g)}{k_e - g}$

$D_0 = (25\% \times 16p) = 4p$
growth $= (0.75 \times 0.18) = 0.135$, i.e. 13.5% and $D_1 = 4p(1.135) = 4.54p$
Share price $= \dfrac{4.54}{(0.15 - 0.135)} = £3.03$

With shareholders seeking a 20% return, share price reduces to: $\dfrac{4.54p}{(0.20 - 0.1350)} = £0.70$

Because the return on reinvestment now is less than the cost of equity, the firm should stop reinvesting, at least in the short term.

CHAPTER 3

3.1 While a capital project may have a high expected return, the risks involved may mean that there is the possibility that it will be unsuccessful – even to the extent of putting the whole business in jeopardy.

3.2 (1) Financial risk; (2) Business risk; (3) Project risk; (4) Portfolio or market risk.

3.3 X has the lower degree of risk relative to the expected returns.

Coefficient of variation: $X = 400/2,000 = 0.2$
$Y = 400/1,000 = 0.4$

3.4 (a) Risk – a set of outcomes for which probabilities can be assigned.
(b) Uncertainty – a set of outcomes for which accurate probabilities cannot be assigned.
(c) Risk-aversion – a preference for less risk rather than more.
(d) Expected value – the sum of the possible outcomes from a project each multiplied by their respective probability.
(e) Standard deviation – a statistical measure of the dispersion of possible outcomes around the expected value.
(f) Semi-variance – a special case of the variance which considers only outcomes less than the expected value.

Appendix A   491

(g) Mean–variance rule – Project A will be preferred to Project B if either the expected return of A exceeds that of B and the variance is equal to or less than that of B, or the expected return of A exceeds or is equal to the expected return of B and the variance is less than that of B.

3.5 Monte Carlo simulation involves constructing a mathematical model which captures the essential characteristics of the proposal throughout its life as it encounters random events. It is useful for major projects where probabilities can be assigned to key factors (e.g. selling price or project life) which are essentially independent.

CHAPTER 4

4.1 To eliminate the risk of, say, a two-asset portfolio, there would have to be perfect negative correlation between the returns from the two assets, and also the portfolio would have to be 'correctly' weighted.

4.2 Expected values:

A: EV = (0.5 × −10%) + (0.5 × 50%) = 20%
B: EV = (0.5 × −20%) + (0.5 × 60%) = 20%

Standard deviations

A: $\sigma_A = \sqrt{[(0.5)(-10\% - 20\%)^2 + (0.5)(50\% - 20\%)^2]}$
$= \sqrt{[(0.5 \times 900) + (0.5 \times 900)]}$
$= \sqrt{900} = 30$, i.e. 30%

B: $\sigma_B = \sqrt{[(0.5)(60\% - 20\%)^2 + (0.5)(-20\% - 20\%)^2]}$
$= \sqrt{[(0.5 \times 1600) + (0.5 \times 1600)]}$
$= \sqrt{1600} = 40$, i.e. 40%

4.3 The expected value = 20% as explained. The standard deviation is:

$\sqrt{[(0.64)^2(30)^2 + (0.36)^2(40)^2 + 0]}$
$= \sqrt{(368.64) + (207.36)}$
$= \sqrt{576}$
$= 24$, i.e. 24%

4.4 To minimise portfolio risk, let α^* = the proportion invested in asset Z. Using the risk-minimising formula 8.4:

$$\alpha^* = \frac{\sigma_Y^2 - \text{cov}_{ZY}}{\sigma_Z^2 + \sigma_Y^2 - 2\text{cov}_{ZY}}$$

$$= \frac{40^2 - (-200)}{200^2 + 40^2 - (2 \times -200)}$$

$$= \frac{1600 + 200}{400 + 1600 + 400}$$

$$= 1800/2400 = 0.75, \text{ i.e. } 75\%$$

4.5 An efficient frontier is a schedule tracing out all the available portfolio combinations that either minimise risk for a given expected return or maximise expected return for a given risk.

4.6 Expected NVP = (0.27 × £30,000) + (0.73 × £24,000)
= £25,620

Standard deviation = $\sqrt{[(0.27)^2(10,000)^2 + (0.73)^2(4,899)^2 + 2(0.27)(0.73)(-20,000,000)]}$
= $\sqrt{7.29\text{ m} + 12.79\text{m} - 7.88\text{m}}$
= $\sqrt{12.22\text{m}}$
= £3,496

4.7 The outright risk-minimiser locates at point B, the portfolio with minimum possible risk. However, risk-averters are willing to accept higher levels of risk if offered sufficient additional rewards, i.e. higher returns. Hence, any portfolio along AB is consistent with risk-aversion. The lower the investor's concern with risk, the nearer to point A he/she will locate.

4.8 With four separate assets to choose from, the investor faces a wider array of available portfolios. The envelope that summarises the investor's opportunities has the same basic shape as in the text, but with an extra 'corner' representing the fourth asset, denoted by point D in Figure A.1. Notice that all sorts of configurations of the envelope are possible, depending on the location of the four assets.

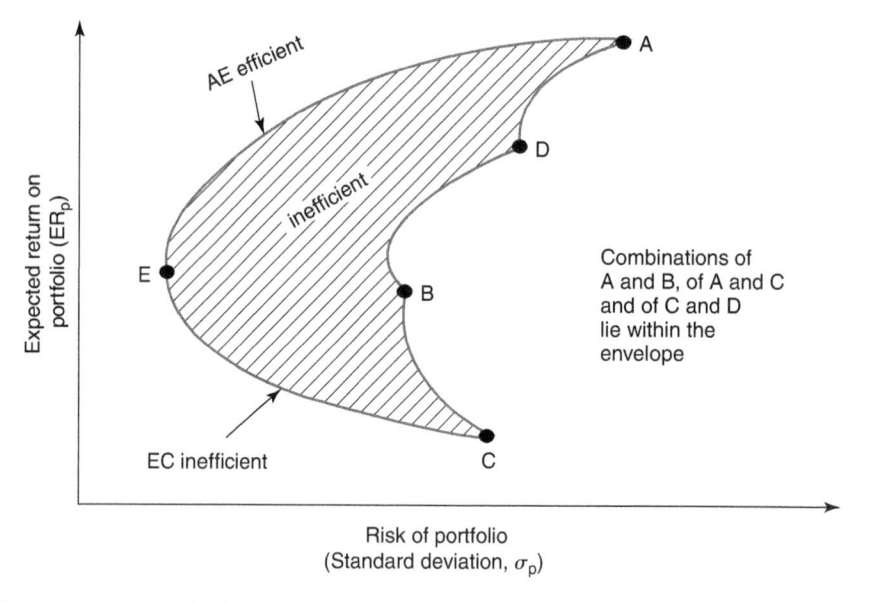

Figure A.1 Portfolio combinations with four assets

CHAPTER 5

5.1 TSR = [Dividend + Capital Gain]/Opening share price, expressed as apercentage.
= [£0.10 + £0.17]/£2.20 = £0.27/£2.20 = 0.123 i.e. 12.3%

5.2 To eliminate the specific risk, the investor would have to hold every share quoted on the markets, i.e. the market portfolio.

5.3

Systematic risk:	political turmoil
	exchange rate fluctuation
	interest rate changes
Unique risk:	labour relations problems
	announcement of a major new contract
	discovery of a defect in a key product

5.4 According to the CAPM, the Beta of Walkley Wagons is 1.2. Hence, the predicted return on its shares would be 1.2 × the predicted market return of 25%, i.e. 30%. (If you believe the experts!)

5.5 Variations around the characteristics line reflect the impact of factors unique to the firm. For BA, this could be due to a pilots' strike, pressure to relinquish landing slots at Heathrow, sale of its stake in Qantas, competition authorities blocking a proposed strategic alliance, etc.

5.6 The Beta values cluster in a relatively narrow range because these are large firms that are, themselves, mostly well diversified, and also because they constitute a major part of the overall market portfolio, which has a Beta of 1.0. Betas below 0.5 and above 1.50 are quite rare.

5.7 The market portfolio has a Beta of 1.0 simply because it varies in perfect unison with itself!

5.8 The SML traces out all combinations of risk and return that are efficient – anything currently located above or below the line represents an aberration from equilibrium that will be eliminated as market players realise the degree of mis-pricing. As they buy or sell, they help to move the market to equilibrium.

In the case of security A, the actual return is 'super-efficient', i.e. in excess of the return warranted by its Beta of 0.3. Conversely, security B is inefficient as it offers too low a return (actually below the risk-free rate) given its Beta. In fact, both securities should offer the same return as they share a Beta. To achieve equilibrium, the price of A must rise, thus lowering its return, and the price of B must fall to raise its return.

5.9 Here, we need a surrogate Beta. Taking the Sainsbury value of 0.86, using a risk-free rate of 3 per cent and the market risk premium of 5 per cent, the required return is:

3% + 0.86(5%) = 3% + 4.3% = 7.3%

This investment would lower the overall Beta of GKN, the effect depending on the relative size of the two areas of activity.

5.10 An investor might outperform the market with this policy, assuming it did actually rise. However, with such a narrowly diversified portfolio, the investor would be unduly exposed to risk factors unique to these five firms.

5.11 The top management team may not be effective in their management of the group as they cannot be experts across a range of businesses.
Extra costs might arise from the group having a management structure that is too hierarchical.
It may be difficult to co-ordinate the different businesses and this may result in inefficiencies.
The company may be too large to be agile and to innovate.

CHAPTER 6

6.1 With EPS = 36p, and the dividend covered three times, the dividend per share must be 12p (36p/12p = 3). Hence, the cost of equity is:

$$k_e = \frac{12p(1 + 3\%)}{£1.80} + 3\% = (6.9\% + 3\%) = 9.9\%$$

6.2 The DGM breaks down totally:

(i) when the firm pays no dividend;
(ii) when the growth rate of dividends exceeds the cost of equity.

6.3 Overall, the required return = 5% + 1.2[6%] = 12.2%
For activity A, it is = 5% + 2.0[6%] = 17%
For activity B, it is = 5% + 0.8[6%] = 9.8%

6.4 Company Beta = (0.65 × Beta of A) + (0.35 × Beta of B)
= (0.65 × 2.0) + (0.35 × 0.8) = 1.58

6.5 The calculation is:

Activity	Weighting	Beta	Weighted Beta
Hotels and Restaurants	85%	1.40	1.19
Costa	15%	0.87	0.13
		Total	1.32

The change in weightings thus tends to raise the calculated Beta, reflecting the higher weighting of the more profitable Hotels and Restaurants division.

6.6 The project Beta = RSF × OGF × divisional Beta
= (0.5 × 0.8 × 1.2) = 0.48

Hence, the required return = 5% + 0.48[6%] = 5% + 2.9% = 7.9%

CHAPTER 7

7.1 The value of a whole company, or enterprise value, is the value of all its assets, whether measured at book value or market value (£5 billion in the case of Innogy plc). The value of the equity is the value of the owners' investment in the firm, or shareholders' funds (£3 billion in the case of Innogy). These are equal only when the firm is financed entirely by equity.

7.2 (i) D.S. Smith's enterprise value is the total value of its assets, i.e. £3,606.3m
(ii) Total liabilities are long-term and short-term creditors, valued at £1,343.3m and £1,178.1m, respectively, total £2,521.4m. Minority interests represent remaining shares in firms previously taken over by Smith. These are neither Smith's liabilities nor Smith's owners' equity. They represent 'outsiders'' share of the total assets. Strictly, the figure given for total assets in (i) should be adjusted for this small item.
(iii) The value of owners' equity = shareholders' funds = net assets = NAV = £1,084.9m. These four terms are synonymous.

7.3 Profit tax = [1 − 30%] × £80m = £56m
EPS = (£56m/100m) = 56p
Implied share value = EPS × surrogate P:E ratio = (56p × 15) = £8.40.

7.4 Break-even value is £1 million, of which £0.361 represents the PV of the rental income. To break even, the resale value must have a PV of (£1m − £0.361m) = £0.639m. Reversing the discounting process, this is a value of £0.639 × $(1.12)^5$ = £1.126m. Hence, the property must rise in value by about 13% to prevent investors from losing out.

7.5 Taxation = 30% × (£25m − £1m) = £7.2m
Free cash flow = Operating Profit + depreciation − interest − tax − investment expenditure
(£25m + £2m − £1m − £7.2m − £3m) = £15.8m.

CHAPTER 8

8.1 (1) A call option gives the owner the right to buy shares (or whatever) at a fixed price within a set period. A put option is the right to sell at a fixed price.
(2) A European option can only be exercised on the expiry date, while an American option can be exercised any time over the life of the option. Most traded options in Europe are actually the American variety.

(3) A wide range including shares, bonds, currency, interest rates, gold, silver, wool, soya beans, etc. Options are also available on interest rates.

(4) (a) The lower the exercise price, the more likely it is that it will be profitable to exercise the call, and therefore the more investors are prepared to pay for the call.

(b) The longer the time that a call has to run to maturity, the greater the scope for the price to drift above the exercise price. Of course, there is also more time for prices to fall below the exercise price. However, the potential gains and losses are not symmetrically distributed. There are limits to the losses but not to the gains.

(c) The price exceeds the profit that can be made immediately by exercising the call, as over its remaining life there will be the opportunity to capitalise on further price movements. These may be upwards or downwards, but we have already noted a bias in the consequence of price changes – this offers a higher expected value of potential gains than losses.

8.2 (1) (a) It has intrinsic value because you could buy the share (exercise the option) for less than the share price.
(2) (a)

8.3 Applying the equation below, we find that the put–call parity relationship holds:

Share price + value of put − value of call = $E/(1 + R_f)$
   44   7   1   = 55/1.10

$$PV\ exercise\ price = 50p$$

8.4 Option value increases with the volatility of the underlying share price because the greater the variability in share price, the greater the probability that the share price will exceed the exercise price. Because option values cannot be negative, only the probability of exceeding the exercise price is considered.

Option values are determined by five main factors:

- share price
- exercise price of the option
- time to expiry of the option
- the risk-free rate of interest
- volatility of the underlying share price

In addition, the payment of dividends and underlying stock market trends have some influence on option values.

CHAPTER 9

9.1 Earnings in Year 0 = £1,000, of which 60%, i.e. £600, are retained. Returns on new investment = (15% × £600) = £90.

Next year's earnings = (£1,000 + £90) = £1,090.

$$\text{Growth rate} = \frac{(£1,090)}{(£1,000)} - 1 = 9\% = (60\% \times 15\%)$$

9.2 Divicut invests £1,000 in Year 1 to return £1,080 in Year 2.
The NPV of this is £1,080/(1.1)² vs. £1,000/(1.1) or £893 vs. £909, thus a negative NPV of £16, because the return on reinvested earnings (8%) falls short of the required 10%.

9.3 Paying out dividends rather than investing in worthwhile projects otherwise inaccessible to shareholders reduces the PV of their future income below what it could have been, i.e. there is an opportunity cost imposed on them.

9.4 Projects A, B and C are all attractive, but C appears unavailable as it would lead to exceeding the budget. However, if C is divisible, the firm should undertake A, B and 3/7 of C; otherwise, it should pay a dividend of £300,000.

9.5 Gordon confuses the risk of the dividends with the risk of the underlying cash flows resulting from new investment. If risk (and any increase in it) is suitably allowed for in the discount rate used to deflate future cash flows, then to discount the more distant future dividend flow would entail double-counting for risk. (If the firm moves into a low risk area, the future dividends could even have lower risk than near-in-time dividends.)

9.6 A clientèle is a set of investors whose interests the firm tries to serve via its particular dividend policy. Investors with short time horizons are likely to include the relatively elderly or infirm, and those with pressing needs for rapid income payments, e.g. to repay debts or to fund a daughter's wedding.

9.7 (i) £1,000/£20 = 50 shares;
(ii) 50 plus 20% = 60 shares.

9.8 Share repurchases may signal that the firm has exhausted investment opportunities or has become too risk-averse to devote funds to R&D. They may also trigger CGT liabilities for some investors. It may also cause embarrassment to directors if share prices subsequently fall.

9.9 A stable dividend policy gives reliability and security. Investors can plan their future income and expenditures more easily. Sharp cuts in dividends, as well as causing alarm, may force investors to sell shares on a weak market. Similarly, a sharp increase in dividends may force investors to reconfigure their portfolios, as well as triggering a CGT liability.

CHAPTER 10

10.1 (i) debt/equity = £50m/£100m = 50%.
(ii) debt-to-debt plus equity = £50m/(£50m + £100m) = 33.3%.
(iii) net debt = debt less cash = (£70m − £10m) = £60m, or as a percentage of equity = (£60m/£100m) = 60%

10.2 Both capital and income gearing are forms of financial gearing, i.e. they stem from the firm's financial structure. Capital gearing is obtained from the Balance Sheet and is measured by the amount of borrowing in relation to owners' equity. Income gearing can be gleaned from the P and L, and is measured by interest cover, or its inverse, the proportion of PBIT accounted for by interest charges.

10.4 Contribution is, of course, unaffected, but operating profit or PBIT would fall by £50,000 to £550,000, and PBT would fall a further £40,000 to £310,000. The two multipliers become:
Contribution/PBIT = (£1,080,000/£550,000) = 1.96
PBIT/PBT = (£550,000/£310,000) = 1.77
The combined multiplier = (1.96 × 1.77) = 3.47

10.5 Scenario A: EV = (0.25 × 5%) + (0.50 × 20%) + (0.25 × 35%) = 20%
Scenario B: EV = (0.25 × 3.3%) + (0.50 × 23.3%) + (0.25 × 43.3%) = 23.3%
Scenario C: EV = (0.25 × 0%) + (0.50 × 30%) + (0.25 × 60%) = 30%

10.6 With 25% gearing, share price = (23.3p/0.25) = £0.93
With 50% gearing, share price = (30p/0.35) = £0.86
It seems that shareholders' demand for a higher return outweighs the increase in EPS as gearing increases.

10.7 Debt/equity ratio of 40% means that debt is 2/7 of the total long-term funds and equity is 5/7. The WACC is thus:

(5/7 × 18%) + (2/7 × 8%) = (12.9% + 2.3%) = 15.2%

10.8 (i) With 11% interest, market value = (£100 × 3.5%/11%) = £31.82
(ii) With 3% interest, market value = (£100 × 3.5%/3%) = £116.67

10.10 (a) Perpetual debt: (30% × £10m debt) = £3m
   (b) 20 years to maturity:
   (20 year annuity of 6% × £10m × T) = (11.4699 × £600,000 × 30%)
   = £2.06m

CHAPTER 11

11.1. Under MM assumptions, firms identical in all respects apart from capital structure (allowing for size) should have the same value. Value is determined by the stream of operating cash flows and the degree of business risk attaching to these, regardless of how the cash flows are 'packaged' or shared out between different classes of investor.

11.2. Arbitrage in pursuit of 'home-made gearing' is restricted by:

- Taxes on capital gains.
- Differences between the borrowing and lending rates available to all parties.
- Different borrowing rates available to firms and private investors.
- Restrictions on some institutions' ability to borrow.
- Transactions costs.

11.3 Value of ungeared firm $= \dfrac{£100m(1 - T)}{0.15} = \dfrac{£70m}{0.15} = £466.7m$

Value of geared firm $= V_u + TB = £466.7m + (30\% \times £200m)$
$= (466.7m + £60m) = £526.7m$

11.4 In the ungeared firm, the overall cost of capital is simply the cost of equity, i.e. 15%. In the geared firm, the overall cost of finance is:

$k_{0u} = 15\%\left(1 - \dfrac{T \times V_B}{V_S + V_B}\right) = 15\%[1 - (30\% \times £200m/£600m)]$
$= 15\%(1 - 1.5\%) = 13.5\%$

11.5 Beta ungeared $= \dfrac{1.45}{\left[1 + (1 - 30\%) \times \frac{1}{2}\right]} = \dfrac{1.45}{1.35} = 1.074$

11.6 The APV is the value of an activity, based on its inherent worth as given by the PV of the stream of operating cash flows, adjusted for any 'special factors' such as tax concessions, financing costs, etc. It is thus the 'basic' NPV plus the PV of non-operating factors.

11.7 In theory, the limit to a firm's taxable capacity is where its interest charge equals the lowest possible level of future cash flows. In reality, it is much less than this. Based on asset-backing, the theoretical limit is where the book value of assets equals the book value of borrowings.

CHAPTER 12

12.1 Managerial motives reduce to the three Ps – power, pay and prestige, all of which are enhanced by size of firm.

12.2 If managers are paid according to growth in EPS, a takeover that exploits synergies may enhance their bonuses. However, if financed by debt, the value of the firm could actually fall. Takeovers that aim to reduce risk rarely benefit shareholders, for whom systematic risk is normally more relevant than total risk.

12.3 Cash is more certain, whereas the value of shares is volatile - by the time payment is made, the share value might have fallen. Investors wishing to liquidate the shares received will incur dealing fees.

12.4 The NPV of the bid for Predator's shareholders = (£1,000m + £200m + £50m) − (£1,000m + £230m) = £20m.
Prey's shareholders benefit by £30m (60 per cent of gains), and those of Predator by £20m (40 per cent), if the bid is completed at this price.

12.5 The strategic approach to takeover analysis and execution involves the following steps:
- Formulate corporate strategy.
- Assess the role of acquisition candidates in achieving that strategy.
- Screen, value and select from among possible candidates.
- Plan for future integration and/or disposals.
- Make informal approach.
- Announce hostile bid if necessary.
- Complete the deal.
- Integrate the acquisition following a detailed resource audit.
- Post-audit the acquisition and integration processes.

12.6 Takeovers fail to achieve the anticipated benefits due to:
- Managerial motivation rather than shareholder orientation.
- Inadequate evaluation of the target.
- Over-payment for the target.
- Failure to plan the integration process.
- Poor integration, e.g. neglect of the human factor.

12.7 There are many motives for divestment, including:
1. Dismantling conglomerates originally created by merger activity through defensive diversification strategies.
2. A change in strategic focus. This may involve a move away from the core business to new strategic opportunities. Alternatively, a business may decide that it is engaged in too wide a range of activities and seek to concentrate its efforts and resources on a narrower range of core activities. Non-core activities will then be divested.
3. Harvesting past successes, making cash flow available for new opportunities.
4. Selling off unwanted businesses following an acquisition. This is called 'asset-stripping'. Such sell-offs are often planned at the time of the bid.
5. Reversing (or learning from) mistakes.

CHAPTER 13

13.1 A speculator deliberately risks losing money by taking a long or short 'position' in a particular currency. A hedger tries to minimise exposure to risk. Nintendo is, at least to some extent, a hedger.

13.2

	Swedish krona (SEK)	Singapore dollar (SGD)	
Spot Forward points Forward outright	10.5895-10.60645 0.0001-0.0016 10.5896-10.6061	2.0499-2.0510 (0.0018-2.0003) 2.0481-2.0507	Remember to add the discount in the case of the currency quoted at a discount, and vice versa

13.3
- Transaction exposure is the risk of loss associated with short-term contractual obligations.
- Translation exposure is the risk of loss when constructing end-of-year financial statements.
- Economic, or operating, or strategic, exposure is the risk of the whole value of the firm falling due to adverse foreign exchange rate changes affecting the PV of future cash flows.

13.4 New York price in one year = $2.00(1.02) = $2.04
London price in one year = £1.00(1.04) = £1.04
Exchange rate under PPP = ($2.04/£1.04) = $1.96 per £1

13.5 Annual interest rate differential of 2.5% = 2.5%/4 over 3 months = 0.625% This is the interest *agio*. Forward rate should be spot less forward *agio* = (£2.0250 × 99.375%) = $2.0123. The US$ trades at a premium of 127 points.

13.6 Langer's assets are now worth (A$100m/1.75) = £57.14m. If all prices inflate at 7% in Australia, Langer's assets will appreciate to A$100m(1.07) = A$107m in one year. The AUD vs. GBP exchange rate should become (1.75 × 1.07/1.02) = A$1.836 per £1. At this rate, the sterling value of these assets = (A$1.07m/1.836) = £58.28m. This is the level to which they would have appreciated had they been located in Britain and experienced 2% UK inflation i.e. £57.14m (1.02) = £58.28m.

13.7 Leading is advancing outflows in a strong currency and advancing inflows in a weak currency. Lagging is delaying inflows in a strong currency and delaying outflows in a weak currency.

13.8 There is no point exercising an option 'at the money'. The purchaser simply loses the premium.

CHAPTER 14

14.1 Broadly, an MNC is a firm whose activities span national borders, but the term usually applies to firms that invest in foreign locations. A global firm both trades and invests abroad.

14.2 FDI differs from domestic investment for many reasons:
- Exposure to FX risk.
- Likelihood of inflation abroad occurring at rates different from home inflation.
- Risk of political intervention, leading to blocked funds, etc.
- Access to concessionary finance and grants.
- Overspill effects on existing operations.

14.3 Beta of project = (1.4 × 1.25) = 1.75
Adjusted for correlation = (1.75 × 0.4) = 0.7
Required return = 5% + 0.7 [11% − 5%] = 5% + 4.2% = 9.2%

14.4 The firm will pay tax only in the United States, i.e. (US$100m × 30%) = US$30m, which is allowable in full against UK tax liability.

14.5 Exposure of US operations = US$(50m − 30m) = US$20m
Exposure in South America = US$100m
Total exposure = US$120m

14.6 The net exposure could be reduced by:
- Producing more output in the United States and shipping direct to South America.
- Sourcing more USD-denominated inputs to support UK production.
- Borrowing in USD.

14.7
- Source materials and services from local suppliers.
- Employ locals in key management posts.
- Invest in training programmes for locals.
- Invest in sports and health facilities, open to the wider population.
- Sponsor local cultural events.
- Undertake joint ventures with local firms.
- Reinvestment rather than repatriation of profits.
- Use local sources of finance.

CHAPTER 15

15.1 **(1)** Some people are simply lucky.
   (2) Some people stay lucky for several time periods, although shrewd ones remember to get out while ahead!
   (3) In any time period, 50 per cent of investors ought to beat the market average.
   (4) Some people deliberately assume high levels of risk for which a relatively high return is appropriate. We should therefore talk about 'risk-adjusted returns' rather than simple returns.
   (5) Some people have access to inside information. This, of course, contravenes strong-form efficiency but it happens, although such information is unlikely to arrive in a steady stream over time.

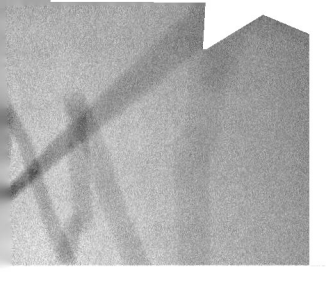

Solutions to selected questions

CHAPTER 1

2 (c) (i) *For the cash offer*

On Day 1, the total value of each firm is:

A: £2 × 2m shares = £4m
B: £3 × 6m shares = £18m

Company B is making an offer of £6 million for Company A which is apparently worth only £4 million – this will reduce the market value of B by £2 million to £16 million or £16 million/6 = £2.67 per share. Against this, the anticipated savings would raise B's value to (£16m + £3.2m) = £19.2m or £3.20 per share (assuming the market accepts this assessment).

1 *Semi-strong form efficiency*

Under semi-strong form efficiency, the market prices will only react when the information about the bid enters the public domain. The advent of new information will produce the following share prices:

		Share price A	Share price B
Day 2	No new information	£2.00	£3.00
Day 4	Takeover bid announced. B appears to be paying £6m for assets worth £4m	£3.00	£2.67
Day 10	Information available which revises the market value of B	£3.00	£3.20

2 *Strong form efficiency*

If the market is strong form efficient, all information is reflected in the share price even if it is not publicly available information. This will mean that on Day 2, when the management of B decides to offer £3.00 for A, the share prices will then react to reflect the full impact of the bid on both shares, perhaps via leakage of information by an informed insider. This will produce the following share prices:

		Share price A	Share price B
Day 2	Full impact of decision to bid and make savings reflected in share price	£3.00	£3.20
Day 4	Public announcement of bid, i.e. information of which the market is aware and therefore has no new information content	£3.00	£3.20
Day 10	Public announcement of savings to be derived from bid, i.e. further information of which the market is aware and therefore has no new information content	£3.00	£3.20

(ii) *For the share exchange*

Prior to the bid, the combined value of the two companies is (£4m + £18m) = £22m. If a share-for-share exchange were made on a one-for-one basis, the value per share of the expanded company would become £22m/8m = £2.75m, until further information about prospective savings emerged. Under semi-strong form efficiency, this will not happen until Day 10, but will leak out on to the market immediately under strong form efficiency. Spread over the whole 8m shares, the savings are worth £3.2m/8m = £0.4 per share.

The sequence of share price movements is thus:

	Semi-strong A	Semi-strong B	Strong A	Strong B
Day 2	£2	£3	£3.15	£3.15
Day 4	£2.75	£2.75	£3.15	£3.15
Day 10	£3.15	£3.15	£3.15	£3.15

(Level of efficiency)

Notice that the ultimate share price under the share exchange is lower than for the cash offer. This is because the benefits of the merger are spread out over a larger number of shares post-bid. In effect, the shareholders of B will have released part of the benefit they expect to receive from the bid to the former shareholders of A.

CHAPTER 2

1 Accounting profit is the excess of income over expenditure. Income and expenses relate to a specific period (e.g. the sales and costs for the month of January) based on accounting conventions such as depreciation. Cash flow is the cash receipts and payments from all operations including capital investment.

2 Using the table in Appendix D, the annuity factor for 10 years and $i = 20\%$ is 4.1925:

PV = £100 × 4.1925 = £419.25

3 Savings: £500,000 × 3.7908 £18,954
   Residual value: £1,000 × 0.62092 £621
   £19,575
   Less: initial cost: (£20,000)
   NPV £(425)

The NPV is negative. Recommend the project is rejected.

7 Free cash flow per share = (£5m/10m) = £0.50 or 50p

(i) $P_0 = (£0.5/0.12) = £4.17$

(ii) $P_0 = \dfrac{50\% \times 50p(1 + [15\% \times 50\%])}{12\% - [15\% \times 50\%]} = \dfrac{26.88p}{0.045} = £5.97$

(iii) $P_0 = \dfrac{50\% \times 50p(1 + [10\% + 50\%])}{12\% - [10\% \times 50\%]} = \dfrac{26.25p}{0.07} = £3.75$

(iv) Present value of dividends over Years 1–3:

Year 1 Dividend = 26.88p, as per part (ii) PV at 12% = £0.239
Year 2 Dividend = 26.88p (1.075) = 28.89p PV at 12% = £0.230
Year 3 Dividend = 28.89p (1.075) = 31.05p PV at 12% = £0.221
PV of dividends beyond year 3:

$= \dfrac{31.05p \,(1.05)}{(12\% - 5\%)} \times \text{(3-year PV factor)}$

= (£4.657 × 0.7118) = £3.315

Share price = Total PV = £4.005

8 (i) £0.37955
  (ii) $(0.6 \times 16\%) = 9.6\%$
  (iii) £0.65
  (iv) £0.20
  (v) $b = g/R = (2\%/10\%) = 0.2$
  (vi) $k_e = ((D_1/P_0) + g) = (£0.054/£0.60) + 8\% = 17\%$

  (vii) As $g = 10.5\%$, and
  $b = 0.7$,
  $$R = \frac{g}{b} = \frac{0.105}{0.7} = 15\%$$

CHAPTER 3

1 While a capital project may have a high expected return, the risks involved may indicate the possibility that the project will be unsuccessful – even to the extent of putting the whole business in jeopardy.

2 Project risk – variability in the projects' cash flows; business risk – variability in operating earnings of the firm; financial risk – risk resulting from the firm's financing decisions, e.g. the level of borrowing; portfolio risk – variability in the returns for an overall portfolio of investments.

3 Woodpulp project

Year	CE	NCF(£)	ENCF(£)	10% DF	PV(£)
1	0.90	8,000	7,200	0.90	6,480
2	0.85	7,000	5,950	0.83	4,938
3	0.80	7,000	5,600	0.75	4,200
4	0.75	5,000	3,750	0.68	2,550
5	0.70	5,000	3,500	0.62	2,170
6	0.65	5,000	3,250	0.56	1,820
7	0.60	5,000	3,000	0.51	1,530
				PV	23,688

NPV = £23,688 − £13,000 = £10,688. Accept the project. ENCF = Expected net cash flow.

4 Meedas Enterprises

Expected value Year 1 (£) = $0.2(400) + 0.3(500) + 0.3(600) + 0.2(700) = £550$
Variance (£) = $0.2(400 - 550)^2 + 0.3(500 - 550)^2 + 0.3(600 - 550)^2 + 0.2(700 - 550)^2 = £10,500$
Standard deviation = £102
Expected value Year 2 (£) = $0.2(300) + 0.3(400) + 0.3(500) + 0.2(600) = £450$
Variance (£) = $0.2(300 - 450)^2 + 0.3(400 - 450)^2 + 0.3(500 - 450)^2 + 0.2(600 - 450)^2 = £10,500$
Standard deviation = £102

Assuming a discount rate of 10 per cent and independent cash flows:

$$\text{NPV} = \frac{£550}{1.1} + \frac{£450}{(1.1)^2} - £800 = £71$$

$$\text{SD} = \sqrt{\frac{(£102)^2}{(1.1)^2} + \frac{(£102)^2}{(1.1)^4}} = £125$$

$$\text{Coefficient of variation} = \frac{£125}{£71} = 1.76$$

CHAPTER 4

1 Portfolio standard deviation $= \sqrt{[(0.5)^2\sigma_X^2 + (0.5)^2\sigma_Y^2 + 2(0.5)(0.5)(r_{XY}\sigma_X\sigma_Y)]}$

$= \sqrt{[(0.5)^2 30^2 + (0.5)^2 45^2 + 2(0.5)(0.5)(0.2)(30)(45)]}$

$= \sqrt{[225 + 506.25 + 135]}$

$= \sqrt{866.25} = 29.4$

This portfolio has a risk only slightly below that of investment X, even though the correlation coefficient is quite low. This suggests that the portfolio weighting involves too little of investment X if the intention is to lower portfolio risk.

2 The appropriate formula is:

$$\text{Proportion invested in asset A} = \frac{\sigma_B^2 - \text{cov}_{AB}}{\sigma_B^2 + \sigma_A^2 - 2\text{cov}_{AB}}$$

Also, remember that $\text{cov}_{AB} = r_{AB}\sigma_A\sigma_B$

(i) The covariance $= -12.6\%$ in A $= 74\%$, in B $= 26\%$
(ii) The covariance is -36% in A $= 29\%$, in B $= 71\%$
(iii) The covariance is 0% in A $= 0.44\%$, in B $= 99.56\%$

3 (a) **China**:

Expected value $= (0.3 \times 50\%) + (0.4 \times 25\%) + (0.3 \times 0) = 25\%$

Growth	Probability	IRR%	Deviation	Squared deviation	Times probability
Rapid	0.3	50	25	625	187.50
Stable	0.4	25	—	—	—
Slow	0.3	0	−25	625	187.50
					Sum = 375.00

Standard deviation $= \sqrt{375.0} = 19.4$, i.e. 19.4%

Scotland:

Expected value $= (0.3 \times 10\%) + (0.4 \times 15\%) + (0.3 \times 16\%) = 13.8\%$

Growth	Probability	IRR%	Deviation	Squared deviation	Times probability
Rapid	0.3	10	−3.8	14.44	4.33
Stable	0.4	15	1.2	1.44	0.58
Slow	0.3	16	2.2	4.84	1.45
					Sum = 6.36

Standard deviation $= \sqrt{6.36} = 2.5\%$

(b) Covariance calculation:
Covariance $= -45$
Expected portfolio return
$= (0.75 \times 13.8\%) + (0.25 \times 25\%) = 16.6\%$
Standard deviation

$= \sqrt{[(0.25^2 \times 19.4^2) + (0.75^2 \times 2.5^2) + (2 \times 0.25 \times 0.75 \times -45)]}$
$= \sqrt{[(23.5) + (3.5) + (-16.9)]}$
$= \sqrt{10.1} = 3.2$, i.e. 3.2%

4 (a) *Ireland*: EV of IRR $= (0.3 \times 20\%) + (0.3 \times 10\%) + (0.4 \times 15\%)$
$= 6\% + 3\% + 6\% = 15\%$

Outcome (%)	Deviation	Sq'd Dev.	p	Sq'd Dev. $\times p$
20	+5	25	0.3	7.5
10	−5	25	0.3	7.5
15	0	0	0.4	0
			Variance = Total	15 $\sigma = 3.87$

Humberside: EV of IRR = $(0.3 \times 10\%) + (0.3 \times 30\%) + (0.4 \times 20\%)$
$= 3\% + 9\% + 8\% = 20\%$

Outcome (%)	Deviation	Sq'd Dev.	p	Sq'd Dev. $\times p$
10	−10	100	0.3	30
30	+10	100	0.3	30
20	0	0	0.4	0
			Variance = Total	60 $\sigma = 7.75$

(b) (i) For a 50/50 split investment:
EV of IRR = $(0.5 \times 15\%) + (0.5 \times 20\%) = 17.5\%$
$\sigma = \sqrt{(0.5)^2(15) + (0.5)^2(60) + 2(0.5)(0.5)(0)(3.87)(7.75)}$
$= \sqrt{[3.75 + 15]} = \sqrt{18.75} = 4.33$

(ii) 75/25 split:
EV = $(0.75 \times 15\%) + (0.25 \times 20\%) = 11.25\% + 5\% = 16.25\%$
$\sigma = \sqrt{(0.75)^2(15) + (0.25)^2(60)}$
$= \sqrt{[8.44 + 3.75]} = \sqrt{12.19} = 3.49$, i.e. lower risk than either project

CHAPTER 5

1 Expected return = $5\% + 1.23[11.5\% - 5\%] = 13\%$. With more pessimistic expectations about market returns, this drops to:

ER = $5\% + 1.23[8\% - 5\%] = 8.7\%$

2 (i) $R_f = 9\%$
  (ii) Beta = 1.71
  (iii) $ER_j = 8.5\%$
  (iv) $ER_m = 19.3\%$

3 The intercept of the Security Market Line is the risk-free rate. It passes through the market portfolio which has a Beta of 1.0. In diagrammatic terms:

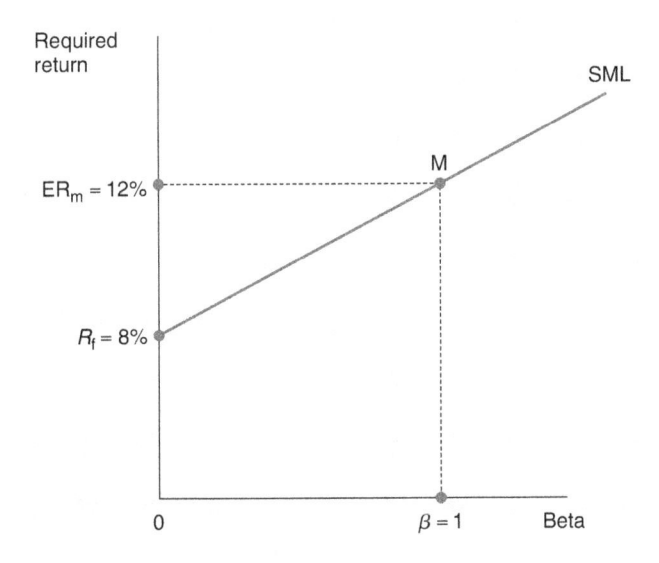

4 $ER_A = 5\% + 0.7[10\% - 5\%] = 8.5\%$
$ER_B = 5\% + 1.3[5\%] = 11.5\%$
$ER_C = 5\% + 0.9[5\%] = 9.5\%$

Comparing the expected returns with those currently achieved, A and C generate returns lower than expected, which suggests they are overvalued. (B looks undervalued.)

5 **(i)** Projecting past returns into the future, the expected return on the whole market is (5% + 7%) = 12%.

(ii)

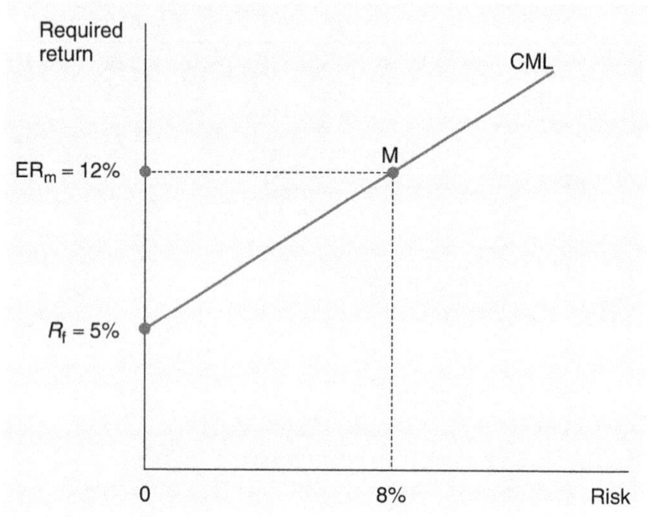

(iii) For a 50/50 portfolio:

$ER_p = (0.5 \times 12\%) + (0.5 \times 5\%) = 8.5\%$

(iv) Bearing in mind there is no correlation between the risk-free rate and the market portfolio, the expression for portfolio risk is:

$$\sigma_p = \sqrt{(0.5)^2 (8)^2}$$
$$= \sqrt{16} = 4, \text{ i.e. } 4\%$$

Alternatively, we could use the weighted average expression:

$(0.5 \times 8\%) + (0.5 \times 0) = 4\%$

(v) As risk increases from 4% (the 50/50 portfolio) to 8% (the market portfolio), the return required increases from 8.5% to 12%, suggesting a risk–return trade-off (assuming it is linear) of:

$(3.5\%/4\%) = 0.875$

Thus, for every one percentage point increase in the portfolio standard deviation, the investor must be compensated by an increase in portfolio return of 0.875%.

6 **(a)** Your graph should show every pair of observations lying along a straight line. This indicates perfect positive correlation between R_j and R_m. The slope of the line, and hence the Beta, is +0.8.

(b) Because all observations lie on the line of best fit, all variation in R_j appears to be explained by variation in R_m, i.e. there is no specific risk.

(c) σ_m^2 = variance of the market return. The mean return on the market portfolio = 2.0. Hence

$$\sigma_m^2 = (5-2)^2 + (-10-2)^2 + \cdots + (6-2)^2 = 306$$

Thus, systematic risk = $(0.8)^2 (306) = 195.84$.
You should expect to find the total risk is also 195.84 because there is no unique risk.

CHAPTER 6

1 The shares are ex-dividend, so the future required return is:

$$k_e = \frac{£0.80(1.045)}{£10.50} + 0.045 = (0.08 + 0.045)$$
$$= 0.125, \text{ i.e. } 12.5\%$$

2 (i) $D_0 = £0.62$
 (ii) $P_0 = £3.64$
 (iii) $k_e = 9.3\%$
 (iv) $g = 6.2\%$

3 Dividend growth is found by solving:

$$11p(1+g)^4 = 20.0p$$
$$(1+g)^4 = \frac{20.0p}{11.0p} = 1.8182$$

From tables, $g = 15.8\%$ approx.

Implied $k_e = \frac{20p(1.158)}{£5.50} + 0.158$
$= 0.042 + 0.158 = 0.20$, i.e. 20%

4 (i) $k_e = 6\% + 0.8[11\% - 6\%] = (6\% + 4\%) = 10\%$

 (ii) Beta = $(0.8 \times 1.25) = 1.0$
  $k_e = 6\% + 1.0[11\% - 6\%] = (6\% + 5\%) = 11\%$

 (iii) Beta = $(0.8 \times 0.75) = 0.6$
  $k_e = 6\% + 0.6[11\% - 6\%] = (6\% + 3\%) = 9\%$

5

Division	R_f	Beta	Market Premium	k_e	% of assets
C	7%	0.7	8.00	12.6%	15
E	7%	1.1	8.00	15.8%	40
R	7%	0.8	8.00	13.4%	20
P	7%	0.6	8.00	11.8%	5
Total	/	0.855	/	13.84%	100

Overall Beta = $(0.15 \times 0.7) + (0.04 \times 1.1) + (0.20 \times 0.8) + (0.25 \times 0.6)$
$= (0.105 + 0.44 + 0.16 + 0.15) = 0.855$

Overall required return = $7\% + 0.855[8\%] = (7\% + 6.84\%) = 13.84\%$

6 (a) EV of return = $(0.6 \times 10\%) + (0.4 \times 20\%) = 14\%$.

Outcome	Deviation	Squared deviation	Prob.	Sq'd × dev. p
10%	−4%	16	0.6	9.6
20%	+6%	36	0.4	14.4
		Variance = Total	24.0	$\sigma = 4.9$

(b) Megacorp ER = 30%   s.d. = 14%   proportion = 80%
Erewhon ER = 14%   s.d. = 4.9%   proportion = 20%

ER = $(0.8 \times 30\%) + (0.2 \times 14\%) = 24\% + 2.8\% = 26.8\%$
S.d. = $\sqrt{[(0.8)^2 (14)^2 + (0.2)^2 (4.9)^2 + 2(0.8)(0.2)(-0.36)(14)(4.9)]}$

(c) The present Beta = 1.20.

$$\text{Beta of project} = \frac{\text{cov}_{jm}}{\sigma_m^2} = \frac{r_{jm}\sigma_j\sigma_m}{\sigma_m^2} = \frac{r_{jm}\sigma_j}{\sigma_m}$$

What is the risk of the market (σ_m)?
Rearranging:

$$\sigma_m = \frac{\sigma_j r_{jm}}{\text{Beta}_j}$$

For Megacorp:

$$\sigma_j = \frac{(14)(0.8)}{1.2} = 9.33$$

$$\text{Project Beta} = \frac{(-0.1)(4.9)}{9.33} = -\frac{0.49}{9.33} = -0.05$$

New Beta for Megacorp = $(0.8 \times 1.2) + (0.2 \times -0.05) = 0.95$. Therefore, the new project lowers Megacorp's Beta.

8 (a) Since the asset Beta is a weighted average of the component segment Betas:

$$\beta_A = \left(\frac{1}{4} \times \beta_N\right) + \left(\frac{1}{4} \times \beta_W\right) + \left(\frac{1}{2} \times \beta_S\right) = 1.06$$

where $\beta_N = \beta$ of North, $\beta_W = \beta$ of West, $\beta_S = \beta$ of South.

Since North is 50 per cent more risky than South, and West is 25 per cent less risky than South, it follows that:

$$\frac{(1.5\beta_S)}{4} + \frac{(0.75\beta_S)}{4} + \frac{\beta_S}{2} = 1.06$$

whence $\beta_S = 1.00$, $\beta_N = 1.50$, $\beta_W = 0.75$.

(b) The asset Beta for East (β_E) is:
$\beta_E = \beta_S \times \text{Relative risk factor}$
$= \beta_S \times \text{Revenue sensitivity factor} \times \text{Operational gearing factor}$
$= 1.0 \times 1.4 \times \frac{1.6}{2.0} = 1 \times 1.12 = 1.12$

(c) The asset Beta for Lancelot after the divestment and acquisition is again a weighted average of the component asset Betas:

$$\beta_A = \left(\frac{1}{2} \times \beta_E\right) + \left(\frac{1}{4} \times \beta_W\right) + \left(\frac{1}{4} \times \beta_N\right)$$
$$= \left(\frac{1}{2} \times 1.12\right) + \left(\frac{1}{4} \times 0.75\right) + \left(\frac{1}{4} \times 1.5\right)$$
$$= 0.56 + 0.1875 + 0.375 = 1.12$$

(d) If we evaluate projects in East on the assumption of all-equity financing, the cut-off rate is:

$R_f + \beta_E (ER_m - R_f) = 10\% + 1.12(15\%) = 26.8\%$

(e) There are numerous problems involved in obtaining tailor-made project discount rates. First, given that we may have to take the Beta from a surrogate company, ungearing the Beta of its shares requires an accurate assessment of the values of the equity and debt. If the company is quoted, the market valuation of equity can be taken, but not all corporate debt is quoted. Thus the debt/equity ratio used will often be a mixture of market and book values, even for quoted companies. Second, decomposing the ungeared Beta into segmental asset Betas strictly requires weighted average calculations based on market values. Since corporate segments are not generally quoted on stock markets, book values invariably have to be used. Third, to measure project Betas requires consideration of whether the project is of a different order of risk from 'typical' projects in the division. If so, the revenue sensitivity factor requires estimation, mainly based on guesswork for unique projects. In addition, the project gearing factor must also be estimated. Fourth, the general problems relating to specification of the risk-free return and the risk premium on the market portfolio still have to be addressed.

CHAPTER 7

3 Free cash flow (£) = Revenue less bad debts less operating costs + depreciation less replacement investment less tax (allowing for relief on bad debts)

$= (0.98 \times 500,000) - (300,000) + (50,000)$
$\quad - (50,000) - (60,000 + [0.3 \times 50\% \times 2\% \times 500,000])$
$= (490,000 - 300,000 + 50,000 - 50,000 - 60,000 + 1,500)$
$= £131,500$

(a) valued at 10% as a perpetuity:

$V = (£131,500/0.1) = £1.315$ million
i.e. $(£1.315m/2m) = £0.6575$ per share (65.75p)

(b) valued over 10 years:

$V = (£131,500 \times 10$ year annuity factor 10%)
$= (£131,500 \times 6.1446) = £808,015m$, or £0.405 per share (40.5p).

CHAPTER 8

1 Companies issue a type of call option when issuing share warrants (giving the holder the right to buy shares at a fixed price) and convertible loan stock (giving the holder the right to exchange the loan for a fixed number of shares).

2 **Gaymore plc**
Traded options give the holder the right, but not the obligation, to buy (a call option) or sell (a put option) a quantity of shares at a fixed price on an exercise date in the future. They are usually in contracts of 1,000 shares and for three, six or nine months.

Holders of a put option in Gaymore plc have the right to sell shares in April at 500p. For this right they currently have to pay a premium of 47p, or £470 on a contract of 1,000 shares.

If the share price falls below 453p (i.e. 500p − 47p), the shares become profitable and the holder is 'in the money'. So if they fall to 450p, the investor can buy shares at this price and exercise his or her put option to sell shares for 500p, a profit of 50p per share which, after the initial cost of the option, gives a net profit of 3p per share or £30 on the contract.

If the share price moves up to 510p by April, the option becomes worthless, and the investor loses his or her 47p premium.

Options such as this one can be used either to speculate or to hedge on share price changes for a relatively low premium.

3 The terms for an exchange traded option are standardised whereas the terms for traditional options can vary from contract to contract. It is the development of standardised options that has facilitated the trading of these instruments.

6 The put–call parity relationship is:

$S + P - C = E/(1 + R_f)$

From this:

$C = S - (E/(1 + R_f)) + P$

where $S = 25$, $P = 15$, $E/(1 + R_f) = 10$.

$C = 25 - 10 + 15 = 30$

The value of the call option is 30p.

7 The put–call parity relationship is:

$S + P - C = E/(1 + R_f)$

$E/(1 + R_f) = 30 + 5 - 19 = 16p$

8 Inputs:

$S_T = 38p \quad X = 40p$

$T = 0.5 \quad r_f = 0.10$

$SD(R) = 0.20$

Valuation equations:

$$C_t = S_t N(d_1) - Xe^{-rT} N(d_2)$$

$$d_1 = \frac{\ln(S_1/X) + (r + VAR(R)/2)t}{SD(r)\sqrt{t}}$$

$$d_2 = \frac{\ln(S_1/X) + (r + VAR(R)/2)t}{SD(r)\sqrt{t}} = d_1 - SD(r)\sqrt{t}$$

$d_1 = [\ln 38/40 + (0.10 + 0.20^2/2)0.5]/0.2/\sqrt{0.5}$
$ = [-0.05129 + 0.06]/[0.2 \times 0.7071]$
$ = 0.06156$

$d_2 = [\ln 38/40 + (0.10 - 0.20^2/2)0.5]/0.2\sqrt{0.5}$
$ = [-0.05129 + 0.04]/[0.2 \times 0.7071]$
$ = -0.07986$

$N(d_1) = N(0.0615) = 0.5245$
$N(d_2) = N(-0.0798) = 0.4682$
$C_1 = 38.00 \times 0.5245 - 40.00e^{-0.10 \times 0.5} \times 0.4682$
$ = 19.93 - 17.81$
$ = 2.12$

Calculations:
The estimated value of the call is 2.12p. This implies that if the call is bought at this price, the share price would have to increase from 38.00p to 40.12p by the end of the six-month period for the investor to break even.

9 Put–call parity

$S + P = C + ke^{-rt}$
$\Rightarrow 420.5 + 38.5 = 50.5 + 420e^{-0.5r}$
$\Rightarrow 0.9726 = e^{-0.5r}$
$\Rightarrow -0.5r = -0.02776$
$\Rightarrow r = 0.0555 = 5.55\%$

10 (a) **Intrinsic value:** The intrinsic value of an option is the difference between the value of the underlying asset and the exercise price of the option. September 800 call is in the money while the April put is out of the money.
Time-value: When options are more valuable, the greater is the likelihood of a significant change in the value of the underlying asset. If an option expires tomorrow, we can certainly say that there is a smaller likelihood of a significant change than if the option expires in six months. Quite simply, the longer the time to expiration, the more opportunity there is for the price to move, and therefore at March the September option is more valuable than the April option.

(b) **Short straddle (written straddle)**
E.g. June 800 call + put: written premiums = 53.5 + 20 = 73.5p
The option writer receives 73.5p. If neither option is exercised, the writer gains all of this. However, this is the outcome only if $S_T = 800$.

If $S_T > 800$ the call is exercised, if $800 < S_T$ the put is exercised.

The writer will gain from the strategy if the intrinsic value of the exercised option is less than the 73.5 premiums received. Hence the writer will only profit if S_T is within the range 726.5 to 873.5.

If $S_T = 726.5$ the put is exercised, the writer must take delivery at 800, therefore losing 73.5, which exactly cancels the written premiums of 73.5, so net profit = 0.

If $S_T = 873.5$ the call is exercised, the writer must deliver the share at price 800, therefore losing 73.5, which exactly cancels out the written premiums, so net profit = 0.

Thus at any share price outside of that range, the writer of the short straddle has an overall loss. If share price at expiration is within the range, the writer makes a net profit.

In general, the profit to short straddle = written premiums − intrinsic value of the option that is exercised.
Losses *could* be very high, e.g. if $S_T = 650$ loss = 76.5 (i.e. 73.5 − 150), if $S_T = 1000$ loss = 126.5 (73.5 − 200). It is extremely risky.

12 Using the Black–Scholes formula:

$$d_1 = \frac{\ln(P_s/X) + 0.5\sigma}{\sigma\sqrt{T}}\sqrt{T}$$

$$= \frac{\ln(3/2.50) + (0.5 \times 0.25)}{0.2 \times \sqrt{0.25}} + (0.5 \times 0.2 \times \sqrt{0.25})$$

$$= \frac{0.1823 + 0.0125}{0.1} + 0.5$$

$$= 1.9982$$

$$d_2 = d_1 - \sigma\sqrt{T}$$
$$= 1.9982 - 0.2\sqrt{0.25}$$
$$= 1.9982 - 0.1$$
$$= 1.8982$$

$$N(d_1) = 0.5 + 0.4767 + \frac{82}{100}(0.4772 - 0.4767)$$
$$= 0.9771$$

$$N(d_2) = 0.5 + 0.4706 + \frac{82}{100}(0.4713 - 0.4706)$$
$$= 0.9712$$

$$P_c = P_s N(d_1) - Xe^{-rT}N(d_2)$$
$$= (3 \times 0.9771) - (2.50e^{-0.05 \times 0.25} \times 0.9712)$$
$$= 2.9313 - (2.50 \times 0.9876 \times 0.9712)$$
$$= 53.35p$$

CHAPTER 9

1 With a residual dividend policy:

Dividends = [Distributable Earnings − Capital Expenditure]

Tom has issued 10 million shares with par value 50p each, giving total book value of £5 million. Total dividends are (20p × 10m) = £2m. Hence, capex = (£10m − £2m) = £8m.

2 As all projects are indivisible, only whole projects with IRR > 20 per cent can be selected, i.e. B + C + E, with total expenditure of £14 million. As this infringes the capital availability constraint of £9 million, Dick is restricted to only B + C, with joint outlay of £7 million, leaving £2 million as a residual dividend.

3 According to Lintner's target adjustment theory, companies only partially adjust their dividends in line with earnings changes. The change in dividend will be half of the difference between current EPS and the last dividend, i.e.

$$\text{Dividend change} = 0.5 \times [0.5 \, \text{EPS}_t - \text{Div}_{t-1}]$$
$$= 0.5 \times [0.5 \times (£3.0) - £1]$$
$$= 0.5 \times £0.5 = £0.25$$

so that the new dividend = (£1.0 + £0.25) = £1.25.

4 Tamas' tax charge = (30% × £30m) = £9m
profit after tax = (£30m − £9m) = £21m
Dividend = (50% × £21m) = £10.5m

i.e. (£10.5m/100m) = 10.5p per share

Net (i.e. post-tax) cash flow = [Pre-tax profit + depreciation − replacement investment − tax]
$$= [£30m + £2m - £2m - £9m] = £21m$$

Value cum dividend = (£21m/15%) + £10.5m
$$= (£140m + £10.5m) = £150.5m$$

Per share, this is (£150.5m/100m) = £1.505 (cum dividend).
The ex-dividend share price is £1.505 reduced by the dividend per share of 10.5p, i.e. (£1.505 − £0.105) = £1.40.

5 (a) The price per share is given by:

$$P_0 = \frac{D_1}{(k_e - g)}$$

where D_1 is next year's dividend, k_e is the shareholder's required return and g is the expected rate of growth in dividends.

The growth rate can be found from the expression:

$5.0p(1 + g)^4 = 7.3p$

where g is the past (compound) growth rate.

$$(1 + g)^4 = \frac{7.3p}{5.0p} = 1.46$$

or

$$\frac{1}{(1 + g)^4} = 0.6849$$

From the present value tables, $g = 10\%$, whence:

$$P_0 = \frac{7.3p(1.1)}{(16\% - 10\%)} = \frac{8.03p}{0.06} = £1.34$$

(b) With D_1 at just 5.0p, using managerial expectations for the investment:

$$P_0 = \frac{5.0p}{(16\% - 14\%)} = \frac{5.0p}{0.02} = £2.50$$

(c) To break even, share price must not fall below £1.34, i.e.

$$£1.34 = \frac{5.0p}{(16\% - g)}$$

Solving for g, we find $g = 12.3\%$, marginally above the assessment of the more pessimistic managers.

(d) Until 2017, Galahad pursued a policy of distributing 40–50 per cent of profit after tax as dividend. Each year, it has offered a steady dividend increase, even in 2016, when its earnings actually fell. This was presumably out of reluctance to lower the dividend, fearing an adverse market reaction, and reflecting a belief that the earnings shortfall was a temporary phenomenon. In 2017 it offered a 12 per cent dividend increase, the highest percentage increase in the time series, possibly to compensate shareholders for the relatively small increase (only 8 per cent) in 2016. It would appear that Galahad has either already built up a clientèle of investors whose interests it is trying to safeguard, or that it is trying to do so.

The proposed dividend cut to 5.0p per share would represent a sharply increased dividend cover of 3.5, on the assumption that EPS also grows at 10 per cent p.a. Such a sharp rise in the dividend safety margin is likely to be construed by the market as implying that Galahad's managers expect earnings to be depressed in the future, especially as it follows a year of record dividend increase. Such an abrupt change in dividend policy is thus likely to offend its clientèle of shareholders at best, and at worst, to alarm the market as to the reliability of future earnings.

In an efficient capital market, with homogeneous investor expectations, the share price would increase by the amount calculated in (b), at least, if the market agreed with the managers' views about the attractions of the projected expenditure. However, in view of the information content of dividends, Galahad's board will have to be very confident of its ability to persuade the market of the inherent desirability of the proposed investment programme. This may well be a difficult task, especially given the stated doubts of some of its managers. The board will have to explain why they feel internal financing is preferable to raising capital externally, either by a rights issue, or by raising further debt finance. While the level of indebtedness of Galahad is not given, the implication is that it is unacceptably high, so as to obviate the issue of additional borrowing instruments. If this is the case, then it seems doubly risky to propose a dividend cut, as it may signal fears regarding Galahad's ability to service a high level of debt.

If the dividend cut is greeted adversely, then the ability of the shareholder clientèle to home-make dividends will be impaired, since, apart from the transactions costs involved, there will perhaps be no capital gain to realise. Any significant selling to convert capital into income will further depress share price.

If the investment programme is truly worthwhile, Galahad's managers perhaps should not shrink from offering a rights issue, since, despite the costs of such issues, shareholders will eventually reap the benefits in the form of higher future earnings and dividends. However, this might suggest a short-term reduction in share price, which may penalise short-term investors, but who still have the option of protecting their interests by selling their rights.

CHAPTER 10

1. LTD/Equity = (£200m/£500m) = 40%
   LTD/(LTD + Equity) = £200m/(£200m + £500m) = 28%
   Total Debt/Equity = (£200m + £50m)/£500m = 50%
   Net Debt = (£200m + £50m) − (£20m + £40m) = £190m.
   Net Debt/Equity = (£190m/£500m) = 38%
   Total Debt/Total Assets = £250m/£800m = 31%
   Interest Cover = (£120m/£25m) = 4.8 times.
   Income Gearing = (1/4.8) × 100 = 21%
   Total Liabilities/Total Assets = (£300m/£800m) = 37.5%

2. Market value of debt = £100 × (£45m/£50m) = £90

   (i) cost of debt = [8% × £100]/£90 = (£8/£90) = 8.9%
   (ii) cost of debt = £8(1 − 30%)/£90 = (£5.6/£90) = 6.2%
   (iii) cost of debt is the solution R to:

   $$£90 = \frac{£8}{(1+R)} + \frac{£8}{(1+R)^2} + \cdots + \frac{£8 + £100}{(1+R)^6}$$

   Solution value for $R = 10.3\%$

   (iv) The cost of debt is the solution R to:

   $$£90 = \frac{£8(1-30\%)}{(1+R)} + \frac{£5.6}{(1+R)^2} + \cdots + \frac{(£5.6 + £100)}{(1+R)^6}$$

   Solution value for $R = 8.25\%$

3 **(a)**   £m

PBIT = (0.3 × £5m) + (0.5 × £50m) + (0.2 × £150m) = £56.5m

Current Structure – £200m equity.

Tax at 30%	(1.5)	(15)	(45)
PAT	3.5	35	105
ROE	1.8%	17.5%	52.5%

Programme (i) – £40m debt/£160m equity.

Interest at 8.5%	(3.2)	(3.2)	(3.2)
Taxable profit	1.8	46.8	146.8
Tax at 30%	(0.5)	(14.0)	(44.0)
PAT	1.26	32.8	102.8
ROE	0.8%	20.5%	64.3%

Programme (ii) – £80m debt/£120m equity.

Interest at 8.5%	(6.8)	(6.8)	(6.8)
Taxable profit	–	43.2	143.2
Tax at 30%	–	(14.0)	(44.0)
PAT	–	30.2	100.2
ROE	(1.5%)	25.2%	83.5%

(b) Risk is measured by the standard deviation of the returns on equity (ROE) around the respective expected values (EVs).

Current Capital Structure.
EV of ROE = (0.3 × 1.8) + (0.5 × 17.5) + (0.2 × 52.5) = 19.8%

Outcome	EV	Deviation	Squared	× probability
1.8	19.8	−18.0	324	97.2
17.5	19.8	−2.3	5.3	2.65
52.5	19.8	32.7	1069.3	213.86
				Total variance = 313.71

Standard deviation = $\sqrt{313.71}$ = 17.7, i.e. 17.7%

Programme (i)
EV of ROE = (0.3 × 0.8) + (0.5 × 20.5) + (0.2 × 64.3) = 23.4%

Outcome	EV	Deviation	Squared	× probability
0.8	23.4	−22.6	510.76	153.228
20.5	23.4	−2.9	8.41	4.205
64.3	23.4	40.9	1672.81	334.56
				Total variance = 491.993

Standard deviation = $\sqrt{491.993}$ = 22.18, i.e. 22.2%

Programme (ii)
EV of ROE = (0.3 × −1.5) + (0.5 × 25.2) + (0.2 × 83.5) = 28.9%

Outcome	EV	Deviation	Squared	×probability
−1.5	28.9	−30.4	924.16	277.248
25.2	28.9	−3.7	13.69	6.845
83.5	28.9	54.6	2981.16	596.230
				Total variance = 880.323

Standard deviation = $\sqrt{880.323}$ = 29.7, i.e. 29.7%

(c) Business risk, exposure to the risk of fluctuations in business activity, can be measured in different ways, e.g. the variability in sales or in some measure of profitability. This example shows how ROE varies under three scenarios. By abstracting from financial risk, the ROE in the all-equity case shows inherent business risk – the ROE varies from 1.8 per cent to 52.5 per cent, with a standard deviation of 17.7 per cent.

Gearing adds a second layer of risk because it imposes an extra fixed cost, i.e. the prior interest charge – the higher the level of gearing, the higher the financial risk. Consequently, we see that the standard deviation of the ROE rises to 22.2 per cent under the relatively modest level of gearing, programme (i), while programme (ii) raises it to 29.7 per cent.

4 (a) (i) Perpetual debt:
$$\text{PV of Tax Savings} = \frac{(T \times i \times \text{Nominal Debt Value})}{i} = \frac{TiB}{i}$$
$$= (30\% \times 10\% \times £100\text{m})/10\%$$
$$= (£3\text{m}/0.1) = £30\text{m}$$

(ii) When debt is repaid in full after 5 years:
PV = £3m p.a. over 5 years at 10% discount rate = (£3m × 3.7908) = £11.37m

(iii) Debt repaid in equal tranches:

Year	Start-year debt	Interest	Tax saving	PV	Repayment
1	100	10	3	2.73	20
2	80	8	2.4	1.98	20
3	60	6	1.8	1.35	20
4	40	4	1.2	0.82	20
5	20	2	0.6	0.37	20
				Total = £7.25m	

(c) The value of the tax shield is higher:
 – the higher the interest rate
 – the higher the tax rate
 – the higher the amount of debt
 – the longer the term of the loan
 – the slower that debt is repaid
 – the greater the firm's taxable capacity

5 Book value weights:

			weight	cost
Equity [£10m + £20m] =	£30m	i.e.	66.7%	20%
Debt	£15m		33.3%	10% pre-tax
	£45m		100%	

WACC = (20% × 66.7%) + (10%[1 − 30%] × 33.3%)
     = (13.3% + 2.3%) = 15.6%

Market value of equity = (20m shares × £4.50) = £90m. The weights become:
Equity: £90m/£105m = 85.7%
Debt: £15m/£105m = 14.3%

$$WACC = (20\% \times 85.7\%) + (10\%[1 - 30\%] \times 14.3\%)$$
$$= (17.1\% + 1.0\%) = 18.1\%$$

CHAPTER 11

1 (i) From MM's Proposition I, the cost of equity is:

$$k_{eg} = k_{eu} + (k_{eu} - k_d)\frac{V_B}{V_S}$$

If the proportion of debt to total finance is 20%, the ratio of debt to equity must be 1:4, i.e. 0.25. Hence,

$$k_{eg} = 20\% + (20\% - 8\%)(0.25) = 23\%$$

2 (i) Because the WACC is constant at 20% at all gearing levels, the figures correspond to the MM no-tax theory.
(ii) This now illustrates the MM with-tax theory, wherein the WACC falls continuously as gearing increases. The cost of equity becomes:

$$k_{eg} = k_{eu} + (k_{eu} - k_d)(1 - T)\frac{V_B}{V_S}$$

The amended table is:

% Debt	% Equity	k_d	k_e	WACC
—	100	—	20%	20%
25	75	5.6%	22.8%	18.5%
50	50	5.6%	28.4%	17.2%
75	25	5.6%	45.2%	15.5%

3 Assume the investor holds 10 per cent of Geared's equity.
Value of stake = 10% × £900 = £90
Personal income initially = 10% × [£100 − (5% × £200)]
= 10% × £90 = £9
Geared's gearing = £200/£900 = 22.2%

Assume the investor sells the stake in Geared for £90, borrows £20 at 5 per cent to duplicate Geared's gearing and invests the whole stake in Ungeared's equity.

Now entitled to earnings of (£110/£950) × £100 = £11.58
Personal interest liability = (5% × £20) = (£1.00)
Net income = £10.58

The investor is better off by (£10.58 − £9.00) = £1.58

9 (a) CAPM
The stated Beta is an equity Beta so that the required return on equity is:

$$ER_j = R_f + \beta_j(ER_m - R_f)$$
$$= 12\% + 1.4(18\% - 12\%) = 20.4\%$$

This is unsuitable as a discount rate because:
(i) It is the required return on equity rather than the required return on the overall company.
(ii) The equity Beta of 1.4 reflects the financial risk of Folten's equity. Wemere's gearing differs from that of Folten, hence their equity Betas will differ.
The inflation adjustment is unnecessary since ER_m and R_f already incorporate the expected impact of inflation.

The equity Beta for Wemere can be estimated by ungearing Folten's equity Beta and regearing to reflect the financial risk of Wemere.

The market value-weighted gearing figures are:

Folten
Equity (138p × 7.2m shares) = £9,936m, i.e. 69.3% of total
Debt = £4,400m, i.e. 30.7% of total
Total = £14.336m

Wemere
Equity (using the takeover bid offer) = £10.6m, i.e. 81.5% of total
Debt = £2.4m, i.e. 18.5% of total
Total = £13.0m

Assuming corporate debt is risk-free, the ungeared equity Beta is

$$\beta_u = \beta_g \times \frac{1}{\left[1 + \frac{V_B}{V_S} \times (1-T)\right]} = 1.4 \times \frac{1}{1 + (0.44)(1-35\%)}$$

$$= 1.089$$

Regearing Beta for Wemere,

$$\beta_g = \beta_u \left[1 + \frac{V_B}{V_S} \times (1-T)\right]$$

$$= 1.089 [1 + 0.23(1-35\%)] = 1.25$$

The cost of equity for Wemere is thus:
12% + 1.25[18% − 12%] = 19.5%

Given the cost of debt is 13%:

WACC = [13%(1 − 35%) × 18.5%] + [19.5% × 81.5%]
= 1.56% + 15.89% = 17.5%

However, the WACC is only suitable as a discount rate if the systematic risk of the new investment is similar to that of the company as a whole.

Dividend Growth Model
The expression for this model relates to the cost of equity, not the overall cost of capital, i.e.

$$k_e = \frac{D_1}{P_0} + g = \frac{14.20p}{138p} + 9\% = 19.3\%$$

No inflation adjustment is required.
The WACC is: [13%(1 − 35%) × 18.5%] + [19.3% × 81.5%]
= 1.56% + 15.73% = 17.3%

(b) Neither method is problem-free. The surrogate company is unlikely to have identical characterisitics, either at an operating level or in terms of financial characteristics. For example, the cost of equity in the Dividend Growth Model is derived from a different set of data regarding dividend policy, growth and share prices.

Folten's managers may have different capabilities, and the company may face different growth opportunities. Before using the estimated WACC, Wemere must be confident that the two companies are a sufficiently close fit.

Even so, the calculated WACC is inappropriate if the systematic risk of any new project differs from that of the company as a whole, and/or if project financing involves moving to a new capital structure.

CHAPTER 12

1 (a) Value of target now:

$$P_0 = \frac{D_1}{k_e - g}$$

$$20 = \frac{80p}{k_e - 6\%}$$

whence $k_e = 10\%$.

Value of target would become

$$P = \frac{80p}{10\% - 8\%} = £40 \text{ per share}$$

Value of equity = £40 × 0.6m = £24m, i.e. an increase of £12m.

(b) Cost of acquisition: (£25 − £20) = £5 per share. In total, £5 × 0.6m = £3m. NPV of acquisition: (£12m − £3m) = £9m. Advise to proceed.

(c) Number of new shares required: 0.6m/3 = 0.2m; new total = 1.2m.

$$\text{Value of new company} = \frac{£90m + £12m + £12m}{1.2m}$$

$$= £114/1.2m = £95 \text{ per share}$$

Cost of acquisition = (0.2m × £95m) − £12m = £7m. NPV of acquisition = (£12m − £7m) = £5m. Again, advise to proceed.

(d) (i) Cost of cash bid unchanged. Pointless to proceed as there are no gains.
(ii) With the share exchange:

$$\text{Value of new company} = \frac{£90m + £12m}{1.2m} = £85 \text{ per share}$$

NPV of acquisition: (0.2m × £85) − £12m = (£5m). Advise not to proceed on this basis.

7 (a) The Balance Sheet net asset value is total assets minus total liabilities, i.e. £620m. Land and buildings have an estimated value of £150m × (1.25)⁴ = £366m, i.e. £216m higher than the book value. Hence, the adjusted NAV is £836m.

Applying Grapper's 12 per cent growth rate, estimated PAT for the coming five years is:

£151(1.12) + £151(1.12)², etc.= £1,074m

This yields a total value of £836m + £1,074m = £1,910m. Grapper's market value is currently (400m shares × share price 470p) = £1,880m. The premium is thus £30m or 7.5p per share.

This is not a sound basis for valuation as it ignores the time-value of money. The premium of 1.6 per cent above the current market price is very small compared with those achieved in many 'real' bids.

Using the Dividend Valuation Model:

$$P_0 = \frac{D_1}{k_e - g} = \frac{D_0(1 + g)}{k_e - g}$$

$$\text{Current dividend per share} = \frac{£76m}{400m} = 19p$$

Hence $D_1 = 19p(1.12) = 21.3p$.
From the CAPM:
$k_e = ER_j = R_f + \beta_j (ER_m - R_f) = 10\% + 1.05(16\% - 10\%) = 16.3\%$

Thus:

$$P_0 = \frac{21.3p}{16.3\% - 12\%} = 495p$$

i.e. 5.3 per cent above the market price.

Restrictive assumptions underlying such a valuation include a constant growth rate, and an unchanged dividend policy. It is more rational to assess the value of Grapper incorporating post-merger rationalisation.

(b) The post-merger sales revenue of Woppit will be over £5,000 million, a size which could deter other takeover raiders, at least from the United Kingdom. However, bids from US and other European sources should not be ruled out. In addition, debt-financed bids from consortia like Hoylake (which bid for BAT) show that size alone is not an adequate protection against a takeover bid.

(c) An indication of the scope for improving Grapper's efficiency can be obtained by examination of key financial ratios.

	Woppit	Grapper
Operating profit margin (PBIT/sales)	20%	16.6%
Asset turnover (sales/total assets)	1.80	1.36
Debtors' collection period	31 days	50 days
Stock turnover	10.3	6.4
Current ratio	1.65:1	2.45:1

There are clear opportunities to improve Grapper's performance by rationalisation and restructuring of activities. For example:

- Grapper's operating profit margin could be brought into line with Woppit's by a price increase and/or cost reduction.
- Grapper's stock level looks high by comparison. There could well be stockholding economies in an expanded operation.
- Grapper's cash holdings look excessive – again, centralised cash management may generate economies.
- Grapper's asset turnover is relatively low. Some assets could well be sold and others worked more intensively.
- Grapper seems to have scope for reducing its investment in debtors.
- Introduction of such economies may well close the gap between Woppit's return on assets of 36 per cent and Grapper's present 22.5 per cent.

CHAPTER 13

1. Remember the bank always wins, so it sells euros at 1.6296, and buys at 1.6320.
   (a) Selling £10 million, its receipts are (10m × 1.6296) = €16.296 million.
   (b) Selling €12 million, its receipts are (12m/1.6320) = £7.353 million.

2. (a) Amount invoiced = (10m × €1.6) = €16m.
   (b) With spot at €1.7 vs. £1, proceeds = €16m/1.7) = £9.412m. Hence, the loss compared to the current spot rate = (£10m − £9.412m) = £0.588m.
   (c) With spot at €1.5 vs. £1, the sale proceeds are (€16m/1.5) = £10.667m. In this case, the exporter gains £0.667m from the exchange rate change.
   (d) If the exporter sells forward, the contracted proceeds are €16m/1.62 = £9.877m.
      (i) The cost of the hedge is thus £0.123m, i.e. 1.2% of the sterling value of the deal.
      (ii) If sterling falls to €1.5 vs. £1, the forward contract guarantees the exporter £9.877 million, but it could have received £10.667 million had it not hedged. There is thus an opportunity cost of (£10.667m − £9.877m) = £0.790m.
      (iii) If sterling rises to €1.7 vs. £1, the forward contract still guarantees the exporter £9.877m, but it would have received £9.412m had it not hedged. The exporter is thus better off by (£9.877m − £9.412m) = £0.465m.
   If the exporter thinks there is an equal chance of a 10 per cent variation in the €/£ exchange rate, it must balance an opportunity cost from hedging of £0.75 million if sterling falls, against being better off by £0.465 million if sterling rises.

3. The forward outrights are:

KRONA	10.960 − 10.967
Less forward premium	(0.025 − 0.011)
Forward outright	10.935 − 10.956
YEN	230.11 − 230.16
Less forward premium	(1.10 − 0.97)
Forward outright	229.01 − 229.19
KRONOR	11.717 − 11.723
Less forward premium	(0.021 − 0.004)
Forward outright	11.696 − 11.719

5 According to Interest Rate Parity,

$$\text{Forward rate} = \text{Spot rate} \times \frac{(1 + \text{US interest rate})}{(1 + \text{UK interset rate})}$$

$$= 1.6000 \times \frac{(1.09)}{(1.10)} = 1.5854, \quad \text{i.e. USD stronger on forward market}$$

The currency of the country in which interest rates are lower (presumably due to lower expected inflation) would be traded at a premium.

6 It is assumed it is desired to hold US$ at the year-end. By lending US$ at 7.625 per cent, the end-year balance will be £1m × 1.07625 = $1,076,250.

If wishing to lend in Swiss francs, the treasurer would convert from dollars at spot of 1.3125 to obtain CHF of $1m × 1.3125 = CHF1,312,500. Over one year, invested at 4.5625 per cent, this would accumulate to CHF1,372,383.

To cover the risk of adverse exchange rate movements, he will then sell CHF forward at the ruling rate of 1.275 to guarantee US$ delivery in one year's time of CHF1,372,383/1.275 = $1,076,379.

The minimal difference of $129 can be attributed to the operation of IRP.

Transactions costs would wipe out any gain from arbitrage.

11 With £1 = S$2.80:

Value of deal at today's spot = S$28m/2.80 = £10.00m

Hedged using a forward contract:

Value = S$28m/2.79 = £10.04m

Money market hedge:

Ashton borrows S$28m at 2%/4 = 0.5%
Borrowing = S$28m/1.005 = S$27.86m
Converts at spot (S$2.8 = £1) to yield S$27.86m/2.80 = £9.95m
Invested at 3%/4 (i.e. 0.0075%) this generates £9.95(1.0075) = £10.03m

The forward hedge is superior.

(a) If future spot is S$2.78 = £1

Value of deal at spot = S$28m/2.78 = £10.07m

Not hedging would have been preferable (with hindsight!)
The OTC option is out of the money and the premium is lost:

Net value = [£10.07m − premium of £0.2m] = £9.87m

(b) If future spot is £1 = S$2.82:

Value of deal at spot = S$28m/2.82 = £9.93m

Hedging would have been preferable (using the forward contract)
The OTC option is in the money.
Net of the premium, Ashton receives:

[S$28m/2.785] − £0.2m = £10.05m − £0.2m = £9.85m

But the forward contract would have been superior to this.

CHAPTER 14

1 In this question, we need to show that the receipts in sterling after adjusting for inflation at both locations remains unchanged.
Current exchange = US$1.50 against £1.
Sterling equivalent of US revenue = $150m/1.50 = 100m

Exchange rate	$ revenue	£ revenue	£ revenue (real terms)
(i) $1.05/1.05 \times 1.50 = \$1.50{:}£1$	$157.5m	£105m	£105m/1.05 = £100m
(ii) $1.02/1.05 \times 1.50 = \$1.457{:}£1$	$153m	£105m	£105m/1.05 = £100m
(iii) $1.05/1.02 \times 1.50 = \$1.544{:}£1$	$157.5m	£102m	£102m/1.02 = £100m

2 (a) (i) With exchange controls:

Year	PAT (SA$000)	OJ share (SA$000)	50% div (SA$000)	Sterling (£000)	PV at 16% (£000)
0	—	—	—	(450)	(450)
1	4,250	2,125	1,062	106	91
2	6,500	3,250	1,625	108	80
3	8,350	4,175	2,088	100	64
			4,775	277	146
			(balance)		NPV = (69)

In this scenario, OJ should reject the project.

(ii) No exchange control:

Year	PAT (SA$000)	OJ share (SA$000)	Sterling (£000)	PV at 16% (£000)
0	—	—	(450)	(450)
1	4,250	2,125	212	183
2	6,500	3,250	217	161
3	8,350	4,175	199	127
				NPV = +21

In this scenario, the positive NPV indicates acceptance, but the project is marginal e.g. the Profitability Index (NPV/Outlay = 21/450) is only 0.047. Given the risk of exchange controls being imposed, this suggests that OJ should treat the project with great caution.

3 PG plc

Year	0	1	2	3	4
Method 1					
C$ Initial investment	(150,000)				50,000
Other cash flows		60,000	60,000	60,000	45,000
Net cash flows	(150,000)	60,000	60,000	60,000	95,000
C$ per £1	1.700	1.785	1.874	1.968	2.066
Sterling	(88,235)	33,613	32,017	30,488	45,983
DF at 14%	1.000	0.877	0.769	0.675	0.592
PV	(88,235)	29,479	24,621	20,579	27,222
NPV = £13,666					
Method 2					
C$ net cash flows	(150,000)	60,000	60,000	60,000	95,000
DF at 19.7%	1.000	0.835	0.698	0.583	0.487
C$	(150,000)	50,100	41,888	34,980	46,265
£ PV at 1.7	(88,235)	29,479	24,621	20,579	27,222
NPV = £13,666					

For the two approaches to generate the same answer, the discount rate applied to the C$ cash flows must be the combination of the sterling discount rate (14 per cent) and the expected strengthening of sterling, according to PPP. This yields:

$$(1.14 \times 1.05) - 1 = (1.197 - 1) = 0.197, \text{ i.e. } 19.7\%$$

A forecast 5 per cent appreciation of sterling against the C$ will be associated with UK inflation rates being 5 per cent less than the rate experienced in Canada. In practice, one might inflate the cash flows in C$ to reflect inflation internal to the Canadian economy.

6 Palmerston plc

Forecast Cash Flow Statement (£m)

Euros per £1	1.65	1.60	1.55
Sales			
UK	200	210	220
Germany	**182**	**188**	**194**
Total	382	398	414
Cost of Goods Sold:			
UK	(120)	(120)	(120)
Germany	(121)	(125)	(129)
Total	(241)	(245)	(249)
Gross Profit	141	153	165
Operating Expenses:			
UK – fixed	(50)	(50)	(50)
UK – variable (20% of total sales)	(76)	(80)	(83)
Total	(126)	(130)	(133)
Net Cash Flow	15	23	32
Firm value at 15%:	(15 × 5.019*)	(23 × 5.019)	(32 × 5.019)
*Annuity factor	= £75.3m	= £115.4m	= £160.61m

The analysis suggests that Palmerston benefits from a strong euro and vice versa. It could further reduce its exposure by shifting its cost base to Germany, or elsewhere in the euro area, preferably to a low-cost location, say, Greece or Portugal.

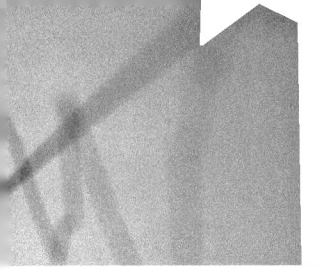

ABC system: a system of stock management that prioritises items accounting for greatest stock value.

Acceptance credit: a facility to issue bank-guaranteed bills (bank bills) by a firm wanting to raise short-term finance. They can be sold on the money market but are unrelated to specific trading transactions. The bank accepts the liability to exchange cash for bills when presented at the due date.

Accepting houses: accepting houses are specialist institutions that discount or 'accept' Bills of Exchange, especially short-term government securities (see Chapter 15).

Accounting rate of return: return on investment over the whole life of a project.

Acquirees: taken-over firms. Also, 'targets' or 'victims'.

Acquirers: firms that make takeovers. Also, 'predators'.

Adjusted NAV: the NAV as per the accounts, adjusted for any known or suspected deviations between book values and market, or realisable values.

Adjusted present value (APV): the inherent value of a project adjusted for any financial benefits and costs stemming from the particular method(s) of financing.

Administration: an attempt to reorganise an insolvent firm under an administrator, rather than liquidate it.

Agency costs: costs that owners (principals) have to incur in order to ensure that their agents (managers) make financial decisions consistent with their best interests.

Aggressive stocks: generate returns that vary by a larger proportion than overall market returns. Their Betas exceed 1.0.

Allocative efficiency: the most efficient way that a society can allocate its overall stock of resources

Alternative Investment Market (AIM): where smaller, younger companies can acquire a stock market listing.

American options: can be exercised at any time up to the maturity date.

Amortisation: repayment of debt by a series of instalments. Also used as a term for depreciation of intangible assets.

Analysis of variance: a statistical technique for isolating the separate determinants of the fluctuations recorded in a variable over time.

Annual percentage rate: the true annual interest rate charged by the lender which takes account of the timing of interest and principal payments

Annual writing-down allowances (WDAs): allowances for depreciation on capital expenditure allowed for tax purposes.

Annuity: a constant annual cash flow for a specific period of time.

Arbitrage: the profitable exploitation of divergences between the prices of goods (or between interest rates), that violate the Law of One Price. Also applied in MM's capital structure analysis to refer to the process of equalising the values of geared and ungeared firms. Hence, **arbitageur**.

Arbitrage Pricing Theory (APT): an extension of the CAPM to include more than one factor (hence, an example of a **multi-factor model**) used to explain the returns on securities. Each factor has its own Beta coefficient.

Arbitrageurs: arbitrageurs attempt to exploit differences in the values of financial variables in different markets, e.g. borrowing in a low-cost location and investing where interest rates are relatively high (interest arbitrage).

Articles of Association: a document drawn up at the formation of an enterprise, detailing the rights and obligations of shareholders and directors.

Asset or activity Beta: the inherent systematic riskiness of a firm's operations, before allowing for gearing. Also known as **firm Beta, company Beta**, or **ungeared Beta**.

Asset-backed securities (ABS): bonds issued on the security of a stream of highly reliable income flows, e.g. mortgage payments to a bank, out of which interest payments are made.

Asset stripping: selling off the assets of a taken-over firm, often in order to recoup the initial outlay.

Asymmetric information: one party to a contract is in possession of more information than the other.

Back-to-back loans: a simple form of a swap where firms lend directly to each other to satisfy their mutual currency requirements.

Balance sheet/statement of financial position: a financial statement that lists the assets held by a business at a point in time and explains how they have been financed (i.e. by owners' capital and by third-party liabilities).

Balloon loan: where increasing amounts of capital are repaid towards the end of the loan period.

Bancassurance: a term coined to denote the combination of banking and insurance business within the same organisation.

Bank loan: usually extended for a fixed term with a pre-agreed schedule of interest and capital repayments. Interest is usually payable on the initial amount borrowed, regardless of the falling balance as repayments are made.

Barter: the simplest form of counter-trade, involving direct exchange of goods with no money being exchanged.

Beta geared: the Beta attaching to the ordinary shares of a geared firm. These bear a risk higher than the firm's basic activity.

Beta ungeared: the geared Beta stripped of the effect of gearing. Corresponds to the activity Beta in an equivalent ungeared firm.

Betas or Beta coefficients: relate the responsiveness of the returns on individual securities to variations in the return on the overall market portfolio.

Bilateral netting: operated by pairs of firms in the same group netting off their respective positions regarding payables and receivables.

Bill of Exchange: a promise to pay at a specific time, issued to suppliers by purchasers in exchange for goods. Bills may be held to maturity or sold at a discount on the money market if cash is required sooner.

Bill of Lading: a document that transfers title to exported goods to the bank that finances the deal when the goods are shipped.

Bird-in-the-hand fallacy: the mistaken belief that dividends paid early in the future are worth more than dividends expected in later time periods, simply because they are nearer in time and viewed as less risky.

Bonds: any form of borrowing that firms can undertake in the form of a medium- or long-term security, that commits them to specific repayment dates, at fixed or variable interest.

Bonus or scrip issues: issues of free shares to existing shareholders *in lieu* of, or in addition to, cash dividends. Reflected in lower reserves (hence the alternative label, **capitalisation issue**).

Book-to-market ratio: ratio of the book value of equity to the market value of the shares.

Boston Consulting Group approach: an approach for assessing capital proposals based on the market growth and market share of the products relating to the proposal.

Break-up value (BUV): the value that can be obtained by selling off the firm's assets piecemeal to the highest bidders.

Building societies: financial institutions whose main function is to accept deposits from customers and lend for house purchases.

Bullet loan: where no capital is repaid until the very end of the loan period.

Business angels: wealthy private investors who take equity stakes in small, high-risk firms.

Buy-back: a method of obtaining payment for building a manufacturing unit overseas by taking the future physical product of the plant in return.

Call option: the right to buy an asset at a specified price on or before expiry date.

Call option: a financial derivative that gives the buyer the right but not the obligation to buy a particular commodity or currency at a specific future date.

Capital: strictly, the funds invested in a firm by shareholders when they purchase ordinary shares, but often used to indicate all forms of equity, and often to refer to any form of finance, whether equity or debt.

Capital allowances: tax allowances for capital expenditure.

Capital asset: any investment that offers a prospective return, with or without risk. However, in finance, the term is usually applied to securities and ordinary shares in particular.

Capital Asset Pricing Model (CAPM): a theory used to explain how efficient capital markets value securities, i.e. capital assets, by discounting future expected returns at risk-adjusted discount rates.

Capital Gains Tax (CGT): paid on realising an increase in share value. Capital gains are currently taxed as income in the United Kingdom depending on the investor's marginal tax rate.

Capital gearing: the mixture of debt and equity in a firm's capital structure, which influences variations in shareholders' profits in response to sales and EBIT variations.

Capitalisation: the procedure of converting (by discounting) a series of future cash flows into a single capital sum.

Capitalisation rate: a discount rate used to convert a series of future cash flows into a single capital sum.

Capital lease/full payout lease: a lease that transfers most of the benefits and risks of ownership to the lessee.

Capital market line: a relationship tracing out the efficient combinations of risk and return available to investors prepared to combine the market portfolio with the risk-free asset.

Capital market line (CML): traces out the efficient combinations of risk and return available to investors when combining a risk-free asset with the market portfolio.

Capital rationing: the process of allocating capital to projects where there is insufficient capital to fund all value-creating proposals.

Capital structure: A firm's mixture of debt and equity resulting from decisions on financing its operations.

Captive firms: subsidiaries of banks and other institutions established to invest in risky but attractive businesses.

Carrying costs: stock costs that increase with the size of stock investment.

Cash flow statement: a financial statement that explains the reasons for cash inflows and outflows of a business and highlights the resulting change in cash position.

Cash operating cycle: length of time between cash payment to suppliers and cash received from customers.

Characteristics line (CL): relates the periodic returns on a security to the returns on the market portfolio. Its slope is the Beta of the security. The regression model used to estimate Betas is called the **market model**.

Chartist: analyst who relies on charts of past share movements to predict future movements (technical analysis).

Classical tax system: a system where dividends are effectively taxed twice – the firm pays profits tax and then investors pay income tax on any dividend payment.

Clientèle effect: the notion that a firm attracts investors by establishing a set dividend policy that suits a particular group of investors.

Commercial paper: a short-term promissory note or IOU, issued by a highly creditworthy corporate borrower to financial institutions and other cash-rich corporates.

Co-movement or co-variability: the tendency for two variables, e.g. the returns from two investments, to move in parallel. It can be measured using either:

(i) the **correlation coefficient:** a relative measure of co-movement that locates assets on a scale between −1 and +1. Where returns move exactly in unison, perfect positive correlation exists, and where exactly opposite movements occur, perfect negative correlation exists. Most investments fall in between, mainly, with positive correlation.

(ii) the **covariance:** an absolute measure of co-movement with no upper or lower limits.

Compound interest: interest paid on the sum which accumulates, i.e. the principal plus interest.

Concentration banking: where customers in a geographical area pay bills to a local branch office rather than to the head office.

Concentric acquisition: undertaken to exploit synergies in marketing of two firms' products, without production economies.

Conglomerate takeover: the acquisition of a target firm in a field apparently unrelated to the acquirer's existing activities.

Contingent claim security: claim on a security whose value depends on the value of another asset.

Contra-cyclical: a term applied to an investment whose returns fluctuate in opposite ways to general trends in business activity, i.e. contrary to the cycle.

Contribution: revenues (turnover) less variable costs, i.e. contribution to meeting fixed costs.

Convertible loan stock: a debenture that can be converted into ordinary shares, often on attractive terms, usually at the option of the holder. Some preference shares are convertible.

Corporate bonds: medium- to long-term borrowing by a company.

Cost centre treasury (CCT): a treasury that aims to minimise the cost of its dealings.

Cost of debt: the yield a firm would have to offer if undertaking further borrowing at current market rates.

Cost of equity: the minimum rate of return a firm must offer its owners to compensate for waiting for their returns, and also for bearing risk.

Costs of financial distress: the costs incurred as a firm approaches, and ultimately reaches, the point of insolvency.

Counterparty risk: the risk that the bank which is party to a hedging transaction such as a forward contract may not deliver the agreed amount of currency at the agreed time.

Counter-trade: a form of trade involving reciprocal obligations with a trading partner, or counterparty, e.g. a commitment to buy from a firm or country that the firm sells to.

Country risk: the risk of adverse effects on the net cash flows of a MNC due to political and economic factors peculiar to the country of location of FDI.

Coupon rate of interest: the fixed rate of interest, as printed on the debt security, which a firm must pay to lenders.

Covariance: a statistical measure of the extent to which the fluctuations exhibited by two (or more) variables are related.

Covered interest arbitrage: using the forward market to lock in the future domestic currency value of a transaction undertaken to exploit an interest arbitrage opportunity.

Credit limits: the maximum amount of credit that a firm is willing to extend to a customer.

Credit risk: the risk that a foreign customer might not pay up as agreed on time or at all.

Crest: an electronic mechanism for settling and registering shares sold on the London Stock Exchange.

Critical mass: the minimum size of firm thought necessary to compete effectively, e.g. to finance R&D.

Cross-currency interest swap: a swap agreement where the parties agree to swap a fixed interest rate commitment for a floating interest rate.

Currency futures contract: a commitment to deliver a specific amount of foreign exchange at a specified future date at an agreed price incorporated in the contract. Contracts can be traded on an exchange in standard sizes.

Currency information system: an information system set up to identify values that are exposed to currency risk, e.g. cash in- and outflows and asset and liability values.

Currency option: the right, but not the obligation, to buy or sell a fixed amount of currency at a pre-determined rate at a specified future date.

Currency swaps: where two or more parties swap the capital value and associated interest streams of their borrowing in different currencies.

Currency switching: where an exporter pays for imported supplies in the currency of the export deal.

Current assets: assets that will leave the balance sheet in the next accounting period.

Current cost accounting (CCA): attempts to capture the effect of inflation on asset values (and liabilities) by recording them at their current replacement cost, i.e. the cost of obtaining an identical replacement.

Current ratio: ratio of current assets to current liabilities.

Days cash-on-hand ratio: cash and marketable securities divided by daily cash operating expenses.

Debenture: in law, any form of borrowing that commits a firm to pay interest and repay capital. In practice, usually applied to long-term loans that are secured on a firm's assets.

Debt capacity: the maximum amount of debt finance, and hence interest payments that a firm or project can support without incurring financial distress.

Debt finance/loan capital: capital raised with an obligation to pay interest and repay principal.

Default: the failure by a borrower to adhere to a pre-agreed schedule of interest and/or capital payments on a loan.

Defensive stock: generates returns that vary by a smaller proportion than overall market returns. Its Beta is less than one.

Derivative: a financial instrument whose value derives from an underlying asset.

Derivatives: securities that are traded separately from the assets from which they are derived.

Direct debit: an automatic payment from a customer's bank account pre-arranged with the bank by both trading partners.

Direct investment: investment in tangible and intangible assets for business operating purposes.

Directors' dealings: share sales and purchases by senior officers of the firm.

Disclosure: release of financial and operating information about a firm into the public domain.

Discount: the amount below the face value of a financial instrument at which it sells.

Discounted cash flow: future cash flows adjusted for the time-value of money.

Discounted cash flow (DCF) analysis: the process of analysing financial instruments and decisions by discounting cash flows to present values.

Discounted payback: period of time the present value of a project's annual net cash flows takes to match the initial cost outlay.

Discounting: the process of reducing cash flows to present values.

Discount houses: discount houses bid for issues of short-term government securities at a discount and either hold them to maturity or sell them on in the money market.

Discount rate: any percentage required return used to convert future expected cash flows into their equivalent present values.

Disintermediation: business-to-business lending that eliminates the banking intermediary.

Diversifiable risk: can be removed by efficient portfolio diversification.

Diversification: extension of a firm's activities into new and unrelated fields. Although this may generate cost savings, e.g. via shared distribution systems, as a by-product, the fundamental motive for diversification is to reduce exposure to fluctuations in economic activity.

Dividend irrelevance: the theory that, when firms have access to external finance, it is irrelevant to firm value whether they pay a dividend or not.

Dividend Valuation Model: a way of assessing the value of shares by capitalising the future dividends. With growing dividend payments, it becomes the **Dividend Growth Model**.

Dividend yield: gross dividend per ordinary share (including both interim and final payments) divided by current share price.

Double tax agreements (DTAs): reciprocal arrangements between countries whereby tax paid in one location is credited in the second, thus avoiding doubling up the firm's tax bill. Hence, Double Tax Relief (DTR).

Earnings before interest and taxes (EBIT): earnings (i.e. profits) before interest and taxation.

Earnings before interest, tax, depreciation & amortisation (EBITDA): a rough measure of operating cash flow, effectively, operating profit with depreciation added back. It differs from the 'Net Cash Inflow from Operating Activities' shown in cash flow statements due to working capital movements.

Earnings dilution: the dampening effect on EPS of issuing further shares at a discount as in a rights issue.

Earnings per share (EPS): profit available for distribution to shareholders divided by the number of shares issued.

Earnings yield: EPS divided by current share price. Sometimes, it refers to expected or 'prospective' EPS, becoming the '**prospective earnings yield**'. It is a simple way of expressing the investor's Return on Investment on the share.

Economic order quantity (EOQ): the most economic quantity to be ordered that minimises holding and ordering costs.

Economic value added (EVA): post-tax accounting profit generated by a firm reduced by a charge for using the equity (usually, cost of equity times book value of equity).

Efficient frontier: traces out all the available portfolio combinations that either minimise risk for a stated expected return or maximise expected return for a specified measure of risk.

Efficient markets: where current share prices fully reflect the information available.

Electronic funds transfer: instantaneous transfer of money from a debtor's bank account to a creditor.

Enhanced scrip dividends: scrip alternatives offered to investors that are worth more than the alternative cash payment.

Enterprise Investment Scheme (EIS): a scheme introduced in the United Kingdom in 1994 offering tax relief to investors who are buying shares in smaller, more risky companies.

Enterprise value: the value of the whole firm.

Entrepreneurial companies: are driven by the growth ambitions and desire of the owners to create significant wealth.

Equity or equity value: the value of the owners' stake in a firm, however calculated.

Equity Beta: indicates the systematic riskiness attaching to the returns on ordinary shares. It equates to the asset Beta for an ungeared firm, or is adjusted upwards to reflect the extra riskiness of shares in a geared firm, to become '**Beta geared**'.

Equivalent annual annuity (EAA): the constant annual cash flow offering the same present value as the project's net present value.

Equivalent loan: the loan that would involve the same schedule of interest and loan repayments as the profile of rentals required by an equipment lessor.

Equivalent risk class: a concept used by MM to include all firms subject to the same business risks (i.e. all having the same Activity Betas).

Eurobonds or international bonds: securities issued by borrowers in a market outside that of their domestic currency.

European options: can only be exercised at the specified maturity date.

Exchange agio: the percentage difference between the spot and forward rates of exchange between two currencies.

Ex-dividend (ex-div. or xd): when subsequent purchasers of a share no longer qualify for the forthcoming dividend payment. Until this point, the shares are quoted **cum-dividend**.

Exercise (strike) price: the price at which the option to buy or sell can be transacted.

Expectations or unbiased forward predictor theory: the postulate that the expected change in the spot rate of exchange is equal to the difference between the current spot rate and the current forward rate for the relevant period.

Expected net present value (ENPV): the average of the range of possible NPVs weighted by their probability of occurrence.

Exporting: sale of goods and services to a foreign customer.

Externalisation: the transfer of key functions and expertise to an overseas strategic partner.

Factoring: a means of obtaining faster cash inflow, and thus increased funds. A firm appoints the factor to collect outstanding accounts payable and to administer debtors' accounts. It also lends money to the client based on the value of the firm's sales.

Factors: organisations that offer to purchase a firm's debtors for cash.

Fair game: a competitive process in which all participants have equal access to information and therefore similar chances of success.

Finance lease: a method of acquiring an asset that involves a series of rental payments extending over the whole expected lifetime of the asset.

Financial distress: in narrow terms, the difficulty that a firm encounters in meeting obligations to creditors. More broadly, it refers to the adverse consequences, e.g. restrictions on behaviour that result, usually from excessive borrowing by a firm.

Financial gearing: includes both capital gearing and income gearing.

Financial intermediaries: institutions that channel funds from savers and depositors with cash surpluses to people and organisations with cash shortages.

Financial leverage: the ratio of profit before interest and tax (PBIT) to profit before tax (PBT).

Financial market: any market in which financial assets and liabilities are traded

Financial Conduct Authority (FCA): a regulatory body for maintaining confidence in the financial markets.

Fixed charge: applies when a lender can force the sale of pre-specified company assets in order to recover debts in the event of default on interest and/or capital payments.

Fixed/fixed swap: a swap agreement where the parties agree to swap fixed interest rate commitments.

Flat yield or running yield: on a bond is the ratio of the fixed interest payment to the current market price of the bond.

Floating charge: applies when a lender can force the sale of any (i.e. unspecified) of a company's assets in order to recover debts in the event of default on interest and/or capital payments. (Ranks behind a fixed charge.)

Floating rate note (FRN): a bond issue where interest is paid at a variable rate (often a Eurobond).

Follow-on opportunities: options that arise following a course of action.

Foreign bonds: loan stock issued on the domestic market by non-resident firms or organisations. In London, called 'bulldogs', in New York 'Yankees'.

Foreign currency swap: a way of extending the delivery date incorporated in a forward contract. A spot/forward swap involves completing the original contract by a spot transaction and entering a new forward contract for the additional of time.

Foreign direct investment (FDI): investment in fixed assets located abroad for operating distribution and/or production facilities.

Foreign exchange exposure: the risk of loss stemming from exposure to adverse foreign exchange rate movements.

Forfaiting: the practice whereby a bank purchases an exporter's sales invoices or promissory notes, that usually carry the guarantee of the importer's bank.

Forward: the forward market is where contracts are made for future settlement at a price specified now.

Forward contract: an agreement to sell or buy at a fixed price at some time in the future.

Forward–forward swap: where the original forward contract is supplemented by new contracts that have the effect of extending the maturity date of the original one.

Forward option: a forward currency contract that incorporates a flexible settlement date between two fixed dates.

Forward rate of exchange: the rate fixed for transactions that involve delivery and settlement at some specified future date.

Franchising: licensing out of a fully packaged business system, including technology and supply of materials, to an entrepreneur operating a separate legally constituted business.

Free cash flow (FCF): a firm's cash flow free of obligatory payments. Strictly, it is cash flow after interest, tax and replacement investment, although it is measured in many other ways in practice, e.g. after all investment.

Fundamental analysis: analysis of the fundamental determinants of company financial health and future performance prospects, such as endowment of resources, quality of management, product innovation record, etc.

Funding: cash and liquidity management, short-term financing and cash forecasting.

Future: a tradable contract to buy or sell a specified amount of an asset at a specified price at a specified future date.

Futures contract: a commitment to buy or sell an asset at an agreed date and price, and traded on an exchange.

FX: abbreviation for foreign exchange.

Gearing: proportion of the total capital that is borrowed.

Generally Accepted Accounting Principles (GAAP): the set of legal regulations and accounting standards that dictate 'best practice' in constructing company accounts.

General valuation model: a family of valuation models that rely on discounting future cash flows to establish the value of the equity or the whole enterprise.

Global companies: serve a range of overseas markets both by exporting and direct investment.

Going concern value (GCV): the value of the assets as stated in the accounts that assume that the firm will continue as a viable entity as it stands, i.e. as an ongoing activity.

Golden handcuffs: an exceptionally good remuneration package paid to executives to prevent them from leaving.

Gross redemption yield: the redemption yield before allowing for income tax payable by investors.

Hedge: a hedge is an arrangement effected by a person or firm attempting to eliminate or reduce exposure to risk – hence to hedge and hedger.

Hedgers: hedgers try to minimise or totally eliminate exposure to risk.

Hedging: attempting to minimise the risk of loss stemming from exposure to adverse foreign exchange rate movements.

Hire purchase (HP): a means of obtaining the use of an asset before payment is completed. An HP contract involves an initial, or 'down-payment', followed by a series of hire charges at the end of which ownership passes to the user.

Home-made dividend: cash released when an investor realises part of his or her investment in a firm in order to supplement his/her income.

Home-made gearing: where an investor borrows to arbitrage between two identical but differently valued assets.

Horizontal integration: the acquisition of a competitor in pursuit of market power and/or scale economies.

Hybrid: a security that combines features of both equity and debt.

Imputation tax systems: taxation systems that offer shareholders tax credits (fully or partially) in respect of company tax already paid when assessing their income tax liability on dividends paid out.

Income gearing: the proportion of profit before interest and tax (PBIT) absorbed by interest charges.

Incremental hypothesis: suggests that firms tend gradually to build their degree of involvement in foreign markets, beginning with exporting and culminating in FDI.

Independent companies: investment companies set up as stand-alone entities by venture capitalists to invest money in risky but potentially attractive businesses.

Information asymmetry: the imbalance between managers and owners of information possessed about a firm's financial state and its prospects.

Information content: the extra, unstated intelligence that investors deduce from the formal announcement by a firm of any financial news, i.e. what people read 'between the lines', or 'financial body language'.

Initial Public Offering (IPO): the first issue of shares by an existing or a newly formed firm to the general public.

Insider trading: dealing in shares using information not publicly available.

Insurance companies: financial institutions that guarantee to protect clients against specified risks, including death, and general risks in return for the payment of an annual premium.

Insured schemes: a pension fund that uses an insurance company to invest contributions and to insure against actuarial risks (e.g. members living longer than expected).

Intangible: intangible assets cannot be seen or touched, e.g. the image and good reputation of a firm.

Interest agio: the percentage difference between interest rates prevailing in the money markets for lending/ borrowing in two currencies.

Interest cover: the number of times the profit before interest exceeds loan interest.

Interest Rate Parity (IRP): asserts that the difference between the spot and forward exchanges is equal to the differential between interest rates prevailing in the money markets for lending/borrowing in the respective currencies.

Interest yield: the annual interest on a bond or similar security divided by its market price.

Intermediaries offer: a placing made to stockbrokers other than the one advising the company making the issue.

Internalisation: the retention by the MNC of key management functions and technology.

Internal rate of return: the discount rate that equates the present value of future cash flows with initial investment cost.

International or Open Fisher Theory: the notion that, because real rates of interest are equalised throughout the world, given freedom of capital mobility, any observed differences in nominal rates between different locations must be due to different expectations of inflation between those locations.

Intrinsic worth: the inherent or fundamental value of a company and its shares.

Investment banks: investment banks are wholesale banks that arrange specialist financial services like mergers and acquisition funding, and finance of international trade fund management.

Invoice discounting: where a factor purchases selected invoices from a client firm, without providing debt collection or account administration services.

IRR or DCF yield: the rate of return that equates the present value of future cash flows with the initial investment outlay.

Irrevocable DLOC: a written authority for a bank to make specified payments to an exporter, whose terms cannot be varied.

Issue by tender: a share issue where prospective investors are invited to bid or 'tender' for shares at a price of their own choosing.

Joint venture: a strategic alliance involving the formal establishment of a new marketing and/or production operation involving two or more partners.

Junk bonds: low-quality, risky bonds with no credit rating.

Lagging: settling as late as possible a payable (receivable) denominated in a currency expected to weaken (strengthen).

Law of One Price: the proposition that any good or service will sell for the same price, adjusting for the relevant exchange rate, throughout the world.

Leading: advancing before the due date a payable denominated in a foreign currency that is expected to strengthen, or advancing a receivable in a currency expected to weaken.

lessee: a firm that leases an asset from a lessor.

lessor: a firm that acquires equipment and other assets for leasing out to firms wishing to use such items in their operations.

Letter of Credit: a credit drawn up by an importer in favour of an exporter. It is endorsed by a bank that guarantees payment provided the beneficiary delivers the Bill of Lading proving that goods have been shipped.

Licensing: involves the assignment of production and selling rights to producers located in foreign locations in return for royalty payments.

Liquidity management: planning the acquisition and utilisation of cash, i.e. cash flow management.

Listed companies: firms whose shares are quoted on the Main List of the Stock Exchange.

Loan Guarantee Scheme: a facility whereby banks are able to lend to firms that would not otherwise qualify for bank finance due to lack of track record, the loan being guaranteed by the Department of Trade and Industry.

Main list: daily list of securities and prices traded on the London Stock Exchange.

Management buy-in (MBI): acquisition of an equity stake in an existing firm by new management that injects expertise as well as capital into the enterprise.

Management buy-out (MBO): acquisition of an existing firm by its existing management usually involving substantial amounts of straight debt and mezzanine finance.

Marginal cost of capital (MCC): the extra returns required to satisfy all investors as a proportion of new capital raised.

Marginal efficiency of investment (MEI): a schedule listing available investments, in declining order of attractiveness.

Market capitalisation: the market value of a firm's equity, i.e. number of ordinary shares issued times market price.

Market model: a device relating the expected (in practice, *actual*) return from individual securities to the expected/*actual* return from the overall stock market.

Market portfolio: includes all securities traded on the stock market weighted by their respective capitalisations. Usually, a more limited portfolio such as the FT All Share Index is used as a proxy.

Matching: offsetting a currency inflow in one currency, e.g. a stream of revenues, by a corresponding stream of costs, thus leaving only the profit element unmatched. Firms may also match operating cash flows against financial flows, e.g. a stream of interest and capital payments resulting from overseas borrowing in the same currency.

McKinsey–General Electric portfolio matrix: an approach for assessing projects within the wider strategic context which focuses on the market attractiveness and business strength of the product and business unit relating to the capital proposal.

Mergers: pooling by firms of their separate interests into newly constituted business, each party participating on roughly equal terms.

Mezzanine finance: covers hybrids such as convertibles that embody both debt and equity features.

Modified internal rate of return (MIRR): the internal rate of return modified for the reinvestment assumption.

Modigliani and Miller's (MM) Capital Structure Theories: (i) MM-no tax, which 'proves' that no optimal capital structure exists, and that the WACC is invariant to debt/equity ratio.
(ii) MM-with tax which suggests that the tax shield should be exploited up to the point of almost 100 per cent debt financing.

Monetary Policy Committee: a body whose members are appointed by the Bank of England, responsible for setting UK interest rates at monthly meetings.

Money market: the market for short-term money, broadly speaking for repayment within about a year.

Money market cover: involves an exporter borrowing on the money market (i.e. creating a liability) in the same currency in which it expects to receive a payment.

Monte Carlo simulation: method for calculating the probability distribution of possible outcomes.

Moral hazard: the temptation facing managers to engage in risky activities when they are protected from the consequences of failure, e.g. by guaranteed severance payments.

Mortgage debenture: a loan instrument under which the ownership of selected assets is mortgaged to the lender – in a default, the title passes to the lender.

Multilateral netting: a central treasury department operation to minimise net flows of currency throughout an organisation.

Multinational company (MNC): one that conducts a significant proportion of its operations abroad.

Natural hedge: where the adverse impact of FX rate variations on cash inflows are offset by the effect on cash outflows, or vice versa.

Natural matching: a natural match is achieved where the firm has a two-way cash flow in the same currency due to the structure of its operations, e.g. selling in a currency in which it sources supplies.

Net advantage of a lease (NAL): the NPV of the acquisition of an asset adjusted for financing benefits.

Net asset value (NAV): the value of owners' stake in a firm, found by deducting total liabilities (i.e. debts) from total assets.

Net asset value approach: calculation of the equity value in a firm by netting the liabilities against the assets.

Net book value: the original cost of buying an asset less accumulated depreciation charges to date.

Net current assets: current assets less current liabilities.

Net debt: a firm's net borrowing including both long-term and also short-term debt, offset by cash holdings. Expressed either in absolute terms, or in relation to owner's equity.

Net present value: the present value of the future net benefits less the initial cost.

Netting: offsetting a firm's internal currency inflows and outflows in the same currency to minimise the net flow in either direction.

Net working capital: current assets less current liabilities.

Neutral stocks: generate returns that vary by the same proportion as overall market returns. Their Betas equal 1.0. Also called 'market-tracking' investments.

New Issue Market: the market for selling and buying newly issued securities. It has no physical existence.

Niche companies: serve a limited segment of their markets, usually offering high-quality, differentiated products at a high margin.

Nil-paid price of rights: the market value of the right to subscribe for new shares offered in a rights issue.

Non-current assets: assets that remain in the balance sheet for more than one accounting period.

Non-recourse (as distinct from recourse): factoring operates where factors are unable to reclaim bad debts from a client's accounts.

Notes: loan securities in general, but often referred to securities that carry a floating rate of interest.

Offer for sale by prospectus: an issue of ordinary shares through an issuing house that promotes the shares in a detailed prospectus aimed at the public in general.

Offset: the requirement for an MNC to undertake a proportion of local sourcing as condition of the award of an export deal (very common in the armaments industry).

Open account: where trading partners agree settlement terms with no formal contract.

Operating gearing: the proportion of fixed costs in the firm's operating cost structure.

Operating gearing factor: a ratio that compares the operating gearing of a particular activity, e.g. a product division within a larger firm, to that of a larger entity such as the whole firm.

Operating/strategic exposure: the risk that adverse foreign exchange rate movements will affect the present value of the firm's future cash flows (effectively, long-term transactions exposure).

Operating/technical efficiency: the most cost-effective way of producing an item, or organising a process.

Operating lease: a job-specific lease contract, usually arranged for a short period, during which the lessor retains most of the benefits and risks of ownership.

Operating leverage: the ratio of contribution to profit before interest and tax.

Operating profit: revenues less total operating costs, both variable and fixed– as distinct from financial costs such as interest payments.

Opportunity cost: the value forgone by opting for a particular course of action.

Opportunity set: the set of investment opportunities (i.e. risk–return combinations) available to the investor to select from.

Optimal capital structure: the financing mix that minimises the overall cost of finance and maximises market value.

Optimal portfolio: the one chosen by an investor to achieve his/her most desired combination of risk and return. This choice depends on the investor's attitude to risk, or risk–return preference, i.e. how he/she rates different combinations of risk and return. If a risk-free asset is available, the optimal portfolio of risky assets is the market portfolio.

Option: the right but not the obligation to buy or sell something at some time in the future at a given price.

Option contract: a contract giving one party the right, but not the obligation, to buy or sell a financial instrument or commodity at an agreed price at or before a specified date.

Option to abandon: choice to allow an option to expire. With a capital investment, abandonment should take place where the value for which an asset can be sold exceeds the present value of its future benefits from continuing its operations.

Overdraft: short-term finance extended by banks subject to instant recall. A maximum deficit balance is pre-agreed and interest is paid on the actual daily balance outstanding.

Over-the-counter: an over-the-counter transaction, e.g. the purchase of an option, where the terms are tailor-made to suit the requirements of the purchaser.

Overtrading: operating a business with an inappropriate capital base, usually trying to grow too fast with insufficient long-term capital.

Owner's equity: in accounting terms, simply the NAV, but can also be expressed in market value terms, i.e. share price times number of ordinary shares issued, or '**capitalisation**'.

Parallel matching: applies where a firm offsets inflows in one currency with outflows denominated in a closely correlated currency.

Participating: preference shares that may qualify for payment of an additional dividend payment in a good year.

Part-payout lease: a lease contract which recovers a return lower than the capital outlay made by the lessor.

Patent: a legal device giving the holder the exclusive right to exploit the technology described therein.

Payback period: period of time a project's annual net cash flows take to match the initial cost outlay.

Pension funds: financial institutions that manage the pension schemes of large firms and other organisations.

Perpetual warrant: a warrant with no time limit for exercising it.

Perpetuity: an infinite series of cash flows.

Placing: an issue of ordinary shares directly to selected institutional investors, who may re-sell them on the stock market when dealings officially commence.

Plant hire: hiring of construction equipment.

Poison pill: a provision designed to damage the interests of a takeover bidder, e.g. handsome severance terms for departing managers, activated on completion of the bid.

Political risk: the risk of politically motivated interference by a foreign government in the affairs of a MNC, that adversely affects its net cash flows.

Portfolio: a combination of investments – securities or physical assets – into a single 'bundled' investment. A well-diversified portfolio has the potential capacity to lower the investor's exposure to the risk of fluctuations in the overall economy.

Portfolio effect: the tendency for the risk on a well-diversified holding of investments to fall below the risk of most, and sometimes all, of its individual components.

Portfolio investment: investment in financial securities such as bonds and equities, with no stake in management.

Post-audit: a re-examination of costs, benefits and forecasts of a project after implementation (usually after one year).

Post-completion audit: audit of a capital project at an agreed time following implementation.

Pre-emption rights: the right for existing shareholders to be offered newly issued shares before making them available to outside investors.

Preference shares: hybrid securities that rank ahead of ordinary shares for dividend payment, usually at a fixed rate, and also in distributing the proceeds of a liquidation. Normally, they carry no voting rights.

Premium: the amount above the face value of a financial instrument at which it sells.

Premium: the difference between the issue price of an ordinary share and its par (or nominal) value.

Present value: the current worth of future cash flows.

Price–earnings multiples: the price–earnings multiple, or ratio (PER), is the ratio of earnings (i.e. *profit after tax*) per share (EPS) to market share price.

Price:earnings ratio (PER): the current share price divided by the latest reported earnings (i.e. profits after tax) per share.

Price variation: adjustment of a firm's pricing policy to take into account expected foreign exchange rate movements.

Pricing/information efficiency: the extent to which available information is impounded into the current set of share prices.

Principal: the principal or face value or par value is the amount of the debt excluding interest.

Principal–agent: the agent, such as board of directors, is expected to act in the best interests of the principal (e.g. the shareholder).

Private placing: an issue of shares directly to a selected number of financial institutions.

Profitability index (PI): ratio of the present value of benefits to costs.

Profit after tax (PAT): profit available to pay dividends to shareholders after tax has been paid.

Profit and loss account/income statement: a financial statement that details for a specific time period the amount of revenue earned by a firm, the costs it has incurred, the resulting profit and how it has been distributed ('appropriated').

Profit centre treasury (PCT): a corporate treasury that aims to make a profit from its dealing – managers are judged on profit performance.

Project gearing factor (PGF): the proportionate increase in a project's operating cash flow in relation to a proportionate increase in the project's sales.

Project risk factor: the product of the Revenue Sensitivity Factor and the Operating Gearing Factor multiplied together.

Proprietorial companies: are run by founders and their heirs to provide a livelihood for their families. They usually have limited growth aims.

Prospectus: a document setting out the existing financial situation of a firm and its future prospects that is published to accompany a share issue.

Provision: a notional deduction from profits to allow for some highly likely future financial contingency. In accounting terms, an appropriation of profit after taxation.

Proxy Beta: used when the firm has no market listing and thus no Beta of its own. It is taken from a comparable listed firm, and adjusted as necessary for relative financial gearing levels. Hence, **proxy discount rate**.

Purchasing power parity (PPP): the theory that foreign exchange rates are in equilibrium when a currency can purchase the same amount of goods at the prevailing exchange rate anywhere in the world.

Pure play technique: adoption of the Beta value of another firm for use in evaluating investment in an unquoted entity such as an unquoted firm, or a division of a larger firm.

Put option: the right to sell an asset at a specified price on or before expiry date.

Quick/'acid test' ratio: current assets minus stocks, divided by current liabilities.

Random walk theory: share price movements are independent of each other so that tomorrow's share price cannot be predicted by looking at today's.

Real assets: assets in the business (tangible or intangible).

Real options: options to invest in real assets such as capital projects.

Rebate clause: an arrangement whereby the lessor pays a proportion of the resale value of an asset to the lessee.

Record Day: the cut-off date beyond which further entrants to the shareholder register do not qualify for the next dividend.

Redeemable: repayable (usually at nominal value).

Redemption yield: the interest yield adjusted for any capital gain or loss if the security is held to maturity.

Re-invoicing centre: a corporate subsidiary set up usually in an off-shore location to manage transaction exposure arising from trade between separate divisions of the parent firm.

Relevant risk: the component of total risk taken into account by the stock market when assessing the appropriate risk premium for determining capital asset values.

Replacement chain approach: the process of comparing like-for-like replacement decisions for mutually exclusive projects with different lives over a common time period.

Replacement cost: the cost of replacing the existing assets of a firm with assets of similar vintage capable of performing similar functions.

Reputation risk: companies now cite reputation risk as one of the greatest threats.

Reserves: the funds that shareholders invest in a firm in addition to their initial subscription of capital.

Residual income: operating profit less the charge for capital.

Residual theory of dividends: asserts that firms should only pay cash dividends when they have financed new investments. It assumes no access to external finance.

Restrictive covenants: limitations on managerial freedom of action, stipulated as conditions of making a loan.

Retail banks: retail banks accept deposits from the general public who can draw on these accounts by cheque (or ATM) and lend to other people and organisations seeking funds.

Retained earnings: reserves represented by retention of profits. Sometimes, labelled 'profit & loss account' on the balance sheet. Also called **revenue reserves**.

Revenue sensitivity: the extent to which revenue of an activity varies in response to general economic fluctuations.

Revenue sensitivity factor (RSF): the revenue sensitivity of a particular activity, e.g. a product division, relative to that of a larger entity, such as the whole firm.

Revenue sensitivity factor (RSF): the sensitivity to economic fluctuations of a project's sales in relation to that of the division to which it is attached.

Revocable DLOC: A Letter of Credit whose terms can be varied without consulting the exporter.

Revolving credit facility: enables a firm to borrow up to a pre-specified amount usually over 1–5 years. As repayments of outstanding balances are made, the loan facility is replenished.

Return on capital employed: operating profit expressed as a percentage of capital employed.

Rights issues: sales of further ordinary shares at less than market price to existing shareholders who are usually able to sell the rights on the market should they not wish to purchase additional shares.

Risk-free assets: securities with zero variation in overall returns.

Risk-minimising policy: a foreign exchange policy designed to eliminate, as far as possible, the firm's exposure to currency risk.

Risk premium: the additional return demanded by investors above the risk-free rate to compensate for exposure to systematic risk.

Risk-sharing: an arrangement where the two parties to an import/export deal agree to share the risk, and thus the impact of unexpected exchange rate movements.

Safety or buffer stocks: stocks held as insurance against stockouts (shortages).

Scale economies: cost efficiencies, e.g. bulk-buying, due to increasing a firm's size of operation.

Scrip dividends: offered to investors in lieu of the equivalent cash payment. Also called a **scrip alternative**.

SEAQ: a computer-based quotation system on the London Stock Exchange where market-makers report bid and offer prices and trading volumes.

Secondary lease: a second lease arranged to follow the termination of the initial lease period.

Securities/capital market: the market for long-term finance.

Securitisation: the capitalisation of a future stream of income into a single capital value that is sold on the capital market for immediate cash.

Security market line (SML): an upward-sloping relationship tracing out all combinations of expected return and systematic risk, available in an efficient market. All traded securities locate on this schedule. In effect, the capital market line adjusted for systematic risk.

Self-administered schemes: a pension fund that invests clients' contributions directly into the stock market and other investments.

Semi-strong form: a semi-strong efficient share market incorporates newly released information accurately and quickly into the structure of share prices.

Sensitivity analysis: analysis of the impact of changes in assumptions on investment returns.

Separation theorem: a model that shows how individual perceptions of the optimal portfolio of risky securities is independent of (i.e. separate from) individuals' different risk–return preferences.

Share repurchase (or buy-back): repurchase by a firm of its existing shares, either via the market or by a tender to all shareholders.

Shareholders' equity: the value of the owners' stake in the business – identically equal to net assets, or equity.

Shareholders' funds or equity capital: money invested by shareholders and profits retained in the company.

Shareholder value analysis (SVA): a way of assessing the inherent value of the equity in a company, taking into account the sources of value creation and the time-horizon over which the firm enjoys competitive advantages over its rivals.

Share premium account: a reserve set up to account for the issue of new shares at a price above their par value.

Share splits (USA: stock splits): a way of reducing the share price of 'heavyweight' shares (prices above £10). Achieved by reducing the par value of issued shares, e.g. two shares of par value 50p to replace one share at £1 is a one-for-one split, halving the share price.

Shortage costs: stock costs that reduce with size of stock investment.

Short selling: selling securities not yet owned (and generally borrowed) in the expectation of being able to buy them later at a lower price.

Sight draft: a document presented to a bank by an exporter seeking payment for an export deal.

Signalling: using financial announcements to deliver more information than is actually spelled out in detail.

Social efficiency: the extent to which a socio-economic system accords with prevailing social and ethical standards.

Special Purpose Vehicle (SPV): a financial vehicle set up to manage the issue of asset-backed securities and arrange for payment of interest and eventual redemption.

Specific risk: the variability in the return on a security due to exposure to risks relating to that security in isolation, e.g. risk of losing market share due to poor marketing decisions.

Speculators: speculators deliberately take positions to increase their exposure to risk, hoping for higher returns.

Spot: the spot, or cash market, is where transactions are settled 'immediately' (in practice, within two days).

Spot–forward swap: a less comprehensive forward swap that involves speculation on the future spot market.

Spot rate: the rate of exchange quoted for transactions involving immediate settlement. Hence, **spot market**.

Spread: the difference between the exchange rates (interest rates) at which banks buy and sell foreign exchange (lend and borrow).

Stock Exchange introduction: where an established firm obtains a stock market listing without selling any shares.

Stockout: where a firm is unable to deliver due to shortage of stock.

Straight or plain vanilla, debt: fixed rate borrowing with no additional features such as convertibility rights or warrants.

Strategic portfolio analysis: assessing capital projects within the strategic business context and not simply in financial terms.

Strong form: in a strong-form efficient share market, all information including inside information is built into share prices.

Sunk cost: a cost already incurred, or committed to.

Synergies: gains in revenues or cost savings resulting from takeovers and mergers, not resulting from firm size, i.e. stemming from a 'natural match' between two sets of assets.

Systematic risk: variability in a security's return due to exposure to risks affecting all firms traded in the market (hence, **market risk**), e.g. the impact of exchange rate changes.

Takeover: acquisition of the share capital of another firm, resulting in its identity being absorbed into that of the acquirer.

Takeover Code: the non-statutory rules laid down by the Takeover Panel to guide the conduct of participants in the takeover process.

Takeover Panel: a non-statutory body set up by, and with the participation of, leading financial organisations to oversee the conduct of takeover bids.

Tangible: tangible assets can quite literally be seen and touched, e.g. machinery and buildings.

Target capital structure: what the firm regards as its optimal long-term ratio of debt to equity (or debt to total capital).

Tax breaks: tax concessions, e.g. relief of interest payments against profits tax.

Tax credit: see **imputation systems**.

Tax shield: the tax savings achieved by setting tax-allowable expenses such as interest payments against profits.

Technical analysis: the detailed scrutiny of past time series of share price or foreign exchange rate movements attempting to identify repetitive patterns.

Term loans: loans made by a bank for a specific period or term, usually longer than a year.

Term structure of interest rates: pattern of interest rates on bonds of the same risk with different lengths of time to maturity.

Theoretical ex-rights price (TERP): the market price to which the ordinary shares should gravitate following the completion of a rights issue.

Times interest earned: the ratio of profit before interest and tax (operating profit) to annual interest charges, i.e. how many times over the firm could meet its interest bill.

Timing/delay option: the option to invest now or defer the decision until conditions are more favourable.

Time-value of money: the notion that money received in the future is worth less than the same amount received today because it could be invested to earn interest over this period.

Total shareholder return (TSR): the overall return enjoyed by investors, including dividend and capital appreciation, expressed as a percentage of their initial investment. Related to individual years, or to a lengthier time period, and then converted into an annualised, or equivalent annual return.

Trade credit: temporary financing extended by suppliers of goods and services pending the customer's settlement.

Traded options: an option traded on a market.

Traditional options: an option available on any security agreed between buyer and seller. It typically lasts for three months.

Traditional theory of capital structure: the theory that an optimal capital structure exists, where the WACC is minimised and market value is maximised.

Transaction exposure: the risk of loss due to adverse foreign exchange rate movements that affect the home currency value of import and export contracts denominated in a foreign currency.

Transfer price: the cost applied to goods transferred between operating units owned by the same firm.

Translation exposure: exposure to the risk of adverse currency movements affecting the domestic currency value of the firm's consolidated financial statements.

Treasury Bills: short-dated (up to three months) securities issued by the Bank of England on behalf of the UK government to cover short-term financing needs.

Treasury operations: financial risk management and portfolio management.

Uncovered arbitrage: interest arbitrage without the use of the forward market to lock in future values of proceeds.

'Underlying' asset: the asset from which option value is derived.

Unit trust: investment business attracting funds from investors by issuing units of shares or bonds to invest in.

Value additivity: the notion that, other things being equal, the combined present value of two entities is their separate present values added together.

Value-based management: a managerial approach where the whole aim, strategies and actions are linked to shareholder value creation.

Value drivers: factors that have a powerful influence on the value of a business, and the investors' equity stake.

Vendor placing/placing with clawback: a placing of new shares with financial institutions where existing investors have the right to purchase the shares from the institutions concerned to protect their rights.

Venture capital (VC): finance, usually equity, offered by specialist merchant banks wanting to take a stake in firms with high growth potential, but involving a high risk of loss.

Venture Capital Trusts (VCTs): stock-market listed financial vehicles set up to invest in a spread of highly risky new or young firms.

Vertical integration: extension of a firm's activities further back, or forward, along the supply chain from existing activities.

Warrants: options to buy ordinary shares at a pre-determined 'exercise price'. Usually attached to issues of loan stock.

Weak form: a weak-form efficient share market does not allow investors to look back at past share price movements and identify clear, repetitive patterns.

Weighted average cost of capital (WACC): the overall return a firm must achieve in order to meet the requirements of all its investors.

White Knight: a takeover bidder emerging after a hostile bid has been made, usually offering alternative bid terms that are more favourable to the defending management.

Working capital: or net working capital is current assets less current liabilities.

Yield: income from a security as a percentage of market price.

Yield curve: a graph of the relationship between the yield on bonds and their current length of time to maturity.

Yield to maturity: the interest rate at which the present value of the future cash flows equals the current market price.

Z-score: a mathematically derived critical value below which firms are associated with failure.

Zero coupon bond: a bond that does not pay interest but is issued at a discount and redeemed at par (full) value.

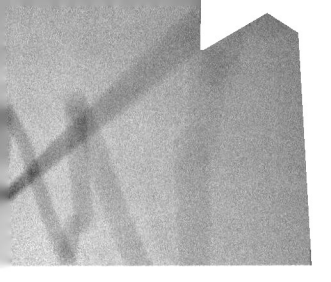

3i *Making an Acquisition*.

3i (1993), *Dividend Policy*, April.

Adams, R. B., A. N. Licht and L. Sagiv (2011) 'Shareholders and stakeholders; how do directors decide?', *Strategic Management Journal*, Vol. 32, No. 12, pp. 1331–1355.

Aggarwal, R., S. Bhagal and S. Rangan (2009) 'The impact of fundamentals on IPO valuation', *Financial Management*, Vol. 38, pp. 253–284.

Ahammad, M. F., V. Leone, S. Y. Tarba, K. W. Glaister, and A. Arslan (2017) 'Equity Ownership in Cross-border Mergers and Acquisitions by British Firms: An Analysis of Real Options and Transaction Cost Factors', *British Journal of Management*, Vol. 28, No. 2, pp. 180–196.

Ahammad, M., S. Y. Tarba, Y. Liu and K. W. Glaister (2016) 'Knowledge transfer and cross-border acquisition performance: the impact of cultural distance and employee retention', International Business Review, Vol. 25, pp. 66–75.

Aharoni, G., B. Grundy, and Q. Zeng, Q. (2013) 'Stock returns and the Miller–Modigliani valuation formula: Revisiting the Fama-French analysis', *Journal of Financial Economics*, Vol. 110, No. 2, pp. 347–357.

Ainley, M., A. Mashayekhi, R. Hicks, R. Rahman and A. Ravalia (2007) *Islamic Finance in the United Kingdom: Regulation and Challenges* (London: Financial Services Authority).

Airmic/Alarm/IRM (2010) *A Structured Approach to Enterprise Risk Management and the Requirements of ISO 31000*.

Akbar, S., B. Kharabsheh, J. Poletti-Hughes and SZA Shah (2017) 'Corporate board structure and risk-taking in the UK financial sector', *International Review of Financial Analysis*, Vol. 50, pp. 101–110.

Akbar, S., SZA Shah, and S. Kalmadi (2012) 'An Investigation of User Perceptions of Islamic Banking Practices in the United Kingdom', *International Journal of Islamic and Middle Eastern Finance and Management*, Vol. 5, No. 4, pp. 353–370.

Alexander, G. J., A. M. Baptista and Shu Yan (2017) 'Portfolio Selection with Mental Accounts and Estimation Risk', *Journal of Empirical Finance*, Vol. 41, pp. 161–186.

Alexandridis, G., K. P. Fuller, L. Terhaar and N. G. Travlos (2013) 'Deal size, acquisition premia and shareholder gains', *Journal of Corporate Finance*, Vol. 20, pp. 1–13.

Alkaraan, F., and D. Northcott (2006) 'Strategic capital investment decision-making: A role for emergent analysis tools? A study of practice in large UK manufacturing companies', *British Accounting Review*, Vol. 38, No. 12 [June], pp. 149–173.

Almazan, A., A. De Motta, S. Titman and V. Uysal (2010) 'Financial structure, acquisition opportunities, and firm locations', *Journal of Finance*, 65, pp. 529–563.

Altman, E. I. (1968) 'Financial ratios, discriminant analysis and the prediction of corporate bankruptcy', *Journal of Finance*, Vol. 23, No. 4 [September], pp. 589–609.

Andersen, J. A. (1987) *Currency and Interest Rate Hedging* (Prentice Hall).

Andrade, G., and S. N. Kaplan (1998) 'How costly is financial (not economic) distress? Evidence from highly-leveraged transactions that became distressed', *Journal of Finance*, Vol. 53 [October], pp. 1443–1493.

Andreadakis, S. (2012) 'Enlightened shareholder value: is it the new modus operandi for modern companies?', in S. Boubaker, B. D. Nguyen and D. K. Nguyen (eds) *Corporate Governance: Recent Developments and Trends*, pp. 415–432 (Springer).

Andres, C., M. Doumet, E. Fernau and E. Theissen (2015) 'The Lintner model revisited: Dividends versus total payouts', *Journal of Banking and Finance*, Vol. 55, pp. 6–69.

Andrews, G. S., and C. Firer (1987) 'Why different divisions require different hurdle rates', *Long Range Planning*, Vol. 20, No. 5 [October], pp. 62–68.

Ang, A., and J. Chen (2007) 'CAPM over the long-run: 1926–2001', *Journal of Empirical Finance*, Vol. 14, pp. 1–40.

Ang, J., T. Arnold, C. M. Conover and C. Lancaster (2010) 'Maintaining a flexible payout policy in a mature industry: The Case of Crown Cork and Seal in the Connelly Era', *Journal of Applied Corporate Finance*, Vol. 22, pp. 30–44.

Ang, J., and P. P. Peterson (1984) 'The leasing puzzle', *Journal of Finance*, Vol. 39, No. 4, pp. 1055–1065.

Angwin, D. (2000) *Managing Successful Post-Acquisition Integration* (FT/Prentice Hall).

Angwin, D. (2004) 'Speed in M&A integration: The first 100 days', *European Management Journal*, Vol. 22, No. 4, pp. 418–430.

Antill, N., and K. Lee (2008) *Company Valuation under IFRS: Interpreting and Forecasting Accounts Using International Financial Reporting Standards*, 2nd (revised) edn. (Harrison House Publishing).

Aretz, K., and S. M. Bartram (2010) 'Corporate hedging and shareholder value', *Journal of Financial Research*, Vol. 33, pp. 317–371.

Arnold, G., and P. Hatzopoulos (2000) 'The theory–practice gap in capital budgeting: evidence from the United Kingdom', *Journal of Business Finance & Accounting*, Vol. 27, Issue 5–6 [June], pp. 603–626.

Arzac, E. R. (2010) *Valuation for Mergers, Buyouts and Restructuring* (Wiley).

Arzac, E. R., and L. R. Glosten (2005) 'A reconsideration of tax shield valuation', *European Financial Management*, Vol. 11, No. 4, pp. 453–461.

Ashkenas, R., L. J. De Monaco and S. C. Francis (1998) 'Making the deal real: How GE Capital integrates acquisitions', *Harvard Business Review*, Vol. 76, No. 1 [January–February], pp. 165–178.

Ashton, D., and D. Acker (2003) 'Establishing bounds on the tax advantage of debt', *British Accounting Review* Vol. 35, No. 4 [December], pp. 385–399.

Asquith, P., and D. Mullins (1986) 'Signalling with dividends, stock purchases and equity issues', *Financial Management*, Vol. 15, Issue 3 [Autumn], pp. 27–44.

Avdis, E., and J. A. Wachter (2017) 'Maximum likelihood estimation of the equity premium', *Journal of Financial Economics*, DOI: https://doi.org/10.1016/j.jfineco.2017.06.003.

Bai, C., and J. Sarkis (2017) 'Improving green flexibility through advanced manufacturing technology investment: Modeling the decision process', *International Journal of Production Economics*, Vol. 188, pp. 86–104.

Bailey, E., and Groves, H. (2014) *Corporate Insolvency: Law and Practice* (Butterworths).

Baker, H. K., S. Dutta and S. Samir (2011) 'Management views on real options in capital budgeting', *Journal of Applied Finance*, Vol. 21, No. 1 [Spring–Summer], pp. 18–29.

Baker, H. K., and G. S. Martin (2011) *Capital Structure and Corporate Financing Decisions: Theory, Evidence, and Practice* (Wiley).

Baker, H. K., and J. R. Nofsinger (2010) *Behavioural Finance: Investors, Corporations and Markets* (Wiley).

Baldeaux, J., M. Grasselli, and Eckhard Platene (2015) 'Pricing currency derivatives under the benchmark approach', *Journal of Banking and Finance*, Vol. 53, pp. 34–48.

Ball, J. (1991) 'Short termism – myth or reality', *National Westminster Bank Quarterly Review*, August.

Ball, R. (2009) 'The global financial crisis and the efficient markets hypothesis: What have we learned?', *Journal of Applied Corporate Finance*, Vol. 21, No. 4, pp. 8–16.

Ball, R., and P. Brown (1968) 'An empirical evaluation of accounting income numbers', *Journal of Accounting Research*, Vol. 6, No. 2 [Autumn], pp. 159–178.

Bank of England (1988) 'Share repurchase by quoted companies', *Quarterly Bulletin*, Vol. 28, No. 3 [August], pp. 382–390.

Barber, B., and T. Odean (2000) 'Trading is hazardous to your wealth: The common stock investment performance of individual investors', *Journal of Finance*, Vol. 55, No. 2, pp. 773–806.

Barber, B. M., and T. Odean (2001) 'Boys will be boys: Gender, overconfidence, and common stock investment', *Quarterly Journal of Economics*, Vol. 116, pp. 261–292.

Barberis, N., A. Mukherjee and B. Wang (2016) 'Prospect theory and stock returns: An empirical test', *The Review of Financial Studies*, Vol. 29, No. 11, pp. 3068–3107.

Barclay, M., and C. Smith, (2006) 'The capital structure puzzle: Another look at the evidence', in J. Rutterford, M. Upton and D. Kodwani (eds) *Financial Strategy*, 2nd edn. (Wiley).

Barclay, M. J., C. W. Smith and R. L. Watts (1995) 'The determinants of corporate leverage and dividend policies', *Journal of Applied Corporate Finance*, Vol. 7, No. 4 [Winter], pp. 4–19.

Bartram, S., G. Brown and F. Fehle (2006) 'International evidence of financial derivative usage', *Social Science Research Network*, October.

Bartram, S. M., G. Brown and F. R. Fehle (2009) 'International evidence on financial derivatives usage', *Financial Management*, Vol. 38, pp. 185–206.

Barwise, P., P. Marsh, and R. Wensley (1989) 'Must finance and strategy clash?', *Harvard Business Review*, Vol. 67, No. 5 [September–October], pp. 85–90.

Baumol, W. (1952) 'The transactions demand for cash: An inventory-theoretic approach', *Quarterly Journal of Economics*, Vol. 66, No. 4 [November], pp. 545–556.

Beck, T., and A. Demirguc-Kunt (2006) 'Small- and medium-size enterprises: Access to finance as a growth constraint', *Journal of Banking and Finance*, Vol. 30, pp. 2931–2943.

Beck, T., A. Demirguc-Kunt and V. Maksimovic (2008) 'Financing patterns around the world: Are small firms different?', *Journal of Financial Economics*, Vol. 89, pp. 467–487.

Becker, B., Z. Ivkovic and S. Weisbeener (2011) 'Local dividend clienteles', *Journal of Finance*, Vol. 66, pp. 655–683.

Beenstock, M., and K. Chan (1986) 'Testing the arbitrage pricing theory in the UK', *Oxford Bulletin of Economics and Statistics*, Vol. 48, No. 2 [May], pp. 121–141.

Bekaert, G., R. J. Hodrick and X. Zhang (2009) 'International stock return co-movements', *Journal of Finance*, Vol. 63, pp. 2591–2626.

Benito, A., and G. Young (2001) *Hard Times or Great Expectations: Dividend Omissions and Dividend Cuts by UK Firms*, Bank of England Working Paper 147.

Bennet, N. (2001) 'One day we will go out of business', *Sunday Telegraph*, 9 December.

Berk, J., and P. Demarzo (2013) *Corporate Finance* (Pearson).

Benartzi, S., R. Michaely and R. Thaler (1997) 'Do changes in dividends signal changes in the future or the past?', *Journal of Finance*, Vol. 52, No. 3 [July], pp. 1007–1034.

Bhattacharya, S. (1979) 'Imperfect information, dividend policy and the bird-in-the-hand fallacy', *Bell Journal of Economics and Management Science*, Vol. 10, No. 1 [Spring], pp. 259–270.

Bierman Jr, H., and J. E. Hass (1973) 'Capital budgeting under uncertainty: A reformulation', *Journal of Finance*, Vol. 28, No. 1 [March], pp. 1119–1129.

BIS (2016) *Triennial Central Bank Survey*. Bank for International Settlements.

Black, F. (1976) 'The dividend puzzle', *Journal of Portfolio Management*, Vol. 2, No. 2 [Winter], pp. 5–8.

Black, F. (1993a) 'Estimating expected return', *Financial Analysts Journal*, Vol. 43, No. 2, pp. 507–528.

Black, F. (1993b) 'Return and Beta', *Journal of Portfolio Management*, Vol. 20, No. 1, pp. 8–18.

Black, F., M. C. Jensen and M. Scholes (1972) 'The capital asset pricing model: Some empirical tests', in M. Jensen (ed.) *Studies in the Theory of Capital Markets* (Praeger).

Black, F., and M. Scholes (1973) 'The pricing of options and corporate liabilities', *Journal of Political Economy*, Vol. 81, No. 3 [May–June], pp. 637–654.

Black, J. R., D. Stock and P. K. Yadav (2016) 'The pricing of different dimensions of liquidity: Evidence from government guaranteed bonds', *Journal of Banking and Finance*, Vol. 71, pp. 119–132.

Blanco, I., and D. Wehrheim (2017) 'The bright side of financial derivatives: Options trading and firm innovation', *Journal of Financial Economics*, Vol. 125, No. 1, pp. 99–119.

Block, S., G. Hirt and B. Danielsen (2017) *Foundations of Financial Management*, 16th edn. (McGraw Hill).

Boakes, K. (2010) *Reading and Understanding the Financial Times* (FT Prentice Hall).

Bodie, Z., and R. Merton (2000) *Finance* (Prentice-Hall).

Borges, L. A., and K. T. Tan (2017) 'Incorporating human factors into the AAMT selection: A framework and process', *International Journal of Production Research*, Vol. 55, No. 5, pp. 1459–1470.

Bowman, R. G. (1980) 'The debt equivalence of leases: An empirical investigation', *Accounting Review*, Vol. 55, No. 2, pp. 237–253.

Bradley, M., G. Jarrell and E. Kim (1984) 'The existence of an optimal capital structure: Theory and evidence', *Journal of Finance*, Vol. 39, No. 3, pp. 857–878.

Bragg, S. M. (2010) *Treasury Management: The Practitioner's Guide* (Wiley).

Branson, R. (1998) *Losing My Virginity* (Virgin Publishing).

Brav, O. (2009) 'Access to capital, capital structure, and the funding of the firm', *Journal of Finance*, Vol. 64, pp. 263–308.

Brealey, R. A., S. C. Myers and F. Allen (2017) *Principles of Corporate Finance* (McGraw-Hill).

Brennan, M. (1971) 'A note on dividend irrelevance and the Gordon valuation model', *Journal of Finance*, Vol. 26, No. 5 [December], pp. 1115–1121.

Brennan, M., and L. Trigeorgis (eds) (2000) *Project Flexibility, Agency and Competition: New Developments in the Theory and Application of Real Options* (Oxford University Press).

Brett, M. (2003) *How to Read the Financial Papers*, 4th edn. (Random House).

Breuer, W., M. O. Rieger, and K. C. Soypak (2014) 'The behavioral foundations of corporate dividend policy: a cross-country analysis', *Journal of Banking and Finance*, Vol. 42, pp. 247–265.

Brickley, J., C. Smith and J. Zimmerman (1994) 'Ethics, incentives, and organisational design', *Journal of Applied Corporate Finance*, Vol. 7, No. 2 [Summer], pp. 20–30.

Brickley, J., C. Smith and L. Zimmerman (2003) 'Corporate governance, ethics and organisational architecture', *Journal of Applied Corporate Finance*, Vol. 15 [Spring], pp. 34–45.

Brigham, E. F., and L. C. Gapenski (2017) *Financial Management Theory and Practice* (Dryden).

Bromwich, M., and A. Bhimani (1991) 'Strategic investment appraisal', *Management Accounting*, Vol. 69 [March], pp. 45–48.

Brooks, R., and L. Catao (2000) 'The new economy and global stock returns', *IMF Working Paper 216*, December.

Brounen, D., A. de Jong, and K. Koedijk (2004), 'Corporate finance in Europe: Confronting theory with practice', *Financial Management*, Vol. 33, No. 4 [Winter], pp. 71–101.

Brown, P. (2006) *An Introduction to the Bond Markets* (Wiley).

Bruner, R., and J. Perella (2004) *Applied Mergers and Acquisitions* (Wiley).

Buchner, A., and N. F. Wagner (2017) 'Rewarding risk-taking or skill? The case of private equity fund managers', *Journal of Banking and Finance*, Vol. 80, pp. 14–32.

Buckley, A. (2004) *Multinational Finance* (Financial Times/Prentice Hall).

Buckley, A. (2012) *International Finance: A Practical Perspective* (FT/Prentice Hall).

Buckley, P. J., and M. Casson (1981) 'The optimal timing of a foreign direct investment', *Economic Journal*, Vol. 92, No. 361 [March], pp. 75–87.

Burton, E., and S. Shah (2013) *Behavioral Finance: Understanding the Social, Cognitive, and Economic Debates* (Wiley).

Butler, K. C. (2016) *Multinational Finance: Evaluating Opportunities, Costs, and Risks of Operations*, 6th edn. (Wiley).

Butler, R., L. Davies, R. Pike and J. Sharp (1993) *Strategic Investment Decisions* (Routledge).

BVCA (2008) *The Economic Impact of Private Equity in the UK 2007* (The British Private Equity and Venture Capital Association).

Byoun, S. (2008) 'How and when do firms adjust their capital structures toward targets?', *Journal of Finance*, Vol. 63, pp. 3069–3096.

BZW (2008) *Equity–Gilt Study*, London.

Caliskana, D., and J. A. Doukas (2015) 'CEO risk preferences and dividend policy decisions', *Journal of Corporate Finance*, Vol. 35, pp. 18–42.

Campbell, J., and T. Vuolteenako (2004) 'Bad Beta, good Beta', *American Economic Review*, Vol. 94, No. 5 [December], pp. 1249–1275.

Campbell, R., K. Koedjik and P. Kofman (2002) 'Increased correlation in bear markets', *Financial Analysts Journal*, Vol. 58, No. 1 [January–February], pp. 87–94.

Carbo-Valverde, S., F. Rodriguez-Fernandez and G. F. Udell (2016) 'Trade credit, the financial crisis, and SME access to finance', *Journal of Money, Credit and Banking*, Vol. 48, No. 1, pp. 113–143.

Carhart, M. (1997) 'On persistence in mutual fund performance', *Journal of Finance*, Vol. 52, pp. 57–82.

Carroll, A., F. O'Brien and J. Ryan (2017) 'An examination of European firms' derivatives usage: The importance of model selection', *European Financial Management* (Accepted Manuscript Forthcoming), DOI: 10.1111/eufm.12115.

Cavaglia, S., C. Brightman and M. Aked (2002) 'The increasing importance of industry factors', *Financial Analysts Journal*, Vol. 56, No. 5 [September–October], pp. 41–54.

Chakravarty, S., and L. G. Rutherford (2017) 'Do busy directors influence the cost of debt? An examination through the lens of takeover vulnerability', *Journal of Corporate Finance*, Vol. 43, pp. 429–443.

Chang, K., and C. Osler (1999) 'Methodical madness: Technical analysis and the irrationality of exchange rate forecasts', *Economic Journal*, Vol. 109, Issue 458 [October], pp. 636–661.

Chen, L., and L. Zhang, (2010) 'A better three-factor model that explains more anomalies,' *Journal of Finance*, Vol. 65, pp. 563–594.

Chesley, G. R. (1975) 'Elicitation of subjective probabilities: A review', *Accounting Review*, Vol. 50, No. 2 [April], pp. 325–337.

Chiou, W. P. (2008) 'Who benefits from international portfolio diversification?', *Journal of International Financial Markets, Institutions and Money*, Vol. 18, No. 5, pp. 466–482.

Chisholm, A. (2010) *Derivatives Demystified* (Wiley).

Choudhry, T., and R. Jayasekera (2013) 'Level of efficiency in the UK equity market: Empirical study of the effects of the global financial crisis', *Review of Quantitative Finance and Accounting*, September.

Clare, A. D., and S. H. Thomas (1994) 'Macroeconomic factors, the arbitrage pricing theory and the UK stockmarket', *Journal of Business Finance and Accounting*, Vol. 21, No. 3 [April], pp. 309–330.

Clark, T. M. (1978) *Leasing* (McGraw-Hill).

Collier, P., T. Cooke and J. Glynn (1988) *Financial and Treasury Management* (Heinemann).

Collier, P., and E. W. Davies (1985) 'The management of currency transaction risk by UK multinational companies', *Accounting and Business Research*, Vol. 15, No. 6 [Autumn], pp. 327–334.

Cooke, T. E. (1986) *Mergers and Acquisitions* (Blackwell).

Cooper, D. J. (1975) 'Rationality and investment appraisal', *Accounting and Business Research*, Vol. 5, No. 19 [Summer], pp. 198–202.

Copeland, T., T. Koller and J. Murrin (2000) *Valuation* (Wiley).

Copeland, T. E., J. F. Weston and K. Shastri (2013) *Financial Theory and Corporate Policy* (Pearson).

Cox, J., S. Ross and M. Rubinstein (1979) 'Option pricing: A simplified approach', *Journal of Financial Economics*, Vol. 7, No. 3, pp. 229–263.

Czinkota, M., T. Ronkainen and M. Moffet (1994) 'International business', in J. Dunning and S. Lundan *Multinational Enterprises and the Global Economy* (Edward Elgar).

Daa, Z., and E. Schaumburg (2011) 'Relative valuation and analyst target price forecasts', *Journal of Financial Markets*, Vol. 14, pp. 161–192.

Damodaran, A. (2012) *Investment Valuation*, 3rd edn. (Wiley).

Damodaran, A. (2015) *The Dark Side of Valuation*, 2nd edn. (FT-Prentice Hall).

Daniel, E., J. Ward and A. Franken (2011) 'Project portfolio management in turbulent times', Vol. 7, No. 2, CIMA Executive Research Summary Series.

Daniels, J. D., L. H. Radebaugh, D. P. Sullivan and P. Salwan (2009) *International Business: Environments and Operations*, 12th edn. (Prentice Hall).

Danis, A., D. A. Rettl, and T. M. Whited (2014) 'Refinancing, profitability, and capital structure', *Journal of Financial Economics*, Vol. 114, No. 3, pp. 424–443.

Daunfeldt, Sven-Olov, and F. Hartwig (2014) 'What determines the use of capital budgeting methods? Evidence from Swedish listed companies', *Journal of Finance and Economics*, Vol. 2, No. 4, pp. 101–112.

David, T., and E. Ginglinger (2016) 'When cutting dividends is not bad news: The case of optional stock dividends', *Journal of Corporate Finance*, Vol. 40, pp. 174–191.

Day, R., D. Allen, I. Hirst and J. Kwiatkowski (1987) 'Equity, gilts, treasury bills and inflation', *The Investment Analyst*, No. 83 [January], pp. 11–18.

DeAngelo, H., and R. Masulis (1980) 'Optimal capital structure under corporate and personal taxation', *Journal of Financial Economics*, Vol. 8, No. 1, pp. 3–30.

Dean, J. (1951) *Capital Budgeting* (Columbia University Press).

DeBondt, W. F. M., and R. Thaler (1985) 'Does the stockmarket overreact?', *Journal of Finance*, Vol. 40, No. 3, pp. 793–805.

Degryse, H., K. Matthews and T. Zhao (2017) 'Relationship banking and regional SME financing: The case of Wales', *International Journal of Banking, Accounting and Finance*, Vol. 8, No. 1, pp. 93–118.

DeLong, J. B., and K. Magin (2009) 'The US equity return premium: past, present and future', *Journal of Economic Perspectives*, Vol. 23, pp. 193–208.

DePamphilis, D. (2013) *Mergers, Acquisitions and Other Restructuring Activities* (Academic Press).

DePamphilis, D. (2017) *Mergers, Acquisitions, and Other Restructuring Activities: An Integrated Approach to Process, Tools, Cases, and Solutions*, 9th edn. (Academic Press).

Department of Trade and Industry (1988) *Mergers Policy* (HMSO).

Devine, M. (2002) *Successful Mergers: Getting the People Issues Right* (The Economist/Profile Books).

Dewally, M., and Y. Shao (2014) 'Liquidity crisis, relationship lending and corporate finance', *Journal of Banking and Finance*, Vol. 39, pp. 223–239.

Díaz, A., and A. Escribano (2017) 'Liquidity measures throughout the lifetime of the U.S. Treasury bond', *Journal of Financial Markets*, Vol. 33, pp. 42–74.

Dimson, E. (1993) 'Appraisal techniques', Proceedings of the Capital Projects Conference, May, Institute of Actuaries and Faculty of Actuaries.

Dimson, E., and R. A. Brealey (1978) 'The risk premium on UK equities', *The Investment Analyst*, No. 52 [December], pp. 14–18.

Dimson, E., and P. Marsh (1982) 'Calculating the cost of capital', *Long Range Planning*, Vol. 15, No. 2 [April], pp. 112–120.

Dimson, E., and P. Marsh (1986) 'Event study methodologies and the size effect: The case of UK press recommendations', *Journal of Financial Economics*, September.

Dimson, E., P. Marsh and M. Staunton (2002) *Triumph of the Optimists* (Princeton University Press).

Dimson, E., P. Marsh and M. Staunton (2008) 'The world-wide equity premium: A smaller puzzle', in R. Mehra, *Handbook of the Equity Premium* (Elsevier).

Dion, C., D. Allay, D. Derain and G. Lahiri (2007) *Dangerous Liaisons: The Integration Game* (The Hay Group).

Dissanaike, G. (1997) 'Do stock market investors overreact?', *Journal of Business Finance and Accounting*, Vol. 24, No. 1, pp. 27–49.

Dixit, A., and R. Pindyck (1995) 'The options approach to capital investment', *Harvard Business Review*, Vol. 73, No. 3 [May–June], pp. 105–115.

Dobbs, R., and W. Rehm (2006) 'The value of share buybacks', in J. Rutterford, M. Upton and D. Kodwani (eds) *Financial Strategy* (Wiley).

Doidge, C., G. A. Karoyli and R. Stulz (2010) 'Why do foreign firms leave U.S. equity markets?', *Journal of Finance*, Vol. 65, pp. 1507–1553.

Donaldson, R. G., M. J. Kamstra and L. A. Kramer (2010) 'Estimating the equity premium', *Journal of Financial and Quantitative and Analysis*, Vol. 45, No. 4, pp. 813–846.

Doyle, P. (1994) 'Setting business objectives and measuring performance', *Journal of General Management*, Vol. 20, No. 2 [Winter], pp. 1–19.

Driessen, J., and L. Laeven (2007) 'International portfolio diversification benefits: Cross-country evidence from a local perspective', *Journal of Banking and Finance*, Vol. 31, No. 6, pp. 1693–1712.

Drucker, P. F. (1981) 'Five rules for successful acquisition', *Wall Street Journal*, 15 October.

Duchin, R., and D. Sosyura (2013) 'Divisional managers and internal capital markets', *Journal of Finance*, Vol. 68, No. 2, pp. 387–429.

Duckett, G. (2010) *Practical Enterprise Risk Management: A Business Process Approach* (Wiley).

Dunning, J. H., and S. M. Lundan (2008) *Multinational Enterprises and the Global Economy* (Edward Elgar).

Economist (2000) 'Making Mergers Work' (The Economist Newspaper Ltd, London).

Eiteman, D. K., A. I. Stonehill and M. H. Moffet (2015) *Multinational Business Finance*, 14th edn. (Pearson).

Elton, E. J. (1970) 'Capital rationing and external discount rates', *Journal of Finance*, Vol. 25, No. 3 [June], pp. 573–584.

Elton, E. J., and M. Gruber (1970) 'Marginal stockholder tax rates and the clientele effect', *Review of Economics and Statistics*, Vol. 52, No. 1 [February], pp. 68–74.

Elton, E. J., M. J. Gruber, S. J. Brown and W. N. Goetzman (2014) *Modern Portfolio Theory and Investment Analysis*, 9th edn. (Wiley).

Emery, D., J. Finnerty and J. D. Stowe (2006) *Corporate Financial Management*, 3rd edn. (Prentice Hall).

Emmanuel, C. R., E. P. Harris and S. Komakech (2008) 'Managerial judgement and strategic investment decisions', Vol. 4, No. 1, CIMA research executive summaries services.

Ehrhardt, M. C., and E. F. Brigham (2017) *Corporate Finance*, 6th edn. (Cengage Learning).

Eun, C. S. (2012) *International Finance*, 6th edn. (McGraw Hill).

Evans, C. (2005) 'Private lessons', *Accountancy*, Vol. 135, No. 1337 [January], pp. 46–47.

Faccio, M., M-T. Marchicab and R. Mura (2016). 'CEO gender, corporate risk-taking, and the efficiency of capital allocation', *Journal of Corporate Finance*, Vol. 39, pp. 193–209.

Fama, E. (1980) 'Agency problems and the theory of the firm', *Journal of Political Economy*, Vol. 88, No. 2 [April], pp. 288–307.

Fama, E. (1998) 'Market efficiency, long-term returns, and behavioural finance', *Journal of Financial Economics*, Vol. 49, No. 3 [September], pp. 283–306.

Fama E. (2014) 'Two pillars of asset pricing', *American Economic Review*, Vol. 104, No. 6, pp. 1467–1485.

Fama, E., and K. French (1993) 'Common risk factors in the returns on stocks and bonds', *Journal of Financial Economics*, Vol. 33, No. 1, pp. 3–56.

Fama, E., and K. French (1995) 'Size and book-to-market factors in earnings and returns', *Journal of Finance*, Vol. 50, No. 1 [March], pp. 131–155.

Fama, E., and K. French (1996) 'Multifactor explanations of asset pricing anomalies', *Journal of Finance*, Vol. 51, No. 1 [March], pp. 55–84.

Fama, E., and K. French (2001) 'Disappearing dividends: Changing firm characteristics or lower propensity to pay?', *Journal of Financial Economics*, Vol. 60, No. 1 [April], pp. 3–43.

Fama, E., and K. French (2002) 'The equity premium', *Journal of Finance*, Vol. 57, No. 2, pp. 637–659.

Fama, E., and K. French (2004) 'The CAPM – theory and evidence', *Journal of Economic Perspectives*, Vol. 18, No. 3 [Summer], pp. 25–46.

Fama, E. F. (1970) 'Efficient capital markets: A review of theory and empirical work', *Journal of Finance*, Vol. 25, No. 2 [May], pp. 383–417.

Fama, E. F. (1991) 'Efficient capital markets', *Journal of Finance*, Vol. 46, No. 5 [December], pp. 1575–1617.

Fama, E. F., and K. R. French (1992) 'The cross-section of expected stock returns', *Journal of Finance*, Vol. 47, No. 2, pp. 427–465.

Fama, E. F., and K. R. French (2006a) 'Profitability, investment and average returns', *Journal of Financial Economics*, Vol. 82, No. 3, pp. 491–518.

Fama, E. F., and K. R. French (2006b) 'The value premium and the CAPM', *Journal of Finance*, Vol. 61, pp. 2163–2185.

Fama, E. F., and K. R. French (2015) 'A five-factor asset pricing model', *Journal of Financial Economics*, Vol. 116, No. 1, pp. 1–22.

Fama, E. F., and K. R. French (2017) 'International tests of a five-factor asset pricing model', *Journal of Financial Economics*, Vol. 123, No. 3, pp. 441–463.

Fama, E. F., and J. McBeth (1973) 'Risk, return and equilibrium: Empirical tests', *Journal of Political Economy*, Vol. 81, No. 3 [May–June], pp. 607–636.

Fama, E. F., and M. H. Miller (1972) *The Theory of Finance* (Holt, Rinehart and Winston).

Favara, G., E. Morellec, E. Schroth and P. Valta (2017) 'Debt enforcement, investment, and risk-taking across countries', *Journal of Financial Economics*, Vol. 123, No. 1, pp. 22–41.

Feldman, S. (2005) *Principles of Private Firm Valuation* (Wiley).

Fenton-O'Creevy, M., N. Nicholson, E. Soane and P. Willman (2003) 'Trading on illusions: Unrealistic perceptions of control and trading performance', *Journal of Occupational and Organizational Psychology*, Vol. 76, No. 1, pp. 53–68.

Ferguson, A. (1989) 'Hostage to the short term', *Management Today*, March.

Fernandez, P. (2004) 'The value of tax shields is NOT equal to the present value of tax shields', *Journal of Financial Economics*, Vol. 73, No. 1, pp. 145–165.

Fernandez, P. (2007) 'Valuing companies by cash flow discounting: Ten methods and nine theories', *Managerial Finance*, Vol. 33, pp. 853–876.

Fernandez, P. (2013) 'Valuing companies using cash flow discounting: Fundamental analysis and unnecessary complications', Working Paper, IESE Business School, University of Navarra.

Fernandez, P., V. Pershin and I. F. Acin (2017) 'Discount Rate (Risk-Free Rate and Market Risk Premium) used for 41 countries in 2017: A survey', Working Paper, IESE Business School University of Navarra (available at: www.ssrn.com).

Ferris, S. P., D. Javakhadze and T. Rajkovic (2017) 'The international effect of managerial social capital on the cost of equity', *Journal of Banking and Finance*, Vol. 74, pp. 69–84.

Finnie, J. (1988) 'The role of financial appraisal in decisions to acquire advanced manufacturing technology', *Accounting and Business Research*, Vol. 18, No. 70 [Spring], pp. 133–139.

Firth, M., P. M. Y. Fung and O. M. Rui (2006) 'Corporate performance and CEO compensation in China', *Journal of Corporate Finance*, Vol. 12, pp. 693–714.

Firth, M., and S. Keane (1986) *Issues in Finance* (Philip Allan).

Fisher, I. (1930) *The Theory of Interest*, reprinted in 1977 by Porcupine Press.

Flavin, T. J., and E. Panapoulou (2009) 'On the robustness of international portfolio diversification switching benefits to regime-switching volatility', *Journal of International Financial Markets, Institutions and Money*, Vol. 19, No. 1, pp. 140–156.

Foley, B. J. (1991) *Capital Markets* (Macmillan).

Forbes, W. (2009) *Behavioural Finance* (Wiley).

Fosback, N. (1985) *Stock Market Logic* (The Institute for Economic Research, Fort Lauderdale).

Franks, J., and J. Broyles (1979) *Modern Managerial Finance* (Wiley).

Franks, J., and C. Mayer (1996a) 'Do hostile take-overs improve performance?', *Business Strategy Review*, Vol. 7, No. 4, pp. 1–6.

Franks, J., and C. Mayer (1996b) 'Hostile take-overs and the correction of managerial failure', *Journal of Financial Economics*, Vol. 40, No. 1, pp. 163–181.

Franks, J. R., and R. S. Harris (1989) 'Shareholder wealth effects of corporate takeovers: The UK experience 1955–85', *Journal of Financial Economics*, Vol. 23, No. 2, pp. 225–249.

Friedman, M. (1953) 'The methodology of positive economics', in *Essays in Positive Economics* (University of Chicago Press).

Frykman, D., and J. Tolleryd (2010) *The Financial Times Guide to Corporate Valuation*, 2nd edn. (Financial Times/Prentice Hall).

Fuller, R. J., and H. S. Kerr (1981) 'Estimating the divisional cost of capital: An analysis of the Pure-Play Technique', *Journal of Finance*, Vol. 36, No. 5, pp. 997–1009.

Galati, G., A. Heath and P. McGuire (2007) 'Evidence of carry trade activity', *Bank of International Settlements Quarterly Review* [September], pp. 27–42.

Galpin, T. J., and M. Herndon (2014) *The Complete Guide to Merger and Acquisitions*, (Wiley).

Gaughan, P. A. (2015) *Mergers, Acquisitions, and Corporate Restructurings*, 6th edn. (Wiley).

Gentry, J. (1988) 'State of the art of short-run financial management', *Financial Management*, Vol. 17, No. 2 [Summer], pp. 41–57.

Geske, R., A. Subrahmanyam and Y. Zhou (2016) 'Capital structure effects on the prices of equity call options', *Journal of Financial Economics*, Vol. 121, No. 2, pp. 231–253.

Ghosh, C., and J. Woolridge (1989) 'Stock market reaction to growth – induced dividend cuts: Are investors myopic?', *Managerial & Decision Economics*, Vol. 10, No. 1 [March], pp. 25–35.

Giddy, I. H. (1994) *Global Financial Markets* (D. C. Heath).

Gilovich, T., R. Vallone and A. Tversky (1985) 'The hot hand in basketball: On the misperception of random sequences', *Cognitive Psychology*, 17, pp. 295–314.

Girerd-Potin, I., S. Jimenez-Garess and P. Louvet (2014) 'Which dimensions of social responsibility concern financial investors?', *Journal of Business Ethics*, Vol. 121, No. 4, pp. 559–576.

Global Treasury Benchmark Survey (2017) 'The "virtual reality" of treasury' (PwC).

Gluck, F. W. (1988) 'The real takeover defense', *The McKinsey Quarterly*, Issue 1 [Winter], pp. 2–16.

Goergen, M., and L. Renneboog (2011) 'Manageral compensation', *Journal of Corporate Finance*, Vol. 17, No. 4, pp. 1068–1077.

Gordon, M. (1959) 'Dividends, earnings and stock prices', *Review of Economics and Statistics*, Vol. 41 [May], pp. 99–105.

Gordon, M. (1963) 'Optimal investment and financing policy', *Journal of Finance*, Vol. 18, No. 2, pp. 264–272.

Goyal, S., and S. Grover (2013) 'A fuzzy multi-attribute decision-making approach for evaluating effectiveness of advanced manufacturing technology – in an Indian context', *International Journal of Productivity and Quality Management*, Vol. 11, No. 2, pp. 150–178.

Grabowski, R. J., C. Nunes, and J. P. Harrington (2017) *International Valuation Handbook – Guide to Cost of Capital* (Wiley).

Graham, B., D. Dodd and S. Cottle (1962) *Security Analysis: Principles and Techniques*, 4th edn. (McGraw-Hill).

Graham, J., and C. Harvey (2002) 'How do CFOs make capital budgeting and capital structure decisions?', *Journal of Applied Corporate Finance*, Vol. 15, No. 1 [Spring], pp. 8–23.

Graham, J. R., and C. R. Harvey (2007) 'The Equity Risk Premium in January 2007: Evidence from the Global CFO Outlook Survey', *Icfai Journal of Financial Risk Management*, Vol. 4, No. 2, pp. 46–61.

Graham, J. R., S. Li, and J. Qiu (2012) 'Managerial attributes and executive compensation', *The Review of Financial Studies*, Vol. 25, No. 1, pp. 144–186.

Grant, L. (2011) *Mergers and Acquisitions* (Siren Publishing).

Grant, R., and L. Soenen (2004) 'Strategic management of operating exposure', *European Management Journal*, Vol. 22, No. 1 [February], pp. 353–362.

Grant, R. M. (2003) 'Strategic planning in a turbulent environment: Evidence from the oil majors', *Strategic Management Journal*, Vol. 24, No. 6, pp. 491–517.

Grant, R. M. (2008) *Contemporary Strategic Analysis* (Basil Blackwell).

Graves, S. B. (1988) 'Institutional ownership and corporate R&D in the computer industry', *Academy of Management Journal*, Vol. 31, No. 2 [June], pp. 417–428.

Greene, W. H., A. S. Hornstein and L. J. White (2009) 'Multinationals do it better: Evidence on the efficiency of corporations' capital budgeting', *Journal of Empirical Finance*, Vol. 16, No. 5, pp. 703–720.

Gregoriu, G., and K. Neuhauser (2007) *Mergers and Acquisitions* (Palgrave).

Gregory, A. (1997) 'An examination of the long-run performance of UK acquiring firms', *Journal of Business Finance and Accounting*, Vol. 24, No. 7–8 [September], pp. 971–1002.

Gregory, A., and S. McCorriston (2004) 'Foreign acquisitions by UK limited companies: Short and long-run performance', University of Exeter Centre for Finance and Investment Working Paper 04/01.

Grice, J. S., and R. W. Ingram (2001) 'Tests of the generalisability of Altman's bankruptcy prediction model', *Journal of Business Research*, Vol. 54, No. 1 [October], pp. 53–61.

Grinyer, J. R. (1986) 'An alternative to maximisation of shareholders' wealth in capital budgeting decisions', *Accounting and Business Research*, Vol. 16, No. 64 [Autumn], pp. 319–326.

Gup, B. E., and S. W. Norwood (1982) 'Divisional cost of capital: A practical approach', *Financial Management*, Vol. 11, No. 1 [Spring], pp. 20–24.

Guthrie, G. (2009) *Real Options in Theory and Practice* (Oxford University Press).

Habeck, M., F. Kroger and M. R. Traem (2000) *After the Merger* (Pearson Education).

Hamada, R. S. (1969) 'Portfolio analysis: Market equilibrium and corporate finance', *Journal of Finance*, Vol. 24, No. 1 [March], pp. 13–31.

Harar, S. (1998) 'Islamic banking: An overview', in J. Rutterford (ed.) *Financial Strategy: Adding Stakeholder Value* (Open Business School/Wiley).

Harrington, D. (1987) *Modern Portfolio Theory, The Capital Asset Pricing Model and Arbitrage Pricing Theory: A User's Guide* (Prentice Hall).

Harrington, D. R. (1983) 'Stock prices, Beta and strategic planning', *Harvard Business Review*, Vol. 6, No. 3 [May–June], pp. 157–164.

Harris, M., and A. Raviv (1990) 'Capital structure and the informational role of debt', *Journal of Finance*, Vol. 45, No. 2, pp. 321–350.

Harris, M., and A. Raviv (1991) 'The theory of capital structure', *Journal of Finance*, Vol. 46, No. 1, pp. 297–356.

Harrison, J. S. (1987) 'Alternatives to merger – joint ventures and other strategies', *Long Range Planning*, Vol. 20, No. 6 [December], pp. 78–83.

Hasan, I., K. Jackowicz, O. Kowalewski and L. Kozłowski (2017) 'Do local banking market structures matter for SME financing and performance? New evidence from an emerging economy', *Journal of Banking and Finance*, Vol. 79, pp. 142–158.

Haspeslagh, P., and D. Jemison (1991) *Managing Acquisitions: Creating Value Through Corporate Renewal* (The Free Press).

Hassan, M. K., and M. K. Lewis (eds) (2005) *Handbook of Islamic Banking* (Edward Elgar).

Hawkins, S. A., and R. Hastie (1990) 'Hindsight: Biased judgments of past events after the outcomes are known', *Cognitive Psychology*, Vol. 107, No. 3, pp. 311–327.

Healy, P., and G. Palepu (1988) 'Earnings information conveyed by dividend initiations and omissions', *Journal of Financial Economics*, Vol. 21, No. 2 [September], pp. 149–175.

Heaton, J. (2002) 'Managerial optimism and corporate finance', *Financial Management*, Vol. 31, pp. 33–45.

Hertz, D. B. (1964) 'Risk analysis in capital investment', *Harvard Business Review*, Vol. 42, No. 1 [January–February], pp. 95–106.

Hexter, O. (2007) 'Positive feeling', *Euromoney* [September], pp. 200–206.

Hirshleifer, D. (2001) 'Investor psychology and asset pricing', *Journal of Finance*, Vol. 56, No. 4, pp. 1533–1597.

Hirshleifer, J. (1958) 'On the theory of optimal investment decision', *Journal of Political Economy*, Vol. 66. No. 4 [August], pp. 329–352.

Hoberg, G., and S. K. Moon (2017) 'Offshore activities and financial vs operational hedging', *Journal of Financial Economics*, Vol. 125, No. 2, pp. 217–244.

Hochberg, Y. V., A. Ljunqvist and Y. Lu (2010) 'Networking as a barrier to entry and the competitive supply of venture capital', *Journal of Finance*, Vol. 65, pp. 829–859.

Hodgkinson, L. (1989) *Taxation and Corporate Investment* (CIMA).

Hopkin, P. (2012) *Fundamentals of Risk Management* (Kogan Page).

Hopkin, P. (2017) *Fundamentals of Risk Management: Understanding, Evaluating and Implementing Effective Risk Management*, 4th edn. (Kogan Page).

Horn, A., F. Kjærland, P. Molnar and B. W. Steen (2015) 'The use of real option theory in Scandinavia's largest companies', *International Review of Financial Analysis*, Vol. 41, pp. 74–81.

Horngren, C. T., A. Bhimani, G. Foster and S. M. Datar (1998) *Management and Cost Accounting* (Prentice Hall Europe).

Howells, P., and K. Bain (2007) *Financial Markets and Institutions* (FT Prentice Hall).

Huang, J., G. M. Mian and S. Sankaraguruswamy (2009) 'The value of combining the information content of analyst recommendations and target prices', *Journal of Financial Markets*, Vol. 12, No. 4, pp. 754–777.

Hull, J. C. (2015) *Risk Management and Financial Institutions*, 4th edn. (Wiley).

Hull, J. C. (2017) *Options, Futures, and Other Derivatives*, 10th edn. (Pearson).

Hunt, J., J. Grumber, S. Lees and P. Vivien (1987) *Acquisition – the Human Factors* (London Business School and Egon Zehnder Associates).

ICAEW (1989) *Accounting for Brands*, P. Barwise, C. Higson, A. Likierman and P. Marsh (Institute of Chartered Accountants in England and Wales, London Business School).

Iqbal, Z. (1999) 'Financial engineering in Islamic finance', *Thunderbird International Business Review*, Vol. 41, No. 4–5 [July–October], pp. 541–560.

Irwin, D., and J. M. Scott (2010) 'Barriers faced by SMEs in raising bank finance', *International Journal of Entrepreneurial Behaviour & Research*, Vol. 16, pp. 245–259.

Jacobson, Tor., and Erik von Schedvin (2015) 'Trade Credit and the Propagation of Corporate Failure: An Empirical Analysis', *Econometrica*, Vol. 83, No. 4, pp. 1315–1371.

Jarvis, R., J. Collis and P. Bainbridge (2000) 'The finance leasing market in the 1990s: A chronological review', Association of Certified and Corporate Accountants Occasional Paper No. 28.

Jenkinson, T., and H. Jones (2009) 'IPO pricing and allocation: a survey of the views of institutional investors', *The Review of Financial Studies*, Vol. 22, pp. 1477–1504.

Jensen, M. C. (1978). 'Some anomalous evidence regarding market efficiency', *Journal of Financial Economics*, Vol. 6, Nos. 2–3, pp. 95–101.

Jensen, M. C. (1984) 'Takeovers: Folklore and science', *Harvard Business Review*, Vol. 62, No. 6 [November–December], pp. 109–121.

Jensen, M. C. (2001) 'Value maximisation, stakeholder theory, and the corporate objective function', *Journal of Applied Corporate Finance*, Vol. 14 [Fall], p. 8.

Jensen, M. C., and W. H. Meckling (1976) 'Theory of the firm: Managerial behaviour, agency costs and ownership structure', *Journal of Financial Economics*, Vol. 3, No. 4 [October], pp. 305–360.

Jensen, M. C., and W. H. Meckling (1994) 'The nature of man', *Journal of Applied Corporate Finance*, Vol. 7, No. 2 [Summer], pp. 4–19.

Jensen, M. C., and R. S. Ruback (1983) 'The market for corporate control: The scientific evidence', *Journal of Financial Economics*, Vol. 11, No. 1–4 [April], pp. 5–50.

Jiang, Z., K. A. Kim, E. Lie, and S. Yang (2013) 'Share repurchases, catering, and dividend substitution', *Journal of Corporate Finance*, Vol. 21, pp. 36–50.

Johanson, J., and F. Wiedersheim-Paul (1975) 'The internationalisation of the firm – four Swedish cases', *Journal of Management Studies*, Vol. 12, No. 3 [October], pp. 305–323.

Johnson, D. T., T. Kochanek and J. Alexander (2007) 'The equity premium puzzle: A new look', *Journal of the Academy of Finance*, Vol. 5, No. 1, pp. 61–71.

Jones, C. S. (1982) *Successful Management of Acquisitions* (Derek Beattie Publishing).

Jones, C. S. (1983) *The Control of Acquired Companies* (Chartered Institute of Cost and Management Accountants).

Jones, C. S. (1986) 'Integrating acquired companies', *Management Accounting*, April.

JPMorgan/Cazenove Ltd (2008) European Listed Private Equity Bulletin.

Junankar, S. (1994) 'Realistic returns: How do manufacturers assess new investment?', Confederation of British Industry, July.

Jupe, R. E., and B. A. Rutherford (1997) 'The disclosure of "free cash flow" in published financial statements: A research note', *British Accounting Review*, Vol. 29, No. 3 [September], pp. 231–243.

Kahneman, D. (2012) *Thinking Fast and Slow* (Penguin).

Kahneman, D., and A. Tversky (1979) 'Prospect theory: an analysis of decisions under risk', *Econometrica*, Vol. 47 [March], pp. 263–291.

Kahneman, D., and A. Tversky (1982) *Judgement under Uncertainty: Heuristics and Biases* (Cambridge University Press).

Kanodia, C., R. Bushman and J. Dickart (1989) 'Escalation errors and the sunk cost effect: An explanation based on reputation and information asymmetries', *Journal of Accounting Research*, Vol. 27, No. 1 [Spring], pp. 59–77.

Kaplan, R. S. (1986) 'Must CIM be justified by faith alone?', *Harvard Business Review*, Vol. 64, No. 2 [March–April], pp. 87–97.

Kaplan, S. N., and J. Lerner (2010) 'It ain't broke: The past, present, and future of Venture Capital', *Journal of Applied Corporate Finance*, Vol. 22, pp. 36–47.

Kaplanis, E. (1997) 'Benefits and costs of international portfolio investments' in *Financial Times Mastering Finance* (FT/Pitman Publishing, London).

Keane, S. (1974) 'Dividends and the resolution of uncertainty', *Journal of Business Finance and Accountancy*, Vol. 1, No. 3 [September], pp. 389–393.

Keane, S. M. (1983) *Stock Market Efficiency: Theory, Evidence, Implications* (Philip Allan).

Kerr, H. S., and R. J. Fuller (1981) 'Estimating the divisional cost of capital: An analysis of the pure-play technique', *Journal of Finance*, Vol. 36, No. 5 [December], pp. 997–1009.

Kester, W. C. (1984) 'Today's options for tomorrow's growth', *Harvard Business Review*, Vol. 62, No. 2 [March–April], pp. 153–160.

Kim, K., S. Patro and R. Pereira (2017) 'Option incentives, leverage, and risk-taking', *Journal of Corporate Finance*, Vol. 43, pp. 1–18.

Kindleberger, C. P. (1978) *International Economics* (Irwin).

King, M. R. (2009) 'The cost of equity for global banks: A CAPM perspective from 1990 to 2009', *BIS Quarterly Review*, September, pp. 59–73.

King, P. (1975) 'Is the emphasis of capital budgeting misplaced?', *Journal of Business Finance and Accounting*, Vol. 2, No. 1 [Spring], pp. 69–82.

Kirilenko, A., A. S. Kyle, M. Samadi and T. Tuzun (2017) 'The flash crash: High frequency trading in an electronic market', *Journal of Finance*, Vol. 72, No. 3, pp. 967–998.

Klemm, M., S. Sanderson and G. Luffman (1991) 'Mission statements: Selling corporate values to employees', *Long-Range Planning*, Vol. 24, No. 3 [June], pp. 73–78.

Klieman, R. (1999) 'Some new evidence on EVA companies', *Journal of Applied Corporate Finance*, Vol. 12, No. 2 [Summer], pp. 80–91.

Koh, P. (2006) 'Leasing gives loans a run for their money', *Euromoney*, October, pp. 90–92.

Koller, T., M. Goedhart and D. Wessels (2015) *Valuation: Measuring and Managing the Value of Companies*, 6th edn. (Wiley).

Kotari, S. P., J. Shanken and R. G. Sloan (1995) 'Another look at the cross section of expected stock returns', *Journal of Finance*, Vol. 50, No. 1, pp. 185–224.

KPMG (1999) Global *M&A survey* (KPMG Group, London).

KPMG (2007) *The Determinants of M&A Success; What Factors Contribute to Deal Success?* (KPMG Group, London).

KPMG (2010) *The Determinants of M&A Success: What Factors Contribute to Deal Success?* (KPMG Group, London).

Kumar, P., and K. Sivaramakrishnan (2008) 'Who monitors the monitor? The effect of board independence on executive eompensation and firm value', *The Review of Financial Studies*, Vol. 21, No. 3, pp. 1371–1401.

Lam, J. (2014) *Enterprise Risk Management* (Wiley).

Lam, J. (2017) *Implementing Enterprise Risk Management: From Methods to Applications* (Wiley).

Lambert, R. A., and D. F. Larcker (1985) 'Executive compensation, corporate decision-making and shareholder wealth: A review of the evidence', *Midland Corporate Finance Journal*, Vol. 2 [Winter], pp. 6–22.

Larcker, D. F. (1983) 'Association between performance plan adoption and capital investment', *Journal of Accounting and Economics*, Vol. 5, No. 1 [April], pp. 3–30.

Lee, E., M. Walker and H. Christensen (2006) *The Cost of Capital in Europe* (Certified Accountants Educational Trust).

Lees, S. (1992) 'Auditing mergers and acquisitions – *Caveat Emptor*', *Managerial Auditing Journal*, Vol. 7, No. 4, pp. 6–11.

Lemon, M. L., M. R. Roberts and J. F. Zender (2008) 'Back to the beginning: Persistence and the cross-section of corporate capital structure', *Journal of Finance*, Vol. 63, pp. 1575–1608.

Lerner, J. (2008) *The Global Economic Impact of Private Equity Report 2008, Globalization of Alternative Investments*, Volume 1 (World Economic Forum).

Lessard, D. (1985) 'Evaluating foreign projects: An adjusted present value approach', in D. Lessard (ed.) *International Financial Management* (Wiley).

Lessard, D. R., and J. B. Lightstone (2006) 'Operating exposure', in J. Rutherford, M. Upton and D. Kodwani, *Financial Strategy* (John Wiley & Sons).

Levich, R. M. (1989) 'Is the foreign exchange market efficient?', *Oxford Review of Economic Policy*, Vol. 5, No. 3, pp. 40–60.

Levinson, M. (2002) *Guide to Financial Markets*, 3rd edn. (London: Economist Books).

Levis, M. (1985) 'Are small firms big performers?', *The Investment Analyst*, No. 76 [April], pp. 21–27.

Levy, H. (2010) 'The CAPM is alive and well: A review and synthesis', *European Financial Management*, Vol. 16, pp. 43–71.

Levy, H. (2012) *The Capital Asset Pricing Model in the 21st Century: Analytical, Empirical, and Behavioral Perspectives* (Cambridge University Press).

Levy, H., and M. Sarnat (1994a) *Portfolio and Investment Selection: Theory and Practice* (Prentice Hall).

Levy, H., and M. Sarnat (1994b) *Capital Investment and Financial Decisions* (Prentice Hall).

Li, J., and I. Tsiakas (2017) 'Equity premium prediction: The role of economic and statistical constraints', *Journal of Financial Markets* (in press), DOI: https://doi.org/10.1016/j.finmar.2016.09.001.

Lim, K-P., and R. Brooks (2011) 'The evolution of stock market efficiency over time: A survey of the empirical literature', *Journal of Economic Surveys*, Vol. 25, No. 1, pp. 69–108.

Lim, S. (2006) 'Do investors integrate losses and segregate gains? Mental accounting and investor trading decisions', *Journal of Business*, Vol. 79, No. 5, pp. 2539–2573.

Limmack, R. J. (1991) 'Corporate mergers and shareholder wealth effects: 1977–1986', *Accounting and Business Research*, Vol. 21, No. 83 [Summer], pp. 239–251.

Lintner, J. (1956) 'The distribution of incomes of corporations among dividends, retained earnings and taxes', *American Economic Review*, Vol. 46 [May], pp. 97–113.

Liu, J., S. Akbar, SZA Shah, D. Zhang and D. Pang (2016) 'Market reaction to seasoned offerings in China', *Journal of Business Finance and Accounting*, Vol. 43, No. 5–6, pp. 597–653.

Liu, Y., H. Szewczyk and Z. Zantout (2008) 'Under-reaction to dividend reductions and omissions?', *Journal of Finance*, Vol. 63, pp. 987–1020.

Longin, F., and B. Solnik (2001) 'Extreme correlation of international equity markets', *Journal of Finance*, Vol. 56, No. 2, pp. 649–676.

Lorie, J. H., and L. J. Savage (1955) 'Three problems in capital rationing', *Journal of Business*, Vol. 28, No. 4 [October], pp. 229–239.

Luehrman, T. A. (1997a) 'What's it worth? A general manager's guide to valuation', *Harvard Business Review*, Vol. 75, No. 3 [May–June], pp. 132–142.

Luehrman, T. A. (1997b) 'Using APV: A better tool for valuing operations', *Harvard Business Review*, Vol. 75, No. 3 [May–June], pp. 145–154.

Madura, J. (2006) *International Financial Management* (West Publishing Co.).

Madura, J., and R. Fox (2017) *International Financial Management*, 4th edn. (Cengage Learning EMEA).

Madura, J., and A. M. Whyte (1990) 'Diversification benefits of direct foreign investment', *Management International Review*, Vol. 30, No. 1, pp. 73–85.

Maksimovic, V., and G. Philips (2008) 'The industry life cycle, acquisitions and investment: Does firm organization matter?', *Journal of Finance*, Vol. 63, pp. 673–708.

Manson, S., A. Stark and M. Thomas (1994) 'A cash flow analysis of the operational gains from takeovers', *ACCA Certified Research Report 35*.

Mao, J. C. T., and J. F. Helliwell (1969) 'Investment decisions under uncertainty: Theory and practice', *Journal of Finance*, Vol. 24, No. 2 [May], pp. 323–338.

Marais, D. (1982) 'Corporate financial strength', *Bank of England Quarterly Bulletin*, June.

Marino, A. M., and J. G. Matsusaka (2005) 'Decision processes, agency problems, and information: An economic analysis of capital budgeting procedures', *The Review of Financial Studies*, Vol. 18, No. 1, pp. 301–325.

Markowitz, H. M. (1952) 'Portfolio selection', *Journal of Finance*, Vol. 7, No. 1 [March], pp. 77–91.

Markowitz, H. M. (1991) 'Foundations of portfolio theory', *Journal of Finance*, Vol. 46, No. 2 [June], pp. 469–477.

Marosi, A., and N. Massoud (2008) '"You can enter but you cannot leave . . .": U.S. securities markets and foreign firms', *Journal of Finance*, Vol. 63, pp. 2477–2506.

Marsh, P. (1982) 'The choice between debt and equity: An empirical study', *Journal of Finance*, Vol. 37, No. 1 [March], pp. 121–144.

Marsh, P. (1990) *Short-termism on Trial* (International Fund Managers Association).

Martin, C., and H. Hesse (2010) 'Islamic banks and financial stability: An empirical analysis', *Journal of Financial Services Research*, Vol. 38, No. 2–3, pp. 95–113.

Mason, C. (2006) 'Informal sources of venture finance', in S. C. Parker (ed.) *The Life Cycle of Entrepreneurial Ventures* (Springer), pp. 259–299.

Mason, C., T. Botelho and R. Harrison (2016) 'The transformation of the business angel market: empirical evidence and research implications', *Venture Capital: An International Journal of Entrepreneurial Finance*, Vol. 18, No. 4, pp. 321–344.

Mason, C., and R. Harrison (2002) 'Is it worth it? The rates of return from informal venture capital investments', *Journal of Business Venturing*, Vol. 17, No. 3 [May], pp. 211–236.

Mason, C., and R. Harrison (2004) 'Improving access to early stage venture capital in regional economies', *Local Economy*, Vol. 19, No. 2, pp. 159–173.

Mason, C., and R. Harrison (2010) 'Annual report on the business angel market in the United Kingdom: 2008/9', British Business Angels Association.

Mason, C., and R. Harrison (2015) 'Business angel investment activity in the financial crisis: UK evidence and policy implications', *Environment and Planning C: Government and Policy*, Vol. 33, No. 1, pp. 43–60.

Mathur, I., and S. De (1989) 'A review of the theories of and evidence on returns related to mergers and takeovers', *Managerial Finance*, Vol. 15, No. 4, pp. 1–11.

McDaniel, W. R., D. E. McCarty and K. A. Jessell (1988) 'Discounted cash flow with explicit reinvestment rates: Tutorial and extension', *The Financial Review*, Vol. 23, No. 3 [August], pp. 369–385.

McDonald, R. L. (2012) *Derivatives Markets*, 3rd edn. (Pearson).

McGowan, C. B., and J. C. Francis (1991) 'Arbitrage pricing theory factors and their relationship to macro-economic variables', in C. F. Lee, T. J. Frecka and L. O. Scott (eds), *Advances in Quantitative Analysis of Finance and Accounting* (JAI Press).

McGrattan, E. R., and E. C. Prescott (2003) 'Average debt and equity returns: Puzzling?', *American Economic Review*, Vol. 93, No. 2 [May], pp. 392–397.

McIntyre, A. D., and N. J. Coulthurst (1985) 'Theory and practice in capital budgeting', *British Accounting Review*, Vol. 17, No. 2 [Autumn], pp. 24–70.

McNeil, A. J., R. Frey and P. Embrechts (2015) *Quantitative Risk Management: Concepts, Techniques and Tools* (Princeton University Press).

McRae, T. W. (1996) *International Business Finance* (John Wiley and Sons).

McSweeney, B. (2007) 'The pursuit of maximum shareholder value: vampire or Viagra?', *Accounting Forum*, Vol. 31, No. 4, pp. 325–331.

Meall, L. (2001) 'Dot.com dot.gone', *Accountancy*, Vol. 128, No. 1296 [August], p. 70.

Mehra, R., and E. C. Prescott (1985) 'The equity premium: A puzzle', *Journal of Monetary Economics*, Vol. 15, No. 2 [March], pp. 145–161.

Meric, I., L. W. Coopersmith, D. Wise and G. Meric (2002) 'Major stock market linkages in the 2000–2001 bear market', *Journal of Investing*, Vol. 11, No. 4 (Winter), pp. 55–62.

Merton, R. (1998) 'Applications of option pricing theory: Twenty five years later', *American Economic Review*, Vol. 88, No. 3 [June], pp. 323–349.

Miglo, A. (2016) *Capital Structure in the Modern World* (Palgrave Macmillan).

Miller, M. (1977) 'Debt and taxes', *American Economic Review*, Vol. 32, No. 2 [May], pp. 261–275.

Miller, M. (1986) 'Behavioural rationality in finance: The case of dividends', *Journal of Business*, Vol. 59 [October], pp. 451–468.

Miller, M. (1999) 'The history of finance: An eyewitness account', in J. M. Stern and D. Chew (2003) *The Revolution in Corporate Finance* (Blackwell Publishing).

Miller, M. (2000) 'The history of finance: An eyewitness account', *Journal of Applied Corporate Finance*, Vol. 13 [Summer], pp. 8–14.

Miller, M., and D. Orr (1966) 'A model of the demand for money by firms', *Quarterly Journal of Economics*, Vol. 80, No. 2 [August], pp. 413–435.

Miller, M. H. (1991) 'Leverage', *Journal of Finance*, Vol. 46, No. 2 [June], pp. 479–488.

Miller, M. H., and F. Modigliani (1961) 'Dividend policy, growth and the valuation of shares', *Journal of Business*, Vol. 34, No. 4 [October], pp. 411–433.

Mills, R. W. (1988) 'Capital budgeting techniques used in the UK and USA', *Management Accounting*, Vol. 61 [January], pp. 26–27.

Mintzberg, H. (1987) 'Crafting strategy', *Harvard Business Review*, Vol. 65, No. 4, pp. 66–75.

Modigliani, F., and M. Miller (1958) 'The cost of capital, corporation finance and the theory of investment', *American Economic Review*, Vol. 48, No. 3 [June], pp. 261–297.

Modigliani, F., and M. H. Miller (1963) 'Corporate income taxes and the cost of capital: A correction', *American Economic Review*, Vol. 53, No. 3 [June], pp. 433–443.

Mollah, S., M. K, Hassan, O. A. Farooque and A. Mobarek (2017) 'The governance, risk-taking, and performance of Islamic banks', *Journal of Financial Services Research*, Vol. 51, No. 2, pp. 195–219.

Morris, C. (2008) *Quantitative Approaches in Business Studies* (Pearson Education).

Mossin, J. (1966) 'Equilibrium in a capital assets market', *Econometrica*, Vol. 34, No. 4, pp. 768–783.

Mun, J. (2016) *Real Options Analysis: Tools and Techniques for Valuing Strategic Investments and Decisions with Integrated Risk Management and Advanced Quantitative Decision Analytics*, 3rd edn. (CreateSpace Independent Publishing Platform).

Murphy, J. (1989) *Brand Valuation: A True and Fair View* (Hutchinson).

Myers, S., and N. Majluf (1984) 'Corporate financing and decisions when firms have information that investors do not have', *Journal of Financial Economics*, Vol. 13, No. 2, pp. 187–221.

Myers, S. C. (1974) 'Interactions of corporate financing and investment decisions – Implications for capital budgeting', *Journal of Finance*, Vol. 29, No. 1 [March], pp. 1–25.

Myers, S. C. (1984) 'The capital structure puzzle', *Journal of Finance*, Vol. 39, No. 3 [July], pp. 575–592.

Myers, S. C., D. A. Dill and A. J. Bautista (1976) 'Valuation of lease contracts', *Journal of Finance*, Vol. 31, No. 3 [June], pp. 799–820.

Narayanaswamy, V. J. (1994) 'The debt equivalence of leases in the UK: An empirical investigation', *British Accounting Review*, Vol. 26, No. 1, pp. 337–351.

Nasona, J. M., and J. H. Rogers (2006) 'The present-value model of the current account has been rejected: Round up the usual suspects', *Journal of International Economics*, Vol. 68, No. 1, pp. 159–187.

Neale, B., A. Milsom, C. Hills and J. Sharples (1998) 'The hostile takeover process: A case study of Granada versus Forte', *European Management Journal*, Vol. 16, No. 2 [April], pp. 230–241.

Neale, C. W., and P. J. Buckley (1992) 'Differential British and US adoption rates of investment project post-completion auditing', *Journal of International Business Studies*, Vol. 23, No. 3 [Third Quarter], pp. 419–442.

Neale, C. W., and D. E. A. Holmes (1988) 'Post-completion audits: The costs and benefits', *Management Accounting*, Vol. 66, No. 3 [March], pp. 27–30.

Neale, C. W., and D. E. A. Holmes (1990) 'Post-auditing capital investment projects', *Long Range Planning*, Vol. 23, No. 4 [August], pp. 88–96.

Neale, C. W., and D. E. A. Holmes (1991) *Post-Completion Auditing* (Pitman).

Neumann, K., and J. Zimmermann (2000) 'Procedures for resource leveling and net present value problems in project scheduling with general temporal and resource constraints', *European Journal of Operational Research*, Vol. 127, No. 2, pp. 425–443.

Nofsinger, J. R. (2008) *The Psychology of Investing* (Pearson Prentice Hall).

Northcraft, G., and M. Neale (1987) 'Experts, amateurs and real estate: An anchoring perspective on property pricing decisions', *Organizational Behavior and Human Decision Processes*, Vol. 39, pp. 84–97.

O'Brien, J., and P. J. Szerszen (2017) 'An evaluation of bank measures for market risk before, during and after the financial crisis', *Journal of Banking and Finance*, Vol. 80, pp. 215–234.

Odier, P., and B. Solnik (1993) 'Lessons for international asset allocation', *Financial Analysts Journal*, Vol. 49, No. 2 [March–April], pp. 63–77.

Oehmke, M., and A. Zawadowski (2017) 'The Anatomy of the CDS Market', *The Review of Financial Studies*, Vol. 30, No. 1, pp. 80–119.

O'Shea, D. (1986) *Investing for Beginners* (Financial Times Business Information).

Otten, R., and D. Bams (2009) 'The performance of local versus foreign mutual fund managers', *European Financial Management*, Vol. 13, pp. 702–720.

Owen, G., J. Black and S. Arcot (2007) *From Local to Global – The Rise of the AIM* (London Stock Exchange Publications).

Owen (Baldock), R., and C. Mason (2017) 'The role of government co-investment funds in the supply of entrepreneurial finance: An assessment of the early operation of the UK Angel Co-investment Fund', *Environment and Planning C: Government and Policy*, 35, No. 3, pp. 434–456.

Payne, A. F. (1987) 'Approaching acquisitions strategically', *Journal of General Management*, Vol. 13, No. 2 [Winter], pp. 5–27.

Peacock, A., and G. Bannock (1991) *Corporate Takeovers and the Public Interest* (David Hume Institute).

Pearce, R., and S. Barnes (2006) *Raising Venture Capital* (Wiley).

Peel, M. J. (1995) 'The impact of corporate re-structuring: Mergers, divestments and MBOs', *Long Range Planning*, Vol. 28, No. 2 [April], pp. 92–101.

Peters, E. E. (1991) *Chaos and Order in the Capital Markets* (Wiley).

Peters, E. E. (1993) *Fractal Market Analysis* (Wiley).

Peters, L. (2016). *Real Options Illustrated* (Springer).

Peterson, P. P., and F. J. Fabozzi (2002) *Capital Budgeting: Theory and Practice* (Wiley).

Pettit, J. (2001) 'Is a share buyback right for your company?', *Harvard Business Review*, Vol. 79, No. 4 [October], pp. 141–147.

Pettit, R. R. (1972) 'Dividend announcements, security performance and capital market efficiency', *Journal of Finance*, Vol. 27, No. 5, pp. 993–1007.

Pike, R. (1996) 'A longitudinal survey on capital budgeting practices', *Journal of Business Finance and Accounting*, Vol. 23, No. 1 [January], pp. 79–92.

Pike, R., N. Cheng and L. Chadwick (1998) *Managing Trade Credit for Competitive Advantage* (CIMA).

Pike, R., J. Sharp and D. Price (1989) 'AMT investment in the larger UK firm', *International Journal of Operations and Production Management*, Vol. 9, No. 2, pp. 13–26.

Pike, R. H. (1982) *Capital Budgeting in the 1980s* (Chartered Institute of Management Accountants).

Pike, R. H. (1983) 'The capital budgeting behaviour and corporate characteristics of capital-constrained firms', *Journal of Business Finance and Accounting*, Vol. 10, No. 4 [Winter], pp. 663–671.

Pike, R. H. (1988) 'An empirical study of the adoption of sophisticated capital budgeting practices and decision-making effectiveness', *Accounting and Business Research*, Vol. 18, No. 2 [Autumn], pp. 341–351.

Pike, R. H., and S. M. Ho (1991) 'Risk analysis techniques in capital budgeting contexts', *Accounting and Business Research*, Vol. 21, No. 83, pp. 227–238.

Pike, R. H., and M. Wolfe (1988) *Capital Budgeting in the 1990s* (Chartered Institute of Management Accountants).

Piketty, T. (2014) *Capital in The Twenty-First Century* (Harvard University Press).

Pilbeam, K. (2010) *Finance and Financial Markets* (Palgrave MacMillan).

Pilbeam, K. (2013) *International Finance* (Palgrave Macmillan).

Pinches, G. (1982) 'Myopic capital budgeting and decision-making', *Financial Management*, Vol. 11, No. 3 [Autumn], pp. 6–19.

Pohlman, R. A., E. S. Santiago and F. L. Markel (1988) 'Cash flow estimation practices of larger firms', *Financial Management*, Vol. 17, No. 2 [Summer], pp. 71–79.

Pointon, J. (1980) 'Investment and risk: The effect of capital allowances', *Accounting and Business Research*, Vol. 10, No. 40 [Autumn].

Poon, S., and S. J. Taylor (1991) 'Macroeconomic factors and the UK stock market', *Journal of Business Finance and Accounting*, Vol. 18, No. 5 [September], pp. 619–636.

Porter, M. E. (1985) *Competitive Advantage* (Free Press).

Porter, M. E. (1987) 'From competitive advantage to corporate strategy', *Harvard Business Review*, Vol. 65, No. 3 [May–June], pp. 43–59.

Porter, M. E. (1992) 'Capital disadvantage – America's failing capital investment system', *Harvard Business Review*, Vol. 70, No. 4 [September–October], pp. 65–82.

Power, M. (2009) *Organized Uncertainty – Designing a World of Risk Management* (Oxford University Press).

Prasad, S. B. (1987) 'American and European investment motives in Ireland', *Management International Review* (Third quarter).

Prelec, D., and G. Loewenstein (1998) 'The red and the black: mental accounting of savings debt', *Marketing Science*, Vol. 17, No. 1, pp. 4–28.

Price, J., and S. K. Henderson (1988) *Currency and Interest Rate Swaps* (Butterworths).

Prindl, A. (1978) *Currency Management* (John Wiley).

Pritchett, P., D. Robinson and R. Clarkson (1997) *After the Merger* (McGraw-Hill).

Pruitt, S. W., and L. J. Gitman (1987) 'Capital budgeting forecast biases: Evidence from the Fortune 500', *Financial Management*, Vol. 16, No. 1 [Spring], pp. 46–51.

Quah, P., and S. Young (2005) 'Post-merger integration: A phases approach for cross-border M&As', *European Management Journal*, Vol. 23, No. 1, pp. 65–75.

Rajan, R., and L. Zingales (1995) 'What do we know about capital structure? Some evidence from international data', *Journal of Finance*, Vol. 11, No. 3, pp. 1421–1460.

Rankine, D., and P. Howson (2014) *Acquisition Essentials* (FT Publishing).

Rappaport, A. (1986) *Creating Shareholder Value: The New Standard for Business Performance* (Macmillan).

Rappaport, A. (1987) 'Stock market signals to managers', *Harvard Business Review*, Vol. 65, No. 6 [November–December], pp. 57–62.

Redhead, K. (1990) *Introduction to Financial Futures and Options* (Woodhead-Faulkner).

Redhead, K. (2008) *Personal Finance and Investments – A Behavioural Finance Perspective* (Routledge).

Reimann, B. C. (1990) 'Why bother with risk-adjusted hurdle rates?', *Long Range Planning*, Vol. 23, No. 3 [June], pp. 57–65.

Risk Measurement Service, London Business School.

Ritter, J. (2006) 'Initial public offerings', in J. Rutterford, M. Upton and D. Kodwani (eds) *Financial Strategy*, 2nd edn. (Wiley).

Robbins, S., and R. Stobaugh (1973) 'The bent measuring stick for foreign subsidiaries', *Harvard Business Review*, Vol. 51, No. 5 [September–October], pp. 80–88.

Rodriguez, R. M. (1981) 'Corporate exchange risk management: Theme and aberrations', *Journal of Finance*, Vol. 36, No. 2 [May], pp. 427–444.

Roll, R. (1977) 'A critique of the asset pricing theory's tests; Part I: On past and potential testability of the theory', *Journal of Financial Economics*, Vol. 4, No. 2 [March], pp. 129–176.

Ross, S., R. Westerfield and J. Jaffe (2002) *Fundamentals of Corporate Finance* (McGraw-Hill).

Ross, S., R. Westerfield, J. Jaffe and B. Jordan (2015) *Corporate Finance*, 11th edn. (McGraw-Hill).

Ross, S., R. Westerfield and B. Jordan (2010) *Corporate Finance Fundamentals*, 9th edn. (McGraw-Hill).

Ross, S. A. (1976) 'The arbitrage theory of capital asset pricing', *Journal of Economic Theory*, Vol. 13, No. 3, pp. 341–360.

Ross, S. A. (1977) 'The determination of financial structure: The incentive signalling approach', *Bell Journal of Economics*, Vol. 8, No. 1 [Spring], pp. 23–40.

Rossi, S., and P. F. Volpin (2004) 'Cross-country determinants of mergers and acquisitions', *Journal of Financial Economics*, Vol. 74, No. 2, pp. 277–304.

Ruback, R. S. (1988) 'An overview of takeover defenses', in A. J. Auerbach (ed.), *Mergers and Acquisitions* (University of Chicago Press).

Rubinstein, M. (2002) 'Markowitz's "portfolio selection": A fifty-year retrospective', *Journal of Finance*, Vol. 57, No. 3, pp. 1041–1045.

Rugman, A., and S. Collinson (2012) *International Business* (Pearson).

Rutterford, J. (1992) *Handbook of UK Corporate Finance* (Butterworths).

Rutterford, J. M., M. Upton and D. Kodwani (2006) *Financial Strategy: Adding Stakeholder Value* (John Wiley & Sons).

Salinas, G. (2015) *The International Brand Valuation Manual: A Complete Overview and Analysis of Brand Valuation Techniques, Methodologies and Applications* (John Wiley).

Sartoris, W., and N. Hill (1981) 'Evaluating credit policy alternatives: A present value framework', *Journal of Financial Research*, Vol. 4, No. 1 [Spring], pp. 81–89.

Saunders, A., and M. M. Cornett (2013) *Financial Institutions Management: A Risk Management Approach* (McGraw Hill).

Savor, P. G., and Q. Lu (2009) 'Do stock mergers create value for acquirers?', *Journal of Finance*, Vol. 63, pp. 1061–1097.

Schepens, G. (2016) 'Taxes and bank capital structure', *Journal of Financial Economics*, Vol. 120, No. 3, pp. 585–600.

Schmidt, B. (2015) 'Costs and benefits of friendly boards during mergers and acquisitions', *Journal of Financial Economics*, Vol. 117, No. 2, pp. 424–447.

Schmidt, K. M. (2017) 'Convertible Securities and Venture Capital Finance', *Journal of Finance*, Vol. 58, No. 3, pp. 1139–1166.

Seasholes, M. S., and N. Zhu (2010) 'Individual investors and local bias', *Journal of Finance*, Vol. 65, pp. 1987–2010.

Shahi, C., and S. Shaffer (2017) 'CAPM and the changing distribution of historical returns', *Applied Economics Letters*, Vol. 24, No. 9, pp. 639–642.

Shanken, J., R. Sloan and S. Kothari (1995) 'Another look at the cross-section of expected stock returns', *Journal of Finance*, Vol. 50, No. 1 [March], pp. 185–224.

Shao, L., C. C. Kwok and O. Guedhami (2010) 'National culture and dividend policy', *Journal of International Business Studies*, Vol. 41, pp. 1391–1414.

Shao, L. P. (1996) (ed.) 'Capital budgeting for the multinational enterprise', *Managerial Finance*, Vol. 22, No. 1.

Shapiro, A. C. (2004) *Capital Budgeting and Investment Analysis* (Pearson).

Shapiro, A. C. (2013) *Multinational Financial Management* (Wiley).

Sharpe, P., and T. Keelin (1998) 'How SmithKline Beecham makes better resource-allocation decisions', *Harvard Business Review*, Vol. 76, No. 3 [March–April], pp. 45–57.

Sharpe, W. (1981) *Investments* (Prentice Hall).

Sharpe, W. F. (1963) 'A simplified model for portfolio analysis', *Management Science*, Vol. 9, No. 2 [January], pp. 277–293.

Sharpe, W. F. (1964) 'Capital asset prices – A theory of market equilibrium under conditions of risk', *Journal of Finance*, Vol. 19, No. 3 [September], pp. 425–442.

Sharpe, W. F., G. J. Alexander and J. W. Bailey (1999) *Investments* (Prentice Hall).

Shefrin, H. (1999) *Beyond Greed and Fear: Understanding Behavioural Finance and the Psychology of Investing* (Harvard Business School Press).

Shefrin, H., and M. Statman (1985) 'The disposition to sell winners too early and ride losers too long: theory and evidence', *Journal of Finance*, Vol. 40, No. 3, pp. 777–790.

Short, T. (2000) 'Should foreign investors buy Polish shares?', in T. Kowalski and S. Letza (eds) *Financial Reform and Institutions* (Poznan University of Economics).

Smith, B. M. (2001) *Toward Rational Exuberance: The Evolution of the Modern Stock Market* (Farrar, Strauss & Giroux).

Smith, K. V. (1988) *Readings in Short-term Financial Management* (West Publishing).

Smith, S. C. (2017) 'Equity premium estimates from economic fundamentals under structural breaks', *International Review of Financial Analysis*, Vol. 52, pp. 49–61.

Solnik, B. H. (1974) 'Why not diversify internationally rather than domestically?', *Financial Analysts Journal*, Vol. 30, No. 4 [July–August], pp. 48–54.

Staw, B. M. (1976) 'Knee-deep in the Big Muddy: A study of escalating commitment to a chosen course of action', *Organisational Behaviour and Human Performance*, Vol. 16, No. 1 [June], pp. 27–44.

Staw, B. M. (1981) 'The escalation of commitment to a chosen course of action', *Academy of Management Review*, Vol. 6, No. 4 [October], pp. 577–587.

Staw, J., and S. Ross (1987) 'Knowing when to pull the plug', *Harvard Business Review*, Vol. 65, No. 2 [March–April], pp. 68–74.

Stoakes, C. (2013), *Know the City* (Christopher Stoakes Ltd).

Stonham, P. (1995) 'Reuter's share re-purchase', *European Management Journal*, Vol. 13, No. 1, pp. 99–109.

Stout, L. (2012) *The Shareholder Value Myth* (Berrett-Koehler).

Strong, N., and X. G. Xu (1997) 'Explaining the cross-section of UK expected stock returns', *British Accounting Review*, Vol. 29, No. 1 [March], pp. 1–23.

Sudarsanam, P., P. Holl and A. Salami (1996) 'Shareholder wealth gains in mergers: Effect of synergy and ownership structure', *Journal of Business Finance and Accounting*, Vol. 23, No. 5–6 [July], pp. 673–698.

Sudarsanam, P. S. (1995) *The Essence of Mergers and Acquisitions* (Prentice Hall).

Sudarsanam, S. (2010) *Creating Value Through Mergers and Acquisitions: The Challenges* (FT/Prentice Hall).

Sudek, R. (2006) 'Angel investment criteria', *Journal of Small Business Strategy*, Vol. 17, No. 2, pp. 89–103.

Swalm, R. O. (1966) 'Utility theory – insights into risk-taking', *Harvard Business Review*, Vol. 44, No. 6 [November–December], pp. 123–136.

Taffler, R. (1991) 'Z-scores: An approach to the recession', *Accountancy*, July.

Takeover Panel (2009) *Code for Takeovers and Mergers*, London.

Taylor, F. (2010) *Mastering Derivatives Markets: A Step-by-Step Guide to the Products, Applications and Risks* (FT Prentice Hall).

Thaler, R. H. (1999) 'Mental accounting matters', *Journal of Behavioral Decision Making*, Vol. 12, No. 3, pp. 183–206.

Thaler, R. H., and C. R. Sunstein (2009) *Nudge: Improving Decisions about Health, Wealth and Happiness* (Penguin).

Thomson Reuters Sukuk Perceptions & Forecast Study 2017.

Tobin, J. (1958) 'Liquidity preference as behaviour towards risk', *Review of Economic Studies*, Vol. 25 [February], pp. 65–86.

Todorov, G. K. (2017) 'Are International Portfolio Diversification Opportunities Decreasing? Evidence from Principal Component Analysis', *International Journal of Economics and Financial Issues*, Vol. 7, No. 3, pp. 639–661.

Tomkins, C. (1991) *Corporate Resource Allocation* (Basil Blackwell).

Tomkins, C. R., J. F. Lowe and E. J. Morgan (1979) *An Economic Analysis of the Financial Leasing Industry* (Saxon House).

Tong, X. Li., and M. R. A. Karim, and Q. Munir (2016) 'The determinants of leasing decisions: an empirical analysis from Chinese listed SMEs', *Managerial Finance*, Vol. 42, No. 8. pp. 763–780.

Travlos, N. G., L. Trigeorgis and N. Vafeas (2001) 'Shareholder Wealth Effects of Dividend Policy Changes in an Emerging Stock Market: The Case of Cyprus', *Multinational Finance Journal*, Vol. 5, No. 2, pp. 87–112.

Tversky, A., and D. Kahneman (1971) 'Belief in the law of small numbers', *Psychological Bulletin*, Vol. 76, No. 2, pp. 105–110.

UNCTAD (2017) *World Investment Report*, United Nations Conference on Trade and Development (www.unctad.org).

Vaga, T. (1990) 'The coherent market hypothesis', *Financial Analysts Journal*, Vol. 46, No. 6 [November–December], pp. 36–49.

Valdez, S., and P. Molyneux (2012) *An Introduction to Global Financial Markets* (Palgrave MacMillan).

Van Binsbergen, J. H., J. R. Graham and J. Yang (2010) 'The cost of debt', *Journal of Finance*, Vol. 65, pp. 2089–2136.

Van Horne, J. (1975) 'Corporate liquidity and bankruptcy costs', Research Paper 205, Stanford University.

Van Horne, J. (2001) *Financial Management and Policy* (Prentice Hall).

Vermaelen, T. (1981) 'Common stock repurchases and market signalling: An empirical study', *Journal of Financial Economics*, Vol. 9, No. 2, pp. 139–183.

Very, P. (2004) *Management of Mergers and Acquisitions* (Wiley).

Wallace, J. S. (2003) 'Value maximization and stakeholder theory: Compatible or not?', *Journal of Applied Corporate Finance*, Vol. 15 [Spring], pp. 120–127.

Walters, A. (1991) *Corporate Credit Analysis* (Euromoney Publications).

Wardlow, A. (1994) 'Investment appraisal criteria and the impact of low inflation', Bank of England *Quarterly Bulletin*, Vol. 34, No. 3 [August], pp. 250–254.

Warner, J. (1977) 'Bankruptcy costs: Some evidence', *Journal of Finance*, Vol. 32, No. 2, pp. 337–347.

Watts, R. (1973) 'The information content of dividends', *Journal of Business*, Vol. 46, No. 2 [April], pp. 191–211.

Wearing, R. T. (1989) 'Cash flow and the eurotunnel', *Accounting & Business Research*, Vol. 20, No. 77 [Winter], pp. 13–24.

Weaver, S. (1989) 'Divisional hurdle rates and the cost of capital', *Financial Management*, Vol. 18 [Spring], pp. 18–25.

Weaver, S. C., D. Peters, R. Cason and J. Daleiden (1989) 'Capital budgeting', *Financial Management*, Vol. 18, No. 1 [Spring], pp. 10–17.

Weingartner, H. (1977) 'Capital rationing: Authors in search of a plot', *Journal of Finance*, Vol. 32, No. 5 [December], pp. 1403–1431.

Weston, J. F., and T. E. Copeland (1992) *Managerial Finance* (Cassell).

Whitaker, S. C. (2012) *Merger and Acquisitions Integration Handbook* (Wiley).

Whittington, R., and L. L. Cailluet (2008) 'The crafts of strategy', *Long Range Planning*, Vol. 41, No. 3, pp. 241–247.

Wilkie, A. D. (1994) 'The risk premium on ordinary shares', Institute of Actuaries and Faculty of Actuaries, November.

Wilkinson, N. (2008) *An Introduction to Behavioral Economics* (Palgrave Macmillan).

Wilkinson, N., and M. Klaes (2012) *An Introduction to Behavioural Economics* (Palgrave Macmillan).

Wilson Committee (1980) 'Report of the committee to review the functioning of financial institutions', Cmnd. 7937, HMSO.

Wilson, M. (1990) (ed.) 'Capital budgeting for foreign direct investments', *Managerial Finance*, Vol. 16, No. 2.

Wood, A. (2006) 'Death of the dividend?', in J. Rutterford, M. Upton and D. Kodwani (eds) *Financial Strategy* (Wiley).

Wright, M., and K. Robbie (1991) 'Corporate restructuring, buy-outs and managerial equity: The European dimension', *Journal of Applied Corporate Finance*, Vol. 3, No. 4 [Winter], pp. 47–58.

Xie, E., K. S. Reddy and J. Liang (2017) 'Country-specific determinants of cross-border mergers and acquisitions: A comprehensive review and future research directions', *Journal of World Business*, Vol. 52, No. 2, pp. 127–183.

Young, D. (1997) 'Economic value added: A primer for European managers', *European Management Journal*, Vol. 15, No. 4 [August].

Young, D., and B. Sutcliffe (1990) 'Value gaps – Who is right? The raiders, the market or the manager?', *Long Range Planning*, Vol. 23, No. 4 [August], pp. 20–34.

Young, S., and S. O'Byrne (2001) *EVA and Value-Based Management: A Practical Guide to Implementation* (McGraw-Hill).

Zenner, M., M. Matthews, J. Marks and N. Mago (2008) 'The era of cross-border M&A: How current market dynamics are changing the M&A landscape', *Journal of Applied Corporate Finance*, Vol. 20, pp. 84–96.

3i (Investors in Industry) 254, 379

ABACUS 103, 143
abandonment options 76–78
ABC system of stock management 523
ABS (asset-backed securities) 523
absolute purchasing power parity (APPP) 397
acceptance credits 523
accepting houses 5, 523
Access 374
accounting
  conventions 361
  creative 15
  profits 233
accounting rate of return (ARR) 523
acid-test ratios 25, 533
Acker, D. 327
acquirees 523
acquirers 523
  acquisitions 5, 334–335. *See also* mergers; takeovers
  behavioural finance and 486
  conglomerate 358
  creation of value 340–343
  criteria 355–356
  integration sequence for 358–360
  post-merger integration 357–360
  reverse 343
  unrelated 358
active management 132–133
activity Betas 154–155, 312, 523
activity ratios 24
adjusted NAV 174, 523
adjusted present value (APV) 318–319, 321–322, 457–460, 523
administration 288, 523
advice, financial 4
agency
  costs 291, 523
  theory 468
agents, corporate managers for shareholders 468–469
aggressive Beta values 119, 120
aggressive stocks 523
agios, foreign exchange rates 401–402, 527
Aglionby, John 474
AIM (Alternative Investment Market) 9, 523
Air France 335

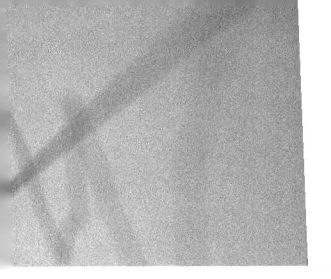

Airbus 448
airlines 68
Aked, M. 114
Akzo Nobel 140, 347
Albertson 335
Alcan 356
Alexander, G. J. 103
Alkaraan, F. 75
All-Share index 16
Alliance Boots 377, 378
Allianz 154
allocative efficiency 11, 523
Alternative Investment Market (AIM) 9, 11, 16, 19, 523
Amazon 179, 335, 431, 436
American Airlines 335
American options 205, 416, 523
amortisation 523
analysis of variance 118, 143–144, 523
anchoring 482
Andrade, G. 289
Andrews, G. S. 166
Anglo American 229–230
Angwin, D. 381
annual percentage rate (APR) 312, 523
annual writing-down allowances 523
annuities 36, 523
  present values 54
  valuation 41
Antill, N. 196
Apache 422
Apollo Tyres 360
Apple 47, 89–90, 93, 299, 317
APPP (absolute purchasing power parity) 397
APR (annual percentage rate) 35, 523
APT (Arbitrage Pricing Theory) 134, 136–137, 523
APV. *See* adjusted present value
arbitrage 7, 12, 301, 523
  currency risks and 401–402
  impediments to 305–306
Arbitrage Pricing Model (APM) 136–137, 473
Arbitrage Pricing Theory (APT) 134, 136–137, 474, 523
arbitrageurs 401, 523
Arcelor 369

Aretz, K. 424
ARR (accounting rate of return) 523
Arriva 336
Articles of Association 523
Arzac, E. 381
Asea Brown Boveri (ABB) 433
Ashton, D. 327
Asquith, P. 258
assessment of political and country risks 451–452
asset Betas 523
asset market approach to exchange rate forecasting 405
asset-backed securities (ABS) 523
asset-stripping 334, 340, 523
assets
  current (*see* current assets)
  fixed (*see* fixed assets)
  monetary 409
  non-monetary 408–409
  real 533
  restructuring 371
  turnover 24
  underlying 203, 535
  values 107
AstraZeneca (AZ) 179, 337
asymmetry of information. *See* information, asymmetry
Audi 410
audits
  post-completion (*see* post-completion auditing)
  resources 359
Authers, John 15, 31, 256, 478, 486
automatic finance. *See* trade credit
availability bias 482
Aviva 250

back-to-back loans 420, 523
backward vertical integration 340, 343
Bailey, J. 103
Baker, H. K. 79, 488
balance of payments (BOP) 405
balance sheets 19, 20, 172, 523
  foreign exchange translation exposure and 407–409
Ball, J. 19
Ball, R. 14, 19
balloon loan repayments 523
bancassurance 524
Bang, Nupur Pavan 101

Bank of England 10, 60, 250, 374, 379, 407, 420
  Monetary Policy Committee 530
Bank of International Settlements (BIS) 393, 415
Banking Reform Bill 5
bankruptcy 287
banks and banking
  bills 524
  clearing banks 4–5
    loans 524
  investment banks 5
  overseas banking 5–6
  retail banking 4–5, 533
  revolving credit facility (RCF) (revolvers) 533
  separation of retail and investment banking 5
  wholesale banks 5
Bannock, G. 361
Barber, B. 488
Barclay, M. J. 325
Barclays Capital 122–123
Barker, Alex 219
barter 524
Bartram, S. M. 424
Basel II and III Accords 5
BAT Industries 249
Becker, B. 258
Beenstock, M. 134, 136
behaviour
  corporate, understanding 468–472
  individual, understanding 467–468
  market, understanding 472–479
behavioural finance 466–467, 479–487
Behavioural Insights Team 484
behavioural studies 467
Belski, Brian 251
Benito, A. 258
Berk, J. 325
Berkowitz, Bruce 101
Berkshire Hathaway 256, 334
Bernatzi, S. 258
Betas 152, 153, 154, 473, 524
  activity 154–155, 312, 523
  analysis 75
  finding 125
  foreign direct investment 439
  geared 524
  key relationships 118
  measurement in practice 118–119
  Modigliani and Miller and 312–313
  proxy 533
  pyramid 155, 156

  security returns and 134
  segmental 156
  systematic risks 115–119
  'tailored' discount rates 154–158
  two-factor model 135
  ungeared 524
BG Group plc 289
Bharti Enterprises 436
Bhattacharya, M. 241, 258
biases, behavioural finance 481–483
bidding, overenthusiastic 369
Bierman, H. Jr. 80
Big Bang 9, 14
Big Mac Index 407
bilateral netting 411, 524
Bills of Exchange 416, 524
Bills of Lading 524
Bin, Xu 445
bird-in-the-hand fallacy 32, 241, 524
BIS (Bank of International Settlements) 393, 415
Black, F. 134, 142, 216, 223, 258, 470
Black-Scholes pricing model 216–217, 224
BlackBerry 475
Blas, Javier 433
Blitz, Roger 396, 402, 406
BMW 410, 444–445, 456
Boakes, K. 19
Bollen, B. 391
Bombardier 175
bond market 2
bonds 42, 44, 524
  in portfolios 114
  valuation 42–44
bonus issues 524
Boo.com 32
book-to-market ratios 524
boot-strapping 345
Boots 341, 377
Boston Consulting Group matrix 164, 524
BP 222, 266, 454
Bradley, M. 325
brand valuation 176–177
  brand contribution method 177–178
  by brand strength 178
  cost-based methods 177
  economic valuation methods 177–178
  market observation methods of 177
  role of NAV in 178
Branson, Sir Richard 60, 183
break-even sensitivity analysis 69–70
break-up values (BUV) 265, 524

breakout points 13
Brealey, R. A. 121, 142
Brennan, M. 223, 235, 258
Brightman, C. 114
British Airports Authority 336
British Airways 335
British Private Equity and Venture Capital Association (BVCA) 378
British Telecom (BT) 355
Brooks, R. 19
Brown, P. 14
Broyles, J. 162
BSA Machine Tools 413
BT 355
BTR 336
bubbles 476, 485
Buckland, Robert 251
Buckley, A. 424, 461
Buckley, P. J. 437
buffer stocks 534
Buffett, Warren 101, 196, 256, 334, 335, 370
building societies 6, 524
bullet loan repayments 524
Bullock, Nicole 170
Busaba Eathai 8
business angels 524
business fit and focus 375
business restructuring 371
business risks 63
buy-backs
  foreign investment projects 450, 524
  shares 250–253, 356–357, 534
buy-ins, management (MBI) 375, 530
buy-outs
  leveraged 357, 373
  management (see management buy-outs)
BVCA (British Private Equity and Venture Capital Association) 378

CAC 40 index 16
Cadbury 336–337, 338
call options 205, 206–208, 416, 524
  covered 210–211
  equity as 218–219
  loan stock, attached to 218
  put-call parity 211–212
  straddles 210
  valuation 211–216
Campbell, R. 114
cannibalisation 437

capital 524
  cost of (*see* cost of capital; weighted average cost of capital)
capital allowances 18, 524
capital asset pricing model (CAPM) 102, 107, 148, 153–154, 473, 524
  arbitrage pricing theory and 136–137
  assumptions of 127–128
  capital market line 128–130
  capital structure theory and 309–311
  criticisms 473
  international portfolio-diversification 112–114
  issues raised by 139–141
  key relationships 130–132
  merger impact assessment 361
  required return 152–154, 162–163
  assessment of 121–126
  reservations about 132–133
  risk and return 108–112, 301
  security market line 119
  security valuation and discount rates 107–108
  taxation 162–163
  testing of 133–134
  worked example 126–127
capital assets 524
capital gains 230
capital gains tax (CGT) 151, 162, 243–244, 347, 524
capital gearing 265–267, 524
capital growth 33–35
capital leases 524
capital market approach to merger impact assessment 361, 362
capital market line (CML) 128–130, 524
capital markets 2, 3, 534
capital rationing 524
Capital Requirements Directive (CRD) 5
capital structure 148, 524
  CAPM and 309–311
  decisions 291
  economic value added (EVA) 287
  financial distress (*see* financial distress)
  measures of gearing 265–269
  Modigliani and Miller theories (*see* Modigliani and Miller (MM) capital structure theories)
  operating and financial gearing 270–276

  optimal 470–472
  target structure 284, 535
  traditional theory 265, 535
  traditional view of gearing and required return 276–279
capitalisation 524
capitalisation rates 277, 524
CAPM. *See* capital asset pricing model
captive venture capital firms 525
carry trade 401, 402
carrying costs 525
cash flows
  foreign exchange transaction exposure and 394, 409–410
  foreign projects 450
  free (*see* free cash flows)
  multi-period 80–82
  perfectly-correlated 81–82
  present values 472
  remittable in foreign investment 438
  single-period 64–68
  valuation of 182–187
cash operating cycle 525
cash takeover offers 346, 347, 348. *See also entries beginning with* cash
Cavaglia, S. 114
CCA (current cost accounting) 175, 526
ceilings 13
central banks 406–407
certainty 60
certainty equivalence 72–73
CGT. *See* capital gains tax
Chan, K. 134, 136
chaos theory 477–479
Chapter 7 bankruptcy, USA 288
characteristics line (CL) 115, 525
charities, investment banks as portfolio managers 5
Charlotte Ransom 87
chartists 13, 405, 406, 525
Chazan, Guy 219
ChemChina 281
Chen, L. 138, 142
Cheque and Credit Clearing Company 4
Chesley, C. R. 165
Chicago Mercantile Exchange (CME) 3, 419, 420
Chilkoti, Avantika 360
China Aviation Industry Corporation 448
Chiou, W. P. 112
Chisholm, A. 424
Choudhry, T. 19
Citigroup 251

City North plc 346
CL (characteristics line) 115, 525
Clare, A. D. 136
classical tax system 18, 244, 525
clearing banks 4–5
clientèle effect 152, 241–242, 525
Cloverleaf 340
CMH (coherent market hypothesis) 479
CML (capital market line) 128–130, 524
CNOOC 455
co-movement 91, 525
co-variability 91–92, 97, 525
Coca-Cola 433, 453
Coefficient of Determination 135
coefficient of variation (CV) 66–67
Coffee Nation 158
coffee shops 158
coherent market hypothesis (CMH) 479
Colley, John 170
Collinson, S 461
Comcast 369
commercial paper 525
commodities in portfolios 114
company Betas. *See* activity Betas
company voluntary arrangements (CVA) 289–290
Compass Group plc 390, 412, 471
competition, foreign direct investment 430–431
Competition Commission 338
Competition and Markets Authority (CMA) 10, 338
competitive advantages 354, 434
compound interest 33–35, 525
computerised dealing, stock markets 14
concentration banking 525
concentric acquisition 525
concentric diversification 341
confirmation bias 483
conglomerate discounts 140
conglomerate takeovers 341, 525
constant dividend valuation model 54–55
consumption preferences 33
Continental 335
contingency crisis plans 453
contingent claim securities 214, 525
contingent value rights (CVR) 347
contra-cyclical returns 88, 525
contraction options 76
contribution 270–271, 525
control
  illusions of 483
  on mergers and acquisitions 359

convertible loan stock 218, 525
convertibles 347
Cooper Tire and Rubber 360
Copeland, T. E. 19, 99, 103, 142, 258, 325
corporate behaviour, understanding 468–472
corporate bonds 42–44, 525
corporate culture 370
corporate finance, options theory application to 218
corporate managers 15
   agents for shareholders 468–469
   behavioural finance and 485–487
   decision making 468
   risk aversion 468
corporate parenting 368–369
corporate restructuring. *See* restructuring
corporation tax 151
   Modigliani and Miller capital structure theories 306–309, 326
correlation
   coefficients 91–93, 112–114, 525
   degrees of 90, 95–96
   intermediate values 96
   negative 93–94
      perfect 90, 95–96
   positive, perfect 95, 96
corruption 452
Corus 336
Costa Coffee 157, 158
cost-based methods of brand valuation 177
cost-centre treasuries (CCT) 525
Costco 245–246
cost of capital 153, 189, 281–284. *See also* weighted average cost of capital
cost of debt 525
cost of equity 147, 148–149, 525
cost of equity capital 182
costs. *See also* opportunity costs
   agency 291, 523
   of debt 279–281
   financial distress 288–289, 525
   fixed 63
   reduction 4
   shortage 534
   sunk 468, 535
   variable 63
counter-trade 450, 525
counterparty risks 414, 525
country risks 450–454, 525
coupon rates of interest 42, 279, 525
covariance 91–93, 97, 98, 525
covered calls 211
covered interest arbitrage 401, 525

Cox, J. 223
creative accounting 15
credit
   ratings 294
   risks 414, 525
   trade (*see* trade credit)
Credit Suisse 256
creditors 288
   order of priority for payment 288
creeping expropriation 451
Crest 525
critical mass 341, 525
Crooks, Ed 422, 435
cross-border takeover activities 336, 337
cross-currency interest swaps 421, 526
cross-default clauses 455
'Crown Jewels' defence 357
culture, corporate 370
cum-dividend 229
currencies. *See* foreign currencies
current assets 20, 172, 526
current cost accounting (CCA) 175, 526
current information 12, 526
current ratios 25, 526
cut-off rate for new investment 305, 326
CV (coefficient of variation) 66–67
CVA (company voluntary arrangements) 289–290
CVC Capital Partners 380
CVR (contingent value rights) 347

Daniels, J. D. 461
Day, R. 121
days cash-on-hand ratios 526
DCF. *See* discounted cash flow
De, S. 363
Dean, J. 50
DeAngelo, H. 325
debentures 526
DeBondt, W. F. M. 482
debt
   capacity 526
   capital 264
   cost of 279–281
   finance 526
   restructuring use 376
   shareholder wealth and 291
   tax advantage of 308
debt/equity ratios 302, 304
debtor days 24
debtors 172, 176
   decision making. *See also* financial decisions
   corporate managers 468–469
   dividends 228–262

default 264, 526
defensive Beta values 119, 120
defensive stock 526
delay options 78, 535
Dell 47
Deloitte 181
DeLong, J. B. 166
Delphi techniques 452
Demarzo, P. 325
demutualisation 89
DePamphilis, D. 381
Department for Business, Innovation and Skills (BIS) 338
Department of Trade and Industry (DTI) 363
deposit-taking institutions 4–6
depreciation 175, 177, 184
deregulation of markets 14
derivatives 3, 203, 526. *See also* forward contracts; futures; hedging; options; swaps
Deutsche Bahn 336
Deutsche Bank 369–370, 471
DGM. *See* dividend growth model
Diageo 177, 252
diminishing marginal utility 61
Dimson, E. 121, 122, 123, 124, 154, 166, 256, 476
Dion, C. 365
direct costs 289
direct debits 526
direct investment 430, 526
Direct Line 254
direct quotes, foreign exchange rates 391
directors' dealings 526
disclosures 526
discount houses 5, 526
discounted cash flow (DCF) 31, 171, 526. *See also* internal rate of return; net present values; profitability, index
   framework 469
   usefulness 469
   in valuation 42, 184–187
   yield 529
discounted payback 526
discounting 35–38, 526
discounts 43, 526
   forward 392
   rates 526
      components 107
      foreign direct investment 438–439
      growth rate exceeding 48–49
      on investment projects 125–126, 320

project 160
    required return and 125, 154–160, 163–164
    risk-adjusted 73–74
    sensitivity analysis 71
    'tailored' 154–160, 163–164
    tables 36–38
disintermediation 8, 526
Disney 369
dispersion of outcomes 64, 65
disposition effect 481
Dissanaike, G. 475
diversifiable risks 526
diversification 88, 468, 526
    concentric 341
    industry 114
    international portfolios 112–115
    need for 139–140
    portfolio theory (*see* portfolios)
    risk averse investors 111
    success judging 354
    by takeovers 343, 344
    theory 90
    unrelated 341
    worked example 97–99
divestments 372
dividend cover 26
dividend discount model. *See* dividend growth model
dividend growth model (DGM) 46–49, 148–152, 184, 234
    limitations 47–49
dividend per share (DPS) 26, 149, 247–248
dividend re-investment plans (DRIP) 250
dividend stream valuation 45
dividend valuation model (DVM) 45–49, 54–55, 230, 233, 526
dividends 22
    alternatives to cash 248–253
    clientele effect 241–242
    conclusions 255–257
    cuts in 234–238, 239, 471
    decisions 228–262
    external equity financing 239–240
    final 229
    foreign direct investment 438–439
    growth (*see* dividend growth model)
    home-made 240, 258–259, 529
    information content of 245–247
    interim 229
    irrelevance 234–236, 471, 526
        objections to 240–245
    legal considerations 232
    paying, taxation and 18

payout ratios 229
policies
    firm value and 232–240
    payment-plus-rights 231
    retention of earnings 231
    stable, case for 254
progressive policies 471
puzzle 253, 255–256
residual theory 238–239, 533
retention ratios 229, 233
scrip 249, 534
shareholders' reliance on 240
shareholders' risks 241
signalling effect 471
smoothing 245–247
special 229
strategic considerations 231
taxation impact 243–244
valuation (*see* dividend valuation model)
worked example 246–248
yields 17, 26, 526
    prospective 148
divisional hurdle rates 164–165
'diworsification' 112
Dixit, A. 223
Dobbs, R. 258
domestic firms, foreign exchange exposure 443, 444
dotcom boom 179
dotcom price bubble 485
double taxation agreements (DTA) 440, 526
doubles 210
Dow Jones Index 16
downside risks 65–66
Doyle, P. 336
DPS (dividend per share) 26, 149
Dresdner Bank 369–370
Driessen, J. 113
DRIP (dividend re-investment plans) 250
Drucker, P. F. 358
D.S. Smith plc 108, 109, 151, 172, 173, 174, 175, 181, 186, 268, 269, 298
Dubai Ports World 336
Duchin, R. 75
Dudley, Bob 222
due diligence 334, 352
Duff and Phelps 175
Dunning, J. H. 461
DVM. *See* dividend valuation model

EAA (equivalent annual annuity) 527
EADS 341

earnings before interest, tax, depreciation and amortisation (EBITDA) 22, 180–181, 186, 269, 527
earnings before interest and taxes (EBIT) 22, 526
earnings dilution 527
earnings per share (EPS) 25, 247, 527
    and takeovers 344–346
earnings stream, valuation of 178–180
earnings yields 54–55, 527
easyJet 158, 379
EBIT (earnings before interest and taxes) 22, 526
EBITDA. *See* earnings before interest, tax, depreciation and amortisation
EC Merger Regulation (ECMR) 338
ECGD (Export Credits Guarantee Department) 453
economic exposures 396, 445, 449
economic order quantities (EOQ) 527
economic policies 437
economic theory and currency risks 399–404
economic valuation methods of brands 177–178
economic value added (EVA) 194–195, 287, 323, 527
Economist, The 407, 424
efficient frontiers 94, 95, 478, 527
efficient market hypothesis (EMH) 12–13, 150, 171, 474–477, 527
    anomalies in 476–477
    chaos theory and 477–479
    criticisms of 475–476
    fundamental analysis and 13–15
    international 404
    semi-strong form 13, 14, 474, 534
    strong form 13, 14, 535
    technical analysis and 13–15
    weak form 12–13, 474, 536
efficient portfolios 473
Egon Zehnder Associates 358
EIS (Enterprise Investment Scheme) 527
Eiteman, D. K. 424
Elan 356
Elay, Jonathan 250
electronic funds transfers 527
Eley, Jonathan 356
Elizabeth Shaw 413
Elton, E. J. 142, 245
Emery, D. 258

EMH. *See* efficient market hypothesis
employee share options 203
enhanced scrip dividends (ESD) 249, 527
ENI 450
ENPV (expected net present value) 61
Enron 289
Enterprise Investment Scheme (EIS) 527
Enterprise and Regulatory Reform Act 2013 338
enterprise value 172, 300, 527
entrapment 487
entrepreneurial companies 527
entry strategies to foreign markets 434–437
E.ON 284, 323
EOQ. *See* economic order quantities
EPS. *See* earnings per share
equity 527
　as call options 218–219
　cost of 147, 148–149, 304, 525
equity Betas 126, 157–158, 527
equity capital 534
equity options 218
equity premiums 124
equity values 172, 527
equivalent annual annuity (EAA) 527
equivalent loans, lease evaluation 527
equivalent risk classes 527
ERM (exchange rate mechanism, European) 404
ESD (enhanced scrip dividends) 249, 527
EU. *See* European Union
Eu, Richard 96
Euro-currency market 2
Eurobond market 2
Eurobonds 527
Euromoney Country Risk Survey 451
Euronext 3, 11, 205
European exchange rate mechanism (ERM) 404
European Investment Bank 521
European options 205, 416, 527
European stock market 11
European Union 437
　Merger Regulation 338
　Takeover Directive 339
European Union stock markets 11
European utilities 174
Eurotunnel 292, 300

EVA (economic value added) 194–195, 287, 527
Evans, C. 486
ex-dividend (xd) 229, 527
exchange. *See* foreign currencies
exchange agios 401, 527
exchange controls 438
exchange rate mechanism, European (ERM) 404
exchange rates. *See* foreign currencies
exchange-traded options 205
executive share options 218
exercise prices 205, 220, 527
existing activities, mergers to reduce dependence on 343
expectations theory 52, 399–400, 527
expected net present value (ENPV) 61, 527
expected values 97
Export Credits Guarantee Department (ECGD) 453
exporting 434, 527
exporting firms, foreign exchange exposure 444
expropriation 451
external equity financing 239–240
external growth 354
external hedging techniques 414–422
externalisation 434, 527

Facebook 170, 187
factor models 134–136
factoring 415, 527
fair game 12, 527
Fama, Eugene 19, 122, 134, 135, 137, 138, 142, 258, 474, 484
FCA (Financial Conduct Authority) 9, 10, 528
FDI. *See* foreign direct investment
FEM (foreign exchange management) strategy 407–410
Fenton-O-Creevy, M. 483
Fernandez, P. 196
Ferranti 352
Ferrovial 336
final dividends 229
finance, raising and taxation 18
Finance Act (1981) 373
Finance Corporation for Industry 379
finance leases 527
financial advice 4, 5
financial characteristics approach to merger impact assessment 361

Financial Conduct Authority (FCA) 9, 10, 528
financial decisions
　financial environment 1–30
　present values and bond and share valuation 31–57
financial distress 287–291, 313–315, 527
　costs of 313, 525
financial environment 1–30
financial gearing 270–276, 527
financial institutions 4
financial intermediaries 4, 528
financial leverage 271, 528
financial management value gaps 369
financial managers 171
　financial markets 2–4, 528. *See also* efficient market hypothesis; *entries beginning with* market
　efficiency of 11–16
financial pages, reading 16–17
Financial Policy Committee (FPC) 10
financial political and country, risks 452–454
financial position, statements of. *See* balance sheets
financial ratios
　acid-test ratios 25
　activity ratios 24
　current ratios 25, 526
　debt/equity ratios 302, 304
　financial statement analysis 23–26
　financing ratios 24–26
　gearing ratios 25, 454–455
　liquidity ratios 24–26
　price:earnings (P:E) ratios (*see* price:earnings ratios)
　profitability ratios 23–24
financial risks 63
Financial Services Authority (FSA) 10
financial services sector 4–8
financial statement analysis 19–27
Financial Times 16, 17
financing ratios 24–26
Finnerty, J. 258
Firer, C. 166
firm Betas. *See* activity Betas
Fisher, I. 50
Fisher effect. *See* Open Fisher theory
Fisons 341
fixed assets 172
　intangible 20, 176
　investments, taxation and 18
　new investment in 191
　tangible 20, 535
　values based on historical cost 175

Index

fixed capital investment 189, 191
fixed charges 528
fixed costs 63
fixed interest bonds 42–44
fixed interest securities 346, 347
fixed/fixed swaps 421
fixed/floating swaps 421
flat yields 528
Flavin, T. J. 113, 114
floating charge creditors 288
floating charges 528
floating rate notes (FRN) 528
floors 13
flow-to-equity (FTE) 192
   geared firms valuation 321, 323
follow-on opportunities 78, 528
Forbes, W. 488
Ford 340, 432, 433, 456
forecast information 12
forecasting 64
foreign bonds 528
foreign currencies
   cocktail 456
   exchange exposures 443–447, 528
      economic 396, 445
      management 399–404
      transactions 393–394, 535
      translation 394–396, 535
   exchange management (FEM)
      strategy 407–410
   exchange rates
      agios 401, 527
      changes 396–398
      direct quotes 391
      forecasting 404–407
      foreign direct investment 437, 443–447
      forward 2, 392, 399, 401, 445, 528
      forward discounts 392
      forward premiums 392
      indirect quotes 391
      interest rate parity (IRP) 400–402, 403, 529
      management strategy 407–410
      outrights 392
      spot 2, 392, 401, 534
      spread 392, 534
      structure of 391–393
   futures contracts 419–422, 526
   information system 409
   options 218, 416–419, 526
   risks
      exchange rate forecasting 404–407
      exposure management 399–404
      external hedging 414–422
      foreign direct investment 435, 438–439, 460

foreign exchange exposure 393–396
foreign exchange management strategy 407–410
   insurance 453–454
   internal hedging 410–414
   swaps 415, 420–422, 526, 528
   switching 448, 526
   transaction exposures 393–394, 535
   translation exposures 394–396, 535
foreign direct investment (FDI) 430, 528
   adjusted present value 457–460
   assessment 456
   borrowing 455
   competition 430–431
   competitive advantages 434
   complexities of 437–438
   country risks 450–454
   currency cocktail 456
   discount rates 438–439
   dividends 438
   evaluation of 437–438, 440–443
   exchange controls 438
   factors in favour of 435–436
   financing of 454–456
   foreign exchange risks 443–447
   hedging foreign project risks 449–450
   interest on loans 438
   investment incentives 437
   management charges 438
   operating exposure 445–449
   political risks 450–454
   profits repatriation and 438
   risks 430
   royalties 438
   strategic significance 430–431
   taxation and 437, 440, 455
   transfer pricing 438
   weighted average cost of capital 457
   worked example 440–443
foreign exchange. *See* foreign currencies
foreign exchange market 2
foreign investment
   direct (*see* foreign direct investment)
   foreign exchange risks 443–447
   multinational corporations 431
   portfolio 430
foreign markets entry strategies 434–437
FOREX (foreign exchange). *See* foreign currencies

forfaiting 528
forward contracts 414, 528
forward discounts 392
forward exchange rates. *See* foreign currencies, exchange rates
forward markets 2, 392
forward options 414, 528
forward premiums 392
forward vertical integration 343
forward-forward swaps 415, 528
Fosback, N. 110
Fox, R. 343, 424
Foy, Henry 433
FPC (Financial Policy Committee) 10
franchising 435, 528
Francis, J. C. 136
Franks, J. 162, 363–364
free cash flows (FCF) 184–185, 233, 301, 528
French, Kenneth 122, 134, 135, 137–138, 142, 258
French, Sarah 389
Friedman, M. 127
FRN (floating rate notes) 528
FRS 10 'Goodwill and intangible assets' 177
Frykman, D. 196
FSA (Financial Services Authority) 10
FTE. *See* flow-to-equity
FTSE indices 16–17
   FTSE 350 16
   FTSE All-Share AIM 16
   FTSE Small Cap 16
full-payout leases 524
Fuller, R. J. 157
Fund houses 8
fundamental analysis 13–15, 528
   in exchange rate forecasting 404, 405
funding 528
future values 33
futures 3, 419–422, 528

GAAP (generally accepted accounting principles) 20, 175, 528
Galpin, T. J. 381
gamblers fallacy 482
Gateway 379
Gaughan, P. 381
GCV (going-concern value) 528
GDP (gross domestic product) 361
geared firms, valuation 321–324
   gearing 264, 528. *See also* leverage
   capital 265–267, 524
   effect on ROE 273–275
   financial 265, 270–276, 527

geared firms, valuation (*Continued*)
  home-made 303, 529
  income 265, 267, 529
  measures of 265–269
  operating (*see* operating gearing)
  project gearing factor (PGF) 159, 533
  ratios 25, 454–455
  traditional view of 276–279
  weighted average cost of capital and 291, 315–318
GEC 250, 355
Geely 410
Geest 379
General Electric 354, 456
general valuation model (GVM) 183, 528
generally accepted accounting principles (GAAP) 20, 175, 528
Gent, Chris 365
Genzyme 347
Ghosh, C. 246
Ghosn, Carlos 433
Gilovich, T. R. 482
Gitman, L. J. 165
Giugliano, Ferdinando 474
GKN 118, 119, 125–126, 135, 152
Glasenberg, Ivan 333
GlaxoSmithKline (GSK) 179
Glencore 267
Glencore Xstrata 333
global brand identity 433
global companies 444, 528. *See also* multinational corporations
Go Fly 379
Godrej Group 195
going-concern value (GCV) 528
golden handcuffs 188, 528
golden parachutes 357
goodwill 177, 361
Google 170, 256
Gordon, Michael 120
Gordon, Myron 241, 258
government loan guarantees 218
government stocks 42–44, 50, 121
Graham, B. 101, 180, 230
Graham, J. 122, 222
Grainger Trust plc 346
Grand Metropolitan Hotels 177
Grant, Jeremy 96
Grant, R. M. 381, 434, 461
Graphic Packaging 181
Greene King 340
Greene, W. H. 75
Gregoriu, G. 381
Gregory, Alan 345, 364, 365
Grene, Sophia 467
gross domestic product (GDP) 361

gross profit margins 23, 285
gross redemption yields 50, 528
growth
  dividends (*see* dividend growth model)
  drivers 361
  external 354
  internal 354
  mergers to restore impetus of 343
  rates 233
  sales 189
Gruber, M. 245
GSK (GlaxoSmithKline) 179
Gup, B. E. 166
Guthrie, G. 80, 223
GVM (general valuation model) 183, 528

Halifax Building Society 89
Hamada, R. S. 310
Hansen, Lars Peter 474
Hanson 336
Harford, Tim 299
Harley-Davidson 413
Harrington, D. R. 166
Harris, M. 325
Harris, R. S. 363
Harrison, Andy 158
Harrison, J. S. 355
Harry Winston Diamond Corporation 341–342
Harvey, C. R. 122, 222
Hass, J. E. 80
Hay Group 365
Healy, P. 258
Heaton, J. 483
hedge funds 7
hedging 3, 7, 209–210, 529
  currency risks and 389, 390–391
  external 414–422
  foreign project risks 449–450
  internal 410–414
  natural 448, 531
  with options 209
  value adding 472
  worked example 417–419
Helliwell, J. F. 80
herding 485
Herndon, M. 381
Hertz, D. B. 71
Hester, Stephen 228
heuristics, behavioural finance 481–483
highly-leveraged transactions (HLT) 289
Hill, Andrew 454
hindsight bias 482

Hinkley nuclear contract 219
hire purchase (HP) 529
historical cost, fixed asset values based on 175
historical information 12
HLT (highly-leveraged transactions) 289
Ho, S. M. 80
holders, options 205
Holmes, D. E. A. 487
home bias when building portfolios 112
home-made dividends 240, 258–259, 529
home-made gearing 303, 529
Hook, Leslie 176
Hopkin, P. 80
horizontal integration 340, 529
horizontal mergers 361
Horngren, C. T. 194
hostile bids, chronology of 339–340
hot hands 482
House Price Bubble 476, 485
Howson, P. 381
HP (hire purchase) 529
Hughes, LIyr 416
Hull, J. C. 80, 223
Hume, Neil 230, 253, 315, 333
Hunt, J. 358
Hunter, Michael 389
hurdle rates 164–165
hybrids 529

Iberia 335
ICAEW 178
ICI 347
IFRS. *See* International Financial Reporting Standards
IKEA 454
illusions of control 483
IMF (International Monetary Fund) 263, 269
impact assessment, mergers 360–368
impairment 175, 177
imperfect markets 471
importing firms, foreign exchange exposure 444
imputation systems 151, 244, 529
in-the-money, options 205, 206, 210
incentives, restructuring 376
income gearing 265, 267–268, 529
income statements. *See* profit and loss accounts
income tax 151
incremental hypothesis 529
incrementalism 468

independent venture capital companies 529
indirect quotes, exchange rates 392
individual behaviour, understanding 467–468
Industrial and Commercial Finance Corporation 379
industrial cooperation joint-ventures 375
industrial logic 341
industry diversification 114
inflation 33
information
  asymmetry 12, 245–247, 292, 468–469, 523, 529
  content 469, 529
  current 12
  dividends, content of 245–247
  efficiency 11, 532
  forecast 12
  historical 12
  published, using 17
  systems, currency 409
initial public offerings (IPO) 529
Innogy 172
inside knowledge 12, 14
insider dealing 12
insider trading 14, 529
insolvency 288, 300
  pre-pack 290
inspection visits 452
institutional investors 11
insurance
  portfolios 210
  as put options 218
insurance companies 5, 6, 529
insured schemes 6, 529
intangible assets 20, 176, 529
Intercontinental Exchange Group 205
interest
  agios 401, 529
  compound 33–35
  cover 25, 268, 529
  on loans, foreign direct investment 438–439
  rates 34
    calculations 41–42
    changes in 291
    coupon rates 42, 279, 525
    factors affecting 44
    options 218
    parity (IRP) 400–403, 443, 529
    risk-free 73
    term structure 44, 50–53, 535
  simple 33
  yields 529
interim dividends 229

intermediaries
  financial 4, 528
  offers 529
internal growth 354
internal hedging techniques 410–414
internal rate of return (IRR) 41, 529
  modified (MIRR) 530
  sensitivity analysis and 68–69
internalisation 433, 434, 436, 529
International Airlines Group 335, 456
international bonds 527
international EMH 404
international financial management 387
  foreign investment decisions 429–464
  managing currency risk 389–428
International Financial Reporting Standards (IFRS) 177
International Fisher Theory. See Open Fisher Theory
International Monetary Fund (IMF) 263, 269
international portfolio diversification 112–115
International Power 172
International Signal Corporation (ISC) 352
Internet bubble 476
intrinsic values, options 211
intrinsic worth of shares 13
Invensys 356
inventories
  economic order quantities 527
  stock-building 185
  stockouts 535
  valuation 176, 190
investment
  financing by dividend retention 234
  foreign (see foreign direct investment; foreign investment)
  incentives foreign direct investment 437
  insurance 453–454
  portfolios 5, 6–7
  risks (see risks)
investment banks 5
investment returns, UK and USA 123
investment trusts 5, 6–7
investor ratios 25
invoice discounting 415, 529
invoice finance 415
IPO (initial public offerings) 529

IRP (interest rate parity). See interest, rates
IRR. See internal rate of return
irrationality 483, 484
irredeemables 51, 279–280
irrevocable documentary letter of credit 529
Isosceles 379
Issuing Houses Association 5
issuing options 204–207
IT4Automation 389

Jacobs, R. 158
Jacoby, Stefan 410
Jayasekera, R. 19
JCB 432
Jensen, M. C. 344, 363, 381, 467, 475
JJB Sports 290
John Wood Group 354
Johnson, Luke 59
Johnson, Miles 180, 202
Johnson, D. T. 122
joint ventures 163–164, 354, 375–376, 436, 453, 529
joint-equity ventures 375
Jones, C. S. 358–360
Jordan, B. 50
Jorgensen, Jon 374–375
junk bonds 530
Jupe, R. E. 186

K-Mart 289
Kahneman, Daniel 467, 480, 482, 488
Kanodia, C. 487
Kaplan, S. N. 289
Kavanagh, Michael 164
Keane, S. 19, 241
Kenning Motor Group 362–363
Kerr, H. S. 157
Keynes, J. M. 476
King, M. R. 166
KKR 377
Klaes, M. 488
Klemm, M. 354
Klieman, R. 196
KLM 335
knowledge, inside 12, 14
Kofman, P. 114
Koh, Annie 96
Kohlberg Kravis Roberts 377
Koller, T. 196, 381
Kothari, S. P. 142
Kothari, Yaresh 360
KPMG 147, 365–366, 368, 381
Kraft 336–337, 338
Kuchler, Hannah 170

Laeven, L. 103, 113
lagging 412, 530
Laura Ashley 379
Law of One Price 12, 396–399, 423, 449, 530
law of small numbers, belief in 482
leading 412, 530
Lee, K. 196
Lees, S. 352, 358, 365
Lerner, J. 378
Lessard, D. R. 461
lessees 530
lessors 530
letters of credit (LOC) 530
  leverage 7. *See also* gearing
    financial 271
    operating 271
leveraged buy-outs 357, 373
Levis, M. 134
Levy, H. 103, 143
Lewin, Joel 236
liabilities
  long-term 265–266
  monetary 408
LIBOR. *See* London Interbank Offered Rate
licensing 354, 434, 435, 530
Lightstone, J. B. 461
Lim, K.-P. 19
Lim, S. 484
limited liability partnerships (LLP) 376
Limmack, R. J. 363–364
LinkedIn 187
Lintner, J. 153, 246, 258
liquid resources 233
liquidation 287–289
liquidity
  dividend policy and 248–253
  management of 530
  preference theory 52
  ratios 24–26
  transformation 4
listed companies 530. *See also* quoted companies
listing rules 9
Lloyds TSB 153
loan capital 526
loan guarantees as put options 218
loan stocks
  call options attached to 218
  convertible 218
loans
  back-to-back 420
  long-term, hedging 409
  short-term, hedging 409
  term 535
LOC (letters of credit) 530
local authority bonds 42

local intelligence 452
Loewenstein, G. 483
logistics, political and country risks 453
London Interbank Offered Rate (LIBOR) 121
London Stock Exchange 2, 9–11, 14
  history 9
  introductions 535
  option market 205
long positions, options 205, 207, 210
long-term borrowings 266
long-term liabilities 265–266
long-term loans, hedging 409
Longin, F. 113
longs 50
L'Oréal 195
Loro Piana 181
loss aversion bias 486
Luehrman, T. A. 325
Lundan, S. M. 461
LVMH 181
Lyceum Capital 375
Lynch, Peter 112

M&A (mergers and acquisitions). *See* acquisitions; mergers; takeovers
Mackenzie, Michael 44
McBeth, J. 134
McCorriston, S. 365
McDonald, R. L. 223
McDonald's 33, 453
McGowan, C. B. 136
McGrattan, E. R. 124
Mackenzie, Michael 44
McKinsey 154, 352, 369
McKinsey-General Electric portfolio matrix 530
McRae, T. W. 408
McReynolds, Malachy 413
Madura, J. 343, 424
Magin, K. 166
main list 530
Majeed, Abdul 360
Majluf, N. 325
Malaysia 96
management buy-ins (MBI) 375, 530
management buy-outs (MBO) 373, 530
management charges, foreign direct investment 438
managers 140. *See also* corporate managers; financial managers
Mannesmann 360, 365
Manson, S. 364
Mao, J. C. T. 80
Marakon Associates 154

marginal cost of capital (MCC) 283, 530
marginal efficiency of investment (MEI) 238, 530
margins, sales 189
market behaviour, understanding 472–479
market capitalisation 22, 530
market efficiency 11–16, 406, 484–485. *See also* efficient market hypothesis
market imperfections 241–242
market model 116–117, 530
market observation methods of brand valuation 177
market portfolios 110, 121–125, 129, 473, 530
market power 343
market prices 171
market regulation 10
market risks 63, 110
market segmentation theory 52–53
market-to-book ratios 473
marketing, political and country risks 452
Markowitz, H. M. 89, 103, 473
Marks & Spencer 17, 75, 210
Marsh, P. 19, 123, 154, 166, 256, 325, 476
Massoudi, Arash 342, 370, 429
Masulis, R. 325
matching 412, 530
  parallel 448, 532
  perfect 449
Mathur, I. 363
maturity, yields to 43, 50, 536
Mauboussin, Michael 190
Mayer, C. 364
MBI (management buy-ins) 375, 530
MBO. *See* management buy-outs
MCC (marginal cost of capital) 283
mean-variance model 473–474
mean-variance rule 67–68
Meckling, W. H. 467
mediums 51
Mehra, R. 122, 123, 124
MEI (marginal efficiency of investment) 238, 530
mental accounting 483–484
Mercedes-Benz 410
Mercer (consultancy) 364
mergers 5, 14, 335, 530. *See also* acquisitions; takeovers
  to fill gaps in product line 341–342
  horizontal 360
  impact assessment 360–368
  integration sequence for 358–360
  post-merger integration 357–360

Meric, G. 114
Meric, I. 114
Merton, R. 223
Metronet 175
Meyer, Gregory 210
mezzanine finance 530
Microsoft 47, 248, 256
Millennium and Copthorne 157
Miller, M. 230, 234, 265, 299, 300, 318, 325, 329, 330, 471
Milne, Richard 410
minimum risk portfolios 93, 98
MIRR (modified internal rate of return) 530
Mittal 369
MMO2 372
MNC. *See* multinational corporations
modern portfolio theory (MPT) 106, 478
modified internal rate of return (MIRR) 530
Modigliani, F. 230, 234, 265, 299, 300–309, 318, 325, 329, 330, 471
Modigliani and Miller (MM) capital structure theories 300–309, 530
   analytical framework 301
   assumptions 301–302
   corporate income tax 306–309
   personal taxation 326–327
   propositions 302–305, 325, 470
Molyneux, P. 19
Mondi 181
monetary assets 409
monetary liabilities 409
Monetary Policy Committee 531
money markets 2, 530
   cover 415–416, 530
money time-values of 32–33, 472, 535
Monte Carlo simulation 71, 530
Moody's 294
moral hazard 289, 530
Morris, C. 90, 116
Morrisons 17, 369
mortgage debentures 530
Moules, Jonathan 195
MPT (modern portfolio theory) 106, 478
Mullins, D. 258
multi-factor models 135
multi-period cash flows and risks 80–82
multilateral netting 411–412, 530
multinational corporations (MNC) 442, 531

advantages of 432–433
operating exposure management 447–449
Muscovy Company 9
Myers, S. C. 318, 325

naked options 207
NAL (net advantage of a lease) 531
Nasdaq OMX Europe 416
National Grid 118, 119
nationalisation 451
natural hedging 448, 531
natural matching 412, 531
NAV. *See* net asset value
Neale, C. W. 437, 487
Neale, M. 482
negative correlation. *See* correlation
negative returns 273
Nestlé 176
net advantage of a lease (NAL) 531
net asset value (NAV) 171, 172, 531
   problems with 175–177
   in valuation 177–178
net book values 20, 531
net current assets 20, 531
net debt 266, 531
net operating income (NOI) 273
net operating profit after tax (NOPAT) 287
net present values (NPV) 37, 531
   certainty equivalence 72–73
   expected (ENPV) 61
   post-tax 151–152
   pre-tax 151–152
   real options and 220–222
   risk-adjustment 73
   rule application 469
   sensitivity analysis and 68–69
net profit margins 23
net working capital 531
netting 411, 531
Netwealth 87
Neuhauser, K. 381
neutral stocks 531
new investment cut-off rate 305, 326
new issue markets 531
new markets 341
Newscorp 357
Nexen 455
Next plc 252
niche companies 531
Nikkei Index 16
Nintendo 390, 391
Nissan 292, 433, 436
Noble Group 314–315
Nofsinger, J. R. 488
Nokia 232
non-current assets. *See* fixed assets

non-monetary assets 408–409
non-recourse 531
NOPAT (net operating profit after tax) 287
Northcott, D. 75
Northcraft, G. 482
Northern Rock 4
Norwood, S. W. 166
notes (securities) 531
NPV. *See* net present values
Nudge Unit 484
'nudging' 484, 488
NYSE Euronext 11, 205

O-Byrne, S. 196
Obama, President Barack 436
objectives harmonisation on mergers and acquisitions 359
Oddbins 290
Odean, T. 488
Odier, P. 112
OEIC (open-ended investment companies) 7
offers for sale by prospectus 531
Office of Fair Trading (OFT) 338
offset 453, 531
Ofwat 164
OGF (operating gearing factor) 159, 531
Oilex 411–412
Oliver, Steve 59, 60
One Price, Law of. *See* Law of One Price
open account trading 531
Open Fisher theory 402–404, 409, 423, 424, 529
open-ended investment companies (OEIC) 7
operating efficiency 11, 531
operating exposure
   extent of 443–444
   management of 447–449
   measurement 445–447
operating gearing 159, 531
   business risks and 63–64
   factor (OGF) 159, 531
   financial gearing and 270–272
operating leases 531
operating leverage 271, 531
operating profits 22, 531
operating risks, foreign direct investment 437
operating strategies, political and country risks 453
OPIC (Overseas Private Investment Corporation) 453–454
opportunity costs 33, 468, 531
opportunity sets 94, 99, 531

optimal capital structure 264, 531
optimal portfolios 93, 94–95, 531
optimal working capital 470
options 5, 531
  abandonment 76–78, 531
  American 205, 416, 523
  call (see call options)
  capital investment 75–79, 218
  contraction 76
  contracts 205, 531
  corporate finance, application to 218
  currency 218, 416–417, 526
  definitions 203
  delay 78, 535
  equity 218
  European 205
  exchange-traded 205
  exchanges 3
  foreign currency 218, 416–417, 528
  forward 414, 528
  hedging with 209
  holders 205
  interest rate 218
  intrinsic values 211
  issuing 204–207
  long positions 205, 207, 210
  naked 207
  OTC 419
  premiums 205–206, 414
  pricing 211–218
  put (see put options)
  real (see real options)
  shares 203–211
  short positions 205, 210
  speculative use of 207–208
  strategic investment 78–79
  strategies 210–211
  terminology 205
  time-values 211
  timing 78, 535
  traded 205, 535
  traditional 205, 535
  values 469–470
  worked example 417–419
  writers 205, 416
ordinary shares risks of holding 109–110
organisational structures revision on mergers and acquisitions 360
OTC. See over-the-counter market
out of the money options 205, 206
outcomes, dispersion of 64
outrights 392
over-the-counter (OTC) market 10, 416, 532
overconfidence 483
overconfidence bias 486, 487

overdrafts 532
overoptimism bias 486
overreaction hypothesis 475
overseas banking 5
Overseas Private Investment Corporation (OPIC) 453–454
overtrading 532
Owen, G. J. 221
owner's equity 532

P&O 336
Pacman defence 357
Palepu, G. 258
Panel on Takeovers and Mergers. See Takeover Panel
Panopoulou, E. 113
parallel matching 448, 532
part-payout leases 532
participating preference shares 532
PAT (profit after tax) 22, 532
patents 434, 532
payback period (PB) 75, 532
payment-plus-rights dividend policies 231
Payne, A. F. 353
payout ratios, dividends 229
PBIT (profit before interest and tax) 271, 301
PBT (profit before tax) 271–272
PCT (profit centre treasuries) 532
P:E. See price:earnings ratios
Peacock, A. 361
pecking order theory 292
pension funds 5, 6, 532
PEP (Personal Equity Plans) 139
PepsiCo 341, 438
perfect matching 449
perfect negative correlation 90, 95–96
perfect positive correlation 95, 96
perfectly-correlated cash flows 81–83
perpetual warrant 532
perpetuities 51, 532
  present values 53–54
  valuation of 40
Perrigo 356
personal consumption, preferences 33
Personal Equity Plans (PEP) 139
personal taxation 326–327
Pessina, Stefano 377
Peters, E. 477
Pettit, J. 258
Pettit, R. R. 258
Pfizer 337
PGF (project gearing factor) 159, 533

Philadelphia Stock Exchange (PHLX) 416, 417
phoenix companies 290
PI (profitability index) 532
Pike, R. 75, 80
Piketty, Thomas 488
Pilbeam, K. 19, 424
Pindyck, R. 223
placing 532
plain vanilla debt 535
planning horizons 189
plans, contingency crisis 453
plans harmonisation on mergers and acquisitions 359
plant hire 532
Plessey 355
Pohlman, R. A. 165
poison pills 357, 532
Politi, James 437
political risks 450–454, 455, 536
pooling finance 4
Poon, S. 134
Porsche 444
Porter, M. E. 190, 354, 361
portfolios 5, 6–7, 11
  analysis
    principles of 89–90
    on project appraisal, reservations 101–102
    risk and return differing 93–95
  bonds in 114
  commodities in 114
  correlation (see correlation)
  diversification and 112–114, 473
  effect 88, 89–90, 532
  efficient 473
  foreign investment 430
  home bias when building 112, 113
  insurance 210
  international diversification 112–114
  investment 430, 532
  meaning 88, 532
  minimum risk 93, 98
  modern theory 478
  more than two components 99–101
  optimal 93, 94–95, 531
  property in 114
  risks 63, 473
    measurement 90–93
  selection 473
  theory 87–105
  worked example 97–99
positive correlation 95, 96
post-completion auditing 358, 532
post-merger implementation 370
post-tax net present values 151–152

PPP. *See* purchasing power parity
pre-emption rights 532
pre-investment negotiation, political and country risks 452–453
pre-pack insolvency 290
pre-tax net present values 151–152
preference shares 347, 532
preferential creditors 288
Prelec, D. 483
Premier Inns 158
premiums 43, 532
　equity 123
　forward 392
　options 205–206, 416
　risks (*see* risks)
　shares 534
Prescott, E. C. 122, 123, 124
present value interest factors for annuities (PVIFA) 36, 39
present value interest factors (PVIF) 36, 39, 523–524
present values (PV) 35–42, 472, 532
　formulae 53–54
Price, Colin 369
price:earnings (P:E) ratios 17, 26, 532
　constant dividend valuation model and 54–55
　meaning 179
　unquoted companies, valuation 187–188
price-to-earnings multiple 171, 178, 532
prices
　bubbles 485
　exercise 205, 527
　market 171
　projects 449
　shares (*see* shares)
　variation 413, 532
pricing
　Black-Scholes pricing model 216–217, 224
　efficiency 11, 532
　options 211–218
primary capital markets 3
principal 42, 532
principal-agent relationship 532
Prindl, A. 410
Pritzker, Penny 437
private equity 376–380
　advantages over public companies 378
　criticisms of 378
　funds 7
　rejoinders 378–379
private placing 532
privatisation 11, 14, 89, 139, 336
probability analysis 75

production, political and country risks 453
profit after tax (PAT) 22, 532
profit before interest and tax (PBIT) 271, 301
profit before tax (PBT) 271–272
profit centre treasuries (PCT) 532
profit and loss accounts 19, 22, 532
profit margins 23
profitability
　index (PI) 532
　ratios 23–24
profits repatriation, foreign direct investment 438
projects
　appraisal portfolio analysis in, reservations 101–102
　discount rates 160
　gearing factors (PGF) 159, 533
　prices 449
　risk factors 160, 533
property in portfolios 114
proprietorial companies 533
prospect theory 480–481
prospective earnings yields 527
prospectuses 533
protective put options 210
provisions 533
proxy Betas 533
Prudential Regulation Authority (PRA) 10
Pruitt, S. W. 165
public equity 379
Publicis 356
published information, using 17
purchasing power parity (PPP) 396–399, 403, 407, 408, 443, 533
pure play technique 157, 533
put options 205, 206, 209, 533
　insurance as 218
　loan guarantees as 218
　protective 210
　put-call parity 211–212
　straddles 210
PV. *See* present values
PVIF. *See* present value interest factors
PVIFA (present value interest factors for annuities) 36, 39

Qinetiq 373
quadratic programming 100
Quah, P. 381
quick assets ratio 25, 533
Quinn, Leo 373
quoted companies, initial public offerings 529

Rajan, R. 325
Ralph, Oliver 228
random walk theory 13, 15, 533
Rank-Hovis-McDougall 177
Rankine, D. 381
Rappaport, A. 19, 188, 190
Raviv, A. 325
RCF (revolving credit facility) (revolvers) 533
re-invoicing centres (RIC) 413–414
Readers Digest 300
real assets 533
real options 75–79, 218, 219–221, 469–470, 533
Really Useful Group 183
rebate clauses 533
receivership 288
Reckitt Benckizer 352
Record Days 229, 533
redeemable preference shares 374
redemption yields 533
Redhead, K. 488
regression analysis 116
regulation of markets 10
Rehm, W. 258
Reimann, B. C. 164, 165, 166
Relative Purchasing Power Parity (RPPP) 397
relevant risks 63, 533
REMM (resourceful, evaluative, maximising model) 467
Renault 292
repackaging finance 4
replacement chain approach 533
replacement cost 175, 533
replacement investment 191–194
reported earnings 233
reporting relationships 359
reputational risks 533
required return 147–169
　assessment of 121–126
　capital asset pricing model 152–154, 162–163
　corporation tax impact 308–309
　dividend growth model 148–152
　divisional hurdle rates 164–165
　'tailored' discount rates 154–160, 163–164
　traditional view of 276–279
　worked example 161–162
reserves 533. *See also* share premium accounts
residual income (RI) 533
residual theory of dividends 238, 533
resistance 13
resource audits 359

resourceful, evaluative, maximising model (REMM) 467–468
restrictive covenants 533
restructuring 5, 371–372
  assets 371
  business fit and focus 375
  businesses 371
  corporate 371–372
  debt use 376
  divestments 372
  incentives 376
  joint ventures 375–376
  management buy-outs 373–374
  strategic alliances 375–376
retail banking 4–5, 533
Retail Price Index (RPI) 136
retained earnings 533
retention of earnings dividend policies 231
retention ratios, dividends 229, 233
return on capital employed (ROCE) 533
return on equity (ROE) 25, 274
return from holding shares 108–109
return on shareholders' funds 25
return on total assets (ROTA) 24
revenue sensitivity 159, 533
revenue sensitivity factor (RSF) 159, 533
revocable documentary letter of credit 533
revolving credit facility (RCF) (revolvers) 533
RI (residual income) 533
RIC (re-invoicing centres) 413–414
rights issues 533–534
  dividends and 239, 240, 242–243
Rio Tinto 253, 267, 356
Risk Measurement Service (RMS) 118–119
risk neutral call option valuation method 215–216
risk-adjusted discount rate 73–74
risk-free assets 128–129, 534
risk-free rates 73, 121
risks
  analysis 74–75
  attitudes to 61–62
  aversion 61–62, 90, 111, 468
  country 450–454
  definition 60
  expected net present value (ENPV) 61
  financial gearing and 272–276
  foreign direct investment 430
  foreign projects, hedging 449–450
  handling methods 68
  management 487

treasuries (see treasuries)
measurement of 64–68
minimisation policies 410, 534
multi-period cash flows 80–82
operating, foreign direct investment 437
political 450–454, 455
premiums 73, 121–125, 534
reduction 4
reputational 533
return and
  concepts of 108–112
  differing 93–95
  security valuation 108–112
scenario analysis 71
sensitivity analysis 68–71, 75
sharing 413, 534
simulation analysis 71–72
stress testing 71
systematic (see systematic risks)
time-value of money and 32
types of 63–64
RMS (Risk Measurement Service) 118–119
Robbins, S. 437
ROCE (return on capital employed) 533
ROE (return on equity) 25, 274–275
Roll, R. 142, 475
Rolls Royce 236, 444, 448
Rosneft 222
Ross, S. 19, 50, 134, 136, 142, 291, 325, 475, 487
ROTA (return on total assets) 24
Rowan, Cheryl 251
Rowntree 176
royalties, foreign direct investment 438
RPI (Retail Price Index) 136
RPPP (Relative Purchasing Power Parity) 397
RSA 228
RSF (revenue sensitivity factor) 159, 533
Ruback, R. S. 363
Rubinstein, M. 103
Rugman, A. M. 461
Rutherford, B. A. 186
Rutterford, J. 258
RWE Ag 172, 174, 283

safety stocks 534
Safeway 335, 369
Sainsbury 125
Sakaldeepi, Khemchand 101
sales
  growth 189

margins 189
Salinas, G. 196
sample size neglect 482
Sang, Eu Yan 96
Sanofi 337, 347
Sarkamies, Sami 232
Sarnat, M. 103
scale economies 341, 534
scenario analysis 71
Schneider Electric 356
Scholes, M. 216, 223, 470
Scottish and Southern Energy plc 229
scrip alternative 249, 534
scrip dividends 249, 534
scrip issues 524
scrips 250
SD (special dividends) 229
SEAQ (Stock Exchange Automated Quotations) system 9, 17, 534
secondary capital markets 3
secondary leases 534
secured creditors 288
securities
  markets 2, 534
  valuation 107–108
    risk and return 108–112
    systematic risks 115–119
securitisation 8, 534
security market line (SML) 119, 152, 473, 534
segmental Betas 156
self-administered pension schemes 6, 534
self-attribution bias 483
self-fulfilling prophecies 13
sell-offs 371–372
semi-strong form of efficient market hypothesis 13, 14, 474, 534
semi-variance 65–66
sensitivity analysis 68–71, 534
  risks 74
Separation Theorem 129, 534
Serco 1
SETS (Stock Exchange Electronic Trading Service) 14
Shao, L. 258
Shapiro, A. C. 424, 461
share premium accounts 534
shareholders
  equity 20, 534
  funds 534
    capital gearing ratios 265–266
    return on 25
  taxation effects on 18
  shareholders value analysis (SVA) 188–190, 469, 534
shares

Index

bonus issues 524
buy-backs 250–253, 534
exchanges for financing takeovers 347
flotation 5
intrinsic worth 13
issues
  by tender 529
  underwriting 218
offers for sale by prospectus 531
options 203–211
ownership 11
preference 347, 532
prices 150
  reaction to news 16
  volatility 205
repurchases 250–253
scrip issues 524
splits 534
Stock Exchange, introductions 535
valuation 45–49, 486
warrants 218
Sharpe, W. E. 100, 103, 107, 153, 289, 473
Shastri, K. 99, 103
Shefrin, H. 481
Shell 71
Shellock, Dave 251
Shiller, Robert 474
short positions, options 205
short-selling 7, 534
short-term loans, hedging 409
short-termism 189
shortage costs 534
shorts 50
Sichuan Airlines 448
Siegel, Jeremy 478
Siemens 188, 355
sight drafts 534
signalling 245–247, 250–251, 291, 469, 471, 534
simple interest 33
simulation analysis 71–72
single farm payment (SFP) 416
single-period cash flows, risk measurement 64–68
Sirkin, Hal 435
Sirower, Mark 369
Skapinker, Michael 370
Skypala, Pauline 133
Slaughter, Matthew 437
small and medium-sized enterprises (SME), securitisation as source of funding 8
small numbers, law of, belief in 482
SME. *See* small and medium-sized enterprises
Smedley, Tim 375

Smith, Alison 248
Smith, C. W. 325
Smith, Terry 112
SML (security market line) 119, 120, 473, 534
Smolin, Lee 477
smoothing, dividends 245–247
Smurfit Kappa 181
Snapchat 170
social efficiency 11, 534
Social Stock Exchange 11
Société Générale 370
Soenen, L. 461
Solnik, B. 112, 113, 439
Sonoco 181
Sosyura, D. 75
South Sea Bubble 476
sovereign wealth funds (SWF) 336
special dividends (SD) 229
special purpose vehicles (SPV) 456, 534
specific risks 110, 140, 534
speculative bubbles 476
speculators 390, 534
spin-offs 371–372
spontaneous finance. *See* trade credit
spot exchange rates 404, 413
spot markets 2
  rates 404, 534
spot-forward swaps 415, 534
spread 404, 534
SPV (special purpose vehicles) 468, 534
SSE 229
Stacey, Kiran 174
Standard & Poor's 294
standard deviation 64–66, 109
statements of financial position. *See* balance sheets
Statman, M. 481
Staunton, M. 123, 154
Staunton, R. 256
Staw, J. 487
Stern Stewart 194–195
Stevenson, Alexandra 232
Stoakes, C. 19
Stobaugh, R. 437
Stock Exchange. *See* London Stock Exchange
Stock Exchange Automated Quotations (SEAQ) system 9, 17, 534
Stock Exchange Electronic Trading Service (SETS) 14
stock markets
  bubbles 476
  computerised dealing 14
  correlation coefficients 113–114
  deregulation 14

  efficiency 369
  listings, mergers to obtain 344
  surges 476
  volatility 113–114
stock splits 534
stock-building 185
stockholding periods 24
stockouts 534
stocks. *See* inventories; shares
straddles 210
straight debt 535
strategic alliances 375–376
strategic exposure 445, 531
strategic financial decisions
  acquisitions and restructuring 333–388
  capital structure
    does it really matter? 299–332
    required return and 263–298
  dividends 228–262
strategic investment options 78–79
strategic portfolio analysis 535
strategic windows 334
strategies options 209–210
Strauss, Delphine 416
stress testing 71
strike prices 205, 416
strong form of efficient market hypothesis 13, 14, 534
Strong, N. 134, 142
Sudarsanam, P. S. 364, 381
Sudarsanam, S. 334
sunk costs 468, 535
Sunstein, Cass 484, 488
supplier credit days 24
support 13
surges 476
Sutcliffe, B. 368
SVA (shareholder value analysis). *See* shareholders value analysis (SVA)
Swalm, R. O. 102, 165
swaps 5
  fixed/fixed 421
  fixed/floating 421
  foreign currency (*see* foreign currencies)
  forward-forward 415
  spot-forward 415
Swatch Group 341
SWF (sovereign wealth funds) 336
switching currencies 448, 526
SWOT analysis 354, 355
synergies 341, 535
systematic returns 117
systematic risks 110, 111, 115–119, 140, 535

'tailored' discount rates 154–160, 163–164
Takeover Code 338–339
Takeover Panel 10, 338–339, 535
takeovers 5, 14, 535
   acquisition criteria 355–356
   activities 335–340
   alternative bid terms 346–348
   bidding 356–357, 369
   cash offers 346, 347, 348
   defence tactics 356–357
   evaluation of bids 348–349
   failures 352, 358, 369–370
   gains expected from 348–349
   hostile bids 339–340
   managerial motives 344
   as market for management control 344
   motives for 340–346
   objectives 354
   regulation of 338–339
   strategies for 351–358
   worked example 349–351
tangible fixed assets 20, 535
target capital structure 283–284, 535
Tata Steel 336
tax breaks 535
tax credits. *See* imputation systems
tax shield 280, 307, 309, 535
taxation
   capital asset pricing model 162–163
   classical tax system 244, 525
   corporation tax (*see* corporation tax)
   dividend growth model and 151–152
   financial decisions and 18
   foreign direct investment and 437, 440, 454
   imputation systems 151, 244, 529
   income tax (*see* income tax)
   personal 326–327
   tax irrelevance thesis 244–245
   as value driver 189
Taylor, F. 424
Taylor, S. J. 134
technical analysis 13–15, 535
   exchange rate forecasting 404, 405
technical efficiency 11, 531
Telefonica 336
tenders, share issues by 529
term loans 535
term structure of interest rates 44, 50–53, 535
TERP (theoretical ex-rights price) 535
Terra Firma 377, 380

Tesco 17
Tett, Gillian 477
Textron 272
Thaler, R. 482, 483, 484, 488
Thames Water 172
theoretical ex-rights price (TERP) 535
Thomas, S. H. 136
Thompson, Jennifer 87
Three-factor model (Fama and French) 137–138
Tianjin Free Trade Zone 448
time-values
   of money 31, 32–33, 472, 535
   options 211
times interest earned 268, 535
timing effects 476
timing options 78, 535
tin parachutes 357
TNK 222
Tobin, J. 103, 365
Tolleryd, J. 196
total shareholder return (TSR) 108–109, 535
TotalFina Elf 450
Toyota 390
Tozer Kemsley Milbourn (TKM) 362–363
trade credit 535
trade-off theory 292
traded options 205, 535
traditional economic model of human behaviour 467
traditional options 205, 535
traditional theory of capital structure 265, 535
traditional view of gearing and required return 276–279
transaction exposures 393–394, 409–410, 535
transfer pricing 414, 432, 438, 535
translation exposures 394–396, 407–409, 535
Transparency International 452
Travelex 379
treasuries operations 535
Treasury Bills 121, 535
Treynor, J. 153
trust of market 139
TSR (total shareholder return) 108–109, 535
Tversky, A. 480, 482, 488
Twitter 170, 176, 187
two-factor model 135–136

Uber 176
UK Listing Authority (UKLA) 9
unbiased forward predictors 400, 527

uncertainty 60
uncovered arbitrage 402, 535
UNCTAD (United Nations Conference on Trade and Development) 442
undated stocks 51
underlying assets 203, 535
ungeared Betas. *See* activity Betas
unit trusts 4, 5, 535
United Airlines 335
United Nations Conference on Trade and Development (UNCTAD) 431
'unknown unknowns' 60, 68
unprofitable projects and strategies 487
unquoted companies valuation 188
unrelated acquisitions 358
unrelated diversification 341
unsecured creditors 288, 290
unsystematic returns 117
US Airways 335
utility 61–62

Vaga, T. 479
Valdez, S. 19
valuation 171
   annuities 41
   bonds 42–44
   brands (*see* brand valuation)
   call options 212–216
   cash flows 182–187
   constant dividend valuation model 54–55
   discounted cash flow in 42, 184–187
   dividend streams 45–46
   dividend valuation model (*see* dividend valuation model)
   earnings streams 178–180
   EBITDA 180–182
   free cash flow and 184–185
   geared firms 321–322
   general valuation model (GVM) 183
   inventories 191
   newly created company 182–183
   perpetuities 40
   problem 171–172
   published accounts, use of 172–178
   securities (*see* securities)
   shares 45–49, 486
   skills 171
   unquoted companies 187–188
   worked example 191–194
value additivity 340, 536
value creation 340–343, 371, 375–376

value drivers 190–191, 536
value gaps 368–370
value, risk and required returns 56
　analysing investment risks 59–86
　capital asset pricing model 106–142
　enterprise value and equity value 170–201
　identifying and valuing options 202–226
　portfolio theory 87–105
　required rate of return 147–169
value-based management 536
Van Binsbergen, J. H. 166
van Horne, J. 128, 289
variable costs 63
variance, analysis of 118, 143–144, 523
VCTs (venture capital trusts) 536
Vector Aerospace 341
vendor placing 536
venture capital 536
venture capital trusts (VCTs) 536
Verizon Wireless 248
Vermaelen, T. 258
vertical integration 340, 536
Virgin Group 183
Vodafone 248, 360, 365
volatility of stock markets 113–114
volcanic eruptions 68
Volvo 410, 470
'VW law' 357

WACC. *See* weighted average cost of capital
Wagstyl, Stafen 455
Walmart 431, 436
War Loan 121, 279
Warner, J. 325

warrants 218, 536
Waterstones 379
Watts, R. 258
WDA. *See* writing-down allowances
weak form of efficient market hypothesis 12–13, 536
wealth measurement 32
Weaver, S. 166
weighted average cost of capital (WACC) 164, 277–278, 536
　calculation of 315–318
　capital structure and 301
　debt/equity ratios and 302
　economic value added and 287
　in European countries 281, 282
　foreign direct investment 457
　geared firms valuation 322
　gearing and 291, 315–318
　Modigliani and Miller on 301
　overall cost of capital 281–284
　required conditions for using 283
　worked example 284–287
Weinland, Don 281
Wellcome Trust 377
Westerfield, R. 19, 50
Weston, J. F. 99, 103
Whitaker, S. C. 381
Whitbread plc 149–150, 153, 156–157, 158
White Knight 357, 536
wholesale banks 5–6
Wieser, Brian 170
Wilkie, A. D. 163
Wilkinson, N. 488
Wilson, James 333
Wilson, M. 437
Wimm-Bill-Dann 341
winning streaks 482
Wise, D. 114

Wood, A. 258
Woolridge, J. 246
work-in-progress 172
working capital 20, 189, 536
　investment in 191
　net 531
　optimal 470–471
WorldCom 175
writers, options 205, 416
writing-down allowances (WDA) 193, 523

xd (ex-dividend) 46, 229, 527
Xstrata 333
Xu, X. G. 134, 142

Yahoo 357
yields 16, 17, 536
　curves 50–54, 121, 536
　dividends (*see* dividends)
　earnings 54–55, 527
　flat 528
　gross redemption 50, 528
　interest 529
　to maturity 44, 536
　prospective earnings 527
　redemption 533
Ying, Liu 445
Young, D. 196, 368
Young, G. 258
Young, S. 196, 381

z-scores 536
Zenner, M. 381
zero coupon bonds 536
zero-sum game, options as 417
Zhang, L. 138, 142
Zingales, L. 325